EXPLORATION

AND

EMPIRE

*The Explorer and the Scientist
in the Winning
of the American West*

BY

WILLIAM H. GOETZMANN

W · W · NORTON & COMPANY
New York · London

Published simultaneously in Canada by Stoddart,
a subsidiary of General Publishing Co. Ltd,
Don Mills, Ontario.

W. W. Norton & Company, Inc., 500 Fifth Avenue, New York, N.Y. 10110

Copyright © 1966 by William H. Goetzmann.
Printed in the United States of America.
First published in the Norton Library 1978 by arrangement with Alfred A. Knopf, Inc.
All Rights Reserved.

Books That Live
The Norton imprint on a book means that in the publisher's
estimation it is a book not for a single season but for the years.
W. W. Norton & Company, Inc.

Library of Congress Cataloging in Publication Data
Goetzmann, William H.
Exploration and empire.
(The Norton Library)
"A note on the sources": p.
Includes index.
1. The West—Discovery and exploration. I. Title.
[F591.G62   1978]   917.8   77-26029

ISBN 0-393-00881-9

4 5 6 7 8 9 0

To

Mewes, Will, Anne, and Stephen

See, vast trackless spaces,
As in a dream they change, they swiftly fill,
Countless masses debouch upon them,
They are now cover'd with the foremost people,
    arts, institutions, known.

WALT WHITMAN, "Starting From
Paumanok," *Leaves of Grass*

INTRODUCTION

THE nineteenth century, for Americans as well as for Europeans, was an age of exploration. During this period all of the islands of the sea were charted, the Antarctic discovered, and the interiors of the continental land masses opened up to the mobile citizens of the Western world, who came to them with Christianity, ideas of progress, new techniques in science, and dreams of romantic imperialism. The nineteenth-century confrontation of the unknown was almost uniquely a Western phenomenon, and as such was primarily important because it helped to create in the centers of dominant culture a series of images which conditioned popular attitudes and public policy concerning the new lands. Out of the charts and the travel literature, the scientific reports, the collections of exotic specimens, the lithographs, the photographs, the adventure novels and popular biographies, the schoolboy geographies, the museums, and even the children's books, emerged a series of impressions—often a series of first impressions unconsciously conditioned by the established culture of the time—which became a crucial factor in shaping the long-range destiny of the newly discovered places and their peoples, and which at the same time altered forever the established culture.

An important part of this latter-day age of discovery was the exploration of the American West, which took place almost entirely within the confines of the last century and reflected many of the characteristics of the broader global phenomenon. Because of its impact upon American culture and in turn upon world culture, this century-long adventure deserves a somewhat different sort of attention than it has hitherto received. Building upon decades of patient and detailed scholarship, it is now possible to attempt the beginning of a new and more general assessment of the role of exploration in the development of the American West, and also, using the American West as a very extensive case study, to inquire more closely into the nature of exploration itself and its consequences as an activity for civilization in general. Such in broadest outlines are the objectives of this book.

A beginning fairly made, however, rests most comfortably upon the reassuring foundations of definition, and in the case of exploration such comfort is difficult to find, for exploration closely analyzed proves, like everything else, to be a very complex phenomenon. It can perhaps best be defined in terms of a concrete example, and then a more general model. For the concrete example let us return to 1868.

On an August day in 1868 the Union Pacific made an unscheduled stop at Antelope Station in western Nebraska. From one of the ornate parlor cars a dignified, scholarly gentleman stepped out upon the prairie. He was Othniel Charles Marsh, a Yale paleontologist, and he was following up a story that had appeared in an Omaha newspaper to the effect that a railroad well-digger had accidentally unearthed the bones of a prehistoric man out there in Nebraska at a place famous only as a way station on the emigrant route to the West. Marsh's own account of the incident captures some of the excitement he felt that day:

"Before we approached the small station where the alleged primitive man had been unearthed," Marsh remembered, *"I made friends with the conductor, and persuaded him to hold the train long enough for me to glance over the earth thrown out of this well, thinking perchance that I might thus find some fragments, at least, of our early ancestors. In one respect I succeeded beyond my wildest hopes. By rapid search over the huge mound of earth, I soon found many fragments and a number of entire bones, not of man, but of* horses *diminutive indeed, but true equine ancestors. . . . Other fragments told of his contemporaries—a camel, a pig, and a turtle . . . perhaps more . . . when I could remove the clay from the other remains secured. Absorbed in this work I took no note of time."*

When ultimately Marsh reboarded the train, he had the first clues to his reconstruction of Protohippus, the miniature three-toed horse of the Pleistocene era. And out of this "find" grew his classic fossil genealogy of the modern horse, one of the most famous pieces of paleontological evidence for the validity of Darwin's theory of evolution through natural selection.

More significantly for the student of exploration, however, Professor Marsh's Antelope Station adventure marked the beginning of the career of still another outstanding explorer of the American West. For Marsh's enthusiasm went far beyond the fossil horse.

"I could only wonder," he wrote, *"if such scientific truths as I had now obtained were concealed in a single well, what untold treasures must there be in the whole Rocky Mountain region. This thought promised rich rewards for the enthusiastic explorer in this new field, and thus my own life work seemed laid out before me."*

The nature of Marsh's adventure in 1868 and his subsequent view of himself as a Rocky Mountain explorer (despite his obvious tender-foot background) highlight one of the most important elements in the history of the American West. The country beyond the Mississippi, as we now know it, was not just "discovered" in one dramatic and color-ful era of early-nineteenth-century coonskin exploration. Rather it was discovered and rediscovered by generations of very different explorers down through the centuries following the advent of the shipwrecked Spaniard Cabeza de Vaca. And this process of repeated discovery was in itself among the most important factors which shaped the develop-ment of culture and civilization in that region.

Usually, however, exploration is not thought of as a process with cultural significance. Rather it is viewed as a sequence of dramatic discoveries—isolated events, colorful and even interesting perhaps, but of little consequence to the basic sweep of civilization. This is be-cause exploration has rarely if ever been viewed as a continuous form of activity or mode of behavior. The words "exploration" and "dis-covery" are most often and most casually linked in the popular imag-ination simply as interchangeable synonyms for "adventure." But exploration is something more than adventure, and something more than discovery. According to Webster, the explorer is actually one who "*seeks* discoveries." He is not simply and solely the "discoverer." In-stead the accent is upon process and activity, with advances in knowl-edge simply fortunate though expected incidents along the way. It is likewise not casual. It is purposeful. It is the seeking. It is one form of the learning process itself, and, as the case of Professor Marsh illus-trates, it was often a branch of science which resulted in a discovery at a place trod many times over by previous generations of explorers bent on other missions in days gone by.

The importance of viewing exploration as activity rather than as a sequence of discoveries is further underscored when one considers the distinction between the explorer and the discoverer in terms of the con-cept of *mission*. Discoveries can be produced by accident, as in the case of the fortunate well-digger at Antelope Station. Exploration, by con-trast, is the result of purpose or mission. As such, it is an activity which, to a very large degree, is "programmed" by some older center of culture. That is, its purposes, goals, and evaluation of new data are to a great extent set by the previous experiences, the values, the kinds and cate-gories of existing knowledge, and the current objectives of the civilized centers from which the explorer sets out on his quest. If Marsh, for example, had not been a paleontologist trained at Yale and in Europe, he might have looked for different things on his trip out West. He might have kept his eye out for mineral deposits perhaps, instead of waxing enthusiastic over a "big bonanza" in bones. He certainly never would have set off with such zest in search of an ancient America in the form of gigantic dinosaurs, exotic pterodactyls, and his own favorites—the extinct toothed birds. Yet, his exploring activity, peculiar as it was, programmed by an older center of culture, had a lasting importance not only in terms of his startling discoveries, but also in terms of the effect it had on the future course of science and public policy in the West, and on the United States as a whole as Marsh rose to prominence in the worlds of science and government. The same might be said in varying degrees for a whole host of other nineteenth-century explorers of the American West—men who synthesized the new sights they saw in the wilderness into projections or images of what the older centers thought the West ought to be. Thus in various periods the West became the great empty continent, Eldorado or Cibola, a barren waste of heathen savages and Spaniards, the passage to India, an imperial frontier, a beaver kingdom, the Great American Desert, a land of flocks and herds, a pastoral paradise, an agricultural Arcadia, a military and administrative problem, a bonanza of gold and silver, a safety valve, a haven for saints, a refuge for bad men, and ultimately, toward the end of the nineteenth century, an enormous laboratory. And so it went —there were many more such images that it might be possible to point out, each demonstrating in some measure the preconceptions that an older culture and its explorers brought to the search for knowledge in the new environment.

With this in mind, my aim has been to focus upon exploration as a meaningful activity and to trace its complex impact not only upon the history of the West but upon the nation as a whole, particularly as it stimulated advances in science and scientific institutions and the evolution, on a national level, of a public policy for the West as a part of the nation. Much of the story necessarily revolves about the role of the federal government in sponsoring the exploration of the West, since it is clear that, contrary to the myth of the rugged independent frontiersman, a good part of the exploration done in the West was done under federal sponsorship. From the early days of Lewis and Clark down to the formation of the United States Geological Survey, the government explorer in one form or another played a vital role. And even when the agents of exploration were not federal servants, their constant referent was nevertheless the national government, and the aid and protection it might be expected to provide.

In addition, the history of Western exploration can serve as a vehicle for demonstrating in a more subtle way some of the larger consequences of the way the West was won. If the region was settled along lines or according to images projected by the older centers of culture, then in the most precise way it was—to borrow a modern concept usually not thought of as being applicable to the nineteenth century of rugged individualism—"other-directed." Men appear to have gone out West to reconstitute the society they had known on countless frontiers to the East—only of course with themselves at the top instead of at the bottom of the social and economic ladder. Even as they came in conflict with the rapidly changing Eastern and national interests, Western men were still largely prisoners of an emulative society. This in turn was not unique to the frontier West. America itself grew up in this emulative and "programmed" fashion. Thus the explorers reflecting national images and plans, and the Westerners who followed their lead, were all part of an "other-directed" pattern. And this perhaps is the major difficulty in defining Western culture itself, for the West, as the history of its exploration clearly shows, has always been in rapid transition. It is, as Frederick Jackson Turner has pointed out, more of a process than a place. But that process has been as much an Americanization process as it has been one of distinctiveness. Contrary to Turner's hypothesis, the Western experience in the main appears not to have brought distinctiveness as such to bear on the country, but instead has offered a theater in which American patterns of culture could be endlessly mirrored.

Thus in a sense the problem of Western culture becomes the problem of American culture, which is itself the rapidly changing offspring of an older, broader society. The two units represent different degrees of the same complex problem which continues to tantalize and elude historians down to our own day. Exploration, by no means the eccentric activity it is sometimes taken to be, does offer, however, a major clue to the shifting relationship of the regional to the national culture in our recent historical experience.

In its broadest terms, the history of nineteenth-century Western exploration can be seen unfolding through three major periods each characterized by a dominant set of objectives, particular forms of exploring activity, distinctive types of explorers, and appropriate institutions which governed these other factors. The first of these periods began with Lewis and Clark and continued down to approximately 1845. It was an era of imperial rivalry in which even the mountain men and fur traders were self-conscious pawns in an international competition for the West. The second was a period of settlement and investment in which numbers and opportunity—"westering"—were all that counted and the explorer was largely dedicated to lending a helping hand in the matter of Manifest Destiny. The third period, from 1860 to 1900, was the era of the Great Surveys, a time for more intensive scientific reconnaissances and inventories. It was also a time for sober second thoughts as to the proper nature, purpose, and future direction of Western settlement. Incipient conservation and planning in the national interest became a vogue, signifying that the West had come of age and its future had become securely wedded to the fortunes of the nation. These three stages or phases of Western exploration form the major parts of the narrative that follows.

Specialists in Western history will readily perceive that in the interests of consolidation and thematic development I have omitted some of the better-known anecdotal material connected with Western exploration, particularly that relating to the fur trade, a subject with which I am not primarily concerned. The numerous voyages up the Missouri River, for example, which are interesting as part of fur-trade history but of less significance to exploration history, I have not attempted to describe at all. Likewise, my excursions into such vast fields as military and mining history, as well as the history of science, have been deliberately, and from a personal point of view, regretfully circumscribed by the requirements of my theme. But since the total story of nineteenth-century Western exploration has never been told before, and one of my primary concerns is to present the reader with a comprehensive and useful reference, as complete as possible within the limitations of space, as to where the explorers actually went, as well as how and why they penetrated the unknown, I have necessarily been forced to include a great deal of geographical detail. It is hoped that the maps inserted at appropriate places will provide the reader with guidance through what is a bewildering geographical maze far greater in scope than any that ever confronted the individual explorer.

And finally, though I have endeavored to go somewhat beyond the descriptive in analyzing the explorer and his activities, I have been continually conscious of him as a man—an individual whose impressions at a particular time and place can only be recaptured by going out with him on his journeys into the unknown and gazing in astonishment at the same wonders he saw, from the same point of view. For in order to understand something of the internal history of exploration it is necessary to understand as fully as possible the explorer himself—to know something of what it felt like to cross the silent wastes of the Great Basin for the first time, or to course down the foaming cataracts of the Green River toward an unknown destination and an unknown fate. It is also necessary to know something of the trivia that affected men's lives in the wilderness, whether it be the limitations of bullboat travel or the discomforts of being caught with a brass surveying instrument on a bald mountain peak in an electrical storm—which is to say that history, to be accurate, must be romantic as well as scientific. So with apologies for many apparent digressions and limitations, herewith is presented a beginning synthesis which is in intent only a reconnaissance in the scientific and at the same time romantic spirit, intended to lay out an imperfect historical trail for others to follow upon, correct, and improve. For me it has been a great but serious adventure of which the reader is invited to partake to the limits of his perseverance and indulgence.

New Haven, Connecticut
Austin, Texas

ACKNOWLEDGMENTS

THE late Yale President, A. Whitney Griswold, once asked rhetorically: "Could *Hamlet* have been written by a committee, or the 'Mona Lisa' painted by a club?" To a large extent the writing of history like the work of the artist is also a solitary occupation, with the responsibility for selection, synthesis, and judgment resting squarely upon the individual. Nevertheless, the present historical adventure would not have been possible without the help of a great number of people and institutions.

First of all I should like to acknowledge the generous financial aid and encouragement granted me by the Executive Committee of American Studies of Yale University, by the Chairman of the American Studies Department, Professor Norman Holmes Pearson, and by former Dean William C. De Vane. Through their agency I was awarded a Susan B. Morse Fellowship and Summer Travelling Grant, which enabled me to complete a large part of the basic research for this book. I am also indebted to the Social Science Research Council for a fellowship granted me in 1961–62 at a crucial stage in my work. In addition I have also benefited from the scholarly generosity of the American Philosophical Society, which awarded me a travel grant in 1959, permitting me to make the first important research trip in connection with this project.

I am indebted in another way to the Yale University Library, which has been my virtual headquarters for some years. I have special reason to thank James T. Babb, former Librarian of Yale, for his breadth of vision that made Yale congenial to the study of Western Americana in the first place; Archibald Hanna, Curator of Western Americana, for his constant and close cooperation with my project; and not the least, Harry P. Harrison, Director of Circulation at the Sterling Memorial Library, whose patient understanding of the scholar's problems most certainly made this book possible. I am also indebted to Miss Judy Schiff of the Yale Historical Manuscripts Collection and to Professor Brooks M. Kelley, Archivist of Yale University and Curator of Historical Manuscripts, for their aid at crucial points in my work.

The list of colleagues, friends, and sometimes even complete strangers who contributed in important ways to this book is very long. Professors Rollin G. Osterweis, Edmund S. Morgan, John M. Blum, Robin Winks, Howard R. Lamar, Norman Holmes Pearson, William H. Dunham, William Lilley, Robert Dalzell, and Peter Bunnell, all of Yale University, in one way or another made helpful suggestions that materially aided my work. Whitfield Bell of the American Philosophical Society and Nathan Reingold of the Library of Congress contributed expert advice in matters pertaining to the history of science. In this aspect of my work, I also benefited greatly by conversations with Professor Carl Waage of the Yale Department of Geology and Professor Thomas Manning of Texas Technological College. Professor Keith Young of the University of Texas Department of Geology assisted me with the scientific illustrations.

Western historians who have come to my aid, if not rescue, in one way or another, are Dale L. Morgan of the Bancroft Library; Robert V. Hine of the University of California at Riverside; William Turrentine Jackson of the University of California at Davis; J. V. Howell of Tulsa, Oklahoma, the forthcoming biographer of F. V. Hayden; Donald Jackson of the University of Illinois Press; the late Edward S. Wallace of Millington Green, Connecticut; the late Robert Glass Cleland; and Wallace W. Farnham of the University of Wyoming. Helpful suggestions in the field of Western history were also furnished me by Fred Nicklason, formerly on the faculty of Amherst College, now in the Yale Graduate School; Michele La Clergue of the University of Texas Graduate School; and the late Newell Remington of Salt Lake City, Utah. Dr. Erwin Raisz, a master cartographer, and my colleague on the National Atlas Project, saved me from many errors through his masterful knowledge of Western topography.

Licenciado Jorge A. Vargas graciously acted as my guide through the Ministry of External Relations in Mexico City. The Marquesa de Zahara generously loaned me family papers which cast light on George Armstrong Custer and John James Abert. She, in fact, served as a spirited guide through the maze of complex "Abertiana," thereby contributing no little enjoyment to my tour. Eugene Kingman and Mildred Goosman made the resources of the very excellent Joslyn Art Museum in Omaha available to me. I am likewise indebted to the Walters Art Gallery, the Kennedy Galleries Inc., the Hudson's Bay Company, the American Geographical Society, the American Museum of Natural History, the Northern Natural Gas Co., the University of Texas Geology Library, and the University of Oklahoma Press for making illustrative materials available to me.

Stewart Richardson, David Horne, Angus Cameron, and Alfred A. Knopf have given me important advice in matters of publishing. Not the least of Mr. Cameron's labors has been the editing of this book for

its publisher. Mr. and Mrs. Robert Perry of Cleveland, Ohio; Mr. and
Mrs. Graham Courtney of Minneapolis, Minnesota; and Dr. and Mrs.
Edward Stit Fleming, of Washington, D.C., all provided forms of encouragement and convivial hospitality that were no less important than
professional advice.

An author's most important critic is often not his wife, but his typist.
Marie Avitable, my typist for many years, has successfully performed
that function, in addition to the many hours of tedious labor connected
with deciphering handwriting and getting words on paper. Additional
contributions in this vein were made by Mrs. Phyllis O'Keefe, Miss Col-
leen Kain, and Mrs. Barbara Norwood. Miss Barbara Greenberg assisted
in the reading of proof, a tedious job at best. And finally, though I cannot
possibly name them all, I am indebted to my closest companions of the
past few years, the Fellows of Jonathan Edwards College, and my students at both Yale and Texas universities in seminars on Romantic
America, American Intellectual History, and Science in American
Culture.

Much to my regret, I am not able to name individually all of the
people at all of the institutions who have contributed so much to my
search for the raw materials out of which this book was fashioned. In
addition to those mentioned above, I am, however, indebted to the staffs
of the following institutions more than I can say: the American Philosophical Society, the Philadelphia Academy of Natural Sciences, the
Pennsylvania State Historical Society, the Yale Peabody Museum, the
Yale Geological Library, the Missouri Historical Society, the Library of
the St. Louis Botanical Gardens, the Oklahoma State Historical Society,
the Library of the University of Oklahoma, the Kansas State Historical
Society, the Gilcrease Institute, the Barker Library of the Texas State
Historical Society, the University of Texas Geology Library, the Denver
Public Library, the Houston Public Library, the San Jacinto Museum,
the Rosenburg Library of Galveston, the Panhandle-Plains Historical
Museum, the William Robertson Coe Library of the University of Wyo-
ming, the libraries and museums at Grand Canyon, Yellowstone, Big
Bend, Zion, Scott's Bluff, and Jackson Hole national parks and monu-
ments, the Jackson Hole Museum (private), the Washington State
Historical Society, the Bancroft Library, the Huntington Library, the
Arizona Pioneers Historical Society, the New Mexico Historical Society,
the John Carter Brown Library, the West Point Museum, the Newberry
Library, the New-York Historical Society, the New York Public Library,
the Torrey Botanical Gardens of New York, the Butler Library of Columbia University, the American Museum of Natural History, the New
York State Library, the New York State Museum, the Archivo Nacional
de Mexico, the Ministerio de Relaciones Exteriores de Mexico, the Li-

brary of Congress Manuscript, Cartographical, and Picture Sections,
the Smithsonian Institution, and the United States Geological Survey.
All of these institutions not only made information and materials available to me, but in addition individual members of their staffs performed
services for me ranging from producing typescripts of documents to
making suggestions concerning obscure collections that I might otherwise have overlooked. In only one instance did I meet with anything
less than full and enthusiastic cooperation. Last of all the institutions,
however, I should like especially to acknowledge the help of the people
in the following branches of the National Archives: the Army Records
Section, the Interior Department Records Section, the Still Pictures
Section, Cartographic Records, and the State Department Records Section. More than anything else, this book is a child of the National
Archives and its dedicated people.

Parts of this book have appeared in somewhat different form in *The
American Quarterly, The Journal of World History,* and *The American
West: An Appraisal* (Museum of New Mexico Press, 1963), to which
acknowledgments are due.

Finally, though it is now fashionable to pay homage to Venus and
Bacchus, or to acknowledge the important services of Zen, Miltown,
and "Pot," I should like to conclude on a more traditional note and ex-
press gratitude to, and admiration for, my wife Mewes, who some years
ago in another book was with me as we went "down the edges, through
the passes, up the mountains steep." She is still with me, though the
edges have grown more precarious, the passes narrower, and the mountains steeper.

CONTENTS

ILLUSTRATIONS

MAPS

Expeditions and Explorations

Prepared especially for this book by William Lacey

Early Maps

PART ONE

Exploration and Imperialism

1805-45

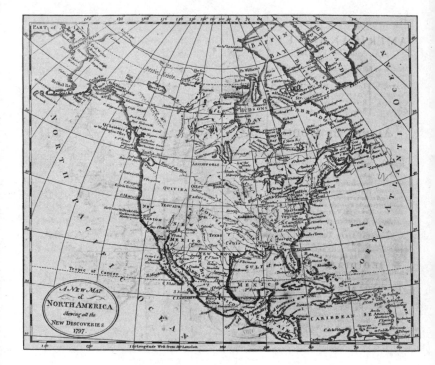

View of North America in Jefferson's time. From Jedidiah Morse's *Gazetteer of America*, 1797. *Courtesy Library of Congress*

CHAPTER I

Westward the Clash of Empires

THE exploration of the American West was never an isolated event. It belongs to world rather than to national history, and never more so than in the opening decades of the nineteenth century. When Captain Meriwether Lewis and Lieutenant William Clark of the United States Army crossed the North American continent from the Mississippi River to the Pacific Ocean between May 14, 1804, and September 26, 1806, they brought to a close nearly three centuries of searching, on the part of European and colonial powers, for a Northwest Passage to India. A new country, the United States, had entered the ancient struggle for control of the trade routes to the Orient, but in so doing, thanks to the work of the Great Captains, it had altered the focus of international rivalry, at least for a time, from the far-off Orient to the Western interior of the North American continent itself. Lewis and Clark had discovered no easy route to Cathay. But theirs had been the final stroke that swept away the eighteenth-century geographers' view that one needed only to cross a single height of land—a ridge of the "Stony Mountains," in Jefferson's terms—before one could look upon the broad Pacific with Cathay on its Western shore.[1] Instead their expedition demonstrated to the world at large the great width of western North America and its potential riches in furs, minerals, fishes, and untold other natural resources. Thus they succeeded in making the

1. The best representation of this view is in Aaron Arrowsmith and Samuel Lewis: *Atlas* (Philadelphia, 1804), especially Map I, Louisiana. The same map is reproduced in Mathew Carey: *American Pocket Atlas* (Philadelphia, 1805), See Carl I. Wheat: *Mapping the Trans-Mississippi West*, 6 vols. (San Francisco, Calif.: Institute of Historical Cartography; 1957–63), Vol. II, pp. 5–11, 13–14. It is instructive to compare the Arrowsmith map with that of Lewis and Clark in 1814 for an idea of Lewis and Clark's overall contribution to a knowledge of the West.

West itself an object of desire—a virgin wilderness that formed a thousand-mile vacuum between the great powers of the world and the United States, and into which, by whatever laws of imperialistic physics prevailed, they must inevitably rush. It was a vacuum that acted, as one historian has pointed out, like a greatly expanded European political frontier with intense pressures on either side.[2] As such, the explorer became more than a mere curiosity-seeker. When he led his nation and his culture into the Western "vacuum" so richly endowed by nature, the buckskin explorer became a vital factor in international diplomacy. For much of the nineteenth century it was the explorer out in the wilderness as much as the diplomats in London and Paris and Washington who took the lead in establishing, through his increased geographical knowledge and his control of the Indians, the practical limits of each nation's frontier on the edges of the vast terrestrial sea that lay between them.

It was not by accident that Lewis and Clark so changed the focus of international rivalry for the West. Rather it was a function of their unique role as explorers with a broad sense of national purpose. They were not fur traders, for example, nor even strictly speaking men of commerce. Instead both men were soldiers with extensive experience in frontier regions, chosen for their general intelligence and knowledge of wilderness skills, and programmed by an elaborate set of instructions from Thomas Jefferson, who saw their mission in the very broadest terms. In his appeal to Congress for funds, Jefferson described the expedition as a commercial one because it thus fell within the limits of his Constitutional powers.[3] Yet privately Jefferson also saw it as a "literary" undertaking, which

2. Howard R. Lamar: "The Concept of Regionalism in the Teaching of the History of the American West," *Reports and Speeches of the Seventh Yale Conference on the Teaching of the Social Studies* (New Haven, 1962), *passim*.

3. Donald Jackson, ed.: *The Letters of the Lewis and Clark Expedition* (Urbana, Ill.: University of Illinois Press; 1962), pp. 10–13, reprints the full text of Jefferson's "confidential" message. See also p. 4, in which Jefferson is quoted by Sr. Carlos Martínez de Yrujo as declaring that "they would give it [the Lewis expedition] the denomination of mercantile, inasmuch as only in this way would the Congress have the power of voting the necessary funds . . ." Jackson, p. 14 *n.*, suggests that Jefferson greatly feared political opposition to his plan, and hence delivered it as a "confidential" message, not to conceal it from the Spanish, French, or British, who already knew about it, but to conceal it from his American political enemies. A plan broadly literary and scientific in scope would have raised opposition from the same strict construction extremists who were to oppose John Quincy Adams's similar plans in 1825. Such opposition, had it gained support, might have made the Louisiana Purchase impossible.

in the parlance of the day meant that it was to collect information covering the whole range of natural history from geology to Indian vocabularies.[4] As explorers, Lewis and Clark might almost be considered a logical extension of the American Philosophical Society, which existed to promote the general advancement of science and "the useful arts."

The repeated attention given to the details of their overland trip has tended to obscure what is perhaps the most important fact about the Lewis and Clark expedition, and that is the degree to which it was "programmed," or planned in advance, down to the smallest detail by Jefferson and his scientific associates in Philadelphia, particularly Caspar Wistar, Benjamin Rush, Andrew Ellicott, and Robert Patterson.[5] After years of collecting information about the West, and several abortive attempts to launch an expedition, Jefferson, who also had some backwoods experience as a surveyor in his native Virginia, had a very clear idea of the kinds of information the explorers should collect. This was first and foremost geographical information of the wide-ranging, nonspecialized kind that characterized the returns of such an eminent scientific man as Alexander von Humboldt. If Jefferson's famous *Notes on Virginia* can be said to constitute a perfect model of the rational eighteenth-century mind organizing the many facts of physical and human nature into a broadly conceived and generally useful pattern, then in equal measure the same can be said for the instructions given to Lewis and Clark.

They were called upon first of all to explore the Missouri and Columbia rivers to locate "the most direct and practicable water communication across this continent for the purposes of commerce." But they were also to "fix" geographical positions by astronomical observations so that a map of the region could be made. Moreover, they were to study the Indian inhabitants very carefully, including their numbers, their relations with other tribes, "their language, dress and monuments," their economic and military pursuits, their food, clothing, and houses, their diseases and remedies, and their laws and customs. In addition Lewis and Clark were to study the "soil and face of the country," particularly its vegetable production, its animals, its fossils, the existing minerals, including metals, limestone, coal, salts, mineral waters, and saltpeter. They were also to take note of volcanic action and to keep statistics on the

4. Jackson: *Letters,* p. 4.
5. See Jackson: *Letters,* pp. 16–18, 21, 23–4, 28–30, 36–40, 44–6, 48–52, 54–60.

weather. In short, though commerce in furs was to be a prime objective, the explorers were to inquire into almost every phenomenon that might prove useful to settlers from the United States.[6] The very strength of Jefferson's instructions was in their broadness and lack of limitations. It was this general approach that called for the study of any and all useful phenomena that set the pattern for much of the early American exploration in the Far West and gave it a tremendous advantage over the more specialized efforts by competing nations. It keynoted what was to be a more flexible and economically mobile American approach to the West. When American explorers, following Lewis and Clark, went out into the West, they characteristically found many more uses for the land than did their counterparts under different flags.

That this was no accident can further be illustrated by a brief glance at the kind of training received by Meriwether Lewis, the nominal head of the expedition. During the summer of 1803 Lewis was in Philadelphia studying natural history with Wistar, Rush, Peale, and other experts.[7] These men also furnished him with advice in the techniques of collecting, and gave him detailed lists of questions to ask the Indians and other people whom he might meet. Part of his time, too, was spent mastering the sextant, the theodolite, and other instruments that were to be used for the careful calculation of longitude and latitude so necessary for the compilation of an accurate map of the unknown region. He also had opportunity to study maps, such as those of John Mitchell and Guillaume De Lisle, in Jefferson's library; and later, in St. Louis, he studied the Spanish maps of Antoine Soulard and the Missouri River charts of John Evans and James Mackay, as well as their journals.[8] In a few short months his head was crammed with the rudimentary outlines of virtually every branch of natural and physical science, and before the expedition got under way, Clark, too, began to master some of these skills. Clark's field notes show, for example, that the bluff frontier soldier had mastered the arts of geography well

6. Jefferson's instructions to Lewis are reprinted in Jackson: *Letters,* pp. 61–6.

7. See footnote 5 above.

8. A discussion of the maps that Lewis and Clark had on hand before starting their trip can be found in Ernest S. Osgood, ed.: *The Field Notes of Captain William Clark, 1802–1805* (New Haven, Conn.: Yale University Press; 1964), pp. 16–17 *n.* Also see Jackson: *Letters,* pp. 28, 53, for indirect evidence that Lewis, as Jefferson's secretary, was also familiar with the maps of Vancouver, Arrowsmith, De Lisle, d'Anville, Thornton, and Ellicott. Also see Jackson: *Letters,* p. 32, which indicates that Jefferson also was familiar with Mitchell's map, and so very probably was Lewis.

enough to be able to calculate with some approximate degree of accuracy the probable distance from Camp DuBois to the Pacific Ocean.[9] Thus, despite their apparent use of erroneous maps of the day that indicated an easy progress over a single mountain ridge from the Missouri to the Columbia, Lewis and Clark, before they started, were able to use the longitude calculations of McKenzie, Vancouver, Evans, and others to determine the magnitude of the trek that lay before them. Had they never made the trip at all, they would at least have added this datum to the existing body of geographical knowledge.

It was as carefully trained agents of a civilized and flexible culture, then, that Lewis and Clark set out into the wilderness and injected the United States into the struggle for a national empire. Their journey took them up the Missouri to Fort Mandan, in present-day North Dakota, where they spent the winter of 1804–05 (see map, p. 23). Then they followed the Missouri along its great bend and down to the Three Forks, where they headed up the Jefferson River and crossed over into Montana's Bitterroot Valley via Lemhi Pass, in one of the most critical stretches of the entire trip. From the Bitterroot they made their way northward to the Clearwater and thence to the Columbia. Then they followed the main Columbia to the Pacific, which they reached on November 7, 1805. In one of the most dramatic moments in the history of exploration, William Clark stood one winter day in a slashing rain and carved on a tall yellow pine overlooking the Pacific: "William Clark December 3rd 1805. By Land from the U. States in 1804 and 1805."

It was in imitation of Alexander McKenzie's announcement of his earlier arrival at the shores of the Pacific far to the north on the Bella Coola River, and a conscious challenge to all other nations who wished to lay claim to the Columbia country. Not only had they collected the required data, filled the notebooks and journals de-

---

9. Osgood: *Field Notes*, pp. 19–21. In footnote 9, pp. 20–1, Osgood points out that Clark's calculations for some stretches of the trip (i.e., from the Continental Divide to the Pacific Ocean) were more accurate than for others (i.e., from the Mandan Villages to the Rocky Mountains). He adds: "For the whole distance from Camp DuBois to the Pacific, Clark's estimate of 3,050 miles was nearly a thousand miles too low; the actual mileage was 3,958 miles." However, the important consideration here would seem to be that Clark, basing his estimates on longitude, had a reasonable understanding of the great distance over which he would have to travel, which stood in sharp contrast to that of the famous geographers of the day, and hence even before starting out Clark was already more sophisticated than most American and many English cartographers, despite the work of the Canadian explorer McKenzie.

manded by Jefferson, but they also had served as diplomatic agents of the United States in establishing a claim to the Columbia.

After wintering at Fort Clatsop, the first American settlement west of the Continental Divide, they returned over a new route, with Lewis leading one party overland from Lo-Lo Pass via the Sun River to the Great Falls of the Missouri, and Clark swinging southward to explore the Yellowstone River. They were reunited at the junction of the Missouri and the Yellowstone and gradually descended the Missouri to St. Louis, where they arrived on September 26, 1806, to the cheers of a small crowd assembled on the bank of the river. The story of their trip, which has been told many times, needs no recapitulation in detail. Its significance for the later history of American exploration lies in the flexible point of view which they brought to the West and which was to set the pattern for the many expeditions to follow. They had sketched in the broad outline of the continent, and they had brought back collections and data enough to suggest the immense value of the interior to all kinds of American enterprise. In so doing, they altered forever the focus and nature of the imperial struggle for North America.

But despite the fact that Lewis and Clark had made known such essentials as the width of the continent, the existence of numerous ranges of high mountains, the location and description of the major rivers of the Northwest and the rich resources of the whole region, what was eventually to become the American West was still largely a geographical mystery in the immediate years after their return. Not until 1814, with the publication of their report (edited by Nicholas Biddle and Paul Allen), was there even a satisfactory cartographic representation of the whole region south and west of the Missouri River. Instead, for a long time the West remained an immense unknown, whose limits were gradually being defined by the explorers sent out into it by the governments and fur-trading companies along its margins.

1

To the north were the British, their interests sustained by two massive economic institutions. The first, Hudson's Bay Company, was founded under a charter from the king in 1670 and stood sovereign over all of Prince Rupert's Land from Hudson Bay to New Caledonia and northward to the Arctic Ocean. The second was the Northwest Company, operating out of Montreal westward via the lakes and portages to the Rocky Mountains and beyond. Engaged in a fierce struggle for control of the Northwest fur trade, both companies were primarily business ventures, concerned with "large" policy only as it affected their financial interests. The Hudson's Bay Company was tightly controlled by a board of directors in London, who in turn authorized a representative (the governor) to meet with a council and see to the practical operation of the fur business under their careful instruction. Profit was the primary concern, and costs were always carefully calculated. At the annual council meetings, such things as the price of salt beef and sausages, the number of pieces of baggage per canoe and their precise weight and content, the daily ration of tea or rum allowed the Indian guides, and the exact circumstances under which the lonely traders at their winter outposts were allowed to cohabit with the Indian women were carefully determined and specified.[1] The object, of course, was to rationalize the trade as much as possible. Under these conditions, exploration was a diversion from the normal business concerns, and was only undertaken when it would yield a clear financial return, or when, due to the pressure of competition, it became a necessity. Even then, the typical Hudson's Bay explorer looked primarily for beaver and portage routes—opportunities for extending the same traditional business pattern as he pushed out into the unknown.

By contrast and undoubtedly by necessity, the Northwest Company, founded in 1787, was far more daring. Blocked by the Americans to the south and the Hudson's Bay posts on the north, and denied access to Hudson Bay itself, the Northwest Company pursued a policy of survival through expansion that involved exploring the country to the westward in search of a northwest passage or a river route to a port on the Pacific. Because of this policy, most of the important Canadian exploration was done by men of the Northwest Company.[2]

Building on the work of the Vérendryes, who as early as 1738 had reached the Mandan Village on the Missouri, the Northwest Company had pushed westward to the Souris and Assiniboine rivers and into the Upper Missouri country, and by the end of 1805 its man, Antoine Larocque, had already explored the valley of the Yel-

1. Harvey P. Fleming, ed.: *Minutes of the Council, Northern Department of Rupert Land, 1821–31* (Toronto: The Champlain Society; 1940), pp. 25–6, 43–4, 56, 94–6, 129–30.
2. Gordon C. Davidson: *The North West Company* (Berkeley, Calif.: University of California Press; 1918), *passim*.

lowstone River, and its traders regularly wintered with the Mandans and other Upper Missouri tribes.[3] Beyond that, in 1789 Alexander McKenzie had crossed through Upper Canada to the Arctic and in 1793 to the Pacific Ocean. And though for a time his monumental work, *Voyage from Montreal Through the Continent of North America to the Frozen and Pacific Ocean in 1789 and 1793 . . .* (1801), had no effect on company policy, eventually its new leader, Duncan McGillivray, persuaded by McKenzie's views, launched a series of probes into the Canadian Rockies and beyond to the Pacific Ocean.[4]

Duncan McGillivray himself had tried to cross the Rockies as early as 1801, and then in 1805 had come Simon Frazer's expedition, the first after McKenzie to cross the northern Rockies and push on to the Pacific.[5] The most important explorer of all was David Thompson, who not only crossed the mountains but explored the entire Columbia River system as well. Though his main concern was perforce the fur trade, and much of his time was spent establishing trading posts west of the mountains, at heart Thompson was an explorer and mapmaker. Before he had joined the Northwest Company in 1797, Thompson had traveled over 9,000 miles in the service of the Hudson's Bay Company, mapping its entire territory as he went along. As he made his maps, and thousands of careful astronomical calculations, they were forwarded to London and there were made available to the civilized world through the maps of the great English cartographer Aaron Arrowsmith. Indirectly, Thompson's early explorations and Arrowsmith's maps led to the launching of the Lewis and Clark expedition, for they were one of the chief sources of inspiration that led President Jefferson to conceive of his policy of transcontinental exploration.[6]

As they reached out to the Upper Missouri and the Columbia River Basin beyond the Rocky Mountains, the Canadian explorers, besides revealing the unknown, defined for a time the northern edge of the wilderness boundary between British interests and those of the United States. In 1807, spurred to activity by the Lewis and

3. François Antoine Larocque: "The Journal of François Antoine Larocque from the Assiniboine River to the Yellowstone 1805," in Ruth Hazlitt, ed.: *Frontier and Midland* (1933–34), Vol. XIV, pp. 241–7, 332–9; Vol. XV, pp. 67–75, 88.
4. Bernard De Voto: *The Course of Empire* (Boston, Mass.: Houghton Mifflin Co.; 1952), p. 530.
5. Ibid., pp. 531–2.
6. For Thompson's life and services, see J. B. Tyrell: Introduction to *David Thompson's Narrative of His Explorations in Western America 1784–1812* (Toronto: The Champlain Society; 1916), pp. xxiii–xxiv.

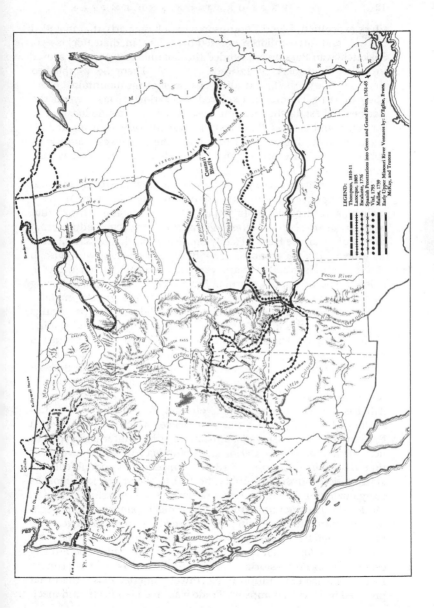

LEGEND:
Thompson, 1810-11
Laroque, 1805
Escalante, 1776
Vial, 1793
Mallet, 1739
Spanish Penetrations into Green and Grand Rivers, 1761-65
Early Upper Missouri River Ventures by: D'Eglise, Evans, McKay, and Truteau

RIVER
MISSISSIPPI
Red River
James
MISSOURI RIVER
Mandan Villages
Arikara Villages
Brandon House
Kullyspell House
Fort Colville
Fort Okanogan
Ft. Vancouver
Fort Astoria
Council Bluffs
Independence
Neosho
Arkansas River
Cimarron
Smoky Hill
Republican
Platte
Niobrara
Cheyenne
Moreau
Belle Fourche
Little Missouri
Yellowstone
Bighorn
Wind
Snake
Owyhee
Humboldt
Walker L.
San Joaquin
Sacramento
Colorado
Taos
Santa Fe
Pecos River
Red River
Canadian
Rio Grande
Green River
Colorado
Little Colorado
Crossing of the Fathers
San Gabriel
SOUTH PASS

Clark expedition, David Thompson with a large party that included
his wife and three children crossed over the Canadian Rockies via
Saskatchewan Pass and ascended the Columbia River to its source
in Lake Windemere at latitude 50° 40′. There he established
Kootenai House, the first trading post west of the mountains. From
1807 to 1810 Thompson explored the various rivers beyond the
Rockies and established trading posts at every strategic location as
far south and east as Thompson's River, thereby securing the allegiance of the Indians and extending the Northwest Company's
sphere of influence among the Flatheads deep into what is now
Montana.

However, during these years, despite his great interest in exploration, Thompson seems to have been primarily concerned with establishing fur-trading posts among the transmontane tribes that
would insure the Northwesters against threatened competition from
their arch-rival, the Hudson's Bay Company. In 1809 he was spurred
on to even greater economic activity by his meeting with Joseph
Howse, a Hudson's Bay man, who was returning from a reconnaissance of the upper Columbia fur preserves. Thus, the following
season, in 1810, Thompson chose not to explore the Columbia to
its mouth. Instead he concentrated on consolidating company gains
by expanding as fast as possible his network of posts and trading
alliances with the friendly Indians who lived west of the Rockies in
the drainage of the upper Columbia. In the summer of 1810 he
headed back to headquarters at Rocky Mountain House on the east
side of the Canadian Rockies, and upon returning in the fall, he was
forced by hostile Blackfeet Indians to detour far to the north via
Athabasca Pass. The mountain crossing in midwinter at a far-
northern latitude was a bitter experience, which was heightened
by even more distressing circumstances at his winter encampment
near the junction of the Canoe and Columbia rivers. The result was
that, though by the spring of 1811 Thompson had undoubtedly decided to descend the Columbia, he had to spend precious months
reorganizing his fur-trade network under the leadership of Finian
McDonald. Thus not until July 3, 1811, did Thompson finally begin
his epic march to the Pacific. As it turned out, this was a year too
late, for when he reached the mouth of the Columbia he found John
Jacob Astor's American fur traders there ahead of him and already
established in Fort Astoria.[7] No greater illustration of the primary
focus of British exploration in Northwest America exists than that
provided by David Thompson. Trade was an end in itself, and meet-

7. Tyrell: *David Thompson's Narrative,* pp. 500-2.

ing the internal competition within the network of the British Empire held priority over everything else.

Despite this orientation, however, the Canadians eventually succeeded in dominating the Northwest largely because of the weakness of American efforts. Thus, thanks to the explorers of the Northwest Company, by the opening of the War of 1812 British interests were in control of the Far Northwest to a point well below the 49th parallel, and there was relatively little save the hostility of the Sioux Indians to prevent them from extending their edge of the frontier even farther southward. Likewise, east of the mountains they were largely in command of the Missouri River north of the Platte. From bases in Wisconsin and Minnesota they regularly used the St. Peter's and Des Moines rivers to tap the Missouri River trade as far downstream as they chose, despite Jay's Treaty and repeated American diplomatic protests. Essentially their intentions were economic rather than political, but at the same time they did not hesitate to resort to military operations when necessary to protect their economic "sphere of influence." No clearer demonstration of this exists than the employment of a man-of-war, the H.M.S. *Raccoon,* to compel the Astorians to surrender their outpost on the Columbia in 1813. Yet, their very role as advance agents of great mercantile combines interested only in the exploitable fur resources, and politically only in the defense of their preserve, gave the Hudson's Bay and Northwest Company explorers a special view of the West. Seldom did they look beyond the trading post and the beaver preserve, and if they did, it was only to lay out portage routes or possible ports of call for sea peddlers on the Pacific Coast. Settlement was anathema to the fur trade, which depended upon an inexhaustible supply of wild animals, and of Indians to catch them. The Canadian explorer, a servant of the company, was conditioned, or "programmed," not to look for future settlement sites but to concentrate on the search for beaver.

2

The American advance into the Northwest came from two directions, the first by sea, as the *Columbia* and other sea-otter traders from New England made landfalls and discoveries on the Pacific Coast, and the second by land, following Lewis and Clark's route out of St. Louis and up the Missouri River. Of these, by far the most important from the point of view of imperial economic rivalries were the various overland excursions northward and westward out of St. Louis.

Even after the success of Lewis and Clark, it was somewhat difficult for would-be American fur traders and entrepreneurs to break into the Mississippi River trade. Consequently, until the 1820's most of the American exploration in the Rocky Mountain West was accomplished as part of the operations of Old World-oriented, St. Louis French trading companies, or on behalf of their hated rival, the bête noire of trans-Mississippia for the next forty years, John Jacob Astor's American Fur Company.

Much has been made of the hustle-and-bustle entrepreneurial spirit of old St. Louis, fur-trading mart of the West, but for a town in the throes of a commercial revolution, St. Louis in the early nineteenth century was remarkably conservative. Its rows of white-washed, verandaed French houses, and its interesting if useless Spanish fortifications, dominated by the crumbling tower of San Carlos, signified its Old World cultural background.[8] Founded in 1764 by Pierre Laclede Liguest as the northern outpost of French Louisiana, St. Louis had been from the beginning a commercial center that attracted French refugees from Illinois and other parts of British America east of the Mississippi. Actually, however, in 1762, to avoid cessation to England, it had been handed over to Spain in a secret treaty, along with all of Louisiana west of the Mississippi, and for the next thirty-seven years it remained a French town under Spanish political rule—a combination involving family economic feudalism and political mercantilism that set the pattern for the town's conservatism.[9]

An outpost of commerce well in advance of the husbandman's frontier, it was viewed by the Spanish as an advanced bastion in the defense of the mines of Mexico. Indeed, to the Spanish all of northern Louisiana, and the great plains to the west, crossed first by Coronado in 1541, and then by the Mallets in 1739 and Pedro Vial in 1792, were one huge buffer that insulated their New World empire from invasion by the profane and aggressive Anglo-Saxons. As a consequence of this view, the Spanish approach to the West was essentially a protective and defensive one, and Spanish ex-

8. James B. Music: *St. Louis as a Fortified Town* (St. Louis, Mo.: R. F. Miller, Printer; 1941), pp. 58–9, 62–7, 70. See also J. Thomas Scharf: *A History of St. Louis City and County,* 2 vols. (Philadelphia: L. H. Everts and Co.; 1883), Vol. I, pp. 268–315.

9. Scharf: *A History of St. Louis,* p. 254. The Spanish rule did not become overt rule until 1770.

plorers, once so bold, became timid and unimpressive. Most of the explorers Spain sent up the Missouri to secure the allegiance of the tribes in defense of the frontier were actually French or Scottish mercenaries. The most successful of these were Joseph Garreau, who in 1787 reached the Arikara Villages near the great loop of the Missouri, and then promptly incurred the enmity of that tribe by his licentious and callous behavior, and Jacques d'Eglise, who reached the Mandan Villages sixty miles above present-day Bismarck, North Dakota.[1]

In 1793, with the permission of the Spanish governor, a trading combine or monopoly entitled the Company for the Exploration of the Upper Missouri was formed under the leadership of Jacques Clamorgan. Its first expedition headed by the schoolmaster Jean Baptiste Truteau was promptly stopped by the Teton Sioux in 1794. In the following year Truteau was allowed to proceed to the Arikara Villages, but that was as far as he got.[2]

The most successful of the Spanish expeditions was led by James Mackay, a former Northwest Company man who had previously visited the Mandans. In 1795 Mackay reached the Omahas on the Missouri before he was stopped, but he had the ingenuity to send his assistant John Evans, a Welshman who was seeking the legendary Welsh Indians, overland to the Mandan Villages, where he thought they might be found. Mackay's instructions to Evans were much more imaginative than those of previous Spanish explorers and were in fact the prototype for the instructions Jefferson issued to Lewis and Clark. Evans was ordered to cross the continent, "in order to discover a passage from the sources of the Missouri to the Pacific Ocean. . . ." And he was further ordered to keep a journal recording latitude, longitude, weather, and winds, and a second

1. A. P. Nasatir, ed.: *Before Lewis and Clark*, 2 vols. (St. Louis, Mo.: St. Louis Historical Documents Foundation; 1952), Vol. I, pp. 82–3. Also see Nasatir: "Jacques d'Eglise on the Upper Missouri, 1791–95," *Mississippi Valley Historical Review* (hereafter *MVHR*), Vol. XIV (1927), pp. 47–56.
2. Nasatir: *Before Lewis and Clark*, Vol. I, pp. 86–91; "Jacques Clamorgan Colonial Promoter of the Northern Border of New Spain," *New Mexico Historical Review*, Vol. XVII (April 1942), pp. 101–12; and "The Formation of the Missouri Company," *Missouri Historical Review*, Vol. XXV (1930–33), pp. 10–22. A more recent account, based on new information, is in Richard Oglesby: *Manuel Lisa and the Opening of the Missouri Fur Trade* (Norman, Okla.: University of Oklahoma Press; 1963), pp. 17-18. Jean Baptiste Truteau: "Journal of Jean Baptiste Truteau, 'première partie,' June 7, 1794–March 26, 1795," *American Historical Review* (hereafter *AHR*), Vol. XIX (1914), pp. 299–333. This Journal is also reprinted in South Dakota Historical Society *Collections*, Vol. VII (1914), pp. 403–74.

journal recording the extent and location of minerals, vegetables, plants, animals, and Indian tribes. All that Evans accomplished, however, was to reach the Mandans and dislodge the British traders from their post for one winter before he returned to St. Louis. With that the Company for the Exploration of the Upper Missouri collapsed, and its guiding spirit, Clamorgan, for a time turned back to the business of trade in areas closer to St. Louis.[3] However, by 1803 the merchants and traders of St. Louis had gained considerable information about the Upper Missouri as single individuals slipped past the Indian blockades and wintered with Upper Missouri tribes or plains Indians as far west as the Black Hills. They knew, for example, of the Yellowstone River and of its tributaries the Powder and Big Horn rivers, and they had heard of volcanic marvels somewhere on the Upper Yellowstone.[4]

The majority of these expeditions were undertaken with the cautious permission of Spanish authority and were financed by the various French trading companies. The most prosperous of these was headed by Auguste Chouteau, whose monopoly of the nearby Osage trade had once been the Lieutenant Governor's prerogative. By and large the French merchants of the city were family-oriented and their firms, with the exception of Clamorgan's combine, were family partnerships with limited capital. Consequently the merchants were reluctant to gamble on long-range, expensive, and far-flung operations. Instead they concentrated on the relatively near at hand and attempted to re-create little feudal empires in the wilderness where, surrounded by servants and relatives, the humble *habitant* could become the *grand seigneur*.

New men, especially Americans, had little chance at first in this bewildering society of Spanish law and interlocking familial directorships where everything pretended to be aristocratic to the core, most of it directed by Madame Chouteau, wife of the founder of the town, who lived to the advanced age of eighty-one, the *grande dame* of frontier society. As if to symbolize their traditionalism and their hold on the town, her sons Pierre and Auguste built what amounted to castles on the edge of the city, their large imposing manor houses surrounded by stone walls, on the inside of which were barns and stables, warehouses, extensive slave quarters, and other buildings

3. Nasatir: *Before Lewis and Clark,* Vol. I, pp. 93–8; and "John Evans, Explorer and Surveyor," *Missouri Historical Review,* Vol. XXV (1930–1), pp. 219–39, 432–60, 585–608.
4. Nasatir: *Before Lewis and Clark,* Vol. I, pp. 91, 101. Also see Annie H. Abel, ed.: "Truteau's Description of the Upper Missouri," *MVHR,* Vol. XIV (1927–28), p. 58.

needed to maintain their domain. At certain times of the year, when the Osage came to town, the grounds of the "castles" would be covered with tepees, and painted chieftains strutting to and fro like noblemen attending some fair of the Middle Ages. It was no wonder that the French of St. Louis, despite their heroic ancestors, were cautious about exploration.[5] They were practical men trying to maintain what they had and re-create something·of the good life of the Old World that their windfall wealth on the frontier afforded them. Exploration was a gamble, and it cost too much. It was really only for desperate men and governments with grandiose designs.

3

One of the most desperate men on the Missouri frontier was a Spaniard from New Orleans named Manuel Lisa. He had arrived in St. Louis in about 1798,[6] and there, in every manner possible for a man with little capital, he sought to make his fortune. The single-mindedness with which he went about it made him one of the most detested and feared men on the entire frontier. A swarthy and sinister man, he was a combination of the conquistador and the frontier opportunist. And it was said by one who knew him that "rascality sat on every feature of his dark complexioned Mexican face."[7] Meriwether Lewis detested him. Governor James Wilkinson feared him, and once ordered him stopped at all costs.[8] His French rivals, particularly the Chouteaus, hated him, and spread rumors about his domestic affairs. On his trips upriver Lisa seldom found it safe to turn his back on his own *engagés*.[9] Yet it was Lisa who, after Lewis and Clark, brought life to Old World St. Louis and

5. Scharf: *A History of St. Louis,* p. 182.
6. Oglesby: *Manuel Lisa,* p. 12. I have also seen the "Official Statement" of Lisa's court dispute with Joseph Robidoux, in the Lisa Papers, Missouri Historical Society, St. Louis, cited by Oglesby in footnote 27, p. 12.
7. Thomas James: *Three Years Among the Indians and Mexicans,* reprint of 1846 edition (Philadelphia: J. B. Lippincott; 1962), p. 22.
8. Gov. James Wilkinson to Zebulon Pike, Aug. 6, 1806, quoted in Walter B. Douglas: "Manuel Lisa," Missouri Historical Society *Collections,* Vol. III (1911), pp. 247–8. See also Zebulon Pike: *The Expeditions of Zebulon Montgomery Pike,* Elliott Coués, ed., 3 vols. (New York: Francis P. Harper; 1895), Vol. II, pp. 574–5.
9. Thomas James: *Three Years,* pp. 5–7, 13–14, 22. Capt. Ruben Holmes: "The Five Scalps," *Missouri Historical Society Glimpses of the Past,* Vol. V (1938).

turned its attention to the Missouri River horizon. His leadership and imagination, along with the financial backing he invariably received, even from his enemies the Chouteaus,[1] provided the initiative that took the Americans up the Missouri River and into the Indian trade. "I put into my operations great activity," he once wrote. "I go a great distance while some are considering whether they will start today or tomorrow. I impose upon myself great privations."[2]

And so he did. Officially thwarted by Governor Wilkinson from opening a trade with Santa Fe, and deprived of his trading rights with the Osage, Lisa immediately grasped the significance of Lewis and Clark's achievement, and turned northward to the Missouri to make his fortune. In April of 1807, backed by William Morrison and Pierre Menard of Kaskaskia, Illinois, he outfitted an expedition of forty-two men, mostly venturesome Americans, and with George Drouillard of the Lewis and Clark expedition as guide, started upriver on the first of his many ventures in that direction— ventures that by the close of the War of 1812 would have won the Missouri River and all the country east of the Rockies for his newly adopted United States of America.[3]

Lisa's plan was to set up forts or trading posts on the upper river that would serve as permanent bases of operation. From these posts, parties of men could move out in every direction to secure the Indian trade at all times in the year. No longer would the traders see the temporary advantage of an annual voyage wiped out by the subsequent trading ventures of their rivals. Moreover, once permanent forts were established, the British to the north would find it more difficult to penetrate his, and the American, domain.

This first expedition up the Missouri River was perhaps the most important of all Lisa's ventures for the history of exploration. Menaced all along the way by hostile Indian tribes—Ponca, Omaha, Sioux, and particularly the Arikara, with whom he narrowly avoided a pitched battle—Lisa made his way far up the Missouri, past the great bend in North Dakota and down the Yellowstone hundreds of miles into virtually unknown territory to the junction of the Big Horn River in central Montana. There

1. Oglesby: *Manuel Lisa,* pp. 67–70.
2. Manuel Lisa to William Clark, St. Louis, July 1, 1817. Quoted in Walter B. Douglas: "Manuel Lisa," Missouri Historical Society *Collections,* Vol. III (1911), p. 382.
3. Ibid., pp. 250–2.

he halted his flotilla and ordered his men to construct a crude fort. Only Antoine Larocque in 1805, William Clark in 1806, and John Colter and his partners the previous winter, had preceded Lisa into this territory. (See map, p. 23.) Unlike the others, however, Lisa had come to stay.[4]

The great significance of Lisa's Fort for the history of exploration is that from it he launched a series of exploring expeditions in all directions that represented in a very real sense the opening up of the Upper Missouri country. In an effort to bring trade to Manuel's Fort, his men visited most of the Indian tribes north of the Wind River Mountains and east of the Continental Divide, and one of his lieutenants, Andrew Henry, crossed over the Divide and established the first American trading post beyond the Rocky Mountains, near Clark's Fork of the Columbia River.[5] In addition to the immense amount of information these men obtained, they established relationships with the Indians which made it possible to secure their allegiance in the crisis with the British in the years to come. They failed only with the Blackfeet, and this was the unavoidable consequence of siding with their traditional enemies, the tribes who were nearer at hand, like the Crows and Flatheads, whose loyalty was apparent and undeniable, and perhaps more useful in the long run than that of the Blackfeet.

Information and trade alliances were the principal objectives of the explorers sent out from Manuel's Fort in the winter of 1807 and in the years that followed. The greatest of these exploring ventures was undertaken by John Colter, one of Lewis and Clark's men. Colter, a Virginian from the Shenandoah Valley, had served the Great Captains as a hunter, and when their expedition reached the Mandan Villages on its way home in 1806, Colter had been honorably discharged to allow him to pursue a hunting-trapping venture on the Yellowstone with William Dixon and Forest Hancock, two traders who had followed the route of the expedition up the Missouri.[6] The previous winter the three partners had trapped the Yellowstone and Big Horn country and then had joined Lisa's company, where, according to Thomas James,[7] most of the men worked on a contract basis, being supplied with powder, shot,

4. Ibid., p. 256. For Larocque, see my footnote 3, p. 10. For Colter, see Burton Harris: *John Colter* (New York: Charles Scribner's Sons; 1952), pp. 53-4.
5. Hiram M. Chittenden: *A History of the American Fur Trade of the Far West*, 2 vols. (Stanford, Calif.: Academic Reprints; 1954), Vol. II, p. 144.
6. Harris: *John Colter*, pp. 36-7.
7. Ibid., pp. 53-4.

traps, and several assistants, in return for a guarantee of their year's catch.

When Colter went out in the winter of 1807, however, he went out alone. Armed with only a pistol and carrying a thirty-pound pack of trade goods, he crossed the wintry peaks of the Big Horn and the Tetons, and as a solitary spectator he looked down upon the windswept beauty of Jackson's Hole, the first civilized man ever to do so. There was no one with him to appreciate the marvels he saw, and since he kept no journal, even his route and the exact object of his mission must remain forever a matter of conjecture. It is known that his first duty was to secure the allegiance of the Indians in the Big Horn Basin to the west of the Fort, but it is also highly probable that Lisa had plans for opening a trade with the Spanish settlements of Santa Fe. Rumor had it, if one is to believe Drouillard's information of that same year, that within several days' march to the south lay Spanish outposts and a great river which led to Santa Fe. By the time Drouillard and Colter were exploring the mountain country to the south and west of Lisa's Fort, Spanish traders out of Santa Fe had been operating as far north as the Green River and possibly the Snake for over forty years.[8] They had also conducted an annual trade with the Arapaho near the North Platte River in Wyoming for an indeterminate period. It is thus highly probable that Colter was in search of the Spanish as well as Indians with beaver skins to trade, and this explains the great range of his trek south and west of the Teton Mountains in 1808.[9]

Further evidence for this conclusion is the fact that in the spring of 1807, at the same time that he launched his first Missouri River expedition, Lisa also formed a secret partnership with Jacques Clamorgan aimed at opening the Santa Fe trade. In December of that year, as Colter was heading for the Yellowstone, Clamorgan and four men entered Santa Fe hoping to trade with the Spaniards.[1] In subsequent years Lisa sent other expeditions south from the Upper Missouri country, and it seems clear that his plan was to establish a transmontane trade route beyond the effective juris-

8. Joseph J. Hill: "Spanish and Mexican Exploration and Trade Northwest from New Mexico into the Great Basin," *Utah Historical Quarterly*, Vol. III (Jan. 1930), *passim*.

9. See map in Nicholas Biddle and Paul Allen, eds.: *History of the Expedition under the Command of Captains Lewis and Clark* (Philadelphia: Bradford and Inskeep; 1814). Harris: *John Colter*, p. 105.

1. Joseph J. Hill: "An Unknown Expedition to Santa Fe in 1807," *MVHR*, Vol. VI (March 1920), pp. 560–2.

diction of the authorities. Colter's expedition must thus have been Lisa's first attempt in this direction.

The evidence for Colter's route is slim. A line on Clark's maps of 1810 and 1814, a blaze on a tree south of Yellowstone Park, and a small stone head found in Pierre's Hole with the name "John Colter" and "1808" carved upon it, plus a few references derived from Colter himself in the works of Bradbury, Brackenridge, and James are all that exists.[2] On the basis of this, historians have assumed that he made a mammoth figure eight to the south and west of Manuel's Fort, extending across the Big Horn Basin and on to the Tetons and what is now Yellowstone Park.[3] He is said to have made his way westward across the Pryor Mountains, a spur of the Big Horns, and then along Clark's Fork of the Yellowstone southwest across the Big Horn Basin to the smaller Sunlight Basin, which lies at the foot of the Absaroka Mountains on the eastern margin of Yellowstone Park. From this point he shifted his direction to southeast and, following the mountains, reached the Shoshone or Stinkingwater River. Then, moving south by southwest past the site of present-day Cody and the extensive and odorous tar pits and thermal springs nearby, which were soon dubbed "Colter's Hell," he worked his way far to the south and around the Absarokas into the Wind River Valley of Wyoming. He was perhaps disappointed at this juncture, having journeyed so many days south, to find no Spanish settlements, or any evidence of the salt caves they were said to have visited.

From this point he turned up the Wind River Valley and crossed into Jackson's Hole over the easy route provided by Togwotee Pass, at the head of the Gros Ventre River. It is not difficult to imagine his emotions as he crossed the pass and saw spread out before him the sublime sight of the Grand Tetons and Jackson

---

2. This evidence is described in Harris: *John Colter*, pp. 73–114.

3. In my account I have generally followed Harris, pp. 73–114, whose investigations of Colter's route have been the most extensive to date. The possibility exists, however, that Colter's progress along the "figure-eight" route was in the reverse direction from that described by Harris. (See Harris's endpaper map.) Colter may well have followed Clark's Fork to the Sunlight Basin, turned *northwest* over the Bannock Trail into the Yellowstone Park area, and from there proceeded southward into Jackson's Hole, over the Tetons, and into Pierre's Hole. This would place him in Pierre's Hole sometime in the winter of 1808, in accordance with the archaeological evidence. From Pierre's Hole he may well have followed the route indicated by Harris, *eastward* instead of westward, around the Absarokas, past Colter's Hell on the Shoshone, down the Shoshone to the Pryor Mountains, and back to Manuel's Fort.

Lake frozen among the pines at the base of the mountains. From Jackson's Hole, however, Colter kept going, now apparently little interested in securing Indians for trade with Manuel's Fort. He crossed over the Tetons via the only pass, and into Pierre's Hole west of the mountains. The date on the carved stone head, 1808, indicates that it must have been late winter or early spring when he made the crossing. Now, however, he swung south again in the direction of possible Spanish settlements on the Rio Colorado to a branch of the Snake, which he mistakenly identified as the Colorado, and which William Clark subsequently named Colter's River. Having gone this far, Colter suddenly turned back and recrossed the Tetons, followed their eastern wall northward past Coulter's (no relation) River, where the slash on the tree was found, and into Yellowstone Park, where he must have discovered Yellowstone Lake.

The principal geyser basins lay west of Colter's route, and he seems to have taken no note of them; instead he followed the western shore of Yellowstone Lake and the Yellowstone River north past the falls and almost to the present-day Mammoth Springs, where he found a much-used Bannock Indian trail that took him over the Snowy Range to the Sunlight Basin once again. At this point the way to Manuel's Fort was clear, but Colter instead retraced his steps of the previous year to the Shoshone River, which he then followed in a northeasterly direction back to Pryor Gap and Manuel's Fort. Thus concluded the first great American exploring trek after Lewis and Clark, and one of the least remembered in history, principally because Colter undertook his expedition alone or accompanied only by wild Indians.

In addition to his great trek of that year, John Colter, while contracted to Manuel Lisa, made four subsequent trips into the Blackfeet country near the sources of the Missouri, each one more dangerous than the last. On one occasion, near the Three Forks, he lay wounded and unable to walk in the midst of a pitched battle between the Blackfeet and the Flatheads. Only the accuracy of his rifle, which he fired while stretched out in a protecting thicket, saved his life and turned the battle in favor of the Flatheads. His success in this battle made it more dangerous than ever for the Americans to trespass on Blackfeet territory. The climax to his adventures came some years later, when at last he was captured by the Blackfeet and forced to run for his life, naked and unarmed, for five miles across a rocky plain between the Jefferson and Madison rivers. He saved himself by plunging into the ice-cold Madison River, where he hid

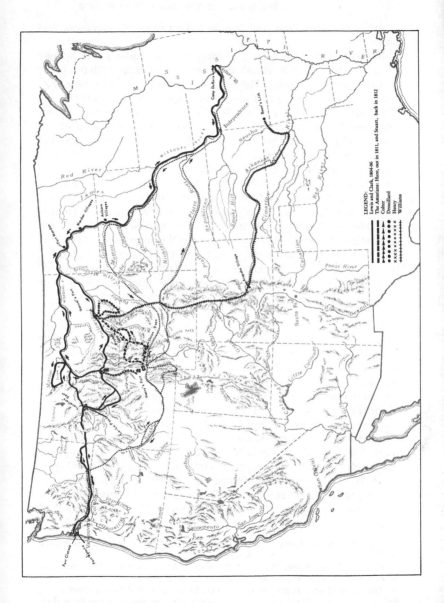

LEGEND:
Lewis and Clark, 1804-06
The Astorians: Hunt, out in 1811, and Stuart, back in 1812
Colter
Drouillard
Henry
Williams

under a tangle of logs and beaver lodges until his pursuers had gone.[4]

In 1810, still in the service of Manuel Lisa, Colter made his last foray into the dreaded Blackfeet country. That year he led a party of thirty-two men to the Three Forks of the Missouri, where they constructed a rude log fort and settled down for the winter's trapping. Almost immediately the Blackfeet fell upon them, and one after another the trappers were massacred. Eventually, after the slaying of the great Drouillard himself, the party broke up, and the remaining men in small bands, Colter included, made their way back to Manuel's Fort on the Yellowstone. The only group that refused to return was the party under Andrew Henry, which crossed over the Continental Divide and established their short-lived but significant first American trading post near Clark's Fork of the Columbia. This post, too, broke up, and the men scattered, but the American frontier had been pushed far to the West, beyond even the Blackfeet. Henry's outpost, though normally deserted, became a landmark for later American trappers. Henry himself, experienced and able, appeared later as a partner in the Rocky Mountain Fur Company. Unlike Colter, he had not had enough of the Upper Missouri.[5]

Other members of Lisa's early venture on the Upper Missouri also made notable contributions to the history of exploration, and to the American advance into the Far West. George Drouillard, who was killed so tragically at the Three Forks in 1810, explored much of the Big Horn Basin and Yellowstone River country in 1808. He conducted two separate expeditions that year into the country south of Manuel's Fort. But the real importance of Drouillard's work lies in the fact that he incorporated his information on a crude but accurate map, the first one known to have been drawn by a mountain man. This proved especially useful to William Clark in compiling his great maps of the West, particularly his unpublished map begun in 1810, which he constantly revised and brought up to date according to the latest information from the traders, and which for this reason is superior to the more famous published version of 1814.[6]

4. John Bradbury: *Travels in the Interior of America* (London: Sherwood Neeley and Jones; 1817), pp. 18–21.
5. Donald McKay Frost: *Notes on General Ashley, the Overland Trail and South Pass* (Barre, Mass.: *Barre Gazette*; 1960), pp. 12–13.
6. The original of this map is in the Yale Collection of Western Americana, Beinecke Library, Yale University. A reproduction of the map has been published by the library.

One especially interesting aspect of Drouillard's map bore on the whole question of frontiers directly. This was the series of notations which he made regarding the proximity of the Spanish settlements to the south. The men of Lisa's expedition in particular, and explorers of the period in general, seemed obsessed with two basic ideas. The first was that all of the great rivers of the West had a common source, which must be found. The second was that from the Upper Missouri, or at least from the Yellowstone, it was but a few days' ride to the hidden citadels of the Spanish empire. Not only the Americans believed this, but the Spanish, having reached the Green River country and the Platte, believed it too.

These two basic ideas regarding the nature of Western geography are perfectly embodied in Drouillard's map, which must thus have been a source of future misconceptions in more famous works. On the Drouillard map are several references to Spanish settlements lying due south, and the number of days which, according to the Indians, it took to reach them. At one point near the Salt Fork is the notation: "Salt Fork is believed to be [illegible] salt, the Spaniards obtain it from this place by crossing over from the river Colorado. . . ." This statement clearly implies the belief that the Colorado River flowed close by, east of the Continental Divide. It further incorporates the idea that a normal commerce was maintained by the Upper Missouri Indians with the Spanish on that river.[7] Undoubtedly because he misunderstood this and similar notations, and because John Colter's discoveries seemed to fit in with it so well, William Clark on his official map of the West made the error of representing the headwaters of the Rio Grande and the Colorado, with their Spanish settlements, in close proximity to the Big Horn and the Yellowstone.[8] The further discoveries of Zebulon Pike only served to add to this misconception, for Pike believed that near the upper Rio Grande was a "grand reservoir" of snows and fountains where all the rivers of the West came together.[9] Thus in this respect the Drouillard, Colter, and Pike expeditions were all of a piece, and together they added up to a remarkable exercise in fictional geography which marred Clark's map and hence, since he was the governor of the whole Louisiana Territory, the government's view of the West, eliminating entirely the Central Rockies. But, more important, it helped to intensify the competition between

7. A reproduction of the Drouillard map appears in Wheat: *Mapping the American West,* Vol. II.
8. Clark map, see footnote 6 on preceding page.
9. Pike: *The Expeditions* . . . , Coués, ed., Vol. II, pp. 523–4.

Section of William Clark's master map of the American West, 1810, one of the most important maps ever made in America. Clark kept this map in his St. Louis office and recorded on it not only his own discoveries but all the information brought into St. Louis by trappers and travelers on the Upper Missouri. It is far more detailed than the 1814 map published with the Biddle narrative of the Lewis and Clark expedition. *Courtesy Yale Western Americana Collection*

Spaniard and American over the entire Rocky Mountain West.
A corrective to this erroneous view of Western geography might
have been supplied by another of Lisa's explorers, the little-known
Ezekial Williams, who in August of 1811 joined a party of twenty-
one trappers led by Lisa's trusted lieutenant Jean Baptiste Champlain, and headed due south from Lisa's Fort on the Big Horn in the
direction of the Spanish settlements.[1] (See map, p. 23.) Apparently, after trapping along the Big Horn mountains, the party eventually broke up on the upper Platte River near Casper, Wyoming.
Williams and a small group continued on to the Arkansas; another
group crossed the Rockies due west from the Platte and perished at
the hands of the Arapaho. Still a third group, led by a man named
Workman, was said to have crossed over the Sangre de Cristo Mountains southwest to Santa Fe and eventually continued on to California. The only record of such an occurrence in either Spanish or
American archives is a notation in the archives of Chihuahua that
four Frenchmen had reached Santa Fe on June 30, 1812, declaring
their "dislike of American rule."[2] The Spaniards, suspicious of their
motives, took them to Chihuahua, then to Arispe, where they were
cast into prison and there presumably remained. Williams, after
spending a season hunting in the Bayou Salade or South Park of
Colorado, was captured by the Arapaho and after many hardships
he was rescued, months later, by two of Manuel Lisa's Indian traders. He arrived at Boon's Lick trading post on September 1, 1813.[3]

The importance of the Williams expedition, despite the scanty
information it furnished, was obvious. For one thing, it established
the existence of a chain of mountains, the Central Rockies, which
now form most of the state of Colorado. The Spanish settlements
of New Mexico and Manuel's Fort on the Yellowstone did not, in

1. For the only reliable account of Williams's travels, see "Ezekial Williams'
Adventures in Colorado," Missouri Historical Society *Collections,* Vol. IV
(1912–13), pp. 194–208, which includes an article from the Kaskaskia
Western Intelligencer for July 9, 1816, and a letter from Ezekial Williams
himself to the editor of the Missouri *Gazette* (Sept. 14, 1816), relating his
adventures. The date of Williams's excursion into Colorado is somewhat uncertain, due to conflicting evidence, as is indicated in this article. I have accepted Williams's own chronology, which is confirmed by Manuel Lisa's letter
of Sept. 8, 1812, to the Spaniards of New Mexico. See Herbert E. Bolton:
"New Light on Manuel Lisa and the Spanish Fur Trade," *The Southwestern
Historical Quarterly,* Vol. XVII (1913–14), p. 62. David Coyner's *The Lost
Trappers* (Cincinnati, Ohio: J. A. and U. P. James; 1847) is a fictionalized
account of Williams's travels.
2. Bolton: "New Light . . . ," p. 61 n.
3. See footnote 1 on this page.

fact, lie on opposite sides of a single mountain ridge. Instead, there was a tremendous country in between, rich in beaver and hostile Indians. Thus, although the best maps of the day indicated that Santa Fe was not far from the headwaters of the Yellowstone, at least one member of Lisa's company survived to say nay. Ezekial Williams had seen the mountain country, explored the Platte, spanned the immense mountain distance from north to south, and, long before anyone else in his profession, floated down the Arkansas to civilization. In effect, he had discovered Colorado. All of this gave him a fairly good idea of the distance between the Mississippi settlements and the Rocky Mountains. He had traversed the beaver kingdom from north to south and from east to west, and his exploration anticipated many of those later adventures which would partially direct the attention of the fur traders away from the Upper Missouri and onto the Central Rockies.

4

For the fur trade, Lisa's ventures to the Yellowstone had a clear significance. They opened the Upper Missouri to the St. Louis traders and indeed advertised its importance as virgin ground for new exploitation. Economically he had brought St. Louis to life, and socially he introduced a new type to its staid backwoods aristocracy, the opportunist of the middle class who had his fortune to make and saw the frontier as the place to make it, not only in the fur trade, but in transportation, land, merchandising, banking, and even government service, in all of which pursuits Lisa had a hand—and after whom the enterprising Americans and even the conservative French would follow.

Knowledge is power, runs the axiom—and after his first few trips to the Upper Missouri, Lisa had both. His explorers furnished him with information about the geography and the Indians which he in turn used and passed on to government officials like William Clark; and this gave him prestige and influence in the community. Policy turned oftentimes on his advice. And, it must be said, Lisa was by the same token grateful to Governor Clark and the United States for his newly won status. "I have suffered enough in person and property under a different government to know how to appreciate the one under which I now live," he wrote in 1818.[4]

So important was Lisa's experience, and the information avail-

4. Douglas: "Manuel Lisa," p. 382.

able to him during the War of 1812, that in 1814 he was made official Indian Agent for the tribes of the Upper Missouri. And his influence among the Sioux, Omaha, and the Poncas thwarted the efforts of Robert Dickson, the British trader in that area, to turn all of the northern Indians against the Americans.[5] As it turned out, this was the last stand by the British in the Near Northwest, and Lisa, thanks to his knowledge of the geography and the Indians, managed to save a fur-trade empire for his adopted United States.

But beyond all this, as Governor Clark's personal manuscript map of the West began to take shape, based on Lisa's information, and that of others, the interconnectedness and the importance of the whole Far Western frontier from the Upper Missouri to the mines of Mexico became more apparent every day. (See map, p. 26.) It was a vast field for enterprise—enterprise of many kinds—and the fur trade would be only a part of it, albeit an important part. But there would be others, merchants, missionaries, soldiers, farmers, miners, artists, scientists,[6] and town builders, who would follow

5. Ibid., pp. 375–9. See also Ernest A. Cruikshank: "Robert Dickson the Indian Trader," Wisconsin Historical Society *Collections*, Vol. XII (1892). So dedicated to his mission was Manuel Lisa that he married Metain, an Omaha squaw, to secure the aid of that tribe against the British. Lisa's wife back in St. Louis seems to have expressed no resentment at this arrangement.

6. Though a detailed account of their activities has been omitted from the narrative, it should be noted that in 1811 the traveler and geographer Henry Marie Brackenridge journeyed up the Missouri River with Manuel Lisa. In addition, that same year John Bradbury and Thomas Nuttall, two botanists of some experience, accompanied Wilson Price Hunt's Astorian expedition upriver to the Arikara Villages. When Hunt turned west on his overland journey, Bradbury and Brackenridge returned to St. Louis. Nuttall continued on with Lisa to the Mandan Villages, thus becoming the first botanist to explore that region. He returned to St. Louis in the early autumn, made his way to New Orleans, and sailed for England just before the outbreak of the War of 1812. Later he returned to the United States and made other notable Western excursions to the Arkansas River in 1819, and to Oregon in 1834–5 with Nathaniel Wyeth. Having begun his career as a collector for Benjamin Smith Barton of Philadelphia, Nuttall ultimately became a professor of botany at Harvard. The most recent account of the work of these early botanists is Susan Delano McKelvey: *Botanical Exploration of the Trans-Mississippi West* (Jamaica Plain, Mass.: Arnold Arboretum; 1955), pp. 103–49. See also John Bradbury: *Travels in the Interior of America in the Years 1809, 1810 and 1811;* and Henry Marie Brackenridge: *Views of Louisiana: together with a journal of a voyage up the Missouri River in 1811* (Pittsburgh: Cramer, Spear and Eickbaum; 1814). Both Bradbury's "Travels" and Brackenridge's "Journal" were reprinted in Reuben Gold Thwaites: *Early Western Travels* (Glendale, Calif., 1904), Vols. V and VI respectively. Nuttall's *A Journal of Travels into the Arkansas Territory During the Year 1819* (Philadelphia: T. H. Palmer; 1821) was also reprinted in Thwaites: *Early Western Travels*, Vol. XIII.

and inherit the West. The old French aristocratic regime was already passing by 1805, and the new men were coming. With them would come a new commercial flexibility and a new sense of mission and government based upon it. This was to be their secret weapon in the struggle for an empire beyond the Mississippi. It would govern almost entirely the way in which they as explorers and settlers viewed the West.

5

Manuel Lisa's explorers, however, were not the only Americans to probe the Rocky Mountain West in the years after Lewis and Clark descended the Missouri. America's leading merchant, John Jacob Astor, a curious, incredibly energetic German immigrant who had parlayed a cargo of flutes into a maritime and fur-trade empire, had conceived a plan for occupying and exploiting the Columbia River and the Rocky Mountains as early as 1808. While on one of his fur-buying trips to Montreal he heard Alexander Henry discoursing on McKenzie's march to the Pacific and the fortune that awaited the man who could establish a port on the Pacific that would tap the fur trade of the interior and carry the goods to market in Canton.[7] By 1810, with Jefferson's tacit approval, Astor had formed just such a company. Spurned in his overtures to the conservative St. Louis traders,[8] he had formed his own combine, the Pacific Fur Company, modeled on the McKenzie and Henry plan, which had grown out of the previous Canadian experience in the West. He himself put up the money, and a group of Canadian and American partners were added to manage the complex field operations of this far-flung enterprise.[9]

By the sixth of September 1810, Astor's ship, the *Tonquin*, had cleared from New York harbor loaded with men and supplies for the establishment of a fur-trading post at the mouth of the Columbia. After an eventful voyage around the Horn and through the Pacific via Hawaii, the *Tonquin* reached its destination, and on April 12, 1811, with the partners Duncan M'Dougal and David Stuart in

7. Kenneth Wiggins Porter: *John Jacob Astor, Business Man* (Cambridge, Mass.: Harvard University Press; 1931), Vol. I, p. 170. For Astor's early career, see pp. 3–164.
8. Ibid., p. 168. See also David Lavender: *Bent's Fort* (New York: Doubleday and Co.; 1954), pp. 32–46.
9. Ibid., pp. 169–70.

charge, the party began the construction of Fort Astoria at the mouth of the Columbia River, which, along with the voyage of the *Columbia* and Lewis and Clark's expedition, established an American claim to the Columbia River and its interior drainage.[1] It seems clear that, from the beginning, trade, rather than a political claim, was Astor's objective. His partners were mostly Canadian, the master of his ship the *Tonquin* was more interested in China than in colonization on the Northwest Coast, and most of the operation on both land and sea was in the hands of men of commerce rather than colonizers.[2] In short, Astor's operation, though he later claimed a patriotic motive for it, was actually an attempt to beat the great Hudson's Bay and Northwest companies at their own game by establishing economic claim to a vast tract of untouched and exploitable beaver country.

The most significant of Astor's operations for the history of exploration were the overland marches between St. Louis and the Columbia led by Wilson Price Hunt and Robert Stuart. In June of 1810, even before the *Tonquin* had left New York, and while Manuel Lisa's men were setting up their post in the Blackfeet country, Wilson Price Hunt, a St. Louis clerk, assisted by Donald McKenzie, a Falstaffian veteran of the Canadian fur trade who weighed some 300 pounds, went to Montreal and began recruiting men for an overland march to the Pacific. By the time they left St. Louis in the early spring of 1811, however, they had exchanged most of their French-Canadians for Americans.[3]

Starting from the Arikara Villages on the Missouri on the eighteenth of July 1811, Wilson Price Hunt's expedition was the second great overland crossing after Lewis and Clark (see map, p. 23). It was accomplished with far greater difficulty, however, since after crossing the Dakotas and the Big Horn Mountains and reaching Henry's Fort on a branch of the Columbia, via Union Pass and Jackson's Hole, Hunt and McKenzie decided to abandon their horses

---

1. The best account of this voyage is Washington Irving: *Astoria, or Anecdotes Of An Enterprise Beyond the Rocky Mountains,* 2 vols. (Philadelphia: Carey, Lea, and Blanchard; 1836). Also see Gabriel Franchere: *Narrative of a Voyage to the Northwest Coast of America in the Years 1811, 1812, 1813, and 1814 . . .*, trans. and ed. by J. V. Huntington (Redfield, N.Y., 1854), which is reprinted in Thwaites: *Early Western Travels,* Vol. VI; and Ross Cox: *Adventures on the Columbia River . . .*, 2 vols. (London: H. Colburn and R. Bentley; 1831).

2. Ibid.

3. Irving: *Astoria,* Vol. I, pp. 131–47. Unless otherwise stated, the account of Hunt's overland expedition is based on Irving.

and set out down the Snake River in boats. They quickly found the Snake River impossible, and the party broke up into smaller groups before they even reached the main Columbia. Starvation was imminent, and dogs, horses, beaver paws, and even skins and roots became providential fare to the stranded explorers. It was the eighteenth of January 1812 before the first of the party led by McKenzie reached Fort Astoria, and February 15, before Hunt and the main party finally came up. Ramsay Crooks and John Day, two other partners, were robbed by Indians and remained stranded in the wilderness until the late spring, when they were finally rescued by one of the Astorian fur brigades.

Despite the disaster that accompanied it, Hunt's overland crossing was significant for several reasons. He had discovered a vital pass around the north end of the Wind River Mountains (Union Pass), which was south of the route taken by Lewis and Clark, and in so doing had opened up the Wind River and the Snake River country to the American fur trade. In addition he had proven that the overland trek to the Pacific, although extraordinarily difficult, was nevertheless possible. But perhaps most important, the incredible hardships of the overland journey had impressed Hunt with the barrenness of the Snake country, and none save McKenzie saw any possibility for future settlement in the area. It was not even regarded at the time as good beaver country. Considerations of this kind undoubtedly were a determining factor in the Astor partners' subsequent decision to abandon Fort Astoria to the British without a fight.

While Hunt was making his way across the continent, the *Tonquin* sailed away from the Columbia and up the Northwest Coast, where its crew were ultimately massacred by Indians, and the ship itself blown up, along with its two hundred Indian conquerors aboard, by a last desperate survivor of the unfortunate crew.[4] In July of 1812 David Thompson arrived at the fort, after having come down the Columbia, and claimed all the interior lands

4. Ibid., pp. 119–20. Also see Franchere, as reprinted in Thwaites: *Early Western Travels*, Vol. VI, pp. 291–2. Both of these accounts are based on a description of the events given by the sole survivor of the disaster, an Indian interpreter. Irving's version, however, mentions the presence on board the *Tonquin* of the ship's clerk Lewis, who was "mortally wounded" and, after inviting the Indians to come aboard, "disappeared," after which the ship blew up along with over two hundred of the Indians. Franchere, who heard the same story from the same Indian interpreter, makes no mention of Lewis. I have followed Irving, principally because of the persuasiveness of his concrete detail in describing other aspects of the incident.

for the Crown.[5] And on June 19, 1812, though Thompson was not yet aware of it, war was declared between Great Britain and the United States. This proved to be a decisive event, for in March of 1813 John George McTavish and a band of ragged Northwest Company men arrived at Fort Astoria and demanded its surrender to the British. They were actually in no position to demand anything. But they expected the arrival of the *Isaac Todd,* an armed English merchantman, which would have supported their claim. Though the *Isaac Todd* failed to arrive, a second Northwest Company brigade appeared and eventually, in November, the H.M.S. *Raccoon,* a British ship of the line, crossed the bar and put in at Astoria, demanding its surrender.[6] By that time, however, the partners, most of whom were Canadian to begin with, had already decided to sell out to the Northwest Company for whatever they could get, and either accept positions with the British company or make their way back to New York. There was thus nothing for the *Raccoon* to conquer, and the first American outpost on the Pacific had collapsed without a fight. West of the Rocky Mountains as far south as they chose to go, the Northwest Company ruled supreme.

The surrender of Astoria did not take place, however, before the most important of Astor's exploring expeditions was launched. On June 29, 1812, Robert Stuart and six men—Crooks, McLellan, Jones, Le Claire, Vallé, and Day—started on the return march across the continent from Astoria to New York.[7] Stuart's route was slightly south of that taken by Hunt on his outward trip (see map, p. 23). With some minor differences, it was the route that later became the Oregon Trail. Like Hunt before him, Stuart found the overland crossing far more difficult than would the later Oregon settlers. John Day went insane and had to be returned to Astoria. After that, they found the Blue Mountains and the valley of the Snake River, as it curved southward through Idaho, extremely difficult to traverse. Then, fearing the Crow Indians, they made a useless detour far to the north, crossing the Tetons into Jackson's Hole, where they reached the point of near starvation before a lone buffalo

5. Franchere, in Thwaites: *Early Western Travels,* p. 253. Also see Tyrell: *David Thompson's Narrative,* p. 501.
6. Franchere, in Thwaites: *Early Western Travels,* pp. 298–9.
7. Unless otherwise stated, the account of Robert Stuart's overland trip is based on Philip Ashton Rollins, ed.: *The Discovery of the Oregon Trail: Robert Stuart's Narratives of His Overland Trip Eastward From Astoria in 1812–13* (New York: Charles Scribner's Sons; 1935). I have also studied Stuart's original manuscript journal and traveling memoranda at the Yale Collection of Western Americana.

bull providentially appeared. The most important part of their trip was their route out of Jackson's Hole. Instead of following Hunt's trail to the north of the Wind River Mountains, they followed an Indian trail to the west of the Mountains, and on Friday, the twenty-third of October, 1812, they discovered the South Pass of the Rocky Mountains at the lower, or southern, end of the Wind River Range. Twenty miles wide, it was a series of mounting hills, which John C. Frémont later declared to be no more precipitous than Capitol Hill in Washington. On the west was Pacific Spring. On the east was the Sweetwater and the Platte. It formed the foremost gateway in the entire West, through which countless thousands of American emigrants would pass on their way to Oregon and California.

After traversing the South Pass, Stuart's party wintered near the Sweetwater and, later in December, on the Platte far out across the Nebraska plains. With the coming of spring they again took up the march, following the Platte River downstream. On the thirteenth of April they met some Oto Indians who told them of the war with England. When they arrived in St. Louis on April 30, 1813, the whole city turned out at the water's edge to greet them. It was like a second coming of the Great Captains Lewis and Clark.

6

The contrast between Astor's fur-trade operation and Lisa's was striking. Whereas Lisa had envisaged a string of posts that would hold the Upper Missouri, Astor had been more interested in the maritime trade of the Pacific, and particularly in exploiting the fur resources of the Columbia for export to Canton. His eye was on the passage to India, with the Pacific Northwest a station on the way. Moreover, in pursuing his aims he hired no free trappers, but instead imitated the operations of the British companies, with which he was so familiar. Furs and profits, not settlement, were his aims. This was reflected in the surrender of Astoria by his partners. They appeared not to have considered a retreat into the interior or into the Willamette Valley, both of which would have been unprofitable but feasible operations. Instead they thought like entrepreneurs and citizens of the world, and sold out of an unprofitable situation rather than defend some "worthless" soil.

Likewise, it was a long time before the importance of the Astorians' discoveries became public knowledge. The journals of

Hunt and Stuart and the others became Astor's personal property, and like a good businessman he shared very little of his "inside" information with the outside world until in his old age he persuaded Washington Irving to write *Astoria* in celebration of the glories of his fur-trade enterprise.[8] In retrospect, however, the information gained by Hunt, Stuart, and the traders who operated out of Astoria in the Columbia Basin was considerable, and had it been made generally available it would have been of real value to the United States in the struggle for the West. Stuart, for example, was clearly aware of his achievement in locating a suitable trail to Oregon and even suggested that wagons might be taken as far west as the Snake River.[9] As it turned out, however, this information remained in the hands of Astor. Among the survivors, there was only the general impression of hardship and starvation. This was not so for McKenzie, however. Upon his rejection by Astor in 1815, he returned to Canada and between 1816 and 1821 opened up the Snake River country to Canadian enterprise by his daring leadership of the fur brigades of the Northwest Company. In the long run, therefore, Astor's adventure on the Pacific, unlike Lisa's operations on the Missouri, added very little to the American advance into the Far West. Instead, paradoxically, it enabled the British to push deep into the heart of the Rocky Mountain West and to dominate for a time all the country west of the mountains and north of the Great Salt Lake, which marked the boundary of the Spanish domain in the heart of the mountain West.

8. Stanley T. Williams: *The Life of Washington Irving*, 2 vols. (New York: Oxford University Press; 1935), Vol. II, pp. 74–5.
9. *Missouri Gazette*, May 15, 1813, quoted in Rollins: *The Discovery of the Oregon Trail*, p. lxvii.

CHAPTER II

The Rediscovery of the Southwest

WHILE Lewis and Clark were making their way to the Pacific, and David Thompson was preparing to cross the Canadian Rockies via the Saskatchewan River, American explorers—fur traders, soldiers, scientists, and gentleman adventurers—had already begun to look toward the Southwest, where rumor had it that the Spaniards were guarding the approaches to a land of gold and silver. In part, the initial impetus to American exploration in this region came from the fact that no one was quite sure of the value and extent of President Jefferson's recent purchase of Louisiana as it stretched away toward the West and South. But from the beginning the primary objective of Americans who went toward the Southwest was Santa Fe, and the commercial wealth in various forms which it appeared to be so jealously guarding.

The Southwest itself, as nineteenth-century Americans viewed it, was a remote area that seemed to hold the destiny of the continent quite as much as the celebrated Northwest Passage. It included present-day Arizona and New Mexico, and parts of Texas, California, Utah, Nevada, Colorado, Kansas, and Oklahoma, but to Americans dependent upon variations of Humboldt's Atlas to his *Political Essay on the Kingdom of New Spain*[1] it was largely a terra incognita and would remain so for some time.

To speak of an American "discovery" of the Southwest is pre-

1. Alexander von Humboldt: *Essai Politique sur le Royaume de Nouvelle-Espagne*, 4 vols. (Paris: F. Schaell; 1811); see Atlas. This map was actually completed in 1809. The most important variation of Humboldt's map was Aaron Arrowsmith's "A new map of Mexico and Adjacent Provinces," published on October 5, 1810. See Wheat: *Mapping the American West: a Preliminary Study* (Worcester, Mass., American Antiquarian Society; 1954), p. 45 *n.*

Zebulon Pike's map of New Spain, based upon Alexander von Humboldt's 1811 map. *Courtesy Library of Congress*

sumptuous. Rather, when the explorers of the nineteenth century reached out from St. Louis and Natchez and Boon's Lick towards the brick-kiln towns of Santa Fe and Taos, they were really entering a region which for nearly three centuries had been the scene of spectacular and almost unbelievable feats of discovery by small parties of clanking Spanish knights and zealous, hard-bitten missionaries. From 1536, when Alvar Núñez Cabeza de Vaca and four companions first stumbled into a camp of slavehunters in northern Sinaloa after a fantastic odyssey across the Southwest from the Gulf Coast of Texas to New Mexico and the Spanish frontier,[2] down through the early years of the nineteenth century, the Spanish had been remarkably active in exploring the whole northern frontier of the Spanish empire, which one historian has aptly called the "Rim of Christendom."[3]

Spurred on by the image of the great Cortez, and by myths of golden lakes and fabled Aztec treasure troves, by stories of lost civilizations and Indians who gave away golden baubles for the asking, and perhaps most of all by visions of the legendary Strait of Anian, expedition after expedition departed into the unknown, to meet disappointment and often death. Nowhere perhaps was the distinctively Spanish "tragic sense of life" better demonstrated than in these expeditions to the northern frontier of mesa and desert and canyon. For though they all failed in their search for the Strait of Anian and for another Tenochtitlán, failed even to hold the country they first discovered, they opened up an immense new land to the forces of civilization. And their failure was on such a grand scale, their heroism so great, that success itself really became irrelevant in the light of history.

By the time the German explorer Alexander von Humboldt published his monumental *Carte Générale de Royaume de Nouvelle-Espagne* in 1811,[4] Spanish explorers had crossed Texas and explored the whole Gulf Coast eastward to Florida and northward as far as Tennessee.[5] They had moved westward across Arizona

2. De Voto: *The Course of Empire*, pp. 11–21. See also Cleve Hallenbeck: *Alvar Núñez Cabeza de Vaca* (Glendale, Calif.: Arthur H. Clark Co.; 1940); and Carl O. Sauer: "The Discovery of New Mexico Reconsidered," *New Mexico Historical Review*, Vol. XII (1937), pp. 270–87.
3. Herbert E. Bolton: *Rim of Christendom: A Biography of Eusebio Francisco Kino, Pacific Coast Pioneer* (New York: The Macmillan Co.; 1936).
4. See footnote 1, p. 36.
5. Frederick W. Hodge and Theodore H. Lewis: *Spanish Explorers in the Eastern United States 1528–1543* (New York: Charles Scribner's Sons; 1907).

and the Colorado River to California, in the course of which
García López de Cárdenas became the first civilized man to view
the Grand Canyon.[6] By 1776, due to the remarkable labors of Padre
Silvestre Vélez de Escalante, they had crossed the mountains and
deserts of northern New Mexico, Colorado, and Utah and reached
the Great Salt Lake Basin at Utah Lake.[7] And from the beginning,
when Coronado marched to Quivira (in Kansas), they had been
familiar with the endless prairies over which the Americans would
come centuries later.[8] The roll of Spanish explorers on which
Humboldt could draw for his map was a resounding list of heroic
and sometimes cruel conquistadors in monks' robes and chain mail.
First came Niza of the fabulous imagination; then down through
the centuries Coronado, De Soto, Cárdenas, Espejo, Rodríguez, the
brothers Zaldivar, Kino, Castaño de Sosa, Oñate, López, Bonilla,
Humaña, Escalante, Miera, Alarcón, Ulloa, Portolá, Serra, Malgares,
and of course, Cabeza de Vaca.[9] But for most men of the nineteenth
century the details of Spanish exploration had been all but forgotten,
so that when the Frenchman Baptiste La Lande and the Americans
James Purcell and Zebulon Pike began their adventures in the
Southwest, the essential task confronting them was one of rediscovery, of regaining the knowledge that had been lost. It proved to
be a task scarcely less exacting than the original discovery itself.

6. De Voto: *Course of Empire*, p. 38.
7. Herbert E. Bolton: *Pageant in the Wilderness, Escalante's Journal* (Salt
Lake City: Utah State Historical Society; 1950). Also published as *Utah
Historical Quarterly*, Vol. XVIII (1950). See also Herbert S. Auerbach:
"Father Escalante's Route," *Utah Historical Quarterly*, Vol. IX (Jan.–April
1941). I have also examined a manuscript copy of the journal of Escalante's
expedition, in the Yale Collection of Western Americana, and an original
copy of Miera y Pacheca's map of the journey.
8. Bolton: *Coronado: A Knight of Pueblos and Plains* (New York: Whittlesey
House; 1949). Also see George P. Hammond and Agapito Rey, eds.: *Narratives of the Coronado Expedition, 1540–1542*, 2 vols. (Albuquerque, N.M.:
The Quivira Society; 1940).
9. Most of these men are considered in De Voto: *Course of Empire*. Also see
Paul Horgan: *Great River*, 2 vols. (New York: Rinehart & Co.; 1954), Vol. I;
and see David Lavender: *Bent's Fort* (New York: Doubleday & Co.; 1954),
p. 13, for a recent brief account of Bonilla and Humaña. Herbert E. Bolton,
ed.: *Spanish Exploration in the Southwest* (New York: Charles Scribner's
Sons; 1916, 1925, 1930) treats some of the more obscure Spanish explorers.

2

The first Americans to venture into the Southwest were not explorers but traders and fortune-seekers. In the spring of 1804, William Morrison of Kaskaskia, soon to become the silent partner of Manuel Lisa, turned his attention to the possibilities of establishing trade between St. Louis and Santa Fe. He outfitted a French Creole named Baptiste La Lande with a small supply of trade goods and sent him in the general direction of the Pawnee Villages on the Platte River, from which point it was hoped La Lande would be able to find his way to Santa Fe. The Frenchman proved to be extremely resourceful. He made his way up the South Platte River to the mountain barrier, and then, as he moved south along the Rocky Mountains he ascertained that Santa Fe was somewhere to the south, and he sent a delegation of Indians into the Spanish stronghold to inform the officials there of his whereabouts and ask them to come for him. As a result he was escorted into the city, introduced to its comforts and pleasures, and in general treated very well—so well in fact that when the time came to think of returning to St. Louis, La Lande looked around at the comely señoritas and the lazy life, and decided to stay. If Morrison wanted his money, let him brave the prairies and the Pawnees and the Spaniards and come collect it himself.[1]

La Lande was not the only American adventurer on the prairies in 1804. An American trader at Natchitoches named Saunders started up the Red River that same year and managed to make it to the southern Pawnee Villages some 500 miles up the river before he was escorted back downstream by Spanish soldiers. In 1805 James Purcell, or "Pursley," as Zebulon Pike called him, cut loose from a band of trappers along the Platte River and made his way to Santa Fe, where he had settled down as a Spanish subject when Pike arrived.[2] How many others, singly or in small groups, drifted across the prairies to the Spanish capital during these years is unknown, for by and large their activities were illegal—a kind of filibustering—and they were kept secret whenever possible. With little private information to go on, therefore, the real initiative for exploration in this direction came from the federal government in

1. Chittenden: *Fur Trade*, Vol. II, p. 491.
2. Ibid., pp. 492–3. Also see Zebulon Pike: *The Expeditions of Zebulon Montgomery Pike*, Elliott Coués, ed., Vol. II, pp. 756–7.

the persons of Thomas Jefferson, the President, and James Wilkinson, the sinister military governor of Louisiana.

3

Jefferson, having just completed the purchase of Louisiana from the French, saw it as the first order of business to learn the nature and extent of his recent acquisition. With a fair amount of historical precedent, he viewed the French claim as including the Mississippi River and all its tributaries as far as their respective sources somewhere in "the Stony Mountains." The Spaniards, who were in actual control in the Southwest, disagreed with this point of view and used whatever means they could to prevent the Americans from exploring the Platte, the Arkansas, the Red, and any other of the western tributaries of the Mississippi which they regarded as being purely Spanish rivers. But Jefferson was determined to have the disputed rivers explored in order to accumulate enough geographical information to be able to bargain intelligently with Spain regarding the southwestern boundary between the two countries.

Accordingly, on July 15, 1803, the President sent a list of seventeen basic questions to important governmental and scientific figures in the Southwest, including Ephraim Kirby, the boundary commissioner; Daniel Clark, United States consul at New Orleans; William Dunbar, a gentleman scientist from Natchez; and W. C. C. Claiborne, the acting governor of the Louisiana Territory. The questions concerned the geography, population, laws, and extent of the newly acquired Louisiana Territory, and were intended to provide Congress with enough information to justify receiving Louisiana formally into the Union.[3]

In answer to his letter Jefferson received replies from Clark, Claiborne, and Dunbar, and an important statistical résumé of the country from John Sibley, a physician who had left Natchez for the frontier settlement of Natchitoches in early 1803 and who in 1805 had explored parts of the Red River.[4] None of these reports, however, gave exact information as to the correct western border of the Louisiana Purchase, and Jefferson, dependent on the vague eight-

3. Paul Leicester Ford, ed.: *The Writings of Thomas Jefferson* (New York: G. P. Putnam's Sons; 1897), Vol. VIII, pp. 252–5. Also see Isaac J. Cox: "The Exploration of the Louisiana Frontier, 1803–1806," *AHR* (1904), p. 152.
4. Cox: "The Exploration of the Louisiana Frontier," p. 152.

eenth-century Spanish maps of the region, soon decided to send out a series of special expeditions to investigate and explore the country.

The first of these expeditions, led by William Dunbar and Dr. George Hunter of Philadelphia, got underway on October 16, 1804.[5] (See map, p. 48.) Originally projected as an exploration of the Red River, it was thwarted by hostile Osage Indians and turned to the Ozark Plateau instead. The expedition took four months in all, and the scientific data, though of limited value, was incorporated into Jefferson's annual message to Congress of February 1805.[6] The same message included important data and maps from the first phase of the Lewis and Clark expedition and indicated the close connection between northwestern and southwestern exploration that existed in President Jefferson's mind. The maps had been drawn by Meriwether Lewis and copied by Nicholas King for the use of the State and War departments. The most significant aspect of these maps was the fact that they showed almost nothing of the central Rockies, indicating the Yellowstone as heading somewhere near Santa Fe.[7]

The following spring Jefferson was able to secure $5,000 from Congress to make another attempt at exploring the Red River to its source, the presumed boundary between Spain and Louisiana. A party under the command of Captain Thomas Sparks was sent out from Fort Adams near the confluence of the Mississippi and Red rivers on April 19, 1806, and marched far up the Red River until at a point some 635 miles upstream they were intercepted by Spanish cavalry and sent back downstream.[8] (See map, p. 48.) By the end of 1806, then, despite the efforts of Jefferson, Louisiana's

5. Ibid., p. 156 n. Also see Thomas Jefferson: *Message from the President of the United States Communicating Discoveries Made in Exploring the Missouri, Red River and Washita by Captains Lewis and Clark, Doctor Sibley and Mr. Dunbar; with a Statistical Account of the Countries Adjacent, Feb. 19, 1806* (Washington, D.C., 1806). I have also examined the George Hunter and William Dunbar Journals, 1804–5, MS., American Philosophical Society. See also Mrs. Dunbar Rowland: *Life, Letters, and Papers of William Dunbar, 1749–1810* (Jackson, Miss.: Mississippi Historical Society; 1930).

6. Wheat: *Preliminary Study*, pp. 64–6.

7. Ibid. Also Doc. 7, Field Notes of Captain William Clark (MS., Yale Western Americana Collections), and Ernest S. Osgood, ed.: *The Field Notes of Captain William Clark* (New Haven, Conn.: Yale University Press; 1964), pp. 20–1 n. 6. Osgood has made an excellent analysis of Clark's calculations as to the probable distance to the Pacific.

8. Thomas Freeman and Peter Custis: *An Account of the Red River in Louisiana Drawn Up from the Returns of Messrs. Freeman and Custis to the War Office of the United States, Who Explored the Same in the Year 1806* (Washington, D.C., 1807).

border was still a mystery. The Spanish garrisons had orders to keep it so, perhaps in accordance with some vague hope of detaching the trans-Allegheny country from the new republic of the United States before the Americans could force the opening of the Mississippi River and thus secure its western drainage forever.

4

By 1805, too, the entire Southwestern frontier had become the scene of intrigue and confusion. A virtual state of undeclared war existed between Spain and the United States. Casa Calvo, the Spanish boundary commissioner, was found to be engaged in espionage, and ordered to leave New Orleans. In retaliation, Casa Yrujo, the Spanish ambassador in Washington, called for his passport and took ship for Europe. All up and down the Mississippi from St. Louis to the Gulf of Mexico, a network of spies and informers kept Spain posted as to the activities of Americans on the frontier.[9] Some of these men, however, acted as double agents, and thanks to their services, the United States was almost equally well informed about Spanish activities. In fact, the master double agent of them all, General James Wilkinson, was chiefly responsible for the hostility and confusion that reigned on the Southwestern frontier.

Since 1787, when he first went West and attempted to detach Kentucky from the newly formed United States, Wilkinson had made a career of stirring up trouble.[1] At this he became a positive genius, being for years in the pay of the Spanish Crown, with the job of reporting on American military movements, which as ranking general in the United States Army he was in a position to initiate. A handsome man of military bearing, Wilkinson seems to have had two aims in life—money and power. The former he needed to maintain his lavish standard of living, and the latter he found irresistible. Likewise the sinuosities of backstairs intrigue were second nature to him, and he never moved toward any objective in a direct manner if a devious alternative was possible.

9. T. P. Abernathy: *The Burr Conspiracy* (New York: Oxford University Press; 1954), *passim*. Also see A. P. Whitaker: "Spanish Intrigue in the Old Southwest," *MVHR*, Vol. XII (1925), pp. 155–76. Also see Dale Van Every: *Men of the Western Waters* (Boston: Houghton Mifflin Co.; 1956), pp. 103–4.

1. Abernathy: *The Burr Conspiracy*, pp. 4–9. See also James R. Jacobs: *Tarnished Warrior, Major-General James Wilkinson* (New York: The Macmillan Co.; 1918), *passim*.

For years Wilkinson had cherished a half-formulated dream of creating a new empire in North America to be carved out of the Western territories of the United States and of Spanish New Mexico—a heartland empire that would control the Mississippi and the Gulf, and through them, the continent. In 1803 he met Aaron Burr, who had similar aspirations, and they devised a plan of action to be executed should the opportunity arise. Wilkinson, in his role as double agent, would bring about a war between Spain and the United States in the Southwest, and then, with the war as a pretext, Burr's private army would seize New Orleans, invade and conquer New Spain, and proclaim an independent Western nation. Then, as Burr put it rather grandly in his coded letter of July 29, 1806: "It will be a host of choice spirits. Wilkinson shall be second to Burr only; Wilkinson shall dictate the rank and promotion of his officers. Burr will proceed westward never to return. . . ."[2]

In the spring of 1805 Wilkinson got his chance. By order of President Jefferson, he was made governor of the Louisiana Territory—which gave him unlimited power in the West. His association with Burr had by this time led him to sponsor Burr's initial reconnaissance of New Orleans.[3] Upon assuming the governorship, Wilkinson also went into partnership with Auguste Chouteau, and together they sponsored a reconnaissance of the Osage country of Kansas and Oklahoma by a party composed of Chouteau's Indian traders and Lieutenant George Peter of Wilkinson's staff.[4] From Lieutenant Peter the General learned much about the road to Santa Fe over which Zebulon Pike was to travel a year later. It is difficult to say just whom this information was intended to benefit, the United States government or the Burr conspirators.

It is also somewhat difficult to assess the significance of Lieutenant Zebulon Pike's expedition to the sources of the Mississippi in the summer of 1805, which was undertaken at Wilkinson's order.[5] Pike's mission was to locate the source of the Mississippi and establish American control of the area, particularly with respect to the British fur traders. And although Pike did not find the true source of the Mississippi, he did succeed in bringing the British traders

2. Quoted in W. Eugene Hollon: *The Lost Pathfinder: Zebulon Montgomery Pike* (Norman, Okla.: University of Oklahoma Press; 1949), p. 96.
3. Abernathy: *The Burr Conspiracy*, pp. 28–9.
4. Jacobs: *Tarnished Warrior*, pp. 220–1.
5. Pike: *The Expeditions . . .* , Coués, ed., Introduction to Vol. I, p. viii.

under American control. He carried out Wilkinson's orders to the letter, ascending the Mississippi by keelboat, and by sled when the river froze over. Since those orders were strikingly similar to the ultimatum issued by the mysterious "Jeremy Pinch" to David Thompson on the Columbia in 1807, some historians believe that Pike himself may have sent the ultimatum to Thompson by means of messages passed along by the tribes of the Upper Missouri.[6] This

6. The identity of the mysterious Lieutenant Jeremy Pinch, or, as he styled himself in an earlier letter to Thompson, Captain Zachary Perch, is one of the intriguing and unanswered questions in Northwest history. Its importance lies in the fact that Pinch, or Perch, represented himself as an officer of the United States government who had established a fort or post in the Pallilo or Palouse Indian country west of the Continental Divide, thus giving the United States priority in that region. Pinch might thus have been the first American explorer after Lewis and Clark to enter the transmontane country, and the first to establish a formal post. The episode reenacts in a microcosmic sense the imperial clash that forms the basic theme of Part I of my book.

My interpretation is based on the following articles: J. Neilson Barry: "Lieutenant Jeremy Pinch," *Oregon Historical Quarterly*, Vol. XXXIII (1937), pp. 323–7; J. B. Tyrell: "Letter of Rouman and Perch, July 10th, 1807," *Oregon Historical Quarterly*, Vol. XXXIII (1937), pp. 391–7; Jessie S. Douglas: "Jeremy Pinch and the War Department," *Oregon Historical Quarterly*, Vol. XXXIX (1938), pp. 425–31; T. C. Elliott: "The Strange Case of David Thompson and Jeremy Pinch," *Oregon Historical Quarterly*, Vol. XXXX (1939), pp. 188–99; W. J. Ghent: "Jeremy Pinch Again," *Oregon Historical Quarterly*, Vol. XXXX (1939), pp. 307–14; and Donald Jackson, ed.: *Letters of the Lewis and Clark Expedition* . . . (Urbana, Ill.: Univ. of Illinois Press; 1962); Morgan: *Jedediah Smith*, pp. 122–3.

The Douglas article establishes the fact that neither Pinch nor Perch were United States Army officers. They must have been, therefore, American impostors who were somewhere in the Upper Missouri country in 1807. And at least one of Pinch's party must have seen or had a copy of the fur-trade regulations issued by General Wilkinson to Lieutenant George Peter in 1805, and Zebulon Pike in 1806, since their letters distinctly parallel Wilkinson's regulations. Pike could not have been Pinch, however, since, as I indicate, Pike was otherwise occupied in Santa Fe at the time. Likewise, Peter accompanied Wilkinson to New Orleans during the same period. Thus, unless Pinch was another of Wilkinson's secret agents as yet unknown to historians, he must have been a member of one of the fur-trading parties who set out from St. Louis in 1807; or he could have been a trader at the Arikara or Mandan Villages who learned of Wilkinson's regulations from one of the St. Louis parties. Four parties are known to have ascended the river in 1807, one of which, and the only one previously identifiable, was Lisa's. Lisa's men, moreover, commenced building forts on the Big Horn that same year, thus fitting in to some extent with the events described in the Pinch letter, except that the western coordinates of Manuel's Fort appear to have been somewhat exaggerated, perhaps deliberately. Thus, it seems likely that Lisa or one of his men, probably not John Colter (see Ghent), forwarded the Pinch ulti-

seems unlikely, however, since by that time Pike was a prisoner of the Spaniards in far off Santa Fe. Perhaps some of Chouteau's traders or even Manuel Lisa's saw a copy of Lieutenant George Peter's similar instructions in 1805, and when they reached the Upper Missouri in 1807 posed as Army officers in an effort to frighten the Canadians away from the fur-trading grounds.[7] In any case, by 1806 Wilkinson by virtue of his two exploring expeditions had established for the United States (or for Burr) a claim to the Mississippi as far as the source, and had secured a diplomatic foothold among the plains Indians on the road to Santa Fe. The time had come for Wilkinson to launch his master plan.

Scarcely had Pike finished his report on the Mississippi expedition when he received orders from Wilkinson which directed him to march into the Southwest, return some Osage Indian captives, make peace between the Kansas and Osage, establish contact with the Comanches, and locate the headwaters of the Red River, which

matum to Thompson in an effort to bluff the Canadians out of the Upper Missouri country. Most of the authorities cited above either concur in this interpretation or offer no refutation of it; hence I have accepted it as the most likely or probable explanation, given the evidence to date.

However, another possibility exists that might reward further detailed research. Pinch's party was said to include two Lewis and Clark men; Lisa's numbered four: Weiser, Potts, Drouillard, and Colter. But there were also two other men on the Upper Missouri who had traveled at least part way with Lewis and Clark, François Rivet and Charles Courtin (for Courtin, see Jackson: *Letters of the Lewis and Clark Expedition*, p. 537 *n.*). It is known (see Barry) that Courtin (and Rivet) established a fort or post somewhere west of the Divide near Clark's Fork and Flathead River (according to Barry) before 1810, when Courtin was killed by Piegan Indians. It is further known that in 1807 Courtin had obtained a license to trap as far up the Missouri as the Great Falls (Jackson), and that in June of 1807 he was at the Arikara Villages. Thus a Courtin and Rivet expedition can, with some justification, be established as one of those leaving St. Louis in the spring of 1807, and with equal justification be presumed to have reached some point beyond the Divide near Clark's Fork, where they established a post. Barry's earlier mention of this event is confirmed by a letter from Finian McDonald to John George McTavish, dated April 5, 1824, and quoted in Morgan, pp. 122–3, in which he says: "I Sa the Masasourey Last fall down as far is the falls an that Part of the Cuntre is rouint of Beaver By the American for they hade fort there fue years agoe about ½ mile beloe Corta is old Fort. . . ." It might be inferred from this that Courtin's (or Pinch's) fort, which was said to be located on the Yellow River, was actually not, as Barry asserts, on Clark's Fork but on the Sun River near its junction with the Missouri just below the Great Falls. Thus, it is highly possible that Courtin, Rivet, or some member of their party was the mysterious Jeremy Pinch, or that Courtin was merely the bearer of a message written by Manuel Lisa.

7. See sources cited in previous footnote.

everyone took to be the boundary between Louisiana and New Spain—everyone, that is, except the Spanish.[8] On the face of it, these orders were innocuous enough, but the suspicion is strong that Pike received secret instructions from Wilkinson to continue on to Santa Fe and spy out its approaches and defenses.

The evidence for this supposition is abundant. First, Pike's own letters made reference to possible military approaches with regard to Santa Fe.[9] Second, when he built his stockade-fort on the Rio Conejos, a small western branch of the Upper Rio Grande near Taos, he must have known that he was in Spanish, not American territory, and nowhere near the sources of the Red River. In fact, when given the opportunity by the Spaniards of being escorted to the head-waters of the Red River, he declined, apparently having lost all interest in the project.[1] And finally, the presence of the mysterious Dr. John Robinson who joined the expedition as surgeon-naturalist some time after its departure, with the ostensible mission of collecting William Morrison's bill from Baptiste La Lande, indicated clearly that Santa Fe, not the Red River, was the primary objective of Pike's expedition.[2]

According to Judge Timothy Kibbey of Louisiana, Wilkinson himself revealed the confidential side of Pike's mission. The expedition was not sent by order of the United States government. Actually, declared Wilkinson, "it was his own Plan and if Mr. Pike suckseeded he the Genl. would be placed out of reach of his enemies and . . . in a situation (if the plan suckseeded) to call his Damned foes to an a/c for their Deeds. . . ." With respect to the risks involved, he added that "Mr. Pike and his party would have documents to shew which would make them as safe as in Philadelphia."[3]

Then with the plan set, and the expedition about to be launched, according to one authority Wilkinson performed a curious final chore. He warned his Spanish friends in Natchez that Pike was to be sent toward Santa Fe.[4] Upon receipt of this information, a large Spanish force under the border captain Don Facundo Malgares marched northward from Santa Fe as far as the Pawnee Villages of Kansas in an effort to intercept the American explorer. The intriguing question thus remains: why did Wilkinson deliberately betray Pike?

8. Pike: *The Expeditions* . . . , Coués, ed., Vol. II, pp. 562–7.
9. Ibid., pp. 571, 588.
1. Ibid., pp. 508–9.
2. Ibid., pp. 498–502. This is also Coués's opinion. See p. 504 *n.*
3. Quoted in Abernathy: *The Burr Conspiracy*, pp. 120–1.
4. Ibid., p. 21.

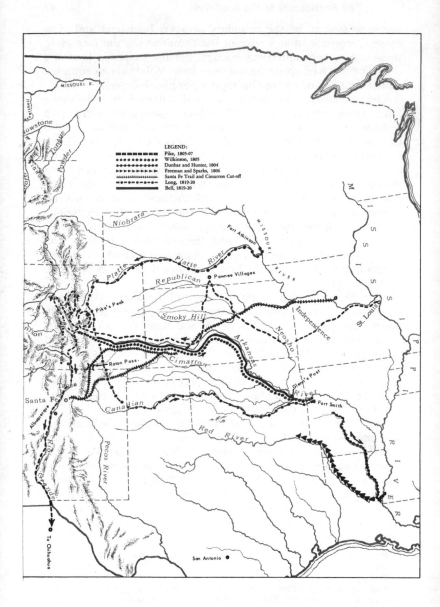

LEGEND:
▪▪▪▪▪ Pike, 1805-07
●●●●● Wilkinson, 1805
━ ━ ━ Dunbar and Hunter, 1804
▶▶▶▶▶ Freeman and Sparks, 1806
✚✚✚✚✚ Santa Fe Trail and Cimarron Cut-off
━ ▪ ━ ▪ Long, 1819-20
━━━━ Bell, 1819-20

The foremost student of the Burr conspiracy believes that as early as June of 1806 Wilkinson had decided to abandon Burr, and therefore he sent Dr. Robinson to make peace with the Spanish so that the Burr plan to start a Spanish war would fail.[5] Presumably Pike and his men were hostages to insure Wilkinson's good faith, and at the same time they were to act as spies, collecting information which Wilkinson could use for his own future reference. It was thus to make certain that the Spanish would contact his secret emissary in time to prevent a border clash that Wilkinson "leaked" the secret of Pike's mission to Spanish agents in Natchez. Meanwhile, innocent or not, Pike led his party out across the prairie, embarked on his grand adventure.

On July 15, 1806, Lieutenant Pike and his twenty-three men disembarked on the Missouri River from Belle Fontaine near St. Louis.[6] His orders took him first to the Osage Villages near the present western border of Missouri and then out across the plains northwest to the Pawnee Villages in Nebraska. After some difficulty with the Pawnees, he turned south to the Arkansas River, following the broad trail left by the command of Lieutenant Don Facundo Malgares, the Spaniard who had been sent out from Santa Fe to intercept him. In following Malgares's trail, Pike was clearly less interested in pinpointing the sources of the Red River than in making a reconnaissance of the whole border area between the two countries, and even of Santa Fe if possible. Given the previous presence of armed Spanish parties in the area, this seems hardly a reprehensible motive.

When Pike reached the Arkansas River, near its great bend in central Kansas, he divided his command, sending Lieutenant Wilkinson (the General's son) downriver with his final dispatches, including a map of the region they had already traversed. Then he turned west to the Rockies, which his men first sighted, looking like "a small blue cloud," on November 15, 1806. Most of November and December Pike spent exploring the Rockies as far north as the sources of the South Platte and as far south as the Sangre de Cristos in southern Colorado and New Mexico. During this time he failed in an attempt to climb Pike's Peak, but he and several of his men did climb Cheyenne Peak some fifteen miles away, and he was thus afforded a panoramic view of the whole of the southern Rockies.

5. Ibid.
6. This account is based on Pike: *The Expeditions* . . . , Coués, ed., unless otherwise stated.

On January 14, 1807, after leaving some of his men in a small fort on the Fountain River, a tributary of the Upper Arkansas, Pike set out with Dr. John Robinson and twelve men southward over the Sangre de Cristos in a bitter midwinter march. Two weeks later, after a terrible ordeal in which six men had to be left behind, crippled with gangrene, the party reached the Rio Grande, which, according to Pike, "we hailed with fervency as the waters of the Red River," but according to the testimony of one of his men everyone recognized perfectly well as a branch of the Rio Grande. Later, on the Rio Conejos they paused and built a small log fort. Then on the seventh of February Dr. Robinson took leave of the party and started off on foot down the Rio Grande (which Pike maintained they all thought was the Red) in an attempt to make contact with La Lande and collect Mr. Morrison's money.[7] Since La Lande was supposed to be in Santa Fe, it was perhaps possible to infer that neither Pike nor Robinson was as hopelessly lost as he pretended to be, and that blue-eyed Lieutenant Pike was only being facetious when he greeted the Spanish cavalry who came to arrest him on February 26 with: "What, is not this the Red River?"

By the first of March 1807, Pike and his men were on the way south toward the New Mexican capital as closely guarded "guests" of the Spanish government. If he was a spy, Pike had an unparalleled opportunity to observe everything about the strategic New Mexican province, and those south of it as far as Chihuahua, where he was taken to the Governor, Don Nemesio Salcedo. In fact, though his papers were confiscated, he was reunited with Dr. Robinson and entertained and informed by all the Spanish military officers in the important northern garrisons. So successful an observer was Pike that when he returned at last to the United States he could give precise data and figures as to just how many and what kinds of troops the Spanish had on hand to defend the northern provinces, and he was well informed as to the character and personalities of all the Spanish military leaders.[8] No more successful espionage operation has ever been conducted in recorded American history.

But Pike's importance lies in more than his role as Wilkinson's agent. His report, compiled mostly from memory, of the march to Santa Fe and of the Mexican tour was the most significant work published up to that time on northern Mexico. It came out in 1810 with an atlas of maps adapted from Humboldt's *New Spain*

7. Pike: *The Expeditions* . . . , Coués, ed., pp. 498–502.
8. Ibid., pp. 718–806. See, for example, pp. 772–3, 793–9.

atlas, which was published the following year in Paris. In this report Pike had several things to say which shaped the course not only of Western exploration, but of Western development and settlement itself.

First of all, he pointed out that the great plains were "sandy deserts" similar to those of Africa. "I saw in my route, in various places," he wrote, "tracts of many leagues where the wind had thrown up the sand in all the fanciful form of the ocean's rolling wave; and on which not a speck of vegetable matter existed."[9] Pike, therefore, not Stephen H. Long, as so many writers have declared, was the originator of the so-called "Great American Desert" myth. But, unlike Westerners of later generations, Pike was not at all disconcerted by the existence of a desert on the Western border. Instead he declared, not without irony in view of the recent Wilkinson-Burr activity:

> But from these immense prairies may arise great advantage to the United States, viz: the restriction of our population to some certain limits, and thereby a continuation of the Union. Our citizens being so prone to rambling and extending themselves on the frontiers will, through necessity, be constrained to limit their extent on the west to the borders of the Missouri and Mississippi, while they leave the prairies incapable of cultivation to the wandering and uncivilized aborigines of the country.[1]

This view of the West, put forth in 1810, set the popular pattern for many years to come. Beyond the Mississippi was prairie, little water, and no timber. It was a paradise for flocks and herds, a never ending game preserve for nomads and Indians, but it was no place for the extension of civilization with farms and towns and mechanical pursuits. Rather the West, and the Southwest in particular, was a barrier which would contain the population and save the Union. At best it was a great prairie ocean which one crossed as quickly as possible to get to Cathay. To facilitate this crossing, Pike found what he considered the virtual equivalent of a Southwest Passage. "By the route of the Arkansas and the Rio Colorado of California," he asserted, "there can be established the best communication on this side of the Isthmus of Darien between the Atlantic and Pacific Oceans."[2] Such a route required, wrote Pike, only 200 miles of land portage between the two great rivers. Moreover,

9. Ibid., p. 525.
1. Ibid.
2. Ibid., pp. 522–3.

since he subscribed to the idea that there was a "Rio Buenaventura" that flowed westward from the Rockies to the Pacific, he left open the possibility of still another westward passage from the heart of the mountain region.[3]

Finally, he pointed out in great detail the trade possibilities of Santa Fe and northern Mexico, which stood as rich ports of call on the far shores of the prairie ocean.[4] These three broad areas of observation concerning the Southwest served to create the American public image of that region for the next fifty years. It was an image not far removed from reality. Certainly in terms of rainfall, grass, and timber resources, the Southwestern plains, especially in the Arkansas River region, were not fit for the agricultural and crude manufacturing culture of that period.

With respect to transportation, by 1853, after the Pacific Railroad Surveys, it became obvious that a Southwestern route roughly between the 32nd and 36th parallels was by far the best route for a transcontinental railroad.

Down to the Mexican War, the trade of Santa Fe and Chihuahua was the lodestone that drew Americans into the Southwest. Indeed, any close examination of the Mexican War and of the whole Manifest Destiny movement will indicate that Santa Fe and its trade was one of the basic American objectives.

So, in practical terms, Pike touched upon all of the important themes that were to command American attention in the Southwest in the early nineteenth century. And though he was often inaccurate, as when he wrote that he could take a position in the Rocky Mountains from whence he could visit the sources of the Platte, the Colorado, the Arkansas, the Red, the Rio Grande, and the Yellowstone rivers in one day—still, as an explorer, he opened up immense vistas to the new American republic. To see this clearly, one need only compare his report with those of his Spanish rivals in the Southwest, which were primarily concerned with frontier defense, or with those of the British in the Northwest, which were narrowly focused upon the interests of the fur trade. It is characteristic of the American experience in Western exploration that from the very beginning, with Lewis and Clark and with Zebulon Pike, explorers and expeditions sent out by the federal government pointed the way to

3. See Pike's "A Map of the Internal Provinces of New Spain," in *The Expeditions* . . . , Vol. III, in which Pike includes Miera y Pacheca's Lake Timpanogos and the Rio Buenaventura. Also see Vol. II, p. 733.
4. Vol. II, pp, 718–806. See especially p. 805.

the broadest considerations of the uses of the trans-Mississippi region, and kept the country as a whole from viewing the West in the narrow terms of the special interests operating in the region at a particular time and place. This emphasis upon a broad public policy was a major point of contrast with the European approaches to the West, and an important factor in the eventual American success in that region.

5

In the years that followed the return of Zebulon Pike, the Spanish with their frontier garrisons at Nacogdoches in east Texas and on the Red River tried desperately to hold the plains frontier against the Americans. Gone was any hope of reclaiming the land east of the Mississippi, and from this point on, particularly after the trial of Aaron Burr, Spanish strategy reverted to an "iron curtain" frontier policy, and an official adherence to mercantilism within the confines of the empire. But despite all Spanish efforts, bands of venturesome American traders entered the Southwestern plains region in ever increasing numbers, and for a variety of reasons. Some, like Manuel Lisa's secret partner Jacques Clamorgan, who reached Santa Fe in 1807, were small clandestine ventures designed to circumvent American regulations governing trade in the Southwest.[5] Others, like Colonel John Shaw, who claimed to have reached the Rocky Mountains in 1809, openly went west in search of gold and silver.[6] Still others drifted into Texas in ever increasing numbers as filibusters.[7] It was thus difficult for the Spanish garrisons to distinguish legitimate from illegitimate pursuits, and since they were under orders to pursue the "hard" line anyway, they arrested almost everyone they could catch.

In December of 1809, J. McLanahan, Reuben Smith, and James Patterson, guided by the Spaniard Emanuel Blanco, left St. Genevieve, Missouri, on a trading expedition to Santa Fe. They got as far as the headwaters of the Red River before they were arrested by

5. Joseph J. Hill: "An Unknown Expedition to Santa Fe in 1807," *MVHR*, Vol. VI (March 1920), pp. 560–2.
6. Col. John Shaw: "Personal Narrative," Wisconsin State Historical Society *Collections*, Vol. II (1859), pp. 197–232.
7. An example of this is seen in John Maley: "Journal," MS., Yale Historical Manuscripts Collection.

the Spanish, taken to Santa Fe and then to Chihuahua, and finally imprisoned for two years.[8]

In the year 1809, too, excitement was generated in the border town of Natchitoches, Louisiana, by the return of Anthony Glass and his men from a winter's trade with the Pawnees and Comanches. They had gone as far west as the headwaters of the Colorado River of Texas near present-day Big Spring, and according to Glass, who must have had "phenomenal" eyesight, they had seen the Rocky Mountains far in the distance. On numerous occasions, too, they had been threatened by Indian emissaries sent to the Pawnees and Comanches by the Spanish comandante at San Antonio, but they had completely won over the Pawnees, who not only protected them and rejected the Spaniards but had also shown them their sacred stone, a mass of malleable metal (obviously a meteorite) some 3 feet 4 inches in length and 2 feet 4½ inches in width, which lay out in the prairie. It was this mass of metal that caused the excitement on Glass's return.[9]

Immediately two rival expeditions, one from Nacogdoches and the other from Natchitoches, were mounted, and in the spring of 1810, first one and then the other had a try at retrieving the mysterious metal. Finally the Natchitoches group triumphed. It was eventually shipped downriver to New Orleans and on to New York City, where authorities pronounced it only iron and nothing more. Benjamin Silliman of Yale, knowing it to be a meteor, ultimately purchased it for his alma mater, where it now resides.[1]

All of these expeditions were the cause of still another venture, the expedition of John Maley up the Red River in 1812. Maley, about whom almost nothing is known except that his friend Judge William Johnson of Charleston, South Carolina, styled him a "wanderer" and Silliman called him "an erratic adventurer,"[2] arrived in Natchitoches in February of 1812 after a fling at filibustering on the Texas border and spent the spring and summer of that year at the Pawnee Villages trying to purchase two other metallic masses. According to his journal,[3] he also managed to discover an aban-

8. Chittenden: *Fur Trade*, Vol. II, p. 496 *n*. See also Phillips: *Fur Trade*, Vol. II, pp. 505–6.
9. "Journal of Anthony Glass," MS., Yale Historical Manuscripts Collection.
1. Ibid. See also Benjamin Silliman Papers, Yale Historical Manuscripts Collection.
2. Silliman Papers.
3. Maley: "Journal." My account of Maley's incredible and hitherto unknown adventures is based on his own manuscript journal, purchased for Yale by Professor Benjamin Silliman. So obscure a figure is Maley that it has been

doned Spanish silver mine and, far out on the prairie, an old Spanish gold deposit. When he returned to Natchitoches for the winter,
he started a virtual gold rush; and the following spring he set off
ahead of all the others, with two companions and $1,500 worth
of supplies, for the gold diggings in what was perhaps the first
American gold rush in the trans-Mississippi West. Out on the
prairie, however, he and his partners were robbed by the Osage and
left with only their knives and their wallets. After a fearsome trek
of nearly two months, during which they were lost for weeks at a
time and one of them nearly died of a copperhead bite, they finally
reached Natchitoches. Maley, after a short trip to the Hot Springs
of Arkansas, appears to have retired from gold hunting for good.
He is last heard from in Nashville, where he spent the winter. Later,
however, he is known to have sold his exciting journal to a New
York bookseller for $500.[4] By 1812, then, expeditions out onto the
plains, particularly along the north bank of the Red River, were
becoming a common occurrence—with or without Spanish permission.

Three more adventurers, James Baird, Samuel Chambers, and
Robert McKnight, went even farther than the Red River. With a
small party they went all the way to Santa Fe in April of 1812.[5]
They were promptly arrested and taken to prison in Chihuahua, where they spent nine long years before being rescued.
Due to the Hidalgo uprising and the Gutiérrez-Magee Texas filibustering expedition in 1812, the Spaniards were in no mood for
welcoming visitors from the United States. Unlike the English to
the north, they chose to leave the beaver in the streams and instead
embarked on a plan to sweep the country of American adventurers.

But even this did not stop the westward advance. In 1814, one
James Philibert led a band of trappers far up the Arkansas on an
expedition. Trapping must have been good, for he returned to
St. Louis for more supplies while his men waited out the win-
ter in a rendezvous on the Huerfano River, a tributary of the
Upper Arkansas. When Philibert did not return at the appointed

impossible to check the veracity of his account on all points. The reader is
therefore warned to accept his story only on the most tentative basis, subject
to confirmation or denial by further detailed research.
4. Silliman Papers.
5. Chittenden: *Fur Trade,* Vol. II, pp. 496–7. Also see Josiah Gregg: *Commerce of the Prairies,* 2 vols. (Philadelphia: J. B. Lippincott; 1962), Vol. I,
pp. 4–5. F. B. Golley: "James Baird, Early Santa Fe Trader," *Missouri Historical Society Bulletin,* Vol. XV (April 1959), pp. 171–93. Thomas James:
Three Years, pp. 57–8.

time, they pulled up their traps and headed over the mountains to Taos, New Mexico, where surprisingly enough they were well received by the Spaniards.

The summer of 1815 passed with Philibert's men enjoying the shady delights of Taos while their leader scouted out supplies and reinforcements in St. Louis. By September he had made an arrangement with Auguste Chouteau and his partner Jules De Mun whereby he would accompany them on a trapping expedition to the Mexican Mountains, and they in turn would purchase the services of all his men for the year's hunt. By this merger Philibert had much to gain and little to lose. Auguste Chouteau, through his position as trader to the southern Osage, dominated whatever Southwestern Indian trade there was, and without his help it was difficult to pass through the Osage tribes and sustain operations far up the Arkansas on the flank of the Spanish Empire.

The relief expedition of Chouteau and De Mun did not fare well, however. After a good season's trapping in the Sangre de Cristo Mountains north and east of Taos, they were arrested by a band of Spanish soldiers on May 24, 1816. All their furs were confiscated and the party was taken before a court of inquiry in Santa Fe, where they were quickly adjudged guilty, forced to kneel and kiss the document sentencing them, and then were thrown into prison for forty-eight days. At the end of that time they were released and sent home across the prairies without weapons or food. The experience so impressed Chouteau that he retired from venturesome operations forever, preferring like Voltaire's hero to "tend his garden" among the Osage.[6]

As late as 1817, neither the Spanish Empire in the Southwest, nor for that matter the western reaches of the new American domain, was open to the enterprise of American citizens. That the United States government submitted so meekly to the Spanish outrages is owing perhaps to the basic uncertainty that prevailed, despite the various probing expeditions and the excellent work of Zebulon Pike, as to the exact limits of American territory in the Far West.

6. Ibid., pp. 497–500. Also see Jules De Mun: "Journals," T. M. Marshall, ed., Missouri Historical Society *Collections,* Vol. V (1927–28), pp. 167–208, 311–26.

6

During and after the treaty of Ghent concluding the War of 1812, the problem of the western limits of the Louisiana Purchase was acute. To the north and northwest the Canadian fur traders continued to dominate the Indian trade as far east as Lake Superior and down into what is now Wisconsin and Minnesota. To make matters worse, in 1816 Lord Selkirk established his ambitious feudal settlement on the Red River of the North.[7] Using the river as an artery of communication, Selkirk's traders could, if they chose, descend into the very heart of American territory, outflank the Missouri River operations, and bring all the northern tribes under their control.

In the period 1815 to 1817 the advantage gained by Lewis and Clark and the Astorians in the Far Northwest was wiped out, and only Manuel Lisa's influence with the northern tribes stood between the weak American foothold beyond the Mississippi and complete British domination. In the Southwest an iron curtain of Spanish chain mail had been lowered over all the country watered by the western tributaries of the Mississippi—or what might be regarded as Mr. Jefferson's "noble" purchase.

Things were not, however, entirely hopeless. Washington retaliated against foreign pressure by requiring all fur traders beyond the Mississippi to have licenses issued by the United States government. Though this proved difficult to enforce, at least it was one weapon to use against commercial infiltration. In addition, the federal government increased the number of its subsidized Western fur-trading posts to nineteen by the end of the War of 1812.[8] Following this, a string of forts was constructed along an interior line from Fort Snelling on the Upper Mississippi to Fort Smith on the Arkansas. These forts were designed to cover all the possible avenues of encroachment into American territory. Thus far, American policy strongly resembled that of the Spanish and British. All of the measures taken were an attempt to protect the Louisiana Purchase territory—still a vaguely defined tract—in the face of determined British attempts to whittle away as much of it as possible before a final boundary settlement would be made.

7. George Bryce: *The Remarkable History of the Hudson's Bay Company* . . . (London: Sampson, Low, Marston and Co.; 1900), pp. 202–14.
8. Paul C. Phillips: *The Fur Trade,* 2 vols. (Norman, Okla.: University of Oklahoma Press; 1961), Vol. II, pp. 67–96.

In 1817 John C. Calhoun became Secretary of War and he brought with him a new and more belligerent policy for the Western frontier. With President Monroe's enthusiastic approval, he proposed to establish a military outpost far up the Missouri River, near the mouth of the Yellowstone, designed to counter Selkirk's moves on the Red River and to check the British advance in that direction while at the same time bringing the Upper Missouri tribes under American influence.[9] This was the genesis of the so-called Yellowstone Expedition of 1819. Calhoun declared: "The expedition ordered to the mouth of the Yellowstone, or rather, to the Mandan village, is a part of a system of measures which has for its objects the protection of our northwestern frontier and the greater extension of our fur trade."[1]

By the spring of 1819 one thousand men under General Henry W. Atkinson were on their way up the Missouri in five ill-constructed steamboats, prepared to establish the crucial outpost. Along with this flotilla was a sixth steamboat, *The Western Engineer,* which carried a corps of scientific explorers under the command of Major Stephen H. Long.

It was the first time steamboats had been used on the Missouri River, and it was also the first time that an official corps of discovery which included trained scientific specialists had ever been sent into the West. One observer, his imagination fired by the scene, declared:

> See those vessels, with the agency of steam advancing against the powerful currents of the Mississippi and the Missouri! Their course is marked by volumes of smoke and fire, which the civilized man observes with admiration, and the savage with astonishment. Botanists, mineralogists, chemists, artisans, cultivators, scholars, soldiers; the love of peace, the capacity for war: philosophical apparatus and military supplies; telescopes and cannon, garden seeds and gunpowder; the arts of civil life and the force to defend them—all are seen aboard. The banner of freedom which waves over the whole proclaims the character and protective power of the United States.[2]

And it *was* an impressive sight, particularly, so the observer grasped, as a demonstration of the extent to which the American government

9. Chittenden: *Fur Trade,* Vol. II, pp. 562–3. Also see Phillips: *Fur Trade,* Vol. II, p. 392.
1. Ibid., p. 563.
2. Ibid., p. 566.

was willing to go to back its claims to the lands west of the Mississippi. Moreover, though the military aspects of the Yellowstone Expedition appeared to be a complete failure, since Atkinson's force
never reached the Yellowstone or any part of the Upper Missouri,
being forced into camp at the Council Bluffs, where the men all
came down with scurvy and fever, still it was an indication of America's seriousness of purpose with regard to the trans-Mississippi
country that could not have failed to impress the British and the
Indians.[3] It indicated that Calhoun, once a War Hawk, was still an
opportunist. He was prepared to take any advantage possible of the
rift between the Hudson's Bay and Northwest companies over Selkirk's colony to insure American control over the Upper Missouri
country. Beyond this, the Yellowstone Expedition finally afforded
the United States an opportunity to explore officially the Southwestern plains region and the limits of Louisiana, still closely connected in the American mind with the Upper Missouri region.

When the military expedition failed at the Council Bluffs, the
scientific contingent too went into winter camp. There the members
of the party—Dr. Thomas Say, the zoologist from New Harmony,
Indiana; Titian Peale, assistant naturalist; Samuel Seymour,
painter; and the Army topographers Lieutenant James Duncan
Graham and Cadet William Swift—spent the winter assembling
collections of rocks, plants, and animals for shipment back to Eastern Seaboard institutions. Eventually most of the specimens were
deposited in Peale's Museum in Philadelphia, where the Lewis
and Clark collections were. There, if they did not serve the cause
of pure science, they at least amused curiosity seekers by the thousands and helped form a popular idea of the Far West.

The leader of the scientific contingent was Major Stephen Harri-
man Long, a Dartmouth graduate who had been an instructor at
West Point, and one of the first members of the Corps of Topographical Engineers.[4] In this role he had become an experienced explorer, having made in 1817 a survey of the inland frontier defenses
from Arkansas to Minnesota, part of which involved his famous
voyage up the Mississippi as far as the Falls of St. Anthony (now
Minneapolis) in a six-oared skiff.[5] His advocacy of the use of
steamboats to explore the West, in a letter to President Monroe of
March 15, 1817, indicates that much of the technology of the

3. Henry Atkinson: *Journal of the Yellowstone Expedition*, MS., Yale Collection of Western Americana.
4. *Dictionary of American Biography*. Hereafter *D.A.B.*
5. Ibid.

Yellowstone Expedition had been his idea.[6] But upon his return
to Washington in the winter of 1819, he found that, as far as the
expedition was concerned, the steamboats were to be abandoned
and his own scientific contingent greatly curtailed. He was ordered
to change direction completely from the Upper Missouri to the Far
Southwest via the Platte River and the Great Plains to the Arkansas
and Red rivers.[7]

With a new botanical assistant, Dr. Edwin James, Major Long's
exploring mission set out from the Engineer Cantonment at the
Council Bluffs on the sixth of June, 1820.[8] (See map, p. 48.) A
curious cavalcade of disgruntled career officers, eccentric scientists,
and artist-playboys, Long's party must have made an amusing spectacle as it struggled west along the north bank of the Platte through
giant herds of buffalo and villages of painted Pawnee and drunken
Otos. On the last day of June they sighted the Rocky Mountains,
though they could not be sure until several days later that it wasn't a
mirage. Pushing onward, they located a large mountain which they
named Long's Peak though they believed it to have been originally
discovered by Zebulon Pike. Six days later they reached the place
where the South Platte leaves the mountains just south of Denver,
and a few days later, on July 18, they climbed Pike's Peak, the first
party ever to do so. Lieutenant Swift measured the height of the
peak above the surrounding plain by means of triangulation, but
since he had no idea of the altitude of the base plain above sea level,
his calculations proved to be virtually useless.

On July 24, after failing to ascend the Arkansas River via the
Royal Gorge, Major Long divided his party and prepared to return
home by two separate routes. One party, commanded by Captain
John R. Bell and including Dr. Say, Mr. Seymour, Lieutenant
Swift, and several riflemen, turned east to descend the Arkansas
to Belle Point in eastern Oklahoma and there await the rest of the
party.[9] Long, accompanied by Titian Peale, Edwin James, and

6. Richard G. Wood: "Exploration by Steamboat," *The Journal of Trans-
port History*, Vol. II (Nov. 1955), pp. 121–2.
7. Edwin James: *Account of an Expedition From Pittsburgh to the Rocky
Mountains Performed In The Years 1819, 20 . . .* , in Reuben Gold Thwaites,
ed.: *Early Western Travels 1748–1846*, 4 vols. [XIV–XVIII] (Cleveland, Ohio:
Arthur H. Clark Co.; 1905), Vol. XIV, p. 13. Hereafter cited as James:
Account of an Expedition, Thwaites ed. See also, for an account of the first
phase of the Long expedition, Titian Peale: "Journal," MS., Library of Congress.
8. James: *Account of an Expedition*, Thwaites ed., Vol. XV, p. 193.
9. John R. Bell: "Journal of the S. H. Long Expedition," in Harlan M. Fuller

seven men, crossed the Arkansas River and headed south in search of the Red River, which he hoped to explore from its source to its mouth, since it was supposedly the boundary between United States and Spanish territory.

The remainder of the expedition constituted a disastrous culmination to what had gone before. Captain Bell's party, after passing through clouds of Cheyenne, Arapaho, and Kiowa Indians, finally came to grief on the Lower Arkansas when three of his men deserted, taking rifles, packs, horses, and most of the expedition's journals and scientific notebooks. They were never heard from again.

Major Long's contingent continued south until they reached a broad river which they took to be the Red. This they followed downstream under conditions of extreme hardship, being forced to subsist for days on the flesh of their own horses. The country was all hostile Indian country seldom penetrated by white men, and whenever they came to a village along the way they were greeted with suspicion and hostility. One village in particular they called the village of the "Bad Heart" Indians. There a strange group of diseased and deformed Indians confronted them with taunts, insults, and noncooperation. But even this occurrence had its lighter side.

> I saw one mother [James recorded in his private notebook] apparently thirty years of age and of the usual stature suckling her infant who *stood* upon the ground. She found it necessary to stoop but little and stood observing us almost erect while the child of about two years was nursing.[1]

Pushing on past the hostile Indians, Long's party finally came to the end of what they had supposed was the Red River, only to find, to their "mortification," that it flowed into the Arkansas River and was not the Red at all but the Canadian. It was somehow a fitting climax to the whole venture, and when, a week later, they met Captain Bell at Belle Point both commanders had frustrating tales to tell. Needless to say, Major Long made no triumphant return to civilization. Moreover, when the account of the expedition was published he judiciously faded into the background, allowing Edwin James to be the official chronicler of their collective misadventures.

and Le Roy R. Hafen, eds.: *Far West and Rockies Series* (Glendale, Calif.: Arthur H. Clark Co.; 1957), Vol. VI.
1. Edwin James: "Journal," MS., Special Collections, Butler Library, Columbia University.

History has not been kind to the Long Expedition. Hiram M. Chittenden declared it to be "an unqualified failure . . . a huge fiasco smothered in elaboration of method."[2] Other authorities have pointed out that in his report Long declared the Great Plains unfit for human habitation, thus launching the "Great American Desert" myth and impeding the progress of Western settlement.[3] Moreover, it was comparatively easy to demonstrate that the scientific results of the expedition were negligible except for Long's important map.

Yet Long's expedition was not all failure. For the first time a team of scientists had surveyed the immense plains region in realistic terms, and taken some measure of the possibilities for settlement in that treeless area. They had revealed the complexity of the river systems in the Southwest, and had visited tribes seldom seen by the white man. But for the misfortune of losing the scientific notebooks to deserters, and the parsimony of the government, they might have produced a monumental scientific report even though they were without the highly developed instruments that explorers would carry as standard equipment a decade later.

In addition, it seems unfair to criticize Long as the perpetrator of the "Great American Desert" myth, though textbooks generally depict him as such. The designation, as previously indicated, clearly belongs to Zebulon Pike, whose report of 1810 was emphatic on this subject. Moreover, both explorers had a point. As of 1820 the Southwestern plains *were* unfit for widespread settlement, given the level of American technology at the time. There was little or no timber for houses and fuel. Surface water was scarce, and light windmills with water pumps had not yet been invented.[4] Much of the soil was sandy and the winters were cold. Huge herds of buffalo, sometimes ten miles long, roamed over the prairies, and hostile Indians jealously guarded their hunting grounds.

A farmer settling these Southwestern plains would have to contend with all these factors and more. Worst of all, he would face them in virtual isolation, since it would be years before means of easy communication with the outside world existed. Pike and Long were among the very few Western explorers who advised against

2. Chittenden: *Fur Trade,* Vol. II, p. 570.
3. Walter P. Webb: *The Great Plains* (New York: Universal Library; n.d.), p. 147. Ray A. Billington: *Westward Expansion* (New York: The Macmillan Co.; 1949), p. 469.
4. Webb: *Great Plains,* pp. 337–9. Light windmills were first manufactured in South Coventry, Conn., in 1854 by the Halladay Windmill Co. But it was not until the 1870's that Fairbanks, Morse and Co. began widespread manufacture and distribution of the machines in the Great Plains.

Stephen H. Long's map, 1821. *Courtesy National Archives*

headlong expansion, and, significantly, they were government explorers with some idea of the overall national needs. They were not promoters, or hunters, or men on the lookout for the main chance, and when they presented the country with cautious reports they were going against the tide of the times.

Long especially has appeared to bad advantage in this respect, since his report came just at the time when Santa Fe (as a result of the Mexican revolution of 1821) was at last opened up to American trade, and John Quincy Adams by a stroke of his pen in 1819 had made America a transcontinental nation in his treaty with Spain. To the north, after the bitter feud between the Northwesters and the Hudson's Bay Company had all but neutralized it, Lord Selkirk's Red River Colony no longer seemed much of a threat. And by 1824 Ashley's mountain men had rediscovered South Pass and opened the Central Rockies to the American advance. Thus, by the time Long (with Edwin James) published his cautious report on the West, the eagle had begun to scream all along the frontier from Canada to Mexico, and a government explorer or public servant of any kind who warned against settling the continent too rapidly seemed somewhat anachronistic, to say the least.

7

The drive toward Santa Fe and the initial opening of the Southwest reached a crucial point in 1821. That year three expeditions set out in the direction of the New Mexican capital. The first was commanded by a citizen of Franklin, Missouri, William Becknell.[5] It was initially advertised in the Franklin *Missouri Intelligencer* as an expedition to collect wild horses on the Great Plains. Starting in early September of 1821, Becknell at the head of about twenty experienced plainsmen rode out over the prairie from Franklin to the Arkansas River, then turned south and crossed Raton Pass on the border of Colorado and New Mexico. There he learned from some Mexican soldiers that independence had been declared and Americans were welcome in Santa Fe. Proceeding to Santa Fe, he traded what goods he had for a rich profit in Mexican silver, and returned as fast as he could to Franklin, where he began preparing

5. Gregg: *Commerce*, Vol. I, p. 5. See also William Becknell: "Journal of Two Expeditions from Boon's Lick to Santa Fe," *Missouri Historical Society Collections*, Vol. II (1906), pp. 55–67.

for an even bigger venture the following year. On the way home he located a new route via the Cimarron River that would enable heavily loaded wagons to reach Santa Fe without crossing over Raton Pass. This route eventually became the Santa Fe Trail. After Becknell's return, the Santa Fe trade never ceased to be the object of public attention in St. Louis and the surrounding towns. It became the subject of a stream of petitions to Congress for aid and protection on the trail.[6]

Besides Becknell's expedition, two more parties are known to have set out for Santa Fe in 1821. The first was led by Thomas James, a veteran of Manuel Lisa's first operations on the Upper Missouri, who was venturing once more into the West to make a stake that would rescue him from bankruptcy back home in Illinois.[7] His partner was Robert McKnight, who besides trading was interested in rescuing his brother John from a Mexican jail where he had languished since his ill-fated venture of 1812. The James-McKnight expedition, after several close calls with the Comanches, finally reached Santa Fe, where James tried with indiffcrent success to sell his trade goods while McKnight journeyed south to rescue his brother from prison in Chihuahua.

A short while after the James-McKnight party reached Santa Fe, still another party, led by Hugh Glenn and Jacob Fowler, came in.[8] They had followed the Arkansas upstream as far as present-day Pueblo, Colorado. There they had gone into encampment while Glenn pushed on to the Spanish settlements to see if his party of Americans would be permitted to enter. He returned with some Spanish emissaries, who, according to Fowler, declared "that the mackeson provence Has de Clared Independance of the mother Cuntry and is desirous of a traid With the people of the united States."[9] With this welcome news, the whole Fowler-Glenn party shouldered their gear and proceeded over the mountains to Taos, where they spread out their goods and commenced trading at last with the "mackesons."

The Fowler-Glenn and the James-McKnight parties returned to

6. See, for example, Alphonso Wetmore: "Petition of Sundry Inhabitants of the State of Missouri Upon the Subject of Communication between the said State and the Internal Provinces of Mexico . . . ," 18th Cong., 2nd sess., Vol. IV, *H.R. Rept.* 79 (1825).
7. Thomas James: *Three Years.*
8. Jacob Fowler: *The Journal of Jacob Fowler,* Elliott Coués, ed. (New York: Francis P. Harper; 1898).
9. Ibid., p. 95.

St. Louis in the summer of 1822, neither of them a financial success.[1] They were almost unique in that respect. So lucrative was the trade that on the way home they passed J. F. Cooper heading over Becknell's trail as fast as he could, with pack mules full of trade goods.[2] Behind him came William Becknell himself at the head of a wagon train, back for a second venture within the year. This marked the real beginning of the rich Santa Fe trade and the first time that loaded wagons were taken over the trail to the Mexican capital.

By the end of 1824 the Santa Fe trade had become so important to Missourians that a young senator from that state, Thomas Hart Benton, rose in the Senate chamber, waving a map which showed the national road from Georgia to New Orleans and which had been given him by the aging Jefferson on Christmas Day, 1824, and demanded a similar favor for the new West—a federally sponsored international road from Missouri to Santa Fe.[3] In presenting this petition, Benton spoke for the new American entrepreneurs, who, in replacing the French, were venturing farther and farther out on the plains. He got his wish on March 3, 1825, when President Monroe signed a bill authorizing $10,000 for surveying and marking the road, and $20,000 for securing the right of way from the Indians.[4] By 1827 the road was completed, and though most trading caravans ignored it in favor of various shortcut versions of the trail, still it symbolized the fact that at long last the way to Santa Fe was clear. The vast prairies had been conquered by the efforts of the trappers and traders and government explorers, and the first great period of American exploration in the Southwest was thus concluded.

8

As the caravans rolled into Santa Fe, the adventurous plainsmen became merchants and shopkeepers whose days were spent haggling over calicoes, or kitchen knives, or copper kettles, and whose nights were an endless round of fandangos, and barroom brawls. Most of the traders grew restless after a short while. Money ran out. And if they were inexperienced traders, and numbers of them were, they

1. Thomas James: *Three Years*, p. 121. Fowler: *Journal, passim.*
2. Fowler: *Journal*, p. 154.
3. Quoted in Kate L. Gregg, ed.: *The Road to Santa Fe* (Albuquerque, N.M.: University of New Mexico Press; 1952), p. 6.
4. Ibid., p. 7.

eventually found themselves with a whole stock of "mulas," or unsalable goods, living off loans from friends—worse off than when they left Missouri.[5] In this case, the fur trade seemed the only answer, and the mountains beyond Santa Fe to the west in all directions, north and south, seemed virtually the answer to a trapper's prayer.

About this time, in February of 1822, while he was vainly trying to dispose of his somber fabrics in Santa Fe, Thomas James received a visit from fifty haughty, hard-riding Ute Indians whose leader said: "Come and trade with the Utahs. . . . We want your trade. . . . Come to our country with your goods."[6] Who could resist such an opportunity, especially if you were saddled with a load of "mulas" and your luck had run out at three-card monte? No wonder, then, that almost immediately parties of American traders and trappers began fanning out in all directions from Santa Fe and the northern outpost at Taos. In the course of their fur-hunting operations, they were to make several important contributions to the knowledge of the soon-to-be American Southwest.

In 1822 William Wolfskill, who had arrived in a caravan that same year, began his career as one of the outstanding men of the Southwestern fur trade. He took a band of men and trapped the Lower Rio Grande as far as the site of El Paso. Then the following year he did it again, with only one companion. In the winter of 1823–24, with Ewing Young and Isaac Slover, he crossed over the Continental Divide west of the Upper Rio Grande and explored the Chama and San Juan country of northwestern New Mexico. By the first of June he was back in Taos with $10,000 worth of furs.[7]

This was the pattern. For the first few years after 1821, the trappers were content to work the valley and the tributaries of the Rio Grande. Some trapped the Upper Arkansas and then made their way back to St. Louis across the prairies. But by 1824 they were ranging farther afield, especially north from Taos into the southern Rockies below the great trade battleground of the Hudson's Bay and Rocky Mountain Fur companies.

In 1824 alone, five parties are known to have traveled north from Santa Fe and Taos through the San Luis Valley and by way of the Uncompagre and Gunnison rivers into western Colorado and eastern Utah as far as the Green River, or else due west from Taos

5. Thomas James: *Three Years*, pp. 88–9, 96, 100.
6. Ibid., pp. 90 ff.
7. J. J. Hill: "Ewing Young in the Fur Trade of the Far Southwest, 1822–1834," *Oregon Historical Soc. Quarterly*, Vol. XXIV (1923), p. 7.

via the Chama, the San Juan, and the Dolores to the Green River. Besides Wolfskill's party, there were groups led by Etienne Provost, Antoine Robidoux, William Huddart, and William Becknell.[8] Possibly there were others. Certainly there were enough so that by the middle of 1824 His Excellency, the Governor of Santa Fe, issued an order which forbade the taking of beaver in the northern provinces.[9] Almost before it had begun, as far as the Americans were concerned, the fur trade appeared to be officially closed. Mexico clearly didn't want its vast heartland explored and its riches tapped by foreign traders and trappers.

This did not stem from lack of interest in the interior, however. One of the great and virtually unknown stories of Western exploration was the story of Spanish penetration westward and northward into the San Juan, the Green, and finally over the Wasatch Range onto the Sevier River and the Great Basin. Between 1761 and 1765 Juan de Rivera, a veteran Spanish frontier fighter, had conducted three expeditions into the southern Rockies. He took his soldiers, traders, and padres north via Taos and the San Juan, past the La Plata Mountains (near Durango, Colorado) to the Dolores River, then to the Uncompagre and finally to the Gunnison in central Colorado. In the vicinity of the Gunnison they met the Utes and other mountain tribes and a brisk trade was established.

After these first expeditions, little is known for the next ten years. From time to time Spanish records show that the veterans of the Rivera expeditions were conducting trade with the northern Indians. In 1775, three of Rivera's men, Pedro Mora, Gregorio Sandoval, and Andrés Muñiz, got as far as the Grand River in western Colorado, possibly farther. And in 1805, when Governor Alencaster dispatched Manuel Mesta, aged seventy, to the Timpanogos River (the Grand) to reclaim some Spanish horses from the Utes, his letter indicated that Mesta had been doing just that for the past fifty years, or ever since Rivera's first venture.[1]

In 1776, in the greatest expedition of all, the Fathers Domínguez and Escalante had led a band of men north from Abiquiu, New Mexico, past the La Plata Mountains and deep into the Rockies

8. Ibid.; Dale L. Morgan: *Jedediah Smith and the Opening of the West* (New York: Bobbs-Merrill Co.; 1953), pp. 147–8; Le Roy R. and Ann W. Hafen: *Old Spanish Trail, Santa Fe to Los Angeles* (Glendale, Calif.: Arthur H. Clark Co.; 1954), pp. 94–101.
9. Phillips: *Fur Trade*, Vol. II, pp. 516–17.
1. J. J. Hill: "Spanish and Mexican Exploration and Trade Northwest from New Mexico into the Great Basin," *Utah Historical Quarterly*, Vol. III (Jan. 1930), pp. 3–23.

across the Grand River to the White River and the Green—farther than any Spaniard had gone before. (See map, p. 11.) Eventually they crossed over the Wasatch Mountains of Utah and descended into the Great Basin near Utah Lake. Then they proceeded south along the mountain wall to the vicinity of the Hurricane Cliffs and present-day Zion National Park, where they turned east once again and crossed the Colorado River near Paria Plateau, just below the Utah-Arizona border. From there they marched south and east through the country of the Moqui and the Zuñi in northeastern Arizona, on their way back to Santa Fe, which they reached on July 29, 1776.[2] It was the most fantastic exploring venture of all those the Spanish conducted in the Southwest, and as late as 1824 Miera y Pacheca's map, a rather fanciful version of the country they traversed, was the basis for all maps of that region, including Humboldt's map of New Spain of 1811, Pike's maps of 1810, and the great Lewis and Clark maps of 1810–20.

But even after that, Spanish exploration in the Great Basin country was not concluded. In an almost forgotten expedition of 1811, Don José Rafael Serracino, the postmaster of New Mexico, led a party out of Santa Fe in an effort to locate a mysterious Spanish settlement, which the Utes asserted lay beyond their territory in a country completely surrounded by wild Indians. Serracino's party traveled for three months northward past the Ute country until they were finally stopped by a "large river," possibly the Snake but probably the Grand, which they could not cross. "There he found," according to the fragmentary account of his trek given by Pino, "many articles manufactured by Spaniards such as knives, razors, and awls; he obtained the same information there, that the manufacturers of those articles lived across the river (somewhere between the north and west)." But, "since they could not tell him exactly where he could cross the river, he decided to return home."[3]

No one knows for certain just where Serracino's exploration took him, but it is possible that he journeyed north and west past the Bear River and the Great Salt Lake to the Snake River, where he met some Indians who had had contact with the Columbia River tribes and others who were familiar with the Spanish coastal opera-

2. See my footnote 7, p. 39.
3. Pedro Bautista Pino: "Exposición sucinta y sencilla de la Provincia de Nuevo Mexico," in H. B. Carroll and J. Villasana Haggard, eds.: *Three New Mexico Chronicles* (Albuquerque, N.M.: The Quivira Society; 1942), p. 134. See also William Davis Robinson letter of March 10, 1821, in *Niles National Register*, Vol. XX (1821), pp. 22–3, which presents a confused account of a Mexican expedition in 1811 similar to and possibly identical with Pino's.

tions at Nootka. If this is the case, then perhaps Serracino was pursuing the same mythical Spanish towns near the Snake that drew John Colter south from Jackson's Hole in 1808. Perhaps, even if he only reached the Grand River, what the Indians were in fact referring to was one of Manuel Lisa's trading parties. In any case, the references in Drouillard's map to Spaniards ten days' march to the south of the Yellowstone no longer seem farfetched, nor do Lewis and Clark's references to Spanish activity just south of Colter's route.

Spanish expeditions north into the Rockies, the Great Basin, and even to the Yellowstone continued well into the nineteenth century. As late as 1851, Brigham Young felt obliged to issue an order expelling all Mexican traders from Utah because they were dealing in captured Indian slaves and children kidnapped from Mormon outposts.[4] Thus, when the American traders trekked north from Abiquiu to the Green River, they were actually not traversing new country, but their achievement was important nonetheless. One of the traders was the portly Etienne Provost, whose band of trappers had been all but annihilated by the Utes under chief Bad Gotcha on the Jordan River in Utah the previous year.[5] Provost, Le Clerc, Becknell, Huddart, Wolfskill, or any of the men who led the swarm of parties that trapped in 1824 on the Green River and into the Great Basin might well have been the first to see the Great Salt Lake (which no Spaniard records having seen), but to this date strict historical evidence awards the honor to Jim Bridger, who was part of Ashley's brigade entering from the east via the Missouri and the Green and Bear rivers.[6]

9

While files of American traders and trappers were meeting on the Green River in what because of its central location would become after 1825 an annual rendezvous, other men from Taos and Santa Fe were branching out to the West along the Gila and its tributaries to California. In 1824 a curious father-and-son combina-

4. See footnote 1, p. 68. Also see Lavender: *Bent's Fort,* pp. 58–61.
5. Morgan: *Jedediah Smith,* pp. 147–8.
6. Ibid., pp. 182–3. See also the letter from Robert Campbell to Lt. G. K. Warren, April 4, 1857, in *Reports of Explorations and Surveys, to Ascertain the Most Practicable and Economical Route for a Railroad From the Mississippi River to the Pacific Ocean* . . . (Washington, 1859), Vol. XI, p. 35.

tion rode into the New Mexican capital at the head of Sylvestre Pratte's trading expedition.[7] In a scene that resembled something out of a novel by Charles Dickens, Sylvestre Pattie of Gasconade, Missouri, despondent over the death of his wife, had left his eight small children with neighbors and relatives. Taking his eldest son, a brash young man named James Ohio, he had shed a tear and turned his back forever on family and civilization, to seek peace and perhaps fortune out West. Ignorant of the intricacies of the fur trade, but excellent woodsmen, the Patties made their way up the Missouri as far as Council Bluffs, where they were turned back for neglecting to obtain a license to trap on the upper rivers. Instead of obtaining the license, however, father and son turned west to the Platte River, where they joined Sylvestre Pratte's train for Santa Fe. Because of his frontier and military experience, the elder Pattie was elected leader of the train.

No sooner had they arrived in New Mexico than fortune favored them. The younger Pattie rescued the beautiful daughter of a former Spanish governor from "a fate worse than death" as a captive of the Comanches. When he deposited the rescued maiden, clad only in his old leather hunting shirt, on her father's doorstep, Pattie received official permission to ignore the governor's edict against American trappers in New Mexico, and his career as an explorer and trapper began.

Pattie's story is a remarkable one.[8] How much is truth and how much is fiction no one will ever know—especially from his romantic *Personal Narrative*, which was published in 1831. Nevertheless, certain facts do emerge. In 1824, thanks to James Ohio's gallant rescue, the Patties were able to trap along the Gila River of Arizona. Then in 1826, while Sylvestre Pattie took charge of the Santa Rita Copper Mines in the Sierra Mimbres of southwestern New Mexico, young James Ohio Pattie, in the face of his father's misgivings, joined Michel Robidoux's party of French-Canadian trappers bound for the Gila River and the Colorado. This party was massacred by normally friendly Papago Indians near the site of present-day Phoenix, Ari-

7. James O. Pattie: *The Personal Narrative of James O. Pattie of Kentucky*, Timothy Flint, ed. (Cincinnati, Ohio: John H. Woods; 1831). Reference based on J. B. Lippincott edition (Philadelphia, 1962), p. 40. Pattie's dates are frequently confused. For an adjustment of his chronology, see J. J. Hill: "New Light on Pattie and the Southwestern Fur Trade," *Southwestern Historical Quarterly*, Vol. XXVI (Jan. 1923), pp. 243–54. Also see Robert Glass Cleland: *This Reckless Breed of Men* (New York: Alfred A. Knopf; 1952), *passim*.
8. Unless otherwise stated, this account is based on Pattie: *Personal Narrative*.

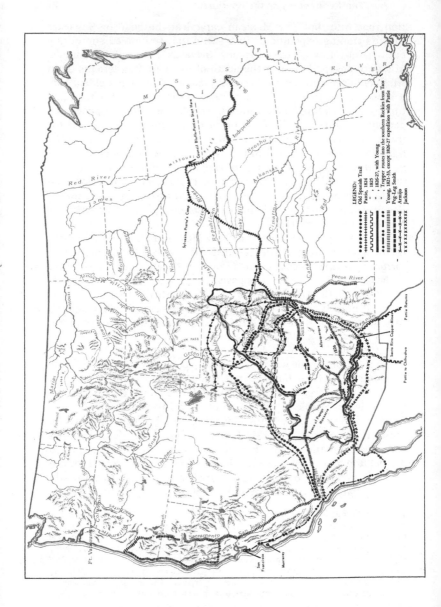

LEGEND:
Old Spanish Trail
Pattie, 1824
        1825
        1826-27, with Young
Young, 1821-33, except 1826-27 expedition with Pattie
Peg-Leg Smith
Armijo
Jackson

Trapper routes into the southern Rockies from Taos

zona, and only Pattie, one companion, and the leader Robidoux escaped alive.

Three days later they joined forces with Ewing Young's party of eighteen, which included George Yount and Tom Smith, soon to be called "Peg Leg," after he amputated his own leg with a butcher knife in the winter of 1827 along the Green River.[9] Ewing Young's party of 1826, with Pattie as chronicler, made one of the greatest of all explorations, if Pattie's geography can be believed (see following note). They trapped down the Gila to the Colorado, then up the Colorado along the rim of the Grand Canyon, where they were the first civilized men since Escalante in 1776 to see its marvels. From Grand Canyon they followed the Grand River to its sources in the Colorado Rockies, and from there they worked the parks northward, according to Pattie, whose geography at this point seems incredible, to the Big Horn and the Yellowstone and then back down the trail east of the mountains and over the passes to Taos and Santa Fe, where they arrived by the summer of 1827. There the new Spanish governor, Armijo, confiscated their year's catch of furs for trespassing in Spanish territory.[1]

9. Ibid.; Hill: "New Light. . . ." Also see Lavender: *Bent's Fort*, pp. 61–62, 75. Smith's memoirs were published in *Hutchings' Illustrated California Magazine*, Vol. V (July 1860–61). See also George C. Yount: "The Chronicles of George C. Yount, California Pioneer of 1826," in Charles L. Camp, ed.: *California Historical Society Quarterly*, Vol. I (April 1923), pp. 3–66.

1. Pattie's alleged trip from the Lower Colorado to Clark's Fork of the Columbia River via the parks of Colorado, the South Platte, the Big Horn, and the Yellowstone, and the return to Santa Fe, all in one season, has usually been taken with skepticism by historians, principally because the time needed to make such a journey does not square with the time Pattie says it took, some three and a half months. There are several possible explanations: (1) Pattie invented the trip, which is not likely since most of his other journeys are known to have basis in fact; (2) Pattie was confused as to the time that elapsed, which is possible since many of his other dates are inaccurate; (3) Pattie actually made a very fast trip (possible but not likely); or (4) Pattie did not reach the Yellowstone or Clark's Fork at all, but became confused about the geography as a result of his summer's wanderings in the Rocky Mountains. The latter possibility, in my opinion, merits further investigation. Pattie's description of his trip (pp. 88–93, Lippincott edition) appears to square reasonably well with the best-known maps of the period, Tanner's map of the United States and Mexico, 1829, and Melish's map of 1816, both of which are largely based on data from the Lewis and Clark and Zebulon Pike expeditions. Indeed, Pike's geography, with its virtual elimination of the country between Taos and the Yellowstone, accords almost perfectly with Pattie's directions, except that a Pike map would have had no reference to Long's Peak, a place mentioned by Pattie (p. 91). It is possible, however, that when Pattie dictated his *Personal Narrative* to Timothy Flint they were both confused as to the geography of the Central Rockies and had reference to one

Later that summer and fall, Pattie made a trip via Chihuahua to Sonora and the west coast of Mexico. He had no sooner returned, to settle down in the Copper Mines with his father, when one of their trusted employees absconded with the firm's capital, and the Patties were once more thrust back on their resources for financial survival. Accordingly, they took the only course possible, another trapping expedition to the Gila to recoup their fortune. This one broke up, however, near the junction of the Gila and the Colorado, where most of the party turned back. Not so the Patties. When they reached the Colorado, the Indians told them of rich Spanish settlements at the mouth of the river, so they headed downstream to the deserted salt flats that mark the river's entrance into the Gulf of California. Only a few white men had ever seen this country before—the Spaniards Ulloa in 1539 and Alarcón in 1540,[2] and recently, in 1825, Lieutenant R. W. H. Hardy of the Royal Navy, who had sailed a comic-opera expedition a short way upriver, where his ship ran aground on a sandbar. Instead of exploring the countryside, the Lieutenant had spent most of his time loading cannon and clumsily attempting

---

of the common maps of the day—circa 1824–30, since Long's Peak is mentioned—most of which were refinements of Pike. Had they done so, they might well have followed Pike's erroneous geography in retracing Pattie's route, and actually placed the expedition much farther north than it had in fact gone. Pattie's own description of the overall geography, which is a virtual paraphrase of Pike, gives strong evidence that this was the case. He says (p. 93): "It will be seen, that all these streams upon which we have been trapping, rise from sources which interlock with each other, and the same range of peaks at very short distances from each other. These form the heads of Red River of the East, and the Colorado of the West, Rio del Norte, Arkansas, Platte, Yellow Stone, Missouri and Columbia." (Compare with Pike's statement in *The Expeditions . . .* , Coués, ed., Vol. II, pp. 523–4.) Had Pattie gone up the Grand River to its head near Long's Peak, and then crossed over to the North Platte (Pattie's South Platte), followed it to the Sweetwater (Pattie's Big Horn) and the Sweetwater to the Big Horn (Pattie's Yellowstone) and the Big Horn to the Green, which he took for Clark's Fork of the Columbia, his summer trip might well have been possible. He would have been just as likely to have found the Green trapped out as he would Clark's Fork, and the round-trip traveling distance is within the realm of the possible. Flint's large library was subsequently destroyed by fire, however, and there is at present no way of determining which maps he possessed, to which the co-authors might have had reference. Thus, the future student of Pattie's adventures is left with a difficult task of detective work. The possibility is intriguing, however. And if the above hypothesis is true, it represents an example of the explorer drawing on the resources of civilization to determine just what, in fact, he had explored or perhaps even discovered.

2. De Voto: *Course of Empire*, p. 31.

to outwit the crowds of curious Indians that lined the riverbank to see his ship. As a capstone to his expedition, he compiled a completely erroneous map of the river and its junction with the Gila.[3]

Near the mouth of the Colorado, the Patties buried their season's catch, and then, starving and thirst-maddened, they followed two Yuma Indian guides across the deserts to California. On March 3, 1828, they stumbled into the Santa Catalina Mission in Lower California, where in short order they were taken into custody and, after several days' forced march, clapped into prison in San Diego. Eventually Sylvestre Pattie, weakened by privation, died in prison; and not until 1830, after further incredible adventures, did James Ohio finally return home to Missouri, sick and penniless—world-weary at the age of twenty-six—to find his brothers and sisters scattered far and wide and everything changed.[4] His had been a remarkable experience, and if in general the narrative he dictated to Timothy Flint in Cincinnati in 1830 is true, and much of it can be substantiated,[5] then few men had seen more of the West than he.

His achievements as an explorer were almost all eclipsed, however. He left no accurate record, or even a description, of his Grand Canyon trip with Ewing Young in 1826. And though he and his father were among the first to cross over from the Rocky Mountains to California, they were nevertheless only the third such American party to do so. By the time the Patties reached Los Angeles, Jedediah Smith, coming down from the rendezvous at Cache Valley, Utah, via the Sevier and the Virgin rivers, had crossed over the desert to the Mojave River and California, and was already moving north along the great interior valleys to the Sacramento River.[6]

In addition, Richard Campbell and a party of thirty-five had also reached California before the Patties by taking a direct route from Zuñi to the Gila and the Colorado and thence across the desert to California. Almost nothing is known of Campbell's expedition except that he opened a feasible route to California and that he reached that country before the Patties.[7]

By 1829 trips to California were becoming a regular occurrence. (See map, p. 72.) In that year the New Mexican trader Manuel

3. R. W. H. Hardy: *Travels in the Interior of Mexico in 1825, 1826, 1827 and 1828* (London: H. Colburn and R. Bentley; 1829), pp. 312–83, and map.
4. Pattie: *Personal Narrative,* pp. 229–30.
5. Hill: "New Light on Pattie." See my footnote 7, p. 71.
6. Morgan: *Jedediah Smith,* pp. 193–216.
7. Alice Bay Maloney: "The Richard Campbell Party of 1827," *California Historical Society Quarterly,* Vol. XVIII (1939), pp. 347–54.

Armijo took a train of loaded mules west out of Abiquiu, New Mexico, and traveling west along the San Juan, crossed the Colorado at Escalante's Paria Plateau Crossing, and continued on over the Kaibab Plateau, through the sites of present-day Kanab and St. George to the Virgin River. At the Virgin he turned south to the meadows at Las Vegas, paused for a time, and then headed out in a southwesterly direction across the Mojave Desert to Cajon Pass, San Gabriel, and Los Angeles. Part of his route lay along the Old Spanish Trail, so called because of the early Green River expeditions.[8]

Also in that year, two more American parties made their way cross-country to the Pacific. Ewing Young, with Kit Carson as one of his trappers, went via Zuñi and the Gila to California.[9] And, though little is known of it, Peg-Leg Smith, now recovered from his ordeal on the Green, led another party down from the Green River to California.[1] In 1830 William Wolfskill finally completed the Old Spanish Trail when he led his grizzled trappers down from the Green River past the future sites of Parowan and St. George, and across the desert to California. His route into the Green River country from the south had been a Spanish caravan route since the days of Rivera, but the western half of the trail was strictly American, and in large measure Wolfskill's most important achievement as an explorer.[2] A final trail was opened up by David Jackson in 1832, when he and eleven men traveled from Santa Fe to California via a southern route through Tucson, San Xavier del Bac Mission, the Gila River, and the Mojave Desert.[3]

In 1832 also, science in the person of the British botanist Thomas Coulter came to the Southwest frontier. Very little is known of his work, but in the spring of that year he made his way alone, or with a small party, from Pala on the San Luis Rey River of California across the desert to the junction of the Gila and the Colorado, where in

8. Hafen: *Old Spanish Trail*, pp. 155–70. Armijo's journal is also reprinted and edited by Hafen in *The Colorado Magazine*, Vol. XXVII (1930), pp. 120–130.
9. Christopher Carson: *Autobiography*, Lakeside Edition, Milo M. Quaile, ed. (Chicago: Donnelley; 1935), pp. 9–13.
1. Hafen: *Old Spanish Trail*, pp. 135–6.
2. George C. Yount: "The Chronicles of George C. Yount, California Pioneer of 1826," in Charles L. Camp, ed.: *California Historical Society Quarterly*, Vol. II (April 1923), pp. 3–66. Also see H. D. Barrows: "The Story of an Old Pioneer, a Biographical Sketch of William Wolfskill," *Annual Publications of the Historical Society of Southern California*, Vol. V (1902), pp. 287–94.
3. Hafen: *Old Spanish Trail*, pp. 175–6.

temperatures ranging as high as 140 degrees Fahrenheit, he attempted to collect suitable specimens of the desert plants.[4]

In a sense, Coulter's entrance into the Southwest marked a turning point in the exploration of this region. By 1832 all of the important trails West had been opened, the beaver streams located, and contact made with the Indian tribes. True, the Colorado River and the Grand Canyon itself still remained somewhat of a mystery and would continue to do so until well after the Civil War, but nevertheless in the Southwest most of the basic work of rediscovery had been done by 1832. The task that remained was a political one, that of opening up the country to American settlers moving West. This would begin in four short years, with the Texan Revolution, and it would be completed by the end of the Mexican War, when most of Spain's northern empire would be eroded away in a wave of aggressive American expansionism. Then a whole new era of exploration would begin.

A new era of exploration would begin, and the process of rediscovery would be resumed, because the new age would ask new questions of the Old Southwest. Despite their tremendous achievements, the Southwestern mountain men and fur traders of this early period left little behind, save their memory of the geography and their special wilderness lore, that would serve the needs of the later generation. They left no maps, for example. As late as 1842, the best map of the Southwest was still Humboldt's "New Spain," and that was all copied from Miera y Pacheca's map of the Escalante expedition, which included such things as the location of primitive Aztec strongholds and tales of the bearded Indians who dwelled on the shores of the mythical Timpanogos. Even the Army mapmakers felt the lack of cartographical records acutely. When Lieutenant William H. Emory constructed his master map of the Southwest in 1844, he was forced to depend on travel books and hearsay for much of the detail of the region. Consequently, in accordance with trapper Alexander Le Grande's meager and possibly apocryphal account of his trip across the arid Staked Plains of Texas in 1827,[5] Emory wrote across that part of his map: "According to Le Grande this region is fertile and well watered."[6]

4. Susan Delano McKelvey: *Botanical Exploration of the Trans-Mississippi West 1790–1850*, pp. 429–30.
5. Raymond Estep: "The Le Grande Survey of the High Plains: Fact or Fancy," *New Mexico Historical Review*, Vol. VII (April 1932), pp. 143–64.
6. William H. Emory: "Map of Texas and the Country Adjacent" (1844), Cartographic Records Section, National Archives.

In addition to the lack of maps, the trappers and traders left few detailed accounts of their travels, so that the story of their achievements must be pieced together from fragments and a few classic stories that appeared in newspapers or obscure books and journals. For the most part, the men of the southern Rockies were extremely reticent about where they had gone and what they had done. After all, most of what they were up to was illegal from the Spanish point of view. Moreover, no one, not even a free soul like the mountain man, was apt to pass on valuable information to a potential competitor. So by and large the vast amount they knew about the Southwest died with them. And though fortunately a few survivors were left to guide the Army explorers of the 1840's and 1850's, most of what the trapper had learned by hard experience had to be learned over again and reinterpreted to suit the needs of a modern generation.

Still, their achievement had not been inconsiderable. They had opened the road to Santa Fe. They had blazed three trails across New Mexico and Arizona to California. They had opened up the heart of the Rockies and helped to discover Great Salt Lake. They had made the first trails from that country to California. They had seen the Colorado from its mouth to its sources, including its stupendous canyon. And they had met every Indian in the whole vast region, from wretched Diggers who lived on worms and bugs to the lordly Pueblos whose complex apartment houses were the largest such man-made structures in the world. Most of all, as their tales filtered back to Missouri and Arkansas and points East, and grew exaggerated, they created a Southwest of the imagination that was exotic and romantic in the extreme—as romantic a vision as any that ever drew Spaniard into the wilderness in search of the Seven Cities of Gold. And so year after year, though it was full of risk and difficulty and frustration, the Southwest trade bulked larger and larger in the eyes of the St. Louis merchant adventurer. It did not matter how bullish or bearish the actual market was in New Mexico. Perennially, it remained one of the powerful attractions, the Venice or Samarkand, as it were, that drew Americans to the Southwest. And it became one of the most immediate objectives of the Mexican War.

CHAPTER III

Canada Moves South

THE 1820's proved to be a crucial decade in the struggle for an empire in the trans-Mississippi West. After 1821, Santa Fe was open to American adventurers, and in the years that followed, caravan after caravan poured into New Mexico, so that, though it was under nominal Mexican control, like Texas it actually became an outpost of American economic interests. To most commercial men in the Valley of the Mississippi, and secretly perhaps in the eyes of the Mexican citizens themselves, it appeared to be only a question of time before the call would go out for the American government to extend its protective and stable system of laws westward over Texas, New Mexico, and California. Trade had brought new life to the "Rim of Christendom," but the new Mexican government, built on the pattern of the Old Spanish regime—unstable and, as it appeared in the northern provinces, blown by whim or caprice— was an unsuitable vehicle for economic progress. What the rising middle-class of traders, planters, and ranchers, Mexican and American alike, needed was some unshakable constitutional guarantee that they would be left free to enjoy their newly won, propertied wealth. The Mexican government offered instead an inadequate legal system remote from the frontier, huge awards of land to aristocratic favorites, little protection from the Indians, and a set of burdensome trade and property restrictions that changed with every change of administering officials.[1] It is not surprising, then, that in the twenties the American filibusters and trader-explorers had begun the process of eroding away the Mexican Empire in the Southwest.

1. See Phillips: *Fur Trade*, Vol. II, pp. 468–509.

2

To the north, too, on the edge of the British Empire the tide began to turn in favor of American enterprise. With the capture of Fort Astoria in 1813, the British Northwest Company was in virtual control of the whole of the Rocky Mountain West as far south as it chose to go. But with the pressure released, operations on the Columbia fell into inefficiency and even decay. Thompson was called back to eastern Canada for good, and there was no one immediately forthcoming, with sufficient daring or imagination, to take his place at the vanguard of exploration on the southern frontier of Canada. Instead, control of the Western Department fell into conservative, and according to Alexander Ross, ridiculously inept hands. Under the shortsighted leadership of John George McTavish, John McDonald, and later James Keith, the Northwest Company turned to the consolidation of its gains at the well-established trading posts along the Upper Columbia, leaving the Snake River frontier unexplored and unexploited. The result was three years of stagnation in which profits fell far below expectations and the Indian tribes grew ever more disenchanted with the white traders. By 1816 matters had deteriorated to the point where men like James Keith and Angus Bethune, who were in charge at Fort George, as Fort Astoria was renamed, began to consider seriously the possibility of abandoning the Pacific outpost and all the trade on the Lower Columbia.[2]

Looking briefly over the period from 1813 to 1816, it is not difficult to see what disheartened them. Nearly every brigade that departed for the interior met with increasing hostility on the part of the Indians, so much so that the Cascades of the Columbia became a virtual gauntlet of Indian wrath through which parties, however strong, had to run at great risk of life and property. The very first expedition sent out by the company in October of 1813 had its difficulties, though it was led by Stuart and McKenzie, veterans of the Astor enterprise.[3] Later that winter, when en route upriver with the annual dispatch for Fort William, Alexander Stuart was

2. Alexander Ross: *The Fur Hunters of the Far West*, Kenneth Spaulding, ed. (Norman, Okla.: Oklahoma University Press; 1956), pp. 32–3. See also Elliott Coués, ed.: *New Light on the Early History of the Greater Northwest . . . The Manuscript Journals of Alexander Henry . . . and David Thompson*, 3 vols. (New York: Francis Harper; 1897), Vol II, pp. 747–916.
3. Franchere: *Narrative*, in Thwaites: *Early Western Travels*, Vol. VI, p. 298.

so severely wounded and his party so harassed that he was forced to
return to Fort George and abandon his trip.[4] A punitive expedition
under McTavish, suffering from his absurd shortsightedness in
neglecting to bring supplies, was virtually at the mercy of the savages, and succeeded in gaining redress from the Indians only by
means of the underhanded stratagem of capturing hostages under a
guise of truce.[5]

On all quarters the news was bad. Alexander Henry ran into
strong Indian resistance when he moved south to the Willamette.[6]
Governor John McDonald found that his men lacked both the in-
centive and the wherewithal to move Fort George upriver to Tongue
Point, where he proposed to erect "the Gibraltar of the West,"
and he left for eastern Canada with the next brigade, a disappointed
man.[7] John Reed, who in a halfhearted gesture had been sent with a
small party to trap on the Snake River, was massacred along with
all his men by angry Indians smarting from the brutal treatment
they had received at the hands of previous company traders.[8]

Setbacks, it seems, came almost with lunar regularity, and often
accompanied with elements of grim humor. On April 17, 1814, the
Isaac Todd finally arrived at the mouth of the Columbia. Her cargo
included a new factor for Fort George, one Donald McTavish, a veteran of the Northwest Company who had come out of retirement
in England to offer his services in cleaning up the mess in the Northwest. Not wishing to cut his last ties with civilization, he brought
along his mistress, a voluptuous blond Portsmouth barmaid, Jane
Barnes, the first white woman to reach the Columbia. Almost from
the outset she raised a stir. Chief Concumly's son, though he already had four wives, felt irresistibly attracted to Jane and offered
the Indian equivalent of a king's ransom for her hand. But McTavish, with what was to the Indian way of thinking incredible self-
ishness, refused the offer. Meanwhile, staid, God-fearing Alexander
Henry offered Jane his "protection," and for a short time she enjoyed the run of his modest quarters. Eventually pride came between McTavish and Henry, and one spring day, despite the fact
that the breakers in the bay were roaring and surging on the verge
of a tempest, and his entire crew was euphoric on rotgut liquor,

4. Ross: *Fur Hunters*, pp. 11–12; Franchere: *Narrative*, pp. 306–8; Coués:
New Light, Vol. II, pp. 790–1.
5. Ross: *Fur Hunters*, pp. 13–15; Franchere: *Narrative*, pp. 308–12.
6. Coués: *New Light*, Vol. II, pp. 810–24; Franchere: *Narrative*, p. 314.
7. Ross: *Fur Hunters*, p. 16.
8. Ibid., p. 13.

McTavish dared Henry to row with him out to the *Isaac Todd*. As a result, all but one of the high-spirited crew drowned when the boat capsized on the Columbia bar, and the fur trade lost one of its few able men in the West, Alexander Henry. It lost something more when Lady Jane sailed on the *Isaac Todd* a few days later, bound for the Far East, where she eventually settled down as the wife of an East India Company official.[9] And the Columbia continued to be a melancholy place for Empire men. At least three ship's doctors committed suicide while their vessels were at anchor off the bar, and every day news came downriver of some rumored disaster.

The company pushed on, however, in its own inept way. On April 4, 1814, two weeks before the arrival of the *Isaac Todd*, the spring brigade left for the interior and managed to make its way through the Cascades and eventually over the Athabasca Pass to safety on the eastern side of the Canadian Rockies.[1] The posts on the Upper Columbia were found to be comparatively prosperous, though at Spokane, as Alexander Ross observed, the men spent most of their time living high and holding stirring horse-racing contests with the Indians.[2] In certain areas the posts were starved for horses, however, and Ross in late April was forced to make a hazardous trip to the Indian stronghold in the Yakima Valley for remounts. There he found the Indians overwhelmingly hostile, and he escaped with his horses only by dint of skillful diplomacy.[3] Later, in July, Ross attempted to locate a direct route to the Pacific between Fort Okanagan and Puget Sound. He was forced to turn back, however, because of the fear of his men.[4] Thus, although furs continued to come in at Fort George, the leaders began to lose faith in the enterprise. It was proving exceedingly difficult to maintain what was already established, and it appeared well-nigh impossible to open up the new country that lay unattended and inviting before them to the South.

9. *Ibid.*, p. 34; Cox: *Adventures on the Columbia,* pp. 140–2; Coués: *New Light,* Vol. II, p. 896; David Lavender: *Land of Giants* (New York: Doubleday and Co.; 1958), pp. 107–8. See also Ross: "Fur Hunters of the Far West," MS., Yale Collection of Western Americana.
1. Franchere: *Narrative,* pp. 336–66.
2. Ross: *Fur Hunters,* p. 96.
3. *Ibid.*, pp. 22–32.
4. *Ibid.*, pp. 36–43.

3

Then in 1816 everything began to change for the better. Donald McKenzie arrived at Fort George from Montreal with orders from the home office to take charge of the inland trade. McKenzie, as previously indicated, had been one of the field partners in the Astoria venture, but because the whole operation had been primarily in the hands of the businessmen rather than the woodsmen, he had exerted little influence on company policy. But he had been greatly underestimated by Astor and his partners. More than any of the Astorians, McKenzie had grasped the possibility of opening up the fur trade in the interior along the Snake River and eastward to the Green. Being a person of some wilderness experience, he found the conditions along the Snake River on the overland march with Wilson Price Hunt more promising than did any of the other traders. So, at the conclusion of the sale of Fort Astoria, he left with the spring brigade for eastern Canada and made his way as fast as possible to New York City, where he offered his services once again to John Jacob Astor.[5]

Astor, however, proved to be shortsighted. Having lost Astoria because of what he considered the perfidy of his Columbia partners, he was not disposed to give McKenzie a second chance. This was made clear in a letter from Robert Stuart to Ramsey Crooks dated March 21, 1815:

> Fat McKenzie is here for the third time since his arrival in the white man's country, he pesters the old Tyger's [Astor's] soul out to employ him again, but he [Astor] dislikes him very much, sometimes says that if he enters into the business upon the meditated large scale he should like to give him a situation in some retired corner where he could do no mischief etc. etc.[6]

This rejection may explain McKenzie's incredible transformation from a reluctant and somewhat ill-disposed partner in the Astor venture into one of the great captains of the Northwest fur trade. From New York he journeyed to Montreal, where the agents of the Northwest Company employed him at the princely sum of £500 a year to take charge of the rapidly deteriorating inland trade in the Northwest.[7] It was a task that he was to discharge with consummate

5. Rollins: *Stuart's Narrative*, p. xxxix.
6. Ibid.
7. Ibid.

skill and with such amazing energy that he was called by Alexander Ross "Perpetual Motion."[8]

In 1816, when he arrived at Fort George, he was not so respected. According to Ross, he was regarded by James Keith and the other business-oriented factors as a man "only fit to eat horseflesh and shoot at a mark."[9] Keith at first refused to give him men and supplies for the necessary reconnaissance of the inland posts which had come under his charge.[1] But eventually, though it was too late in the year to do much, McKenzie was blessed with a crew of derelict Iroquois, Abenakis, and Hawaiians, and allowed to depart upriver to do his worst. He was given no company man to second him in the field, and, as his only supporter Alexander Ross remarked: "Never . . . had a person for the interior left Ft. George with such a motley crew, nor under such discouraging circumstances."[2]

McKenzie was up to the task, however, and after overcoming some Indian hostility at the Dalles, he wintered among the Company's fiercest enemies at the Cascades of the Columbia, completely winning them over with presents and a constant show of kindness. So captivated were the Cascade Indians that McKenzie gave a canoe-load of supplies to the Chief for safekeeping and was able to reclaim it from the same Indians six months later, completely intact.[3]

On his first reconnaissance, McKenzie managed to visit all the Upper Columbia posts, Okanagan, Shus-Whaps, Spokane, and numerous other trading centers. Much of his activity involved marches through country where the winter snow had not yet melted and the temperature was still near the freezing point. By June, his first mission was finished, and he returned with the spring brigade to Fort George.[4]

In 1817 he had a similar frustrating experience at Fort George. Neither able men nor adequate supplies were forthcoming, and he was forced to depart with the summer brigade in the same hopeless conditions as the previous year.[5] But gradually his plans were taking shape. His policy was to be firm with the Indians, but to do whatever possible to conciliate them. He devised a new system of defense for his men while they were on the march, and like a small-time politician in a rural election contest, he gained the Indians'

8. Lavender: *Land of Giants*, p. 112.
9. Ross: *Fur Hunters*, p. 58.
1. Ibid., pp. 69–70.
2. Ibid., pp. 70–1.
3. Ibid., pp. 78–81.
4. Ibid.
5. Ibid., p. 83.

confidence by admiring their children. "When men stood aloof," remembered Ross, "he caressed their children, which seldom failed to elicit a smile of approbation from the rudest."[6]

In addition to devising means to trade with the Indians more adequately, McKenzie also considered broader strategy. After his second visit to the inland posts, he became convinced that two changes were needed. First, the headquarters of the inland trade either at Fort George or at Spokane served no purpose. Second, the method of securing furs would have to be changed. The Indians, regarding fur trapping as undignified work, were at best only casually interested in bringing furs to the trading posts. Therefore, the Company itself would have to organize brigades of men to go into the field and do the actual trapping. Moreover, as he was to learn in the Snake country, they could not always depend on the river and the canoe to provide the means of supplying their parties and getting the furs to market. They would have to travel great distances in every direction overland by horseback.[7]

Such logic seems simple enough, but at the time it amounted to a revolution in the fur trade. Only the Americans on the Upper Missouri had tried a similar operation, and they were still largely bound to the river system.[8] At about the same time, Chouteau and De Mun were also experimenting in like manner on the Southwestern plains, but their endeavors were soon terminated by the Spaniards, who arrested them.[9]

When McKenzie finally returned to Fort George in the spring of 1818, he returned with more than a plan and a plea for help. He brought with him a wealth of experience gained in the inland country, including a novel method for thwarting attempts on one's life, which he had tested in action when he was forced to stun two Iroquois would-be assassins with a tent pole.[1] Most important, he brought an ultimatum from the Company Council at Fort William, directing the officials at Fort George to give him one hundred men and whatever assistance he required to establish a post among the Nez Percé (Walla Walla) at the junction of the Snake and the Columbia rivers.[2]

On July 11, 1818, McKenzie and a party of ninety-six, with Ross as second in command, reached a point on the right bank of the

6. Ibid., p. 90.
7. Ibid.
8. Thomas James: *Three Years, passim.*
9. See my Chapter 2, p. 56.
1. Ross: *Fur Hunters*, p. 110.
2. Ibid., p. 117.

Columbia a few miles below its junction with the Snake, and commenced preparations to build a fort. According to Ross, the site was an admirable one overlooking the broad Columbia to the west, the barren plains to the north, and the foothills of the Blue Mountains to the east and south.[3] In point of practical fact, however, this was far from an ideal location. There was no wood available for construction purposes; it had to be hauled great distances through hostile Indian country.[4] And if John Mix Stanley's drawing of the post, made for the Northern Pacific railroad survey in 1853, is accurate, it was a somber, dreary place flanked by mountains on one side and looking out over the basalt scablands on the other.[5]

McKenzie, however, did not pause to admire the view. Instead, he set about placating the local Indians, and started his men to constructing the fort. Eventually a palisade of hewn, flat-sided timbers was erected, with a blockhouse on each of the four corners, and huge water tanks atop the blockhouses to defend the structure against assault by fire. The Indians were not allowed in the fort and were forced to do their trading through a small window eighteen inches square. The fort was placed under the charge of Alexander Ross, and as soon as possible McKenzie departed for the first of his three important Snake country explorations. His party numbered 55 men, 195 horses, and carried 300 beaver traps.[6]

Due to McKenzie's understandable reluctance to engage in paper work while in the field, it is impossible to be certain of his exact line of march. (See map, p. 90.) Initially he took his men across the Blue Mountains into the Snake country and probably followed the Snake River, which ran south on the other side of the mountains. Very early upon his arrival in the Snake country, McKenzie was forced to allow twenty-five of his Iroquois to trap on their own, and to his dismay he later found that they had traded all their equipment, rifles, traps, blankets, beaver skins, and whatever else they could find, for the transitory delights of local Indian life, particularly the enjoyment of female companionship.[7]

Ultimately McKenzie's party reached the Skamnaugh or Boise River in western Idaho, which was to be a landmark on their route, and then pushed on for twenty-five days south and east of the Snake

3. Ibid., pp. 117–19.
4. Ibid., p. 120.
5. See *Pacific Railroad Reports,* Vol. XII, Pt. I, p. 152.
6. Ross: *Fur Hunters,* p. 125.
7. Ibid., pp. 127–8.

River into the region between the Snake and the Green rivers. They found the country rich in beavers and hostile Indians, both virtually untouched by the hand of the white man. During the course of this march, McKenzie returned at least once to Fort Nez Percé, his outpost at the junction of the Snake and the Columbia, making the trip alone in the winter on showshoes.[8]

After four months in the farthermost regions of the Snake country, McKenzie returned to the Fort via a circuitous route which probably took him north from Green River into Jackson's Hole and across the Tetons to the vicinity of Henry's Fort. Then he proceeded down the Snake to the Boise and over the Blue Mountains to Fort Nez Percé. Much of the route he remembered from his harrowing experiences with Wilson Price Hunt's overland Astorians in 1811.[9]

Once again, he did not pause long at the Fort. Having ascertained that Ross had matters well in hand, he set out with six men to determine the possibilities of using the Snake River for navigating supplies and equipment to his men in the Snake country. On April 15, 1819, he reported jubilantly that as far as "Point Successful head of the narrows," probably some miles downstream from Caldron Linn, the river was entirely "safe and practicable."[1] Moreover, to strengthen his operations in the field he ordered Ross to send a supply expedition to meet him on June 5, 1819, on the Boise River.[2] Not the least of his achievements was the traversing by water of Hell's Canyon on the Snake River, a feat performed by no white man before McKenzie and by few men after him.

The man selected to head the supply party was a relatively inexperienced newcomer, William Kittson, who had just arrived at Fort Nez Percé from Fort George. Kittson's early efforts in the Snake country were distinguished chiefly by his carelessness. Ignoring Ross's orders to be alert and cautious at all times, he advanced toward the Boise rendezvous without taking the precaution to post night guards. As a result, on two separate occasions the Indians stole his horses. After the second foray, he was left stranded with forty-one men and all his supplies, several days short of the rendezvous. Only McKenzie's foresight saved him. Just as he was about to give up hope and abandon the supplies, ten men from McKenzie's party arrived at his camp with the captured horses, which they had

8. Ibid., pp. 135–8.
9. Ibid.
1. Ibid., pp. 138–9.
2. Ibid.

reclaimed from the Indians, and the whole party was then able to proceed to the Boise.[3]

On his return to Fort Nez Percé, however, Kittson was not quite so fortunate. Indians attacked his party, and killed two stragglers.[4] At the same time McKenzie himself, left at the Boise rendezvous with only three men to guard the supplies, barely escaped disaster when he stood off a Snake war party by holding a match to a keg of powder and threatening them all with oblivion. Having escaped this danger, he was then forced to hide for three days on an island while roving war parties canvassed the vicinity.[5] Twenty-two days later, Kittson's second relief expedition reached him, and a new year's exploration of the Snake River country was under way.

In the late summer and fall of 1819, McKenzie sent trapping parties all over the country between the Snake and the Green rivers, north as far as Blackfoot Lake, and south as far as Bear Lake in eastern Utah.[6] This was the deepest penetration into the central mountain area made by Canadian or American explorers to date. McKenzie's men appear to have trapped the Bear River and camped on Bear Lake, but not to have followed the Bear River downstream to its outlet in the Great Salt Lake. It was left to the Americans to discover the Lake and its immense basin in the heart of the West. In terms of the fur trade, however, the second Snake expedition was a complete success. McKenzie arrived back at Fort Nez Percé with 154 loads of beaver pelts, followed like the Pied Piper of Hamelin by a colorful cavalcade of nearly five hundred Cayuse Indians, extending for two miles through the defiles of the Blue Mountains.[7] By prodigious effort in the savage and dangerous Snake country, McKenzie had resurrected the lifeless Western Department and had explored an immense unknown wilderness.

Before he retired from the fur trade at the expiration of his contract in 1821, McKenzie made one more spectacular march into the Snake country, but of this, little is known.[8] Thus, we have only glimpses of his great achievements, but these are enough to establish him as one of the West's most significant explorers, a man who rose from adversity and disgrace to revolutionize the fur trade in the Far Northwest. Of all the men who explored be-

3. Ibid., pp. 139–43.
4. Ibid., p. 142.
5. Ibid., pp. 147–8.
6. Ibid., pp. 152–3.
7. Ibid., p. 176.
8. Ibid., pp. 182–3, 185.

yond the Rocky Mountains, Donald McKenzie clearly deserves to be counted among the greatest. When he returned eastward to York Factory and the eventual command of the Red River Colony, thanks to his energy and his imagination, which revitalized and revolutionized the Columbia and Snake river trade, British fortunes in the Northwest stood higher than they had ever been. Then came the twenties, and the clash of empires, British and American, began anew.

4

McKenzie's successors in the Snake country brigades operated from a new base, called Flathead Post, far to the north and east on Thompson's River in what is now Montana. In so doing, they hoped to tap new trade territory, to take advantage of the friendly Indians nearby, to use the portage route via the Upper Columbia rather than the ocean-going harbor on the Lower Columbia, and most of all to push their sphere of influence as far east as possible, occupying, so to speak, as much of the vacuum between them and the Americans as they could. This shift was made possible by the merger of the Northwest and Hudson's Bay companies in 1821. which ended the bitter Red River War that had severed the transportation line of the Northwest Company, forcing it to supply the Western posts by means of a ship to the Columbia and Fort George. After 1821, the Saskatchewan and Athabascan Pass routes were opened once more, providing an actual surplus of men and supplies for the Northwestern posts. Between 1822 and 1824, therefore, three brigades were sent down from the north (Flathead Post) into the great arc made by the Snake River (see map, p. 90). In 1822 Michel Bourdon led his men as far south as Bear Lake in Utah and as far east as Blackfoot River in southeastern Idaho. He had spectacular success in securing furs, but due to Indian troubles he was forced to cache them somewhere out in the Snake country.[9] The next year Finian McDonald, Thompson's former lieutenant and Bourdon's superior, led the Snake Brigade. His expedition seems to have consisted of one long skirmish with the Blackfeet, during which Bourdon was killed. To follow his exact route south to the Snake River is perhaps tedious, but it is worthy of note that according to his letters he got "as far as the Croe Indian Cuntre

9. Morgan: *Jedediah Smith*, pp. 120–1.

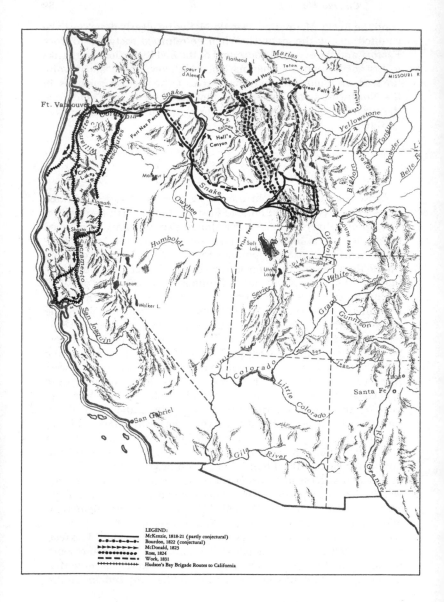

LEGEND:
McKenzie, 1818-21 (partly conjectural)
Bourdon, 1822 (conjectural)
McDonald, 1823
Ross, 1824
Work, 1831
Hudson's Bay Brigade Routes to California

on the rail Spanish river." By this he undoubtedly meant the Green. Moreover, his letter added: "Sa the Musasoury Last fall down as far is the falls," which indicates that from the Green he made his way north as far as the Great Falls of the Missouri. Most interesting perhaps of all, he wrote "that Part of the Cuntrie is rouint of Beaver By the Americans for they hade fort there fue years agoe about ½ mile beloe Corta is old Fort."[1] In speaking of "Corta is old Fort," he was perhaps referring to the activities of a veteran French-Canadian trader named Courtin who had penetrated the Upper Missouri country shortly after Lewis and Clark.[2]

The third of McKenzie's successors was his friend Alexander Ross, whose *The Fur Hunters of the Far West* is the only account of many of his adventures. Ross, in leading his brigade, experienced the greatest hardship of all, being snowbound near present-day Sula, Montana, for over a month, with starvation and mutiny ever imminent. More important, Ross inadvertently brought the British fur trade back into direct contact with the Americans when on October 12, 1824, a party of his Iroquois hunters returned to camp with eight American trappers who had saved their lives. The Americans were led by Jedediah Smith, and before the season was over they accompanied Ross and his men back to the Flathead Post —all the while reconnoitering the British operation completely.[3] The Company's home office called it a colossal blunder; after he served a short term at Flathead House, it rudely sent Ross off to retirement on the Red River.[4] Smith's expedition was the opening pressure of an American wedge that would eventually drive the British from the Snake and the Columbia. Before this happened, however, it would be 1811 all over again and the battle for the continent would have to be fought once more.

1. Ibid., pp. 122–3; Ross: *Fur Hunters*, p. 208.
2. See my Chapter 2, footnote 6, p. 45.
3. Ross: *Fur Hunters*, pp. 208–93. See also the manuscript version of Ross's book, in the Yale Collection of Western Americana. Ross described Smith and his trappers as "shrewd, well-meaning men," but his English editor, who appears to have censored as well as edited the manuscript, struck out the adjective "well-meaning," leaving Jedediah and his men merely "shrewd" to the readers of Ross's printed account. See especially p. 285.
4. Lavender: *Land of Giants*, p. 125; Frederick Merk: *Fur Trade and Empire* (Cambridge, Mass.: Harvard University Press; 1931), pp. 46, 351.

5

Fortunately for the Hudson's Bay Company, it had a number of officers who were equal to the task, and for nearly twenty years they managed to obstruct the American advance. One man in particular made a vital contribution. This was George Simpson. Only thirty-two years old in the spring of 1824, Simpson had had an amazing four-year career in the Hudson's Bay Company, rising from a raw recruit to the position of joint governor of the entire Company. In 1824, partly as a result of information gained on his whirlwind tour of the Western outposts, but primarily on the basis of instructions from London that were similar in nature to those sent to the Royal Governors in the eighteenth-century American colonies, Simpson began the reorganization of the Western Department.[5]

Since the overall Company strategy appears to have been based upon the expectation of an eventual American triumph in the Far West, Simpson set about developing the coastal trade by establishing a new port at the mouth of the Frazier River, in the event that they would have to pull back from the Columbia. Then he established a new base, Fort Vancouver, farther inland along the Columbia River. Moreover, all other posts were either abandoned or forced into the strictest economy. As a final stroke, he appointed the ruthless Peter Skene Ogden leader of the Snake River brigade, with orders to range as far south as possible and to take the maximum amount of beaver wherever he went. Scorched earth was the policy. Ogden was to create a fur desert, a burned-over district into and beyond which it would not be profitable for rival American traders to pass. In the process, the Company would of course take maximum profits.[6]

The appointment of Ogden had great importance for the history of exploration, since he proved to be the greatest of all the British fur-trader explorers. The son of an American Loyalist who fled to Canada during the Revolution, Ogden was born in Quebec in 1797.[7]

5. Merk: *Fur Trade and Empire, passim.* See also Lavender: *Land of Giants,* pp. 117–18, for a colorful description of Simpson's visit to the Western outposts.

6. Morgan: *Jedediah Smith,* pp. 131–2; Merk: *Fur Trade and Empire,* pp. 44–8, 252; E. E. Rich, ed.: *Peter Skene Ogden's Snake Country Journal* (London: Hudson's Bay Record Society; 1950), pp. xxxvii–li.

7. Biographical details based on T. C. Elliott: "Peter Skene Ogden, Fur

At the age of seventeen, he joined the Northwest Company as a clerk and during the years of conflict with the Hudson's Bay Company he gained a reputation as the meanest and most ruthless of antagonists. Just for fun, he once forced a companion to climb a tree and then set fire to its lower extremities. On another occasion he assaulted a Hudson's Bay official in his own post, leaving him at the point of death; and later, when he captured the post, he imprisoned twenty men, women, and children on starvation rations and with no sanitary facilities. So bad had his reputation grown that by 1820 he had been forced to flee to the Northwest country to stay beyond reach of the law. With the merger of the Hudson's Bay and Northwest companies, his name was dropped from the employment roll with what seems to have been very little regret. Thus, when Simpson personally saw to his reinstatement and assignment to the Snake River Brigade, it was clear that the "Honorable Company" meant to turn its "ultimate weapon" loose on the Americans.

6

Whatever he had been before, however, Ogden led his outcast Snake Brigade with honor and skill for the next six years. Beginning with his first expedition into the Snake country, he repeatedly faced disaster and survived. On December 20, 1824, he left Flathead House with a party of fifty-eight people, including the *engagés* and their wives and children. By the time he reached the Hell Gate on the Bitterroot River, near Missoula, Montana, he also had Jedediah Smith and his seven men for company. Then followed nearly two months of leapfrogging southward to the beaver country, with first Ogden, then Smith trapping out ahead. When they reached Bear River on April 26, near the present-day town of Grace, Idaho, Smith and his men departed for good, leaving Ogden to move farther south into Cache Valley. On the march south, according to William Kittson, who kept a journal, one of Ogden's trappers, Thomas McKay, climbed a high mountain and saw far to the west "a large lake which Bear River falls into."[8] It was the first con-

---

Trader," *Oregon Historical Quarterly,* Vol. II (March–Dec. 1910), pp. 229–78; and Rich: *Snake Country Journals,* pp. xi–lxxix.
8. Rich: *Snake Country Journals,* Appendix A, p. 232. Rich speculates that Ogden's first camp on Bear River "may have been near Grace, Idaho" (p. 40, *n.* 1).

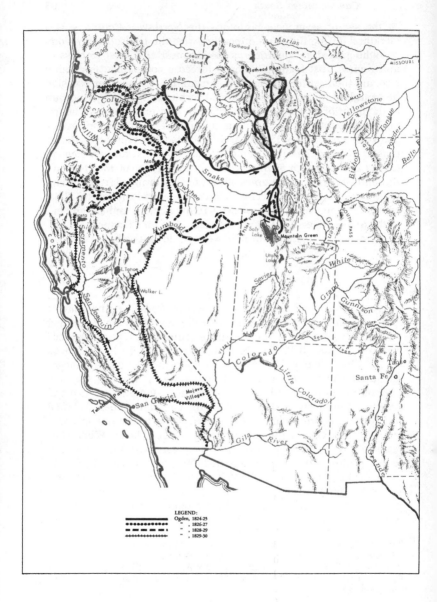

LEGEND:
Ogden, 1824-25
  "   , 1826-27
  "   , 1828-29
  "   , 1829-30

temporary record of the sighting of Great Salt Lake, although American trappers are known to have seen it the previous fall of 1824.[9]
In addition to this, Ogden also learned that "Bear River has nothing
to do with the Spanish River," indicating that this was the first
time a Canadian brigade had pushed far enough south along Bear
River to determine its outlet into the Salt Lake.[1] Ogden also speculated on information he received from the Indians concerning a
large river at the west end of the Great Salt Lake, concluding it
must be the Umpqua River, which flows through Oregon to the
Pacific and had been observed by McKay the previous year.[2] In
this instance he was merely adding to one of the West's most persistent and influential geographical myths, that of the Rio Buenaventura that was supposed to flow from the Salt Lake to the Pacific.[3]
Of all the Western explorers, however, Ogden came the closest to
finding it, when in 1828 he discovered what is now called the Humboldt River of Nevada.[4]

   Disaster struck his first expedition on May 23, 1825, when Johnson Gardner and a party of free-lance American trappers invaded
his campsite at Mountain Green, just east of Salt Lake. They
promptly raised an American flag and informed Ogden that he was
trespassing on American territory, completely ignoring the fact
that both parties were below the 42nd parallel and hence technically in Mexican territory. At this point Ogden's party fell to pieces.

9. Morgan: *Jedediah Smith,* pp. 182–5.
1. Rich: *Snake Country Journals,* p. 50.
2. Ibid.
3. The best and most recent discussion of the myth of the Rio Buenaventura,
or San Buenaventura, is Gloria Griffin Cline's *Exploring the Great Basin*
(Norman, Okla.: Oklahoma University Press; 1963), *passim.* The river was
"discovered" and named by Escalante in 1776 and first appeared on Miera y
Pacheca's map of his expedition. In incorporating Escalante's data into his
map of New Spain (1811), Humboldt included the San Buenaventura. His
atlas was copied so many times by American and European cartographers
that the San Buenaventura myth grew powerful enough to offset, throughout
the first half of the nineteenth century, actual proofs that the Rio Buenaventura did not exist.
4. Again, the most recent description of Ogden's discovery of the Humboldt
River is in Cline's *Exploring the Great Basin,* pp. 112–24, which is based
on Ogden's actual journal in the Hudson's Bay Archives. See also T. C.
Elliott, ed.: "Journals of the Snake Expeditions, 1827–28; 1828–29," *Oregon
Historical Quarterly,* Vol. XI (1910), pp. 355–97, especially p. 384. Agnes
Laut's transcript of Ogden's journal, which forms the basis for Elliott's
work, differs in numerous instances from the original that Cline saw, suggesting that the transcript was not a literal one. For example, compare p. 116
in Cline's work with p. 384 in Elliott's, both dealing with Ogden's first view
of the Humboldt.

Led by an errant Iroquois, John Grey, his trappers deserted to the Americans, who apparently encouraged them to finish the job by attacking Ogden and his few loyal men for their furs and whatever other booty they could find. Captain Bligh cast adrift in the South Seas could have been no more disconsolate than Ogden on the night of May 26, 1825. "Here I am," he wrote in his journal, "surrounded on all sides by enemies and our expectations and hopes blasted for returns this year." There was nothing else to do but turn north as fast as possible.[5]

When he finally returned to Fort Nez Percé (Walla Walla) on November 2, 1825, Ogden had seen more of the West in one season than any other trader. Besides reaching the Salt Lake, he had gone north to Clark's Fork of the Columbia, then southwest via Lemhi Pass to the Boise, the Payette, and finally Fort Nez Percé.[6] All of this country was traced on William Kittson's excellent manuscript map.[7] It provided the first cartographic representation of the Snake and Bear river country, which by now had become familiar to Hudson's Bay men, and also the first representation of the Great Salt Lake after that by Escalante in Miera y Pacheca's map of 1776. A cartographic landmark, Kittson's map is perhaps the best documentation now available of the status of the fur trader's knowledge of the mountain West at that time.

7

In all, Ogden made five more trips south into the country beyond the Columbia and the Snake, and in so doing pushed the Canadian frontier into the very heart of Mexican Utah and California (see map, p. 94). In the winter and spring of 1825-26, he once again trapped the Snake country as far east as the Portneuf River in Idaho.[8] Then, after only two months' rest, he set off again in September of 1826 on an expedition that took him south through Oregon via Malheur Lake, the headwaters of the Des Chutes, and ultimately the Klamath, which he followed into California. Though his route south from Klamath Lake is not certain, it is probable that

5. Rich: *Snake Country Journals,* pp. 51–6, especially p. 54.
6. Ibid., pp. 5–93.
7. Ibid. See reproduction of Kittson's map.
8. Ibid., pp. 95–205.

Ogden got as far as the Modoc lava beds and the Pit River before
turning back to the Rogue River. Somewhere along the way he
sighted and named Mount Shasta, which he called "Mt. Shasty."
Along with the "Nasty" and the "Shasty" rivers, it appears as part
of the confused geography of this region on Aaron Arrowsmith's
map of 1831.[9]

By August of 1827 he was again leading a brigade east to the
Snake River and the Portneuf of Idaho, where that winter he got
the better of Samuel Tullock's band of American trappers and
they apologized for Johnson Gardner's transgressions at Mountain
Green.[1]

The most significant of Ogden's expeditions, however, took place
the following season, in 1828–29, when he discovered the Humboldt, or, as he called it, the "Unknown" River.[2] Though he was not
aware of it at the time, he had found one of the great links in the
immigrant road that would take his rivals the Americans on to the
Pacific and California.

Besides his discovery of the Humboldt River, Ogden recorded his
first view of the Great Salt Lake, on Friday, December 26, 1828.[3]
By the end of December he had explored much of the north side of
the lake, coming to the conclusion that the country was barren and
"destitute of everything."[4] One other interesting observation he made
modified his earlier statement concerning the river which was said
to flow westward from the lake. "Beyond these mountains," he
wrote from Promontory Point, "west tho' the lake has no discharge,
there must be a large river in a barren country."[5] It was clear that
he was not referring to the Humboldt, since by this time he knew it
well, but rather to another version of the mythical Buenaventura.
But, as if to counterbalance his contribution to fantasy with regard
to the Buenaventura, Ogden also produced, as a result of this expedition, a crude though accurate sketch map which traced the entire
course of the Humboldt River, including its termination within the
Great Basin at the Humboldt Sinks east of present-day Reno, Ne-

9. T. C. Elliott: "Peter Skene Ogden, Fur Trader," *Oregon Historical Quarterly*, Vol. XI (1910), p. 249. See also Carl I. Wheat: "Preliminary Report,"
p. 87.
1. Elliott: "Journals of the Snake Expeditions, 1827–28, 1828–29," p. 367.
2. See footnote 4, p. 95.
3. Elliott: "Journals of the Snake Expeditions, 1827–28, 1828–29," p. 389.
4. Ibid.
5. Ibid., p. 392.

vada, where he put down the ominous notation: "280 Indians camp attacked."[6]

Though little-known, the most intriguing of Ogden's explorations in the American West was his last one, made in 1829–30. (See map, p. 94.) It is the one for which the least information exists, since all his journals were lost, along with nine of his men, in a whirlpool on the Columbia River just before he reached Fort Vancouver on the return home. Late in October 1829 he set out at the head of a band of thirty experienced men southward from the Columbia for the Humboldt Sinks that he had visited the previous year. According to his letter of March 31, 1831, he had a sharp exchange with the Indians at the Humboldt Sinks, and then turned southwest, and after six days discovered "a fine large river" which discharged into a large salt lake. Then, he continued in the same letter, "I still however persevered in advancing and reached the Great Sandy desert of Great Salt Lake."[7] Clearly this would have been impossible had he turned southwest from Humboldt Sink; his direction must have been southeast. Eventually he came out on the "South West Branch of the Rio Collorado."[8] His description of the march in Traits of American-Indian Life and Character indicates that he was at that point on the Colorado River where Jedediah Smith had been attacked by Mojave Indians in 1827, or approximately at Needles, California. Moreover, his description of the forced march across the barren desert country, during which he and his men ate their dying horses for food and drank their blood to slake their thirst, also indicates that they had traversed the Great Basin rather than the California Valleys. And finally, upon encountering Indians near the Colorado, he was able to identify them as the same Mojave tribe who had attacked Smith. Like Smith, he too had an encounter with these Indians, with more

6. Cline: Exploring the Great Basin, p. 124. Cline does not mention the phrase "280 Indians camp attacked," but it is mentioned in Carl I. Wheat: Mapping the Transmississippi West, Vol. II, p. 116.
7. Sources for Ogden's expedition of this year are: Eugene Duflot de Mofras: Duflot de Mofras' Travels on the Pacific Coast, Marguerite Wilbur, ed. (Santa Ana, Calif.: The Fine Arts Press; 1937), 2 vols.; Peter Skene Ogden: Traits of American-Indian Life and Character. By a Fur Trader (London: Smith, Elder and Co.; 1853); Alice Bay Maloney: "Peter Skene Ogden's Trapping Expedition to the Gulf of California in 1829, '30," California Historical Society Quarterly, Vol. XIV (1940), pp. 308–16; Eugene Scaglione: "Ogden's Report of His 1829–30 Expedition," California Historical Society Quarterly, Vol. XXIV (1949), pp. 117–24; J. J. Hill: "Ewing Young in the Fur Trade of the Far Southwest 1822–1834," Oregon Historical Quarterly, Vol. XXIV (1923), pp. 1–35.
8. Scaglione: "Ogden's Report," p. 121.

fortunate results, however. When the Indians charged his party, he ordered his men to fire a volley into them, and then charge with home-made spears. "The first, however, sufficed," he remembered, "for on seeing the number of their fellows who in a single moment were made to lick the dust, the rest ingloriously fled, and we saw no more of them. Twenty-six remained dead on the field." If nothing else, this was probably the first of innumerable sad instances in recorded history where Indians officially "licked the dust."[9]

From the Needles, according to Ogden's later account, his brigade marched south down the Colorado to the Gulf of California, making him the first civilized man to traverse the American West from north to south. According to Duflot de Mofras's map, Ogden's party then moved northwest from the Gulf of California and crossed through Cajon Pass near San Bernardino and then followed either Tehachapi or Walker's Pass into the San Joaquin Valley.[1] Coursing northward up the San Joaquin, Ogden apparently kept to the eastern foothills and away from the missions and the presidios, so that he was not discovered by the Spaniards. Somewhere along the way he joined forces for a time with Ewing Young's brigade and they continued on together as far as Pit River.[2] Eventually, following his old trail of 1826–27 via Klamath Lake and the Des Chutes, Ogden made it back to Fort Vancouver, but not before nine of his men and all of his records were lost to the rapids of the Columbia, a tragedy made all the more poignant by the hardships they had come through.

As an explorer, Ogden deserves to be ranked with the giants of the West. In the course of his six expeditions between 1824 and 1830 he completely explored the Snake River country, north and south, Oregon, the Salt Lake and Bear River region, and much of California north of San Francisco Bay. He had helped to discover the Great Salt Lake, and he had discovered the all-important Humboldt River. Though Jedediah Smith, and perhaps the Spaniards, had preceded him across the Great Basin, Ogden was one of its first explorers. And, as mentioned before, he was the first to traverse the transmontane West from north to south.

Almost as important as the exploits themselves were his reports and maps submitted to the Hudson's Bay office in London. Unlike so much of the information gathered by the lonely mountain men,

9. Ogden: *Traits*, p. 20.
1. See footnote 7 on preceding page.
2. Maloney: "Ogden's Expedition," p. 313; Hill: "Ewing Young."

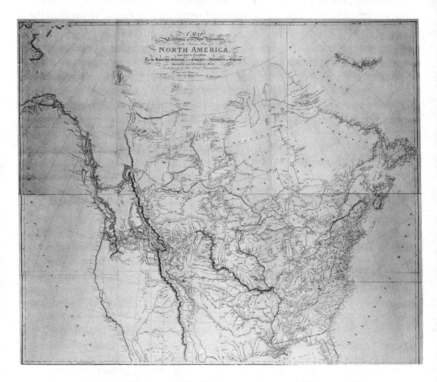

Aaron Arrowsmith's map of North America. *Courtesy Library of Congress*

Ogden's discoveries, with the exception of his march to the Gulf of California, were not consigned to oblivion. Instead his knowledge was passed on to the world-famed cartographers Aaron Arrowsmith and Sons and A. H. Brué of Paris, where, along with other data collected by the brigade leaders of the period, it formed the basis of their commercial maps for several decades.[3] Most of what was known about the Northwest was derived from the work of Lewis and Clark, David Thompson, and Peter Skene Ogden. That he was included in such select company is some measure of Ogden's achievement as an explorer. But, ironically enough, perhaps the greatest significance that can be attached to the discoveries of Ogden and the other Canadian explorers of his day is that as their findings became known and recorded on the maps of Arrowsmith and Brué they became important sources of information if not inspiration for Americans who were bent on driving the British off the Columbia and out of the Northwest.

8

After the era of Peter Skene Ogden, the history of British exploration in the Northwest is largely anticlimactic. His successor, a Scotch-Irishman named John Work who hated everything about the country and resented having to spend his life there, led four expeditions as Snake Country Brigade leader, one of which explored San Francisco Bay.[4] For the most part, these added nothing but detail to what was already known. In all, eleven separate expeditions were sent out under Work, McLeod, Laframboise, and Ermatinger after 1830. That year, however, proved to be the high-water mark of British discovery in the Northwest.[5] Thanks to the magnificent efforts of the brigade leaders, the frontier had been pushed far south into Spanish territory—as far even as the Gulf of California—and east beyond the Great Salt Lake to the Bear River of Idaho, though by 1830 the Americans had already begun to push back this frontier.

The question arises then why, after all their magnificent efforts in exploration and exploitation, did the Hudson's Bay Company

3. Cline: *Exploring the Great Basin,* pp. 123, 200–1.
4. William S. Lewis and Paul C. Phillips, eds.: *The Journal of John Work* (Cleveland, Ohio: Arthur H. Clark Co.; 1923). See also Alice Bay Maloney, ed.: *Fur Brigade to the Bonaventura* (San Francisco: California Historical Society; 1945), *passim.*
5. Herbert E. Bolton: Introduction to Maloney: *Fur Brigade,* pp. iii–vi.

eventually lose the Columbia and all its empire on the Pacific south of the 49th parallel of north latitude? The importance of such factors as the positive efforts of American missionaries, settlers, and statesmen, and the exigencies of European politics and diplomacy, are obvious. But the history of Canadian exploration in the Northwest itself provides a further insight into the loss of the Pacific domain, for it focuses clearly the strengths and weaknesses of the contrasting cultures that first bid for its control.

Viewed in one way, the Hudson's Bay men like Ogden, Work, and their predecessors were harbingers of civilization who removed the clouds of mystery and fable from the Pacific Northwest, and their findings were available to geographers and men of science who could make the proper use of them. But viewed in another way, these explorers were merely fur traders, employees of a gigantic and semifeudal governing monopoly which was the product of the English mercantile civilization itself, and as an institution embodied its values. As such it was primarily interested in profit, and only secondarily interested in such things as settlement, order, and broad economic development—and then only as they contributed to the primary purpose of the Company.

Commerce, therefore, controlled the brigade leader's function as an explorer. He was an agent of a *fur* company. He did not look for wagon routes, or places for permanent settlement. He was not interested in the potentialities for the development of a Western civilization based upon agriculture, minerals, or lumbering, except as such activities were necessary to support some distant and isolated trading post, or to supplement the Company's income. Invariably he looked for beaver. This was the information the Company appreciated, and it governed the policies of even the most enlightened of Company leaders. Since the Hudson's Bay Company had complete control over all Canadian exploration in its domain, there was little room for variety of purpose or motive in those undertakings. By the time the Company officers realized the value of diversification and founded the Puget's Sound Agricultural Company in 1839, it was too late.[6] The result was inevitable stultification. Brigade leaders, able men though they were, found only what the Company wanted them to find, and the Company in turn geared its policies toward what its explorers had found. When the brigade leaders began reporting that the beaver were scarce, there was no real reason

6. For the story of this venture, see John S. Galbraith: *The Hudson's Bay Company as an Imperial Factor 1821–1869* (Berkeley, Calif.: University of California Press; 1957).

to remain in the Northwest. For two decades the Company and its servants had succeeded brilliantly in their commercial objectives, but only rarely did anyone ask why, if the beaver are destroyed, do the Americans keep coming, and how?

Only Governor Simpson appeared to be mindful of such a question, and then primarily in the interest of protecting the Company's fur preserves. In the spring of 1829 he interrogated Jedediah Smith on the possibilities of an American migration to the Columbia for purposes of "agricultural speculation." And he uncritically accepted the answer that Smith gave him to pass on to his superiors in London, which was that Smith had "discovered difficulties . . . which are likely to deter his Countrymen from attempting that enterprize." He referred to the "impassible" sandy desert, and the rugged mountains that lay between the Mississippi and the Willamette, and concluded that no such attempt at settlement was likely to be made— at least according to the American, Jedediah Smith.[7]

But Smith himself reported in quite different terms to the Honorable John H. Eaton, American Secretary of War. In a letter headed St. Louis, October 29, 1830, Smith and his two partners, David E. Jackson and William L. Sublette, concluded that it was possible with relative ease to take not only wagons, but herds of cattle and milk cows, by way of South Pass as far as the Great Falls of the Columbia, along what was to become the Oregon Trail. They further implied, by means of Smith's glowing description of the agricultural possibilities at Fort Vancouver, that the Oregon country was a fine one for farming.[8] This kind of information inspired migration, and made settlement in the Far West seem possible. It was *not* the kind of information that Simpson and the other Hudson's Bay leaders received from their own men, nor was it the information they really desired to hear.

The eyes of the British Empire were therefore blinded, and despite the magnificent achievements of the giants Thompson, McKenzie, Simpson, Ross, McDonald, Ogden, Work, and Laframboise, despite the careful cartography of the brothers Arrowsmith, the course of commerce rather than empire governed the British in the Northwest. And failing to expand their horizon of knowledge with flexi-

7. Quoted in Morgan: *Jedediah Smith*, pp. 287–8. See also *Part of Dispatch from George Simpson Esq. Governor of Ruperts Land to the Governor & Committee of the Hudson's Bay Company London* (London and Toronto: The Champlain Society), pp. 67–8.
8. Quoted in Morgan: *Jedediah Smith*, pp. 343–7. It was originally printed in 22nd Cong., 2nd sess., *Sen. Doc.* 39 (1832–33), pp. 21–3.

bility in all directions—imprisoned, as it were, within their own particular values and institutions—they achieved comparatively little that was permanent in the Northwest. Long before the beaver hat went out in London, the gentlemen of the Canadian fur trade had taken their departure from that region where they had expended so much blood and treasure for so many years.

CHAPTER IV

The Mountain Men

AN advertisement in a frontier newspaper began the final process that carried the Americans into the Central Rockies and swept the British and Spanish from the inland empire. On February 13, 1822, at the same time that Becknell and others were opening the Santa Fe Trail, General William Henry Ashley placed his famous call in the St. Louis, Missouri, *Gazette and Public Advertiser* for "Enterprising Young Men . . . to ascend the Missouri to its source, there to be employed for one, two, or three years."[1] With these recruits he launched the first of a series of expeditions into the West that led to the discovery of new routes across the Rocky Mountains, over which American adventurers and emigrants would cross to the Pacific. Before the chain of events begun by Ashley and his advertisement was concluded, the first great climax in the struggle for a trans-Mississippi empire had been reached, and the Spanish and British horizon pushed back from the Central Rockies and the Pacific shores.

As Thomas Hempstead of the old Missouri Fur Company pointed out almost immediately, and not without misgivings, Ashley's venture was a comparatively new one. His hunters and trappers were not *engagés* or servants of the company; they were free men under short-term contract to Ashley. "I am told," wrote Hempstead, "the hunters and trappers are to have one half of the furs and they make the Company furnish them with Gun Powder Lead etc etc., they are only to help build the fort and defend it in case of necessity. . . ."[2] The men that Hempstead was referring to were free trappers, soon

1. Quoted in Morgan: *Jedediah Smith*, pp. 19-20.
2. Ibid., pp. 28-9. See also Thomas Hempstead to Joshua Pilcher, April 3, 1822, Thomas Hempstead Letterbooks, Yale Collection of Western Americana.

to become known as "mountain men," a much-celebrated but often misunderstood breed.

2

Historians fond of romanticizing the exploits of these mountain men as folk heroes have usually projected them in terms of two vivid stereotypes, each containing more than a measure of reality. On the one hand, they are seen as Byronic types—outcast banditti, veritable misanthropes of the plains and Rockies who loved only the freedom of the hunt and the chase, and scorned civilization. Everyone, from Washington Irving, who described their "wild, Robin Hood kind of life," to Bernard De Voto, who thought of them as "Odysseus Jed Smith and Siegfried Carson and the wingshod Fitzpatrick" living in a "province of fable," has seen them in terms of what is largely a European literary convention that somehow seemed to make their wilderness wanderings exotic and attractive to the world outside.[3]

On the other hand, the mountain man has also been portrayed as the saddest of all American heroes. Remote as Neanderthal and sometimes as inarticulate, these men were "stared at as though they were bears," wrote Rudolph F. Kurz, Swiss artist who traveled the Upper Missouri.[4] In this guise the mountain man became a member of the backwoods proletariat enslaved and exploited by ruthless company masters. A wild free spirit who was after all not free, he was really bringing about his own destruction as he searched out the beaver in all of the secret places of the mountain West in obedience to his betters in the world of commerce. Dependents of the London dandy and his foppish taste in hats, the mountain man was Caliban—symbol of a wilderness fast disappearing before the crush of civilization.[5]

3. For two examples, see Washington Irving: *The Rocky Mountains: or, Scenes, Incidents, and Adventures in the Far West,* 2 vols. (Philadelphia: Carey, Lea, and Blanchard; 1837), Vol. I, p. 27; and Bernard De Voto: Introduction to *The Life and Adventures of James P. Beckwourth,* T. D. Bonner, ed. (New York: Alfred A. Knopf; 1931), p. xxvii.

4. Quoted in Dorothy O. Johansen: Introduction to *Robert Newell's Memoranda* (Portland, Oregon: Champoeg Press; 1959), p. 2.

5. See, for examples of this view, Ray Allen Billington: *The Far Western Frontier* (New York: Harper & Brothers; 1956), pp. 46–7; Cleland: *This Reckless Breed,* pp. 24–5; Bernard De Voto: *Across the Wide Missouri* (Boston: Houghton Mifflin Co.; 1947), pp. 96–104; Henry Nash Smith: *Virgin Land* (Boston, Mass.: Harvard University Press; 1950), pp. 59–70, 81–9.

As most effective stereotypes do, these contain much that is true. They have highlighted the distinctive aspects of the mountain man and made him come to life in a special way. But they have neglected an equally important facet of the portrait—one that had great bearing on the mountain man's role as an explorer—his close resemblance to the common business-oriented people of the time all across the country. It was this set of values that General Ashley was counting on when he made his appeal to them as men of "enterprise."

Instead of being simply and solely exotic primitives, they very often shared the convictions of most of the other plain republican citizens of the Jacksonian era, though they had perhaps more than their share of courage and daring. The Jacksonian man (whatever his politics), according to one recent historian, "was an expectant capitalist, a hard-working ambitious person for whom enterprise was a kind of religion . . . the master mechanic who aspired to open his own shop, the planter, or farmer who speculated in land, the lawyer who hoped to be a judge, the local politician who wanted to go to Congress, the grocer who would be a merchant."[6] To these one must emphatically add the free trapper who hoped someday, if he hit it lucky and avoided the Indian tomahawk, to be one or all of these, or perhaps better still, a landed gentleman of wealth and prestige like those who had been the dominant figures in the world he left behind back on the Cumberland or the Valley of the Shenandoah or the Hudson. He went out to the frontier, like many another man of those days of laissez-faire individualism, to seek his fortune. In short, though he may have looked quaint or even outlandish, the mountain man was no simple primitive. When he went out West, he did so as a prospector on the broadest scale. He too was an expectant capitalist.

As an expectant capitalist (in contrast to the British or Spanish explorer), the mountain man had several other distinguishing characteristics. Though his primary business was the fur trade, he was not confined by its horizon, and in fact remained alert for other possibilities that would make his fortune, whether it be farming, the mines of Mexico, the transportation and supply business, or simply real estate. He looked with imagination and flexibility upon the West, and this enabled him to regard as "discoveries" things that other explorers had simply passed over. With the experience of previous frontiers in Virginia, Pennsylvania, Kentucky, Tennessee, and

6. Richard Hofstadter: *The American Political Tradition* (New York: Alfred A. Knopf; 1948), Vintage Edition (1955), p. 59.

western New York to guide him, it was second nature for the mountain man to regard the wilderness as simply a stage in the civilizing process—a place to be settled and developed in the future. Whereas for the Spaniard it was a country to be conquered, and for the English, a land to exploit, for the mountain man the West was ultimately a place to live.

Moreover, as these men confronted their Spanish and British counterparts out in the wilderness, each skirmish appeared to carry international importance, and the mountain men and frontiersmen came to identify their own interests with the nation and the government. Witness, for example, James Clyman's homely but revealing epitaph for Moses "Black" Harris, who once offered to lead a company of 700 mountain veterans into Oregon to "sweep it clear of the British and Indians."

> Here lies the bones of old Black Harris
> who often traveled beyond the far west
> and for the freedom of Equal rights
> He crossed the snowy mountain Hights
> was free and easy kind of soul
> Especially with a belly full.[7]

The triumph of the American fur trade was thus self-consciously seen as the triumph of American enterprise itself, and with it automatically came settlement and, it was assumed, sooner or later— and this was important—the dominion of free economic and political institutions.

Given this close identification with the national destiny, it was particularly fortunate that under the system of frontier republicanism the mountain men had direct access to their government. They were, in fact, friends and advisors to Governor Clark, Indian Agent O'Fallon, and Senator Benton. What they as explorers had to say, grammar notwithstanding, made a difference. Sometimes, as in the case of Ashley or Sublette, they became important political figures in their own right. In any event, they could be heard in the highest political circles of the land, and they did not hesitate to resort to this privilege often—and to good national advantage, as in the case of the Smith, Jackson, and Sublette report on the Oregon Trail to the Secretary of War, mentioned in the previous chapter. Like the older generation of Jeffersonian laissez-faire advocates on frontiers to the

7. Charles L. Camp, ed.: *James Clyman, Frontiersman* (Portland, Oregon: Champoeg Press), 1960 edition, p. 64.

East, they often called upon the central government or its representatives to aid them in their march to the West.[8]

With such familiarity possible, the vital role of republican government in safeguarding equal rights to property and in aiding the entrepreneur on the frontier was taken for granted (in the present day as well as in theirs). Western men were invariably surprised when some senator from South Carolina or Massachusetts rose to question its extension, for it was always the basic condition for whatever success they hoped to achieve. It is thus not surprising, then, that as explorers the mountain men, like other frontiersmen, looked on the West not as a desert, or an Indian refuge, or even a vast game preserve, but as a place to be lived in, to succeed in, and most of all a state to be governed so as to encourage its citizens in these pursuits. Their vision of the West as the *American* West had thus to them a kind of inevitability about it that was incomprehensible to outsiders, but which nonetheless in countless subtle ways governed what they looked for and what they found as explorers of the unknown. It led them, for example, as in the case of Ashley and his successors of the 1820's and 1830's, to look instinctively for emigrant routes over the mountains to Oregon and California and, having found them, to seek federal protection for the citizens who would use them.

3

General Ashley himself represented the archetype of Jacksonian merchant adventurer. Born in 1778 in Chesterfield County, Virginia, he had come west to Missouri sometime before 1805, settling in St. Genevieve, the old French colony below St. Louis. There he rather quickly attained prominence as a militia captain and, incongruously enough, a Justice of the Peace. Later, in partnership with his friend Andrew Henry, he became a munitions maker. Henry owned the lead mine and Ashley had been fortunate enough to discover a saltpeter cave on Cave Creek in Texas County, near Potosi, in the heart of the Missouri mining country. When the extraordinary demand created by the War of 1812 was terminated, Ashley aban-

8. A more complete discussion of my reinterpretation of the mountain man's role in the West, including statistical data, can be found in William H. Goetzmann: "The Mountain Man as Jacksonian Man," *American Quarterly*, Vol. XV (Fall, 1963), pp. 402–15.

doned his gunpowder works and came to St. Louis, where he became a surveyor and real-estate speculator.

A man of honor and distinguished bearing, though slightly built and hardly handsome, with his thin nose and hawk-like features, Ashley commanded respect wherever he went, and before long he had risen from militia captain to brigadier general of the state militia. With the organization of Missouri as a state in 1821, he became the lieutenant governor and presiding officer of the legislature. Like so many other frontier Americans of his peculiarly flexible type, Ashley bound himself to no one trade or calling, though he liked politics the best, and he was to be most successful in the fur trade. Instead he appeared to desire most of all the prestige and esteem of the community, even of the state, whose governorship he sought unsuccessfully in 1824. He was thus no different from most Americans who went West in search of the main chance. Resourceful, honorable, opportunistic, flexible, he was willing to risk everything on a venture that promised to advance his fortune. Above all, unlike the merchants of the Hudson's Bay to the north, and the Spaniards to the south, he was not tied to a traditional line of endeavor. He could change his life overnight. He proved this in 1822, when with his partner Andrew Henry, he quit the real-estate business and entered the fur trade.[9]

4

As a result of his advertisement, Ashley assembled a prime crew of "enterprising" men and sent them up the Missouri to a post at the mouth of the Yellowstone River. From the beginning, however, the General suffered grave misfortune. On the way upriver, one of his trading barges sank, with a resulting loss of $10,000.[1] Then in June of 1823 a second flotilla of keelboats suffered a disaster at the Arikara Villages far up the Missouri. Most of Ashley's best men, including Jedediah Smith, James Clyman, Edward Rose, Bill Sublette, and Hugh Glass, were pinned down by murderous fire from rifles

9. Biographical information on William Ashley can be found in Harrison C. Dale, ed.: *The Ashley-Smith Explorations and the Discovery of A Central Route to the Pacific, 1822–1829* (Glendale, Calif.: Arthur H. Clark Co.; 1941), pp. 57–63; Morgan: *Jedediah Smith*, pp. 25–9. The most recent and complete biographical data on Ashley, however, are in Morgan: *The West of William H. Ashley* (Denver, Colo.: Fred A. Rosenstock–The Old West Publishing Co.; 1964), pp. xv–xxvii.
1. Dale: *Ashley-Smith*, p. 64.

and arrows on the sandy beach opposite the Arikara town and only escaped by throwing away their rifles and equipment and swimming downstream to the safety of the fast-retreating keelboats. Before the battle was over, fourteen of the trappers, or one sixth of Ashley's entire force, lay dead at the water's edge. James Clyman, one of the survivors, declared:

> Before meeting with this defeat, I think few men had stronger ideas of their bravery and disregard of fear than I had but standing on a bear and open sand barr to be shot at from bihind a picketed Indian village was more than I had contracted for and somewhat cooled my courage.[2]

After the battle, the Missouri River remained closed above the Indian villages, and a subsequent military campaign in August 1823, under Colonel Henry Leavenworth, though it discomfited the Arikara somewhat, did nothing to open the river.[3] By the fall of 1823, Ashley, $100,000 in debt, was a desperate man, and in an effort to recoup his losses he decided to abandon the river and send his expeditions overland to the mountains, thereby officially initiating the Central Rocky Mountain fur trade.[4]

In September, the two partners Ashley and Henry took what was left of their men and launched two expeditions out from Fort Kiowa, their temporary headquarters and the last outpost between Council Bluffs and the Yellowstone. The first expedition, consisting of thirteen men, was led by Henry himself, and headed overland across present-day Nebraska and the Dakotas for the Yellowstone outpost (see map, p. 114). Along the way, two of the men were killed by Mandans, encouraged by the success of their allies, the Arikara, to strike back at the white traders heading for the country of their enemies upriver.

When Henry reached his fort on the Yellowstone, where he had established a post the previous year, he ran into further bad luck. The Indians had stolen most of his horses and were not bringing furs into the post as expected. In desperation, he moved his base south up the Yellowstone to its confluence with the Powder River. Later

2. Camp's *James Clyman*, pp. 7–13, contains the best account of the Arikara fight. The quotation appears on p. 12.
3. Dale: *Ashley-Smith*, pp. 75–82; Donald McKay Frost: *Notes on General Ashley: The Overland Trail and South Pass* (Barre, Mass.: Barre *Gazette*; 1960), pp. 20–1. See also Appendix B, pp. 65–144, of Frost's *Notes on General Ashley* for correspondence and newspaper comments relating to the Leavenworth expedition. See also Morgan: *Jedediah Smith*, pp. 63–77.
4. Dale: *Ashley-Smith*, pp. 82–7.

he moved once again to the Big Horn, not far from the site of Lisa's old fort (see pp. 18–19). Nothing worked, and in one last effort he sent one of his lieutenants, John H. Weber, south and west over the Big Horn Mountains, into the valley of the Big Horn River, and over the Owl Creek Mountains at its southern edge into the Wind River Basin, to winter among the Crows. The same path had been followed by Henry's old friend Drouillard nearly thirteen years before.[5]

5

The other party sent out from Fort Kiowa that fall of 1823 produced more important results. It was led by Jedediah Strong Smith, one of the giants of the fur trade and one of the greatest of all American explorers. Smith, who was only twenty-four years old in 1823, was perhaps the youngest captain in the history of the fur trade, and also one of the most able. Born on January 6, 1799, at Jericho, in the Susquehanna Valley of southern New York, Jedediah Smith came into the world with a tradition of Westering. His father had been on the move westward almost continuously since the close of the Revolutionary War, when he left New Hampshire and proceeded south and west across New York almost to the borders of Pennsylvania. In 1810 the Smiths moved on again over the border into Erie County, Pennsylvania. There, as a youth, Jedediah Smith learned the usual wilderness skills of shooting and stalking and in addition he received the rudiments of a good education from a family friend, Dr. Titus Simons. Family tradition has it that Dr. Simons gave Jedediah a copy of the 1814 Biddle account of the travels of Lewis and Clark, which launched him on his career in the Far West.[6]

Smith first entered on the Far Western scene in the spring of 1822. He had passed the winter of 1821–22, as he states in his journal, on the Illinois frontier near the Rock Rapids of the Mississippi, and that spring he came down to St. Louis, heard of Ashley's first expedition bound for the Upper Missouri, and signed on.[7] Thus,

5. Ibid., pp. 84–5; Morgan: *Jedediah Smith*, pp. 42, 81, 87, 96–106; Frost: *Notes on Ashley*, pp. 29–34, 56–60. See also Charles L. Camp: "The D. T. P. Letters," *Essays for Henry Raup Wagner* (San Francisco: California Historical Society; 1947), pp. 24–5.
6. Morgan: *Jedediah Smith*, pp. 23–6.
7. Maurice S. Sullivan, ed.: *The Travels of Jedediah Smith* (Santa Ana, Calif.: The Fine Arts Press; 1934), p. 1.

he gained his first experience in the West as a member of Major Henry's first Yellowstone party, a detachment of which Jedediah accompanied as far west as the Musselshell River in central Montana before turning back to Fort Henry on the Yellowstone.[8] A month after Smith's departure, the Blackfeet sent the whole party back to the Yellowstone, four of its members lost to the Indians.

By the summer of 1823 Smith had come back down the river just in time to take part in Ashley's fight with the Arikara. In the course of these travels he had become a seasoned mountain man and developed into a natural leader. Despite his comparative youth, he had proved himself on the Upper Missouri and on the beaches before the Arikara Villages.

The details of Smith's first expedition West are known primarily through the narrative of James Clyman, who was one of the party, along with Thomas Fitzpatrick, William L. Sublette, Thomas Eddie, and seven others. According to Clyman, the party left Fort Kiowa on the last day of September, guided by a member of the French (Missouri) Fur Company, who continued as far west as the Sioux Villages on the edge of the Black Hills. Their line of march was along the White River (White Clay Creek, to Clyman), through the South Dakota badlands, where they nearly died for lack of water, past the Sioux Villages, and on into the Black Hills proper. Here they ran into bad luck. An enraged grizzly bear burst from a thicket and "sprung upon the Capt. taking him by the head first," and pitching him to the earth. By the time the bear was dispatched, Smith lay broken and bleeding on the ground, but miraculously still conscious and in full possession of his senses. Here is Clyman's account of what followed:

> I asked the Capt. what was best he said one or 2 [go] for water and if you have a needle and thread git it out and sew up my wounds around my head which was bleeding freely I got a pair of scissors and cut off his hair and then began my first job of d[r]essing wounds upon examination I [found] the bear had taken nearly all of his head in his capuous mouth close to his left eye on one side and clos to his right ear on the other and laid the skull bare to near the crown of the head leaving a white streak whare his teeth passed one of his ears was torn from his head out to the outer rim after stitching all the other wounds in the best way I was capable and according to the captains directions the ear being the last I told him I could do nothing

8. *Ibid.*, pp. 2–10.

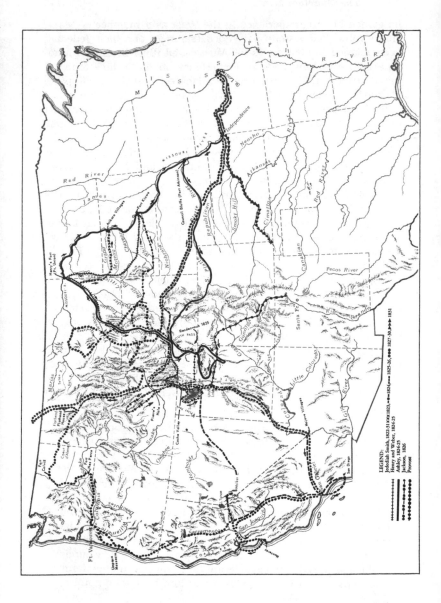

LEGEND:
Jedediah Smith, 1822-31 ***; 1823, **** 1825-26; *** 1827-30, ►►► 1831
Henry and Weber, 1824-25
Ashley, 1824-25
Jackson, 1826
Provost

for his Eare O you must try to stick up some way or other said he then I put in my needle sticking it through and through and over and over laying the lacerated parts together as nice as I could with my hands water was found in about one mille when we all moved down and encamped the captain being able to mount his horse and ride to camp whare we pitched a tent the onley one we had and made him as comfortable as circumstances would permit.[9]

It took Smith ten days to recover from his wounds, during which time his men explored the Black Hills. Then they were on their way across the Belle Fourche, and a southern tributary of the Powder River (the Little Powder River), over a ridge and into the valley of the Powder River itself, where they met Edward Rose, who had gone ahead to make contact with his friends and blood brothers, the Crows. Gradually, trapping beaver along the way, they worked across the Big Horn Mountains via Granite Pass and into the Big Horn Basin, which they found to be beautiful, fit for cultivation, and filled with game. Not so the valley of the Wind River, which they reached in late November. It offered little in the way of game or campsites until they moved north to a point just east of Frémont's Peak, or at present-day Dubois, Wyoming, where they found a village of Crow Indians and Captain Weber's band of traders from Henry's Fort. Together they all went into a bleak winter encampment in the skin lodges of the Crow Village.

6

The winter of 1824 was a severe one, and Wind River Valley was aptly named. On at least one occasion, Clyman and Sublette nearly perished while on a hunting expedition because the wind blew so hard they could not get a fire started to protect themselves from the numbing cold. Yet, despite the weather, the regular pursuits of life went on. The Crows, naked to the waist and almost contemptuous of the sub-zero weather, made two tremendous buffalo hunts, in one of which Clyman estimated they slaughtered over a thousand buffalo. So many were killed that most of the village remained out all night guarding the individual carcasses from the wolves. Clyman and a small band of Indian sharpshooters by themselves had ac-

9. Camp: *James Clyman,* pp. 15–29. See especially p. 18 for an account of Smith's encounter with the bear.

counted for seventy kills in one afternoon of a mad stampede, and they were on foot and relatively immobile.

But it wasn't buffalo robes they were after, it was beaver, and so early in February, 1824, they moved up Wind River to its head near Union Pass and attempted to cross over the Continental Divide and into Jackson's Hole the way the Astorians had done in 1811. The snow was too deep, however, and they were forced to turn back to the Crow Villages once again. There they spread out a deerskin on the ground and, using piles of sand for mountain ranges, inquired of the Crows just how they might get over or around the Wind River Mountains and into the Valley of the Seedskeedee (Green River), which the Crows had assured them was rich in the beaver they sought. It is not entirely clear whether Jedediah Smith and his men knew of the existence of the Seedskeedee before they questioned the Crows. Their attempt to cross over Union Pass suggested they knew of the treks made by the Astorians, who had seen the Green, though their lack of knowledge concerning the southern route around the Wind River Mountains suggests that they knew very little of Robert Stuart or his crossing of South Pass in October of 1812 (see pp. 33–4). Perhaps the bulk of their knowledge came from Andrew Henry, and when they headed for Union Pass they were aiming for the Tetons and Henry's old outpost on Clark's Fork (see p. 24), rather than following the Astorians. At any rate, from a deerskin and sandpile map which they made at the Crow Villages, they learned from the Indians (as had Robert Stuart) of the existence of a pass over the mountains at the extreme southern end of the Wind River range, and by the end of February they had packed up and were headed for this point. (See map, p. 114.)

No one has recorded just how long it took them to travel down the Popo Agie and over the Divide to the Sweetwater, but almost all the way they were accompanied by freezing winds and heavy snowfall. They reached the Sweetwater in withering sub-zero weather; the wind coming down the valley blew so hard that it was impossible to light a campfire. Finally they sought refuge in a valley somewhat lower down on the Sweetwater and in the opposite direction from that in which they were heading. There they made camp and waited out the blizzards, subsisting on mountain sheep. After two weeks, when game ran out, they cached what equipment they could and headed west up the Sweetwater, agreeing to meet in the valley on or about June 1. For six days they toiled forward through snowdrifts and without any water other than melted snow. Food, too, was scarce. That sixth day was noteworthy in that Clyman and

Sublette were able to bag an antelope caught in a snowdrift, and the party had its first fresh meat in several days. The occasion was also remarkable, however, in that for the second time in history (Robert Stuart's party being the first) American trappers had crossed over the broad low ridge that was the South Pass of the Rocky Mountains. A day later, when he saw the waters flowing in the opposite direction, Jedediah Smith realized what they had done.[1] And though no account of their trek indicates that they viewed the moment as a solemn one in the history of exploration, they clearly recognized its importance, for from that point on Ashley men, and later other parties, used it as the main avenue of approach and departure from the Central Rockies. In the years to come, half a continent's worth of people would pour through this gap, making it as famous and important as the one discovered by Virginia hunters back on the Cumberland.

7

For Smith and his men, not much mattered but getting water on the Little Sandy and heading for the beaver country on the Seedskeedee. They reached this long-sought destination on March 19, and immediately divided up into parties which trapped the tributaries up and down the river.[2] Smith, with seven men, went south almost to the foot of the Uinta Mountains and trapped in the vicinity of Black's Fork and possibly as far south as Henry's Fork. At this point the patterns of discovery were on the verge of meeting, as just over the Uintas to the south, also on the tributaries of the Green, was Etienne Provost and his party of trappers working north out of Santa Fe. The Green south of the Uintas was of course familiar territory after 1822 for Americans from New Mexico (see Chapter 2).

By June, Jedediah Smith and his men had all had a successful spring hunt and they headed for the rendezvous on the Sweetwater. There, however, though Smith and Fitzpatrick made connection, they missed James Clyman. He was forced to hide, and then flee for his life, from an Indian war party out on a summer hunt of its own.[3] In fact, the area picked for a rendezvous, as Frémont later

1. Ibid. The narrative of Smith's expedition presented here is based on Clyman, unless otherwise stated. See also Morgan: *Jedediah Smith*, pp. 78–92.
2. Morgan: *Jedediah Smith*, pp. 93–5.
3. Ibid. See also Camp: *Clyman*, pp. 27–9.

pointed out, was a famous Indian war ground where the tribes of the Central Rockies met and fought.[4]

The final phase of Smith's first expedition into the West was beset by a number of difficulties. Clyman, fleeing from the Indians, had to make it back down the Platte alone to Fort Atkinson on the Missouri near Council Bluffs. Fitzpatrick and two comrades, Stone and Branch, started down the river with their year's catch in a buffalo-hide bullboat. They capsized and ended up caching their furs near Independence Rock, after which they hiked the 500 or so miles back to Fort Atkinson. They arrived—according to Clyman, who himself had had an incredibly harrowing time of it— "in a more pitible state if possible than myself."[5] Jedediah Smith and the rest of his men stayed out on the Green River exploring its course north to the Blackfoot Fork of the Snake, near which they fell in with a band of Iroquois trappers from the Hudson's Bay Company and made their historic contact with Alexander Ross's party (see Chapter 3).

Meanwhile, exploration was carried forward by Captain Weber's party, which had wintered with Jedediah Smith and his men in the Wind River Valley. In July they followed Smith's party across the South Pass and on to a rendezvous near Rock Springs on the Green River (see map, p. 114). Then the Weber party separated, turning north to Bear River, which they trapped in the fall, before wintering in Cache, or, as it was then called, Willow Valley in Idaho. Sometime during this period—from the existing evidence, no one can be quite sure whether it was the late fall of 1824 or the early spring of 1825—two trappers in Weber's party made a wager as to the destination of Bear River, and young Jim Bridger was sent down the course of the river to decide their bet. "This took him," wrote his friend Robert Campbell in 1857, "to where the river passes through the mountains, and there he discovered the Great Salt Lake." Campbell added, apparently following Bridger's own account of his activities: "He went to its margin and tasted the water, and on his return reported his discovery. The fact of the water being salt induced the belief that it was an arm of the Pacific Ocean. . . ."[6]

4. See Charles Preuss: *Topographical Map of the Road from Missouri to Oregon . . . in VII Sections . . . from the Field Notes and Journal of Captain J. C. Frémont . . . by Order of the Senate of the United States* (Baltimore, 1846), section IV.
5. Camp: *Clyman*, p. 29.
6. Robert Campbell to Lt. G. K. Warren, April 4, 1857, in *Pacific Railroad Reports*, Vol. XI, p. 35. This is derived from Bridger's own statement.

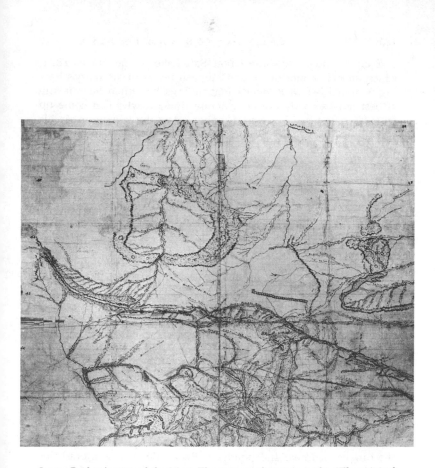

James Bridger's map of the West. The note on this map reads: "The original made by James Bridger for Col. Wm. Collins. First drawn in the earth or sand with a stick—then in detail on the skin of an animal with charcoal, then given to Col. W. O. Collins by Bridger; Collins then made this exact map—Casper Collins gave it to John C. Friend (Rawlins, Died June, 1922) who gave it to Grace Raymond Hebard." *Courtesy William Robertson Coe Library, University of Wyoming*

Even if Bridger saw the Great Salt Lake in the fall of 1824, which appears doubtful, since Campbell refers to the party's having wintered before Bridger's feat is described, then he was still at best only a co-discoverer. Etienne Provost, who had come up from Taos and in 1824 was trapping below the Uintas, made his way in the fall of that year down the Weber River Canyon, through the Wasatch Mountains, to what must have been a view of the lake. His claim, unlike Bridger's, lacks any real documentation, and Bridger has traditionally been considered the discoverer of the lake. Inference alone awards Provost priority, though among the trapping fraternity, if William Marshall Anderson was any judge (see his remarks in *The American Turf Register* for 1837), Provost was clearly the discoverer.[7]

Shortly after Bridger and Weber's party saw the Salt Lake, Jedediah Smith and his men, following Weber, saw it too,[8] and then in May of 1825 Peter Skene Ogden and his Hudson's Bay brigade happened into the Valley,[9] so that by the end of 1825 the great inland sea was well known to the trapping fraternity. It would be another year, however, before the lake was fully explored. All told, 1824 had been a most important year in the history of Western exploration, especially in the Central Rockies.

8

Back in St. Louis, Ashley learned of the experiences of Clyman, Fitzpatrick, and Smith, and chose to regard what he heard as good news. While Fitzpatrick headed back over the prairies to reclaim the furs cached near Independence Rock, Ashley began outfitting a new expedition for the Seedskeedee which he proposed to lead himself.

Ashley's expedition bound for the Rocky Mountains got underway from Fort Atkinson on approximately the first of November 1824.[1] Five days later the General, who had stayed behind winding

7. Morgan: *Jedediah Smith*, p. 182. Anderson actually stated: "Tis believed the credit, if there is any in the accidental discovery of a place is due to Weaver (Weber?) or Provost"—implying, if Weaver is indeed Weber, that Bridger, who was part of Weber's party, could have been its discoverer. Morgan, however, adds that Anderson "became an impassioned advocate of Provost. . . ."

8. Ibid., p. 184.

9. See my Chapter 3, p. 95.

1. Unless otherwise stated, the account of Ashley's expedition of 1824–25 is based on Dale: *Ashley-Smith*, pp. 115–57; Dale L. Morgan, ed.: "The

up his affairs, joined his men. They were already well along the
way to the mountains. The expedition consisted of twenty-five men,
all outfitted by Ashley; fifty pack horses; and several wagons and
teams, the first to be used in the Central Rocky Mountain trade,
although at least two years previously William Becknell had taken
his heavily loaded wagons south over the Santa Fe Trail. Among
the twenty-five men in Ashley's party were Clyman, Fitzpatrick,
and a boastful mulatto blacksmith named Jim Beckwourth who
became known after a short while as the greatest liar in the whole
West—a figure, as Bernard De Voto has pointed out, of pure
mythology, larger than life and never shy about acknowledging
the fact.

Begun in desperation, Ashley's winter march across the prairies
and mountains in 1824–25 was a daring feat. As the trappers
marched along through the wind and snow north of the Platte, they
found the going more and more difficult. Wagons had to be discarded, and the horses nearly starved, before a supply of cottonwood bark was located along the river. Fortunately the Indians
were friendly. The trappers spent eleven days with the Pawnees
near the forks of the Platte, securing new horses and resting the
ones who had come this far. Then they pushed on up the South
Platte to the Rocky Mountains proper, crossing over the front range
in three days of difficult going. On the other side of the front range,
they were confronted by the Medicine Bow Range of southern
Wyoming, whose streams they trapped in leisurely fashion before
finally crossing this second barrier between Elk Mountain and
Medicine Bow on March 25, 1825. (See map, p. 114.) From this
point on, they skirted the Red Desert area of south-central Wyoming, moving along the Platte and then crossing westward south
of South Pass via Morrow Creek, Pacific Creek, and the Big and
Little Sandy rivers, to the Green River, which they reached on
April 15.

On the Green River, Ashley wasted no time. He set his men to
work constructing a bullboat in which he proposed to take a detach-

---

Diary of William H. Ashley," Missouri Historical Society *Bulletin*, Vol XI
(1954–55), pp. 9–40, 158–86, 279–302; T. D. Bonner, ed.: *The Life and
Adventures of James P. Beckwourth* (New York: Alfred A. Knopf; 1931).
Of these, I have relied most heavily on Morgan. I have also examined the
manuscripts of Ashley's "Narrative," as reproduced in Dale, and Ashley's
"Diary," published in the Missouri Historical Society *Bulletin*. They are de-
posited in the Ashley and William Sublette Collections, respectively, in the
Missouri Historical Society, Jefferson Memorial Building, St. Louis, Missouri.

ment and explore the Green as far south as possible. The rest of
his party he split into three groups. Fitzpatrick and six men were
sent south down the Green River to trap the tributaries coming out
of the Uinta Mountains, notably Henry's Fork. Clyman, with six
men, was sent north, "to the sources of the Shetskedee." And
Zacharias Ham was designated leader of a party of seven men
which was sent to trap beaver in the mountains to the west, toward the Bear River.[2] In sending out his men in all directions into
the wilderness, Ashley made provision for their return meeting,
which has since been called the first "rendezvous" in fur-trade
history.[3] This designation ignores the wilderness meetings of
McKenzie and his men of the Snake Country Brigades, and the
annual Grand River trading "fairs" which the Spaniards up from
Taos held for the benefit of the Utes and other tribes of the
interior. Nevertheless, Ashley's instructions of 1825 which ordered
his men to meet him down Green River about fifty miles, at a
"place of randavoze for all our parties on or before the 10th of
July next," have been considered the beginning of the American
rendezvous system and somewhat of a revolution in the fur trade.
From 1825 on, parties of free trappers ranged far and wide and
then every summer returned to a designated spot in the heart of
the mountains. There they met a company trader who exchanged
whiskey, guns, knives, and other productions of civilization for
their annual catch in beaver. After a time, the trader who used
supply wagons instead of pack horses became the main beneficiary
of all the Rocky Mountain trapping activity.

9

Having dispatched his men in all directions, Ashley set out
on an exploring expedition of his own.[4] At nine o'clock on the
morning of April 22, the General loaded (six) men and baggage
on his bullboat and, though he himself was unable to swim,
launched out on the dangerous rapids of Green River in a daring
southward reconnaissance (see map, p. 114). For day after day
Ashley and his men drifted down the Green River through immense
canyons and past short stretches of staggeringly beautiful meadows
that formed Indian camping places on the edge of the river.

2. Morgan: "Diary of Ashley," p. 34.
3. Morgan: *Jedediah Smith*, pp. 171–2.
4. Morgan: "Diary of Ashley," pp. 35–40, 158–86, 279–302.

No one in his party knew what to expect of the river, except that they had heard of an immense whirlpool somewhere far off, among its lower canyons, which "sucked" everything down into the center of the earth. They had heard the same tale, however, about the Great Salt Lake. Back East in the United States, a certain Captain Symmes was soon to enlarge upon this nineteenth-century preoccupation with whirlpools and advocate a theory of gigantic polar whirlpools toward which all global water was rushing, taking with it ships, fish, walruses, icebergs, and everything that floated, down into the center of the earth. It was a good theory and furnished writers like Edgar Allan Poe and Jules Verne with material for many a story. But in 1825, on the Green River, when Ashley's boats suddenly began to capsize in the whirlpools of the Colorado, the mulatto James Beckwourth—according to his own modest account—instantly recognized it as the much advertised great "suck" and miraculously dove in to save the General, who was "no swimmer," from an unwelcome descent into the mysterious Colorado River maelstrom.[5]

The party plunged onward down the river, portaging the falls at Red Canyon, where Ashley painted his name on the canyon wall, then coursing on again through the Flaming Gorge, Lodore Canyon, which cuts for twenty miles through the Uintas, and the narrow confines of Split Mountain Canyon, until on May 16 they made their first contact with white men other than members of their own party. On that day, near the mouth of what has come to be called Ashley's Fork, they met two Frenchmen from Etienne Provost's party of trappers up from Taos, who gave them bad news about the country below.[6]

Ashley's party traveled for thirty-one days down the river, about twenty miles past the point where they met Provost's men, to

5. Bonner: "Beckwourth," pp. 35–6. Beckwourth on Beckwourth is not usually a trustworthy source, and in this case he clearly exaggerates, declaring that the bullboat actually capsized and that Ashley was thrown struggling into the water, from which he was rescued by the valiant Beckwourth. For a more accurate version, see Morgan: "Diary of Ashley," pp. 170–1, in which Ashley clearly indicates that the craft did not actually capsize, though he, along with the boat, was rescued by "two of the most active men," who "leaped in the water took the cables and towed her [the boat] to land just as from all appearances she was about making her exit and me with her for I cannot swim & my only hope was that the boat would not sink. . . ." In my text I have deliberately refrained from stating that Beckwourth pulled Ashley from the water, though I have attempted to catch the flavor of the moment and something of Beckwourth's own character.
6. Morgan: "Diary of Ashley," p. 173 and footnote.

the mouth of Minnie Maud Creek just north of Desolation Canyon in eastern Utah. Then he and his men turned back up the river to the Uinta, or Duchesne, River, which flows into the Green from the West, and proceeded up that river and its upper tributary, Strawberry Creek, toward the Wasatch Mountains to the west. For the next month they marched in company with Etienne Provost and his men overland to the north and west around the Uinta Mountains, and then east again, where on the time appointed they appeared at the designated rendezvous on Green River, twenty miles above the mouth of Henry's Fork. There all of Ashley's parties assembled, plus that of Etienne Provost and Johnson Gardner. All told, some 120 men camped on the Green that season, and Ashley did business with all of them, including the twenty-five Iroquois deserters from Peter Skene Ogden's Canadian brigade.[7] Then, the rendezvous over, the General packed up his precious furs, concluded his exploring activity, and headed north through South Pass, over the Big Horn, and down the Yellowstone to its junction with the Missouri. There he met, as he knew he would, an expedition led by Colonel Leavenworth and Major Benjamin O'Fallon which had pushed that far up the Missouri in hopes of reopening the river to the Indian trade. Under the protection of the Leavenworth-O'Fallon expedition, Ashley embarked down the Missouri River with all his furs. He returned home with enough beaver to take him completely out of debt and put him on the way to becoming a wealthy man.[8] More important, however, under his direction, and in part as a result of his own experiences, the whole of the Central Rockies had been opened up to the fur trade, the Green River explored, and the significance of the South Pass underscored. The first permanent American wedge had been driven into the transmontane West.

10

Along with Ashley when he floated back downriver to St. Louis was Jedediah Smith coming home from the wilderness for the first time in four years. At the rendezvous on Green River, Smith had informed Ashley of his experiences with the Hudson's Bay men in the fall and winter of 1824–25, during which, while Ashley

7. Morgan: *Jedediah Smith,* pp. 171–2.
8. Ibid., pp. 173–4.

was making his way out across the plains and over the front range of the Rockies, Smith and his men had accompanied Alexander Ross and his frightened band from the Snake River northward all the way to the Flathead Post near Clark's Fork in northern Montana.

During his stay, Smith had observed the Hudson's Bay operation very closely, and was able to report accurately on the number of Canadians employed in the country north of the Snake. Then, too, at the rendezvous of 1825 Ashley obtained more information from Etienne Provost, who had been present on Weber River when Johnson Gardner, scarcely two weeks earlier, had ordered the Hudson's Bay Company out of the Rockies for good. But he did not need to get an account of the activities from Provost. Johnson Gardner, too, was present at the rendezvous, as well as the twenty-five Canadian trappers who had mutinied against Ogden. Clearly, then, Ashley and Smith had much new information to digest as they cruised down the Missouri to St. Louis in the fall of 1825.

The result of their meeting was to elevate Jedediah Smith to the status of Ashley's partner—a clear step upward on the road to entrepreneurial success.[9] He replaced Andrew Henry, who desired to leave the mountains while he still had his scalp. Smith was to serve as the "field partner," the leader of the Rocky Mountain brigades, while Ashley, who married Miss Eliza Christy in a St. Louis society wedding on October 26, 1825, settled down grandly in the fur-trade capital as senior partner, marketer of beaver, and sometime politician and public figure. He was eventually to reach the Congress of the United States, where along with Thomas Hart Benton he was the chief spokesman for the fur-trade capitalists of the Missouri frontier.

11

In the spring of 1826, after his first winter out on Bear River as field commander, Smith sent his trapping parties in all directions in search of beaver. He himself turned his attention to the Great Salt Lake and the possibility, which he had heard of from the Ute Indians, of its having a western outlet to the Pacific. Following William Clark's map, which in turn derived in part from those of Humboldt and Pike, General Ashley believed that the rivers he

9. Ibid., pp. 175–6.

crossed coming around the Uinta Mountains all came together at the Great Salt Lake to form the source of the Multnomah (Willamette), or southern tributary of the Columbia. As yet neither he nor any other mountain man, American or Canadian, had any idea of the nature and extent of the Great Basin. However, he had learned from the Hudson's Bay deserters at the Green River rendezvous that whatever the river was that flowed west from the Salt Lake, it was not the Multnomah. That was far away to the West and flowed in a different direction.[1] Significantly, they had no idea of the Humboldt River, which might have served the purpose, for it was of course not until the winter of 1828–29 that it was discovered by Ogden. Lacking any real knowledge, then, Ashley had persisted in believing that a river flowed west out of the Salt Lake, and he called it, following Escalante, the Buenaventura. In the spring of 1826, therefore, though he was not able to go himself, Smith sent out an expedition under David E. Jackson to investigate the unknown country north and west of the lake.[2]

Little is known of Jackson's trek except that he moved around the north shore of the lake, past Promontory Point, to its northwest corner, where four men from his party, said to be James Clyman, Louis Vasquez, Henry Fraeb, and Moses (Black) Harris, embarked in a bullboat on a circumnavigation of the mysterious lake. They coasted its western shoreline for twenty-four days without finding the outlet that marked the Buenaventura, although, as an article in the *Niles Register* for December 9, 1826, pointed out they "passed a place where they supposed it must have been."[3] Instead of discovering anything, however, they returned to Smith's party tired and exceedingly thirsty after twenty-four days afloat on unpalatable salt water. But at least they had found no whirlpool.

Jackson continued his explorations of that season up into the Snake River country to the north, rather than turning south and following around the shore of Great Salt Lake. Just where he went is not clear, but at any rate he was in country already explored by the Hudson's Bay men, and he was back in time for the rendezvous of 1826 at Cache Valley.

One other party that wintered with Smith that year also made exploring history. It was supposedly led by William L. Sublette, and left the rendezvous late in July, heading due north across the

1. Ibid., pp. 181–2.
2. Carl I. Wheat and Dale L. Morgan: *Jedediah Smith and His Maps of the American West* (San Francisco: California Historical Society; 1954), p. 59.
3. *Niles's National Register*, Dec. 9, 1826.

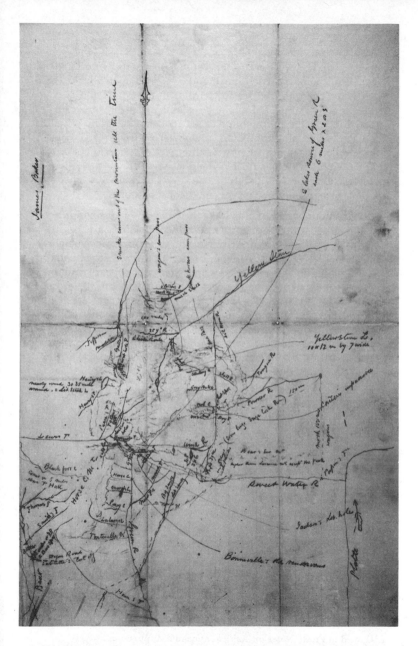

James Baker's map of the Yellowstone region, circa 1856–57. One of the few surviving maps of the West made by a mountain man, discovered by the author. *Courtesy New York State Museum*

Snake and up Henry's Fork to the Tetons, then across into Jackson's Hole. At this point it turned north and happened upon a large fresh-water lake "one hundred by forty miles in diameter, and clear as crystal": Yellowstone Lake. Sublette and his men were the first civilized men after John Colter to set foot in what is now Yellow-stone Park. One of the obscure members of the party, Daniel T. Potts, immortalized himself by writing a letter home to his brother in Philadelphia which as it turned out survived through publication in a newspaper (the Philadelphia *Gazette and Daily Advertiser*) as the first account of the marvels of the Yellowstone.

> On the South border of this Lake [he wrote], is a number of hot and boiling springs, some of water and others of most beauti-ful fine clay, resembling a mush pot, and throwing particles to the immense height of from twenty to thirty feet. The clay is of a white, and of a pink color, and the water appears fathom-less, as it appears to be entirely hollow underneath. There is also a number of places where pure sulphur is sent forth in abundance. One of our men visited one of these whilst taking his recreation—there at an instant the earth began a tremend-ous trembling, and he with difficulty made his escape when an explosion took place resembling that of thunder. During our stay in that quarter I heard it every day.[4]

Curiously enough, Potts, Sublette, and party did not tarry long near the Yellowstone, nor do they appear even to have followed the river as far as the falls, for Potts does not mention it. Perhaps they were frightened of the explosions, or of Blackfeet. At any rate, they pushed on and, as Potts says, "by a circuitous route to the North West we returned" [to Bear Lake]. Along the way, he added, they narrowly escaped from Blackfeet war parties who were on their trail.[5]

12

If the spring of 1826 had been a momentous one in terms of ex-ploration, the rendezvous of that year in Cache Valley proved to be equally important for the history of the fur trade. At the rendezvous, Ashley, who had come West with reinforcements for the brigades and a load of trade goods, sold out his interest in the Rocky Moun-

4. Quoted in Frost: *Notes on Ashley*, Appendix A, pp. 60–1.
5. Ibid.

tain Fur Company to Jedediah Smith and two partners, David E. Jackson and William L. Sublette. Smith, Jackson, and Sublette proposed to continue trapping operations out in the mountain valleys while Ashley retired from the scene, to serve exclusively as the middleman who would supply them with trade goods and market their beaver.[6] This would afford the General the leisure to pursue the social and political career he had always desired. And why not? In the four short years he had been in the fur trade, Ashley had done more than any other man to revolutionize the trade and reopen the West to American enterprise. Moreover, both in his personal excursions through the mountains and down the Green River, and in the expeditions he was responsible for sending out, Ashley had performed a crucial service in the cause of Western exploration. His men had effected the rediscovery of the South Pass. They had discovered and explored the Great Salt Lake. And they had opened up the marvels of Yellowstone Park for interested readers of the Philadelphia *Gazette and Daily Advertiser*. Of prime importance, Ashley and his men had begun to point the way West for American emigrants as well as fur traders. Nowhere is the consciousness of this fact better demonstrated than in Charles Keemle's remarks of November 8, 1826, in the *Missouri Herald and St. Louis Advertiser*. Keemle, himself a former mountain man, wrote:

> The recent expedition of General Ashley to the country west of the Rocky Mountains has been productive of information on subjects of no small interest to the people of the Union. It has been proved, that overland expeditions in large bodies may be made to that remote region without the necessity of transporting provisions for man or beast. Gen. Ashley left St. Louis in March last, and returned in September. . . . The whole route lay through a level and open country, better for carriages than any turnpike road in the United States. Wagons and carriages could go with ease as far as General Ashley went, crossing the Rocky Mountains at the sources of the north fork of the Platte, and descending the valley of the Buenaventura towards the Pacific Ocean.[7]

This, perhaps as well as anything else, sums up Ashley's most important contributions to exploration and what might be called the "public policy" of encouraging settlement in the West. It also

6. Morgan: *Jedediah Smith*, pp. 188–9.
7. Ibid., p. 192. For further comment on Ashley, see Frost: *Notes on Ashley*, Appendix B, pp. 131–44.

indicates the limits of his achievement. By the late summer of 1826, the way into the Rocky Mountains as far as the Great Salt Lake had become well known thanks to his efforts and those of his men. But there was no certainty as to what lay beyond to the Far West. Was it really, as Ashley believed, the Buenaventura and a new highway to the Pacific?

13

While his new partners, Jackson and Sublette, conducted the fall hunt of 1826, Jedediah Smith determined to find out just what did lie beyond the Salt Lake to the south and west. He put it quite simply in a letter to General William Clark, then Superintendent of Indian Affairs at St. Louis:

> I started about the 22nd of August, 1826, from the Great Salt Lake, with a party of fifteen men, for the purpose of exploring the country S.W. which was entirely unknown to me, and of which I could collect no satisfactory information from the Indians who inhabited this country on its N.E. borders.[8]

At the outset, then, his object was, not to reach the Pacific, but to open up and explore new country.

Sometime after August 15 and before August 22, 1826, which was his stated date of departure, Smith and sixteen men left Cache Valley and headed down the Bear River to the valley of the Salt Lake.[9] Besides Smith, there were Harrison G. Rogers, his clerk, quar-

8. Reproduced in Morgan: *Jedediah Smith,* p. 335. Data on Smith's march out to the mountains in 1825–26 are contained in William Fayel: "A Narrative of Colonel Robert Campbell's Experiences in the Rocky Mountain Fur Trade from 1825–1835," St. Louis, July 1886, the original of which is in the Bancroft Library Manuscript Collections P-W22. A typescript copy of this document was very generously loaned to me by Mr. Dale L. Morgan.

9. Smith gives his date of departure as August 22, 1826 (see Morgan: *Jedediah Smith*). But Morgan also points out, on p. 195, that the actual starting date may well have been August 15, when Harrison Rogers declares he issued a gill of rum to each man. Presumably this was preparatory to starting out.

My account of Smith's expedition of 1826 is based on the following: Harrison G. Rogers' "Journal," as reprinted in Dale: *Ashley-Smith,* pp. 193–319, the original manuscripts of which I have examined at the Missouri Historical Society; Morgan: *Jedediah Smith,* including Smith's letter in the Appendix; and Morgan and Wheat: *Jedediah Smith and His Maps.* The latter volume somewhat modifies the conclusions drawn by Morgan in his

termaster, and jack-of-all-trades; Peter Ranne, "a man of color"; Nappasang, a "Nippising Indian from Canada"; and Manuel Eustovan, Arthur Black, Robert Evans, Daniel Ferguson, John Gaster, Silas Gobel, John Hanna, Abraham Laplante, Manuel Lazarus, Martin McCoy, James Reed, John Wilson, and John Reubascan. Of this group, fifteen, including Smith, made the trek to California. "Nappasang" and Manuel Eustovan appear to have accompanied the expedition only as far as the Virgin River, where they dropped from sight as far as history is concerned.

Smith's route southward took him past the Great Salt Lake and down to Utah Lake, where he met the Ute Indians and distributed presents to them. From there he marched south, with the Wasatch Mountains on his left and the desert on his right, to the Sevier River of central Utah, which he named "Ashley's River." From its direction he assumed that it flowed into Utah Lake. (See map, p. 114.) On the Sevier River he questioned the "Sampatch" (San Pete Ute) Indians that he met, but learned nothing of the country ahead. It was obviously a land of scarcity (starvation, as he put it), with little else besides dust-dry alkali plains and mesquite. But he kept on anyway over a range of mountains and down onto still another river, which he called Adams River in honor of the President. This was actually the Virgin River, which flowed south out of the mountains and into the Colorado below Grand Canyon. Here Smith paused to rest his men and purchase supplies from a tribe of primitive Paiute Indians who lived along the Virgin and its tributaries. When they took up their march, they followed the Virgin through what is now Zion National Park and then turned south by southwest through more stark deserts until they reached the Colorado River, which Jedediah Smith immediately recognized, no one knew how, as the same Seedskeedee that they were all so familiar with in its northern reaches.

By this time they had passed completely out of the beaver country and into the Colorado Plateau area of mesa and canyon traversed previously only by the Spaniards Escalante and Garcés. However, neither of these hardy men had seen precisely the same part of the plateau province that Smith saw.

Upon reaching the Colorado, Smith took his men and horses across to the east bank and then rode south through the twisted difficult Black Mountain country of Arizona for many days until

earlier work and appears to have achieved greater accuracy of geographical detail.

suddenly they descended from the plateaus and emerged out into a beautiful valley that ran for miles along the river, its green vegetation sparkling in the sunlight. This was Mojave Valley, and its inhabitants, the Mojave Indians, were one of the most curious and exotic of all the tribes in the West. The men were nearly naked, but painted and tattooed all over; the women wore short bark skirts that stood out like Hawaiian hula skirts and gave them a plump, pleasant appearance. "Ammuchabas," Jedediah called them, and was glad to make friends. He and his men were worn out and emaciated with hunger. More than half their horses had died, and the rest were too exhausted to carry anything, so the whole party came down out of the mountains on foot, alive and not much more.

They remained with the Mojaves for more than two weeks, regaining their strength and asking questions about the strange unknown country that surrounded them. Smith learned from two Indians who had escaped from a mission that California was not far to the west, and he therefore resolved to survey the desert country all the way to the Mexican lands. On November 10, 1826, they set out across the Mojave Desert for California, guided by the two mission Indians. The route they followed was an old Indian trade route that linked the shell-collecting tribes of the coast with the primitive tribes of the interior. It was the one followed by Padre Garcés to California in 1776. They traveled west along this aboriginal caravan route for fifteen days, following much of the time along the course of the Mojave or, as Jedediah Smith called it, the Inconstant River. Eventually they crossed over the San Bernardino Mountains, following the headwaters of the Mojave River, and entered the green paradise of flocks and herds that was California. They were the first Americans to make the trip overland to California through the Southwest, and with their arrival in that pastoral province the American wedge had been driven deeper into the West. The frontier in that direction, heretofore only a thousand miles of wilderness, had suddenly become a border, with the Mexicans in California, and the Americans pushing on aggressively just over the Sierras.

When Smith and his trappers arrived in California, they were well received by the people and the clergy, but Governor Echeandia viewed them with suspicion, regarding them as intruders and possible filibusters. They were made to wait two weeks before the Governor would see them at all, and then they were detained from December 8 until mid-January before being allowed to depart with fresh supplies. This long delay, however, worked to the government's disadvantage since Smith and his men had a chance to look over California's pastoral paradise, which convinced some at least of its possibilities for future settlement by Americans. Harrison Rogers, Smith's clerk, noted that at San Gabriel (now Los Angeles) "upwards of 1000 persons" were employed in making various and sundry articles including blankets, whiskey, and food products. The cattle herd nearest at hand numbered 30,000, with "Horses, sheep, Hogs, etc. in proportion."[1] Fiestas and fandangos went on for weeks, the mission-made aguardiente flowed freely, and the women were, in Harrison Rogers's laconic style, "very unchaste." Two of Smith's Americans, Ferguson and Wilson, decided to stay.[2]

14

The rest of the party, led by Smith, headed out from San Gabriel on January 18, 1827. When they reached the San Bernardino Valley they turned north and continued the search for the Buenaventura just out of reach of the Spaniards in California. Eventually they crossed the Tehachapi Mountains and entered the San Joaquin Valley of California. Their northward march was along the foothills of the Sierra Nevadas, where they passed the great marshy lakes of Tulare, and trapped beaver along all of the tributaries of the San Joaquin. When they could, they traded with the friendly Indians.

By the first week in May they had reached the American River in northern California and were attempting to cross eastward over the Sierras by this route. They failed in this first attempt, however, as the snow in the passes was still too deep and the temperature freezing cold. After losing five horses, and seeing his men nearly freeze to death, Smith gave up and returned back down the western slope of the mountains. Completely unaware that he was in prime gold country, Smith was concerned primarily with his men and their survival, so he moved them south to the Stanislaus River, and saw them securely encamped under the command of Rogers. Then with two men, Silas Gobel and Robert Evans, he headed east up the Stanislaus and into the towering Sierras for one more attempt at a crossing. Starting on May 20, 1827, it took the three men eight days to cross over the mountains via Ebbetts Pass, and when they arrived on Walker's Fork, which flowed eastward into the Great Basin, they

1. Dale: *Ashley-Smith,* p. 196.
2. Ibid., pp. 216 *n.*, 217, 223 *n.*

had already lost two horses and one mule, and the trip had only just begun.[3]

Before them stretched the Great Basin, hundreds of miles of desert and desolation, dotted here and there by isolated mountain peaks and a few brackish springs. Even the Indians avoided it when they could, and only a few miserable Diggers—figures out of the Stone Age who lived on rats and bugs—called the Basin home. Almost nothing is known of Jedediah's exact route across the Basin, but it is assumed from the David H. Burr map of 1839, based on Smith's sketches, that from a point south of Walker's Lake he proceeded almost due east, parallel to or following almost identically what is now Highway 6 through Tonopah, Ham Springs, and Ely, Nevada.[4] Shortly after he passed the site of present-day Ely, Nevada, he began turning north, so that when he entered Utah he was proceeding in a northeasterly direction toward the Salt Lake. At this point, on June 22, 1827, his fragmentary journals begin:

North 25 Miles. My course was nearly parallel with a chain of hills in the west, on the tops of which was some snow and from which ran a creek to the north east. On this creek I encamped. The Country in the vicinity so much resembled that on the south side of the Salt Lake that for a while I was induced to believe that I was near that place. During the day I saw a good many Antelope, but could not kill any. I, however, killed 2 hares which when cooked at night we found much better than horse meat.[5]

They had been out thirty-two days from the camp on the Stanislaus, and still the Salt Lake was not in sight. With Gobel and Evans in a state of near despair, and food and water running low, Smith pushed on as fast and as far as he could, making as much as forty miles a day over the burning salt plain. On the twenty-fifth of June, in the bright sun of ten o'clock in the morning, Robert Evans gave out, and Smith and Gobel were forced to leave him stretched out on the plain under the shade of a small cedar tree. As Smith put it:

We could do no good by remaining to die with him and we were not able to help him along, but we left him with feelings only

3. Morgan and Wheat: *Jedediah Smith and His Maps*, p. 69. Francis Farquhar: "Jedediah Smith and the First Crossing of the Sierra Nevada," *Sierra Club Bulletin*, Vol. XXVIII (June 1943), pp. 36–53.
4. Morgan and Wheat: *Jedediah Smith and His Maps*, pp. 69–70.
5. Sullivan: *Travels of Smith*, p. 19. My account is based on Smith's journal, which is reproduced in Sullivan: *Travels of Smith*.

known to those who have been in the same situation and with the hope that we might get relief and return in time to save his life.[6]

Fortune favored them. After traveling for about three miles they reached a mountain, "and there," Smith recalled, "to our inexpressable joy we found water. Gobel plunged into it at once, and I could hardly wait to bath my burning forehead before I was pouring it down . . . regardless of the consequences."[7]

As soon as they could, they hurried back and revived Evans, then once again they pushed forward into the unknown. At last, on June 27, they came to a ridge, and ascending it they saw before them the Great Salt Lake. They had done what no other white man, and probably no Indian, had ever done before. They had crossed the continent at its most difficult, over its highest mountains and across its largest desert, the vast, primeval lake bed that was the Great Basin. For Jedediah Smith it was almost like a homecoming.

Their troubles were not over, however, once they reached the lake. Crossing the Jordan River near its mouth took two days, and Smith almost drowned. Then they marched through Indian country past the lake, up the Bear River, and on July 3 they rode suddenly down out of the hills and into the trappers' rendezvous, where, as Smith put it: "My arrival caused considerable bustle in camp, for myself and party had been given up as lost. A small Cannon brought up from St. Louis was loaded and fired for a salute."[8]

15

Jedediah's achievement as an explorer had been considerable. Not since Escalante had anyone penetrated the country west of the Colorado and south of the Great Basin. Smith and his men, following the intricate canyons of the Virgin River as far as the lower Colorado, had all but laid out what was to become in a few years "the Old Spanish Trail" to California. They were the first after Garcés to follow the ancient Indian trading route over the Mojave Desert on into California. And they were the first Americans, perhaps even the first white men, to explore the great interior valleys of that pastoral province, and in so doing they discovered for them-

6. Ibid., p. 21.
7. Ibid.
8. Ibid., p. 26.

selves California's potential as a promised land for American settlers. But the greatest achievement of all belonged exclusively to
Smith and his two companions Gobel and Evans. They were the
first to cross eastward over the High Sierras, and they were the first
to conquer the sandy wastes of the Great Basin. In only one respect
had Jedediah failed. He had not found the Buenaventura, or any
other easy highway to California across the arid wastes west of the
Salt Lake.

However, when he crossed the Sierras and headed into the Great
Basin he had turned east at a latitude so far south that he could
not be certain that a river did not cross the mountains farther north
and flow down into the Sacramento, which he had come to call the
Buenaventura. In point of fact, he had missed what would become
the great immigrant highway of the future—the Humboldt River,
which Peter Skene Ogden discovered a few years later.

But Jedediah Smith was, after all, a fur trapper and his prime
concern at the summer rendezvous was the party of men and the
cache of beaver that he had left out in California in charge of Harrison Rogers. As soon as he could, he assembled a new party of
eighteen men and started south past the Salt Lake and up over the
rim of the Great Basin for the Mojave Villages on the lower Seedskeedee.[9] His route south on the second expedition varied slightly
from that of his first, and when he reached the Mojave Villages his
reception was completely different. During the months that had in-
tervened between this and his last visit, the Mojaves had suffered
a defeat at the hands of another party of white men—trappers from
Taos led by Sylvestre Pratte who had killed a number of their tribe
in a pitched battle.[1] The atmosphere was definitely ominous when
Smith and his men arrived at the Mojave Villages, but the Indians
did not make their move until the final day, when they caught Smith
and his whole party engaged in ferrying their supplies across the
Colorado River. In a sudden attack they killed ten men and captured
two squaws, destroying the entire party on the eastern bank of the
Colorado. Smith and eight men were left stranded on a raft in mid-
river with only five guns, few supplies, and very little ammunition.
Miraculously, they made their escape by drifting downstream and
constructing a fort on the opposite riverbank, where they were able
to hold off the Indians until nightfall and then made their escape
westward into the desert.

Even here they were not out of danger, for they were far south

9. Morgan and Wheat: *Jedediah Smith and His Maps*, pp. 70–1.
1. Morgan: *Jedediah Smith*, p. 239.

of the old Indian caravan route and it required all of Smith's skill to bring them north again and locate the Mojave River, with its life-giving water. They made it, however, and on August 28, 1827, they crossed over Cajon Pass and descended into the San Bernardino Valley, to throw themselves once more on the hospitality of the Spaniards.

This time Smith and his men were not well received at all by the Mexican authorities, and a delay of two months ensued. Only after an American ship captain agreed to act as his sponsor was Smith allowed to depart. Ultimately, however, he went by sea aboard the ship *Franklin* and met his men near San Francisco, where they had been held in protective custody by the comandante while Smith awaited the Governor's pleasure. On December 30, 1827, he and his men took up the trail again, and this time made their way north up the Sacramento and out of California. They had, in Smith's words, "returned again to the woods, the river, the prairie, the Camp and the Game."[2] In retrospect, they would have been better off, had they stayed in California.

Smith's route north took him to the head of the Sacramento, then west, probably via the Trinity River, to the coast, which he followed more or less, at times being forced inland by the terrain, until he reached the Umpqua River, on July 13, 1828. His route was such that it remained an open question whether the Buenaventura or any river like it in fact existed, for at the head of the Sacramento he turned toward the coast and thus did not explore the Pit River country, through which such a river might possibly flow. Instead, traveling via the coast, they reached the Umpqua, where they learned from the Indians that the Multnomah, or Willamette, was not far to the north. On the verge of reaching civilization, in the Hudson's Bay domain, they relaxed, made camp, and set their beaver traps. Smith and two men set out upstream in a canoe to look for game. He had not gone far when Indians swarmed over his camp and in a brutal hand-to-hand fight overwhelmed and massacred all his men except Arthur Black, who, though wounded by a tomahawk, fled into the woods and escaped, carrying with him unforgettable scenes of his companions of the trail being beaten to death or scalped by the savages.

2. My account of Smith's 1827 expedition is based primarily on Smith's Journal, published in Sullivan: *Travels of Smith,* pp. 26–105; and Harrison G. Rogers's second Journal, published in Dale: *Ashley-Smith,* pp. 242–75. These are supplemented by Morgan: *Jedediah Smith,* and Morgan and Wheat: *Jedediah Smith and His Maps.*

Smith, too, nearly lost his life when his Indian guides set on him, but he and his two men managed to escape. Hurrying back to camp, they ascended a low hill and, looking down on their camp-site, saw nothing but the battered remains of their companions. Knowing that their Indian enemies were all around, Smith and his men headed into the woods and, like Arthur Black, eventually made it in safety all the way to the Hudson's Bay Company head-quarters at Fort Vancouver. Back on the Umpqua lay his massacred band, men worth remembering: Rogers, Gaster, Hanna, Laplante, Lazarus, McCoy, Ranne, Reed, Daws, Lapoint, Marechal, Palmer, Swift, and Virgin. It was the worst disaster in the history of the fur trade. Altogether in his operations of 1827 Smith had lost twenty-six men in two massacres, almost twice as many as Ashley had lost in the Arikara disaster which had closed the Missouri River in 1823.

16

At Fort Vancouver Smith and his men were treated with cour-tesies far beyond those required of protocol between two interna-tional business rivals. In the fall of 1828 Dr. McLoughlin dispatched an expedition south under Alexander McLeod to recover Smith's furs and equipment. Amazingly enough, a large part of the furs and much of the equipment, such as Jedediah Smith's own journal in Harrison Rogers's notebook, were eventually recovered from the Indians. The furs were sold to the Hudson's Bay Company at a rea-sonable price, and the notebooks Smith retained when he returned to United States territory in the spring and summer of 1829.

Smith remained at Fort Vancouver until March 12, 1829, when he took his departure in a boat bound upriver to Fort Colville near the Kettle Falls of the Columbia. During his stay at Fort Vancouver, Smith had had the opportunity of meeting the energetic Governor Simpson and of being present at the beginning of the construction of the new Fort Vancouver. Though Simpson was inclined to con-sider Smith an uncouth American, relations were cordial and Smith, in addition to passing on a certain amount of misinformation con-cerning the interior country, also apparently drew a map for Dr. McLoughlin, which has not yet been found.[3] Most significant of all, as his letter of October 29, 1830, to the United States Secretary of

3. Morgan and Wheat: *Jedediah Smith and His Maps,* p. 15.

War indicates (see p. 103), he kept his eyes open and noted the possibilities for a permanent agricultural and commercial settlement in the Northwest. In addition he passed on to the Secretary of War such data as the number of cattle and horses possessed by the British, the yield of corn and grain, and the number of cannon guarding Fort Vancouver. It was an excellent intelligence report. His long letter, co-signed by his partners, David E. Jackson and William Sublette—chronicling the ease with which loaded wagons and even milk cows could be taken over the prairies, through the Rocky Mountains via the South Pass, and from there all the way to the Pacific—was one of the most important contributions to a practical knowledge of the West ever made.[4]

This letter by Smith, Jackson, and Sublette gained national prominence as Senate Document 39 of the second session of the Twenty-first Congress of the United States. Along with it appeared two other documents of the greatest significance which point up clearly the vital role of the mountain-man explorer in creating an image of the Far West and its destiny for the nation as a whole. The first of these was a report by William H. Ashley himself, calling for federal aid to the hazardous fur trade in the form of reduced tariffs on trade goods and a company of mounted riflemen to protect the trappers and traders.[5] As such, it was symptomatic of the instinctive reliance of the Western entrepreneur on government aid in settling the West, as was mentioned at the outset of this chapter.

The other document was a report by Joshua Pilcher, another mountain man and head of the Missouri Fur Company. Pilcher had spent the years 1827–30 out in the mountains, and he had made a thorough reconnaissance of all the British trading posts from Fort Vancouver north to Fort Colville and east across Canada to Lake Superior. His report was, if anything, more authoritative than that of Smith, Jackson, and Sublette. Pilcher's theme was simple. He described Fort Vancouver as a paradise for farming, cattle raising, and shipbuilding, a place "where a great city and powerful nation will eventually grow up," and he voiced strong fears that the British would grasp this potential before the United States. Then, as if to point the way west for his countrymen, he declared that "nothing is more easily passed" than the Rocky Mountains. By the "head of the Platte," he wrote, "I have crossed . . . often, and always without delay or difficulty. It is in fact one of the best passes and presents

4. See my Chapter 3, pp. 103–4, for a discussion of this document. It is reproduced in Morgan: *Jedediah Smith,* pp. 343–8.
5. 21st Cong., 2nd sess., *Sen. Doc. 39* (1831).

the best overland route from the valley of the Mississippi to the mouth of the Columbia. . . ."[6] Taken together, these three documents —Ashley's letter on the fur trade; that of Smith, Jackson, and Sublette; and Pilcher's report on the suitability of Oregon for settlement and the easy overland road thereto—constituted what might be called the first emigrant guide to the Far West. Though it lacked the all-important map and precise instructions as to the trail, it presented an accurate picture of the Far West and its potential, and in general indicated the way in which this paradise could be reached. And as a final touch it called upon the federal government to see to it that American emigrants did reach the Columbia and that it would be secured to the United States. No clearer evidence of the mountain-man explorer's sense of national mission exists.

17

When Smith departed from the Hudson's Bay post at Fort Colville, his days as an explorer were not yet finished. From Colville he went north all the way to the Canadian border and beyond. Then he turned south and met his partner David E. Jackson just north of Flathead Lake. From there the two moved south through the now familiar Bitterroot Valley and crossed over Monida Pass to Henry's Fork of the Snake, where they met Sublette and accompanied his party to the rendezvous at Pierre's Hole just west of the Tetons. In the fall of 1829 Smith and Sublette coursed north and then east, passing just south of the Yellowstone Park area. An attack by Blackfeet scattered their party, and some of the men were reunited, picturesquely enough, according to Joe Meek, right in the midst of one of the geyser basins.[7]

No fur-trade party tarried long in Yellowstone Park, however, and this was no exception. Smith and his men crossed the ranges due east of the park area, just as John Colter must have done twenty-two years before, and then headed down into the Big Horn Basin. Eventually they trapped their way south across the Basin, over the Owl Creek Mountains, and into the Wind River Valley, which they found unsuitable for a winter encampment. Ultimately they moved north once again, to a winter encampment on the

6. Ibid.
7. Morgan and Wheat: *Jedediah Smith and His Maps,* pp. 77–8; Francis Fuller Victor: *The River of the West* (Hartford, Conn.: R. W. Bliss & Co.; 1870), pp. 75–7.

Powder River, probably where it enters the mountains east of the Big Horn Basin.[8]

In the spring of 1830 Smith led one more hunt, this time west into the heart of the Blackfeet country around the Judith River tributary of the Missouri. But the Blackfeet were everywhere and trapping was not profitable.[9] By summer rendezvous time, he had had enough of the mountains. His letters of the previous year indicated that he longed for home and the companionship of what was left of his family and old friends.[1] So that summer, at the rendezvous on the Popo Agie, or Upper Wind River, where Sublette brought his loaded wagons for the first time, Jedediah Smith sold out his interest in the fur trade and left the mountains forever. He purchased a farm, and a town house with two servants in St. Louis, intending to enjoy the civilized affluence of an Ashley or a Chouteau. He had not turned entirely away from the West, however. The following spring of 1831, in one more attempt to add to his fortune before he settled down as a merchant with his brother, he headed into the Southwest at the head of a caravan bound for Santa Fe. While looking for water on the ever dangerous Cimarron crossing, he met his death at the hands of Comanche warriors.[2] With his passing, at the age of thirty-two, was lost one of the greatest of all American explorers.

18

When Jedediah Smith died, much of his knowledge of the West died with him—as happened with so many of the great fur-trade explorers. In the case of Jedediah Smith, this was an immense loss, for he had seen more of the West than any other man, and with a natural genius for geographic detail, greater even than that of Lewis and Clark, he had understood much of what he saw in geographic terms. It had been his intention when he returned from Santa Fe to bring together this knowledge, so painfully acquired, in the form of a journal and master map of the whole West,

8. Morgan and Wheat: *Jedediah Smith and His Maps*, pp. 78–9.
9. Ibid., pp. 79–80.
1. See Morgan: *Jedediah Smith*, Appendix B, pp. 349–66, where these letters are reproduced. I have also examined the original letters, which are in the Kansas State Historical Society, Topeka, Kansas. One other letter is in the possession of Mr. Floyd Risvold of Minneapolis, Minnesota. I saw a copy at the Kansas State Historical Society.
2. Morgan: *Jedediah Smith*, pp. 329–30.

which he hoped to publish.[3] Instead, his journals passed into the hands of Ashley, who did not publish them, although he did preserve them. All of Smith's maps, however, disappeared. Thus, only fragments of what he had learned passed on to the generations immediately succeeding him, and this in widely scattered and ineffectual ways. His letters received widespread notice, especially that of July 12, 1827, to General William Clark, which was eventually published in France in the *Nouvelle Annales des Voyages*.[4] Some of the information he communicated to Dr. McLoughlin at Fort Vancouver found its way into the maps of Aaron Arrowsmith and A. H. Brué in Paris.[5] General William Ashley passed on his copy of a Jedediah Smith map to David Burr, the official cartographer of the House of Representatives, and Burr's map of 1839 was perhaps the best representation of Jedediah's geographical knowledge made public before modern times.[6] Somehow, too, knowledge of Smith's trek across the Great Basin reached the aged Albert Gallatin in New York, and Gallatin incorporated Smith's march on his "Map of the Indian Tribes of North America," published as part of the *American Antiquarian Society Transactions* in 1836.[7] And finally, as recently as 1953, the scholar Carl I. Wheat discovered perhaps the most thorough evidence of Smith's mastery of Western geography, a Frémont map of 1845 on which Dr. George Gibbs of Oregon, apparently using a Smith manuscript map, had sketched in almost all of the geographical knowledge that Smith had had, even adding notes made by Smith himself on his map.[8] From this it is possible to make a fair assessment of what Smith and his contemporaries had learned of the West—a vital part of the intellectual history of its time.

In its broadest terms, the Frémont-Gibbs-Smith map fills in the entire country between the region covered by the Lewis and Clark map of 1814 and that covered by Zebulon Pike's maps of the Southwest, and where it overlaps the other two maps it offers a correction of their geography. Its main contributions are:

3. Morgan and Wheat: *Jedediah Smith and His Maps*, p. 15.
4. "Excursion a l'ouest des Monts Rocky, extrait d'une lettre de M. Jedediah Smith . . . Saint Louis . . . 11 Oct. 1827," *Nouvelles Annales des Voyages*, Vol. XXXVII (second series, Vol. VII), Paris, 1828, pp. 208–12.
5. Morgan and Wheat: *Jedediah Smith and His Maps*, pp. 15–26.
6. Ibid.
7. Albert Gallatin: "Map of the Indian Tribes of North America," American Antiquarian Society, Archaeologica Americana, *Transactions and Collections*, Vol. II (1836).
8. Morgan and Wheat: *Jedidiah Smith and His Maps*, pp. 38–9.

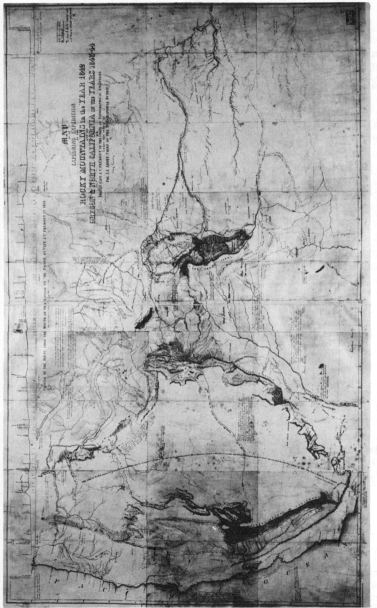

Frémont-Gibbs-Smith map of the West. A copy of Frémont's famous map of 1845, with Jedediah Smith's notations on it. The only known map which indicates Smith's knowledge of Western geography.

Discovered by Dale L. Morgan and Carl I. Wheat. Note the clear indication of Smith's trek across the Great Basin. *Courtesy Library of Congress and American Geographical Society*

1. A correct redrawing of the Big Horn River and its tributaries.

2. The first accurate characterization of the North Platte, the Sweetwater, and the all-important South Pass, along with Scott's Bluff and Chimney Rock, important landmarks along the future emigrant route to the Far West.

3. A more correct version of the sources of the Colorado, the Rio Grande, and the Arkansas rivers, which Pike had heretofore seen as coming together in one "Grand reservoir of snows and fountains."

4. Colorado's four great interior "parks" are represented for the first time.

5. The Rio Grande is indicated with some accuracy.

6. The Green River and its tributaries, thanks to Ashley's information, are included for the first time on any American map.

7. Great Salt Lake, Bear Lake, Sevier Lake, Utah Lake, together with the Bear, Weber, Sevier, and Virgin rivers, are accurately placed, and some idea is given of the Great Salt Lake's "self-contained drainage." This, however, was easy to do on a Frémont map since it was one of Frémont's chief conclusions concerning the lake.

8. The Sierra Nevadas and the Great Central Valley of California are also included, and some idea given of a Great Basin. Again, Frémont's map is ideal for the purpose, as it attempts to depict, as he thought for the first time, the Great Basin as a distinctive geographical phenomenon.

9. All of the rivers flowing west out of Oregon to the Pacific were shown and named by Smith. The Willamette, and its relationship to the Cascades and the Columbia, is shown correctly for the first time.

In short, the map reveals—in Carl I. Wheat's words—"the fur trader's West portrayed at a moment of climax."[9]

The era of William H. Ashley and Jedediah Smith had been a classic one in the history of Western exploration. Most of the important features of Western geography had been revealed and the Rocky Mountain heartland had been opened up to American exploitation. For sheer enterprise and pristine discovery there would never be anything to match those days when General Ashley coursed down the Seedskeedee in a hastily made bullboat and his

9. Ibid., *passim.* My assessment of the importance of Smith's explorations is based in large part, though by no means exclusively, on Morgan and Wheat. In some cases I have modified their views and in other cases I have introduced conclusions of my own.

men first gazed on the marvels of the Yellowstone and the silent lonely shores of the Great Salt Lake, and crossed the wastelands of the Great Basin for the first time from California's pastoral landscapes to the earthier environs of a trapper's rendezvous in the Rocky Mountains. General Ashley and his men, turned aside from the Missouri River artery by the Arikara disaster, had opened up the Great West for all time, and much of what they knew and what they described guided generations of future emigrants. Of all the explorers, they had been the first to describe Oregon and California as a paradise for settlers. But though they had opened up the West, found the South Pass, gone to the Pacific Coast and touted its glories, they had not yet blazed an effective trail for Westbound emigrants. They had only called attention to the existence of a feasible trail. And when Ashley retired and died young (in 1838), and Jedediah Smith was killed so tragically in 1831, much of their specialized information went with them. As the 1830's began, a second set of fur-trader explorers appeared—an eccentric French captain on special leave from the American Army, a Boston ice dealer, a Tennessee trapper, a Harvard botanist, and the first of a new breed, the wagon-train scout. These men would take up where Ashley and Smith left off, as explorers of a central path to the Pacific and harbingers of the era of Manifest Destiny.

CHAPTER V

Something More Than Beaver

BY the early 1830's the fur trade had reached its height, and bands of trappers in fierce competition with one another searched out every hidden park, glade, and beaver stream in the Rocky Mountain region. After the work of Ashley, Smith, and others of the earlier generation of trapper-explorers, the Central Rockies from the great bend of the Missouri to the Southern Sierras of New Mexico became a familiar place to the men of the fur trade. South Pass was the all-important gateway, and without it the commerce of the Rockies could hardly have existed at all. Farther west, the Seedskeedee was the crossroads for parties of north- and southbound hunters. North by northwest was the Snake River, the road to Oregon, and then due north the two sets of Tetons, which served as landmarks to parties bound for the Blackfeet and Flathead country. Jackson's Hole and Pierre's Hole, on opposite sides of the easternmost, or Grand Tetons, saw mountain rendezvous of various kinds, some grim, some hilarious, as trapper bands crossed and recrossed those beautiful valleys that John Colter had first seen in solitude scarcely twenty years before. To the trapper and the Crow Indian who frequented them, Absaroka or the Big Horn and Wind River basins were a paradise, "just exactly," as a Crow chief put it, "in the right place."[1] Even the marvels of Yellowstone Park, Colter's Hell, and Beer Springs on the Bear River were well known, and their merits contrasted among the trapping fraternity over and over again in the same high seriousness in which vacationers at Newport or Saratoga or White Sulphur Springs compared their spas a decade or so later. Perhaps the clearest statement of the familiarity with which the trapper had come to regard the mountains was made

1. Irving: *The Rocky Mountains*, Vol. I, p. 214.

by Jedediah Smith himself just as he concluded his trek across the Great Basin. Coming upon the Salt Lake "surrounded by a wilderness of More than 2000 Miles," Smith claimed to be excited by "those feelings known only to the traveler, who after long and perilous journeying comes again in view of his home." He added: "I had traveled so much in the vicinity of the Salt Lake that it had become my home of the wilderness."[2]

Even so, as the 1830's began, the trapper-explorers, great travelers though they were, had not yet completed the basic work of exploration in the West. They had crossed the Great Basin to California, and they had made their way to Oregon, but they had not as yet laid out trails clear enough for others to follow. The most significant achievements of the 1830's were to be those of the men and expeditions that blazed a trail over the mountains to the Pacific, enabling the American people who came after them to "fan out," as it were, into the West, and exploit the geographical breakthrough made by Smith at the South Pass.

2

Of these explorers, one of the most interesting was Captain Benjamin Louis Eulalie Bonneville, who in 1831 obtained a leave of absence from the United States Army and went West to become a fur trader and explorer. Thanks to Washington Irving, who immortalized him in one of his romantic histories, Captain Bonneville has come down through time as the very picture of the dashing cavalier of the West. "A history-made man" puffed up all out of proportion, asserted Hiram M. Chittenden, historian of the fur trade, whose own interpretation of the period leaned heavily toward the Gilded Age business hero rather than the dashing cavalier of an earlier era.[3] And yet a glance at Bonneville's career is sufficient to prove otherwise.

Born in 1793 in France, Bonneville was the son of a rather outspoken political journalist whose strictures against Napoleon caused him to be sent with his entire family to bleak exile in America.[4] Far from grieving, however, the senior Bonneville soon re-

2. Sullivan: *Travels of Smith*, p. 23.
3. Chittenden: *Fur Trade*, pp. 396–433. See especially pp. 396–7.
4. Bvt, Maj. Gen. George W. Cullum: *Biographical Register of the Graduates of the U. S. Military Academy* . . . , third edition (Boston: Houghton Mifflin Co.; 1891), Vol. I, pp. 146–50.

vived his old friendship with Tom Paine (who had returned to America) and retired to a pleasant life of the mind, leaving his family to shift more or less for themselves. As one writer put it: "Almost on any summer's day he was to be seen book in hand, under one of the Battery trees, or in the shadow of St. Paul's Church, little heeding, in his poetic dreams, the passing throng or the passing hour."[5] His son Benjamin was somehow admitted to West Point, graduated in December of 1815,[6] and embarked on a life of action which, however, was never very far removed from the grandiose dreams that had so mesmerized his father.

The first ten years of Bonneville's military career were a constant tour of civilized and frontier outposts and one long stretch in the old Southwest on the national road-building project between Washington and New Orleans.[7] While serving at Fort Gibson in the Indian Territory, the jumping-off point for southern expeditions bound for a year's hunt in the Rocky Mountains, Bonneville got the idea for his own excursions in those distant parts. With seemingly ridiculous ease, the Captain, who apparently had "connections," obtained leave from the Army and financial backing from Alfred Seton, friend and associate of John Jacob Astor and an old Astoria hand.[8] The next five years Bonneville spent leading bands of hardy trappers through the Rocky Mountain wilderness.

Historical opinion as to the true motives for Bonneville's Western expedition has been sharply divided. Chittenden, Bancroft, and even his fellow officers at Fort Gibson asserted that Bonneville's sole motive was commercial.[9] He himself made no secret of the fact that he hoped to do some trading, and yet there is some evidence that Bonneville's mission encompassed a good deal more than commerce.

5. Ibid.
6. Ibid.
7. Ibid. See also "Statement of the Military Service of Benjamin L. E. Bonneville," in Appointment, Commission and Personal Branch File Relating to Benjamin L. E. Bonneville, Adjutant General's Office, R.G. 94, National Archives. Hereafter referred to as Bonneville File R.G. 94.
8. Ibid. See also Washington Irving: The Adventures of Captain Bonneville . . . , Edgeley U. Todd, ed. (Norman, Okla.: University of Oklahoma Press; 1961), p. xxvi. Hereafter cited as Todd: Bonneville.
9. Chittenden: Fur Trade, p. 399; H. H. Bancroft: History of the Northwest Coast (San Francisco: A. L. Bancroft & Co.; 1884), Vol. I, pp. 516–17; Vol. II, pp. 390, 585. Letter of November 3, 1835, from the officers of Fort Gibson, and letter of November 4, 1835, from Brig. Gen. Mathew Arbuckle to Secretary of War, in Bonneville File R.G. 94, National Archives. See also Todd: Bonneville, p. xxxvi.

In the summer of 1831, when he went to St. Louis, he was armed with explicit and detailed instructions from the War Department as to how to spend his "leave of absence." He was to explore the country to the "Rocky Mountains, and beyond with a view of assertaining the nature and character of the various tribes of Indians inhabiting those regions: the trade which might profitably be carried on with them: the quality of the soil, the productions, the minerals, the natural history, the climate, the Geography and Topography, as well as the Geology of various parts of the Country within the limits of the Territories belonging to the United States, between our frontier, and the Pacific. . . ."

Moreover, in his spare time he was to devote his attention to what has come to be called the strategy of "small wars." That is, he was to note the number of warriors in each Indian tribe, their alliances, their state of war or peace, etc., and most important, their manner of making war: "of the mode of subsisting themselves during a state of war, and a state of peace, their Arms, and the effect of them, whether they act on foot or on horse back, detailing the discipline, and maneuvers of the war parties, the power of their horses, size and general description; in short, every information which you may conceive would be useful to the Government."[1]

Perhaps the most significant thing about his official instructions was the fact that he was commanded to collect information about such a wide variety of subjects—far beyond the needs of commerce, the fur trade, or even the requirements of a military campaign against the Indians. Thus, in an "unofficial" capacity, Bonneville was to serve the cause of national expansion.

He was to do all of this, General Macomb's letter of instructions made clear, at his own or his backer's expense. The government would have no official part in it.[2] In short, there appears to be strong evidence for believing, as Bernard De Voto and others believe, that besides being in the fur business Captain Bonneville was also a "spy" in the same sense as Lewis and Clark, Zebulon Pike, and somewhat later, John C. Frémont.[3] More consciously than Pike,

1. Maj. Gen. Alexander Macomb to Capt. B. L. E. Bonneville, Washington, July 29, 1831. Bonneville File R.G. 46, National Archives. Also reprinted in Todd: *Bonneville*, pp. 379–80.
2. Ibid.
3. De Voto: *Across the Wide Missouri*, pp. 58–60; Cleland: *This Reckless Breed*, pp. 278–9. Todd, in *Bonneville*, p. xxv, is more cautious than De Voto or Cleland, declaring that "the known records do not furnish conclusive support" for the "spy hypothesis." However, given General Macomb's explicit instructions calling upon Bonneville to gather information about the West,

and as much as Frémont and Lewis and Clark, he was an instrument of American policy, and a further example of the federal government's interest in the development of the Far West frontier.

3

On the first of May 1832 he set out from Fort Osage, bound for the mountains, at the head of a caravan of wagons, the first such vehicles to cross the Continental Divide. His course was out along the North Platte via the now-familiar emigrant route through South Pass and past the Little Sandy to the Green River, where he went into a "grand encampment" that included his own party and that of Lucien Fontenelle of the American Fur Company.[4]

Seeking a permanent base of operations in the mountains, he moved his entire party north along the Green River to a point five miles above the mouth of Horse Creek. There, on the west bank of the river, he built a stout log fort complete with palisade and twin bastion towers. "Bonneville's Folly," the trappers called it because it was so far north on the Green that it was useless in winter and, in fact, untenable for most of the spring and fall.[5] Yet—as one historian has pointed out—though it may have been in a bad location for the beaver business, as a potential military post it was perfectly situated for guarding the approaches to South Pass, Union Pass, Jackson's Hole, the Snake River, the Bear River, and the Great Salt Lake. Moreover, it stood guard on the edge of the Blackfeet country. Thus, it was a highly strategic location for a military observer.

As soon as he could, however, Bonneville divided his party and sent one band of trappers to Bear River, under the command of a trusted lieutenant.[6] Then, with the main corps, he moved north through Pierre's Hole, where he passed the site of the bitter battle

including areas under foreign sovereignty, for which he was issued a passport, it would seem that his mission in the Far West was indeed an intelligence mission comparable to those of Lewis and Clark, Zebulon Pike, and John C. Frémont. Furthermore, Bonneville's "cover" as a fur trader might be valid grounds for considering him technically a spy since he was gathering information in a clandestine manner.

4. Unless otherwise stated, this account is based upon Irving: *The Rocky Mountains.*

5. De Voto: *Across the Wide Missouri*, pp. 58–60; Todd: *Bonneville*, p. 44 *n.*

6. Irving: *The Rocky Mountains*, Vol. I, p. 98.

between the trappers and the Blackfeet that had taken place just after the summer rendezvous, scarcely a month before, and ultimately he went into winter camp on the Salmon River.

By the following summer of 1833, when he reached the annual rendezvous, Bonneville had little to show for a season's trapping in the mountains. But at rendezvous that year he made his most significant decision as an explorer. He sent the veteran Tennessee trapper Joseph Walker[7] and a party of forty of his own men and twenty or more free trappers westward beyond the Salt Lake to trap, and eventually to locate a trail to California. In his account of the expedition, Irving declared Walker's mission to be a simple reconnaissance of the western shores of the Salt Lake,[8] but it seems clear from the statement of Walker's clerk, Zenas Leonard, that from the beginning the party was bound for California. "The other division," wrote Leonard, "under the command of a Mr. Walker, was ordered to steer through an unknown country, towards the Pacific, and if he did not find beaver, he should return to the Great S. L. in the following summer. . . . I was anxious to go to the coast of the Pacific, and for that purpose hired with Mr. Walker as clerk for a certain sum per year."[9] Perhaps, since much of the country through which Walker passed was below the 42nd parallel and hence was Mexican territory, Irving, who had after all been a professional diplomat, did not find it expedient to publish Bonneville's true intent in a book scheduled for wide distribution just after the Texas crisis in 1837.

But, intentionally or not, Walker and his men marched on to California. They struck the Humboldt, or Mary's River, after more than a month's traveling over the barren plains west of the Salt Lake, and they followed it down, just as countless emigrant trains would do ever afterward, as far as the marshy lakes referred to as the Humboldt Sinks. Walker's men, and Bonneville's subsequent map, referred to them as "Battle Lakes,"[1] however, because at this point Walker's party of nearly sixty men drew themselves up in a line behind a breastwork of their baggage and let fly with a withering volley from their rifles into a band of curious Digger Indians

7. Ibid., pp. 195–200.
8. Ibid., pp. 209–10.
9. Zenas Leonard: *Narrative of the Adventures of Zenas Leonard . . .* , John C. Ewers, ed., under the title of *Adventures of Zenas Leonard Fur Trader* (Norman, Okla.: Oklahoma University Press; 1959), pp. 64–5.
1. Irving: *The Rocky Mountains.* See map in Vol. II.

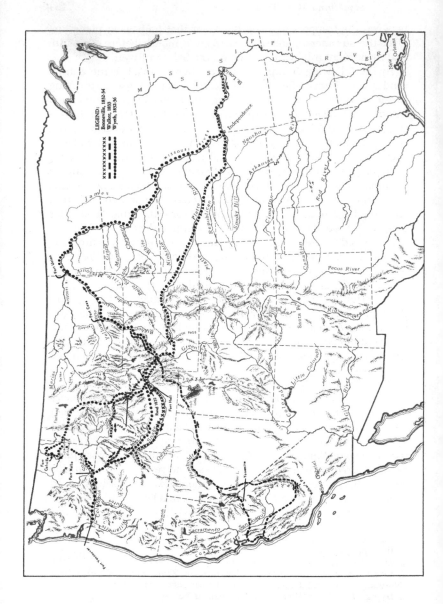

LEGEND:
Bonneville, 1832-34
Walker, 1833
Wyeth, 1832-36

who appeared to menace the party, killing or wounding several dozen while the rest fled in terror. Leonard adds: "Captain Walker then gave orders to some of the men to take the bows of the fallen Indians and put the wounded out of misery. The severity with which we dealt with these Indians may be revolting to the heart of the philanthropist; but the circumstances of the case altogether atones for the cruelty."[2]

Just where Walker and his men crossed over the Sierras into California is not entirely certain. The strong probability, based on Leonard's narrative, is that they moved up a fork of Walker's River, through Mono Pass, then along the Divide between the Merced and Tuolumne rivers, where they were the first civilized men to see the sky-high falls in what is now Yosemite National Park.[3] The trip through the mountains took twenty days of the toughest possible trail breaking. On occasion, both men and horses gave out after plunging and flailing away at the deep snow in the mountain passes. Food was scarce (they hadn't killed anything larger than a rabbit since leaving the Salt Lake, except of course the several dozen Digger Indians). Tempers were short, and once the whole party threatened to mutiny and turn back to the Great Basin. They were pacified by a huge feast of choice roast horse.

Finally, however, about the first week in November they began to come down from the Sierras via the valley of the Merced River. As they approached the interior of California, they were continually dazzled by the kind of marvels that later colored many an emigrant's letters back home. First were the giant redwood trees, measuring "sixteen to eighteen fathom round the trunk."[4] Then, as they were camped on the Merced, there came an earthquake, which Walker told them must be the roar of the Pacific near at hand.[5] On the night of November 12 they were further astounded by a meteor shower. And finally there was the ocean itself, first its arm at Suisun

2. Leonard: *Narrative,* p. 72. Another important account of Walker's expedition is George Nidever: *The Life and Adventures of George Nidever* [1802–1883], William Henry Ellison, ed. (Berkeley, Calif.: University of California Press; 1937). This is a "recollection" of events dictated by Nidever to E. F. Murray in 1878 when he was seventy-five years old, over forty years after Walker's expedition took place. It represents for the most part a vivid and accurate confirmation of the account given by Leonard, though Nidever's description of killing two Indians with one bullet (p. 33) smacks of the tall tale.
3. Leonard: *Narrative,* p. 79 *n.*
4. Ibid., p. 83.
5. Ibid., p. 89.

Bay, then the broad open coasts of the Pacific south of San Francisco Bay, where they stared in amazement at stranded whales lying like helpless Gullivers washed up on a Lilliputian beach.

Once in California, they followed the suggestion of Captain Bradshaw, skipper of an American sea-otter vessel, whom they met on the coast south of San Francisco, and made for the capital at Monterey, where they hoped to obtain supplies.

Walker's band proceeded to Monterey by cautious stages, well aware of the rough treatment accorded Jedediah Smith and other American parties in the past. But when they reached the capital they were treated kindly by Governor Figueroa, and spent most of December sightseeing and recuperating from their long journey.

On January 13, 1834, however, they set out for home, leaving behind six men who preferred to stay in California and exchange the life of a trapper for that of a ranchero or mechanic, the latter being much in demand.[6] On his homeward route, Walker moved down the San Joaquin Valley to what came to be known as Walker's Pass, a low, easy gateway through the southern end of the Sierras that would soon become one of the important emigrant highways into California (see map, p. 152). From Walker's Pass they proceeded north, lost and suffering so greatly from thirst that they drank the blood of their slaughtered animals. But finally they reached familiar territory at the Humboldt Sinks. According to Leonard, they had lost sixty-four horses, ten cows, and fifteen dogs, but no men.[7]

At the Battle Lakes they again engaged in one-sided combat with the Diggers, killing fourteen and wounding many more "as," said Zenas Leonard fiercely, "we rode right over them."[8] The way back was slightly different from their outward route and approximated more closely the future emigrant trail. They followed the Humboldt as far as they could to its source and then struck out overland north to the Snake River, thereby avoiding the Salt Desert due west of Great Salt Lake. From the Snake it was a routine matter by this time to follow its course to a convenient point and then turn off for the Bear River, where on the twelfth of July they were reunited at last with Captain Bonneville and the rest of the party. Their remarkable trek was over. In a sense they had completed what Ashley and Smith started, in that they had traced out what became

6. Ibid., p. 119.
7. Ibid., p. 125.
8. Ibid., p. 13.

the great emigrant trail to California. Their achievement was the most important of the whole Bonneville adventure, and the Captain so recognized it, claiming it ever after as his own.[9]

Of all the results of the expedition, however, perhaps the most important was that, like Jedediah Smith's men before them, Walker's (and Bonneville's) men saw California as a land of abundance that was potentially the province of the American settler. Still in competition with the Spanish, British, and Russians, the mountain men, even the rudest of them, took a "public" or nationalistic view of the Far West. Looking north from San Francisco Bay, Zenas Leonard asserted:

> Much of this vast waste of territory belongs to the Republic of the United States. What a theme to contemplate its settlement and civilization. Will the jurisdiction of the federal government ever succeed in civilizing the thousands of savages now roaming over these plains and her hardy freeborn population here plant their homes, build their towns and cities, and say here shall the arts and sciences of civilization take root and flourish? Yes, here, even in this remote part of the Great West before many years will these hills and valleys be greeted with the enlivening sound, of the workman's hammer, and the merry whistle of the ploughboy. But this is left undone by the government, and will only be seen when too late to apply the remedy. The Spaniards are making inroads on the south— the Russians are encroaching with impunity along the seashore to the north, and further northeast the British are pushing their stations into the very heart of our territory, which even at this day, more resemble military forts to resist invasion than trading stations. Our government should be vigilant. She should assert her claim by taking possession of the whole territory as soon as possible—for we have good reason to suppose that the territory *west* of the mountain will some day be equally as important to a nation as that on the east."[1]

9. Lt. Gouveneur Kemble Warren: "Memoir," in *Reports of Explorations and Surveys for the Most Practicable and Economical Route For A Railroad From the Mississippi River to the Pacific Ocean,* 33rd Cong., 2nd sess., *Sen. Ex. Doc. 78,* Vol. XI (1859), pp. 33–4. Hereafter cited as *Pacific Railroad Reports.*
1. Leonard: *Narrative,* pp. 94–5. Leonard also indicated his association of Walker's expedition with the national interest when he wrote that upon reaching California "the idea of being within hearing of the *end* of the *Far West* inspired the heart of every member of our company with a patriotic feeling for his country's honor . . . ," p. 89.

Clearly the future that Leonard envisaged for the Far West involved more than the fur trade. He saw, as did most men of his time, a diversified settler's frontier, protected by the United States Government, that was in actuality an extension or copy of the previous American frontier cultures across the country.

4

Bonneville's own efforts during 1833–34, while Walker was in California, added little to the history of exploration. Indeed, his whole operation after the summer rendezvous of 1834 has little significance as exploration since it merely repeats what the mountain trappers had been doing for over a decade. Two aspects only of his work deserve further mention. During the winter season of 1833, while Walker was following the Humboldt to California, Bonneville traveled along the Astorians' route to the Columbia, which he reached at Fort Walla Walla. There he was rebuffed by Pambrun, the Hudson's Bay Company factor, and instead of continuing on to Fort Vancouver retraced his steps once again to his base camp on the Portneuf River of Idaho. It was June 1 when he arrived there, and a month later he was reunited with Walker's party on the Bear River.[2]

The following season, in the fall of 1834, he sent still another party, under his lieutenant Montero, into the Crow country and himself took up the trail to Fort Walla Walla, again without success.[3] Ordinarily, it would be somewhat difficult to account for these two treks to Oregon. But quite obviously Bonneville was probing British strength and observing their operations in the Northwest, as well as attempting to establish contact with the Indians of the region.

He returned from the Northwest in the fall of 1834, went into winter encampment at the upper end of Bear River Valley, and in the following spring of 1835 made one last hunt. After that he attended the annual rendezvous at the forks of the Wind River at the end of June and the first part of July. Then, following an extended tour of the Crow country, he paid off his men, packed up his gear, and left the mountains for civilization.[4] Lucien Fontenelle, viewing him only as a meddlesome Easterner trying to be a

2. Irving: *The Rocky Mountains*, Vol. II, pp. 97–104.
3. Ibid., p. 127.
4. Ibid., p. 151.

fur trader, heaved a sigh of relief and declared that the mountains at last "were clear of him."[5] But, as it turned out, Fontenelle was wrong. For the next twenty-five years Bonneville served at various stations throughout the West, on two occasions commanding the Department of New Mexico, and at other times visiting Fort Vancouver and the San Francisco base at Benicia, California, on tours of duty.[6] Though Andrew Jackson was personally pleased with his maps of the West, and Congress reinstated him in the Army at his former rank despite the fact that he had overstayed his leave by two years, the men of the old Army never forgave him, and for the rest of his career Bonneville was shuttled from one disagreeable assignment to another—wherever there was a Botany Bay that needed an army commander. His only rewards for services rendered were a brevet received in the Mexican War and his immortalization in Washington Irving's Western classic, *Scenes and Adventures in the Rocky Mountains.*

In 1835, at the Senate inquiry concerning his petition for reinstatement in the Army, however, Bonneville's accomplishments in the Far West were amply demonstrated, though apparently never widely broadcast. While in the field he had forwarded two reports to the War Department, only one of which reached its destination. Delivered to General Macomb himself by Michael Cerré, Bonneville's most trusted man, the first report of July 29, 1833, from Wind River—a copy of which survives—is detailed and follows the General's instructions exactly in its composition. It includes information about the year's activities, the geography, topography, weather, Indians, wildlife, the fur trade, and most important of all, British activity in Oregon. Bonneville described the Oregon country and particularly the Willamette as "one of the most beautiful, fertile and extensive vallies in the world, wheat, corn and tobacco country." And he added: "If our Government ever intend taking possession of Origon the sooner it shall be done the better." As a field intelligence report, it ranks with the best that the government had ever received from the West.[7]

When he returned, Bonneville also presented the War Department with his extensive journals and maps, which were soon lost, and until recently have been disregarded by historians.[8] Had the

5. Chittenden: *Fur Trade,* Vol. I, p. 427.
6. See my footnotes 4 and 7 on pp. 147 and 148.
7. Bonneville's report is contained in Bonneville File R.G. 46. It is also reprinted in Todd: *Bonneville,* pp. 381–90.
8. See Washington Irving to Maj. Gen. Alexander Macomb, Sept. 20, 1835, Bonneville File R.G. 94. Todd, in *Bonneville,* pp. xx–xxi, is the first historian

journals been published without benefit of Washington Irving,
Bonneville's reputation as an explorer might perhaps have been
more secure. As it was, his maps made public through Irving's account, which came out in 1837, were among the first to represent
the mountain West and particularly the Great Basin. Though Albert
Gallatin's "Map of the Indian Tribes of North America," published
in 1836, is generally considered to have preceded Bonneville's in
showing the Great Basin, it is clear from information that Bonneville gave Irving the year before, while Irving was writing *Astoria*,
that Bonneville had already made his maps of the West and therefore had the prior claim to the title of first cartographer of the
Great Basin.[9]

As late as 1840, however, these two maps, along with those of
Lewis and Clark and Zebulon Pike, remained among the best American maps of the period. There were only a few others of any importance—Humboldt's map of New Spain based on Spanish
exploration, Zebulon Pike's map of 1810, Stephen H. Long's map
of 1821, A. H. Brué's map of 1833, Aaron Arrowsmith's map of
1834, a revised version of his earlier master map which included
Hudson's Bay data and some Jedediah Smith material, and David
H. Burr's map of 1839, perhaps the most accurate of all, since it
was clearly based on the travels of Jedediah Smith. All other maps
of the period—which were to have such a profound impact on the
American mind—stemmed from this handful of early maps. Perhaps the prime example of an imitator was Captain Washington
Hood of the Topographical Engineers, who, when he published
his "Map of the United States Territory of Oregon West of the
Rocky Mountains," so slavishly copied Arrowsmith that he included
the British cartographer's *rectangular* version of the Great Salt
Lake.[1] Though Hood had learned enough by 1839 to question the
trappers who had actually seen the country, his map of that year,
"Exhibiting the Practicable Passes of the Rocky Mountains," is
almost equally incorrect. Contemporary cartography as of 1840
was clearly of little value to the Westbound emigrant, for few of the
map makers even troubled to show the South Pass. Indeed, as
Washington policy makers would discover in the years ahead,

to take serious note of the fact that Bonneville did present his journals to the
government. His treatment of the whole Bonneville affair in fact reopens the
Bonneville case for future historians.
9. Todd: *Bonneville*, p. xxii.
1. Carl I. Wheat: "Preliminary Report," pp. 87–8. Also compare maps.

faulty cartography could become the source of prime international and domestic confusion.

5

If Bonneville, the romantic soldier-adventurer, and Walker, the mountain man, had at last pointed the way to California, the location of the trail to Oregon was the work of a somewhat different type of explorer. As early as 1815, Hall J. Kelley, a recent graduate of Middlebury College, teacher, and founder of, among other things, the Penitent Female Refuge Society and the Boston Young Men's Education Society, began advocating, wherever he could get a hearing, the termination of the Oregon joint occupation treaty with England, while at the same time he urged the forthright American occupation of Oregon. Initially aroused by Nicholas Biddle's 1814 edition of *The Lewis and Clark Expedition,* the Boston schoolmaster went on to read all he could about Oregon and the West. Indeed, if one can believe John B. Wyeth, he went even further afield. According to Wyeth, Kelley had "read all the books he could get on the voyages and travels in Asia, Africa, Europe, and America, until he had heated his mind to a degree little short of the valorous Knight of La Mancha."[2] Like John Jacob Astor before him, and the Humboldtean scientists of his generation, Kelley had a global, romantic imagination abounding in schemes for aiding and abetting the course of empire. In short order he began sending plans and petitions to Congressmen, who were soon (in 1818) to deliberate the Oregon question. In these he called for the Americanization of the whole Northwest. More than a trace of the rhetoric and logic of the imaginative Boston schoolmaster is evident in the proposals of Benton and Linn, and other enthusiasts of the "Oregon lobby."

When Congress failed to do more than extend the joint occupation agreement in 1818, Kelley turned to other expedients, notably the planning and assembling of his own Oregon Colonization Society, which he believed was destined to sail forth like the Pilgrims across the continent to Oregon and there construct the New England outpost that would make the country American.[3] One of the

2. John B. Wyeth: *Oregon* (Cambridge, Mass., 1833; private printing), reprinted in Thwaites: *Early Western Travels,* Vol. XXI, p. 24.
3. F. G. Young, ed.: "The Correspondence and Journals of Captain Nathaniel J. Wyeth, 1831–6," *Sources of the History of Oregon* (Eugene, Oregon: Oregon University Press.; 1899), Vol. I, pp. 8–10. Hereafter cited as Young: *Wyeth Journals.* Wyeth's party was also to be a joint stock venture.

people most aroused by Kelley's scheme was Nathaniel J. Wyeth of Cambridge, Massachusetts. Wyeth was an ice dealer who cut ice in blocks out of various Cambridge Ponds and shipped it to the Caribbean and other parts of the world where such a commodity was needed. When Kelley assembled his party for Oregon, Wyeth signed on to go along, thinking to establish himself at the mouth of the Columbia, where so many Boston merchantmen stopped to call and collect sea otter and beaver skins. In short, though it was scarcely two decades later, the shades of Astor's scheme began to rise once more in the mind of the Boston entrepreneur. The project represented, however, not the temporary commercial enterprise of Astor, but rather the carrying of New England culture in all of its phases out to the Far Northwest.

6

By December of 1831 Wyeth became convinced that Kelley, being too idealistic, was never going to get his company into the field at all. And if by chance he ever did, it would never make it, since Kelley envisioned a veritable Noah's Ark procession of men, women, children, and animals all bound for Oregon.[4] So Wyeth broke with Kelley and began assembling his own company of men, dressing them in standard uniforms consisting of "coarse woolen jacket and pantaloon, a striped cotton shirt and cowhide boots," and training them under rigorous midwinter wilderness conditions on an island in Boston Harbor. In addition he had amphibious wagons especially constructed so that river crossings would be a simple matter. The wagons, which were handsome if strange vehicles, cost him no end of ridicule as he took them past the jeering students in the Harvard Yard on the way to their shakedown cruise in Boston Harbor.[5] Not unmindful of the cause of science, too, Wyeth took the trouble to seek the advice of Professor Thomas Nuttall of Harvard, that eccentric who had once visited the Upper Missouri with Wilson Price Hunt in 1811.[6] By this time, Nuttall, having explored Arkansas and the Ozarks, had settled down to a curious existence as a Harvard professor, living on the second floor of a house near the botanical gardens whose only entry was by means of a rope ladder, which he seldom lowered to would-be

4. Ibid.
5. De Voto: *Across the Wide Missouri*, p. 66.
6. Young: *Wyeth Journals*, p. 12.

visitors.[7] Wyeth, however, was an exception, and so, fortified with the good professor's advice in matters of science, and assisted by his brother Dr. Jacob Wyeth and his nephew John B. Wyeth, Nathaniel Wyeth and company set sail from Boston Harbor on March 10, 1832, bound for Baltimore on the first leg of their journey.[8]

Their route from Baltimore was due west over the Alleghenies and via the Ohio rivers to St. Louis, where Wyeth learned from William Sublette of the Rocky Mountain Fur Company, and Kenneth McKenzie of the American Fur Company, just how much knowledge of the Far West the mountain men had acquired since the days of Lewis and Clark and the Astorians. It was a revelation, but it did not change his plans very much. Still keeping to his flexible scheme to engage in the fur trade and take advantage of whatever other opportunities might arise, he sold his amphibious wagons to greenhorns as quickly as possible and secured pack animals to take his party overland to the Pacific.[9]

They left Independence, Missouri, on May 3, 1832, in company with William Sublette and his party of Rocky Mountain traders. But almost from the outset dissension prevailed. Six men deserted before the caravan was fairly underway. Then, when they reached the Pierre's Hole rendezvous in July, John B. and Jacob Wyeth led a revolt against Nat's leadership and seven more men turned back to the states and comparative civilization.[1]

But before either party could make much progress in their respective directions, an advance guard of trappers stumbled on some Gros Ventre, and in a truce parley shot down their chief in cold blood. Thus began the celebrated fight at Pierre's Hole in which the trapper Sinclair [St. Clair] and two others were killed and William Sublette and seven men were wounded. The Indians, holed up in a log fort and cleverly protected by buffalo- and deer-hide screens, fought unbelievably well against the larger number of Rocky Mountain sharpshooters bent on massacre. Had the trappers not listened to their Flathead allies (who wanted plunder more than revenge), however, and set fire to the log fort, they might have gained a complete victory. As it was, the Indians deceived them into thinking there was an attack on their main camp, causing a delay in the trappers' advance until the following morning. That night the Indians left the fort and their dead behind and retreated to safety,

7. McKelvey: *Botanical Exploration,* p. 141 *n.*
8. Young: *Wyeth Journals,* p. 47.
9. De Voto: *Across the Wide Missouri,* p. 66; John B. Wyeth: *Oregon,* p. 44.
1. John B. Wyeth: *Oregon,* pp. 64–8.

thereby gaining a "moral victory." A few days later they added to
their laurels by catching, killing, and mutilating two of Wyeth's
greenhorn deserters, who were heading back to the states with the
wounded William Sublette and his party.[2]

After the Battle of Pierre's Hole, in which Nat Wyeth distinguished himself, he headed west across the Snake River plains.
His route was a chord subtended by the great southward arc of the
Snake River, a country already well trapped by the Hudson's Bay
brigades.[3] (See map, p. 152.) For part of the way, as a protection
against the Blackfeet, Wyeth and his men accompanied Milton
Sublette's party. Then, when they reached the Snake River once
again, they split up, with Wyeth's men working the streams to the
south and west of the river and Sublette's men staying north and
east of the river. Eventually, about the fourteenth of October 1832,
Wyeth and his men made their way northward and across the Blue
Mountains to Fort Walla Walla near the junction of the Snake and
the Columbia. On October 29 Wyeth arrived at Fort Vancouver,
where he met the great Dr. "McGlauglin" as he noted in his journal.[4]
At this point he discovered that his ship, the *Sultana*, had been
wrecked at sea, somewhere off the Society Islands. With all his
careful plans dashed to pieces, even Wyeth began to give up hope,
and his party broke up, some joining the Hudson's Bay Company,
others preparing to catch the next ship bound for Boston. Wyeth
himself spent a gloomy winter at Fort Vancouver.[5]

The following spring (1833), he and two remaining men accompanied Francis Ermatinger's brigade as it moved northward up
the Columbia to Fort Colville, past the old Spokane House, and over
to the Flathead Post on Thompson's River in Montana, where they

2. There are numerous accounts of the Battle of Pierre's Hole, including:
Young: *Wyeth Journals*, pp. 158–9; John B. Wyeth: *Oregon*, p. 63; George
Nidever: *Life and Adventures*, pp. 26–30; Zenas Leonard: *Narrative*, pp.
43–5; William L. Sublette, Missouri *Republican*, Oct. 16, 1832; William F.
Wheeler: "Louis Rivet, 1803–1903, Personal History. . . ," *Montana Historical
Society Contributions* X, p. 252; Warren A. Ferris: *Life in the Rocky Moun-
tains*, Paul C. Phillips, ed. (Denver, Colo.: The Old West Publishing Co.;
1940), pp. 154–5, 201–2; Irving: *The Rocky Mountains*, pp. 88–98; Charles
Eberstadt, ed.: *The Rocky Mountain Letters of Robert Campbell* (New York:
Edward Eberstadt and Sons; 1955), pp. 7–11. John C. Ewers, in Zenas
Leonard: *Narrative*, p. 45 *n.*, has pointed out that the Indian enemies were
Gros Ventre, not Blackfeet as most of the participants seemed to think. This
opinion is confirmed by Wyeth. See Young: *Wyeth Journals*, p. 210.

3. Young: *Wyeth Journals*, pp. 163–77. Wyeth really begins his westward
trek in August (p. 163).

4. Ibid., p. 176. Wyeth also spells McLoughlin as "McGlaucland" (p. 181).

5. Ibid., pp. 177–80.

arrived on April 7, 1833. Wyeth's trip south from this point took him to the Three Tetons near Pierre's Hole, where he made contact with one of Bonneville's lieutenants. Eventually, on July 2, Wyeth joined Bonneville's party near Henry's River and the two began making plans for an expedition to be captained by Wyeth himself which would penetrate the country south of the Snake River and west of the Great Salt Lake as far as California, or, in other words, the same area later traversed by Joseph Walker under Bonneville's orders.[6]

For some reason, however, by July 4 Wyeth had changed his mind and decided to head back home to Cambridge.[7] On July 7 he left Bonneville's camp and eight days later reached the site of the annual summer rendezvous at Bonneville's Fort near the upper Green River.[8] From this rendezvous the Captain dispatched Walker on his expedition to California. Wyeth, however, headed the other way, via the Big Horn and Yellowstone rivers to the Upper Missouri. En route he paused to build a bullboat on the Little Big Horn and while so engaged, on August 14, 1833, he made an agreement that changed his plans for the following year. He contracted with Milton Sublette, who acted on behalf of the Rocky Mountain Fur Company, to bring the annual load of merchandise and trade goods to the company's summer rendezvous the next year.[9] Then he floated down the rivers, past Fort Cass, Samuel Tullock's establishment on the Yellowstone, to Fort Union at the junction of that river with the Missouri.

Fort Union was the American Fur Company's headquarters on the Upper Missouri, and as such it was the residence of Kenneth McKenzie, the ruthless, energetic, but withal, where his wife was concerned, strangely sentimental leader of the Upper Missouri Outfit (no relation to Donald McKenzie of the Northwest Company).[1] At the very time that Wyeth landed at the log-palisaded fort which guarded the approaches to the Blackfeet and Crow country, McKenzie was readying a "secret weapon" for use against the competi-

6. Ibid., pp. 58–60, 62–3, 65–6, 181–205.
7. Ibid., pp. 68–9. Wyeth's letters of July 4, 1833, discussing his plans to go to California (pp. 62–6), are all marked "not sent," which indicates that he changed his mind about the Bonneville venture sometime between July 4 and July 18, 1833, possibly after seeing Bonneville's poor showing at the rendezvous.
8. Young: *Wyeth Journals*, p. 205.
9. Ibid., pp. 83, 205–9.
1. See Letters of Kenneth McKenzie to his wife, McKenzie Collection, Missouri Historical Society. An especially good example is his letter of Oct. 29, 1844, from Fort Pierre.

tion in the Indian trade. The "weapon" was a distillery designed to manufacture liquor locally, thereby enabling the company to get around the government's edict against the shipment of alcohol up the Missouri into Indian country.[2] During Wyeth's stay at the fort he learned all about the "still," perhaps from McKenzie himself, who felt justifiably proud of his ingenuity. Directly he reached Fort Leavenworth, however, Wyeth, with that reforming zeal that has stirred generations of New Englanders, went straight to the authorities and reported his friend McKenzie. In one stroke he nearly accomplished what the entire Rocky Mountain Fur Company had been unable to do for years, the ejection of Astor's monopoly from the mountains.[3] Ultimately, thanks to judicious lobbying by company men in Washington, the Astor men were able to stay, though McKenzie was ruined and forced to retire from the trade.[4]

7

By this time, however, Wyeth was in Cambridge preparing for his second and even more elaborate venture into the mountains. On the strength of his contract with the Rocky Mountain Fur Company, Wyeth was able to secure backing from his Cambridge partners for a second expedition to the West, this one to be based on an even more complex plan than the first. His plan involved sending a ship, the *May Dacre*, with trade goods to the mouth of the Columbia, where it would take on a load of furs secured from the Indians and also a load of salmon that had been obtained from the Columbia during the season. Meanwhile, Wyeth himself would go overland to rendezvous in the Rocky Mountains, his caravan bearing the trade goods so desperately needed by the mountain men. The first year he would supply the Rocky Mountain Fur Company; in later years he would obtain control of all the carrying trade to the Rocky Mountains *on both sides*, and the fishing business to boot.[5] Essentially, then, Wyeth's was a transportation venture which, in contrast to Kelley's scheme, involved little in the way of a permanent establishment in the Far West and yet yielded a maximum profit on the investment. It was a considerable refinement of Astor's more romantic plan, and yet, though several decades had

2. Chittenden: *Fur Trade*, Vol. I, pp. 356–9.
3. Ibid., pp. 360–2.
4. Ibid.
5. Young: *Wyeth Journals*, pp. 73–8.

passed, the essential technique and the objectives of the two ventures were the same. Like the Astorians, Wyeth was essentially a commercial explorer.

But he was not entirely a man of commerce. During the winter of 1833–34 his interests began to broaden and change, in keeping perhaps with the new era of learning and expansion that was beginning to engulf Cambridge, and indeed all of Jacksonian America. He persuaded his friend from Harvard, the eccentric Dr. Nuttall, to make one more trip to the West, this time to collect plants for the Harvard Botanical Garden. In addition, he secured the services of Dr. John Kirk Townsend of Philadelphia to be the official ornithologist on the expedition. Then, to top everything else scientific, Wyeth began taking lessons himself in mathematical astronomy and surveying, so that he could successfully map the regions he explored and determine geographical points with accuracy. To insure his success in this undertaking, he hired as his second in command, Captain Joseph Thing, a retired sea captain who was presumably experienced in the use of the sextant and the compass.[6]

Still another dimension was added to Wyeth's venture when the Methodist missionary Jason Lee and his nephew Daniel Lee signed on. A tall, powerful outdoorsman from Vermont, Jason Lee had been teaching a church school in Stanstead, Quebec, when he was selected by the Mission Board to answer the call of the Indians in *The Christian Advocate* and go and minister to the Flatheads, who according to the *Advocate* so desperately needed him out beyond the Rocky Mountains. To raise money for his mission, Lee engaged in a round of public sermons and camp meetings, the first one being held at Cambridge, where Nat Wyeth and a poor deformed Indian boy who served as a Flathead were his most effective drawing cards. Then later he repeated the performance all the way across the backcountry as far as St. Louis, where he and his entourage nearly missed the expedition in trying to give one last series of "sermons."[7] In a sense, the primary importance of Wyeth's expedition, though not its main purpose, was that it opened up the Oregon Trail and the Northwest to the two chief forces of contemporary civilization, science and organized Protestant Christianity.

Much of the detail of Wyeth's expedition is unimportant.[8] At the

6. Ibid., pp. 101–2, 103–4, 106–7, 128.
7. De Voto: *Across the Wide Missouri*, pp. 181, 185; Young: *Wyeth Journals*, p. 130.
8. It can be followed in Young: *Wyeth Journals*, pp. 221–5.

head of a large party of men, he made one of the fastest overland trips between Independence, Missouri, and the Green River rendezvous on record. He left Independence on April 28, 1834, and reached rendezvous fifty-one days later, on June 19. But this was not quite fast enough. A rival party under William Sublette made the trip faster, and when Wyeth arrived at rendezvous, he learned that Fitzpatrick and company had gone back on their bargain and dealt with Sublette instead, leaving him with thousands of dollars worth of trade goods and no buyers, not even Indians. According to Joe Meek, who was there, Wyeth turned to the Rocky Mountain partners and declared: "Gentlemen, I will roll a stone into your garden that you will never be able to get out."[9] Then he left the rendezvous with all his men (Jason Lee was glad to go, as the unbridled licentiousness and drinking scandalized him)[1] and headed north to the Snake River, where he commenced work on a fur-trading fort at the junction of the Snake and the Portneuf.

For several weeks all hands fell to and aided in the construction of the fort. Then, when the heavy cottonwood logs were all in place and the various cabins and sheds built, Wyeth and most of his company marched off across the Snake River scablands for Oregon, leaving behind a garrison of twelve inexperienced men to hold the fort and dispose of his trade goods to the friendly Bannocks and Snakes. To those left behind, Fort Hall, according to Osborne Russell, represented no glorious achievement as the first permanent American outpost beyond the Continental Divide. Instead it was, Russell wrote, "the most lonely and dreary place I think I ever saw—not a human was to be seen excepting the men about the fort."[2]

When Wyeth arrived at last at Fort Vancouver, he found that marine disaster had struck again. This time it was lightning. And though the *May Dacre* was not a total loss, as was the *Sultana*, still she arrived too late for the fishing season and Wyeth labored in vain through the fall and winter of 1834–35 to establish a fur-trading foothold in the Northwest. Wherever he went, the Hudson's Bay monopoly outsold, outgave, and outsmarted him.[3]

Meanwhile, on the Upper Columbia, Jason Lee on the way out had abandoned his plan to minister to the Flatheads and turned

9. Francis Fuller Victor: *River of the West*, p. 164.
1. De Voto: *Across the Wide Missouri*, p. 203.
2. Osborne Russell: *Journal of a Trapper* (Boise, Idaho: Syms Fork Co.; 1914), p. 13.
3. De Voto: *Across the Wide Missouri*, p. 208.

instead toward the Willamette.[4] When he arrived there with Wyeth, he was welcomed by Dr. McLoughlin of the Hudson's Bay Company and with his nephew he began the establishment of a farm and a sawmill in the Willamette Valley—seeing it as his first duty to minister to the white men already out there, and leaving the Flatheads, who were, in his words, "savages," to others, like Marcus Whitman and Father De Smet, who would follow. The Lees, then, with their assistants and the men of Wyeth's party who remained when his venture broke up, set about establishing what amounted to a permanent American colony south of the Columbia, in what was undisputed territory. In effect, though the fur-trade and fishing ventures both failed, Wyeth succeeded in rolling stones into two gardens—the first with his post at Fort Hall on what was soon to become the Oregon Trail, the second when Jason Lee and his brethren formed the nucleus of an American settlement in the Northwest.

In a fine, fitting irony, the architect of the project was there to see its beginning. Hall Jackson Kelley arrived at Fort Vancouver one morning in March of 1835, with some refugees from justice, including the great Ewing Young. They were accused of stealing cattle in California. Kelley arrived sick and in disgrace, and when he was carried into Fort Vancouver by Michel Laframboise, he was refused admission to the "gentlemen's table" and hustled away to an unused shack.[5] Neither a blue-blood, nor a gentleman of the cloth, nor even a tradesman, Kelley was simply a schoolteacher suspected of cattle rustling. No one recognized him as the man of vision who had planned the American settlement of Oregon in the first place. But then, what did a shack, or for that matter a "gentlemen's table," matter to a true Romantic—"a knight," as John B. Wyeth had said, "of La Mancha"? He was probably more comfortable where he was, anyway.

8

In the fall of 1836 Wyeth returned to Fort Hall, replenished its supplies, and proceeded to his outpost on the Willamette in the spring. After placing it in charge of an agent, he headed East again.[6] He paid one more visit to Fort Hall and then headed south down the Green River and through Ute country to Taos, from whence

4. Ibid., pp. 208–9.
5. Young: *Wyeth Journals*, p. 250.
6. Young: *Wyeth Journals*, p. 255.

he returned home via the Upper Arkansas and the Santa Fe Trail.[7]
Presumably, even after the disasters at the rendezvous of 1834 and
on the Columbia, Wyeth was not yet willing to give up and made
one last swing into Taos to see if the carrying trade to the southern
mountains might not be worth his while. Ultimately, however, he
returned to Cambridge and became the ice king of the country—a
tradesman to the end. Before settling down, he had seen more of
the Far West than most other mountain men of his day. True, he
had broken no trails that were really new, but he had clearly established the trail to Oregon. He had mapped the Multnomah, or
Willamette, for the first time with instruments,[8] and he had brought
the first American scientists to the country beyond the Rockies. In
so doing, he had ushered in a new era of exploration—an era in
which, in the words of one overenthusiastic newspaper editor of
the time, the traveler would no longer wander "bewildered in a cloud
of fables prepared to see marvels," but would be able to secure the
advantages of the positive and permanent advance of scientific
knowledge.[9] This was achievement enough for any man, particularly an ice-cutter from Cambridge, Massachusetts.

And, as if to add a postscript to Wyeth's achievement and that
of Jason Lee in establishing the Willamette settlements, President
Andrew Jackson in the fall of 1836 signified official interest in the
fate of Oregon. He sent a personal representative, William A.
Slacum, to observe conditions in the new American outpost.[1] What
most Westerners considered a lengthy period of not-so-salutary
neglect was about to come to an end. Indeed, in the summer of
1835, even before Wyeth returned from the West, and before
Slacum ever set foot in Oregon, Colonel Henry M. Dodge and a
party of United States Dragoons headed out along the Platte River
to the Rocky Mountains on a reconnaissance in force, designed to
awe the plains Indians and open up the trail to Oregon for parties
of settlers who were already beginning to crowd frontier communities, waiting for their chance to embark on the way West.[2]

7. Ibid.
8. Ibid., *passim*.
9. Washington *National Intelligencer*, Oct. 12, 1855.
1. William A. Slacum: "Report on the Territory of Oregon to Accompany
H. R. Bill No. 976," 25th Cong., 3rd sess., *H. R. Rept. 101* (1839).
2. Lt. T. B. Wheelock: "Journal of Colonel Dodge's Expedition from Fort
Gibson to the Pawnee Pict Village," 23rd Cong., 2nd sess., *Sen. Ex. Doc. 1*
(Dec. 1835), pp. 73–93. Also see James Hildreth: *Dragoon Campaigns to the
Rocky Mountains . . .* (New York: Weber and Long; 1836); Louis Pelzer:
Marches of the Dragoons in the Mississippi Valley (Cedar Rapids, Iowa:

9

By the end of the 1830's a turning point had been reached in Western history. The Oregon Trail had been clearly established. Forts Laramie, Hall, and Boise existed as points of respite along the way, and within a few years Fort Bridger would be added to their number. In 1835 the Rocky Mountain Fur Company collapsed, and by 1839 the yearly rendezvous was a thing of the romantic past. The free trappers were all company men working out of trading posts, or else they had begun to put their knowledge to work in the most important enterprise of the next decade—guiding the countless wagon trains westward to Oregon and California over trails which they themselves had helped to establish. The final opening of practical emigrant trails to California was in fact the climax of the "mountain man" era of Western exploration. It demonstrates more clearly than anything else the ultimate utility of their knowledge, and their settler-oriented point of view.

The first important emigrant party to take the trail to California was the Bartleson-Bidwell company of 1841.[3] Organized by John Bidwell, a frontier schoolteacher and farmer who had recently been robbed of most of his worldly possessions by a band of Missouri gunmen, the party was captained, at least for ceremonial purposes, by wealthy John Bartleson, who refused to go at all unless he was voted to command. It was guided as far as Soda Springs on Bear River by the mountain veteran Thomas "Broken Hand" Fitzpatrick, who taught the settlers most of what they came to know about the plains and the mountains, and then pointed them with vague geographical directions toward the Great Basin and California. From that point they were on their own.

A comparatively youthful group, the Bartleson-Bidwell party had

Torch Press; 1917); Lt. G. Kingsbury: "Journal of the March of a Detachment of Dragoons, Under the Command of Colonel Dodge, during the summer of 1835," 24th Cong., 1st sess., *Sen. Ex. Doc.* 209 (1836).

3. The major accounts of this party are John Bidwell: *Echoes of the Past* (Chico, Calif.: Chico *Advertiser;* n.d.); John Bidwell: *Journey to California* (San Francisco: J. H. Nash, Printer; 1937); Nicholas Dawson: *Narrative of Nicholas "Cheyenne" Dawson Overland to California in '41 and '49, and Texas in '51* (San Francisco: Grabhorn Press; 1933). The most recent historical treatment is George R. Stewart: *The California Trail* (New York: McGraw-Hill Book Co.; 1962), to which I am indebted for the overall structure of the narrative dealing with the California Trail.

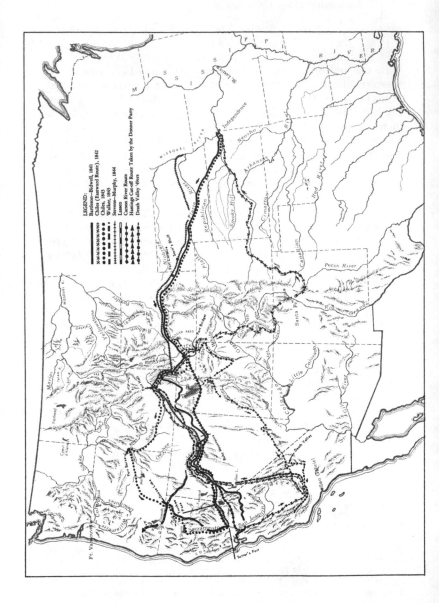

had no real experience in the Far West with its mountains and deserts, but it did number a family of Kentucky hunters, a few frontier veterans, and some border adventurers. It also included five hardy women and ten children. Setting out into the unknown with no maps, no familiarity with landmarks, and only vague hearsay directions to guide them, they nevertheless persevered through heat and thirst and near-starvation, to blaze a first crude emigrant trail into California.

From Soda Springs they followed the Bear River south almost to Great Salt Lake and then turned west into the barren desert-like country north of the lake. Guided by Indians, they swung south at a point just below the Idaho border and reached Rabbit Spring, a forlorn spot. There the real hardships began as they failed to find the headwaters of Ogden's River, their only guide to California. When they reached Pilot Peak, a prominent landmark due west of Salt Lake, they had begun to abandon their wagons and supplies, and by the time they crossed the Ruby Mountains, which jutted up out of the desert south of Ogden's (Humboldt) River, they had left all their wagons behind and converted to pack mules.

In mid-September, however, they reached Ogden's River, and from that point on followed it as far as the Sinks forty miles east of the Sierras. Their trail across the mountains was via Sonora Pass and the Stanislaus River into central California, a difficult and dangerous route that proved to be generally impractical for anything but pack trains. Finally, however, on October 30, 1841, worn out by the mountain country and much reduced by a starvation diet of mule meat, coyote, and acorns, they came at last to the Valley of the San Joaquin and their destination—Marsh's Ranch. They were the first emigrant party to reach California, proving, with incredible perseverance and hardship, that it could be done.

The experience of the Bartleson-Bidwell party proved valuable. J. B. Chiles, one of the group, headed back East the following year, determined to lead another party to California. His return route took him via Tejon and Walker's Pass across the southern flank of the Sierras into the Great Basin, then north to the Humboldt River. He followed the Humboldt as far as he could, then struck out overland to Fort Hall in Idaho. From Fort Hall he made a personal exploration of the Rocky Mountain West on a grand scale, heading due south to the headwaters of Bear River, then across to the Green, and then to the Old Spanish Trail, which he followed into Santa Fe. He reached Independence, Missouri, via the Santa Fe Trail, which by 1842 had become a well-marked avenue of commerce.[4] (See map, p. 48.)

In 1843 Chiles made use of the experience he had gained as he led another emigrant party West to California. However, when he got as far as Fort Hall he abandoned the Humboldt River–Great Basin route and continued on to Fort Boise in western Idaho. From there he blazed a trail due west via the Malheur River of Oregon and the forbidding country which surrounded it, to the Pit River country of northern California. By the time he and his party reached the coastal province, they too had been forced to abandon their wagons. With great hardship, they made their way, sometimes hopelessly lost, across the lava beds and through the rough timbered country around Mt. Shasta, down into the Sacramento Valley. In attempting to turn the northern flank of the Sierras, Chiles had not been much more successful than had the leaders of the Bartleson-Bidwell party in their march to the south.[5]

Also in 1843, however, the mountain veteran Joseph Walker led a party on a more direct route to the Humboldt River via Thousand Springs Creek. Continuing south past the Humboldt Sinks, the Walker party entered Owens Valley and successfully crossed over Walker Pass into the San Joaquin Valley. However, despite Walker's great experience and unsurpassed knowledge of the country, this party too was forced to abandon its wagons and hence could not claim the distinction of being the first to lay out a true emigrant trail to California.[6]

This objective was attained by the Stevens-Murphy party in 1844 in what could be called the most important of all the overland trail explorations of the early emigrant period.[7] The party, which formed at Council Bluffs, Iowa, in the spring of 1844, was composed of twenty-three men, eight women, and fifteen children. More than half of this number consisted of the numerous members of the family of Patrick Murphy, a Missouri farmer. But, most important, it also included at least three experienced mountain men: Caleb Greenwood, who had been to Oregon with the Astorians; Isaac Hitchcock, a veteran of forty years in the fur trade, who may have

4. Stewart: *California Trail*, pp. 32–5.
5. Ibid., pp. 36–46.
6. Ibid., pp. 42–51.
7. Ibid., pp. 53–74. See also George R. Stewart, ed.: *The Opening of the California Trail* (Berkeley, Calif.: University of California Press; 1953), which reprints the reminiscences of the Stevens-Murphy party of 1844.

been one of Bonneville's men; and Elisha Stevens. Stevens was chosen the leader, and his knowledge and resourcefulness seems to have been chiefly responsible for the success of the expedition.

They left Council Bluffs on about May 18, taking what was later called the Mormon Trail north of the Platte River. By the fourth of July they had passed Fort Laramie and reached Independence Rock in time for an appropriate celebration. After they crossed South Pass and descended the Little Sandy, which flows to the Pacific, Isaac Hitchcock, who knew something of this particular stretch of the country, persuaded them to strike out due west across the sage plain of western Wyoming toward the Green River (see map, p. 170). This required several days of hard travel, and then more difficult days from the Green to the Bear River, where they again struck the Oregon Trail. In making this forced march, they had laid out what came to be known as Sublette's Cut-off. A famous and important variation of both the Oregon and the California trails, this was essentially the track followed by numerous parties of early Rocky Mountain trappers as they headed for the beaver grounds of the Green and Bear rivers.

At Fort Hall, Stevens and his party learned nothing of the fate of the expeditions, such as Walker's, which had preceded them the year before. They were able to follow Walker's tracks to the Humboldt River, however, after which they coursed down the Humboldt to the now familiar Sinks. On this part of the trail, neither Greenwood nor Hitchcock was much help, but at the Sinks they met an old Indian chief named Truckee who directed them westward to a pass over the Sierras. With Stevens and two other members of the party riding out ahead as scouts, the emigrants headed directly across Forty Mile Desert and into the mountains. This was the first of a series of crucial decisions that resulted in the final breaking of the California Trail.

Following the Truckee River, they passed Truckee Meadows, the site of modern Reno, and began the climb to Donner Lake high in the mountains. By the time they reached the lake, the party had split into two sections. One small band, under Dr. John Townsend, mounted on horseback, headed due south and reached Lake Tahoe, from which point they easily crossed over to the American River and arrived at Sutter's Fort. The main force, under Stevens, decided to abandon six wagons and most of the nonessential supplies at Donner Lake, leaving three men behind in a winter cabin to guard them. Then, with tremendous labor, they pushed and hauled the rest of the wagons over the steep granite wall north of the lake that marked the crest of Donner Pass and the final entry into California. Thus they were the first to take wagons down into the promised land, marking a clear but difficult trail for others to follow. It was a feat of exploration which because of the number of people involved has never been recognized as such. Stevens, Greenwood, Hitchcock, Murphy, and the others have, of course, received wide recognition as pioneers in California migration, but only rarely have they been classed as the important explorers that simple justice entitles them to be.

The rest of their story has little to do with exploration, but it does reflect something of the measure of the men (and women). Partway down the western slope of the Sierra, with snow descending in great quantities, the emigrants set up a winter camp. The women, one of whom had just been delivered of a baby, settled down to await the spring thaw. Most of the men marched off to Sutter's Fort, where they took part in the Micheltoreña uprising that eventually culminated in the Bear Flag Revolt. At Donner Lake, the three men left with the wagons and property found themselves virtually buried by the deep snows that covered their cabin. Two of the men, who were adept at manipulating snowshoes, set out for California, leaving behind Moses Schallenbarger, a teen-age member of the party who volunteered to sit out the long winter by himself rather than take to snowshoes. By the time spring came, most people had given up Schallenbarger for lost, but when Dennis Martin, who risked death himself in the still deep snows of Donner Pass, reached the lakeside cabin, he found Schallenbarger alive and in good condition. The young pioneer had managed to feed himself on foxes, which he trapped, and to keep his sanity by reading all of Dr. Townsend's many books left in the cabin. And so, unlike the later expedition of 1846, which gave Donner Lake and Donner Pass their names, this one had a happy ending.[8]

By the end of 1844 the trail to California was a fact, and members of the Stevens party, such as Caleb Greenwood, returned East to lead more emigrants over the route the following year. In 1845 two parties took the Stevens trail, one led by Greenwood, another by Lansford W. Hastings, a scout who had come to California by way of Oregon.[9] Frémont, too, pioneered a trail across the Great

8. Ibid., pp. 74–80. The reminiscences of Moses Schallenbarger are included in Stewart: *The Opening of the California Trail.*
9. Ibid., pp. 84–105.

Basin in that year, though it proved to be of little immediate use to emigrants.[1] Also in 1845, Hastings published his famous *Emigrant's Guide to Oregon and California*, based on material gleaned from Frémont's reports and data compiled from his own Western wanderings.[2] It became for a time the most famous of all emigrant guides and gained Hastings sufficient prestige as a scout to enable him to lead several parties west directly across the Great Basin Desert on a route that he improvised as he went along. There followed the disastrous crossing of the Donner party in 1846, however, in which under Hastings' leadership the emigrants became trapped in the winter snows of Donner Pass and were reduced to starvation and cannibalism. By 1849 Hastings' reputation as a guide and explorer had sunk to a proper level of insignificance, if not disgrace.[3]

As the 1840's passed, new overland routes were opened up almost every year (see map, p. 170). In 1846 Jessie Applegate and a company of Oregonians searched out a trail from southern Oregon to Lassen's Meadows in northern California.[4] The Aram company of emigrants laid out a new version of the Truckee Trail over the mountains via Coldstream and Emigrant canyons.[5] And also in 1846, T. H. Jefferson produced a map based on his experiences with Hastings which provided an accurate rendering of all the trails he had seen.[6]

In 1848 Peter Lassen laboriously blazed a trail northward from the Humboldt to Black Rock in northern Nevada and thence via the Pit River, Mt. Shasta, and over Lassen's Pass into northern California.[7] In 1849 this became a much used, though somewhat impractical, trail to the gold fields. The most important new route

1. John Charles Frémont: *Memoirs of My Life* (Chicago: Belford, Clarke and Co.; 1887), Vol. I, pp. 430 ff. See also Thomas Salathiel Martin: "Narrative of John C. Frémont's Expedition to California in 1845–46, and Subsequent Events in California Down to 1853, Including Frémont's Exploring Expedition of 1848," dictated to E. F. Murray (Sept. 5, 1878), Bancroft Library, Berkeley, California.
2. Lansford W. Hastings: *The Emigrant's Guide to Oregon and California* . . . (Cincinnati, Ohio: George Conclin; 1845).
3. The best accounts of the Donner party are Stewart: *The California Trail*, pp. 176–84; George R. Stewart: *Ordeal By Hunger: The Story of the Donner Party* (New York: Henry Holt and Co.; 1936); and De Voto: *Year of Decision* (Boston: Houghton Mifflin Co.; 1942), *passim*.
4. Stewart: *The California Trail*, p. 144.
5. Ibid., pp. 174–6.
6. This map is mentioned in Stewart: *The California Trail*, p. 148. See also Carl I. Wheat: *Mapping the American West*, Vol. II.
7. Ibid., pp. 215–16.

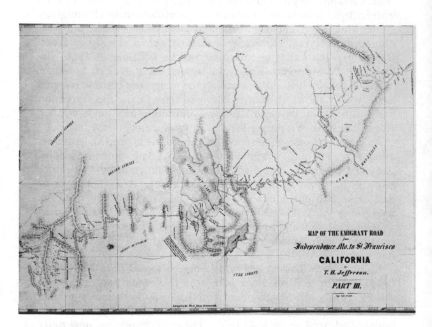

A portion of T. H. Jefferson's map of the Emigrant Road to San Francisco, Part III, the best of the privately made emigrant maps. Shown is a portion of Utah. The legend to the right of the Desert of Utariah reads: "To accomplish the long drive grass and water must be carried from Hope Wells and the journey performed night and day making short & regular camps. Not more than five waggons should go in company and the cattle should be continually guarded." *Courtesy Library of Congress*

was also located in 1848 when a company of eastbound Mormons, fresh from the discoveries at Sutter's Mill, trekked out the Carson River Trail over the mountains from Placerville. This soon became the most widely used emigrant road.[8]

In 1849 came the location of the Hudspeth Cut-off to the Humboldt River, and William Lewis Manley's heroic march into California via Death Valley, which was discovered in the course of that difficult journey.[9] Then, in the 1850's, every California town and hamlet had its pioneer company in the mountains searching for a wagon road over the Sierras that would direct emigrants and business its way. Nobles' Wagon Road from Honey Lake to Shasta City, Jim Beckwourth's trail from Bidwell's Bar, the Henness Pass Road from Marysville, the Placer County Emigrant Road out over Squaw Valley, Johnson's Cut-off from Placerville to Lake Tahoe, the Big Trees Road from Stockton, and the Sonora Road, laid out and discovered by Joseph C. Morehead, a veteran of Crabb's filibustering expedition to Mexico, were the most prominent of many such trails blazed eastward over the mountains, each with the idea that it would become the western terminus of an eventual transcontinental wagon road.

Frequently seen as a great and inevitable folk movement to the Pacific shores, these early pioneer expeditions were also important in the history of Western exploration. And despite the fact that few of the trail blazers stand out as great individual, classic explorers, what they accomplished nevertheless had immense practical value. Their achievements as explorers were largely derived from the mountain man's flexible view of the West and drew on the knowledge and experience of such men as Walker, Greenwood, Hitchcock and Stevens; yet they added up to something more. They were the capstone of four decades of previous exploration in the West and at the same time the beginning of a new national era.

8. Erwin R. Gudde, ed.: *Bigler's Chronicle of the West* (Berkeley, Calif.: University of California Press; 1962), pp. 112–29.
9. Stewart: *California Trail*, pp. 251–3. For the Death Valley Forty-Niners, the best account is William Lewis Manley: *Death Valley in '49*, Milo Milton Quaife, ed. (Chicago: R. R. Donnelley and Sons; 1927). See also Carl I. Wheat: "Trailing the Forty-Niners through Death Valley," *Sierra Club Bulletin*, Vol. XXIV, No. 3 (June 1939); and "Pioneer Visitors to Death Valley after the Forty-Niners," *California Historical Society Quarterly*, Vol. XVIII, No. 3 (Sept. 1939).

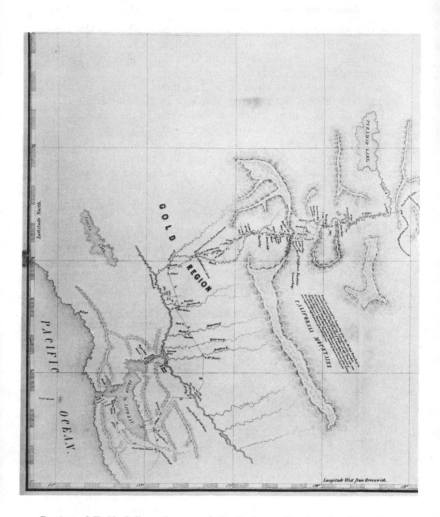

Portion of T. H. Jefferson's map of the Emigrant Road to San Francisco, Part IV, showing the California Gold Region. Legend above California Mountains reads: "It was six miles east of the Truckey Pass of the Cal. M[ts] that Reeds Party in November encountered snow ten feet deep and half the party perished. Emigrants who reach this Pass by the first of October are safe. Those who come later and encounter snow should at once retreat to Grass Valley of the mouth of the Truckey River and winter there or to the southward on the streams of the eastern base of the California Mountains. The western descent of these mountains is the most rugged and difficult portion of the whole journey." *Courtesy Library of Congress*

10

With the opening of the trails to Oregon and California, one great period in Western exploration had ended and another had all but begun. Though the clash of imperial systems had not yet reached its climax—the Oregon Boundary Settlement of 1845 and the Mexican War of 1846—as far as the explorer was concerned, the forces that would lead to that climax had already been generated. The West was no longer an unknown wilderness, a stepping stone on the road to India. Its potential in resources had become apparent, along with its vast dimensions and great difficulties. The basic overland routes were located, and the continental outlines figured in crude maps drawn from heartbreaking experience. Above all, due to the efforts of this first generation of explorers the West was no longer merely a vacuum between empires. Neither a game preserve to be exploited nor a northern mystery beyond the rim of Christendom, it had become by 1840 a place to move into—to occupy and settle and develop. It was a frontier of process as well as place. This had been due in large measure to the vision of the first American explorers, the mountain men and soldiers and wagon-train scouts who with the aid of the federal government looked beyond the fur trade to the future.

Thus, from the vantage point of 1845, it is possible to interpret the previous decades of Western history in a somewhat different fashion than has been traditional. Lost in the detail of the fur trade, and content with tracing economic behavior back solely to motives of profit and loss, historians have seen this period only as the era of the fur trade.[1] They have generally been satisfied to write the business history of the competitive wars of the beaver kingdom and not much more. The common struggle of the little traders against Astor's "monster monopoly," American Fur;[2] the shameful exploitation of trappers by middlemen, and Indians by whiskey; and the cutthroat tactics of William Sublette as he gained control of and slowly extinguished the grand old Rocky Mountain Fur Company have been common approaches to the period. In its least parochial treatment, the fur trade has been related in part to the

---

1. For example, see Katherine Coman: *Economic Beginnings of the Far West* . . . , 2 vols. (New York: The Macmillan Co.; 1912); Chittenden: *Fur Trade;* Phillips: *Fur Trade.*
2. See Don Berry: *A Majority of Scoundrels* (New York: Harper & Brothers; 1961), pp. 271 ff., 348 ff.

commerce of the London Strand and the worldwide market in beaver hats and winter coats.[3] All of this is valuable, but it tends to emphasize a single factor, albeit a most important one, to the exclusion of others. It fails to answer a number of vital questions such as why the British and Spanish and Russians failed in the Far West, and the Americans succeeded, and further what this meant in terms of the civilization to follow. It does not explain why a man like Jedediah Smith ever braved the rocky wastes of the Far Southwest and the deserts of the Great Basin, where the largest fur-bearing animal was a rat that the Diggers ate for food. Nor does the fur trade really account for the whole massive impulse that started the caravans of white-topped wagons on the trail to Oregon and California and a hundred other places in the American West. The explanation lies in factors above and beyond any single phenomenon such as the fur trade, and the period cannot therefore be characterized solely in terms of that economic enterprise. Rather, it was a continuation and extension of the great clash of empires in North America, at first thought to have ended with the French and Indian War and then finally with Lewis and Clark's discovery of a substitute for the Northwest Passage. The fact is, however, that Lewis and Clark's discovery was really only the beginning of another act in that imperial drama, perhaps not even a final one at that. And the true focus for the period must be on the clash of cultures on a grand scale, in all their complexity, both in the wilderness and back in civilization.

In this clash, the explorer was virtually an anthropological type. He was the gatherer of knowledge, "programmed" consciously or unconsciously by his civilization and his previous experience, who was then sent out to satisfy a whole range of cultural desires by his discoveries in the unknown. As such, he was a unique reflector of the cultures and their aspirations—a tracer element, as it were, in the North American imperial body politic. Through him the clash of empires was joined. In his story is the clue to why one culture prevailed and the others retired from the field. The American as flexible man, republican, and expectant capitalist stands clearly revealed. Hidden as yet, but discoverable through the story of future explorers asking new questions and undertaking new tasks in the West, are the weaknesses in this man and the problems inherent in his cultural ambitions.

3. Phillips: *Fur Trade, passim.* Berry: *A Majority of Scoundrels,* pp. 296–310.

CHAPTER VI

The Romantic Horizon

ANOTHER side of Western exploration in this period is presented by the work of the scientists and artists who accompanied expeditions to that remote region. Taken together, these men and their work illustrate not only the comparatively broad range of American interests and approaches to the West, but also a new kind of contrapuntal image of the West that began to arise out of the impact of European ideas upon American "high culture," the effect of which was to generate a series of ambiguities in the headlong march of empire across the continent. To the artist and the scientist, European and American alike, the West was important not as a place for settlers and civilization; it was important as a source of new experiences, new data, new sensations, and new questions. Governed by the abstract, ordered framework of eighteenth-century science and a paradoxical Lockian psychology of sense impressions, both the scientist and the artist in the West dedicated themselves to the concrete and the particular, with the result that they suddenly found themselves romantics breathing the life of exoticism into the remote extremities of the body of nature. For as one looked upon the frontier from Europe or the outposts of European culture along the Eastern Seaboard, one almost automatically assumed an idealistic and pastoral view of nature and nature's noblemen. Trans-Mississippia represented the unspoiled horizon beyond the crush of civilization continually hypothesized by European philosophers. It was a virtual international park for collectors of nature's wonders in all their gorgeous plumage and pristine freshness. For many who had no need to hack house and farm out of the sod, it represented the very symbol of the good life. The effect of all this was to cast serious doubt, at least for a time, upon the validity of the slogans of Manifest Destiny.

2

Before 1820, the botanists Nuttall, Bradbury, and the geographer-historian Henry Marie Brackenridge, who ascended the Missouri as far as the Mandan Villages under the protection of Wilson Price Hunt and Manuel Lisa, stood almost alone, along with David Thompson, as scientific investigators of the frontier. Their works were important pioneer efforts. Nuttall's *Genera of North American Plants* (1818) was an attempt at a comprehensive work in the Linnaean tradition, as was Frederick Pursh's *Flora Americae Septentrionalis* (1814), based on Bradbury's Missouri River specimens, which had been confiscated by the British in the War of 1812. Bradbury's *Travels in the Interior of America* . . . (1817) and Brackenridge's well-known *Views of Louisiana* . . . (1814) were further impressive contributions to the beginning of a systematic description of the West and its natural phenomena. Nuttall continued his work in later years, traveling through Arkansas Territory in 1819, and accompanying the second Wyeth expedition to Oregon. Of the work of the early scientists, his was the most important. It formed the basis for the first Harvard College botanical garden, and his publications were well-received in Europe, so that despite his eccentricities and his frontier orientation, Nuttall became a man of renown on both sides of the Atlantic.[1]

These pioneers were followed by the scientists of the Long expedition. Most of Long's civilian assistants were professionals trained in Philadelphia, with the exception of Thomas James, substitute botanist of the expedition and its official chronicler, who was a student of John Torrey and Amos Eaton at the Albany Academy. William Baldwin, the original botanist, was a graduate of the University of Pennsylvania Medical School and a contributor to the *Transactions* of the American Philosophical Society. Thomas Say

1. Thomas Nuttall: *Genera of North American Plants,* 2 vols. (Philadelphia: D. Heath; 1818). Frederick Pursh: *Flora Americae Septentrionalis,* 2 vols. (London: White, Cochrane and Co.; 1814). John Bradbury: *Travels in the Interior of North America.* Henry Marie Brackenridge's *Views of Louisiana: The Journal of a Voyage Up the Missouri River, in 1811* is reprinted in Thwaites: *Early Western Travels,* Vol. VI. See also Thomas Nuttall: *A Journal of Travels into the Arkansas Territory, During the Year 1819* (Philadelphia: Thomas H. Palmer; 1821), also reprinted in Thwaites: *Early Western Travels,* Vol. XIII. The best general account of early naturalist activity in the West during this period is Susan Delano McKelvey: *Botanical Exploration of the Trans-Mississippi West.*

was a founder of the Philadelphia Academy of Natural Sciences and perhaps the most brilliant zoologist in the country. As early as 1818 he had pointed out in an article in the first issue of *Silliman's Journal* the value of fossil evidence in determining the relative age of rock strata. He was the first American scientist to do so, and his article came at a time when even the Europeans were not yet fully convinced of the validity of the fossil method. Out of his collections made on the Long expedition and other field trips he produced *American Entomology*, published in three volumes in Philadelphia (1824–28), for decades the classic work on the subject. Augustus E. Jessup, the geologist of the Yellowstone Expedition, also came from Philadelphia and was an early member of the Academy of Natural Science. Titian Ramsey Peale served as scientific illustrator, and another Philadelphian, Samuel Seymour, painted genre scenes and landscapes intended to illustrate the general report. Peale's careful drawings of the animal life observed along the line of march were noteworthy contributions in the field of scientific art, which had developed as part of the eighteenth century age of global exploration, in which even English warships began to carry artists and naturalists. Peale later accompanied the United States Exploring Expedition to the South Seas and the Antarctic.[2]

Most of Long's scientists were representative of a school of naturalists that centered in Philadelphia, then the scientific capital of the country. Drawing their inspiration and advice from the famous Edinburgh "naturalist circle," with which they had direct contact both in person, as students, and by correspondence, the Philadelphians by means of such institutions as Peale's Museum, the Academy of Natural Sciences, and the American Philosophical Society created a center for the study of geography and natural history that provided the men and the training for a series of scien-

2. Edwin James: *Account of an Expedition from Pittsburgh to the Rocky Mountains, performed in the Years 1819, 1820 . . . under the Command of Maj. S. H. Long*, 2 vols. (Philadelphia: H. C. Carey and I. Lea; 1823). Thwaites reprints the three-volume London edition of 1823 in *Early Western Travels*, Vols. XIV–XVII. See especially Vol. XIV for biographical data on the members of his expedition. See also Thomas Say: "Observations on Some Species of Zoophytes, Shells etc. Principally Fossils," *American Journal of Science*, Vol. I (1818), p 382; and *American Entomology*, 3 vols. (Philadelphia, 1824–28). The best sketch of the life of Titian Peale is Jessie Poesch: *Titian Ramsey Peale, 1799–1885, and His Journals of the Wilkes Expedition* (Philadelphia: American Philosophical Society; 1961). I have examined Titian Peale's original animal drawings at the office of Edward Eberstadt and Sons, New York City, and Peale's journals in the Library of Congress.

tific explorations of the West.[3] From Meriwether Lewis, who took lessons in that city before his departure for his transcontinental march, to Dr. John Kirk Townsend, an ornithologist who accompanied Wyeth to Oregon in 1834–35, the important civilian scientific training and expertise available to the Western explorers came in large measure from Philadelphia. The Military Academy at West Point supplied most of the engineers and topographers. Only with the foundation of the Smithsonian Institution, in 1846, did the national scientific center move to Washington.

As a group, the early naturalists, particularly those who worked in the West, were a special breed. They were in search of an orderly knowledge of nature—as orderly, let us say, as the Linnaean or binomial-sexual system which was just coming into use and into the framework of which they tried to fit their new data. But they were also interested in the unusual and the exotic, particularly since almost everything they found in America was new to the Old World. The study and description of the thousands of new species that abounded in America was the life work of all of them. And for the artist, such as Peale, or John James Audubon and Alexander Wilson, the chance to draw, or paint, or somehow represent the exotic novelties of America was irresistible and a clear path to success both at home and abroad. Thus their labors resulted in many novelties but few new theories, though the eccentric Constantine Rafinesque, prowling the backwoods of Kentucky, clearly foreshadowed Darwin's hypothesis.[4] Rather, as Americans were to do for many decades, they provided the background research, the collection, classification, and description of plants and animals and minerals that were to make the sweeping generalizations of mid-century comprehensible to the scientific world.

3

The greatest of the American explorer-naturalists, however, was not, strictly speaking, a natural scientist at all until late in his life. He was a painter and an ethnologist. Nevertheless, George Catlin

3. Brooke Hindle: *The Pursuit of Science in Revolutionary America, 1735–1789* (Chapel Hill, N.C.: University of North Carolina Press; 1956) deals with Philadelphia and the naturalist circle.
4. Bernard Jaffe: *Men of Science in America* (New York: Simon and Schuster; 1958), pp. 104–29.

deserves to be ranked in the forefront of those who contributed to the organized knowledge of the country beyond the Mississippi. He combined all of the traits of the naturalists—the passion for organized information, a genius for accurate and meaningful observation, the collector's instinct, an eye for novelty, and most of all a love for the primitive and exotic.

Born in 1796 in Wilkes-Barre, Pennsylvania, the scene of the comparatively recent Wyoming massacre, George Catlin grew up in a frontier community where the Indian was a recent and ever-present memory.[5] His mother, in fact, had been a captive in the Wyoming massacre and had fortunately escaped. From her presumably he acquired his early interest in Indian lore. But Wilkes-Barre was a community like most others on the frontier, oriented toward civilization, and Catlin was sent to Tapping Reeve's law school in Litchfield, Connecticut, where his father had studied, and where such famous men as John C. Calhoun and the Maya explorer John Lloyd Stephens had also studied. After two years, Catlin went into practice, as he put it, in "Nimrodical" fashion, for most of his youth had been spent "with books reluctantly held in one hand, and a rifle or fishing pole firmly and affectionately in the other."[6] Eventually, the romantic life got the better of the practical life and he abandoned the law in favor of painting. Around 1824 he moved to Philadelphia and began to work seriously as a portraitist, though he had had no formal instruction except the advice of Thomas Sully and Rembrandt Peale.

The turning point in Catlin's life came when he saw a delegation of Indian chiefs who came to Philadelphia en route to Washington for a visit. "In silent and stoic dignity," he remembered, "these lords of the forest strutted about the city for a few days, wrapped in their pictured robes, with their brows plumed with the quills of the war-eagle, attracting the gaze of all who beheld them." He saw them instantly as the exotic subjects for the kind of painting he wished

5. The most recent biography of George Catlin is Harold McCracken: *George Catlin and the Old Frontier* (New York: Dial Press; 1959). See also Lloyd Haberly: *Pursuit of the Horizon* (New York: The Macmillan Co.; 1948), and the masterful short biography of Catlin by Van Wyck Brooks: *Fenellosa and His Circle* (New York: E. P. Dutton and Co.; 1962), pp. 157–96.
6. George Catlin: *Illustrations of the Manners, Customs, and Condition of the North American Indian with Letters and Notes Written During Eight Years of Travel and Adventure Among the Wildest and most Remarkable Tribes Now Existing*, ninth edition, 2 vols. (London: Henry G. Bohn; 1857), Vol. I, p. 2. Hereafter referred to as Catlin: *North American Indians*.

to do. By painting the vanishing redmen as they really were, he could make a contribution to knowledge comparable to that of the naturalists and scientific illustrators he knew so well in Philadelphia. He resolved to devote his life to "the production of a literal and graphic delineation of the living manners, customs, and character of an interesting race of people who are rapidly passing away from the face of the earth—lending a hand to a dying nation, who have no historians or biographers of their own to pourtray with fidelity their native looks and history. . . ."[7]

Unable to embark on his plan to paint the Western Indians immediately, he spent several years in Albany painting portraits of its leading citizens, including De Witt Clinton, and making sketches of the Erie Canal. Whenever he could, he visited the nearby Indian reservations and painted Senecas, Tuscaroras, Oneidas, Ottawas, and Mohicans. His first famous Indian portrait was of Red Jacket standing on a cliff overlooking Niagara Falls. Catlin depicted him in rather awkward fashion, pointing to the falls and the mist that rose above them in which he believed his ghost would hover after death.

By 1830, Catlin had made up his mind to go West. Armed with letters of introduction from government officials in Washington, he went to St. Louis. There he was befriended by Governor William Clark and was able to accumulate funds for a trip to the Indian country by painting portraits of the Governor and other fashionable people of the city. In 1832 he secured passage on the American Fur Company steamer *Yellowstone*, the first such craft to ascend the Missouri River to its upper reaches. On the *Yellowstone* he traveled upriver to Fort Union, observing and painting the river and the country along the way. At Fort Pierre, where the boat stopped for an extended time, he painted wild Indians, including Ha-won-je-tah, "The One Horn," chief of the Sioux; Tchan-Du, "Tobacco of the Oglalas"; and many others, gaining a reputation as a powerful medicine man among the Indians, who crowded into his makeshift studio to watch him work.[8]

He also painted the Indian dances, feasts, and ceremonies, and paid close attention to their tribal customs. His description of Indian medicine ceremonies and the role of the medicine man and his charms and amulets proved to be particularly valuable in understanding Indian life. In addition he became a connoisseur of Indian

7. Ibid., pp. 2–3.
8. Ibid., Vol. I, *passim*. See also McCracken: *George Catlin*. My account is based on Catlin: *North American Indians*, unless otherwise stated.

clothing, often swapping something of his own for a set of beaded leggings or a feathered headdress. His greatest coup was bargaining for a medicine man's entire costume, including his bearskin mantle and all the assorted bats' wings, feathers, and small animal-skin totems that went with it.

It was the same wherever he went. Among the Blackfeet he painted their chief Four Bears and dozens of other dignitaries, as well as their gaudy ceremonies. In painting the Indians, Catlin exchanged his rather slick portraitist's style for a more primitive one dictated by the limitations of his working conditions. Painting out-of-doors, or in crude forts and lodges, with a choice of about ten hand-mixed colors and whatever brushes and canvas he could carry on his back, Catlin became a primitive limner of the redman's world, not only documenting in concrete detail everything he saw, but managing to capture the romanticism and nobility of an Indian culture as yet unspoiled by the white man. In a sense, his great talent was to see the Indian as he saw himself, in a kind of grand simplicity —with the unself-conscious pride of the unvanquished.

When he journeyed back down the Missouri, Catlin took a canoe, and along the way he visited all of the river tribes except the hostile Arikara. This included the Mandans, who lived in the same earthen lodges in the same villages where Lewis and Clark had wintered on their trip upriver. He also recorded on canvas and in letters back home the revolting details of the scalp dance and the O-kee-pah (Okipa) ceremony of the Mandan. In the latter, men were strung up by skewers stuck through their muscles and rotated by their fellow warriors. When they fainted from shock, they were let down, and upon recovering crawled about dragging buffalo skulls from the skewered muscles. From time to time a brave would climax the ceremony by hacking a finger from his hand as an offering to the gods. At other times the braves were strung up and forced to gaze directly into the sun until a kind of blindness descended upon them and they fainted from loss of blood. In recording these scenes, Catlin rarely passed judgment, and few people back home believed his accounts were the truth until they were substantiated by later observers.

Most important of all was Catlin's skill as a scientific recorder. And he happened to be at the right place at the right time, especially in the case of the Mandans, who were wiped out by smallpox within three years after Catlin's visit. At times, however, Catlin's passion for recording detail led him into error. Taking the Mandan's myth of their origin—the story of a Noachian flood and a birchbark ark —at face value, Catlin concluded that they were indeed the descendants of Madoc and his Welsh emigrants whom John Evans had tried to find in his trip up the Missouri in 1795.[9]

For the next eight years, from 1832 to 1840, Catlin painted Indians wherever he could find them, at Fort Snelling in Minnesota, at the Pipestone Quarry in South Dakota, in Wisconsin and in Florida, in Georgia, where he met and painted the noble Osceola, on the Southwestern Plains, where he accompanied Colonel Dodge's Dragoons to the Rocky Mountains, and even back in civilization whenever a visiting tribal dignitary was available. In all, he traveled thousands of miles by canoe, on horseback and muleback, in steamers, keelboats, and bullboats.[1] At the end of eight years as an explorer-painter and ethnologist of the West, he could say:

> I have visited forty-eight different tribes, the greater part of which I found speaking different languages, and containing in all 400,000 souls. I have brought home safe, and in good order, 310 portraits in oil, all painted in their native dress, and in their own wigwams; and also 200 other paintings in oil, containing views of their villages—their wigwams—their games and religious ceremonies—their dances—their ball plays— their buffalo hunting and other amusements (containing in all over 3000 full length figures); and the landscapes of the country they live in, as well as a very extensive and curious collection of their costumes and all their other manufactures, from the size of a wigwam down to the size of a quill or a rattle.[2]

4

Catlin was interested in the Indians not only as curiosities and scientific specimens, however. As he witnessed the advance of the white man into the Indian domain, he came to lament the passing of the Indian civilization, which he regarded as equal to that of the intruder, and in most respects superior. In recording Indian life at this particular time and place, Catlin caught, as it were, on a historical slide the almost total effacement of one civilization by another—what the modern ethnologist calls euphemistically "accul-

9. Catlin: *North American Indians*, Vol. II, Appendix A.
1. Ibid., Vols. I and II. But see also McCracken: *George Catlin*, who effectively disputes Catlin's claim that he went to the Great Salt Lake in 1833 (pp. 130–1).
2. Catlin: *North American Indians*, Vol. I, p. 4.

turation." Catlin, however, was more romantic in his description, which echoes Rousseau and Chateaubriand.

I have viewed man in the innocent simplicity of nature, in the full enjoyment of the luxuries which God has bestowed upon him . . . happier than kings and princes can be, with his pipe and little ones about him. . . . I have seen him shrinking from civilized approach, which came with all its vices, like the dead of night, upon him . . . seen him gaze and then retreat like the frightened deer. . . . I have seen him shrinking from the soil and haunts of his boyhood, bursting the strongest ties which bound him to the earth and its pleasures. I have seen him set fire to his wigwam and smooth over the graves of his fathers . . . clap his hand in silence over his mouth, and take the last look over his fair hunting ground, and turn his face in sadness to the setting sun. All this I have seen performed in nature's silent dignity . . . and I have seen as often the approach of the bustling, busy, talking, elated, and exultant white man, with the first clip of the plough share, making sacriligious trespass on the bones of the dead. . . . I have seen the grand and irresistible march of civilization . . . this splendid juggernaut rolling on and beheld its sweeping desolation. And I have held converse with the happy thousands, living as yet beyond its influence, who had not been crushed, nor have yet dreamed of its approach. I have stood amidst these unsophisticated people and contemplated with feelings of deepest regret the certain approach of this overwhelming system which will inevitably march on and prosper; reluctant tears shall have watered every rod of this fair land; and from the towering cliffs of the Rocky Mountains, the luckless savage will turn back his swollen eyes on the illimitable hunting-grounds from which he has fled, and there contemplate, like Caius Marius on the ruins of Carthage, their splendid desolation . . . all this is certain . . . and if he could rise from his grave and speak, or would speak from the life some half century from this, they would proclaim my prophecy true and fulfilled.[3]

Catlin thus became something more than an explorer. He became a critic of the civilizing process itself, and a reformer. Wherever he went, he spoke for the Indian, defending him and, by implication, nature itself against the very forces that most of the

3. Quoted in McCracken: *George Catlin*, pp. 15–16.

other explorers were helping to promote. In 1834, for example, in Pensacola, Florida, he met John Howard Payne, the composer of *Home, Sweet Home*, and accompanied him north to protest the removal of the Cherokee Indians from Georgia. When Payne was arrested by the military at the home of John Ross for his activities on behalf of the Indians, Catlin, for whom a warrant was also issued, indignantly journeyed to Washington and took his case directly to President Andrew Jackson. "I . . . went to the 'White House,' " Catlin remembered, "and was admitted to the presence of Genl Jackson who was in his office alone. I asked him for what cause an order had been issued for our arrest—to which he replied, 'it is none of your business, Sir.' Of course my interview ended there."[4] But Catlin never ceased to put his researches to practical use in the cause of the Indian.

In an attempt to influence public opinion, he tried to promote a national park in Washington which would preserve nature and nature's noblemen in all their authenticity. As the cornerstone of this project, he offered to sell his paintings and collections to the federal government, but his proposal failed in Congress by one vote. So instead he took his materials to New York and began what was the first wild West show in history.

He opened at the Stuyvesant Institute on Broadway with Ioway chief Keokuk, and an assemblage of Sioux and Sacs and Foxes who did war dances and shot bows and arrows. It was a tremendous success. Then in 1839 he traveled to England and set up his show in the Egyptian Hall on Piccadilly Circus, and was repeatedly received by the Queen and the Prince Consort. In London in 1841 he published *Letters and Notes on the North American Tribes*, the collection of all his articles written during eight years in the West. So well, in fact, was he received in England that he stayed five years and came to regard it as home.

Then in 1845 he moved on to Paris and erected his wigwams and set up his paintings in the Louvre, capturing the Rousseauistic imagination of the French, and particularly of King Louis Philippe, until the revolution of 1848 made further shows under the auspices of the French monarch difficult, if not impossible. The death of his wife and only son in Paris caused him to grow despondent for a time, but in 1851, with the encouragement of Alexander von Humboldt, he embarked on a new career as an explorer, departing to paint the Indians of South America. For the rest of his life Catlin

4. George Catlin to William H. Brewer, Brussels, Jan. 18, 1869, Brewer Papers, Yale Historical Manuscripts Collection.

roamed the Western Hemisphere from Tierra del Fuego to Kamchatka, painting Indians and recording the details of their lost civilization. When he died, in 1872, Catlin had returned to America after an absence of thirty-one years and had been accorded official recognition by Joseph Henry himself, who provided him with an office in one of the towers of the Smithsonian.

Eventually the Smithsonian acquired his Indian paintings through private donations, and though until recently George Catlin lay forgotten in Brooklyn's Greenwood Cemetery, his paintings of the 128 tribes of the Western Hemisphere represent perhaps the most important and authentic view of Indian life at the high tide of their civilization, before the era of the white man's Manifest Destiny. Catlin was, indeed, a naturalist who loved nature—the perfect embodiment of the romantic as scientist.[5]

5

Essentially, the kind of romantic ethnology that Catlin's work represented, especially his view that nature was exotic and pristine, appealed more to Europeans than it did to Americans, who were preoccupied with the march of empire. Humboldt, with his monumental geographical exploration of South and Central America. set the scientific tone of the era. By Catlin's day the two dominant figures in the field of world geography were Humboldt and Karl Ritter, whose *Erdkunde* (1818) was the first important attempt at a scientific study of the world's population. Humboldt in particular stimulated a whole generation of German explorers to visit the American West. Beyrich, a Prussian botanist, accompanied Colonel Dodge's dragoons in 1835 and died of fever on that unfortunate expedition in which Catlin, too, almost died.[6]

Fredrick Paul Wilhelm, Duke of Württemberg, was one of the earliest Humboldtean explorers of the American West. Well-educated by a pupil of Cuvier at the Stuttgart Gymnasium, and a student of Humboldt, Duke Paul was a recognized geographer-naturalist before he came to America, having traveled extensively in the Near

5. Biographical details of Catlin's later life are based on George Catlin: *Last Rambles Amongst the Indians of the Rocky Mountains and the Andes* (New York: D. Appleton and Co.; 1867); McCracken: *George Catlin;* Brooks; *Fenellosa;* and Haberly: *Pursuit of the Horizon* (see footnote 5, p. 185).
6. "Monsieur Beyrick" (sic) is mentioned in Lt. Thomas Wheelock: "Journal of Colonel Dodge's Expedition," pp. 76, 80.

192 EXPLORATION AND EMPIRE

East, Algeria, Russia, and the Caribbean. He held membership in the Royal Leopold Academy of Vienna, the Société Imperiale Zoologique d'Acclimation of Paris, the Society of Natural Science of Athens, and the academies of London and Petersburg, which amounted to recognition by most of the scientific societies of Europe.[7]

On the sixteenth of October 1822, he sailed from Hamburg on his first journey to North America. This trip took him first to New Orleans, then up the Mississippi and its various tributaries, including the Red River, the Yazoo, and the Ohio. Upon reaching St. Louis, he began an extensive tour of the fur-trade country, going west to the Platte and the Kansas rivers and up the Missouri as far as Council Bluffs. Along the way he made extensive collections of plants, animals, and Indian artifacts, taking great care to identify and classify his specimens according to the canons of Linnaeus. Duke Paul's first expedition to America lasted over two years, from 1822 to 1824, and some time after he returned he published his important book, *First Journey to North America in the Years 1822 to 1824*, in Stuttgart.[8]

In all, Duke Paul made four journeys to North America, of which very little is known. In 1829–31 he returned to the West, traveling up the Missouri River to the Mandan Villages and Fort Clark. He then journeyed to the Rocky Mountains and the Three Forks country, where he studied the Blackfeet and Assiniboin. On his return downstream to St. Louis, he was rescued by a Sioux and spent some time in their villages.[9]

Most of 1831 was taken up with a trip to Mexico, the scene of Humboldt's mighty labors. Then he returned to Germany via New Orleans, Cincinnati, Buffalo, Lake Erie, Niagara Falls, and the East Coast. From 1849 to 1856, and in 1857 and 1858, he made two further Western forays but of these virtually nothing is known. By 1860 he had traveled over more of the American West than any other foreign explorer, but because he took along no artist on his travels, he has been largely neglected by students of Western exploration.

The same has not been true for Duke Paul's friend and fellow

7. The primary source of information concerning Duke Paul of Württemberg is the reprint of his "First Journey to North America in the Years 1822 to 1824," translated by William Bek, with notes and appendix by Friedrick Bauser, in *South Dakota Historical Collections*, Vol. XIX (1938), pp. 7–474.
8. First published by J. G. Cotta, Stuttgart and Tübingen, in 1828.
9. *South Dakota Historical Collections*, Vol. XIX, pp. 472–3.

Humboldtean, Prince Maximilian of Wied-Neuwied. In 1833, accompanied by his faithful servant Dreidoppel and the twenty-three-
year-old artist Karl Bodmer, Prince Maximilian steamed 2,000 miles
up the Missouri River to Fort Union, and then took a keelboat to
Fort McKenzie, the American Fur Company's advanced outpost
among the Blackfeet, near the headwaters of the Missouri. At each
of the major forts along the way the Prince and his painter stopped
to make careful studies of Indian life, and while at Fort McKenzie
he witnessed a surprise attack on a Blackfoot Village by the Assiniboin. Bodmer managed to capture it on canvas in perhaps the only
painting ever made of an Indian battle by an eyewitness.[1] Like Duke
Paul, from whom he received advice prior to his trip, Maximilian
was a serious naturalist who had also explored South America.[2]
His field notes indicate that he paid close attention to the description of natural phenomena that he observed, and in some cases the
notes were enhanced by Bodmer's sketches and those of the Prince
himself made right on the spot.[3]

The most important ethnological work of Prince Maximilian's
expedition was done during his winter's stay with the Mandans,
who were wiped out by the following year. The Prince's notes, and
Bodmer's accurate paintings, made from careful pencil sketches,
furnish the most complete record of that vanished tribe. Bodmer's
rendition of the dimly lit interior of a Mandan hut is the only such
painting of its kind. There the Indian family sits, surrounded by dogs
and horses stabled inside on the fringe of the living quarters. Buffalo
robes, baskets, shields, lances, bows and arrows, medicine bags,
pipes—all the accouterments of war and peace are represented
in Bodmer's painting, which is thus an important ethnological record. This painting was accompanied by numerous other drawings
and sketches of Mandan life.

Maximilian is remembered in part because of Bodmer's magnifi-

1. Prince Maximilian of Wied-Neuwied: *Travels in the Interior of North
America in the Years 1832 to 1834* (London: Ackerman and Co.; 1843). Reprinted in Thwaites: *Early Western Travels*, Vols. XXII–XXV. I have also
seen the original German edition, published in Coblenz in 1839, and the
French edition of 1840–43.
2. See Prince Maximilian: *Travels in Brazil in the Years 1815, 1816,
1817* (London: Henry Colburn and Co.; 1820).
3. "Scientific Journal," Maximilian Papers, Joslyn Art Museum, Omaha,
Nebraska. The Maximilian Papers, including his manuscript diaries, correspondence, and scientific journal, along with the originals of many of
Bodmer's paintings, have been presented by the Omaha Northern Natural
Gas Company to the Joslyn Art Museum, where I had the privilege of examining them.

cent paintings. By far the most talented artist to depict the American West in its earliest days, Bodmer not only portrayed Indian life in striking portraits and genre groups, but also rendered the Missouri landscape as it had never been rendered before. The vast ranges of white hills and immense stretches of prairie that lined the river, a buffalo crossing on the upper river overshadowed by ranges of romantic peaks and a brilliant Barbizon sky, the distinctive white castle formations, and all the snags and sandbars and twisted forest growth along the lower river were re-created by the young Swiss artist in what amounted to perhaps the most exotic image of Western America ever done.

Then, too, since the Prince was also interested in the pockets of German emigrants in America and the possible routes West for future emigrant parties, the artist and his patron traveled from the Eastern Seaboard to St. Louis. Bodmer painted New Harmony, Indiana, and Bethlehem, Pennsylvania, the headquarters of the renowned German naturalist Bishop Muhlenberg. The expedition wintered in New Harmony and the Prince was able to compare scientific notes with Thomas Say and Charles Alexander Le Sueur, an important French émigré scientist who had joined that utopian community. Bodmer, temporarily released by the Prince, went alone to New Orleans and, as a result of this trip, produced a series of striking pictures of the Lower Mississippi and the Deep South.[4]

Bodmer's best paintings—the Indian portraits, the landscapes, the ethnological and artifact groups, the representations of fur-trade posts and outposts of civilization from New York to St. Louis and New Orleans—were all made into magnificent engravings for Maximilian's *Travels in the Interior of North America in the Years 1832 to 1834,* published at the Prince's expense in his home city of Coblenz in 1839–41. A large elephant folio volume which accompanied Maximilian's excellent narrative displayed Bodmer's engravings, improved versions of his paintings touched up here and there in his German studio. The Prince's sumptuous work clearly outshone in sheer attractiveness even the best efforts of the great Humboldt himself. It provided a masterful record of life on the Missouri frontier that confirmed much of Catlin's revelations.

Still another German who explored the mountain West was Frederick Wislizenus, a physician of liberal persuasion who had been forced to flee Frankurt because of his part in the abortive revolution

4. Maximilian: *Travels,* in Thwaites: *Early Western Travels,* Vol. XXII, pp. 13, 197.

of 1833. Like most of his European colleagues, Wislizenus was well educated, having studied at Jena, Göttingen, Tübingen, and Zurich, where he finally received his medical degree under the tutelage of the great German romantic scientist and philosopher Oken, who was also at that time a refugee. In 1835 Wislizenus arrived in Mascoutah, Illinois, not far from St. Louis, and there set up his practice and quickly became friendly with the St. Louis German community, particularly with Dr. George Engelmann, the West's leading botanist.[5]

To a European who had been educated in the romantic naturalist tradition, the Rocky Mountains were an irresistible attraction, so in the spring of 1839 Wislizenus invested his savings in explorer's paraphernalia and joined a fur-trading party under the leadership of Black Harris heading for the last Green River rendezvous. His reconnaissance of 1839 took him from Westport out along the Platte to Fort Laramie, then on through South Pass to the rendezvous. When the July assembly broke up, Wislizenus accompanied a party to Fort Hall and there decided to turn back. From Fort Hall he journeyed south to Bear River, up that river, over the Uinta Mountains, across the Green, and into Brown's Hole in Colorado. Eventually he came out on the South Platte and, penetrating the front range of the Rockies, turned south to Bent's Fort on the Arkansas River. From that point he took the Santa Fe Trail back to Missouri. His account of the year's journey contains some interesting observations and a crude map, but it is primarily a romantic travel book rather than a careful scientific study of the West that he had seen. It draws but little upon his talent for science.[6]

Early in 1846 Wislizenus, by now a working partner of George Engelmann, decided to make a more serious scientific exploration of the Southwest. He joined the last traders' train to leave for Santa Fe before the outbreak of the Mexican War, and in company with the traders he got as far south as Cosihuiriachi, where he was imprisoned by the Mexicans. Taking advantage of a parole that allowed him the freedom of the countryside two leagues around the town, the naturalist made a thorough study of the region. His report on northern Mexico, which was later published as a government docu-

5. Biographical data on Wislizenus may be found in F. A. Wislizenus: *A Journey to the Rocky Mountains in the Year 1839*, translated . . . with a sketch of the author's life by Frederick A. Wislizenus, Esq. (St. Louis, Mo.: Missouri Historical Society; 1912), pp. 5–13.
6. Ibid., *passim*. See map reproduced at end of book.

ment, was the most important geographical and economic survey of that almost unknown region then published.[7] Like all of his European counterparts, Wislizenus found the mountains and the Southwest, and later California, highly romantic. But unlike many German observers who were returning to Europe with vivid impressions, Wislizenus, who had become an American, saw the West largely in terms of the march of empire and civilization. "A transformation of this remarkable country seems then at hand," he wrote in 1840. "It is perhaps only a few years until the plow upturns the virgin soil, which is now only touched by the lightfooted Indian or the hoof of wild animals. Every decade will change the character of the country materially, and in a hundred years perhaps the present narratives of mountain life may sound like fairy tales."[8]

6

Besides the Germans, the English also showed considerable interest in the West during this period, but they were far less studious. Sir George Gore went hunting on the Lower Yellowstone. Captain Frederick Ruxton (very possibly a British spy) explored the central parks of Colorado and lived with the mountain men. He was a great traveler, and covered most of the mountain West, and Mexico besides. When he returned to England he wrote one of the classics of early Western literature, *Life in the Far West* (1849), a fictionalized account of the authentic adventures of the trappers Killbuck and La Bonte that stamped them forever in the Robin Hood "banditti" image.[9]

The most famous of all the British sportsmen was Sir William Drummond Stewart, a Scotsman who had been with Wellington on the Spanish Peninsula Campaign. Stewart, too, had been to the West in that busy year of 1833. There he had met and become fast friends with William Sublette, Robert Campbell, and many other

7. F. A. Wislizenus: "Memoir of a Tour to Northern Mexico, Connected with Col. Doniphan's Expedition in 1846 and 1847," 30th Cong., 1st sess., *Sen. Misc. Doc.* 26 (1848). This memoir also contains a geological sketch, a profile of his route, a botanical appendix by George Engelmann, meteorological tables, and a map.
8. Wislizenus: *Journey in 1839,* p. 162.
9. George Frederick Ruxton: *Life in the Far West,* LeRoy R. Hafen, ed. (Norman, Okla.: Oklahoma University Press; 1951). See also Hafen, ed.: *Ruxton of the Rockies* (Norman, Okla.: Oklahoma University Press; 1950).

prominent mountain men.[1] In 1837, having inherited Murthley Castle in Scotland on the condition that he would live there the rest of his life, Stewart went back to the West for one last hunt along the Seedskeedee—the only proper sport in the world. So that he would not forget his days in the mountains he too took along an artist, Alfred Jacob Miller of Baltimore, and Miller became the third of the great triumvirate of early Western painters.

Working mostly with pencil and watercolors, though he occasionally used oils, Miller recaptured the dramatic life of the fur trade with wit and tremendous romantic verve. Resembling somewhat, in his use of colors, the English school of Turner and Constable, Miller caught the wild swirl of an Indian camp, the frantic motion of the buffalo hunt, and best of all the minute details of trapper life such as the setting of beaver traps in the evening, the picketing of the horses, a quiet encampment by a moonlit lake, and the evening campfire with the teller of tall tales holding forth like some Indian chieftain at a council fire. He also sensed something of the quaint attractiveness of the Indians. Almost never are they fierce in his pictures. Rather, they are companions in a pastoral frolic. There were girls bathing naked in a mountain stream—reminiscent of Herman Melville's Typee maidens—or brides newly purchased from a proud and slightly humorous old chief. Lacking the skill of Bodmer and the furious dedication and scientific interest of Catlin, Miller nevertheless made a contribution both to art and to history. In the latter cause he rendered invaluable service in preserving a record of the rugged life of the mountain men just before they too, like the Mandan Indians, passed from the stage of Western history.

Significantly, for almost all of these early explorers, except perhaps Catlin, the West was a picturesque and romantic wilderness abounding in the exotic and the marvelous. It was a sportsman's and naturalist's paradise destined to remain undisturbed perhaps for centuries. When these men returned to civilization, they wrote about it in novels like Stewart's *Altowan* and brilliantly illustrated travel books like those of Maximilian. Duke Paul established a whole museum dedicated to Western artifacts and curiosities. For most of them, even the scientists, the West was over the horizon, a remote part of Humboldt's Cosmos like the Amazon Valley of South America or the Pampas or Cotopoxi in the heart of the Andes. Even many of the educated Americans tended to share this European view and

1. See, for example, De Voto: *Across the Wide Missouri*, and correspondence between Stewart and William Sublette in Sublette Papers, Missouri Historical Society.

produced works and even wild West shows that emphasized remote and fantastic America. While they were doing this, a very different group of American explorers, less conscious of Europe, were turning their hands, or at least contributing their experience, to another and quite distinct literary genre—the emigrant guide and the railroad report.

The coming generation of explorers, for the most part soldier-engineers trained at West Point, were already moving out into the West to build on what they could learn of the mountain man's knowledge, which along with their new and more accurate maps and topographic surveys would make it easy, perhaps all too easy, for the tide of settlement to sweep on to the far Pacific.

The Romantic Horizon

THE primary function of the artist who accompanied the explorers into the American West was reportorial. He was to record and document the new lands and the new people, and his medium was the most dramatic means of conveying to the public at large just what the country was like beyond the edge of the great frontier. But since the spaces were so vast, the scenery so grand and terrifying, and the Indians so exotic, the documentary art of the explorer-artists inevitably fused romanticism with realism. Even the most detailed and ethnologically exact painting, the most faithfully executed landscape, had a freshness and spirit that bore witness to a common image of the American West as the "romantic horizon."

It is the thesis of this book that explorers, as they go out into the unknown, are "programmed" by the knowledge, values, and objectives of the civilized centers from which they depart. They are alert to discover evidence of the things they have been sent to find. Similarly, in large measure, the artists who accompany them also see what they are trained to see and in the way they are trained to see it. The new sights and subjects offered by the West were represented in terms of the artistic conventions dominant in the civilized culture of the day. Fortunately for the explorer-artist, the nineteenth century had a passion for the far-away, the exotic, and the sublime—in short, for the kind of romanticism to which the Far West quite naturally lent itself. The explorer-artist fitted in with and fulfilled the expectations of a popular taste that was ultimately European in origin. Whether in water-colors, oils, drawings, or mass-produced lithographs, the work of the artist in the American West of the nineteenth century was primarily an extension of the vision of Poussin, Claude Lorrain, the Barbizon

School, the painters of the Swiss Alps, Turner, Delacroix, and the dozens of illustrators who accompanied the great English voyages of discovery in the late eighteenth and early nineteenth centuries. This work most closely resembled the "practitioner art" of men like George Edwards, who drew exotic creatures "from life" on the Spanish Main in 1755, or William Hodges and John Webber, who painted the noble savages and the romantic discoveries of Captain Cook to such effect that they were even translated into wallpaper and household decorations by the tastemakers of the early nineteenth century. Thus, for the cultural historian, *things*—in this case, paintings and drawings—represent an additional source of evidence for conclusions derived from a study of the written acounts of adventure and discovery in the unknown West.

I

The Exotic West

First view of the Rocky Mountains. Watercolor sketch by Samuel Seymour, a Philadelphia artist with Major Stephen H. Long's expedition of 1819–20. *Courtesy Yale Collection of Western Americana*

A view of the Upper Missouri in 1833. Engraving from a painting by Karl Bodmer, artist to the expedition of Prince Maximilian of Wied-Neuwied. Bodmer was one of the major figures of the Barbizon School and the teacher of Millet. He was, however, no geographer. Though he called this painting "View of the Rocky Mountains," from this point on the Upper Missouri he could not possibly have seen the Rocky Mountains. *Courtesy Northern Natural Gas Co. and Joslyn Art Museum*

"Wild Scenery—Making a Cache." Watercolor by Alfred Jacob Miller. Painted by Miller in his Baltimore studio in 1858 from sketches made on his Western trip in 1837, this picture, with its sublime landscape of bottomless gorges, towering crags, and celestial light, is a carry-over from Miller's European training and the epitome of romantic conventionalism. *Courtesy Walters Art Gallery and University of Oklahoma Press, copyright 1951*

George Catlin painting Mah-to-tah-pa, the Mandan chief: the documentary artist at work on an exotic subject. Compare with Bodmer's portrait of the Chief, p. 205. The debate as to whether Catlin was a primitive or a romantic seems pointless, for primitivism was very much a part of the romantic aesthetic. *Courtesy American Museum of Natural History*

"The Mandan Torture Ceremony." Painting by George Catlin, 1832. A privileged view of a secret savage rite, this is one of Catlin's most valuable ethnological contributions. *Courtesy American Museum of Natural History*

"The Interior of the Hut of a Mandan Chief." Engraving from a painting by Karl Bodmer, 1833. Note the wealth of ethnological detail. This, along with Catlin's studies of the same tribe, is of rare value, for by 1835 the Mandans had been wiped out by smallpox. *Courtesy Northern Natural Gas Co. and Joslyn Art Museum*

"Mato-Tope, a Mandan Chief." Engraving from a painting by Karl Bodmer, 1833. *Courtesy Northern Natural Gas Co. and Joslyn Art Museum*

"Abdih-Hiddisch, a Minatarre Chief." Engraving from a painting by Karl Bodmer, 1833. The chief's headgear shows that the process of acculturation had begun. *Courtesy Northern Natural Gas Co. and Joslyn Art Museum*

"The Buffalo Dance of the Mandans." Engraving from a painting by Karl Bodmer, 1833. This and the scene that follows give Bodmer's impressions of the terror and mystery of Indian life. The cultural importance of the ceremony is suggested by the formal composition of the work. A pyramidal structure of solid, almost classical figures is balanced by the skillful paralleling of lines represented by poles, gun barrels, and spears. *Courtesy Northern Natural Gas Co. and Joslyn Art Museum*

"Scalp Dance of the Minatarres." Engraving from a painting by Karl Bodmer, 1833. A mingling of Indian barbarism and romantic symbolism. *Courtesy Northern Natural Gas Co. and Joslyn Art Museum*

II

Some Western Versions of Pastoral:
the Painter as Mythmaker

The next seven plates are the work of Alfred Jacob Miller, the European-trained Baltimore artist employed in 1837 by Sir William Drummond Stewart to document his adventures among the mountain men and Indians of the Rocky Mountains. Miller was the second person to paint the Rocky Mountains (see p. 200), but his favorite subjects were the mountain trappers and their Indian companions. He seldom depicted hostile Indians. Rather, his redmen were noble savages in a sentimentalized, pastoral landscape reminiscent of the work of Turner, with whom he studied. Miller's mountain men, painted realistically in their everyday pursuits, likewise became, at the same time, creatures of myth. Figures in a misty pastoral landscape in situations fraught with danger, they were allegorical nature-gods, the epitome of the "wild Robin Hood kind of life" described by Washington Irving in *The Adventures of Captain Bonneville* and by Stewart in his novel *Altowan*, both of which derived from the romantic banditti tradition in European literature and art.

Mass slaughter of buffalo by Plains Indians. Watercolor by Alfred Jacob Miller done in 1858 from a sketch made in 1837. *Courtesy Walters Art Gallery and University of Oklahoma Press, copyright 1951*

The Indian at home. Watercolor by Alfred Jacob Miller done in 1858 from a sketch made in 1837. *Courtesy Walters Art Gallery and University of Oklahoma Press, copyright 1951*

"Indian Women Swimming." Watercolor by Alfred Jacob Miller done in 1858 from a sketch made in 1837. A forest idyll that calls to mind Melville's *Typee*, or the works of Gauguin; the Indian girls seem virtually part of nature itself in all its innocence and freshness. *Courtesy Walters Art Gallery and University of Oklahoma Press, copyright 1951*

"Trapping Beaver." Watercolor by Alfred Jacob Miller done in 1858 from a sketch made in 1837. Perhaps the best representation ever made of the trapper at work. *Courtesy Walters Art Gallery and University of Oklahoma Press, copyright 1951*

"Escape from Blackfeet." Watercolor by Alfred Jacob Miller done in 1858 from a sketch made in 1837. A Turneresque view of the mountain man in a moment of danger. *Courtesy Walters Art Gallery and University of Oklahoma Press, copyright 1951*

"Breakfast at Sunrise." Watercolor by Alfred Jacob Miller done in 1858 from a sketch made in 1837. The wilderness campfire, an important pastoral image, is presided over by Miller's patron, Stewart, in a broad-brimmed hat, center foreground. Around campfires such as these, Jim Bridger, Black Harris, and other mountain men told the tall tales that created their own myths. *Courtesy Walters Art Gallery and University of Oklahoma Press, copyright, 1951*

Man in nature: a trapper confronting a moonlight buffalo stampede. Sepia wash by Alfred Jacob Miller, 1837, a sketch made on the spot. It recaptures almost perfectly the mountain man as the simple powerful man of nature. *Courtesy Joslyn Art Museum*

The Romantic Reconnaissance

Beginning in 1842, a second generation of artists entered the American West. Sponsored largely by the federal government and attached to the various army expeditions, these artists made thousands of pictures of virtually every aspect of the West, and since their works were widely distributed, in the form of lithographs published in government reports, they can be credited with presenting the scenes and wonders of the West for the first time to a mass audience. A mixture of amateur and professional, European and American, their work was no less romantic than that of the previous generation. With certain exceptions, the level of competence places these artists closer to the "practitioner artists" of the European tradition than to the masters of the nineteenth century. The quality of the work is less important, however, than the subjects depicted and the images projected.

First view of the Southwest. Lithograph from a drawing by John Mix Stanley published in William H. Emory's *Notes of a Military Reconnaissance* (1848). Stanley accompanied Col. Stephen Watts Kearny's command in its march from Santa Fe to the Pacific during the Mexican War. His drawings, such as this one of a pass through the mountains of southern Arizona, were the first graphic representations of what is now the American Southwest. *Courtesy University of Texas Library*

Natural obelisks, drawn by Edward or Richard Kern in 1848–49 and reproduced in the publisher's prospectus for Frémont's *Memoirs* (1886). The drawing depicts John Charles Frémont's expedition in the Rocky Mountains. *Courtesy Henry E. Huntington Library and Art Gallery*

Lt. Whipple's expedition crossing the Colorado River near the Mojave Villages. Watercolor by Heinrich B. Möllhausen, 1853. Möllhausen (see Chapter 9), a German scientist, artist, and writer, was the personal representative of Alexander von Humboldt on Whipple's Pacific Railroad Survey of 1853. Note, in the lower left-hand corner, the men skinning an animal. The boat was made of bundles of rushes or reeds. *Courtesy Oklahoma Historical Society*

A moonscape of mountain peaks. Watercolor by Heinrich B. Möllhausen: a surrealistic view of the Southwest by the German "Fenimore Cooper." Möllhausen never allowed facts, or the demands of literalism, to interfere with his romantic imagination. Whipple once wrote that the only thing Möllhausen painted accurately was a Navaho blanket. *Courtesy Oklahoma Historical Society*

"Fort Massachusetts." John Mix Stanley, from a sketch by R. H. Kern: a lithograph from the Pacific Railroad Survey *Reports*, 1853. Fort Massachusetts was a military outpost in the San Luis Valley of Colorado and New Mexico, visited by Captain John W. Gunnison's expedition. *Courtesy University of Texas Library*

"A View of the Ancient Lake Bed of the Great Basin." A. H. Campbell, lithograph, Pacific Railroad Surveys, 1853. *Courtesy University of Texas Library*

"Camp of the Red River Hunters." John Mix Stanley, lithograph, Pacific Railroad Surveys, 1853. *Courtesy University of Texas Library*

"Herd of Bison, Near Lake Jessie." John Mix Stanley, lithograph, Pacific Railroad Surveys, 1853. This North Dakota scene was made on the Isaac I. Stevens expedition. Stanley also took photographs on this trip, but none appears to have survived. *Courtesy University of Texas Library*

"Old Fort Walla Walla." John Mix Stanley, lithograph, Pacific Railroad Surveys, 1853. *Courtesy University of Texas Library*

"Crossing the Hellgate River, May 5th, 1854." Gustave Sohon, lithograph, Pacific Railroad Surveys, 1854. Sohon was an enlisted man in the U.S. Army who clearly had had previous training in art, probably in Europe. He stayed in the Northwest, made illustrations for the Mullan Road *Report*, and painted or sketched many of the Indians and early outposts of the area. This representation is reminiscent of Poussin or Claude Lorrain. *Courtesy University of Texas Library*

"Franklin Valley." C. Schumann, from a sketch by F. W. von Egloffstein, steel engraving, Pacific Railroad Surveys. An allegorical nature-god looking out across the Great Basin, drawn by Egloffstein, a Prussian cartographer and artist who accompanied Lt. Beckwith's expedition in 1854, this is still another European-inspired romantic image of the American West. *Courtesy University of Texas Library*

"Camp Scene in the Mojave Valley of Rio Colorado." Lt. J. C. Tidball, 2nd Artillery, lithograph, Pacific Railroad Surveys, 1853. *William H. Goetzmann*

"South End of Lake Guzman." A. B. Gray, lithograph from his *Survey of a Route on the 32nd Parallel for the Texas Western Railroad, 1854.* Courtesy *Barker Center for Texas History, University of Texas*

Crossing the Pecos River. A. B. Gray, lithograph from his *Survey of a Route on the 32nd Parallel for the Texas Western Railroad, 1854. Courtesy Barker Center for Texas History, University of Texas*

Co-Co-Pa Indians. Drawn by Arthur Schott; lithograph from the *Report on the United States–Mexican Boundary Survey, 1850–53*. Schott was German and had, it appears, a sense of humor. *Courtesy University of Texas Library*

Hualpais. Drawn by Heinrich B. Möllhausen; lithograph from J. C. Ives's report of his Colorado River expedition of 1857. These and the Indians in the following plate are more realistic than the usual Indian portraits, and not in Möllhausen's typical style. Perhaps he was so shocked by their wretched condition that he painted them realistically for once. However, Möllhausen wanted to bring one of the Grand Canyon Hualpais back to civilization pickled in a jar. *William H. Goetzmann*

Chemehuevis. Drawn by Heinrich B. Möllhausen; lithograph from J. C. Ives's report of his Colorado River expedition of 1857. *William H. Goetzmann*

"Moquis Pueblos." J. J. Young, from a sketch by F. W. von Egloffstein; lithograph, Ives's *Report*. This is the first picture of the Hopi pueblos of Arizona, executed in a style reminiscent of the allegorical works of Thomas Cole or Gustave Doré. Note that the natural setting of the pueblos as conventional picturesque ruins is more important to the artist than the details of their structure. The Indians appear to be Greek shepherds tending a flock of indeterminate animals. In the distance, pilgrims wend their way upward from the nether regions to what might be the court of Kubla Khan or a ruined Greek temple. *William H. Goetzmann*

First view of the Grand Canyon. J. J. Young, from a sketch by F. W. von
Egloffstein; steel engraving from J. C. Ives's report on the Colorado River
expedition. A Dorésque landscape that bears little resemblance to reality.
The Grand Canyon is fitted into a European stereotype of Gothic verticality.
William H. Goetzmann

222

"Crossing the Great Salt Lake Desert." Original watercolor by J. J. Young from a sketch by H. V. A. Von Beckh. Capt. James Hervey Simpson's expedition starting out across the Great Basin: a realistic view of the landscape, with typical isolated mountain ranges in the distance. *Courtesy National Archives, Cartographic Records Section*

"Genoa, East Foot of Sierra Nevada." Original watercolor by J. J. Young from a sketch by H. V. A. Von Beckh. Capt. Simpson's expedition arriving at the Mormon settlement on the western edge of the Great Basin. Genoa soon gave way to the great mining towns of the big bonanza years. *Courtesy National Archives, Cartographic Records Section*

The Sublime Replaces the Pastoral

After the Civil War, the process of Western exploration resumed on an even grander scale. Great surveys covering hundreds of square miles and entire regions replaced the single reconnaissance. The increasing scale of Western exploration was also reflected in the work of the artists who accompanied the expeditions. Men like Albert Bierstadt, Thomas Moran, Sanford Robinson Gifford, and Gilbert Munger produced huge canvases, sometimes as much as fifteen feet in length and covering vast Western panoramas.

In part, the vastness of these Western paintings can be attributed to the new physical vantage points from which the artists saw the country—in company with surveying parties atop lofty mountains (see Portfolio III). But there were other factors as well. A demand for the monumental in domestic as well as in public architecture created a market for larger, more impressive paintings. The artists mentioned could sell virtually anything they painted at prices roughly commensurate with the number of square feet of canvas covered. In addition, the portable wet-plate camera enabled photographers in the field to encompass immense vistas (see Portfolio III), and this in turn had an effect on the painters who worked with them. It influenced Moran's career decisively, for instance, as his paintings of the Yellowstone, derived in part from W. H. Jackson's photographs, proved to be a tremendous success. And, finally, of equal importance was the fact that tastes and styles changed in the centers of culture, particularly the European centers in which virtually every American painter of prominence had his training. The grandioseness of the Düsseldorf School in Germany, and tours of the Alps, had a formative influence on Bierstadt. Turner, who had earlier influenced Miller, had a different and more profound impact on the work of Moran, whose rainbow coloration of Western scenes became his stock-in-trade. The sublime, picturesque aesthetic of Ruskin had a marked effect on Clarence King, which in turn affected that explorer's choice of the painters who accompanied him into the field—notably, Gifford and Munger. Even a relatively obscure artist such as Thomas Hill, who painted the California Sierras almost at the same time that they were being explored by the California Geological Survey parties, received his training under Meyerheim at Fountainbleau. Thus, a different view of the West emerged through a complex combination of circumstances that were rooted primarily in the tastemaking centers of civilization. The latter-day West lost its sense of the simple pastoral, and to some extent its terror and mystery. It became sublime and picturesque—a wonderland for the tourists and nature lovers who poured into the parks at Yellowstone and Yosemite, gazed into the Grand Canyon from Inspiration Point, and invaded the magnificent parks of Colorado seeking a reality that had been created for them before they ever left home. The pictures that follow provide a sampling of that new image of the American West.

"Dawn at Donner Lake, California." Oil painting by Albert Bierstadt, 1872–1873. Bierstadt had a studio overlooking the Hudson River and extended this view into his Western work, but he also saw the West in terms of his European experience. Edward Tuckerman and Harold McCracken quote the following letter by Bierstadt from the Rocky Mountains as evidence of his European view of the Western landscape: "The mountains are very fine: as seen from the plains they resemble very much the Bernese Alps; they are of granite formation, the same as the Swiss mountains, their rugged summits covered with snow and mingling with the clouds . . . the colors are like those of Italy." *Courtesy Joslyn Art Museum*

"Grand Canyon of the Colorado." Oil painting by Thomas Moran. This is a good example of Moran's contrived picturesqueness. *Courtesy Joslyn Art Museum*

"Indians and the North Dome of Yosemite." Oil painting by Thomas Hill, 1880. Though Hill did not accompany the exploring expeditions, he was painting the Yosemite about the same time that King and Whitney were exploring it, and his aesthetic is the same as theirs. This is a later example of his work, which resembles that of Bierstadt and Moran. *Courtesy Kennedy Galleries, Inc., New York*

"Summits of the Wasatch Range, Utah." Chromolithograph from a painting by Gilbert Munger. Munger was a guest of Clarence King's Fortieth Parallel Survey and made this painting about 1871. It appeared as an illustration in King's *Systematic Geology. Courtesy Professor Keith Young, Dept. of Geology, University of Texas*

The Mount of the Holy Cross. Woodcut engraving from a sketch by William H. Jackson. This appeared in many places, first in F. V. Hayden's annual report of his survey of Colorado. It is typical of the mass-produced Ruskinian picturesqueness of the day, in which art took on religious overtones and provided inspiration to the public. Compare this picture with Jackson's photograph in Portfolio III. *Courtesy Yale University Library*

PART TWO

---

*The Great Reconnaissance
and Manifest Destiny*

1845-60

CHAPTER VII

When the Eagle Screamed
The Explorer as Diplomat
in the Final Clash of Imperial Energies

WITH much of the basic work of discovery accomplished by 1840, exploration in the American West entered a new phase which was concerned with the problems of settlement on the widest possible scale. The cultural and economic aims implicit in the previous period now became explicit national political objectives. And the government itself, always a partner in discovery, began to assume a major responsibility in launching expeditions into the Far West designed to aid its citizens in the conquest and development of the region. Emigration, successful emigration, which implied rapid economic growth and the establishment of republican political institutions, thus became an official national aim. It was to facilitate this aim that the United States Government, under the leadership of Colonel John James Abert, reorganized the Army's Corps of Topographical Engineers in 1838 and made it into a separate branch of the military whose primary duties were the exploration and development of an underdeveloped continent.[1] Few governments in the past had ever allocated national resources in men and material so unambiguously dedicated to long-range social considerations.

1. For a history of the Corps of Topographical Engineers, see William H. Goetzmann: *Army Exploration in the American West, 1803–1863* (New Haven, Conn.: Yale University Press; 1957), Chapter I, pp. 3–21. Additional details concerning Col. John James Abert may be found in the De Zahara Collection, Yale Western Americana Collection.

The next great period of exploration in the American West was thus characterized by its clear relationship to national political and economic aspirations and by the increased sophistication of the questions that its explorers would put to the West. The professional explorer and scientist began to take to the field in the 1840's, and with his appearance came a new and significant refinement, not only in the scientific approach to the West, but in all aspects of the search for knowledge. The basis of geographical discovery shifted from the simple notation of landmarks and natural wonders, of settlement sites and overland trails, to the scientific assessment of basic resources, the serious study of primitive cultures different from our own, and the application to the West of the engineer's calculations so necessary to the advent of a complex and technical civilization into that pristine region. The essence of the new era of exploration that began about 1840 and continued on to the Civil War is thus the story of the increasing involvement of the explorer in serious national concerns. It is perhaps best told in terms of the explorer's relation to three major categories of national concern with the West that emerged during this period: (1) the final diplomatic definition of the West; (2) the crucial technological problems of transportation; and (3) the necessity for a great scientific inventory of the natural and human resources of the new domain.

1

One of the characteristics of the era of Manifest Destiny is that the explorer played an unusually prominent part in the diplomatic maneuvers for the American West. Negotiations at every level depended upon a specialized knowledge of the unfamiliar wilderness country that only the explorer possessed. Consequently he was frequently called on to play a part far beyond his normal pursuits. Or, if his direct participation was not required, the information he possessed—data often gathered for quite different purposes—was pressed into service by statesmen deciding the fate of a continental empire. During the two decades before the Civil War, then, the explorer and his findings figured importantly in at least three significant diplomatic crises: the Oregon dispute with England, the Mexican War, and the final boundary dispute with Mexico which led to the Gadsden Purchase. In these episodes the explorer, perhaps as much as anyone else, helped to shape the exact contours of America's Western domain.

Given this important role, it is not surprising that the explorer was often a controversial as well as a heroic figure. And in this period, none was more controversial than Lieutenant Charles Wilkes of the United States Navy and Captain John C. Frémont of the Corps of Topographical Engineers. Each had a vital, if somewhat indeterminate, role in bringing about a settlement of the Oregon boundary. Both these men, public figures of their day—one a presidential candidate and founder of a new political party—have been at the same time overpraised and underesteemed.

Historians long accustomed to scoff at the pretentiousness of Frémont, the boyish pathfinder of the High Sierras, have overlooked his significant contributions to an organized knowledge of the Far West—an organized knowledge that does not seem so spectacular with a modern map or geography book at hand, but which for its day was remarkable and in fact opened up the unknown West to much of destiny-conscious America. In the same fashion, Charles Wilkes, who sailed a United States Exploring Expedition around the world and in the process discovered a new continent, the Antarctic, was also, to many, pretentious and absurd. Yet to others he was the embodiment of the wide-ranging energies and aspirations of the American people. In the eyes of President John Tyler, however, he was not worthy of notice and deserved at most the court-martial he received after his return from a grueling five years at sea. Controversial and often puzzling, and in so many ways alike, these two men were the first of the explorer-diplomats of the 1840's and 1850's. Their work was distinctly related to and so intimately connected with the acquiring of Oregon that an assessment of their contributions is vital to any history of American expansion, and especially to one that has for its focus the role of exploration in this process.

2

Since the expedition of Lieutenant Charles Wilkes to the Northwest Coast, or what was then called Oregon, is not part of the agrarian and overland tradition, it has always had an uncertain place in the history of Western exploration. Originally conceived of as a small part of the much larger work undertaken by the great global Exploring Expedition, the reconnaissance of the Northwest Coast was almost an afterthought to the grandiose dream of the expedition's chief architect, Jeremiah N. Reynolds. Reynolds, an Ohio newspaperman whom posterity chiefly remembers as being the last person mentioned by Edgar Allan Poe as he lay dying in a Baltimore hospital, was also the author of "Mocha Dick," a whaling story that Melville used as the basis of his classic *Moby Dick*. In addition, Reynolds was a follower and advocate of the geographical theories of Captain John Cleves Symmes, who believed that the earth was hollow and composed of five concentric spheres which could be entered through vortices at each of the poles.[2] The discovery of land in the Antarctic by the Stonington sealer Nathaniel Palmer in 1819[3] appeared to offer some confirmation of this theory and Reynolds began agitating for an official, government-sponsored, scientific expedition that would have as its duty the exploration of the South Polar Seas. This coincided with the aspirations of numerous New England and New York businessmen with maritime interests, who being mostly Federalists or Whigs, firmly believed that the government ought to provide the same kind of support for the maritime frontiersman as for the men of the West.

Wherever Reynolds went in the East, he found his sentiments echoed and his project backed by interested people. Soon the plans for the exploring expedition were broadened to include a survey of the South Sea Islands and the various ports of call in South America and the Far East, as well as a charting of the chief directions of the world-wide whale migrations. It was inevitable that eventually a survey of the Northwest Coast would be included, since for thirty years the coastal harbors had been ports of call for the New England sea-otter hunters.

Though Reynolds's plan received enthusiastic acceptance almost from the beginning, it fell victim to Whig-Democrat politics. Not until May of 1836, shortly after Reynolds had addressed both houses of Congress in a patriotic speech which lasted some three hours and was one hundred pages long, was the expedition finally authorized.[4]

2. R. F. Almy: "J. N. Reynolds: A Brief Biography with Particular Reference to Poe and Symmes," *The Colophon* (1937), Vol. II, pp. 227–45. See also J. N. Reynolds: *Voyage of the United States Frigate Potomac . . . During the Circumnavigation of the Globe, in the Years 1831, 1832, 1833 and 1834* (New York: Harper & Brothers; 1835).

3. *D.A.B.*

4. J. N. Reynolds: *Address on the Subject of a Surveying and Exploring Expedition to the Pacific Ocean and South Seas, Delivered in the Hall of Representatives on the Evening of April 3, 1836* (New York: Harper & Brothers; 1836). See also Reynolds: *Exploring Expedition Correspondence Between J. N. Reynolds and the Hon. Mahlon Dickerson . . . Touching the South Sea Surveying and Exploring Expedition*, reprinted from *The New York Times* of July, Aug., and Sept., 1837 (New York, 1838).

Two more years, and several bitter feuds later, it finally got under-way.

Charles Wilkes came late to all this political skirmishing. An able navigator and enthusiastic naval scientist, he was appointed commander at almost the last moment by Joel Poinsett, the acting Secretary of the Navy, who ultimately saw to the assembling, staffing, and launching of the expedition.[5] Wilkes had served with the Mediterranean Squadron and he had established the first naval observatory in the United States in Washington, D.C. At the time of his selection he was official keeper of the national charts and instruments, hence the most important naval scientist. It was therefore not as surprising as it might seem that he was chosen over several senior officers to head the expedition.

Wilkes and his squadron left Hampton Roads, Virginia, on August 18, 1838, bound first for the island of Madeira and then for the South Atlantic.[6] His flotilla consisted of six ships, the frigates *Vincennes* and *Peacock*, the sloop *Porpoise*, the store ship *Relief*, and two small New York City pilot boats, the *Sea Gull* and the *Flying Fish*. The latter was especially picked for work among the Antarctic ice floes. In addition to the naval officers, many of whom had some sort of scientific training, there was a core of professional scientists and naturalists. This included James Dwight Dana of Yale, the geologist; Timothy Pickering and Titian Peale, naturalists; Horatio E. Hale, philologist; John Pitty Couthouy, conchologist; William Rich, botanist; William D. Brackenridge, horticulturist; and Messrs. Joseph Drayton and Alfred T. Agate, draftsmen. Men of varied and uneven talents; with the exception of Dana, by no means the best scientist the country had to offer, all of them had hopes of becoming a Humboldt, or a Darwin, to whose recent cruise aboard the *Beagle* (1831–36) they had frequent reference. Together they were to assemble the first of the enormous scientific collections that characterized the age of Humboldtean science in America. Their work in the Northwest was part of the great scientific reconnaissance of the whole Western region.

From 1838 to 1841 the men of the Exploring Expedition were

5. Daniel Henderson: *The Hidden Coasts* (New York: William Sloane Associates; 1953), pp. 35–7.
6. Unless otherwise stated, this account is based on Charles Wilkes: *Narrative of the United States Exploring Expedition During the Years, 1838, 1839, 1840, 1841, 1842*, 5 vols., with an Atlas (Philadelphia: Lea and Blanchard; 1845).

occupied in the Southern Hemisphere. They rounded the Horn and headed for Palmer's Land and their unsuccessful try at the deadly Antarctic ice floes, after which one night, on a routine mission, the *Sea Gull* was lost with all hands aboard. By this time the squadron had turned northward to Valparaiso for new supplies and overhauling. This accomplished, they sailed on to the South Pacific, to Fiji, Tahiti, Samoa, the Gilberts, and finally Sydney for a winter's berth in New South Wales, where the scientists studied the aborigines. From December 26, 1839, to February 21, 1840, the *Vincennes*, the *Porpoise*, the *Peacock*, and the *Flying Fish* headed south and coasted the frozen white cliffs of the Antarctic for 1,500 miles, enough to convince them and most of the world that it was indeed a new continent, though English geographers, out of jealous pique, refused to accept Wilkes's findings until well into the twentieth century. From the Antarctic they coursed north again to Sydney and revisited the South Pacific. When they finally all met again at Hawaii, Wilkes and his men had seen and experienced a good deal of the primitive and exotic life of the South Seas.

But above all they had mapped the broad Pacific so accurately that nearly a hundred years later their charts could be used by marine divisions landing at Makin and bloody Tarawa.

The important part of their cruise for the student of Western history, however, was not the "thousand Patagonian sights and sounds" of the Southern Hemisphere, but their work in the Northwest, which began when Captain Wilkes and the *Vincennes* arrived off the bar of the Columbia on April 28, 1841. They were greeted that day by an unbroken line of crashing surf which presented no opportunity for entering the river's mouth, so Wilkes turned north to Juan de Fuca Strait and Puget's Sound, there to continue his explorations under more favorable conditions. During those first months the *Vincennes* and the *Porpoise* divided their labors, the *Porpoise* going north past Vancouver Island and the San Juan Archipelago into the Straits of Georgia, while Wilkes took the *Vincennes* south into Puget's Sound to a temporary landing at Nisqually. Then began a series of overland expeditions under various officers, including Wilkes himself. One party marched east to Okanagan and Fort Colville near the Kettle Falls of the Columbia, and crossed overland to Wailaptu and Walla Walla at the juncture of the Snake and the Columbia. Another connected Nisqually on Puget's Sound with the Columbia directly to the south. A third party went by whaleboat to examine the possibilities of Gray's Harbor at the base of the Olympic Peninsula. Everywhere they went, from Bellingham Bay to Similkameen, they met Indians who were every bit as exotic and strange as the tribes of the South Seas. War canoes, fifty feet long and hideously carved, totem poles glaring blood red, leaping salmon speared by ambidextrous fishermen and dried by the hundreds of thousands, potlatches, taboo burial grounds, rumors of massacre, a language of clicks and klings, superb boatmen, dumpy women, deformed flat-headed children, the civilized and the savage all greeted the naval officers turned terrestrial explorers and amateur ethnologists.

Meanwhile the second part of the flotilla, which included the *Peacock* and the *Flying Fish*, had also arrived off the Columbia bar and met disaster. On July 18, 1841, the *Flying Fish* crossed the bar safely, but due to a vicious crosscurrent the *Peacock* stuck fast and fell to the mercy of thunderous tides and breakers. Eventually the ship was lost, but due to good luck and conspicuous heroism on the part of the crew, no men and very few of the scientific notes went down with the ship. The wreck of the *Peacock* on the Columbia bar, however, did more than volumes of admonition to dramatize to Americans back home the inadequacy of the Columbia Bay as an ocean port. As such, this was perhaps the most significant aspect of the whole Northwest Coast experience.

Eventually Wilkes and Captain Hudson of the *Peacock* joined forces at Fort Vancouver, and a new ship, the *Oregon*, was secured. Despite Wilkes's interest in the coastal harbors, he also explored the Columbia River and the interior, suggesting the importance both to him and to the United States of the existence of a westward-flowing river which was navigable, and thus suitable for commerce. Before he left the Northwest for San Francisco Bay, Wilkes went up the Columbia to test its possibilities. He also dispatched Lieutenant George Emmons and a party of officers and scientists overland via the Willamette Valley to California,[7] in an attempt to verify the fact that no other major river (except the unsuitable Umpqua) flowed west to the sea and made a harbor north of Spanish California.

Despite the invaluable data Wilkes had assembled—the hundreds of maps and charts, the drawings and paintings, the thousands of specimens, and the all-important personal experience—when he and his men arrived back home they were greeted with silence and

7. See George F. Emmons: "Journals, Aug. 12, 1838–June 10, 1842," Vol. III, Yale Western Americana Collection, for an account of the overland trip to California. Also see Titian Peale: "Journals," MS., Library of Congress. Peale's Journals have also been published in Jessie Poesch: *Titian Peale.*

indifference. Their data were scattered and misused and, because of the delicate nature of the pending Webster-Ashburton negotiations, Wilkes's report was transmitted to Congress by President Tyler as a confidential message. The Antarctic explorers got no toll of the bell or medals or torchlight parades, and even today Wilkes is more often remembered as the Yankee skipper who took the Confederates Mason and Slidell off a British ship and nearly lost the Civil War singlehanded.

Recent scholarship, perhaps redressing the balance, has accorded Wilkes a crucial role in determining the 49th parallel as our Northwest boundary. His reports, along with the works of Mofras and Greenhow, are credited with convincing the American commercial class (the Whigs?) that the Columbia harbor was useless and that the primary object of any settlement with England should be Puget Sound and its magnificent harbors.[8] And yet, despite his magnificent labors, there is no clear link between the information Wilkes had to convey, the sentiments of the merchant class, and the policy-making of stubborn old President Polk. And the fate of Wilkes's data is a good example of how an explorer's knowledge, vital though it may be, can be ignored or misused.

From the beginning his statements about the Columbia Bar were in dispute. Midshipman James Blair (son of Montgomery Blair of Missouri), an officer of the *Flying Fish*, presented the sworn testimony of veteran New York pilots, who, though they had never seen the Columbia, deemed its harbor far safer than, and superior to, that of New York. Wilkes's attempt to reply only heightened the confusion, and his subsequent court-martial on another matter further served to discredit his findings.[9]

Eventually, however, it seems clear that the possibility of securing a good ocean port north of the Columbia but south of the 49th parallel did influence Secretary of State Webster's decision to offer a compromise of United States–British difficulties at the 49th parallel, a position which had been taken by earlier American negotiators for quite different reasons.[1] Webster's offer was quickly

8. Norman Graebner: *Empire on the Pacific* (New York: The Ronald Press; 1955), pp. 28–9.
9. See James Blair: *Notices of the Harbor at the Mouth of the Columbia River: By the Commander and Other Officers of the Exploring Expedition* (Washington, 1846), Yale Collection of Western Americana.
1. Clyde A. Duniway: *Daniel Webster: Secretary of State*, in Samuel Flagg Bemis, ed.: *The American Secretaries of State and Their Diplomacy* (New York: Alfred A. Knopf; 1928), Vol. V, pp. 57–8. See also Bemis: *A Diplomatic History of the United States* (New York: Henry Holt and Co.; 1953), pp. 275–7.

rejected, as he doubtless suspected it would be, and the delicate diplomacy of the Northwest passed into the period of "masterful inactivity" favored by the Carolinian John C. Calhoun.[2] There it rested, somewhere between the compromising attitude of commercial Whigs and the bellicose agrarianism of Western neo-war hawks, when President Polk took office. Contrary to recent speculation, however, President Polk appears to have ignored Wilkes's data entirely when he conducted his very personal negotiations with Britain. Wilkes's name appears only once, for example, in Polk's lengthy diary, and there is no reference to Puget Sound ports.[3] Buchanan, the Secretary of State, made reference to the ports only twice and never to Wilkes as such.[4] Unfortunately for the history of exploration, Wilkes, though he helped to establish Webster's original line at 49 degrees, very quickly dropped into oblivion thereafter.

Polk appears to have based his policy on an indifference to geographical information, and a fine sensitivity to domestic political sentiment. A perusal of his diary indicates that the actual value and utility of the territory in dispute between the United States and Britain never entered his calculations, yet he steadfastly opposed all propositions that would grant Canadians perpetual free navigation of the Columbia River. He seemed more concerned with simply winning the diplomatic struggle with England—looking John Bull straight in the eye, as it were—and securing whatever quantity of territory he could, in order to placate the more militant 54° 40′ agrarian and fur-trade faction in Congress, which, after all, made up the majority of his political supporters.[5] The acquiescence of this faction in the final 49th parallel treaty, however, was undoubtedly influenced in large measure by Polk's refusal to barter away the Columbia, which, it was fast becoming evident, was the only great avenue of approach to a future inland continental empire. Thus, perhaps in an ironic way, the Wilkes expedition helped to prepare Congress and the public for an appreciation of the Columbia, not as a port, but as an interior avenue of communication to the inland empire. Ultimately, however, far fewer people read or were convinced by the rather expensive and hard-to-get reports of the Exploring Expedition than they were by the widely circulated accounts

2. Bemis: *A Diplomatic History of the United States*, p. 277.
3. See Milo M. Quaife, ed.: *The Diary of James K. Polk . . .* , 4 vols. (Chicago: A. C. McClurg and Co., 1910). Vol. I deals especially with the Oregon question.
4. See John Bassett Moore, ed.: *The Works of James Buchanan*, 12 vols. (Philadelphia: J. B. Lippincott Co.; 1908), Vol. VI.
5. *Polk Diary*, Vol. I, *passim*.

of the exploits of another explorer—Captain John C. Frémont, the
boy hero of the Rockies and protégé of the all-powerful Senator
Thomas Hart Benton of Missouri.

3

The genesis of John C. Frémont's career as an explorer might be
said to have taken place on Christmas Day, 1824. On that occasion
Thomas Hart Benton,· then a young senator from the new West,
visited Thomas Jefferson at Monticello, where for hours, while a
gentle Virginia mountain snowstorm fell outside, they compared
plans, strategies, and political views of the West.[6] Benton always
regarded the meeting with mystical reverence. To him it was a lay-
ing-on of hands—a mission and a commission.

Shortly afterward, as evidence of the extent of their discussion,
he was able to wave the map that Jefferson gave him and make his
demands for the national road to Santa Fe.[7] And when he began
thinking of an exploring expedition to Oregon with Frémont at its
head, he was only repeating the strategy practiced by Jefferson long
ago when he sent out Lewis and Clark as an advance guard into
Louisiana and across the "Stony Mountains." Next to the Lewis and
Clark expedition, and perhaps surpassing it in this respect, the
explorations conducted by John C. Frémont between 1842 and 1845
are the outstanding examples, in American history, of the calculated
use of exploring expeditions as diplomatic weapons.

Nominally under the direction and control of the War Department and the Topographical Bureau, since Frémont held his lieutenant's commission under that agency, they were actually, in
Benton's words, "conceived without its [the government's] knowledge, and executed upon solicited orders, of which the design was
unknown."[8] In short, all three times that he went out into the West in
1842–45, Frémont was on secret missions that nevertheless committed the government to a position and a policy far beyond anything publicly acknowledged. Yet as expeditions they were designed
to be public. That is, their chief objective was to dramatize the West

6. *Register of Debates in Congress*, 1824–25 (Washington: Gales and
Seaton; 1825), pp. 109–10. This meeting is also mentioned in Kate L. Gregg:
The Road to Santa Fe (Albuquerque, N.M.: University of New Mexico Press;
1952), p. 6.
7. Ibid.
8. Thomas Hart Benton: *Thirty Years View*, 2 vols. (New York: D. Appleton and Co.; 1854–56), Vol. I, pp. 468–9.

as the American destiny, and to provide a vast range of scientific and economic information about the West that would underscore its value and encourage overland emigration. In this way, while Calhoun was dreaming of "masterful inactivity" on the Pacific, Benton and his expansionist colleagues, so long frustrated in their attempts to get federal action on the Oregon question, took steps to provide the settlers and the "thirty thousand American rifles" that would secure Oregon for the United States. It was a Jeffersonian strategy up to a point. Then it passed on into the grandiose symbolism of an age of romantic expansionism.

Frémont, if anyone ever did, fitted perfectly the requirements of the romantic hero-symbol of an age of expansionism. Handsome, intelligent, mercurial, born of an uncertain liaison and therefore with something of a Byronic legacy, he was a self-made cavalier. Famous as a lover, eager as a student, admired and befriended by his elders, he could command the allegiance of an astonishing range of people from congressmen and savants to mountain men and Indians. Characteristically, when he was offered the command of Benton's Western expedition he accepted with the idea of advancing knowledge and conquering nature. "In this interview [with Benton]," he wrote, "my mind had been quick to see a larger field and differing and greater results. It would be travel over a part of the world which remained the new—the opening up of unknown lands; the making unknown countries known; and the study without books—the learning at first hand from nature herself; the drinking first at her unknown springs—became a source of never-ending delight to me."[9] Beneath his charm and enthusiasm, too, one saw sometimes a glimpse, sometimes more, of the incredible tough-mindedness and endurance that were to make those dreams a reality for a time.

If he was a symbol and a romantic cavalier, Frémont was also an experienced explorer by the time he undertook to lead Benton's expeditions into the West. In 1836–37 he had accompanied Captain William G. Williams of the Topographical Engineers on a reconnaissance of the Cherokee country of Georgia, North Carolina, and Tennessee.[1] In 1838 he joined the immigrant French scientist Joseph N. Nicollet on an expedition westward from Fort Snelling on the Mississippi in Minnesota west to the Red Pipestone Quarry in present-day Minnesota. Thus began his training under that illustrious explorer.[2] Nicollet himself had been engaged in explor-

9. Frémont: *Memoirs*, p. 65.
1. Ibid., pp. 24–5.
2. Ibid., pp. 30–54.

ing parts of Louisiana and the Upper Mississippi country under the auspices of the fur trader Pierre Chouteau since 1835. In 1835–36 he ascended the Mississippi, mapping its course as he went. Skilled in the physical sciences, especially mathematics, geodesy, and the exacting arts of cartography, the Frenchman was the first to introduce into the scientific exploration of the West such techniques as the use of fossils to correlate various geological strata, and the use of the barometer to measure altitudes. As a mentor and tutor he supplied what Frémont essentially lacked at first—disciplined scientific training.[3]

Frémont made two expeditions with Nicollet, the one out of Fort Snelling on the Upper Mississippi to the Pipestone Quarry, and another, more extensive tour in the year 1839 up the Missouri River to Fort Pierre and thence northward overland along the Couteau des Missouri to Devil's Lake in North Dakota and across to Red River, down that river to Renville's station near Lake Traverse, South Dakota, and back to the Mississippi via the Minnesota River route. On the latter expedition Frémont first met mountain men and began to learn the explorer's trade from such veterans as William Dixon, Louison Frenière, and Etienne Provost.

By 1842, experienced in the ways of science and politics, he had married the senator's daughter and secured the position as leader of Benton's "secret" expedition to the Rocky Mountains. When he arrived in St. Louis on May 22 he had with him Charles Preuss, a curious, red-faced German who hated the West and the outdoors, but who was nevertheless to be his excellent cartographer and partner in many wilderness adventures.[4] On the way upriver to Chouteau's station, he also met Kit Carson and thus began their famous lifelong friendship.

By the time Frémont was ready to set out over the prairies for the mountains, he had assembled a prime crew of experienced mountain men and hunters. At the head of this band, he journeyed out along the Oregon Trail, branched off on the South Fork of the Platte, and explored the mountain wall northward from St. Vrain's

3. Joseph N. Nicollet: *Report Intended to Illustrate a Map of the Hydrographical Basin of the Upper Mississippi River* . . . (Washington: Blair and Rives; 1843). Also issued as 26th Cong., 2nd sess., Sen. Doc. 237 (1843).
4. For a sketch of Preuss, see Charles Preuss: *Exploring With Frémont*, translated and edited by Erwin G. and Elisabeth K. Gudde (Norman, Okla.: Oklahoma University Press; 1958), pp. xix-xxix. I have also studied the original manuscript of the Preuss diaries, now at the Library of Congress.

Fort in Colorado to Fort Laramie in Wyoming, where he assembled all his men for a direct assault on the emigrant trail over the Rockies.[5] Ignoring the rumors of an imminent Indian uprising, Frémont marched west along the Sweetwater through South Pass and north to the Wind River Mountains, where, instead of turning his energies to the mapping of an emigrant route across the mountain barrier, he climbed what he took to be the highest peak of the Wind Rivers and planted a home-made eagle flag symbolizing American sovereignty.[6] (See map, p. 245.) Monumentally impractical, his gesture had almost no scientific value. He even lost his plant and mineral specimens shooting the canyons of the Sweetwater. And yet it appeared to be from the first a part of his design and indeed the culminating objective of his expedition. Clearly, he calculated to light a signal fire in the Rocky Mountains— a beacon, as it were, atop the continental spine that would dramatize Benton's rhetoric and lead people west to Oregon. Everything else was incidental.

And when he wrote up his report, which was rushed into print for the next session of Congress, he further dramatized the mountain episode by contrasting the grandeur and sublimity of the mountain peaks with the flight of a "weary little brown bee" that he found buzzing there.[7] The high and the low, the sublime and the humble, the hero and the commoner, the mysterious workings of nature all conspired with the Pathfinder and his mentor to topple forever the fabled god Terminus and open the way to the West. The 1842 expedition, which was after all only a somewhat shallow gesture, nevertheless had great significance for the American people and did more than all the ventures of the mountain men to point the way West. Here is Joaquin Miller, for instance, remembering its impact on his boyhood on an Ohio farm:

> I fancied I could see Frémont's men, hauling the cannon up the savage battlements of the Rocky Mountains, flags in the air, Frémont at the head, waving his sword, his horse neighing wildly in the mountain wind, with unknown and unnamed

5. Unless otherwise stated, this account is based on John Charles Frémont: *Report on an Exploration of the Country Lying between the Missouri River and the Rocky Mountains on the Line of the Kansas and Great Platte Rivers* (Buffalo, N.Y.: Derby Co.; 1851). Hereafter cited as Frémont: *1842 Exploration*.

6. A picture of the flag appears in Frémont: *Memoirs*, p. 152.

7. Frémont: *1842 Exploration*, pp. 104 ff.

empires at every hand. It touched my heart when he told how a weary little brown bee tried to make its way from a valley of flowers far below across a spur of snow, where he sat resting for a moment with his men; how the bee rested on his knee till it was strong enough to go on to another field of flowers beyond the snow; and how he waited a bit for it to go at its will.

I was no longer a boy . . . now I began to be inflamed with a love for action, adventure, glory, and great deeds away out yonder under the path of the setting sun.[8]

Exact details mattered little. Frémont's first expedition was a success. As rhetoric and symbol it was sublime. The Senate ordered a thousand extra copies of his report to be printed and distributed throughout the land.

The following year Frémont was determined to accomplish even more. At Benton's request he was ordered to "connect the reconnaissance of 1842 with the surveys of Commander Wilkes on the coast of the Pacific Ocean, so as to give a connected survey of the interior of *our* continent."[9] The maritime and the interior interests in the West were to be linked by an exploring expedition, and their mutual interests made self-evident. This time, however, the Oregon Trail was to be carefully mapped and the road laid out for emigrant parties. Moreover, details on the location of campsites, wood, water, and Indians were to be assembled and presented in a final report. Also, data for the possible location of a string of forts were to be collected, a move timed to coincide with certain bills that the expansionists were urging in Congress. As it turned out, Frémont's expedition went far beyond what had been expected.

He left St. Louis in the early spring of 1843 at the head of a party of thirty-nine men, including Charles Preuss and the famous mountain man Tom Fitzpatrick.[1] Along the way he was joined by Alexis Godey and Kit Carson, who came up from Taos. When he journeyed west out of St. Louis in 1843, however, Frémont was no longer in the vanguard of discovery. He was part of a mass movement, the first of the great migrations to Oregon and California. Ahead of him

8. Joaquin Miller: *Overland in A Covered Wagon*, Sidney G. Firman, ed. (New York: D. Appleton and Co.; 1930), pp. 42–3.

9. Goetzmann: *Army Exploration*, p. 85. This is based on Abert to Benton, March 10, 1843, L.S., T.E., R.G., 77, National Archives; and Frémont: *Report of the Exploring Expedition to the Rocky Mountains in the Year 1842, and to Oregon and North California in the Years 1843–44* (Buffalo, N.Y.: Derby Co.; 1851), p. 123. Hereafter cited as Frémont: *1843–44 Exploration*.

1. Unless otherwise stated, this account is based on Frémont: *1843–44 Exploration*.

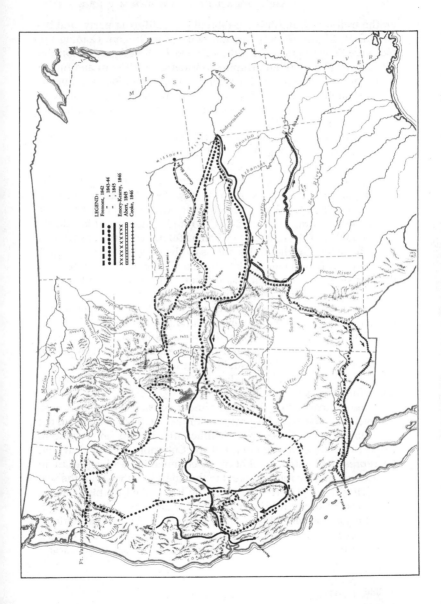

on the trail was J. B. Chile's trailbreaking California party, and beyond that, Elijah White's caravan bound for Oregon. Coming up, too, were Belgian priests bound for Father De Smet's mission in the Bitterroot Valley; William Gilpin, an itinerant politician and future governor of Colorado; and Sir William Drummond Stewart, out for his last hunt along the Seedskeedee before returning to his castle in Scotland. As far as one could see, travelers and their accouterments dotted the landscape.

In an effort to break a new trail, Frémont took his men south along the Kansas rather than the Platte River, crossed the mountains at the Cache de la Poudre River in central Colorado, and picked up the emigrant trail at the Sweetwater after crossing over the barren Laramie Plain (see map, p. 245). On September 6, they sighted the Great Salt Lake "stretching in still and solitary grandeur far beyond the limits of our vision," wrote Frémont. And he added: "I am doubtful if the followers of Balboa felt more enthusiasm when from the heights of the Andes, they saw the great Western Ocean."[2] Unaccountably believing the lake to be unexplored, they paused and devoted several days to that task. Then they pushed on via Fort Hall and the Snake River to the Columbia and Oregon.

In traversing this country, Frémont made highly significant observations. He termed the barren Salt Lake benches "a bucholic place" and declared it a fine location for a settlement.[3] Fort Hall he found a nuisance in British hands, but an American military post in that vicinity, he asserted, "would naturally form the nucleus of a settlement."[4] In short, as an official explorer he was always alert to possibilities for settlement.

When he reached the Dalles, Frémont considered his basic task completed, and leaving his party encamped, he pushed on down the Columbia to Fort Vancouver. Significantly, he did not trouble to inspect the harbor at the mouth of the Columbia. It was clear that he represented interests that were commercial and agrarian in orientation and therefore related to the interior rather than the sea.

Having reached Fort Vancouver, he had linked up his searches with those of Captain Wilkes and symbolically as well as scientifically his job was done. But this time Frémont had greater ambitions. He decided to turn south and explore the country between Oregon and California and in so doing perhaps to locate the Buenaventura,

2. Ibid., p. 198.
3. Ibid., p. 213.
4. Ibid., p. 217.

another avenue of inland commerce that supposedly led to the sea. Though most maps of the day showed the Buenaventura quite clearly, no one had seen it, and there were rumors and even books, notably one by Washington Irving and Benjamin Bonneville, that said it didn't exist at all except in the cartographers' imagination.[5] Frémont saw it as his job to move south and find out if it existed. If it did not, then the Columbia, being the only river of its kind, took on added significance in the current negotiations with England.

On November 25, 1843, he and his men marched south down the Des Chutes River and eventually, after several days of travel, came out on the western edge of the Great Basin, which Frémont clearly recognized as such, thereby becoming in a real sense its discoverer, though he was of course not the first to traverse its barren wastes.

Near Lake Tahoe they found a likely avenue of approach to the Sierras and despite the fact that winter was already upon them they began a crossing of the mountains. The crossing took thirty days in all and was a fantastic test of endurance and courage. The Indian guides deserted, others gave up and began chanting their death songs, at least one man went mad from fear and exposure. Another wandered off into the woods and was lost for years until one spring day years later he emerged back in Jefferson, Missouri.[6] Every day the group faced cold and fatigue and hunger, and there was no respite from the everlasting trailbreaking through drifts as high as a man. Eventually, however, man by man and mule by mule they struggled down from the mountains and emerged at Captain John Sutter's idyllic ranch on the American River. There, among other things, they met J. B. Chiles and his party, who had earlier found an easier route over the mountains.[7]

Frémont's view of California was important. He was one of the first and certainly one of the most widely read observers to point out its agricultural virtues. Mountain men such as Jedediah Smith and Zenas Leonard were well aware of California as a pastoral paradise, but their impressions had nothing like the circulation of Frémont's report and his work was one of the most important factors in per-

5. Washington Irving: *The Rocky Mountains*, Vol. II (see map).
6. The Jefferson, Missouri, *Inquirer* for Saturday, Nov. 22, 1845, carried the following item: Frémont's Baptiste De Rosier, "arrived in this city on yesterday, bringing with him a certificate from Captain Sutter, dated Upper Helvetia, California, May 18th 1845, which states that Rosier having lost himself upon the plains, wandered about many days, he at last reached Sutter's settlement on the Rio Sacramento."
7. See my Chapter 6, p. 172.

suading emigrants to come there. It was avidly read, in every one of its six printings, and passed around by would-be overland parties. Many set out for the West "guided," as Sarah Royce remembered, "only by the light of Frémont's travels."[8]

After a stay in California, Frémont and his men moved down the San Joaquin Valley and crossed over the Tehachapi Pass (which they believed to be Walker's Pass) into the desert country of the Great Basin. Their course east took them over the Old Spanish Trail laid out ten years before by Smith, Wolfskill, Amijo, and the mountain men and traders out of Santa Fe. When they reached the Las Vegas meadows, they were joined by Joseph Walker, the former Bonneville lieutenant, and thanks to his masterful grasp of mountain geography they made their way east by means of the Duchesne and White rivers, that run across northeastern Utah and northwestern Colorado, respectively, and via Robidoux's station, the Green River, and the parks of Colorado. In so doing, they traversed some of the wildest country in North America—country that had long been the familiar haunt of Spaniards and trappers out of Taos, but which would need continual reexploration in the years to come, before its details finally became fixed in the civilized mind.

All in all, Frémont's trek of 1843–44 had been a great and epic journey, one that would have secured his place in history forever had he done nothing else. As a result of his labors, he had accumulated a large collection of scientific specimens and data, and created a matchless cartographical picture of the West which was all the more valuable because it was largely based on fact.

The first of his tasks was to draw all of this into tangible form as a report and map that could be distributed throughout the country to promote the West and provide information to westbound emigrants. With the help of Charles Preuss, who drew his first great map of the West to supplement the report, and Jessie, whose prose style made his report read like the romance it really was, Frémont completed this task in masterful fashion. Though his report made few original contributions to geographical science, it was comprehensive in scope and monumental in its breadth—a classic of exploring literature. Most important of all, it was widely influential. To would-be emigrants like the Joaquin Millers and the Sarah Royces, it provided a guide and inspiration. In Europe the great Humboldt noted its data in his *Aspects of Nature* and accorded Frémont the highest of praise as a geographer and explorer.[9] And Brigham Young, reading

8. Sarah Royce: *A Frontier Lady*, Ralph H. Gabriel, ed. (New Haven, Conn.: Yale University Press; 1932), p. 3.

the report amid the disastrous breakup of Nauvoo, decided that since the Salt Lake Valley was remote, and at the same time "bucholic," it was indeed "the place" of Mormon destiny.[1]

Despite his widespread success, however, one of the ironies of Frémont's career was his failure either to move President Polk to activity in Oregon or to secure the enthusiastic backing of the Whigs, whose only interest in the West was still the Pacific ports. In terms of executive and congressional policy, Frémont's report seems to have had little direct effect. Polk had already made up his mind to secure California, and Frémont's findings which indicated there was no Buenaventura or interior river besides the Columbia failed to move him to more aggressive action in Oregon. "Like the Secretary [of War] he found me 'young,'" wrote Frémont in disappointment, "and said something of the 'impulsiveness of young men,' and was not at all satisfied in his own mind those three rivers [alternatives to the Columbia River] were not running there as laid down."[2]

In the last analysis, therefore, Frémont's contributions do not appear to lie in the field of pure science, or even in the field of high political strategy. Rather, as in the case of his 1842 expedition, his work was symbolic—a rallying point of Manifest Destiny that in the long run made Polk's aggressive trans-Mississippi policy seem acceptable and even inevitable to large numbers of Americans. *Littell's Living Age* perhaps caught the symbolic Frémont best—an American self-image at mid-century:

> His name is identified forever with some of the proudest and most grateful passages in American history. His 20,000 miles of wilderness explorations, in the midst of the inclemencies of nature, and the ferocities of jealous and merciless tribes; his powers of endurance in a slender form; his intrepid coolness in the most appalling dangers; his magnetic sway over enlightened and savage men; his vast contributions to science; his controlling energy in the extension of our empire; his lofty and unsullied ambition; his magnanimity; humanity, genius, sufferings and heroism, make all lovers of progress, learning, and virtue, rejoice. . . .[3]

9. Alexander von Humboldt: *Aspects of Nature*, Elizabeth J. Sabine, trans. (Philadelphia: Lea and Blanchard; 1849), pp. 51, 219.
1. Brigham Young, in an interview for *The New York Times*, quoted in Frémont: *Memoirs*, pp. 415–16.
2. Frémont: *Memoirs*, p. 419.
3. "John Charles Frémont," *Littell's Living Age*, Vol. XXVI (July, Aug., Sept., 1850), p. 208.

These sentiments were duly, if not appropriately echoed by John L. O'Sullivan in the *Democratic Review*.[4] At last the imperial struggle for the West had been dramatized and broadcast to the people.

4

The Mexican War presented new opportunities for exploration in the Southwest, and the army explorers who went out as a result of the conflict returned with new data, and new points of view concerning the West that shaped national policy for years to come. Preliminary to any conflict with Mexico was the necessity for (1) quieting the Indian tribes; (2) locating supply routes to the West; (3) generally reconnoitering the possible battleground to be contested by the two countries. All of these objectives were sustained by three army expeditions sent out into the West in 1845.

In the summer of 1845 Colonel Stephen Watts Kearny, a veteran frontier cavalryman, took five companies of the First Dragoons and made a great circular patrol across the prairies to Fort Laramie, the South Pass, then along the mountain wall to St. Vrain's, then Bent's Fort on the Arkansas River, and back to St. Louis again. The purpose of Kearny's expedition was to test the capacity of cavalry for sustained operations in the field far from a base of supply, and at the same time to awe and pacify the Indians.[5] He accomplished both tasks admirably, and in his report he advocated the annual cavalry foray, patterned after the French in Algeria, as a far superior method of controlling the Indians than having a string of expensive forts along the Oregon Trail, a policy advocated by Benton and Frémont. As a hardened frontier soldier, Kearny had a strictly military viewpoint. Any thought of the army post as a nucleus of settlement, as Frémont suggested it might be and as the Spanish presidio had been for centuries, would have brought only a smile of derision to his face. But if his view of the West was somewhat one-sided, his brief recon-

4. John L. O'Sullivan: "Annexation," unsigned article in *United States Magazine and Democratic Review*, Vol. XVII (July–August 1845), pp. 797–8. Also see his more popular statement in the New York *Morning News*, Dec. 27, 1845.
5. This account is based on Stephen Watts Kearny: "Report of a Summer Campaign to the Rocky Mountains . . . in 1845," 29th Cong., 1st sess., *Sen. Exec. Doc. 1* (1846), pp. 211 ff. Also see James Henry Carleton: *The Prairie Logbooks*, Louis Pelzer, ed. (Chicago: The Caxton Club; 1943); and Philip St. George Cooke: *Scenes and Adventures in the Army* (Philadelphia: Lindsay and Blakiston; 1857).

naissance had clearly demonstrated that cavalry was not only feasible but indispensable to any sustained operation in the immense plains of the West and Southwest.

In February of 1845, too, Frémont himself was ordered into the field and commanded to

> strike the Arkansas as soon as practicable, survey that river, and if practicable, survey the Red River within our boundary line, noting particularly the navigable properties of each . . . and determine as near as practicable, the points at which the boundary line of the United States, the 100th degree of longitude west of Greenwich, strikes the Arkansas and the Red River. It is also important that the Arkansas should be accurately determined.[6]

He was to avoid long journeys to isolated points, and to so time his operation that his party would come in before the end of 1845. For once, Frémont was to be used on a tactical rather than a strategic mission. However, as soon as his party reached Bent's Fort on the Arkansas, Frémont ignored his orders and divided his command, boldly sending the Colonel's son, James W. Abert, down the Canadian River to complete the tactical mission, while he took a picked company of mountain sharpshooters and blazed a trail through the Central Rockies and across the Great Basin to California.

Leaving camp on August 9, 1845, Lieutenant James W. Abert, assisted by the mountain men John Hatcher and Caleb Greenwood, conducted his difficult reconnaissance of the Canadian and Arkansas rivers with great skill and daring. It was not an easy mission. He had to lead his men straight through the heart of the dangerous Comanche and Kiowa country. Only the fact that Greenwood and Hatcher were adopted members of the Kiowa tribe saved the expedition from massacre by the Indians who menaced them all along the way.[7]

Frémont, assisted by the redoubtable Carson, Godey, and Joseph Walker, turned up the Arkansas River, skirted the Royal Gorge, crossed over the Tennessee Pass, and made his way via the White River, across the Grand and the Green, down the Duchesne and the

6. J. J. Abert to Frémont, Feb. 12, 1845, L.S., T.E., R.G., 77, National Archives.
7. James W. Abert: "Journal of Lieutenant James W. Abert from Bent's Fort to St. Louis in 1845," 29th Cong., 1st sess., *Sen. Exec. Doc. 438* (1846). The De Zahara Collection at the Yale Western Americana Collection contains some letters from James W. Abert revealing his background and personality.

Timpanagos rivers to the shores of the Great Salt Lake.[8] Once again he had crossed the Continental Divide, and he had done it dramatically at its most difficult latitude (see map, p. 245). From Great Salt Lake he headed west directly across the Great Basin, first to Pilot Peak, then the Humboldt Mountains, then dividing his party he cut diagonally southwest with a small force to the Humboldt Sinks. It was a new transcontinental route, and in a letter to Jessie, Frémont wrote: "By the route I explored, I can ride in thirty-five days from the Fontaine-qui-Bouille River [Fontain River above Bent's Fort] to Captain Sutter's; and for wagons the road is decidedly better."[9] He was again thinking of strategic, long-range considerations and the best means to get settlers out to the Far West as fast as possible. That he was in Mexican territory did not seem to bother him at all. He regarded its destiny as inevitably American. Indeed, once in California he bid defiance to Mexican authorities as he moved leisurely north through the Salinas Valley, past Sutter's Fort, and into the Klamath country. There he received the famous and controversial visit from Marine Lieutenant Archibald Gillespie and turned south into California in time to assist in the Bear Flag Revolt. He now would have a direct influence on the course of international affairs, whether for better or for worse.

Though a controversy has persisted concerning Gillespie's mission and whether Frémont received presidential orders to turn south into California—the latest evidence being Jessie Benton's letter of March 21, 1847, which asserted that Frémont was "revenging a personal insult" and "knew nothing of the war"[1]—still it seems clear that in undertaking his strategic mission far beyond the scope of his orders Frémont must always have had the subversion of California in mind. Hence his instant and perhaps instinctive, if not impetuous, reaction in the Bear Flag situation. In the last analysis, not much more can be said for Frémont. He was a romantic, stormy figure in his own day, a man of many moods and differing fortunes and attitudes, yet withal attractive to many in his time. He perhaps disintegrates on close historical scrutiny, yet he was a representative figure of his time whose posture has perhaps more to tell us about the 1840's and 1850's than do his actual achievements.

8. Frémont: *Memoirs*, pp. 432 ff. Unless otherwise stated, the account is based on this work. However, see also Thomas Salathiel Martin: "Narrative of John C. Frémont's Expedition to California in 1845–46. . . ."
9. Quoted in Frémont: *Memoirs*, p. 452.
1. Jessie Benton Frémont to John Torrey, March 21, 1847, Torrey Papers, New York Botanical Gardens.

5

As the Mexican War developed, Army Topographical Engineers were assigned to each of the major field commands. The exception was the command of Alexander Doniphan, marching south from El Paso, which as it turned out, in the light of the future difficulties in determining the true location of the Mexican border, might well have been the one with which the engineers and surveyors should have been most concerned. The officers serving the field armies supplied much information, not only about the immediate theaters of operation, but also about the Indians and generally about life and its possibilities in the arid Southwest. Captain George W. Hughes, for example, in his report of the operations of Wool's Army, sketched out the entire pattern of inner and outer Texas frontier defenses that later was adopted by the War Department.[2] Hardcastle's survey of the Valley of Mexico, in another case, was used as propaganda by those who favored the annexation of all Mexico.[3] But, of all the reconnoitering done in the Mexican War, perhaps the most important was Lieutenant William Hemsley Emory's reconnaissance of the Far Southwest with Kearny's Army of the West.[4]

Realizing that some force beyond Frémont's would be needed to secure California once the Mexican War had begun, President Polk, at Senator Benton's suggestion, ordered Colonel Stephen Watts Kearny to continue overland from New Mexico to California and complete its conquest. Accordingly, on September 25, 1846, Kearny set out from the conquered capital of Santa Fe with 300 Dragoons and a topographical unit headed by Lieutenant William H. Emory bound across the Southwest for San Diego. A party of Mormon soldiers who volunteered for United States service was led by Captain Philip St. George Cooke and followed some days behind as a

2. George W. Hughes: "Report . . . Communicating . . . a Map Showing the Operations of the Army of the United States in Texas and the Adjacent Mexican States on the Rio Grande; Accompanied by Astronomical Observations, and Descriptive and Military Memoirs of the Country," March 1, 1849, 31st Cong., 1st sess., *Sen. Exec. Doc. 32* (1850).
3. H. L. F. Hardcastle and M. L. Smith: "Map of the Valley of Mexico . . . ," 30th Cong., 2nd sess., *Sen. Exec. Doc. 19* (1848–49).
4. William Hemsley Emory: "Notes on a Military Reconnaissance from Fort Leavenworth in Missouri to San Diego in California, Including Parts of the Arkansas, Del Norte, and Gila Rivers," 30th Cong., 1st sess., *Sen. Exec. Doc. 7* (1848). Unless otherwise stated, the account is based on this source, hereafter referred to as Emory: "Notes."

reinforcement.[5] Despite the fact that most of the country had been traversed at one time or another by Spanish conquistadors, Santa Fe traders, and mountain men, and that it had been mapped by the great Humboldt in 1811, it was still, cartographically speaking, virtually unknown. The two best maps of the region, Mitchell's map of 1846, and Tanner's map of the same year, had been compiled largely from Frémont's and Wilkes's maps, but since neither Mitchell nor Tanner had seen the country, and Humboldt too had done his map from conjecture, the entire Southwest remained to be accurately mapped.

Emory, bluff, blunt, picturesque cavalry man though he appeared to be, was actually the perfect man for the task. He was a Maryland aristocrat and friend of Jefferson Davis; the army was his career; but he was particularly interested in the scientific aspects of military life. Hence his preference for the Topographical Engineers. Like many another Topographical Engineer, he considered himself one of a company of savants, and among his friends were numbered leading scientists of the day such as Louis Agassiz, Asa Gray, George Engelmann, Spencer F. Baird, and Joseph Henry.[6] Emory embodied the outdoorsman and military man of action as Western savant. He was another Frémont, ready to use his explorer's skill to help shape the national destiny.

Kearny's route took him down the Rio Grande, where he met Kit Carson coming overland from California with the news of its early conquest. Thereupon Kearny dispatched 200 troopers back to Santa Fe and hastened on ahead with 100 men and the topographers. At the Santa Rita del Cobre copper mines in the Sierra Mimbres of southwestern New Mexico he stopped to parley with the Apache Chieftain Mangus Colorado, then moved on to the Upper Gila River, which he followed west through rough country to the beginning of its great bend in Arizona. Guided by a Maricopa Indian, the Army of the West marched crosscountry to the villages of the Pima and Maricopas, once fierce warriors who massacred the Robidoux trapping party, now peaceful farmers working the flood plain of the Gila River near the site of modern Phoenix. From the Pima Villages they pushed on to the junction of the Gila and Colorado,

<hr>

5. Philip St. George Cooke, W. H. C. Whiting, and Francis X. Aubrey: *Exploring Southwestern Trails 1846–1854*, Ralph P. Bieber and A. B. Bender, eds., Southwestern Trails Series (Glendale, Calif.: Arthur H. Clark Co., 1938), Vol. VII.
6. For a biographical sketch of William H. Emory, see Goetzmann: *Army Exploration*, pp. 128–30. Also see *D.A.B.*

and Emory fixed its position accurately for the first time. Kearny's command suffered greatly crossing the California desert, but finally after several days his army reached Warner's Ranch in California, where it was met by a detachment of marines under Lieutenant Archibald Gillespie, who had come east from the Pacific Coast.

A few days later, just beyond Warner's Ranch, near the Indian village of San Pascual on the road to San Diego, Kearny's army had its first major clash with the Mexican troops. It was a classic cavalry charge in which saber and pistol were pitted against lances and flintlock. After the first bold rush, individual combat was the order of the day, and before the battle was over, eighteen Americans had been killed and thirteen wounded, while the Mexicans who retired from the field lost but two. Gillespie lay at the point of death, Kearny was badly wounded, and one third of all the American officers were casualties of one kind or another. Victorious only by the merest technicality, the Army of the West found itself barricaded at a place called Snooks Ranch, in serious danger of annihilation. Only the arrival of reinforcements brought by Kit Carson saved the day and enabled Kearny's Army to "walk out" to the Pacific.[7]

When they reached the Pacific, which one mountain man thought was "a great prairie without a tree,"[8] Emory's task as an explorer was temporarily ended. He had completed one of the important reconnaissances of the decade and his data were of both long-range and immediate significance. His map, which, except in one instance, was based solely on personal observation of the terrain, immediately rendered all others, such as Mitchell's, Tanner's, and even Humboldt's, obsolete.[9] It became a standard reference on the Southwest and guided countless overland parties to the Pacific. It also provided the Army with the vital geographical information needed to begin containing the savage tribes which would be inherited with the new domain at the end of the war.

In addition to his cartographic labors, Emory broadened his researches to encompass geology, botany, and zoology, but most important were his endeavors in what might be called the early science of man. Almost singlehandedly, he began the study of Southwestern archaeology with his careful examination of the Pecos ruins, and

7. Arthur Woodward: *Lances at San Pascual* (San Francisco: California Historical Society; 1948) is the best secondary account of the battle. See also Emory: "Notes," p. 108; and Edwin L. Sabin: *Kit Carson Days*, 2 vols. (New York: The Press of the Pioneers; 1935), Vol. II, p. 529.
8. Emory: "Notes," pp. 112–13.
9. See map in Emory: "Notes."

the Casas Grandes along the Gila River. Inspired by Prescott's recently published *Conquest of Mexico* (1843) and John Lloyd
Stephens's *Incidents of Travel in Central America, Chiapas, and
Yucatan* (1841), Emory speculated at great length on the origin of
the Pueblo tribes whose ruins dotted his line of march. He concluded, quite correctly in the modern view, that no direct connection
existed between the ancient Pueblo tribes and the Mayas and Aztecs
farther south.[1] It was a scientific rather than a romantic conclusion
and contrasted sharply with the views advanced by the long series of
soldier-anthropologists and scholars who followed in his wake. For
the next decade the Army, in the person of the officers of the Topographical Corps and other officers at lonely outposts, took the lead
in promoting and developing the serious study of the ancient monuments of the Southwest.

In a more contemporary approach to the science of man, Emory,
who was himself a Maryland slaveholder, wrote:

> No one who has ever visited this country and who is acquainted
> with the character and value of slave labor in the United States
> would ever think of bringing his slaves here with any view to
> profit, much less would he purchase slaves for such a purpose.
> Their labor here if they could be retained as slaves among peons
> nearly of their own color, would never repay the cost of trans-
> portation much less the additional purchase money.[2]

It was a sentiment that Webster would echo in his famous seventh
of March speech on behalf of the Compromise of 1850.

More important perhaps in the long run for Western history,
Emory observed: "In no part of this vast trail can the rains from
Heaven be relied upon, to any extent for the cultivation of the soil.
. . . The cultivation of the earth is therefore confined to the narrow
strips of land which are within the level of the waters of the streams
and wherever practised in a community, or to any extent, involves a
degree of subordination and absolute obedience to a chief, repug-
nant to the habits of our people."[3] He thus anticipated the approach
to the problem of arid lands taken some thirty-two years later by
John Wesley Powell in his *Report on the Lands of the Arid Region*,
even to the extent of proposing new settlement patterns based on
water resources rather than 160-acre grid patterns traditionally

1. Ibid., pp. 131–4.
2. Ibid., p. 99.
3. Ibid., p. 98.

staked out against the landscape on the earlier frontiers.[4] From the beginning, too, Emory recognized, as Powell never did, that such a system would hardly be democratic, but must involve some unpleasant degree of authority and coercion. Indeed, the only such successful applications of planned water use before the twentieth century appear to have been carried out under authoritarian Spanish and Mormon systems of government. From the beginning, a planned approach to the West ran headlong into the basic Jeffersonian agrarian philosophy of the independent entrepreneur. The Topographical Engineers, as the years passed, were the first to experience this clash of frontier values in the West.

One other result of Emory's reconnaissance was all-important and had a direct impact on diplomatic relations between the United States and Mexico for the next decade. As soon as Emory returned to Washington, he advised Secretary of State Buchanan that any Southern boundary line should include territory below the Gila River, since all hope of building a transcontinental railroad through the Southwest depended upon securing a route that ran as far south as 32 degrees north latitude.[5] The Mormon expedition led by Captain Philip St. George Cooke, which took a more southerly route through Guadalupe Pass and Tucson, tended to confirm this judgment, except that, lacking instruments, Cooke failed to note that the only suitable route actually ran south of 32 degrees and thus more territory would be needed. This innocent oversight generated no little sectional antagonism during the succeeding decade, and was responsible to a large degree for future American diplomacy.

6

The final important impact of the explorer upon the diplomacy of American continentalism came with the actual settlement of the boundary line between the United States and Mexico. Here, because the disputed region was largely unmapped and hence unknown in precise terms, the explorer's knowledge was a vital factor in the ultimate diplomatic agreement which set limits to American continental expansion.

When Nicholas P. Trist composed the Treaty of Guadalupe-

4. John Wesley Powell: *Report on the Lands of the Arid Regions of the United States* (Washington, D.C.: U.S. Government Printing Office; 1878).
5. James Buchanan to Nicholas P. Trist, Washington, July 19, 1847, in Moore: *Buchanan*, pp. 368–9.

Hidalgo, he did so almost entirely in ignorance of the geography of
the country through which the boundary line between the two nations would run. His researches had been largely confined to the erroneous commercial maps of Mitchell, Tanner, and Disturnell and
a report compiled by Captain Robert E. Lee based on the works of
Moscaro, Antonio Barriero, and José Agustín de Escudero.[6] These
works were likewise for the most part inaccurate, as Trist himself
realized. "All of these geographical notes," he wrote in a memo to
himself, "are replete with errors; for nothing is positively known and
the only basis for them consists of ill-formed conjectures and worse
information."[7] Nevertheless, with time pressing hard upon him
after Polk's order of recall, he managed to create a version of the
boundary line which satisfied the Mexican negotiators. Article V of
the Treaty of Guadalupe-Hidalgo, which described the boundary
line, specified that it should run from a point three marine leagues
out in the Gulf of Mexico, up the Rio Grande along its deepest chan-
nel, to the point where the river struck the southern boundary of
New Mexico. Thence it would run westerly along the traditional
southern boundary of New Mexico, "which runs north of the town
called Paso" (now Juarez), to its western termination, and thence
northward along the western line of New Mexico until it intersected
the first branch of the Gila River, or to the point on the line nearest
such branch, and then down it to the Gila, down the Gila to the
Colorado, and then in a straight line to a point on the Pacific Ocean
designated as one marine league south of the southernmost point of
the port of San Diego as laid down by Juan Pantoja in 1802 in his
atlas to the voyages of the schooners *Sutil* and *Mexicana*. The
southern and western limits of New Mexico were to be those specified on J. Disturnell's "Map of the United States . . . 1847," a map
known at the time to be inaccurate, as were all others available, but
nonetheless pressed into service as an arbitrary definition of the
limits of New Mexico.[8] The use of this map and the difficulty of
deciding on the true boundary of New Mexico caused the most
trouble in the final negotiations between the United States and Mexico. Because of this, the explorer as boundary surveyor was called
upon to exercise maximum influence on the course of American history.

6. Nicholas P. Trist: Memorandum, Jan. 1848, Vol. 29 (Jan. 28–Feb. 13,
1848), Trist Papers, Library of Congress.
7. Ibid.
8. "The Treaty between the United States and Mexico . . . ," 30th Cong.,
1st sess., *Sen. Exec. Doc.* 52 (1848), pp. 43–5.

According to the treaty, each country was to appoint a commissioner and a surveyor who were to meet in San Diego one year from the signing of the agreement and jointly see to the running and marking of the boundary line upon the earth. Because so many provisions of the treaty depended on matters of geographical interpretation, it was evident from the beginning that the commissioners and surveyors would have a quasi-diplomatic status. Moreover, they were political appointees, which interjected still another complication into what already promised to be a difficult and ambiguous situation.

From the beginning, the Army's exploring corps, the Topographical Engineers, was associated with the boundary survey, but at first in a capacity subordinate to that of the civilian commissioner and surveyor. The first American commissioner was John B. Weller, a defeated Democratic senatorial candidate from Ohio. He received his appointment in January of 1849, in one of the last acts of Polk's administration. Something of a midnight appointee, with no obvious qualifications for a boundary commissioner, he was extremely unpopular with Zachary Taylor's incoming Whig administration. The surveyor was A. B. Gray of Texas, a railroad enthusiast and freelance explorer who had served on Memucan Hunt's Texan contingent on the U.S.–Texas Sabine River Boundary Survey.[9] Various officers of the Topographical Engineers, including Lieutenants William H. Emory and A. W. Whipple, were assigned to the commission to see to the actual execution of the exacting tasks of geodesy and surveying.

After a long delay due to difficulties in securing transportation north from the Isthmus of Panama, the American Commission finally arrived in San Diego, and on July 3, 1849, the Mexican Commission under General García Condé also arrived. From that date commenced the active boundary-survey operation.[1]

9. Goetzmann: *Army Exploration,* pp. 157–8. See also Paul Neff Garber: *The Gadsden Treaty* (Philadelphia: University of Pennsylvania Press; 1923), pp. 11–12.
1. José Salazar Ylarrequi: *Datos de los trabajos astronómicos y topográficos dispuestos en forma de diario. Practicados durante el año de 1849 y principio de 1850 por la Comisión de límites Mexicana en la linea que divide esta república de la de los Estados Unidos, por el geómetra de dicha comisión, José Salazar Ylarrequi* . . . (Mexico, 1850), p. 12. See also "Diario del Genl. Pedro García Condé sobre los límites de las dos California . . . En relación con los trabajos astronómicos y topográficos," MS. Archives del Ministerio de Relaciones Exteriores, Mexico City. General Condé's diary has been hitherto unknown to historians, and I am indebted to the Mexican government for aid in locating it and for permission to examine its contents and quote from it.

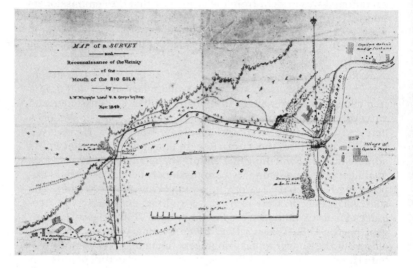

Lt. Amiel Weeks Whipple's field sketch map of the junction of the Gila and Colorado rivers. Made for the Mexican Boundary Survey. *Courtesy Oklahoma State Historical Society*

The running of the line across California to the Gila and Colorado was beset by numerous difficulties. Some of these were technical and diplomatic, such as the necessity for coming to an agreement on the length of a marine league, or the attempt made by Mexico, and thwarted by the United States, to demand the port of San Diego in trade for additional land along the Lower Colorado, which was already United States territory. These were minor difficulties compared to those arising from the gold rush and from political interference in Washington. The gold rush, in addition to pushing prices of food and supplies sky-high, also provided a strong temptation to the men on the survey to desert and seek easy wealth. Moreover, the tremendous influx of gold seekers, most of them exhausted and destitute, put a new responsibility on all government officials and taxed their resources severely.[2] And finally, at a crucial time in the survey, Weller found it impossible to secure operating funds, as his removal from office was rumored to be imminent. Only the presence of the military, with their ability to secure rations from army posts, gave the commission the stability needed to survive.[3] Then, ultimately, Weller was removed on trumped-up charges and the survey operation would have collapsed, but in fact it had just managed to complete its work on the western end of the line in time.[4]

When work resumed on the eastern end of the line in the summer of 1850, it was under the direction of a new boundary commissioner, John Russell Bartlett of Providence, Rhode Island, and New York City. Aside from the fact that he was a Whig and had friends in Washington, Bartlett, like Weller, had no qualifications beyond his enthusiasm for travel and travel books.[5] With a characteristic disdain for things Western, the Whigs had appointed as commissioner a bibliophile and bookstore proprietor who was the very epitome of visionary impracticality.

For years, in partnership with Charles Welford, Bartlett had run a bookstore in the Astor Hotel, which was a favorite meeting place for globe-trotters and lovers of the exotic. Here, among the rows of leather-bound books, the aged Albert Gallatin used to hold forth on the ancient and primitive races of mankind, and John Lloyd Stephens and E. G. Squier swapped stories about Central America.

2. Goetzmann: *Army Exploration*, pp. 161–2.
3. Ibid., pp. 163–4.
4. Ibid.
5. John Russell Bartlett: "Autobiography," MS. Bartlett Papers, John Carter Brown Library, Brown University, pp. 32–3, 59.

Brantz Mayer spoke long and often of Mexico as it was and as it is, and worried aloud about how he was going to feed his family of six daughters without another government job. Edgar Allan Poe, too, was an occasional visitor at Bartlett's, and it was perhaps there that he met Jeremiah N. Reynolds and absorbed the fascinating theories of Captain Symmes which run through so much of his writing and which held such a powerful hold on his imagination even to the end.[6]

With all of this "experience" behind him, Bartlett set out for Texas in the spring of 1850, and after a series of misadventures, which included three murders committed by his men, habitual drunkenness, insubordination, mutiny, and an attempted quartermaster's fraud by his own brother, he finally arrived in El Paso. There he met the Mexican Commissioner García Condé, who was prepared to do battle over the interpretation of the treaty provision concerning the southern boundary of New Mexico.[7] The confusion arose over the fact that according to the coordinates on the map the southern boundary of New Mexico was only one degree of latitude long and cut the Rio Grande "north of the town called Paso" so far north as to give both the Mesilla Valley and the Santa Rita Copper Mines to Mexico. By the scale of the map, and by the internal logic of the landmarks portrayed, the boundary line ran only eight miles north of "the town called Paso," and tradition had always carried the boundary line three degrees of longitude west from the Rio Grande. Confronted by this problem, Bartlett and Condé agreed to compromise. They would run the line the traditional three degrees west of the Rio Grande and then north to the Gila, but it would cut the Rio Grande at 32° 20′ north latitude, or some thirty miles north of "Paso."[8] Having settled this, they commenced work on the line, and made progress despite continual harassment by Apache and Comanche Indians.

On July 19, 1851, A. B. Gray, the surveyor, arrived at the Santa Rita del Cobre headquarters, and refused to concur in Bartlett and Condé's agreement.[9] All work was stopped on the line and the difficulty became an impasse. At stake was more than the Mesilla Valley. It was the right of way for a Southern transcontinental railroad, which Gray, and later most of the army explorers on the sur-

6. Ibid. Also see Jerry E. Patterson: Introduction to MS. "Journal of Brantz Mayer," Yale Collection of Western Americana.

7. Goetzmann: *Army Exploration*, pp. 169–73.

8. Ibid., pp. 173–6.

9. Ibid., p. 176

vey, believed was within the disputed territory. Sectional politics immediately came into play. And the dismissal of Gray by the Whig Secretary of the Interior W. H. H. Stuart only served to heighten the controversy, especially since his replacement was the experienced but contentious Southerner Major William H. Emory.

The controversy concerning the boundary line finally came to a head on the floor of Congress when John B. Weller, now a senator from California, produced the testimony of A. B. Gray, Colonel J. D. Graham, Lieutenant A. W. Whipple, and Major William H. Emory to the effect that the Bartlett-Condé agreement surrendered the only Southwest (and national) railroad right of way.[1] Weller then demanded an investigation. He was seconded by the entire Texas delegation and most of the Democratic Party. Senator James Y. Mason finally pushed through a measure withholding all funds until the boundary line "error" was rectified.[2] In all the heat of the political conflict no one paid any attention whatsoever to the long and detailed letter from Nicholas P. Trist, the original negotiator, to the New York *Evening Post*, upholding Bartlett's position completely.[3] Instead, Bartlett and his agreement were used as a rallying cry to focus demand for a further slice of territory in the Southwest that would provide a route for the railroad. Aided and encouraged by the military explorers of the Topographical Corps, who told them just how big a slice to demand, and backed by aggressive military action under Governor William Carr Lane on the Rio Grande, the expansionists practiced their brinkmanship with such effectiveness that the Gadsden Purchase was completed to satisfy their demands in December of 1853.[4] The episode represents perhaps the most dramatic use of explorer's data to secure a diplomatic victory in the annals of the country.

With the Gadsden Purchase, the outlines of the continental United States (with the exception of Alaska) had been drawn and the first phase of the great imperialistic struggle for the West had been completed. The explorer as gatherer of knowledge, as dramatist, symbol, politician, and even diplomat had played many significant roles in the final enactment of America's "Manifest Destiny." For the most part soldiers in blue and politically appointed

1. Ibid., pp. 186–9.
2. Ibid.
3. Nicholas Trist to the New York *Evening Post* draft, Vol. 32, 1848 misc. letters, Vol. 34 (June 20, 1849–Feb. 23, 1853), Trist Papers, Library of Congress. Also quoted in Goetzmann: *Army Exploration*, p. 190.
4. Ibid., pp. 189, 193–5.

government officials after 1840, these explorers had completed the work begun by Lewis and Clark and sustained by the mountain men and traders in the first decades of the century. Now, with the empire won, a new set of tasks implicit in the imperialistic adventure came to the fore. The first of these was the necessity for locating vital transportation routes into the West, and particularly a practicable path for the transcontinental railroad.

CHAPTER VIII

In Search of an Iron Trail

THE acquisition of a Pacific empire in California and Oregon forced Americans to think primarily in terms of transcontinental transportation when they addressed themselves to the problem of populating, developing, and defending their new Western domain. Pioneers and scouts had already laid out the wagon road through South Pass and its subsequent variations, but the construction of a railroad to the Pacific was inevitable. Since 1844, when Asa Whitney first officially proposed to cross Lake Michigan and span the Northwest with steel rails, the question had been not whether a railroad was coming, but how and where. Both considerations were of vital concern to the nation and they divided Congressional opinion so sharply as to render all agreement virtually impossible. Apart from the complicated issue of financing the railroad, the greatest divisive factor was the location of the line, particularly its eastern terminus in the Mississippi Valley. If every emigrant wagon trail formed a potential roadbed, every city, town, and crossroads hamlet in the entire Mississippi Valley was a potential eastern terminus—the emporium of transcontinental trade, or a port on the vast inland sea of Western commerce whose ultimate destination, as Senator Thomas Hart Benton never tired of saying, was "India." With the railroad terminus, so it was believed, would come control of the entire caravan trade of the West. Hence, since more than one road was considered financially unthinkable, competition over railroad routes and termini was fervent and bitter. Not only was North pitted against South, but within each section, up and down the Mississippi Valley, local rivalries flourished. Memphis and Vicksburg vied with one another, and both were concerned to divert river traffic away from New Orleans. St. Louis, St. Joe, and Springfield were bitter interstate rivals, and none had much use for Cairo, the proposed southern terminus of the Illinois Central. To the north, Chicago looked west by northwest to St. Paul and a Northern transcontinental route, and there were promoters such as Stephen Douglas who protected his Illinois interests by acquiring the site of modern Duluth, the natural jumping-off spot for a Far Northern route. Each time a faction appeared to be gaining the upper hand in the race for the road, the others would combine to thwart it. Boosterism was rampant, and railroad conventions charged with the fervor of evangelical camp meetings were annual occurrences.[1]

2

With customary perspicacity, Senator Benton of Missouri quickly realized that the city that seized the initiative and made a dramatic effort on its own toward building the route would ultimately secure the necessary federal support. Accordingly, in the summer of 1848 he persuaded his old friend Robert Campbell and two other St. Louis businessmen to finance an exploration of a central, or 38th parallel, route that would run west from St. Louis to San Francisco. The expedition, quite naturally, would be led by his son-in-law, John C. Frémont, the Pathfinder himself.

Frémont, bitter over his court-martial at the hands of General Stephen Watts Kearny and the West Point officers of the Old Army, was eager to redeem himself. If he could blaze the trail over the Rockies for the iron horse, he would be a hero once more. Meanwhile, in July of 1848, Benton fought a rear-guard action in the Senate. He opposed Connecticut's Senator Niles on his proposal for a land-grant road along Whitney's Far Northern, or "New England," route, and he declared: "We must have surveys, examinations, and explorations made, and not go blindfolded, haphazard into such a scheme."[2]

By the first week in October Frémont was already in action. He

1. For a general discussion of the railroad struggle, see Robert Russel: *Improvement of Communication with the Pacific Coast as an Issue in American Politics, 1783–1864* (Cedar Rapids, Iowa: Torch Press; 1948); Goetzmann: *Army Exploration*, pp. 262–6; Allan Nevins: *Ordeal of the Union*, 2 vols. (New York: Charles Scribner and Sons; 1947), Vol. II, pp. 86–7; F. H. Hodder: "The Railroad Background of the Kansas-Nebraska Act," *MVHR*, Vol. XII (1925–26).

2. *Congressional Globe*, 30th Cong., 1st sess., p. 1011. Also quoted in LeRoy and Ann Hafen, eds.: *Frémont's Fourth Expedition* (Glendale, Calif.: Arthur H. Clark Co.; 1960), pp. 17–18.

had journeyed to Westport, Missouri, and there assembled a crew of thirty-five men, veterans of his previous expeditions such as Alexis Godey, Charles Preuss, and Ned Kern. He was ready to assault the Rockies once again. His plan was to follow the 38th parallel as closely as possible and locate a new pass over the Continental Divide in the vicinity of the Cochetopa Pass, which led out of the San Luis Valley of Colorado over the San Juan Mountains and into the valley of the Green River. He and Benton both seemed to believe that there was indeed a clear pass in this vicinity, on the other side of which was an easy route to California. In this they were ignoring a great deal of Western geography, as Frémont was soon to discover.

The party left Westport on October 20, 1848, and followed first the Kansas River then its Smokeyhill Fork.[3] The monotony of the journey over the autumn prairie was broken when they reached the Arkansas River and met Thomas Fitzpatrick, now an Indian agent and currently in council with the Comanches and Cheyennes at the Big Timbers. From the Big Timbers they followed the south bank of the Arkansas River upstream past the site of Bent's Fort to the Pueblo, where the experienced mountain men warned them of an unusually hard winter to come. At the Pueblo Frémont took on Old Bill Williams as a guide and then moved on, past Lancaster Lupton's Hardscrabble Post, over the Sangre de Cristos at Mosca Pass, and down into the Upper Rio Grande in the San Luis Valley. Here Bill Williams was presumably in familiar country where he had trapped beaver for over 30 years. It was now December and heavy snow had begun to fall. Crossing Mosca Pass, the explorers' beards and hair had turned to icicles.

It is not entirely clear whether Frémont wanted to cross the mountains at Cochetopa Pass or whether he was deliberately searching for a pass that branched off from farther up on the Rio Grande.

3. My account of Frémont's expedition is based on the following: Hafen: *Frémont's Fourth Expedition,* which reprints most of the major documents relevant to the expedition and includes biographical sketches of the participants; "The Fort Sutter Papers," a typescript copy of which is in the Yale Western Americana Collection; "The Narrative of Thomas Salathiel Martin," MS., Bancroft Library; The Charles Preuss Diaries, Library of Congress, and their translation; Gudde and Gudde: *Exploring with Frémont;* William Brandon: *The Men and the Mountain* (New York: William Morrow Co.; 1955); Allan Nevins: *Frémont;* Frederick Dellenbaugh: *Frémont and 49;* and Robert Hine's excellent *Edward Kern and American Expansion* (New Haven, Conn.: Yale University Press; 1962). The Preuss diaries, especially, throw new light on the responsibility for the disaster, and as such tend to support Frémont. See especially Gudde and Gudde: *Exploring with Frémont,* p. 144.

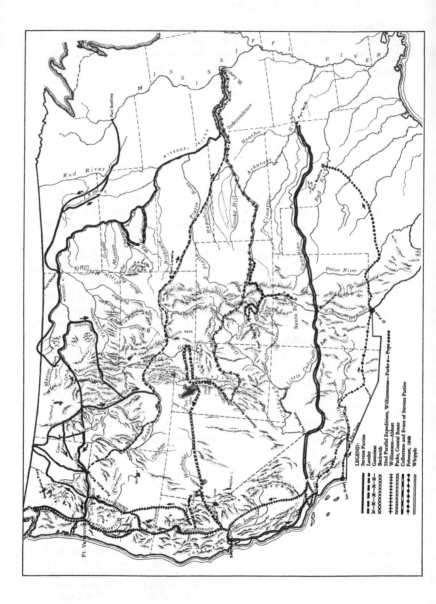

Bill Williams thought the objective was simply to reach California and he wanted to circle south out of the valley entirely around the mountains. But Frémont wanted to go across the mountains. Accordingly, in mid-December, Old Bill led the party north up Alder Creek, a tributary of the Rio Grande, right into the San Juan Mountains, an impassable wintry waste where the snow was more than ten feet deep and the temperature fell to 20 degrees below zero. Somewhere in the snow Bill Williams lost his way and they turned north fifteen miles too soon, to reach what later ironically became known as Bill Williams Pass. By December 17, five days later, they were 12,327 feet high, on Pool Table Mesa near Wanamaker's Creek in southern Colorado, caught in a blinding snowstorm, the mules falling one by one, frozen to death. Old Bill Williams, himself numb with cold, had sunk into near insensibility. In desperation Frémont decided to turn back. The day after Christmas, from a camp on Bellows Creek in the foothills of the mountains, Frémont dispatched four of his stoutest men, King, Brackenridge, Creuzefeldt, and Bill Williams, back to the Taos settlement for supplies. Then he waited.

Sixteen days later his party had heard nothing and Frémont himself determined to go for help. Taking Godey with him, he left Lorenzo Vincenthaler in charge of the main camp, with orders to bring the equipment and follow him back to civilization. That was the beginning rather than the end of the ordeal. One by one the men failed in the bitter cold. Some lay down by the trail, exhausted, and froze to death. Others starved. Morain, a French-Canadian, went back up the trail to help his old friend Sorrel, and when he found him, he too sank into despair and stayed and slowly died with him. After several days, the main party broke into two segments. One, headed by Vincenthaler and consisting of the strongest men, determined to wait for no one. It was survival of the fittest. The other party, which included the Kerns, C. C. Taplin, Andrews, Cathcart, McGehee, and Stepperfeldt, decided to proceed more slowly, share whatever food they had, and not to leave anyone in distress. Neither plan worked with complete success.

Disaster had already overtaken Bill Williams's advance guard. They had run out of food, and caught in the open on a vast plain, they were on the verge of starvation. Henry King died and according to some accounts was eaten by the three survivors, Creuzefeldt, Brackenridge, and Williams.[4] When Frémont found them, they were in an extremity of pain and exhaustion.

4. Brandon: *The Men and the Mountain*, p. 254.

Eventually Frémont and Godey, with the help of some Ute Indians, reached a settlement and Godey returned with a rescue party while the Pathfinder pushed on to Taos in a totally exhausted condition. One by one, Godey rescued the various clots of men strung out on the wintry trail behind him, and by January 28 they were on their way to survival. Manuel, an Indian, who was the first to give out, was found alive, but ten other explorers had perished. In all, it was one of the greatest disasters in the history of American exploration, made all the worse by the charges of cannibalism and the reprehensible conduct of Vincenthaler and his comrades.

Frémont, however, was not entirely downcast. In fact, he was soon declaring: "The result was entirely satisfactory. It convinced me that neither the snow of winter nor the mountain ranges were obstacles in the way of a [rail]road."[5] Then, taking the Southern, or 32nd parallel, stage route, he pushed on to California, leaving the remnants of his band in Taos under the painful necessity of shifting for themselves.[6]

3

Though Benton refused to believe it, and as late as February 7, 1849, rose in the Senate to propose a grand plan based on Frémont's "discoveries," the first Pacific railroad expedition had been a total and even tragic fiasco.[7] This deterred no one, and efforts to locate a railroad route continued more strongly than ever. Because of the weather, however, and because the Mexican War had focused attention on it, the Southern, or 32nd parallel, route along the Gila River began to command the greatest national attention. Military necessity, complicated by the eleventh article of the Treaty of Guadalupe-Hidalgo, which made the United States responsible for restraining the Comanches and Apaches from raiding Mexico, demanded a border road. And there were even broader considerations. In an open letter to Francis Markoe of the State Department, Colonel Abert of the Topographical Engineers de-

5. Quoted in Hine: *Edward Kern* . . . , p. 61.
6. Hine: *Edward Kern* . . . , pp. 61–6, records the unhappy plight of the survivors of the party who were left behind in New Mexico. Benjamin Kern and Bill Williams were killed by Ute Indians in an attempt to collect some of Frémont's abandoned supplies.
7. Benton's plan is in Hafen: *Frémont's Fourth Expedition*, pp. 49–73. It is taken from the *Congressional Globe*, 30th Cong., 2nd sess., pp. 470–4.

clared: "The consequences of such a road are immense. They probably involve the integrity of the Union. Unless some easy, cheap, and rapid means of communicating with these distant provinces be accomplished, there is danger, great danger, that they will not constitute parts of our Union."[8]

In further open letters to the St. Louis Railroad Convention of 1849 and the Memphis Convention of 1851, Abert urged a plan that incorporated a road and eventually a railroad along the Southern, or 32nd parallel, route, which would help police the border and at the same time link up with California. It would run east from the Rio Grande below Santa Fe, across Texas, cutting all of its principal rivers at the head of navigation, and come to a great fork at Nacogdoches, where one branch of the road would continue on to Vicksburg, Savannah, Charleston, Wilmington, Norfolk, and Washington. The other fork would slant north to Little Rock, St. Louis, Pittsburgh, and New York. Thus, in Abert's view, it was to be a truly national road, a great compromise in which everyone, North and South, would get something. Moreover, in addition to transporting goods laterally across the country, the road would also connect all the southward-flowing rivers of Texas and thereby create a great economic network with the Texas Gulf ports, which in turn would lead to the establishment of a Caribbean empire.[9]

As head of the Topographical Engineers, Colonel Abert was in a position to implement these plans, and as early as the spring of 1849, in response to the urgent pleas of the Congressional delegates of Arkansas and Texas, he dispatched an expedition westward out of Fort Smith, Arkansas, bound for Santa Fe. The expedition, which generally followed Josiah Gregg's Canadian River Trail of 1839, was led by Captain Randolph Barnes Marcy of the Fifth Infantry, who was just beginning his career as a prominent Western explorer.[1] Along with Marcy were two companies of the Fifth In-

8. Col. John James Abert to Francis Markoe, May 18, 1849, L.S., T.E., R.G. 77, National Archives.
9. Ibid. See also Abert to J. Loughborough, St. Louis, Sept. 24, 1849, and Abert to Glendy Burke, New Orleans, Dec. 17, 1851, L.S., T.E., R.G. 77, National Archives.
1. See Randolph B. Marcy: "Report of a Route from Fort Smith to Santa Fe," 31st Cong., 1st sess., *Sen. Exec. Doc.* 64 (1850); and James Hervey Simpson: "Report and Map of the Route from Fort Smith, Arkansas, to Santa Fe, New Mexico," 31st Cong., 1st sess., *Sen. Exec. Doc.* 12 (1850). Also see Grant Foreman: *Marcy and the Gold Seekers* (Norman, Okla.: University of Oklahoma Press; 1939). For a recent biography of Marcy, see W. Eugene Hollon's

fantry, one company of the First Dragoons, and Lieutenant James Hervey Simpson of the Topographical Engineers. Simpson had arrived at Fort Smith on a steamboat crammed with eager gold-seekers and he was well aware of the urgency of his mission. The route west followed closely along the Canadian River, past the Antelope Buttes on the border of the Texas Panhandle—observed by Lieutenant Abert in 1845—and then cut south across the Llano Estacado of Texas, which Marcy termed "the great Zahara [sic] of North America," to Cerro Tucumcari in New Mexico. They crossed the Pecos River at Anton Chico on St. John's Day, June 24, 1849, and four days later rode into Santa Fe (see map, p. 276).

Generally this was a highly feasible route, and emigrant parties bound for California were already beginning to use it. Simpson called it "superior" and "practicable" for a railroad, though he felt that "the time has not yet come when this or any other railroad can be built over this continent." He felt that centers of population must precede the railroad rather than the converse, and that natural resources must be exploited and made available.[2] In the face of headlong and grandiose plans for Western development, his was a sobering and practical voice. His conservatism does not seem so startling if one remembers that he predicted in 1849 that it would be twenty years before a transcontinental railroad would, in fact, be constructed. When it was constructed in 1868-9, however, he was one of its engineers.[3]

Marcy on the other hand declared enthusiastically: "I am, therefore, of the opinion that but few localities could be found on this continent which (for as great a distance) would present as few obstacles for the construction of a railway as upon this route."[4]

He was even more enthusiastic, however, about his return route, which took him east from Doña Ana on the Lower Rio Grande, across the southern rim of the Llano Estacado, to Big Spring, Preston, and Fort Wachita. Though this route passed right through the territory of the fierce Comanches and Kiowas (who murdered one of his men), it was closer to Colonel Abert's plan and had the advantage of a link with the Gila River route which terminated at El Paso or Doña Ana.[5]

---

excellent *Beyond the Cross Timbers* (Norman, Okla.: University of Oklahoma Press; 1955).

2. Simpson: "Report and Map . . . ," pp. 21-2.
3. Ibid., pp. 22-3.
4. Marcy: "Report . . . Fort Smith to Santa Fe," pp. 191-2.
5. Ibid., pp. 196 ff.

4

Marcy's early expeditions across Texas were supplemented in 1850–52 by the work of a special task force of explorers commanded by Lieutenant Colonel Joseph E. Johnston, one of the highest-ranking officers in the Topographical Corps. Stimulated by the civilian explorations undertaken in the summer of 1848 by John Coffee Hays and Captain Samuel Highsmith, who with a party of thirty-five Texas Rangers attempted to locate a trail across West Texas,⁶ Colonel Johnston launched a series of expeditions out of San Antonio designed to lay out dual-purpose military and emigrant roads across the tortuous landscape of the Edwards Plateau and the Davis Mountains.⁷ Besides connecting the inner and outer rings of defensive fortifications in Texas, these expeditions also linked central Texas and a possible railhead with the Rio Grande, and they clearly were important for a Southern transcontinental railroad.

Essentially two routes were explored—a northern trail which cut directly across the Edwards Plateau of central Texas and crossed the Pecos River at the Horsehead Crossing, and a southern trail which struck the Rio Grande near the mouth of the Pecos River and then followed the Pecos north to the strategic Horsehead Crossing and a link with the northern route (see map, p. 276). The northern route was first discovered by Major Robert S. Neighbors, a federal Indian agent, and John L. Ford of the Texas Rangers and was later resurveyed by Lieutenant F. T. Bryan of Colonel Johnston's Topographical Engineers.⁸ The lower, or southern, route was discovered in the winter of 1849 by Lieutenant W. H. C. Whiting of the Army Engineers and his assistant Lieutenant W. F. Smith of the Topographical Corps, who were also attached to Johnston's command.⁹ The latter route, which led first to Presidio on the Rio Grande, was the route taken by the Colonel himself when he accompanied Major Jefferson Van Horn's command to El Paso.¹ Numerous

6. Averam B. Bender: "Opening Routes Across West Texas, 1848–1850," *Southwestern Historical Quarterly*, Vol. XXXVII (1933–34), p. 119.
7. W. F. Smith: "Report . . . of Routes from San Antonio to El Paso," 31st Cong., 1st sess., *Sen. Exec. Doc.* 64 (1850), contains most of the reports of Colonel Johnston's exploring corps in Texas.
8. Bender: "Opening Routes Across West Texas," pp. 119–20. See also Lt. F. T. Bryan, in Smith: "Report," pp. 23 ff.
9. Smith: "Report," pp. 4–7 ff.
1. Joseph E. Johnston, in Smith: "Report," pp. 26–9. See also S. G. French, in Smith: "Report," pp. 40–54.

other army trails were laid out in Texas in the 1850's, but these two routes, along with Marcy's, proved to be the most practicable. Only the hostile Indians and the lack of timber and water were important drawbacks. To provide water, Colonel Abert exiled one of his most disagreeable young officers, Lieutenant John Pope, on a three-year tour of duty (1855–58) prospecting for water by means of artesian wells drilled into the Llano Estacado. Though Lieutenant Pope was characteristically optimistic, the poor man spent most of his time in frustration, chasing Indians, replacing makeshift equipment, braving the elements, and drilling dry holes.[2] Clearly, there was not much water on the Staked Plains, and the technology of the 1850's could barely produce what little there was.

5

In the continued search for trails across the Southwest, two other important military expeditions were launched in the Ninth or New Mexico Military Department. The first of these was under the command of Colonel John M. Washington and left Santa Fe on August 15, 1849. Primarily it was a punitive expedition against the Navaho Indians, whose daring raids on outlying New Mexican settlements had become particularly irksome. But accompanying the Washington expedition was Lieutenant Simpson, whose orders from Colonel Abert specified that he was to take whatever opportunity he could find to explore the Old Spanish Trail from Santa Fe via Abiquiu, St. Joseph's Springs, and across the Upper Colorado to Los Angeles. Colonel Abert was purposely vague in his instructions because he, like everyone else in official Washington, knew very little of these interior trails. And the Spanish Trail in particular was somewhere between mystery and legend for even the most informed civilized geographers.

Simpson's travels with Washington's command in the summer of 1849 took him out of Sante Fe, north and west to the Chaco River near the 36th degree of north latitude.[3] (See map, p. 276.)

2. Col. Andrew Atkinson Humphreys: "Report of the Office of the Pacific Railroad Explorations and Surveys, Nov. 29, 1856," 34th Cong., 3rd sess., H. R. Exec. Doc. 1 (1856–57), p. 212. See also the correspondence between Pope and Humphreys: Pope to Humphreys, Sept. 14, 1855; Nov. 16, 1855; Feb. 10, 1856; June 30, 1858; June 24, 1859; and Pope's Reports to Humphreys, 1857–58, all in L.R., Bureau of Explorations and Surveys, R.G. 48, National Archives.
3. J. H. Simpson: "Journal of a Military Reconnaissance from Santa Fe, New Mexico to the Navajo Country Made with the Troops under Command

There Colonel Washington's troopers successfully invaded the Chaco Canyon stronghold of the Navaho. A few days later the entire command marched westward into the Canyon de Chelly, another Navaho citadel. After a sharp, one-sided skirmish with the Indians, the Navaho power was broken forever and Lieutenant Simpson was free to explore the Canyon de Chelly. He was the first white man to discover and describe its spectacular prehistoric Indian pueblos.

The return march from the Canyon de Chelly was via the Pueblo Bonito and Fort Defiance, thence due east past Zuñi, Inscription Rock, and the Puerco River towns of New Mexico. Along the way Lieutenant Simpson examined some of the most important archaeological sites in the entire Southwest (see Chapter 9). With respect to the railroad, Simpson, supplementing his own observations with information given him by the mountain man Richard Campbell (see p. 75), concluded that a good route existed from the Rio Grande due west past Zuñi and across the Colorado to California. In effect, though his findings were not conclusive, he had located a new Southwestern trail that complicated the railroad problem by presenting a clear alternative to the road discovered by Lieutenant Emory.

His suggestions for a road west of Zuñi were followed up in an expedition sent out in 1851 under the command of Captain Lorenzo Sitgreaves of the Topographical Corps. The Sitgreaves expedition, which also made significant contributions to archaeology and ethnology, marched along the Zuñi and the Little Colorado westward across Arizona, past the San Francisco Mountains, to the Mojave Villages on the main Colorado.[4] (See map, p. 276.) Despite the presence of the skilled mountain-man guide Antoine Leroux, the group ran afoul of Indians and suffered a number of casualties, including Leroux himself, who was so badly wounded by a Yampais arrow that he eventually was unable to function as guide. The surgeon, Dr. Woodhouse, who kept a notebook recording his duties on the expedition, was faced with virtually every medical problem, from poisoned-arrow wounds to rattlesnake bites, before Sitgreaves's battered

of Brevet Lieutenant Colonel John M. Washington, Chief of the Ninth Military Department and Governor of New Mexico," 31st Cong., 1st sess., *Sen. Exec. Doc. 64* (1850), pp. 55–168. Unless otherwise stated, my account is based on this source.

4. This account is based on Lorenzo Sitgreaves: "Report of an Expedition Down to the Zuñi and Colorado Rivers," 32nd Cong., 2nd sess., *Sen. Exec. Doc. 59* (1853); and Dr. S. W. Woodhouse: "Journals," MS., Philadelphia Academy of Natural Sciences.

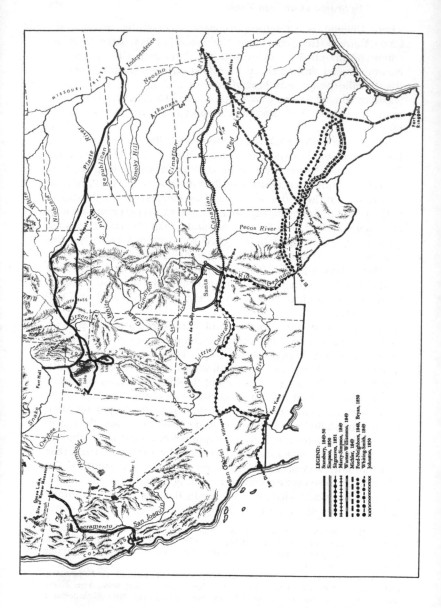

LEGEND:
Stansbury, 1849-50
Simpson, 1850
Sitgreaves, 1851
Marcy-Simpson, 1849
Warner-Williamson, 1849
Michler, 1849
Ford-Neighbors, 1848; Bryan, 1850
Whiting-Smith, 1849
Johnson, 1850

command marched into the remote Colorado River outpost at Fort Yuma.[5] Though they eventually continued on to California, it was clear that Sitgreaves and his men had discovered no easy highway to the Pacific. Not only was the country rough and water scarce, but the Indians were decidedly hostile. Emigrants would have trouble making the trek, and the country offered, at that time, very little inducement for a railroad, though today the Santa Fe Railroad actually follows his route.

If these Southwestern explorations laterally across the country from Texas to the Pacific had as yet located no easy way for the first transcontinental railroad, they had at least firmly focused national and official government attention on such a project in this area. As a result of their efforts and the diplomatic maneuvers arising from the Mexican Boundary Survey, the South seemed by 1853 to be on the verge of securing the transcontinental road as its own. Climate, security, and all scientific investigation to date seemed to point to the Southwest as the focus for the future development of the country. Where it would end, short of South America itself, no one could properly say.

6

Other sectional interests were hardly satisfied with this scheme, however, and the Topographical Bureau, as a national agency, was forced to respond to demands for exploration at a more northern latitude. Accordingly, in the early spring of 1849, Captain Howard Stansbury of the Topographical Corps was ordered to make a reconnaissance along the Platte River Trail and due west across the Wasatch Mountains to Salt Lake City.[6] There he was to map the Salt Lake and its environs, make a report on the Mormon settlements, and march as far north as Fort Hall. Ever mindful of the Southwestern route, Colonel Abert ordered Stansbury to return via the Old Spanish Trail and Santa Fe. Stansbury and his assistant, Lieutenant John Williams Gunnison, were to accompany Colonel

5. Woodhouse, in his "Journals," gives a vivid account of the trials and tribulations of Sitgreaves's command. As surgeon to the expedition, Woodhouse was in a good position to record the casualties from disease and Indian attacks on the line of march.
6. My account is based on Howard Stansbury: "Exploration and Survey of the Valley of the Great Salt Lake of Utah," 32nd Cong., spec. sess., *Sen. Exec. Doc.* 3 (1851). Abert's orders to Stansbury are in Abert to Stansbury, April 11, 1849, L.S., T.E., R.G. 77, National Archives.

William Wing Loring's regiment of mounted riflemen, who were heading west over the Oregon Trail, but they arrived at Fort Leavenworth, Kansas, after Loring's command had left and so formed their own independent expedition.

Their march took them over the now familiar Oregon Trail past Fort Kearney, its adobe buildings still unfinished, to Fort Laramie, where they forded the Sweetwater on a ferry run by an enterprising man who charged them two dollars a head. Civilization had come West, at least as far as Fort Laramie. Beyond this point, things were less civilized, but there was still Fort Bridger, to which they were taken by Bridger himself, who served as their guide. From Bridger's fort the problem resolved itself into a search for suitable railroad passes over the Wasatch Mountains. While Gunnison took the supply train over the main emigrant route via Fort Hall, Stansbury and Bridger attempted to locate a railroad pass via Ogden's Creek. When they finally reached the shores of the Salt Lake, Stansbury concluded that no good route existed in the area they had come through. A railroad would have to cut through the mountains farther north, via Cache Valley and Blacksmith's Fork, a conclusion subsequently confirmed by the Union Pacific engineers nearly fifteen years later.

Once out at the Salt Lake, Stansbury spent the rest of the season making a thorough survey, including a reconnaissance for the first time of the western shores. Lieutenant Gunnison mapped Utah Lake and the south-central parts of the Mormon Empire. In their work, the first scientific reconnaissance of the Basin Kingdom, they were assisted by the able Mormon scout, Albert Carrington.[7]

After a season in the field, they spent the winter in Salt Lake studying the Mormon people. As a result, Gunnison wrote the first objective study of the Mormons ever done by a gentile.[8] Stansbury's official report also revealed much about the Mormons, and was decidedly friendly. Moreover, he was the first person to recognize the Great Basin for what it was—a prehistoric lake bed. "There must," he wrote, "have been here at some former period a vast *inland* sea, extending for hundreds of miles and the isolated mountains which now tower from the flats forming its western and southern shores were doubtless huge islands similar to those which now

7. Ibid., pp. 121–2.
8. *The Mormons or Latter Day Saints in the Valley of the Great Salt Lake, a History of Their Rise and Progress, Peculiar Doctrines, Present Conditions and Projects* (Philadelphia: Lippincott, Grambo and Co.; 1852).

rise from the diminished waters of the lake."[9] He thus anticipated both Clarence King and Grove Karl Gilbert, whose classic works described prehistoric Lake Bonneville and Lake Lahonton some thirty years later.[1]

The following spring of 1850 Stansbury finished his survey of the lake and in the fall he concentrated on locating a railroad route due east from Salt Lake.[2] Ignoring Colonel Abert's instructions to explore the Spanish Trail, he sought Bridger's help in finding a suitable central route through the Wasatch and Rocky mountain barriers. He followed the Weber River to Echo Creek, threaded its canyons to the Bear River, Muddy Creek, and Fort Bridger (see map, p. 276). From that point he skirted the South Pass and traced a path across Bridger's Pass, and the Great Sage Plain of south-central Wyoming. Most important, he located Cheyenne Pass, at the head of the Chugwater River, which suggested that a railroad could indeed crack the mountain barrier far south of the traditional emigrant trail.[3] All the explorations were cut short, however, by Captain Stansbury's severe injury sustained in a fall from his horse. As a result, the Captain was unable to do much to promote his route, beyond submitting his report, and his discoveries went largely unnoticed. Yet the Union Pacific was later built to a large extent along the trail he had traversed.

7

Meanwhile, at the other end of the Central line, out in California, another expedition was in progress which had obvious reference to Stansbury's. On June 27, 1849, Captain William H. Warner, T.E., a veteran of Kearny's Army of the West, was ordered to lead a reconnaissance from the Upper Sacramento River over the Sierras to the Humboldt (see map, p. 268). The main object of his foray was "to discover a railroad route through that section of the country"—a route which would follow the emigrant trail and connect with the one being laid out by Stansbury across the Great Basin to the East.[4]

9. Ibid., p. 105.
1. See G. K. Gilbert: *Lake Bonneville*, United States Geological Survey Monograph 1 (Washington, D.C.: Government Printing Office; 1890). Also see my Chapter 12.
2. Stansbury: "Report," pp. 217–61.
3. Ibid., p. 261.
4. Robert S. Williamson: "Report of a Reconnaissance of a Route through

Warner's mission took him north out of Benicia and up the Sacramento River. After several days he arrived at Peter Lassen's ranch on Deer Creek, and there Lassen gave him directions to the famous trail which he had discovered and over which three hundred argonauts a day were currently entering California. Warner subsequently marched his command up Deer Creek but when he reached Lassen's Pass he found it too steep for a railroad route. What would do for emigrant wagons with their log pulleys and chains would not do for the railroad. He then turned north toward the Pit River, hoping to find a pass near its headwaters. This was the same dangerous country where nearly every party of mountain trappers coming down from Oregon had been menaced by Indians, and where in 1846 Frémont lost his good friend of the trail, Basil Lajeunesse.

On September 20, due to the lateness of the season, Warner took a small advance party and pushed on ahead, leaving his aide Lieutenant R. S. Williamson to follow. He discovered and crossed Madeline Pass, a good railroad throughway, and approached the shores of Goose Lake in northeastern California. There, suddenly, he was ambushed by a sizeable party of Pit River Indians and almost immediately riddled with arrows. One of the survivors reported the scene.

> The Captain's mule turned with him and plunged down the hill; and having been carried about two hundred yards, he fell from the animal, dead. The guide [Bercier] dismounted and prepared to fire, but finding he could not aim his rifle he succeeded in remounting and retiring down the hill. He died the next morning. The party was thrown into confusion and retreated at once.[5]

Of the wounded, at least one more died in the succeeding retreat from the lake. Lieutenant Williamson was able to recover Warner's body and his valuable maps, but the search for a railroad route had proved hazardous and difficult, not to say futile. Despite the brave efforts of Warner and Williamson, little mention was made of the suitable Sierra Pass their expedition had located, in the long and desperate debates over the proper location for a Pacific Railroad that occupied the 1850's.

the Sierra Nevadas by the Upper Sacramento," 31st Cong., 1st sess., pt. II, *Sen. Exec. Doc.* 47 (1849–50), p. 17.
5. Ibid., pp. 17–20.

8

On March 2, 1853, the Thirty-second Congress authorized a final solution to the Pacific railroad problem—an important governmental survey of all the principal routes, to decide which was the "most practicable and economical." The surveys were to be under the command of Jefferson Davis, the Secretary of War, and he was to submit his report by the first Monday in January of 1854, that is, within ten months.[6] At the outset it looked like an impossible task, but fortunately a reconnaissance, rather than a detailed mile-by-mile study of grades and curves, was all that was required. Moreover, an analysis of the Congressional debates suggests that the surveys may well have been a stratagem to take the decision out of the hands of an indecisive Congress and consign it to the Secretary of War. Davis's actions in instituting the plan indicate that this may indeed have been the case. For most of the work he planned to use the officers of the Topographical Corps, but instead of placing the surveys under Colonel Abert's authority, he established a separate Bureau of Explorations and Surveys, accountable to him and with his old friend Major Emory as its commander.[7] In cooperation with Emory and his successor, Captain Andrew Atkinson Humphreys, the initial routes to be explored were selected. In general the routes considered for the surveys were those that appeared to have the most political backing in Congress rather than those most scientifically feasible. Four main parties were sent into the field, each corresponding to an important sectional interest.

The Northern survey, which was to explore the country between the 47th and the 49th parallels, was led by Isaac I. Stevens, an ambitious young army officer who had just resigned his commission to become governor of the new Washington Territory. Stevens was a friend and protégé of Senator Stephen Douglas, who backed the Northern venture. The route he was to survey led from the Great Lakes westward via the great bend of the Missouri River to Puget Sound.[8] As the new governor of Washington Territory, it was in Stevens' direct interest to report favorably on the Northern route.

6. *Congressional Globe*, 32nd Cong., 2nd sess. (1853), p. 841.
7. For more detailed discussion, see Goetzmann: *Army Exploration*, pp. 266–275.
8. Ibid., p. 265. See also Nevins: *Ordeal of the Union*, Vol., II, pp. 86–7, 201; and Hodder: "The Railroad Background of the Kansas Nebraska Act," pp. 3–4.

Projected routes for the Pacific Railroad Survey, 1854. *Courtesy National Archives*

Dead in the center of the map, along Senator Benton's 38th parallel route, another expedition was launched. It was to follow a trail roughly similar to that taken by Frémont in 1848, except that it aimed for Cochetopa Pass instead of Bill Williams Pass. Moreover, though Benton filibustered mightily, it was not led by Frémont. Its commander was Captain John Williams Gunnison, who had served with Stansbury on the survey of the Salt Lake—a good choice, since the expedition was eventually to pass through Mormon country. It appears, however, that Gunnison and his men, even before they started out, believed the route to be impractical. There is some indication that Davis sent the party into the field with the object of proving Benton wrong, rather than locating a railroad route.[9]

Thwarted in his efforts to have Frémont appointed to command, Benton again arranged a private survey and sent Frémont into the field on the heels of Gunnison's party. And again Frémont came to grief in the San Juan Mountains. Before he reached civilization on the other side of the mountains, the Pathfinder saw his entire expedition disintegrate, and on the verge of rescue one of his men perished, frozen to death in the snow.[1]

Fortunately, however, Senator Benton backed up this venture by securing a princely appropriation of $250,000 and the appointment of Edward Fitzgerald Beale as Indian Commissioner to California. Beale quite naturally adopted the 38th parallel route as the "shortest" and most "practicable" route West, and he took along his kinsman, a newspaperman named Gwin Harris Heap, to publicize the advantages of the road. As a result of the trip, which in itself was relatively uneventful, they produced a privately printed report which made the Cochetopa Pass route seem almost incredible in its economic possibilities. This report was distributed throughout the country.[2]

To the south, along the 35th parallel—the route scouted by Sitgreaves in 1851—an expedition led by Lieutenant Amiel Weeks Whipple took the field. Strenuously advocated by Representative

9. R. H. Kern to J. S. Phelps, Pittsburgh, May 29, 1853, Yale Collection of Western Americana.
1. Nevins: *Frémont*, pp. 408–20. For a first-hand account, see S. N. Carvalho: *Incidents of Travel and Adventure in the Far West with Colonel Frémont's Last Expedition*, B. W. Korn, ed. (Philadelphia: The Jewish Publication Society of America; 1954), first published by Derby and Jackson, in New York, in 1857.
2. Stephen Bonsal: *Edward Fitzgerald Beale* (New York: G. P. Putnam's Sons; 1912), pp. 65–6; Gwin H. Heap: *A Central Route to the Pacific . . .* (Philadelphia: Lippincott, Grambo and Co.; 1854).

Phelps of Springfield, Missouri,[3] the 35th parallel route was a compromise route that promised to satisfy the citizens of Arkansas, Tennessee, and Mississippi, as well as those of Illinois, since it would connect with the Illinois Central at Cairo. It was, moreover, direct, and it ran through country with good year-round climate.

On these counts, however, the 32nd parallel route appeared to be the best. So convinced of this was Davis that he did not at first even deem it necessary to send expeditions out to explore it. Ultimately, he yielded to political pressure and sent two missions into the field to survey the 32nd parallel line—one from the West, led by the veteran explorer of New Mexico, Lieutenant John G. Parke, and the other from the East, commanded by Captain John Pope, who even at this early stage of his career was addicted to self-advertisement from his "headquarters in the saddle."[4]

In California, other expeditions coursed north and south between the Coast Range and the Sierras looking for passes over the mountains and a connection between California and the Far Northwest.[5]

There was at least one interesting omission from the routes selected. This was the 41st parallel route, parts of which had been explored earlier by Stansbury and the Warner-Williamson expedition. This route had the advantage of being on a direct line to San Francisco, and its central location gave it a good potential as a compromise route. In his final evaluation of the survey reports, Davis claimed that the Stansbury and Warner surveys, along with Frémont's in 1843, had provided enough information.[6] But these missions had not included railroad engineers or provided much data on grades, curves, or costs.

When the exploring parties took to the field they included not only Army Topographical Engineers and military escorts, but teams of civilian scientists as well. Taking advantage of the opportunity offered by the great federal reconnaissance, the various scientific societies and colleges had lobbied vigorously in Washington, first to persuade the Secretary to take a broad scientific approach to the

3. Goetzmann: *Army Exploration*, p. 287. For the source of Phelps's enthusiasm, see John Pope to J. S. Phelps, Oct. 28, 1852, copy L.S., T.E., R.G., 77.
4. John Pope: "Report of Exploration of a Route for the Pacific Railroad, near the Thirty-second Parallel of North Latitude, from the Red River to the Rio Grande," *Pacific Railroad Reports*, Vol. II, Pt. IV, pp. 51 ff.
5. Robert S. Williamson: "Report of Exploration in California for Railroad Routes to Connect with the Routes near the 35th and 32nd Parallels of North Latitude," *Pacific Railroad Reports*, Vol. V.
6. *Pacific Railroad Reports*, Vol. I, Pt. I, pp. 12–16.

railroad problem, and second to secure positions for their representatives on the surveys.[7]

The most elaborate expedition was Isaac I. Stevens's Northern-survey party. It was composed of two main sections. One, led by Stevens himself, headed up the Missouri by boat to its jumping-off point at Fort Union on the Yellowstone and Missouri rivers.[8] A second major party, under Captain George B. McClellan, moved east across the Cascade Mountains of Washington searching for passes on the western end of the line. From time to time these major parties were subdivided into smaller units and the entire country between the 47th and the 49th parallels was surveyed (see map, p. 268). The three principal problems were: (1) locating a pass across the Continental Divide; (2) turning the northern flank of the Bitterroot Mountains; and (3) crossing the Cascade Mountains. Relying on data from Lewis and Clark's journals, the parties located no less than five passes over the Divide: Marias, Lo-Lo, Hell-Gate, Cadotte's Pass, and Lewis and Clark's Pass. Turning the northern flank of the Bitterroots proved to be easier than expected, much of the way consisting of the old routes taken by Canadian fur traders down from lakes Coeur d'Alene and Pend d'Oreille. They failed to locate a proper pass over the Cascade Mountains, however, because Captain McClellan, displaying the same overcautious attitude that was to cost him victories in the Civil War, refused to test the snows in Snoqualmie Pass.[9] Had he done so, he would have discovered the desired railroad route, since the snow in the passes was not as deep as was generally believed.

In his report to Davis, Stevens was highly enthusiastic, as might be expected. He claimed to have located two routes, depending on which terminals and which passes were used. The cost of construction would range between $90,338,649 and $95,927,880, and the winter snows at that latitude "would not present the slightest impediment to the passage of railroad trains."[1] Whenever he could, Stevens took the occasion to promote the potentialities of the North-

7. Goetzmann: *Army Exploration*, pp. 307–8.
8. Isaac I. Stevens: "Narrative and Final Report of Explorations for a Route for a Pacific Railroad near the Forty-Seventh and Forty-Ninth Parallels of North Latitude from St. Paul to Puget Sound," *Pacific Railroad Reports*, Vol. XII, pp. 32–3.
9. Ibid., p. 146. Also see Philip Henry Overmeyer: "George B. McClellan and the Pacific Northwest," *Pacific Northwest Quarterly*, Vol. XXXII (1941), pp. 3–60.
1. Ibid., p. 351.

ern route, maintaining that the country "far surpassed" the Empire of Russia for the "cultivation of the great staples."[2]

Others, including many citizens of Washington Territory, and members of his own exploring party, did not share Stevens's views. His naturalist, Dr. George Suckley, wrote to his brother from Fort Steilacoom in January of 1854:

> The general feeling here is in favor of a railroad route through the South Pass having a Y-shaped bifurcation, the one branch to San Francisco, the other Puget Sound. The extreme northern route to the mind of all who went over it; including that of our railroad estimating engineer, who were unprejudiced seems *impracticably expensive*. A road *might* be built over the tops of the Himaleyah mountains—but no reasonable man would undertake [it]. I think the same of the Northern route. Tunnels of two miles in length are not our only obstacles; gullies, steep grades and deep cuts are bad enough, but the almost innumerable heavy and strong high bridges required and the large number of short and sudden curves, frequently of less than 1,000 feet radius, are very serious obstacles.[3]

Such was its dissatisfaction with Stevens's views that the legislature of Washington Territory commissioned Frederick West Lander, a civilian engineer, to survey another route from Puget Sound to South Pass which branched off from the main emigrant trail. His report, which was favorable, was included in the final edition of the *Pacific Railroad Reports*.[4]

9

Captain John W. Gunnison of the Topographical Engineers launched his 38th parallel expedition from Fort Leavenworth on June 23, 1853. (See map, p. 268.) His party included several veterans of Frémont's 1848 disaster, including Richard Kern, the topographer, and Frederick Creuzefeldt, the German botanist, who was one of those accused of cannibalism.[5] The crucial phase of

2. Ibid., p. 331.
3. George Suckley to John Suckley, Fort Steilacoom, Washington Terr., Jan. 25, 1854, Suckley Papers, Yale Western Americana Collection.
4. For Lander's report, see *Pacific Railroad Reports*, Vol. II, Pt. III, pp. 5–44.
5. See E. G. Beckwith: "Report of Exploration for a Route for the Pacific Railroad, by Capt. J. W. Gunnison, Topographical Engineers, near the 38th and 39th Parallels of North Latitude, from the Mouth of the Kansas River,

Gunnison's expedition was the survey of Cochetopa Pass in southern Colorado and the location of a railroad route westward out of the San Luis Valley. In this endeavor they were only partially successful. Menaced continually by belligerent parties of Ute Indians, they nevertheless, with the help of Antoine Leroux, managed to cross over the San Juans via a good wagon road and reach the valley of the Grand River. From there they made their way across Green River and through the Wasatch Mountains down into the valley of the Sevier River. At this point Gunnison assumed his major task was completed, and the danger from Indian attack was over. But when they reached the Mormon town of Manti they found its citizens barricaded in their houses, fearful of an Indian attack. In a letter to his wife, Gunnison wrote from Manti:

> There is a war between the Mormons and the Indians and parties of less than a dozen do not dare to travel. We did not know what a risk we have lately been running until coming here for I have been riding carelessly in the mountains hunting roads ahead and other curious capers.[6]

It was his last letter. Early on the morning of October 26, 1853, as the cook was stirring the embers of the morning fire and Gunnison was returning from his morning ablutions in the Sevier River, a party of Paiutes struck the camp from all sides. In the wild confusion of the Indian attack, Gunnison fell, riddled with arrows. Creuzefeldt pitched forward beside the fire, and the troopers were massacred as they fled in all directions. Only four escaped. It was two days before the main survey party reached the scene of the massacre, and by that time the animals had made short work of what the Paiutes left.[7] The massacre of Captain Gunnison and his command was the worst disaster suffered by the Army in the West up to that time, and the publicity it received was a severe blow to advocates of a central railroad route through Paiute territory. Some,

---

Mo., to the Sevier Lake, in the Great Basin," *Pacific Railroad Reports*, Vol. II. See also Nolie Mumey: *John Williams Gunnison* (Denver, Colo.: Artcraft Press; 1955), which includes a translation from the German of Dr. James Schiel's narrative and, most interesting, the Indian versions of Gunnison's massacre, on which my account is largely based. See also the Gunnison Papers, Henry E. Huntington Library, San Marino, California; Josiah Gibbs: "Gunnison Massacre," *Utah Historical Quarterly*, Vol. I (1928), pp. 67–75; and Hine: *Edward Kern and American Expansion*, pp. 96–7.
6. Lt. John W. Gunnison to wife, City of Manti, Oct. 18, 1853, Gunnison Papers, Henry E. Huntington Library.
7. See footnote 5 on preceding page.

however, blamed the Mormons rather than the Indians for the massacre, and it became one more grievance between the United States and Deseret that helped to bring on the Mormon War of 1857.

The command of the expedition devolved upon Lieutenant E. G. Beckwith of the 3rd Artillery, who took the survivors into winter encampment in Salt Lake City. Beckwith was genuinely interested in locating a central railroad route, and early the following spring he led a party which re-explored Stansbury's trails over the Wasatch Mountains. He found the Weber River and the Timpanogos Canyons ideally suited for a railroad.[8]

After exploring the Wasatch Mountains, Lieutenant Beckwith increased the size of his party by signing on several veterans of Frémont's second disaster who had staggered into Salt Lake City the previous winter.[9] Then he turned west to locate a route across the Great Basin and into California. This phase of the 38th parallel survey had been his own idea and he had obtained clearance from the Secretary of War in February of 1854.[1] It proved to be an enormously successful operation. From Salt Lake City he swung north to the 41st parallel and crossed the Great Basin via Pilot Peak and the Humboldt River to the base of the Sierra Nevadas near Mud Lake. Then he located two suitable passes over the mountains and into the valley of the Sacramento River: Madeline Pass, and Nobles Pass, which originated at Honey Lake and was already a wagon route (see map, p. 268).

In completing Gunnison's survey, Beckwith had actually laid the direct central route that linked Warner's California reconnaissance with Stansbury's discovery of a pass near Lodgepole Creek in the front range of the Rocky Mountains. In so doing, he had anticipated the actual route taken by the first transcontinental railroad. But since he was an artillery officer and not an engineer, he neglected to include cost estimates for the road and his report was virtually ignored by Davis and Humphreys in their final evaluation of the surveys.

10

Though the Union Pacific eventually followed a central route, this was not necessarily the best route for the United States as of mid-century. Lieutenant Amiel Weeks Whipple led a party west

8. Beckwith: *Pacific Railroad Reports*, Vol. II, pp. 113–14.
9. Carvalho: *Incidents of Travel and Adventure*, pp. 205–12.
1. Beckwith: *Pacific Railroad Reports*, Vol. II, pp. 113–14.

from Fort Smith, Arkansas, in July of 1853 along what may well have been the most practicable route at that time—the 35th parallel route (see map, p. 268). Whipple's party included Dr. Jules Marcou, a Swiss geologist, and Heinrich Baldwin Möllhausen, an artist-naturalist who had been sent to America by Baron Von Humboldt, the great Prussian geographer. Möllhausen eventually returned to Germany, where he wrote so many novels based on his travels in the American West that he became known as the "German Fenimore Cooper."[2]

The route taken by Whipple's party was essentially the Canadian River trail laid out by Josiah Gregg in 1839 and surveyed by Abert, and later Marcy and Simpson in 1849.[3] West of Albuquerque they headed for Zuñi; and from Zuñi they were guided by Antoine Leroux, who had been with Sitgreaves in '51 and only recently with the Gunnison party as far as Grand River. Whipple's trail west of Zuñi swung south of that taken by Sitgreaves and followed the Bill Williams Fork across Arizona to its junction with the Colorado River. Then, reversing Sitgreaves's directions, Whipple took his men up the Colorado as far as the Needles and then across the Mojave Desert to San Bernardino.

"There is not a doubt remaining," Whipple reported, "that for construction of a railway the route we have passed over is not only practicable but in many respects eminently advantageous."[4] When he reported his cost-estimates for the road, however, Whipple made a serious error. He nearly doubled the true costs, submitting an incredible figure of $169,210,265 when in actuality the costs should have been $93,853,605, as he realized when he made his final estimates.[5] Because of the confusion over the costs, Whipple's route,

2. Preston Barba: *Baldwin Möllhausen, the German Cooper* (Philadelphia: University of Pennsylvania and D. Appleton and Co.; 1914). See also Heinrich Baldwin Möllhausen: *Diary of a Journey from the Mississippi to the Coasts of the Pacific with a United States Government Expedition,* trans. Mrs. Percy Sinnett, 2 vols. (London: Longman, Brown, Green, Longmans & Roberts; 1858).

3. See pp. 271–2.

4. Amiel Weeks Whipple: "Report of Explorations for a Railway Route near the Thirty-Fifth Parallel of North Latitude from the Mississippi River to the Pacific Ocean," *Pacific Railroad Reports,* Vol. III, Pt. II, p. 132. See also the Whipple Papers, Oklahoma State Historical Society.

5. Ibid., p. 76. Compare with earlier estimate in A. A. Humphreys and G. K. Warren: "An Examination by Direction of the Hon. Jefferson Davis, Sec. of War of the Reports of Explorations for Railroad Routes from the Mississippi to the Pacific, Made under the Orders of the War Department in 1853–54 . . . ," 33rd Cong., 1st sess., *H. R. Exec. Doc. 129* (1855), p. 57.

the only one with a real chance as a compromise route before the Civil War, appeared in a far less favorable light than it deserved. Nevertheless, it continued to have numerous supporters.

Somewhat anticipated by A. B. Gray's civilian survey of the Southern route in 1853,[6] the official surveys of the 32nd parallel route by Lieutenant John G. Parke and Captain John Pope were important and they more than confirmed the enthusiastic expectations of the Topographical Bureau. In the winter of 1854 Parke surveyed a trail through the Chiracahua Mountains of Arizona via Nugent's Wagon Road, and in the spring of 1855 he improved the route by locating still another pass.[7] The interesting thing about Parke's trails is that they were located after the negotiation of the Gadsden Purchase. Had he been sent into the field earlier, the purchase would not have taken place, and there would not have been the related Boundary Survey difficulties.

At the eastern end of the line, in Texas, Captain Pope explored the Guadalupe Mountains of New Mexico in search of a suitable railroad pass and then led his command along the southern border of the dreaded Staked Plains of Texas. When it became necessary to cross the plains, Pope sent his subordinates out instead, while he "explored" Lieutenant Bryan's trail via Horsehead Crossing of the Pecos and Big Springs. Pope was extremely enthusiastic about the Southern route in his report and even went so far as to speculate at some length about its potentialities for tapping the entire trade of northern Mexico.[8]

11

Out in California, Lieutenant Williamson performed the crucial service of exploring the southern passes over the Sierra Nevadas, and he reluctantly concluded that no feasible railroad pass existed

6. See A. B. Gray: *Southern Pacific Railroad, Survey of a Route for the Southern Pacific R.R. on the Thirty-Second Parallel by A. B. Gray, for the Texas Western R.R. Company* (Cincinnati, Ohio: Wrightson and Co; 1856).
7. John G. Parke: "Report of Explorations for That Portion of a Railroad Route, near the Thirty-Second Parallel of North Latitude Lying between Dona Ana, on the Rio Grande, and Pimas Villages, on the Gila," *Pacific Railroad Reports,* Vol. II, Pt. V. See also *Pacific Railroad Reports,* Vol. VII, Pt. I, pp. 19–42.
8. John Pope: "Report of Exploration of a Route for the Pacific Railroad, near the Thirty-Second Parallel of North Latitude, from the Red River to the Rio Grande," *Pacific Railroad Reports,* Vol. II, Pt. IV.

at the western end of the 32nd parallel line. Instead, he recommended a route from Fort Yuma via Cajon or San Gorgonio Pass to Los Angeles, rather than San Diego, and a subsequent swing north through Tehachapi Pass into the San Joaquin Valley.[9] Williamson's report should have been a severe blow to the advocates of the 32nd parallel route, for his discoveries tended to reinforce the claims of Lieutenant Whipple, who had surveyed the 35th parallel line. Even today the Southern Pacific Railroad into San Diego is forced to dip southward into Mexico before it reaches its destination.

The final phase of field operations on the Pacific Railroad Surveys was the Williamson-Abbott expeditions north from California in search of coastal routes between California and the Northwest.[1] Despite some difficulty with Indians, the Army Topographers located two practical coastal routes, one east of the Cascades, and one to the west of them. The west one, which closely approximated the old Hudson's Bay brigade trail, would involve a difficult series of ridges between the Upper Sacramento and the Des Chutes River— the rough country where Klamath and Pit River Indians were accustomed to ambush the trappers—but the survey engineers were ultimately able to circumvent the Klamath country by way of suitable passes on either flank. The effect of the Williamson-Abbott coastal surveys was to strengthen the position of San Francisco as the logical Western terminus for the railroad, since it was now certain that from it in either direction, north or south, branches of the railroad could run.

12

The evaluation of the Pacific Railroad Surveys took place in two stages. A preliminary report was issued by the War Department in 1855,[2] and then beginning in 1857, in a series of large quarto volumes, the final report was issued. The two reports differed considerably. In the 1855 version, Davis and Humphreys dismissed the Stevens, Gunnison, and Whipple reports rather easily in favor of the 32nd parallel line. And, indeed, the Secretary's ready conclusion

9. Robert S. Williamson: "Report of Exploration in California for Railroad Routes to Connect with the Routes near the 35th and 32nd Parallels of North Latitude," *Pacific Railroad Reports*, Vol. V, pp. 41–3.
1. Henry L. Abbott: "Report upon Explorations for a Railroad Route from the Sacramento Valley to the Columbia River," *Pacific Railroad Reports*, Vol. VI.
2. See footnote 5, p. 289.

was that "the route of the thirty-second parallel is, of those surveyed, 'the most practicable and economical route for a railroad
from the Mississippi River to the Pacific Ocean.'"[3] The surprising
fact was that on close examination not one but a number of feasible
routes had been discovered, including Lander's South Pass line,
Beckwith's trail along the 41st parallel, and Whipple's compromise
line along the 35th. Moreover, the obvious advantage of the 32nd
parallel route had begun to fade as a result of Williamson's failure
to locate a good pass into San Diego. As a result of the surveys, then,
the confusion that confronted Congress was actually heightened.

Davis did his best to dispel that confusion by continuing to advocate the 32nd parallel route, despite its poor points, in the final
version of the survey reports. In reviewing the claims of the other
sectional routes, he stressed their disadvantages, uncritically accepted reports condemning them—such as McClellan's erroneous
belief that impossible snows blocked Snoqualmie Pass—and paid
scant attention to such newly discovered routes as Lander's and
Beckwith's, though he ultimately termed Beckwith's 41st parallel
route the best after the Southern route.[4]

The result, of course, was failure. In the face of such obvious
partisanship, no Congress could agree to build the road, and the
debate continued. As Zedekiah Kidwell of Virginia concluded, Davis,
by his failure to adjust to the winds of politics and shift his support
to a compromise route such as the 35th parallel route, had "harmed
the South he sought to serve."[5] No one at that time, however, considered the reasons for Davis's refusal to compromise in the interests of national expediency. But, in the light of history, the reasons
are clear. For nearly ten years since the Mexican War the Topographical Bureau and its trained engineer-explorers had concentrated the bulk of their attention on the Southwest. Science itself,
in the persons of countless army engineers, had pointed the way to
a Southwestern route. Davis, well aware of this backlog of evidence
gained from experience in the field, could not bring himself to yield
to what he considered political expediency. Blinded by his long experience in military affairs, and emotionally committed to the South
besides, Davis stood on the scientific evidence derived from the

3. *Pacific Railroad Reports*, Vol. I, Pt. I, p. 29.
4. For a detailed analysis of Davis's conclusions, see Goetzmann: *Army Exploration*, pp. 295–304.
5. Ibid., p. 303. See also Zedekiah Kidwell: "Supplementary Report in Reply
to the Comments of the Sec. of War," 34th Cong., 3rd sess., *H. R. Misc. Doc.*
44 (1857), p. 6.

years of Topographical Engineer reports. His position was made clear in a speech to the Senate in 1858. "If the section of which I am a citizen has the best route, I ask who that looks to the interest of the country has a right to deny it the road."[6] Thus ended the last real opportunity for a compromise between North and South over the development of the West. The responsibility for this failure has rested primarily on Davis, but it was also a function of the very explorations and explorers themselves. In this case, knowledge only served to increase the already existing confusion.

13

Even after the failure of the Pacific Railroad Surveys of 1853, the search for a transcontinental railroad route continued. In the summer of 1859, Captain James Hervey Simpson, who had been attached to the United States expeditionary force in Utah, made an extensive reconnaissance across the Great Basin from Camp Floyd in Utah to Carson City and Genoa at the base of the Sierra Nevadas.[7] His guide, John Reese, had taken him along a new trail south of any explored previously, and when he returned to Camp Floyd, Simpson had laid out such an improved route that the Chorpenning Mail Line and the Russell, Majors, and Waddell Company adopted it instantly (see map, p. 307). But it was not suitable for a railroad.[8] What was practical for stagecoaches and wagons would not do for the locomotive. In taking the jouncing stage over the Sierras from Genoa to Sacramento, Simpson had given very little thought to the finer points of railway engineering.

Still the need for a transcontinental railroad persisted. By 1860 there were over 300,000 people in California, the vast majority of whom demanded a link with the East, for economic and political reasons, but also for other motives such as homesickness and the simple desire for closer contact with their past. The craving for a "window to the East" was also enhanced by the great mineral strikes recently made in Nevada, at such places as the Comstock on the

6. Jefferson Davis: "Remarks on Pacific Railroad Bill, Dec. 14, 1858," in Dunbar Rowland, ed.: *Jefferson Davis: Constitutionalist,* 10 vols. (Jackson. Miss.: Mississippi State Historical Society; 1923), Vol. II, p. 317.
7. James H. Simpson: *Report of Explorations Across the Great Basin of the Territory of Utah for a Direct Wagon-Route from Camp Floyd to Genoa, in Carson Valley in 1859* (Washington, D.C.: Government Printing Office; 1876).
8. Ibid., p. 35.

eastern slopes of the Sierras. Any railroad line that crossed the Sierras even as far as Nevada was certain to be a paying proposition. Therefore, from the California point of view—and because of the discovery of gold and the heroic efforts of the wagon-trail scouts, who had seen to the population of the region, there was a California point of view—the railroad was no longer a grandiose dream. It was a practical necessity.

Almost coincidental with this realization had come a shift in technology that made a new approach to the problem feasible. This was the emergence of the railroad specialist. Whereas in 1853 the army had dispatched artillerists and topographers and fortification engineers to search out railroad routes, by the end of the decade there were enough men trained and experienced in railroading to make railroad exploration a vastly more practical undertaking. Once again, new questions and new techniques needed to be applied to an old problem.

Typical of the new men was Theodore D. Judah of Bridgeport, Connecticut.[9] Judah, unlike so many engineers of his day, was not an alumnus of West Point. He had attended Rensselaer Polytechnic Institute in Troy, New York. And afterward he made a distinct career of railroading, working first on the New Haven, Hartford, and Springfield, then on the Connecticut River Railway, which with its hilly terrain and steep slopes was a foretaste of things to come, out West. Before he was thirty, Judah had planned and built the sky-high Niagara Gorge Railroad and he had served as head of construction for the important Buffalo and New York Railway. By 1854, when he was called West to California to build a line eastward into the Sierras from Sacramento, Judah was a thoroughly experienced railroad man. Indeed, he was almost a genius in his special trade.

In the course of constructing the Sacramento Valley Railroad eastward to Folsom on the western slopes of the Sierras, between 1854 and 1856, Judah, like most other men in California, became interested in the transcontinental railroad to the point of obsession. After he had completed the line to Folsom, he struck out on his own to explore the passes over the Sierras. In 1857 he published an extensive pamphlet entitled *A Practical Plan for Building the Pacific Railroad,* and he became known locally as "Crazy Judah." With these qualifications, he was deemed, at the 1859 Railroad Conven-

9. Biographical data on Judah based on Oscar Lewis: *The Big Four* (New York: Alfred A. Knopf; 1938).

tion in San Francisco, the ideal man to go to Washington and present the case for California.

In 1860 he returned to California to gather additional data about railroad passes over the Sierras. In all, he explored five basic routes over the mountains: one from Folsom via the Middle Fork of the American River, a continuation of the Sacramento Valley Railroad; another via Nevada City and the Yuba River, known as the Henness Pass Road; a third via Yuba Pass, Downieville, and the Truckee River; and a fourth via Beckwith's Pass, which had been located during the great reconnaissance of 1853. But he rejected all of these in favor of a fifth line that he had located with the help of a frontier druggist, "Doc" Strong of Dutch Flat, California. Early in the spring of 1860 he received a letter from Strong and as soon as he could he hurried to Dutch Flat to look over the druggist's proposed route. Together they discovered a massive monocline, or inclined ramp, rising upward unobstructed between the Yuba and Bear rivers into the Sierras all the way to Donner Pass. This was the ideal route over the first and steepest crest of the Sierras, and though they didn't stop to examine it closely at that time, they were certain that the valley of the Truckee River would take them over the second crest and down into Nevada.

In "Doc" Strong's drugstore they excitedly drew up the articles of association for a Pacific Railroad and, in the months that followed, attempted to sell shares to finance a thorough and scientific survey of the Donner Pass–Truckee routes. By the end of the summer they had succeeded, and the Central Pacific Railroad Company was unofficially formed. The subscribers were the now famous big four, Leland Stanford, Charles Crocker, Collis P. Huntington, and Mark Hopkins, and some lesser-known men, Lewis A. Booth, Charles Marsh, and James Bailey. The money provided by these men enabled Judah to make a thorough engineering survey of the road in 1861, complete with barometric profiles, calculation for grades, curves, tunnels, bridges, etc., a vastly more sophisticated survey than those conducted by the Topographical Engineers. His only miscalculation was in underestimating the amount and effect of the snowfall.

The Central Pacific Railroad Company was formally organized in June of 1861 with Leland Stanford as its president, and Judah was sent to Washington to secure federal backing for the road. It seems clear that at the outset Stanford and his partners professed a desire to secure federal aid for a transcontinental railroad, while in fact they intended to push the line only as far as the lucrative

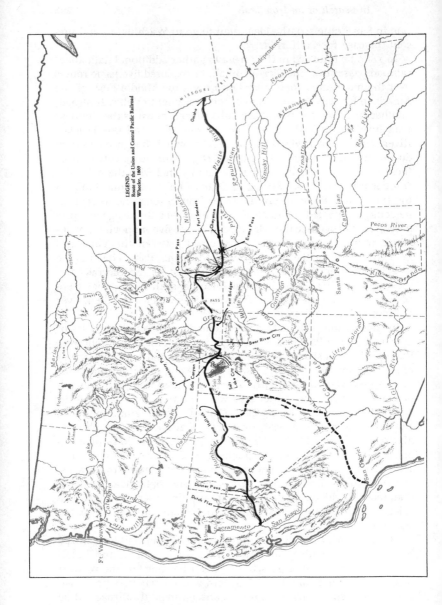

LEGEND:
Route of the Union and Central Pacific Railroad
Wheeler, 1869

Nevada mines. At this early stage they might possibly even have settled for a wagon road. At the same time it was obvious that the first railroad line over the Sierras would have a head start over all others toward securing the transcontinental franchise, should it appear profitable. The Central Pacific was in an excellent position to acquire official support from Washington, since its leaders were all staunch Republicans. Stanford became governor of the state, and Representatives John C. Burch and Aaron A. Sargent, both of his party, saw to it that Judah was made clerk to both the Senate and the House Railroad Committees, with full speaking privileges on the floor of both houses. He was also given a large office in the Capitol, which he turned into a public railroad museum. No other body of railroad entrepreneurs in California was in a position to challenge the Central Pacific, and so, right or wrong, Judah's route was the one most likely to be selected—especially after the firing at Fort Sumter and the secession of the Southern states removed all objections from that quarter, and at the same time thoroughly discredited the Democrats. On June 20, 1862, when the Pacific Railroad Bill was passed, it was a mere formality that the Central Pacific was selected to build eastward over the Sierras to the Nevada line. The new technology, which enabled Judah to locate and thoroughly report on the best route; the new national politics; and the new Western state had led the way in launching a final connection between East and West.

14

The location of the Union Pacific route westward over the Rockies to Promontory Point, Utah, was a more complex operation. For one thing, the old problem of competing eastern termini still existed. Chicago, St. Louis, Memphis, Vicksburg, and Cairo were old contestants. In addition, by 1859 new cities like Kansas City and Council Bluffs also figured prominently. Thus, while the selection of San Francisco seemed an inevitability for the western end of the railroad line, any attempt to select an eastern terminal met with fierce resistance. The deadlock was eventually broken, however, and in a similar way as at the western end of the line, by a combination of technical know-how, private initiative, and political leverage.

The most famous explorer for the Union Pacific route was Colonel Grenville M. Dodge—like Judah, a railroad specialist. Dodge, who was born in Danvers, Massachusetts, in 1831, was also something of a prodigy.[1] He attended the Norwich Academy of Science, and in July of 1851 he received a diploma as a "military and civil engineer" from Partridges Private School. After a brief apprenticeship on the Illinois Central, he met Peter A. Dey, the famous railroad engineer, and began seriously to learn his trade. When he moved over to the Mississippi and Missouri, Dey took young Dodge along and made him his assistant in charge of the survey from Davenport, Iowa, to Iowa City. By November 22, 1853, Dodge had pushed the survey to completion at Council Bluffs on the Missouri.

For a few years after that, Dodge turned to other pursuits, one of which was making a series of reconnaissances west of the Missouri River along the old Mormon Trail in an effort to locate a proper transcontinental route. By 1859, though he was only twenty-eight, Dodge had gained a local reputation as one of the best-informed railroad men on the Western frontier. According to Dodge, it was with wonderful astuteness that Abraham Lincoln questioned him about possible railroad routes during his visit to Council Bluffs in 1859. In a single meeting on a hotel verandah near the steamboat landing, Dodge recalled, Lincoln had quizzed him to the fullest extent of his knowledge concerning the transcontinental routes, and as a result the road terminus had been secured for the Iowa city. That this meeting ever took place has, however, been questioned. Professor Wallace Farnham has recently noted that nothing in Dodge's own papers, or any other contemporary account, substantiates Dodge's story beyond the fact that Lincoln was indeed in Council Bluffs in 1859. Moreover, certain statements made by Dodge

1. Biographical data on Dodge is based on Grenville M. Dodge: *How We Built the Union Pacific Railway and Other Railway Papers and Addresses* (privately printed in New York, 1910); and J. R. Perkins: *Trails, Rails and War, The Life of General G. M. Dodge* (Indianapolis: Bobbs-Merrill Co.; 1929). Both of these accounts of Dodge's career—Perkins being based on Dodge—must be used with extreme caution. Prof. Wallace D. Farnham, in "Grenville Dodge and the Union Pacific: A Study of Historical Legends," an unpublished address to the Mississippi Valley Historical Association, May 1963, has used the Dodge Papers to show in convincing fashion that Dodge created his own legend, which did not always accord with the facts. In the particular case of the discovery of Evans Pass, Farnham makes clear. that Evans, not Dodge, was the discoverer and that Dodge did not just come upon the pass while fleeing a band of Indians as he states. In all cases where there is a discrepancy between Dodge's account and Farnham's, I have followed Farnham. The scholarly generosity of Prof. Farnham in lending me a copy of his unpublished paper, which is part of his forthcoming book on the Union Pacific Railroad, is hereby gratefully acknowledged.

concerning his later associations with Lincoln in connection with railroad policy are demonstrably false.[2] It seems likely, therefore, that Dodge in later years magnified his role in the creation of the Union Pacific on several counts. Undoubtedly, on his tour in 1859 Lincoln managed to convey to the state Republican delegates—soon to be bound for the Chicago convention—his interest in an Iowa city as a possible starting point for the railroad. And Dodge was one of these delegates.

When the Union Pacific Railroad Company was formed, under the leadership of Thomas C. Durant, Dodge was no longer surveying Western railroad routes. Instead he was serving with the 4th Iowa Infantry in the Civil War, at battles such as Pea Ridge, and later Atlanta, where he was severely wounded.[3] In the fall of 1863, however, while on sick leave he went to Washington, where as Durant's assistant he met with Lincoln and helped Durant convince the President that the best route for the Union Pacific was via the old Mormon Trail and up the Valley of the Platte River.[4] In later years Dodge was fond of claiming that he was the first to note the possibilities of that route, but in Jefferson Davis's *Pacific Railroad Reports*, Captain A. A. Humphreys had clearly pointed out its merits, which had been revealed by Captain Howard Stansbury as early as 1850. Later, in 1856, Lieutenant F. T. Bryan of the Topographical Engineers had laid out a wagon route along the same line.

After his report to Lincoln, Dodge went back to the front while his old mentor Peter A. Dey, now chief engineer for the Union Pacific, supervised a reconnaissance of the line from the Missouri River to the Great Salt Lake. This reconnaissance included extensive surveys of the mountain wall behind Denver, including Berthoud Pass (located by Berthoud and James Bridger in 1861), and a survey by James T. Evans of the entire Lodgepole Creek–Cheyenne Pass region and westward through Bridger's Pass to the Wasatch Mountains.[5] Out in Salt Lake City, Samuel Reed was in charge of the survey parties and he searched the Green River country and the canyons of the Wasatch Mountains for a suitable

2. Lewis: *The Big Four*. See also Farnham: "Grenville Dodge and the Union Pacific. . . ."
3. Dodge: *Union Pacific, passim*, D.A.B.
4. Farnham: "Grenville Dodge," *passim*.
5. Wesley S. Griswold: *A Work of Giants* (New York: McGraw-Hill Book Co.; 1962), p. 96. See also John Debo Galloway: *The First Transcontinental Railroad* (New York: Simmons-Boardman Co.; 1950), pp. 236–7.

route. He also proceeded as far west as the Humboldt River. So enthusiastic were the Mormons about the project that Brigham Young sent his son Joseph to search the mountains for a trail into Salt Lake City.[6] The importance of Dey's surveys was chiefly negative. They eliminated the South Pass emigrant trail and the Denver–Berthoud Pass line from consideration.[7] Moreover, he and his men managed to narrow the range of possible routes to a line through the Black Hills, the present-day Laramie Range of Wyoming, across the Red Desert, over Bridger's Pass, and through either the Timpanogos or Weber River canyons to Salt Lake. Then in 1864 Dey resigned.[8]

Dodge, meanwhile, had continued as consultant to the road, even while serving on active duty. In 1865 he was transferred to a Western Plains command, and it was in that year, he later claimed, that while leading a cavalry reconnaissance he made his great discovery. According to his own account, he was scouting the Lodgepole Creek area in Wyoming with "a few cavalrymen and guides," when he noticed a band of Indians who had worked themselves in between his scouting party and the main command and were preparing for a surprise attack. "I therefore immediately dismounted," he remembered, "and giving our horses to a couple of men with instructions to keep on the west side of the ridge between Crow Creek and Lone Tree Creek, keeping it and holding the Indians away from us, as our arms were so far-reaching that when they came too near our best shots would reach them. . . .

"We made signals for our cavalry, but they did not seem to see them. It was getting along in the afternoon, as we worked down this ridge, that I began to discover that we were on an apparently very fine approach to the Black Hills, and one of the guides has stated that I said, 'If we saved our scalps I believed we had found a railroad line over the mountains.'"[9] Actually, neither in his personal diary nor in his letters does Dodge state that he saw any hostile Indians or discovered the pass he was looking for. His own papers reveal that the day in question was a rather routine, "tedious" day, with no Indians and no dramatic discovery of the railroad pass.[1]

6. Ibid.
7. Ibid.
8. Griswold: A Work of Giants; Galloway: The First Transcontinental Railroad, pp. 236–48.
9. Dodge: Union Pacific, p. 17.
1. Farnham: "Grenville Dodge."

The pass in question—Lone Tree Pass— was actually located and surveyed by Dodge's assistant James Evans in the summer of 1866 and it has since been named in his honor, for it was a considerable discovery—one fully as important as the South Pass, found by Robert Stuart some fifty-three years earlier.[2]

By the time Dodge assumed actual command as Union Pacific Engineer in 1866, most of the basic reconnoitering for the railroad line had been completed and the remaining work was largely detail. But it was nonetheless important, demanding the expertise of specialists. It could also be dangerous. In 1867, six miles east of Cheyenne, an exploring party under L. L. Hills was attacked by Indians and Hills was killed. Later in July of the same year, Percy T. Brown, another chief surveyor, and one of his men, a nephew of the infamous Thurlow Weed, were killed by the Sioux on the Laramie Plains.[3] Still the survey work continued, and the line was finally laid out westward over the Wasatch Mountains via Echo and Weber river canyons to Ogden, rather than Salt Lake City, and on past the famous meeting spot at Promontory Point. Graders and track-laying parties, brawny Irishmen under tough General Dan Casement, followed, and on May 10, 1869, the transcontinental railroad was at last completed. Over a thousand miles long, and scaling two immense mountain ranges and the vast stretches of the Great Basin, it was the engineering wonder of the age. It was also a significant achievement in the history of exploration—one that has often been overlooked because it was conducted by teams of surveyors and engineers rather than individual military heroes like Frémont.

With the laying out of the Pacific Railroad a new age had begun for the West, and one of the aims of Manifest Destiny had been well-nigh accomplished. A whole new population moved into the West over the iron rails, and city after city sprang up along its path—each at first usually and appropriately named "Hell on Wheels." Cheyenne, Rawlings, Ogden, Corinne, Elko, and Reno were just a few of the many points of settlement created by the railroad, and from it in either direction new centers were spawned. A figment of the transcontinental imagination, in actual practice the railroad was the instrument for settling the vast Western interior. With the great influx of people into the mountains and deserts of the West began still another era in the history of that region. And just as they had a hand in the solution of the fore-

2. Ibid.
3. Griswold: *A Work of Giants*, pp. 217–18.

most technical problems of the age, so too the explorers of the era of Manifest Destiny undertook to provide a broad base of general information about the country they had helped to develop. Their massive scientific inventory of the 1850's was one of the basic works of the Great Western Reconnaissance.

CHAPTER IX

The Great Reconnaissance

WHILE the Pacific Railroad commanded the most public attention, perhaps the chief Western preoccupation of the national government during the era of Manifest Destiny was a grand national reconnaissance of the entire trans-Mississippi country. Virtually every expedition conducted by the Corps of Topographical Engineers operated under orders to make a general examination of the plants, animals, Indians, and geological formations of the country traversed. Together, these many expeditions, and their data, were meant to comprise a total geographic inventory of the West which would have meaning and utility for Westbound Americans, whatever their needs. Most of the expeditions were under the ultimate supervision of the Topographical Bureau, which was in turn advised by the best scientists in America. The learned societies, such as the Philadelphia Academy of Natural Sciences, the Albany Academy, and the Smithsonian Institution, sponsored the trained fieldmen who went out into the wilderness and collected specimens, and back home, platoons of scientific analysts devoted their lives to organizing and classifying the materials brought in by the government expeditions, whether it be ancient Silurian mollusks or sun-bleached Comanche skulls.

Whereas the pioneers and settlers looked upon the West as a place to live, and the prospector saw it as a place to exploit, to the government scientist the West was a vast natural laboratory —a bonanza of exotic specimens and wonders of nature whose meaning and interconnectedness it had been the job of science to describe since the eighteenth century. Humboldtean and romantic in their general approach, the best American scientists sought inspiration from Europe, as they had for decades. Their duty, as they saw it, was to relate all the new Western phenomena to a great cosmic and Linnaean chain of order out of which was derived all that man needed to know of a universe which, as Louis Agassiz pointed out, was really "the thoughts of the Creator . . . a system that is His, not ours."[1] Theirs was thus the same inspiration that moved the great Humboldt himself to write from his camp high up in the Andes of South America:

> The ultimate aim of physical geography is . . . to recognize unity in the vast diversity of phenomena. . . . I have conceived the mad notion of representing, in a graphic and attractive manner, the whole of the physical aspect of the universe in one work, which is to include all that is at present known of celestial and terrestrial phenomena, from the nature of the nebula down to the geography of the mosses clinging to a granite rock. . . .[2]

Classification—collection, classification, and organization—of the unique and the marvelous, from time-stained ruins hidden away in canyons lost for centuries, to specimens of volcanic ash or exotic Indian vocabularies, commanded the attention of government explorers, whether or not they also looked for emigrant wagon trails or mountain passes over which to march an army. It was the essence of civilization come to the wilderness, and the record of these explorers, so often overlooked, is almost equal to the marvels they found and collected.

At the same time a countervailing demand persisted throughout the West. Almost unnoticed, the earlier efforts of explorers to conduct citizens out to the West had succeeded. After the Gold Rush, California filled up rapidly with hundreds of thousands of citizens, some of whom spilled over into Nevada following the big bonanza at Comstock and Washoe. Then mineral strikes broke out all over the West during the 1850's, from the remote Fraser River in Canada to the desert silver mines of Arizona. Idaho and Montana experienced rushes, and consequent population explosions, and three mountain men turned miners and citizens in 1858 laid out the new metropolis of Denver, Colorado, after the abortive rush to nearby Cherry Creek.

In equally spectacular fashion, but for different reasons, Utah continued to prosper and grow as the kingdom of Deseret. To the south, intrepid parties of Mormons moved into the great, silent

1. Louis Agassiz: *Methods of Study in Natural History*, seventeenth edition (Boston: Houghton Mifflin Co.; 1886), p. 64.
2. Quoted in Victor W. Von Hagan: *South America Called Them* (New York: Alfred A. Knopf; 1945), p. 145.

canyons of Zion. In October of 1854 the Mormon scout W. D. Huntington led a party of twelve men through hostile Indian country to the San Juan and north of that river discovered the ancient Indian ruins of Hovenweep Canyon.[3] In addition Jacob Hamblin, another Mormon scout, crossed over the Colorado near Escalante's trail and opened the Monument Valley country of the Hopi—or "Moki," as they were called—to civilization.[4]

Everywhere in the West, as the fifties wore on, makeshift towns with schools and saloons sprang up in unlikely places. Comparative abundance and a new way of life came with them—an economy based, not on land or agriculture, but on minerals. This meant that while government exploring parties backed by the foremost Eastern and European scientists were searching through the great empty laboratory of the West for nature's marvels and something on which to base the future march of empire, the process of civilization had in reality long since begun and a new set of explorer's criteria had come to the fore. Essentially, these came down to one theme, a demand for expeditions that would have local social and economic utility. Thus by mid-century clashing themes of some importance began to emerge: localism vs. nationalism or, as the case may be, internationalism; practicality vs. theory; science vs. common sense; private interests vs. broad public policy; settlers vs. soldiers; and soldiers in turn vs. politicians; white men vs. Indians; East vs. West; and in the broadest sense a clash of contrasting images of the West vastly oversimplified—the Garden (meaning a belief in the economic potential of the West) and the Desert (meaning the belief that the West was a land of scarcity that would take centuries to develop). As the men of the Great Reconnaissance went out into the West to search for nature's wonders and to do what they could for the march of empire, the clash between these two views was everywhere apparent. And the clash did not abate throughout the lengthened shadows of the nineteenth century. It was a fundamental ambiguity in American culture— an unavoidable consequence of attempting the rapid conquest of an underdeveloped continent.

3. Le Roy Hafen: "The Discovery of Prehistoric Ruins in Colorado, 1854," *The Colorado Magazine of History,* Vols. XXX–XXXI (1953–54), pp. 275–80.
4. Paul H. Bailey: *Jacob Hamblin Buckskin Apostle* (Los Angeles: Westernlore Press, 1948), pp. 195–210.

2

In addition to the Pacific Railroad Surveys numerous other Western expeditions were conducted by officers of the Topographical Engineers during the period 1853–60—all of which brought back scientific information similar in nature to that gathered by the railroad surveys. As a result of the Mormon War, that abortive clash between Deseret and the United States that took place in 1857, a series of parties were sent out with orders to locate trails which converged on the Mormon kingdom from all sides and over which supplies might be sent to General Albert Sidney Johnston's Army of Utah. The most important result of these expeditions was not the location of new mountain trails into Utah but the introduction of professional geologists and other scientists to the hitherto unknown country of mesa and canyon and basin.

One of the most important of these Mormon War expeditions was led by Lieutenant Joseph Christmas Ives. A poor boy who was raised in a boardinghouse in New Haven, Connecticut, and later attended Yale and West Point, Ives became a Confederate officer and social arbiter of beleaguered Richmond society during the Civil War.[5] In 1857, however, he was primarily interested in furthering his army career by opening up the unknown Colorado River and by being the first to undertake a scientific exploration of the great canyon of that river. He and his men landed at the mouth of the Colorado River in November of 1857 and there assembled a 54-foot paddle-wheel steamboat in which, after numerous adventures and feuds with local steamboat captains, they ascended the Colorado to the head of navigation in Black Canyon.[6] On the trip upriver they had passed through the country of the Yuma, the Chemihuevis, and the fierce Mojaves who had massacred Jedediah Smith's party of mountain trappers. Ives and his men had also managed to fend off a party of Mormon scouts sent to spy on their activities. But, scientifically speaking, the most

5. Goetzmann: *Army Exploration*, p. 379. Also see New Haven *Register*, Jan. 22, 1956.
6. Unless otherwise stated, this account is based on Lt. J. C. Ives: "Report upon the Colorado River of the West," 36th Cong., 1st sess., *H.R. Exec. Doc.* 90 (1861). Hereafter cited as Ives: "Report." Also see Arthur Woodward: *Feud on the Colorado* (Los Angeles: Westernlore Press; 1955); and Edward S. Wallace: *The Great Reconnaissance* (Boston: Little, Brown; 1955). Also see Lt. J. L. White: "Report on the Colorado River," L. R. Bureau of Explorations and Surveys, R.G. 48, National Archives.

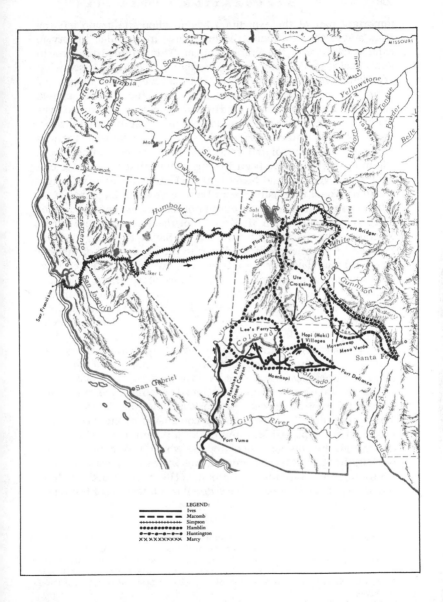

LEGEND:

———————	Ives
— — — —	Macomb
+++++++++	Simpson
●●●●●●●●●	Hamblin
●–●–●–●–●	Huntington
××××××××	Marcy

important part of the expedition began when the group left the river and headed overland, the first party in recorded history to explore the floor of the Grand Canyon. This afforded the expedition's geologist, Dr. John Strong Newberry, a chance to see what no scientist had ever seen before, the massive eroded plateaus of northern Arizona and southern Utah, and the titanic exposed gorges of the Grand Canyon. His work on this expedition was among the most important ever done in the West. It far surpassed, for example, the work of Heinrich Baldwin Möllhausen, the personal representative of the great Humboldt, whose primary contribution seems to have been the suggestion that they pickle one of the local Indians and bring him back to civilization in a jar.[7]

Almost equal in importance to Ives's first scientific exploration of the Grand Canyon was an expedition conducted in the summer of 1859 by Captain John M. Macomb of the Topographical Corps. Macomb led a party northward out of Santa Fe along the Old Spanish Trail.[8] Then he crossed over to the headwaters of the San Juan and marched due west from that river, past the southern edge of the Sierra de la Plata Mountains of southern Colorado, where he and his men found the ruins of numerous ancient Indian villages near what is today Mesa Verde National Park. Eventually they emerged from the mountains out onto the Colorado Plateau and after a difficult march through rugged country made their way to a view of the junction of the Green and Grand rivers (see map, p. 307). It was a sight no civilized man, not even a mountain man, had ever described before. At last the whole complex drainage of the Colorado River system had been made clear and one more blank spot on the map of the West filled in. Dr. Newberry, who remained in the West after the conclusion of the Ives expedition, also accompanied Macomb to the junction of the Green and the Grand, and his geological report, which linked up with his work in the Grand Canyon country, was by far the most important contribution of Macomb's expedition.[9] (His work in both of these regions will be considered in more detail in a later part of this chapter.)

7. Ives: "Report," p. 98.
8. Unless otherwise stated, this account is based on Capt. John Macomb: *Report of the Exploring Expedition from Santa Fe, New Mexico, to the Junction of the Green and Grand Rivers of the Great Colorado of the West in 1859* (Washington, D.C.: U. S. Engineer Dept.; 1876). Hereafter cited as Macomb: *Report*. The manuscript of his report is in R.G. 77, National Archives.
9. Macomb: *Report*. See especially Part II.

A final consequence of the Mormon War that had important scientific implications was the Great Basin expedition of Captain James Hervey Simpson, previously mentioned in connection with the Pacific Railroad. Simpson's work, especially his exploration of the Wasatch Mountains and his march from Camp Floyd to Carson Valley, was important because it afforded the St. Louis geologist Henry Engelmann an opportunity to make a complete transcontinental profile from the Mississippi to the Pacific.[1] Engelmann had accompanied Lieutenant F. T. Bryan on his expedition of 1856 across the front range of the Rockies via Lodgepole Creek and over the Medicine Bow Mountains at Bryan's Pass as far as Green River.[2] He was thus in a position to link his geological findings with those of Newberry to the south and Hayden and Meek to the north in a further effort at arriving at a comprehensive geologic picture of the West.

While the Mormon War explorations were being conducted, other expeditions of equal importance were sent out to open up the Dakotas to the march of settlement. There, because of the hostility of the Sioux, the prime necessity was a transportation network that led into the Sioux country over which troops and supplies could be sent. The first of these forays was conducted by Lieutenant Gouverneur Kemble Warren, a handsome, boyish soldier who somewhat resembled Frémont in his marked ability and his dashing enthusiasm. In 1855 he steamed up the Missouri River to Fort Pierre at the head of a survey expedition, and then at great risk he crossed overland, accompanied only by a few fur trappers, to join Colonel W. H. Harney's command in time for the Battle of Blue Water Creek.[3]

In 1856 he was accompanied by Ferdinand Vandiveer Hayden, who was already famous as one of the first paleontologists to work in the West. Hayden, still another protégé of James Hall of Albany, had first seen the West when he was sent up the Missouri along with Fielding Bradford Meek on a fossil-collecting mission in 1853.

1. James H. Simpson: *Report of Explorations across the Great Basin of the Territory of Utah for a Direct Wagon-Route from Camp Floyd to Genoa, in Carson Valley, in 1859* (Washington, D.C.: U. S. Engineer Dept.; 1876). For Engelmann's report, see especially Appendix I.
2. "Report of Secretary of War for 1857," 35th Cong., 1st sess., *H.R. Exec. Doc.* 2 (1857–58), pp. 455–520.
3. G. K. Warren: "Explorations in the Dacota Country in the Year 1855," 34th Cong., 1st sess., *Sen. Exec. Doc.* 76 (1856). Also see W. H. Harney: "Report of the Battle of Blue Water," 34th Cong., 1st sess., *H.R. Exec. Doc. 1* (1855–56); and G. K. Warren: MS. "Journal," Warren Papers, New York State Library, Albany, New York.

He had promptly run afoul of the Culbertson-Evans party of the Pacific Railroad Surveys attached to Stevens' command, and only the skillful arbitration of Professor Louis Agassiz, who happened to be in St. Louis at the time, enabled him to remain in the field.[4] In 1854, on his own, Hayden had gone up the Missouri as far as Fort Benton just below Great Falls and explored the whole country for paleontological specimens.[5] He had wintered upriver; then in 1855 he had gone with Meek to explore Kansas.[6] By 1856, when he accompanied Warren to the Yellowstone and Powder River country, Hayden knew more about the paleontology of the northern plains than any man alive.

He learned still more on the Warren expedition of 1856 and even more the following year. In 1857 he accompanied Warren to the Loup Fork–Niobrara River country of northern Nebraska—soon to be made famous as a paleontological gold mine by O. C. Marsh of Yale—then on to the Black Hills of South Dakota, also fertile country for the geologist.[7] In all, that year he made two trips to the fringes of the Black Hills, each from a different direction, and he dug up numerous fossil specimens, which he sent back to Meek in his laboratory in one of the Smithsonian's Gothic towers, or to Dr. Joseph Leidy at the Philadelphia Academy of Natural Sciences.[8]

A final expedition of the period, led by the fastidious Captain William F. Raynolds across the northern plains and into the Wind River Mountains in 1859–60 in an unsuccessful attempt to penetrate the Yellowstone Park region, was also accompanied by Hayden (see map, p. 311). On this march, guided personally by Jim Bridger, Hayden survived a mutiny, a mid-winter excursion into the towering Wind River Range, and months of boredom at an abandoned

---

4. F. B. Meek to James Hall, St. Louis, May 19, 1853, Box 5, James Hall Papers, New York State Museum, Albany, New York. See also F. B. Meek: "Journal of Nebraska Expedition," Field Book 3, Fielding B. Meek Papers, Smithsonian Institution.

5. George P. Merrill: *The First One Hundred Years of American Geology* (New Haven, Conn.: Yale University Press; 1927), pp. 501–3.

6. Ibid., p. 504. See also Hayden-Meek correspondence, Vol. III, Fielding B. Meek Papers, Smithsonian Institution. Meek's notebook for 1855 is not among his papers, but his notebooks for the Kansas expedition of 1858 shed light on his earlier activities. See Field Books 5 and 6, Meek Papers, Smithsonian Institution.

7. Warren: *Preliminary Report of Explorations in Nebraska and Dakota in the years 1855–56–57* (Washington, D.C.: U. S. Government Printing Office; 1875).

8. See the extensive correspondence between Hayden and Meek in Vol. III, Meek Papers, Smithsonian Institution.

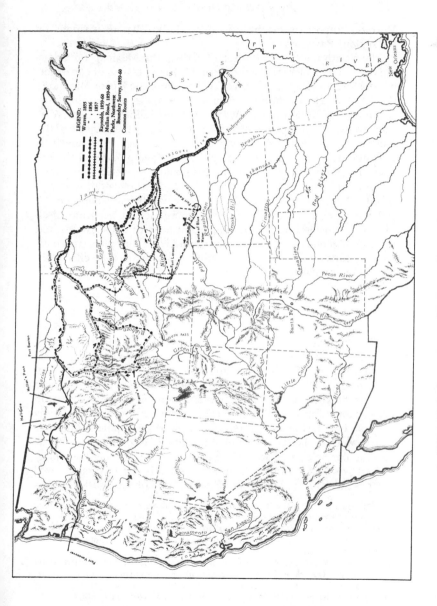

Mormon outpost, where he was given daily religious sermons by the zealous Raynolds.[9]

Along with the Pacific Railroad Surveys, the Mexican Boundary Surveys, and incidental discoveries made in the course of constructing the Mullan Road from Fort Walla Walla to the Upper Missouri,[1] these latter-day expeditions comprised the major opportunities for scientific exploration in the American West before the Civil War. They were all exciting and important, and largely the projects of the federal government. Taken together, their findings, particularly in the fields of science and art, afford the best idea possible of the impact of what might be called "the Humboldtean world view" upon the development of the West. For this reason, the overall scientific results of these expeditions of the 1850's will be considered in the following pages according to their emergence as separate disciplines. A consideration of the important scientific discoveries and their ambiguous consequences for the march of empire is perhaps a fitting capstone for the era of Manifest Destiny as it is reflected in the history of Western exploration.

3

The first task of the Humboldtean scientific explorers of the 1840's and 1850's was the compiling of an overall map of the West based upon actual exploration and trigonometric and astronomical surveys. David Burr's map of 1839 encompassed virtually a sum total of the knowledge of the mountain men which had survived in cartographic form, but it was hardly scientific and had few if any accurately determined points. The early Topographical Engineer charts were no better. Captain Washington Hood's map, with its rectangular Salt Lake, derived whatever accuracy it had from plagiarized portions of Aaron Arrowsmith's Hudson's Bay maps. And even as late as 1844 Lieutenant Emory's map of the Southwest was

9. William F. Raynolds: "Report on the Exploration of the Yellowstone and the Country Drained by that River," 40th Cong., 2nd sess., *Sen. Exec. Doc.* 77 (1868). See also Raynolds's diaries for the expedition, in Yale Western Americana Collection, in which Raynolds recounts his attempts to convert Hayden to Christianity.

1. See John Mullan: "Report and Map of Capt. John Mullan, United States Army, of his Operations While Engaged in the Construction of a Military Road from Fort Walla Walla, on the Columbia River, to Fort Benton, on the Missouri River," 37th Cong., 3rd sess., *Sen. Ex. Doc. 43* (1863).

compiled from hearsay sources little better than those used by Humboldt back in 1811.

Joseph N. Nicollet, in his surveys of the Dakotas and the Mississippi, had shown the way. His "Map of the Hydrographic Basin of the Upper Mississippi River" was based on some 90,000 instrument readings and 326 distinctly determined astronomical points.[2] With its overall regional concept of a "hydrographic basin," Nicollet's map and the accompanying report were years ahead of their time. Had he lived one more decade, Nicollet would undoubtedly have become the official government cartographer of the whole trans-Mississippi West. But he died suddenly in 1843, alone and relatively unknown except to the scientific community.

His protégé Frémont carried on the cartographical work assisted by the moody German, Charles Preuss. As a result of the Pathfinder's epic marches through the West, several highly important Western maps emerged. Most significant was the map accompanying his report of 1843–44. The first with any scientific basis to portray the West comprehensively, it charted only the country observed along the line of march, except for one erroneous departure. Frémont, in an understandable guess, made Utah Lake, a freshwater body, part of the Great Salt Lake. Frémont's map also indicated the Great Basin, with the resounding descriptive legend: "The Great Basin; diameter 11° of latitude, 10° of longitude; elevation above the sea between 4 and 5000 feet; surrounded by lofty mountains; contents almost unknown, but believed to be filled with rivers and lakes which have no communication with the sea, deserts, and oases which have never been explored, and savage tribes which no traveler has seen or described."[3] It was a cartographic landmark and guided thousands of travelers westward to the Pacific. Various adaptations of the map found their way into privately printed emigrant guides and thus it had an even greater, though unmeasurable, secondary influence.

The most useful "Frémont map" was printed in seven sections in 1846. It was drawn by Charles Preuss from Frémont's data and followed the emigrant trail westward providing information on weather, grass, terrain, Indians, and wildlife. It was studded with descriptive comments from Frémont's narrative of his expedition of

2. J. N. Nicollet: "Report Intended to Illustrate a Map of the Hydrographic Basin of the Upper Mississippi River," 26th Cong., 2nd sess., *Sen. Exec. Doc.* 237 (1840–41).
3. See map in Frémont: *Report.*

1843–44 and provided the most authentic guide for the Western traveler until the various cut-offs and alternative trails began to emerge.[4]

After Frémont's maps, the most practical of the day were those drawn by Lieutenant, later Major, William Hemsley Emory. His map of the Far Southwest, made while marching across New Mexico and Arizona to California with Kearny's Army of the West, in fact constituted the first instrumental survey of that region.[5] It was accurate for the most part, considering his rather crude instruments and the little time available to an army on the march. Its one failing was that it did not note properly the great bend of the Gila River. This made little difference, however, to the thousands of argonauts who used the map as published by Congress, and took the Gila Trail to California.

But it mattered to Emory, and on the Mexican Boundary Survey of 1850–57 he was greatly concerned to compile an accurate map. This seemed especially urgent because of the obvious errors in Disturnell's map which played such a vital part in the treaty negotiations with Mexico, and because of the necessity for a chart showing the true boundary between the United States and Mexico as the American and Mexican commissions were struggling to lay it out. Emory's map which ultimately came out in 1853 was the most accurate rendering of the Southwest ever made up to that time, though it still had certain faults and omissions. Particularly, it failed to show the possible East-West railroad passes north of the 32nd parallel.[6]

The most important of the maps drawn by the Topographical Engineers was Lieutenant Gouverneur Kemble Warren's map of 1857, which accompanied Jefferson Davis's final report on the Pacific Railroad Surveys.[7] A monumental work which encompassed the whole West, Warren's map was, in a sense, the culminating achievement of the Great Reconnaissance period. For the first time, a reasonably accurate, instrument-based outline of the entire complex geography of the West was available. Only twenty-six when he produced the map, Warren was something of a cartographic genius. In order to construct the master map of the West, he had to

4. See Charles Preuss: *Topographical Map of the Road from Missouri to Oregon . . . In VII Sections* (Baltimore: E. Weber and Co.; 1846).
5. See map in Emory: "Notes."
6. See map in Emory: "Report on the United States and Mexican Boundary Survey," 34th Cong., 1st sess., *H.R. Exec. Doc. 135* (1857).
7. See Warren's map in *Pacific Railroad Reports*, Vol. XI.

Lt. G. K. Warren's great map of 1857. Made for the Pacific Railroad Survey Report, Warren's is the first sophisticated map of the trans-Mississippi West, and one of the most important maps of the West. *Courtesy National Archives*

collate all the work of the previous decades, including the innumerable computations and celestial observations made by the many parties engaged in the railroad surveys themselves. In the thousands of cases where duplications or variations existed, he made a thorough check of the instruments used by the survey parties, their comparative quality, and the experience of the surveyor. Even then, he was often forced to base his decision on a mean between two previous versions.[8] Nevertheless, despite inevitable difficulties and some occasional crudities, Warren produced one of the climactic maps in the history of American cartography. After his work, as Carl I. Wheat has written, everything else was a matter of filling in detail.[9]

One of the most important detailed maps drawn before the Civil War was the work of the Prussian topographer F. W. von Egloffstein, who accompanied Lieutenant Joseph Christmas Ives on his exploration of the Colorado River and the first descent into the Grand Canyon in 1857. In order to represent the rugged topography of the canyon and plateau country that the Ives party traversed, Egloffstein devised a new contour map which resembled a sand table model, making the mountains appear to stand out in sharp relief.[1]

The great achievement, cartographically speaking, of the 1840's and 1850's, however, was not the careful representation of detail exemplified in Egloffstein's map, but rather the compiling of the first comprehensive picture of the West. This fitted in with the Humboldtean, cosmic approach to geography, and it also had real practical value to would-be Western settlers. It represented, for one thing, the immense distances to be spanned and, for another, the complexities and relationship of river systems, mountains, valleys, basins, and vast giant-step plateaus. A base upon which scientist and settler alike could work, it constituted a progressive step in the nineteenth-century tradition at a moment when the demands of theory and practice were for once almost entirely complementary.

8. Warren: "Memoir to Accompany the Map of the Territory of the United States from the Mississippi to the Pacific Ocean," *Pacific Railroad Reports,* Vol. XI. This is reprinted in Goetzmann: *Army Exploration,* pp. 440–60.
9. Wheat: *Preliminary Report,* p. 103.
1. See map in Ives: "Report."

4

Closely related in spirit to the work of the cartographers was the effort of the geologists to fill in a comprehensive geological map of the West. At first, in the Frémont and Abert expeditions, the Topographical Engineers, armed with Parker Cleaveland's *Handbook of Mineralogy*, acted as amateur geologists. They noted coal deposits, or possible mineral veins, and on occasion brought back fossils. Soon, however, the professional geologists took advantage of a scientific lobby that began to crystallize with the foundation of the Smithsonian Institution, to secure employment with the Western expeditions. They thus had opportunity to see the new country for themselves. Ultimately this made all the difference. But at first the geologists vied with one another to be first to survey the field comprehensively. When the results of the Pacific Railroad Surveys were published, not one but three highly speculative geologic maps of the West were produced—one by the rugged individualist W. P. Blake, who had personally seen only the Southwest and the Pacific Coast, and another by the contentious Swiss geologist Jules Marcou, whose map was based on a single transcontinental reconnaissance with Lieutenant Whipple's 35th parallel survey. In addition, James Hall, consultant to the Mexican Boundary Survey and paleontologist of New York State, though he had never seen the West at all, produced a third, which was claimed to supersede all others. It was clear that in this area, too, despite the sometimes heroic labors of Blake and Marcou out in the field, Humboldtean enthusiasm had somehow overcome scientific common sense.[2]

However, as professionals like Blake and Marcou and especially James Hall's star pupil John Strong Newberry ventured out into the West, the geologists' interests began to change and become less comprehensive. They concentrated upon earth-shaping processes such as erosion, glaciation, wind sculpture, vulcanism, and mountain-making. Newberry, for example, while accompanying the Ives expedition of 1857—the first geologist ever to see the Grand Canyon country—took a position atop a mesa just to the west of the Little Colorado River and, looking out over the plateau landscape, saw it in startling perspective. "Like the great canyons of the Colorado,"

2. Goetzmann: *Army Exploration*, pp. 323–6. See also the correspondence between James Hall and W. P. Blake, 1856–57, Boxes 7 and 9, James Hall Papers, Albany Museum; and Merrill: *Geology*, pp. 315–16, and Appendix pp. 675–81.

James Hall's geological map of the West. Made to accompany the reports
on the Pacific Railroad Surveys, Hall's is the first attempt at a geological map
of the West. *Courtesy National Archives*

he wrote, "the broad valleys, bounded by high and perpendicular walls belong to a vast system of erosion, and *are wholly due to the action of water.* Probably nowhere in the world has the action of this agent produced results so surprising. . . ." He added that it had "a topographical character more complicated than that of any mountain chain."[3]

W. P. Blake, taking note of the immense alluvial fans and clear evidence of ancient beaches visible in the Great Basin, speculated, in the *Pacific Railroad Reports,* as to whether the Basin was due to "oceanic action or to subsequent aqueous modifications."[4] And, looking to the south, Blake reasoned that perhaps the Great Basin was all that was left of a great arm of the sea that had extended northward from the Gulf of California and had subsequently been choked off by the silt piled up from the ancient overflows of the Colorado River.[5]

Newberry, like most of the other geologists, was fascinated by the Colorado River. In an attempt to account for its deep chasms, he reasoned that the river had once been a series of catch basins which were somehow tilted by uplifting until the water ran over the lip of each basin into another, cutting canyons laterally across entire mountain chains.[6] It was an exquisite piece of deduction on a grand scale and the best theory of Colorado River erosion to date before it was superseded for a time by the work of John Wesley Powell. (See further discussion, pp. 563–4.)

Perhaps as important as the earth-shaping forces, to the geologists of the Great Reconnaissance, was the reconstruction of the geologic past. Here they learned to rely upon fossil evidence as well as stratigraphical conformities, and like the European scientists, they constructed or defined stratigraphic columns that went deep into the earth and far back into the ages. An example of such a reconstruction was Newberry's description of the levels visible in the Grand Canyon.[7] Another was Hayden's and Meek's description of the Badlands of Dakota. Later on, these same Cretaceous formations were traced farther south and west by the St. Louis geologist Henry Engelmann in 1856 and 1859 in his work along the 41st parallel, first with Lieutenant F. T. Bryan of the Topographical Corps, and later with Captain Simpson in Utah. By 1860 the various strati-

3. Ives: "Report," Pt. II, p. 45.
4. *Pacific Railroad Reports,* Vol. V, Pt. II, p. 220.
5. Ibid., p. 232.
6. Ives: "Report," Pt. II, pp. 19–20.
7. Ibid., p. 42.

graphic core samplings were beginning to have some relationship to one another and whole formations could be traced from the Dakota Badlands to the Llano Estacado of Texas. More important, the sequence of deposition, and hence the comparative ages of the mountain ranges and upland plains, was fast becoming known.

One of the most spectacular advances in Western geology was made in 1849 when John Evans led an expedition to the White River of present-day South Dakota and returned with a supply of pre-historic bones that marked the beginning of the serious study of Western paleontology.[8] By far the most effective paleontologists, however, were Hayden and Meek and their Eastern collaborator Joseph Leidy. As a result of this combination of Western energy and Eastern intelligence, it was discovered that animals such as pre-historic camels, elephants, rhinoceri, and even horses had existed in the West long before the beginning of the modern era. Leidy's book, *The Ancient Fauna of Nebraska*, besides being a classic work in the science of paleontology, somehow caught in its very title the excitement that must have been experienced by these early geologists as they uncovered animals, plants, and even whole historical horizons long since passed away. The existence of these ancient creatures in America raised doubts throughout the scientific world about the migration of creatures outward from a common center of creation. Perhaps, as the evidence now suggested, there had been simultaneous separate creations and then concomitant evolution along the lines suggested by Lamarck and hinted at by Leidy's primitive horse cycle. Under the influence of Hayden, Meek, and Leidy, and stimulated by the great Western explorations, the science of paleontology in America began to have worldwide consequences.[9]

In geology more than in cartography, the split between the objectives of the sophisticated scientific culture of the East and the felt needs of the West became apparent. The settlers out on the frontier had very little use as of 1859 for a geologic map of the West, nor did they really care for complex analyses of stratigraphy or paleontology, even when such findings were available to them in free government publications. The background approach of the "pure" scientist in the field of geology, with his feeling for order and historical time sequences for their own sake, seemed irrelevant

8. Merrill: *Geology*, pp. 275–6. Evans's fossil discoveries are described in David Dale Owen: *Report of a Geological Survey of Wisconsin, Iowa, and Minnesota; and Incidentally of a Portion of Nebraska Territory* (Philadelphia: Lippincott, Grambo and Co.; 1852).

9. See more extended discussion on pp. 492–4.

to the harsh necessities of frontier life. The inherent weakness of the Great Reconnaissance geologists was not their devotion to the esoteric, but rather their failure in addition to provide practical data in mineralogy, especially in the location and careful description of coal and salt deposits and veins of the precious metals that provided the stimulus for Western development. In short, the task was really simpler than they imagined. It was left to amateurs and more perceptive, if opportunistic, scientists of a later generation to complete.

5

Virtually every Western expedition of the period had a botanist who collected specimens for careful examination back in the Eastern centers of learning. Most of the scientific classification was done by the eminent Princeton botanist John Torrey or by his pupil and protégé Asa Gray of Harvard. Of the two, Gray was perhaps the more interesting because he was in constant contact with the latest developments in European science.[1] In fact, so close was this contact that in 1859 Charles Darwin sent him an advance version of his *Origin of Species*. And in the spring of that year, in a dramatic confrontation in Cambridge, Gray—using Darwin's idea, and plant data collected by the various Western expeditions and Perry's visit to Japan—demolished forever the separate-creation theories of his more eminent colleague Louis Agassiz.[2] As his biographer observes, however, Gray, though he had a brilliant mind, had very little time for theory.[3] Instead Gray and Torrey, and the various specialists like W. W. Bailey at West Point, the expert on fresh-water infusorae, and George Engelmann of St. Louis, an expert on cacti, were deluged with thousands of specimens from out of the West whose classification took up most of their time.

The most important of these works of plant classification, also in the Humboldtean tradition, were the "Botany of the Mexican Boundary" and the botanical volume of the Pacific Railroad Surveys. The "Botany of the Mexican Boundary" alone included the classification and careful description of some 2,648 species brought back by the five field collectors of the Mexican Boundary Survey, C. C.

1. A. Hunter Dupree: *Asa Gray* (Cambridge, Mass.: Belknap Press; 1959). See especially pp. 185–96.
2. Ibid., pp. 252–63.
3. Ibid., pp. 211–12.

Parry, Arthur Schott, George Wright, George Thurber, and J. M. Bigelow, all under the supervision of John Torrey. It also included the past work of free-lance field collectors such as Ferdinand Lindheimer, Augustus Fendler, Jean Luis Berlandier, and Lieutenant Darius M. Couch, who spent his spare time from army garrison duty collecting Texas plants.[4] In this work, as in the later volume on the Pacific Railroad botany, there was very little attempt at generalization or formulation of broader theory. Following the example of Humboldt's studies of South America, Newberry, Bigelow, Cooper, and some of the other railroad survey botanists attempted to relate plant types to altitude, geological formations, weather belts, and geographical regions. Bigelow even went so far as to devise a profile chart depicting various trees and plant growths characteristic of different altitudes.[5] But this was not really speculative or theoretical. It was simple induction. The botanical efforts of the Great Reconnaissance, then, resulted in catalogues and inventories that organized masses of data for use by later, more theoretically oriented scientists.

Only Dr. Parry, in the "Botany of the Mexican Boundary," addressed himself to practical questions of settlement and he concluded that lack of rainfall made most of the boundary country west of the Rio Grande impractical for settlers with agricultural ambitions—a generalization that should have been but was not always obvious to most men who moved into the region.[6] This was characteristic. In all the careful botanical work done by the exploring parties and their colleagues back home, there was little more than superficial thought given to the specific problems of the traditional agricultural settler. Lieutenant Pope's abortive experiments with artesian wells, and the continuing attempts by the Army to use camels in the West, not to mention the reiterations by Warren and Davis and Simpson that most of the country west of the Mississippi basin was desert, all added up to an official opinion that farming was impossible in the West. Except for the "bucholic" regions of Oregon and California, the West was seen as a picturesque, indeed an exotic, wasteland that would not really be settled profitably by agriculturists for years to come. Given the level of technology of the day, this was not an unwarranted conclusion. It was hardly acceptable to Westerners, needless to say, and bred an attitude of skepticism toward all official explorers and their conclusions.

4. Emory: "Report," Vol. II, Pt. III.
5. *Pacific Railroad Reports*, Vol. III.
6. Emory: "Report," Vol. II, Pt. III, pp. 15–16.

6

In zoology, too, the emphasis was upon cataloguing, description, and classification—now often referred to as "background research." Most of the specimens brought back by the Western expeditions were forwarded to the Smithsonian Institution, where they came under the direct supervision of Spencer F. Baird. The most important of his works were the zoological volumes of the Pacific Railroad Surveys. In four impressive tomes, Baird and his assistants, Charles Girard and the team of John Cassin and George N. Lawrence tried to encompass all the known species of animals, birds. and fishes in the West. Baird, who had been a student of John James Audubon, thought of his works as successors to Audubon's *Birds of America* and *Viviparous Quadrupeds of North America*, and indeed they were.

Baird personally saw to the production of the three volumes on animals and fishes, and in the volume on animals alone he added some seventy new species to those portrayed by Audubon and Bachman scarcely a decade before. The volume on birds was done with the help of John Cassin and George N. Lawrence, and there too Audubon was surpassed in number of new species by 232. Though it was not as beautifully illustrated as Audubon's book, the work of Baird, Cassin, and Lawrence was monumental. For the first time such a study could be done at leisure from museum specimens collected in one place and available for inspection by other scientists, which added immensely to its scientific accuracy. Baird, Cassin, and Lawrence's work on birds exerted, according to Elliott Coués, "an influence stronger and more widely felt than that of any of its predecessors . . . and marked an epoch in the history of American ornithology."[7]

But, despite the accuracy and comprehensiveness of the zoological surveys of the period, they left much work to be done. There was, of course, not a hint of Darwinian speculation or even of evolution in general. There had been no interest in such questions on the part of Americans, who were bent on description and classification. Likewise, the explorer-scientists, and their Washington partners, had very little, if any, idea of ecology or the relationship of the birds and animals to their environment and the corresponding life and food cycle. Unlike similar ventures among whalers on the high

7. For zoological volumes, see *Pacific Railroad Reports*, Vols. VIII, IX.

seas, where the routes and migrations of the great mammals were carefully studied, no one concerned himself with the habits of the buffalo and other wild game. Even the beaver was largely ignored, as were the migratory fowl. In short, there was no attempt at all to relate animals and men on any level—either in the Darwinian realm of evolution or in the practical realm of human and animal ecology.

7

The most romantic achievements of the Great Reconnaissance were not, however, in the realm of the natural sciences, but rather in the newly emerging science of man. Throughout the eighteenth century, physical geography had been queen of the sciences and the study of man an exercise in moral theory demonstrated usually by anthropological models—fiction absolutes like the Indian and the Negro used by Jefferson in his *Notes on Virginia,* or like Crevecoeur's famous American farmer. The great exploring expeditions of the late eighteenth and early nineteenth centuries began to change all this. As men like Captain Cook and Humboldt and Mungo Park came into actual contact with the primitive and exotic peoples of the earth, concrete studies based on collections of empirical data replaced deductive speculation. The unique types of mankind began to be studied and appreciated for their own sake or, alternatively, as part of the great riddle of the descent of man from his Biblical forebears. Humboldt's physical geography was soon supplemented by the work of Karl Ritter, whose *Erdkunde,* which came out in 1817–18 in two volumes, was the first work to integrate the study of man with the study of physical phenomena. A central work of the German romantic renaissance, Ritter's book systematized the work of Herder, the folklorists, and the artists, and made it relevant to the disciplines of science. Before it was finished, *Erdkunde* ran to some twenty-three volumes, which paralleled Humboldt's equally lengthy *Aspects of Nature* as the romantic encyclopedia of its day.

Something of the same spirit prevailed among American intellectuals and explorers of the Great Reconnaissance. The romantic histories and travel books of Prescott and John Lloyd Stephens opened new and exciting lost worlds. Scholars of the day, and even the soldier-explorers, dipped back into works by obscure Spanish chroniclers, like Clavigero, and Vertancourt and Torquemada, in search of data on America's primitive past and exotic present. Albert

Gallatin's American Ethnological Society was founded in 1842. It served as a rallying point for students of the science of man, and also as an avenue of publication. Bartlett's bookstore supplied the literary wants of the globe-travelers and explorers and also served as a lobby for would-be explorers seeking government positions afield, whether they were Democrats or Whigs.

In Philadelphia, at the Academy of Natural Sciences, Samuel George Morton engaged in earnest studies of his fellow man that required the collection, comparison, and calibration of the skulls of all mankind. His friend George R. Gliddon, once United States Consul to Egypt, had the largest collection of skulls in the world and he happily supplied Morton with considerable raw material. Too, it was a rare week which passed without Dr. Morton's receiving at least one skull from a party of Western explorers. Almost all the learned men of his day took him quite seriously and many of them listened attentively one evening at the Philadelphia Academy as he demonstrated his theories by carefully measuring the lips, hair, cranium, and buttocks of a rather nervous Hottentot boy. No one was more interested in his work than Dr. Josiah Nott of Mobile, who passed Morton's conclusions on to John C. Calhoun, who in turn used them in his famous speeches as arguments for Negro inferiority.[8]

Meanwhile, out West, Henry Rowe Schoolcraft, explorer of the Mississippi, had begun work on his six-volume compendium of all knowledge concerning the American Indian. E. G. Squier and Edwin H. Davis had produced a study of the moundbuilders of the Mississippi Valley,[9] and by 1845 George Catlin, as previously mentioned, had brought countless Indian tribes to life with his vivid brush and precise pen.

The government explorers, too, made important contributions to the study of man. As a result of their Mexican War reconnaissances, Lieutenants Emory and James W. Abert of the Topographical Corps were afforded the opportunity to study the Indian ruins of the Southwest at first hand. Emory, building on the crude observations of Josiah Gregg and his own studies of Pecos and the Casas Grandes of Arizona, countered the claims of Humboldt that these sites marked the path of Aztec migrations southward into Mexico. He

8. For a well-written, detailed account of this activity, see William Stanton: *The Leopard's Spots* (Chicago: University of Chicago Press; 1960).

9. E. G. Squier and E. H. Davis: *Ancient Monuments of the Mississippi Valley* (New York and London: Bartlett and Welford; 1848), also published as Vol. I, *Smithsonian Contributions to Knowledge* (Washington, D.C.: Smithsonian Institution; 1848).

was supported by Gallatin himself as he asserted that the Pueblo peoples of the past, despite the evidence of stone dwellings, were the direct forerunners of the Pueblos of the present.[1]

Lieutenants Abert and Peck, on detached duty from the Army of the West, set out in search of the Seven Cities of Cibola—a quest that intrigued everyone who studied Southwestern archaeology and history. They believed they had found them in the cities of the Puerco Valley. Especially did the sky-high pueblo of Acoma, perched on its mesa, seem the city mentioned by so many Spanish chroniclers.[2]

These two expeditions had been the pioneer efforts in the field of Southwestern archaeology, but they were somewhat hurried reconnaissances, compared to the expeditions that followed. In the summer and fall of 1849, Lieutenant James Hervey Simpson, along with R. H. and E. M. Kern, the artist-draftsmen from Philadelphia, accompanied Colonel John M. Washington on a punitive expedition into Navaho country. They marched up the Chama River and there discovered the Chaco Canyon. Lieutenant Simpson and Richard Kern spent days in the canyon, excavating, collecting, mapping, and in their mind's eye reconstructing the lost Indian cities. Kern, following a suggestion first advanced by Josiah Gregg, reconstructed the largest of the pueblos, Hungo Pavie, as a gigantic stepped-back apartment house which presented a blank wall to the outside on three sides and faced inward on a court. Except for the precision of his angles and the number of levels in height, Kern's reconstruction was essentially correct. In all, Simpson and Kern mapped and diagrammed ten major sites in the Chaco Canyon. They had seen all but one.[3]

From the Chaco they pushed on to the Navaho stronghold at Canyon de Chelly and opened its archaeological wonders to the outside world too. Though they explored less than one fourth of the entire canyon, they located and charted many of the ruined citadels until then unknown to civilized man. The most spectacular of

1. Emory: "Notes."
2. "Report of the Secretary of War, Communicating in Answer to a Resolution of the Senate, a Report and Map of the Examination of New Mexico Made by Lieutenant J. W. Abert, of the Topographical Corps, Feb. 10, 1848," 30th Cong., 1st sess., *Sen. Exec. Doc.* 23 (1848), pp. 73–5.
3. James Hervey Simpson: "Journal of a Military Reconnaissance from Santa Fe, New Mexico to the Navajo Country Made with the Troops under Command of Brevet Lieutenant-Colonel John M. Washington, Chief of the Ninth Military Department and Governor of New Mexico," 31st Cong., 1st sess., *Sen. Exec. Doc.* 64 (1850), pp. 55–168. See also Hine: *Edward Kern.*

these was the Casa Blanca, or white house, which nestled precariously under a huge overhanging wall of rock. In its exploration of the Chaco Canyon and the Canyon de Chelly, in addition to the examination of the Pueblo Bonito and Inscription Rock near Zuñi, the Simpson expedition ranked as the major archaeological endeavor undertaken in the Southwest before the days of William Henry Jackson and W. H. Holmes.[4] No serious student of these sites can afford to neglect Simpson's pioneer report even in the present day.

And after Simpson there were others who made noteworthy explorations. Sitgreaves, in his expedition of 1851, investigated the Wupatki ruins of Arizona, and he wrote one of the best of all possible descriptions of Zuñi. Even his encounters with the Yampais, Apaches, and the Cosninos had some anthropological value. R. H. Kern's drawings made on this expedition were especially useful.[5] Then, too, Macomb's sighting of the ancient citadels of Mesa Verde in 1859 have long remained obscured by the later work of W. H. Jackson and the Hayden Survey.[6]

Even the regular line officers of the Army conducted archaeological explorations. Lieutenant Henry B. Judd in 1850 reinvestigated Pecos and the sites southward to the Rio Grande,[7] and in December of 1853 Dragoon Major James H. Carleton made a reconnaissance of the Upper Rio Grande in which he explored the ruins of Abó, Quarra, and Grand Quivira.[8] All of these reports were published by the Congress of the United States and opened up a new and fascinating lost world to beneficiaries of the federal franking privilege. Many were reprinted and thus competed with the gaudier works of John Russell Bartlett, Brantz Mayer, and William Hickling Prescott on the parlor tables of literate America.

Fascinated though they were with the romantic past, the ex-

4. Simpson: "Navajo Country."
5. Lorenzo Sitgreaves: "Report of an Expedition Down the Zuñi and Colorado Rivers," 32nd Cong., 2nd sess., *Sen. Exec. Doc.* 59 (1853). The originals of Kern's drawings are in the Philadelphia Academy of Natural Science.
6. See Macomb: *Report*, p. 106.
7. 33rd Cong., 2nd sess., *Sen. Exec. Doc.* 78 (1850). Also see Averam B. Bender: *The March of Empire* (Lawrence, Kansas: University of Kansas Press; 1952), p. 98. Also see Bender: "Government Explorations in the Territory of New Mexico, 1846–1859," *New Mexico Historical Review*, Vol. IX (1934), pp. 12–13.
8. "Diary of an excursion to the ruins of Abó, Quarra and Gran Quivira in New Mexico, under the Command of Major James Henry Carleton, U.S.A.," 33rd Cong., 2nd sess., *Sen. Misc. Doc.* 24 (1853). See also Bender: "Government Explorations in the Territory of New Mexico, 1846–1859," pp. 18–20.

plorers did not devote themselves entirely to ancient Indian civilizations. Indeed, if they were army officers, one of their prime duties
was to collect information on the living Indians, especially their
numbers and war-making potential. Much of Schoolcraft's gigantic
compendium derived from the reports of army explorers with whom
he was in contact. And the official government reports themselves
provided immense amounts of data on the redmen. Emory's study
of the Pima and Maricopa was classic. Ives in his Grand Canyon
Report presented an account of tribes so primitive and so remote
they had never been seen by white men—the splay-footed Hualpais
of the Grand Canyon. He also furnished data on the Yuma, Chemihuevis, and Mojaves. And he made a pilgrimage to the citadels of
the Hopis, which stood remote as Xanadu on the northern rim of
Monument Valley.

In the *Pacific Railroad Reports,* both Stevens and Whipple included essays on the Indians. The latter's report, actually written
by Thomas Eubanks and W. W. Turner, was most important. It
included twenty-one separate tribal vocabularies, and classified the
various tribes according to six basic linguistic groups which are
largely in use even today—the Algonkin, Pawnee, Shoshone,
Apache, Keres, and Yuma. Moreover, Turner reopened an old controversy by conclusively linking the Apache linguistically with the
Athabascas of Canada, which, of course, suggested a line of southward migration from the Bering Sea land bridge.[9]

In their studies of the Indians, the explorers touched upon the
practical only occasionally. Emory recommended aid to the Maricopas.[1] Raynolds deplored the corruption and wretched conditions
of the vermin-infested Missouri River tribes.[2] Hughes recommended
extermination as the best policy in Texas.[3] And Warren, though he
sympathized with the Sioux, who were beginning the forty years'
war that would be their last stand, saw no alternative but to brush
them aside in the march of civilization.[4] Most of the real work with
the Indians was left to mountain veterans like Kit Carson and
Thomas Fitzpatrick, who served as first-class Indian agents, or else
to the cavalry, who had what might be called in modern parlance
the "final solution" to the Indian problem.

To most men of the day, the Indian was merely one of the many

9. *Pacific Railroad Reports*, Vol. III, Pt. III, p. 84.
1. Emory: "Notes," p. 68.
2. Raynolds: "Report," p. 21.
3. Hughes: "Report," p. 109.
4. Warren: *Preliminary Report*, p. 52.

Western wonders—marvels, freaks, and exotics, all the more interesting because they were sometimes dangerous. They were grass-skirted Mojaves, wretched dirt-daubed Diggers, Mokis from the painted-desert courts of Kubla Khan, Assiniboin buffalo hunters, implacable Sioux, Pueblo apartment-house dwellers. They were Navaho with their gaudy blankets, Comanche, centaurs of the plains and canyons, and Klickitats from the great north paddling carved war canoes fifty feet long. With few exceptions, they were, to most observers, not men at all. In the 1850's they were not even an acute problem. They were marvels—the very symbol of romantic America.

8

All across the whole range of human knowledge—in cartography, geology, paleontology, botany, zoology, archaeology, and ethnology —the direction and achievement of the Great Western Reconnaissance was clear. It was a search for the broad outline, the comprehensive catalogue that was basic to any long-range scientific consideration of the region. With Warren's map and Torrey's plants and Newberry's stratigraphy, the West began to be related to a larger totality of cultural knowledge. Though it was replete with marvels and wonders, it could be comprehended in civilization's centers of learning. For most scientist-explorers working within a European orientation, this was achievement enough—though of course in many cases, for example the geological map, it was superficial and incomplete. Most of all, despite the inductive methods employed, their work was still philosophical and metaphysical rather than scientific in its emphasis. As late as 1860, what was called science was still an attempt, pre-Darwinian in nature, to comprehend in Louis Agassiz's terms a vast system that was the mind of God. The search was for unity, totality, oneness with the whole "Kosmos." Multiplicity had only just begun to appear as a preoccupation of some scientists such as Hayden and Meek with their specific researches into the problems of paleontology, or Hall with his interest in vulcanism and mountain-making, or Leidy with his primitive horse cycle, but these were mere diversions from the search for unity that prevailed among the explorers and scientists of the Great Reconnaissance.

In addition, since the system they were tracing out reflected the complex mind of the Creator, they were constantly alert to signs and wonders. As romantics they appreciated the moonscapes depicted by survey artists like F. W. von Egloffstein.[5] Immensity— sublime, endless, empty immensity with here and there an Indian or a buffalo as allegorical nature god—was most often depicted by the explorer-artists of the day. They were more appreciated at home. Likewise verticality was prized. When Egloffstein drew his first pictures of the Grand Canyon they reached to the heavens and dropped to the depths like gorges out of Doré's underworld.[6] Man, especially civilized man, whenever he did appear, was usually only a figure in the foreground, almost insignificant in the face of the immensity of nature and nature's wonders. This philosophy, or point of view, characterized the entire romantic era and indeed carried over into the post-Civil War years, culminating finally, at its happiest and best, in the creation and preservation of such natural wonderlands as Yellowstone Park and Yosemite.

It might be argued, however, that despite the storehouse of information produced and the satisfying series of overarching relationships that were forthcoming, the science of the Great Reconnaissance was really, for the most part, noncumulative. That is, it led nowhere. It was stored up for an eventuality that never came. In its cosmic orientation, it followed a blind lead and in the long run added little but detail to man's understanding of the universe. Darwin in his *Origin of Species*, and Lord Kelvin with his studies of heat and energy, had led mankind off in a different direction—a direction that left most of the science of the Great Reconnaissance far behind. Even Mendel, growing sweet peas in an obscure Austrian monastery, penetrated deeper into nature's secrets than did John Torrey with his endless catalogues of Western plants. Only Joseph Leidy and Asa Gray, thanks to their contacts with Darwin, emerged on the side of scientific progress. The day of the metaphysical naturalist was clearly over and a great scientific fault line had occurred that rendered his work obsolete. If the Western experience was a fair example, the course of science, even sophisticated science, was not invariably in the direction of greater and more useful knowledge.

The cosmic point of view in the Great Reconnaissance, which sustained philosophical speculation and scientific endeavor, also had its repercussions in public policy. In the broad case of the Pacific Railroad, it was clear that the grandiose vision of a passage to India actually impeded the construction of the road. Construc-

5. See, for example, *Pacific Railroad Reports*, Vol. XI.
6. Ives: "Report." See especially p. 80.

tion was only possible when short-range, specific problems, such as the location of a pass out of Dutch Flat, were considered. The clash between the nationally oriented, scientific point of view and local, practical demands was most clearly illustrated when in 1856 Senator John B. Weller of California presented a leather-bound petition from 75,000 California freemen calling for a road over the Sierras. He asked that the construction of the road not be entrusted to the engineer-explorers, but to "practical men"—"stage contractors, who, instead of taking instruments to ascertain the altitude of mountains take their shovels and spades and go to work and they overcome the difficulties of the mountain, while an engineer, perhaps, is surveying the altitude of a neighboring hill."[7] In an age of sudden expansion, when the West was rapidly filling up, few representatives of the people could afford to have much patience with background science. For them the earth was more important than the cosmos.

Likewise, the Westerner had little patience with the long-range public image of the West that developed in official Washington as a result of the numerous army explorations. Whereas Jefferson Davis and his military advisors saw the West as a desert—an Algeria to be policed by a camel corps or squadrons of cavalry who would keep the tribes in the hills—the Western citizen projected it as a land of civilization and potential plenty, especially if federal help were forthcoming. Not content to be a caravan station on the windswept road to India, as G. K. Warren saw the villages of Nebraska and Dakota, the citizens of those and other territories within a short while became boosters and promoters. Despite their apparent lack of immediate promise, towns like Yankton and Pierre, and all the local citizens, vied with great enthusiasm for a place in the economic and political sun.[8] Heated disputes broke out all over the West about the location of wagon roads, and county seats, stagecoach mail franchises, and territorial legislatures. In all of this, the federal explorer with his scientific and cosmic orientation was somewhat anomalous. By the 1860's a new day had come in the West, and though explorers would still be needed, after the Civil War and the construction of the Pacific Railroad, they would be a very different breed of men.

7. *Cong. Globe*, 34th Cong., 1st and 2nd sess. (1855–56), Vol. XXV, pp. 1297–1298.
8. For an example of this, see Howard R. Lamar: *Dakota Territory* (New Haven, Conn.: Yale University Press; 1956), pp. 177–244.

PORTFOLIO II

Scientific Art and Western Exploration

IN addition to the necessity of representing the Western scene in drawings, paintings, and lithographs for public consumption (the subject of Portfolio I), the process of exploration also generated another, and perhaps more important, artistic problem. This was the problem of how to describe new scientific discoveries that could not be adequately described on a printed page. The scientists and artists who accompanied the Western expeditions resorted to many conventional, and some unconventional, devices in an effort to convey their scientific truths. In the former category, the map immediately comes to mind. This, of course, was a very old device. But during the nineteenth century it was undergoing considerable refinement and was being used in increasingly ingenious and flexible ways, as the series of maps reproduced in this book indicates.

In addition to maps, however, numerous other artistic devices were either adapted or invented to convey the various scientific discoveries of the explorers. These included simple, and not so simple, charts and graphs; incredibly detailed drawings of fossils, plants, and animals; vast, artificially contrived panoramas that were nevertheless more exact than photographs; geological maps, cross-sections, stratigraphic columns, schematic cut-away drawings, and various kinds of landform maps that resemble modern paintings. These devices were of varying degrees of effectiveness and displayed at times a certain lack of skill, but often, in contrast to the paintings and drawings seen in the previous portfolio, they represented an aspect of technical experimentalism not found elsewhere. They constituted a different form of "practitioner" documentary art that revealed, in a significant way, historical changes that were taking place in American scientific endeavor. Moreover, they had important influences on the work of conventional artists. Thus, these scientific artists form an important part of the history of American art and of the story of Western exploration.

The concept of scientific art as such is not new, though its excellence often goes unrecognized. One only has to look to the anatomical studies of Da Vinci or the fortification drawings of Vauban for precedents, or to the engineering blueprints or molecular models of today for recent examples of the tradition which is an important one, particularly for a technologically oriented civilization. The following plates are examples of the scientific art and ingenuity produced by the process of Western exploration.

I

The Complexities of Western Landscape: a Scientific View

Panoramic drawing of the main chain of the Rocky Mountains. Engraving by John Mix Stanley after a drawing by Gustave Sohon, 1854. It would be virtually impossible to take up a position that would encompass this sweeping view of the Rocky Mountains. The artist has composed his view from a number of sketches, indicating the major passes by means of lines and legends. It thus becomes a kind of topographical map. This appears to be a European technique, since it is here introduced by Sohon, and in the Pacific Railroad *Reports* was brought to a high degree of perfection by F. W. von Egloffstein. It was also employed by the Austrian John E. Weyss on the United States–Mexican Boundary Survey. *Courtesy University of Texas Library*

A field sketch for a panoramic drawing. Sketch by Henry Elliott of the Hayden Surveys. The view is of the Sweetwater River Valley, with the Devil's Gate in the distance. *Courtesy National Archives*

The greatest of the panoramic-scientific artists was William H. Holmes (for biographical sketch, see Chapter 14), who was employed first as a topographer for the Hayden Surveys. He become an accomplished geologist and ethnologist, as well as a topographer, while serving with Hayden, and then joined the United States Geological Survey, where he did his greatest work as illustrator for Clarence Dutton's *Tertiary History of the Grand Canyon District,* examples of which are included here. Like the earlier panoramic artists, Holmes had a talent for creating his own artistic perspective which enabled him to portray hundreds of miles of rugged landscape. In addition, he brought to his work a thorough knowledge of topography and geology which enabled him to depict in his drawings the features of physical geology better than any camera study ever could. His pictures were thus visually exciting and also scientifically valuable. They helped, as much as anything else, to form the theories concerning the physical geology of the "Plateau Province" of Utah and Arizona.

View of Green River basin, looking west from Green River. Lithograph from a drawing by W. H. Holmes. A comprehensive view of the mountain man's country, and the Eocene lake beds which were the scene of the Cope–Marsh dinosaur hunts. In the left background are the Uintas; to the right, the Bridger Group. *Courtesy Yale University Library*

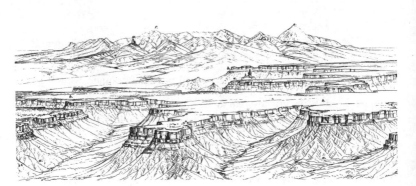

Southwestern border of the Mesa Verde, showing the Sierra El Late in the distance. Lithograph from a drawing by W. H. Holmes, from F. V. Hayden's annual report for 1876. This view looks west across Mancos Canyon, with the southwestern border of Mesa Verde in the distance. *Courtesy Yale University Library*

"The Temples and Towers of the Virgen [Virgin]." Lithograph from a drawing by W. H. Holmes. This and the following three drawings are from the Atlas to Clarence Dutton's *Tertiary History of the Grand Canyon District*. They represent Holmes at his most magnificent. This view looks across the plateau region to the canyons of Zion. *Courtesy University of Texas Library*

"Views Looking East and South from Mt. Trumbull." Lithograph from a drawing by W. H. Holmes. Compare these with the painting by Moran in Portfolio I. Holmes's legends to these pictures read as follows:

"Upper View looking east; the Grand Cañon in the distance. Upon the horizon is the summit of the Kaibab. Glimpses of the Cañon in the Kaibab are given at distances varying from 45 to 85 miles. The opening of Kanab Cañon is seen on the left. On the right Cataract Cañon is seen coming from the South. In the foreground is the upper part of the Toroweap Valley."

"Lower View looking south from a different standpoint: the Grand Cañon in the distance with the opening of the inner gorge. Upon the brink of the gorge stands the crater Vulcan's Throne. The lower Toroweap Valley is on the left. South of the Cañon is another lateral Valley along which runs the Toroweap fault dropping the platform on the west (right). The fore and middle grounds are filled with many basaltic craters. The darkly shaded spots are very recent outpours of basalt." *Courtesy University of Texas Library*

"The Grand Cañon at the Foot of the Toroweap—Looking East." Lithograph from a drawing by William H. Holmes. This is one of a series of drawings of the Grand Canyon which, when placed side by side, cover its entire sweep. The figures in the foreground give an idea of the scale of Holmes's drawing. Note, too, his careful portrayal of the various rock strata. *Courtesy University of Texas Library*

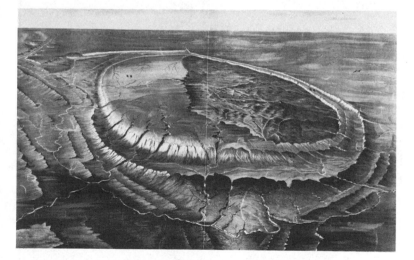

"Bird's Eye View of the Black Hills, to Illustrate the Geological Structure." Lithograph from a drawing by Henry Newton. Halfway between a chart and a panoramic drawing, this unusual schematic picture appeared in Newton and Jenney's report on the Black Hills (see Chapter 11). *Courtesy National Archives*

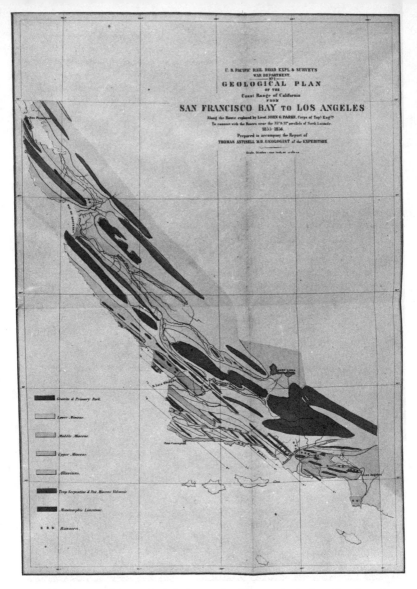

Early geological map of 1856. Drawn by Thomas Antisell, a Scotch geologist who accompanied Lt. J. G. Parke's Pacific Railroad Survey party. Antisell located only two basic formations: Granite or primary rock, and the Miocene. Though working at a rapid pace with a survey party on the move, he was able to map these formations over a considerable area and even to suggest their relationships. Historically, however, the chief significance of this map is that it indicates for the first time deposits of bitumen, or oil, in California. (See Chapter 10 concerning the California oil controversy.) *William H. Goetzmann*

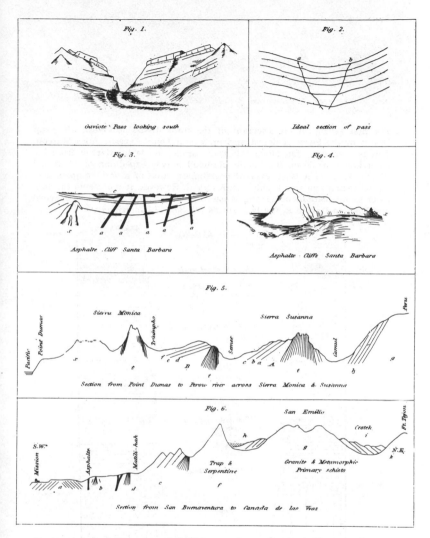

Early geological diagram, 1856. This was drawn by Antisell to supplement the geological map of California. He presents, in Figs. 1–4, external and internal views of geological phenomena in order to suggest their structure. Note his portrayal of the "Asphalte Cliff" at Santa Barbara, where Benjamin Silliman claimed to have discovered oceans of oil. Figs. 5 and 6 are a crude attempt to suggest the relationships of various rock strata by means of a cross-sectional diagram. *William H. Goetzmann*

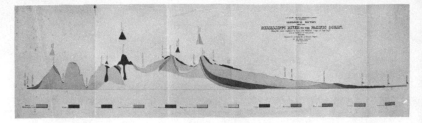

The first geological cross-section of the trans-Mississippi West, 1853–54. Drawn by the Swiss geologist and protégé of Louis Agassiz, Jules Marcou. This is a cross-section along the 35th parallel, made by Marcou from his observations while on the Pacific Railroad Survey expedition of Lt. Amiel Weeks Whipple. It is an evident oversimplification of a very complex geological region and was highly controversial. However, it represents the limits of sophistication concerning Western geology before the work of Hayden and Meek in Dakota in the late 1850's. *William H. Goetzmann*

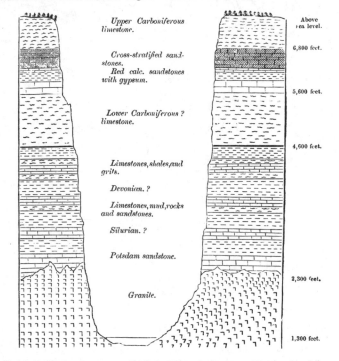

The first geological cross-section of the Grand Canyon. Drawn by John Strong Newberry for Lt. J. C. Ives's report on the Colorado River expedition of 1857. Newberry assembled this stratigraphic column from his own observations while on the Ives expedition. It was one of the most important columns in the history of American geology. Newberry, Hall, and the team of Hayden and Meek are principally responsible for beginning the compilalation of a stratigraphic column for the American West. *William H. Goetzmann*

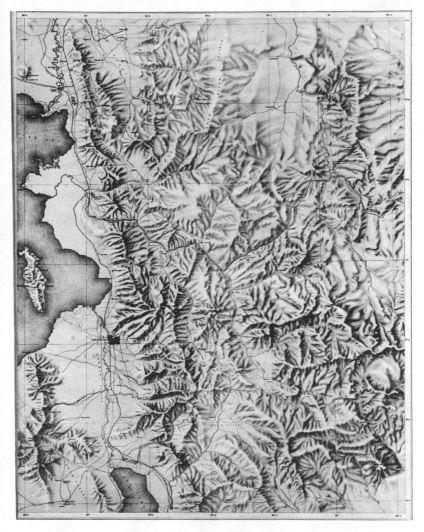

Topographical map of the Wasatch Mountains. Drawn by James Terry Gardner for the Fortieth Parallel Survey, this map, in its attempt to indicate landforms, is a work of art in and of itself. The process of suggesting landforms was introduced in America by F. W. von Egloffstein in his maps for the Ives expedition report. Gardner undoubtedly learned the technique from C. F. Hoffmann, the German topographer of the California Geological Survey. This technique was soon displaced by the more efficient system of contour lines. *Courtesy National Archives*

Geological map of the Wasatch Mountains. This is also from the Atlas to the Fortieth Parallel Survey and indicates the relationship between the topographical map, with its contour lines, and the portrayal of geological data —a vast improvement over the map by Antisell shown above. *Courtesy National Archives*

The Varieties of Natural History

Another aspect of scientific work in the West was the collection of specimens of plants, animals, and fossils. All the new species discovered had to be carefully analyzed, classified, and then depicted in accurate drawings that could be referred to by other scientists in the field. This was important work and required highly specialized skills. The artist not only had to be able to draw and to transfer these drawings onto lithographic stones. He also had to know something about his subject, so as to know what to draw. And he had to envision the specimens as live, rather than dead and therefore inert. Often he achieved this effect by portraying his subject in its typical habitat. Thus almost unconsciously the artist began to introduce the concept of ecology so conspicuously lacking in the work of the scientists themselves. (See pp. 323–4.) In view of the demands placed on the artists, it is not surprising that the best work was done in Europe, particularly in Paris, where J. H. Richard was one of the masters. In the 1850's a few good artists had been trained in America, and the paleontologist F. B. Meek became one of the best illustrators of his own works on invertebrate fossils. The following plates are typical of the exacting and difficult art of scientific illustration in the mid-nineteenth century.

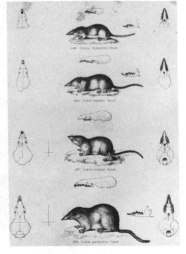

Prairie dog. Pacific Railroad *Reports. Courtesy University of Texas Library*

Views of the shrew. Pacific Railroad *Reports. Courtesy University of Texas Library*

Cactus. Pacific Railroad *Reports*.
Courtesy University of Texas Library

Invertebrate fossils. Pacific Railroad
Reports. This is an example of F. B.
Meek's excellent detailed work. *Cour-
tesy University of Texas Library*

Reptile. Pacific Railroad *Reports*. An example of J. H. Richard's work. *Courtesy University of Texas Library*

Numenius Occidentalis. Sitgreaves *Report*, 1853. Drawn by Edward Kern, artist to the expedition. *Courtesy University of Texas Library*

Skeleton of Phenacodus Vortmani, Cope. From E. D. Cope's "Bible," Vol. III of Hayden's *Final Reports of the United States Geological and Geographical Surveys of the Territories*. The caption reads: "Found in place in the Wasatch Eocene of the Big Horn Basin by J. L. Wortman." *Courtesy University of Texas Geology Library*

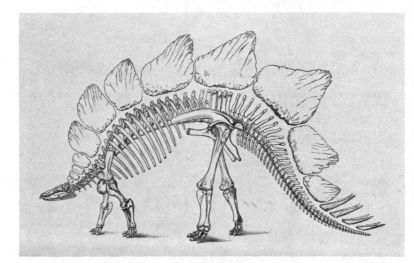

Restoration of Stegosaurus Ungulatus, Marsh. From O. C. Marsh's "The Dinosaurs of North America" in *Sixteenth Annual Report of the United States Geological Survey, 1895. Courtesy University of Texas Geological Library*

Limning the Lost Civilizations

Still another form of scientific art had to do with ethnology and the new science of archeology. Before the camera, the only way of recording and presenting studies of prehistoric Indian cultures was by means of drawings, which, even in the late nineteenth century, were highly romantic in style. Portfolio I presents examples of ethnological art. The illustrations in this section are examples of the artist as archeologist.

Reconstruction of the Pueblo of Hungo Pavie. Lithograph from a drawing by R. H. Kern made on the Simpson expedition to the Navajo country in 1849. This is a reasonably accurate reconstruction. *Courtesy Barker Center for Texas History, University of Texas*

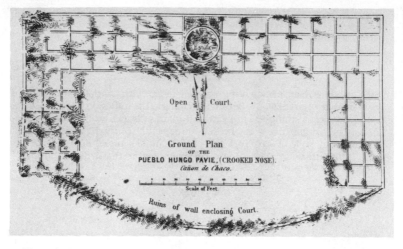

Plan of Hungo Pavie. Kern drawing from the Simpson *Report*. *Courtesy Barker Center for Texas History, University of Texas*

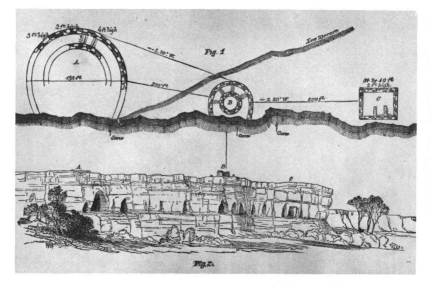

Group of cave dwellings and towers on the Rio San Juan. Lithograph from a drawing by W. H. Holmes published in F. V. Hayden's annual report for 1876. This is from Holmes's report of his exploration of the San Juan sites in 1875 with W. H. Jackson. This work launched Holmes on his illustrious career as an ethnologist. *Courtesy University of Texas Geology Library*

Ruins in the Cañon de Chelly. Lithograph from a drawing by William H. Jackson, published in Hayden's annual report for 1876. *Courtesy University of Texas Geology Library*

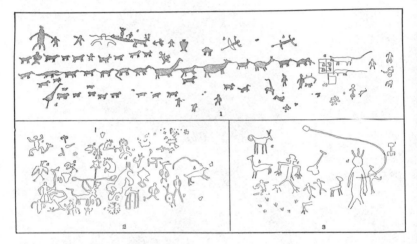

Figures of the Rio San Juan about ten miles below the Rio La Plata. Holmes.
These prehistoric Indian drawings, carved in rock, were copied by Holmes
in 1875. *Courtesy Yale Western Americana Collection*

PART THREE

Exploration

and the Great Surveys

1 8 6 0 - 1 9 0 0

CHAPTER X

The New Mountain Men
California's Geological Survey

THOUGH the federal government and the Army Topographical Engineers had dominated Western exploration in the 1850's, by the end of that decade the civilian scientist had begun to come into his own as Western explorer. No longer the general-purpose naturalist who accompanied the army expeditions, the new scientific explorer tended to be a specialist—most often a geologist or a metallurgist; and he had been trained either in Europe or in the new scientific schools attached to the prominent Eastern colleges like Yale and Harvard. With him, too, came a new technique worked out in the older and more settled regions of the country—the state geological survey. Since 1830, when Professor Edward Hitchcock of Amherst began his classic work in Massachusetts, the state geological survey, with its civilian chief and its corps of consulting experts, had been a standard institution in the older states of the East and South.[1] It was a hallmark of enlightened state administration, a source of local cultural pride, and the means whereby exploitable resources might be cheaply located and advertised to would-be investors. The latter motive, which usually appealed most to legislatures, seldom prevailed in the minds of the survey scientists, however, and the classic model of the state survey was that of New York, which featured as its outstanding contribution James Hall's substantial volumes on the *Palaeontology of New-York*.[2] During the 1850's, teams of scientists worked in Ohio, Illinois, Wisconsin, Michigan, Missis-

1. Merrill: *Geology*, pp. 127–499.
2. James Hall: *Palaeontology*, 8 vols. in 13 (New York: C. Van Benthuysen and Sons; 1847–94). This was part of the Natural History Survey of New York State, of which Hall was a geologist.

sippi, Alabama, Tennessee, and Louisiana. By the end of the decade they had even crossed the Mississippi into Texas, and Iowa, and Kansas, where rich fossil deposits revealed whole new horizons of ancient life.[3] With these surveys, too, the dual image of what the West was and was destined to be assumed even more complex proportions. The geologists and topographers were members of a newer elite community which was fast replacing that formed by the old army. As such, they often saw the West in terms of the scientific rather than the military problems involved. And where they were called upon to apply their knowledge, they thought largely in terms of efficiency and waste. This was in sharp contrast to the ideas of Western legislators and the demands of Western citizens, who had always thought of the West as a place to live in and develop and exploit. To them the geologist was not much different from a fur trader's guide, or a wagon master. His job was to lead them to the promised land and show them the way to its riches.

There arose then in the 1860's still another West to be placed beside the passage to India, the imperial domain, the beaver kingdom, the Great American Desert, the paradise of flocks and herds, the empty Algeria, Arcadia, Golconda, and the Creator's mighty firmament. These had been revealed by explorers in the past. The new West was, by implication, the "resource West," to be revealed by the scientific explorer, but also to be guarded when the occasion demanded against reckless exploitation and the rampant, often illicit speculation that came to characterize the Grant administration, both in the East and in the West. Thus it became clear that in an age which depended upon and demanded exploitation and speculation, the explorer was once again ahead of his time and even running counter to it. Out of his Western experience came conservation and the first great national agencies dedicated to that proposition. It was, however, a sequence of events far more complex than the often portrayed conflict between the "interests" and the guardians of the public domain.

In the 1860's, however, conservation on a national level still lay in the future, obscured by the more immediate concerns of the Civil War. The state survey in the Far West during this period formed a bridge between the old days of army exploration and planning in the West and the more famous era of the national surveys under Clarence King, F. V. Hayden, and John Wesley Powell. And in this respect the California Survey was by far the most important. Ex-

3. Merrill: *Geology*, pp. 293–390.

tending in time from 1860 to 1874, it embodied perfectly the techniques and conflicts of the new era of exploration and exploitation, and it produced many of the men, such as Clarence King, who went on to future greatness in the national surveys. Often overlooked by Western historians and governmental historians alike, the California Survey was not only a model for the later federal surveys. In scope and importance it deserves to be ranked as the first in the series of great surveys that characterized post-Civil War exploration in the Far West.

Moreover, in terms of the explorer's experience, it embodied rich contrasts which paralleled the contrasts of California itself. Monotonous if not depressing surveys of quartz mills and washed-out hydraulic mining sites were more than matched by the moonscapes of Inyo and Owens Valley and by the Big Trees or Lassen's lonely cone. And everything else was capped by the Ruskinian sublimity and breathtaking grandeur of the towering Sierras which these college-bred explorers revealed for the first time to the outside world. For by some twist of fate the men of Yale and Harvard, Freiburg and the École des Mines, helped history to repeat itself—they became, in the 1860's a new generation of mountain men.

1

The California Surveys as such began with the ambitious plans of Josiah Dwight Whitney, their eventual chief, as early as December of 1848. Shortly after the first rush to California, Whitney, who had been running a survey of the Lake Superior copper regions, wrote to his brother William:

California is all the rage now and poor Lake Superior has to be shoved into the background. We are already planning to secure the geological survey of that interesting land, where the farmers can't plough their fields by reason of the huge lumps of gold in the soil.[4]

By mid-January he was at work on a plan to present to the American Academy. But that same year he was called upon to succeed Dr. C. T. Jackson as co-director of the Michigan Surveys, and the Cali-

4. J. D. Whitney to W. D. Whitney, Boston, Dec. 11, 1848, Whitney Papers, Yale Historical Manuscripts Collection. Hereafter referred to as Whitney Papers. Also quoted in Edwin Tenney Brewster: *Life and Letters of Josiah Dwight Whitney* (Boston: Houghton Mifflin Co.; 1909), p. 101.

fornia project had to be abandoned. It was taken up by Philip T. Tyson, who in 1849 toured the gold regions and sent back a report to the Topographical Bureau in Washington which, in attempting to check the gold fever, greatly underestimated the value of the California mineral deposits. His report, when printed as a federal document in 1850, failed, however, to deter any Argonauts.[5]

In 1853, the Senate of California called upon Dr. John B. Trask to submit a further report on the geology of the state. He produced a thirty-one page pioneer work entitled *On the Geology of the Sierra Nevada or California Range*, although he had never really explored the Sierras himself.[6] The California Senate was pleased and urged him on to greater efforts. Eventually, in a series of eight papers, he superficially outlined the geology of California.[7] The Pacific Railroad explorers W. P. Blake, Thomas Antisell, and Jules Marcou also made contributions, but most of their work, like Trask's, was primitive and inadequate.[8] The geology of California was a complex phenomenon, perhaps the most complex of any state, and it demanded more than a few months of hasty reconnaissance to yield up its secrets.

By 1859 Whitney was again interested in the survey and that year he marshaled most of the leading scientists in the country, including Agassiz, Dana, Bache, Joy, and Brush, to support both the project and his directorship of it.[9] On the political side, family connections assured him the support of Judge Stephen J. Field, then the most powerful figure in California politics. Eventually, on April

5. Philip Thomas Tyson: *Geology and Industrial Resources of California* (Baltimore: W. Minafie and Co.; 1851); and *Report of the Sec. of War, Communicating Information in Relation to the Geology and Topography of California by Philip T. Tyson* (Washington, D.C.: U.S. Government Printing Office; 1850).

6. John Boardman Trask: "Report on the Geology of Northern and Southern California, Embracing the Mineral and Agricultural Resources of those Sections . . . ," California Legislative Assembly Session of 1856, *Doc. 114*. Other reports by Trask appear as Calif. Legislative Assembly Documents 9, sess. 1854; *14*, sess. 1855; and a 31-page report in sess. 1853, which is the report referred to in the text.

7. Ibid.

8. *Pacific Railroad Reports*, Vol. VI, Pt. II, pp. 276–7, for Blake; Vol. VII, Pt. II, pp. 35–6, for Antisell; Vol. III, Pt. II, pp. 166 ff.

9. Brewster: *Josiah Dwight Whitney*, p. 186. Also see James D. Dana to J. D. Whitney, New Haven, Jan. 12, 1859; Alexander D. Bache to J. D. Whitney, Washington, Jan. 3, 1859; Chas. A. Joy to J. D. Whitney, Jan. 10, 1859; J. D. Whitney to W. D. Whitney, Jan. 11, 1859; Chas. A. Joy to J. D. Whitney, Jan. 15, 1859; J. D. Whitney to W. D. Whitney, Jan. 13, 1859—all in the Whitney Papers, Yale Historical Manuscripts Collection.

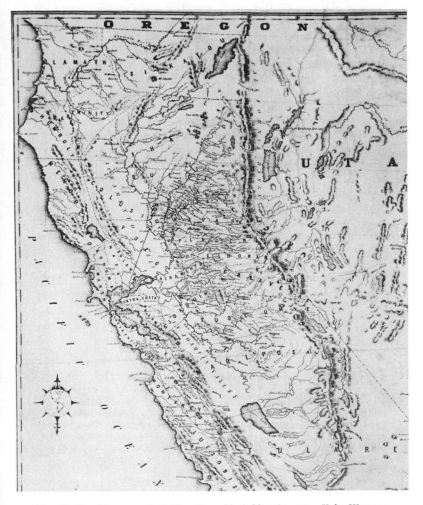

John B. Trask's map of California gold fields. *Courtesy Yale Western Americana Collection*

21, 1860, the geological survey bill became law.[1] Whitney called it "a most enlightened measure," and it must have been especially gratifying since he himself drafted the bill that described the nature and extent of the survey.[2]

The task before him, as he set it down for the legislature, was "to make an accurate and complete Geological Survey of the State, and to furnish . . . proper maps, and diagrams thereof, and with a full and scientific description of its rocks, fossils, soils, and minerals, and of its botanical and zoological productions. . . ."[3] Significantly, no mention was made of a practical survey of resources, for, as Whitney later told the legislature, "it was not the business of a geological surveying corps to act to any considerable extent as a prospecting party."[4]

His salary was $6,000 a year and he was allowed to appoint as many assistants as he saw fit, within the limits of the $20,000 appropriated for the first year's work.[5] Accordingly, on November 14, 1860, he landed in San Francisco with a team that included William H. Brewer, an agricultural chemist; William Ashburner, a relative of Stephen Field; and Chester Averill, a near-sighted Yale student who was being exiled from New Haven for a "college prank."[6] Interestingly, one of the great strengths of Whitney as leader of the Survey was his ability to choose excellent men as assistants.

2

Whitney himself was the epitome of the scientific- and conservation-oriented explorer. A bearded man of medium height, forty-one

1. Brewster: *Josiah Dwight Whitney*, p. 184. Also see Osgood Putnam to J. D. Whitney, San Francisco, Feb. 18, 1859; Feb. 4, 1860; Feb. 22, 1860; Mar. 5, 1860; Mar. 12, 1860; April 4, 1860; April 19, 1860; April 25, 1860; and Henry M. Field to J. D. Whitney, Jan. 12, 1860, Whitney Papers, which present the inside story of Whitney's appointment. Osgood Putnam was Whitney's brother-in-law and served as his campaign manager in California.
2. Brewster: *Josiah Dwight Whitney*, p. 185.
3. Ibid., pp. 184–5.
4. Josiah Dwight Whitney: *Geology*, Vol. I (Philadelphia: Sherman and Co.; 1865), p. xix. This statement is taken from Whitney's address to California Legislature. See J. D. Whitney: *Letters of the State Geologist Relative to the Progress of the State Geological Survey*, 8 vols. in one (San Francisco, 1862, 1863, 1866–67), p. 8.
5. Brewster: *Josiah Dwight Whitney*, pp. 184–5.
6. Ibid., p. 190.

years old, with an aristocratic bearing and a reputation as a wit, Whitney brought to the task the highest qualifications in terms of education and experience that it was possible for a nineteenth-century American to have. He had been educated at George Bancroft's Round Hill School and Yale College, where he was graduated in 1839, a Phi Beta Kappa.[7] Wishing to be a chemist, he had studied long years in Europe—in Paris and Berlin, and eventually at Geissen with the great Liebig himself.

Then he had come home to a job on the New Hampshire State Geological Survey secured for him by his more practical and somewhat impatient father, a banker in Northampton, Massachusetts. Whitney worked on the New Hampshire Survey as assistant to Dr. C. T. Jackson, a rather eccentric man who took time out from his geological work to help invent anesthesia—a mistake which involved him in a long law suit with Wells and Long and other claimants to the invention. As a result, Jackson's achievements were obscured and he was driven to eventual confinement in an asylum. Before this, however, when Jackson became the state geologist of Michigan, Whitney followed as his assistant and together they surveyed the rich copper deposits of the peninsula and the shoreline of Lake Superior. In later years Whitney drew on his extensive experience as a chemist to analyze the ore deposits of Iowa, Illinois, and Wisconsin, incurring the enmity of the citizens of Wisconsin by his refusal to tout the mineral potential of their state.

As a result of this experience, and because of his firm conviction that what was most needed in the mid-century age of mineral booms was a compilation of sober statistical fact, he wrote and published in 1854 *The Metallic Wealth of the United States*.[8] A classic work of Gilded Age scholarship, and the standard reference for twenty years on metallic wealth, it probably helped, more than anything else, to secure legislative support for his directorship of the newly promoted California Survey. Thus, though he was just entering on the major phase of his career, Whitney was already an experienced metallurgist, chemist, and geologist—an able man, hard and uncompromising, with a gruff manner and a whiplash tongue. By virtue of his ability, integrity, and experience, he was already well thought of in the highest scientific circles of the country.

7. Unless otherwise stated, biographical details are based on Brewster: *Josiah Dwight Whitney.*
8. J. D. Whitney: *The Metallic Wealth of the United States* (Philadelphia: Lippincott, Grambo and Co.; 1854).

Whitney's assistant, William H. Brewer, came from a similar background.[9] A graduate of Yale, member of the first class of the Sheffield Scientific School, along with George J. Brush and W. P. Blake, Brewer had likewise studied in Europe—at Heidelberg with Bunsen, in Munich with Liebig, and in Paris with Chevreul. Though most of his training was in chemistry, Brewer's primary interest was in agricultural chemistry, which he taught at Washington College and later for many years at Yale. A brawny, rawboned Dutchman with an easygoing manner and a strong sense of integrity, Brewer was one of the greatest men of the California Survey. He had never met Whitney, and obtained his job through the intercession of Brush. His reason for going to California was to forget the recent death of his young wife and only child.[1]

Ashburner, who was competent, though never up to the rigors of field work, served as the "inside man" who worked up the mineralogical samples. In 1862 he resigned from the Survey to take the less difficult and more lucrative job of mine superintendent. He remained loyal to the Survey, however, and gave his help to it throughout the 1860's. Averill, too, pulled his weight, as packer, instrument man, and topographer even in the highest Sierras.[2]

Later additions to the Survey were William Moore Gabb, a rather conceited but able invertebrate paleontologist; and C. F. Hoffmann, a young German who had been a protégé of Frederick West Lander, the wagon-road surveyor, and who was destined to become one of the great pioneer topographers of the West. In its later stages the Survey was joined by the famous mountaineering pair Clarence King and his friend James T. Gardner. Through the years there were others, but none who figured so prominently or contributed so much as these.

3

Although Whitney deplored superficiality, he saw it as his first task to make a thorough reconnaissance, as quickly as he could, of the whole state of California. With the overall region surveyed, he could then settle down to the long pull of detailed geological

9. William H. Brewer: *Up and Down in California*, Francis Farquhar, ed. (New Haven, Conn.: Yale University Press; 1930), pp. xvii-xxx. This biographical sketch is based on the above and also on the papers of William H. Brewer, Yale Historical Manuscripts Collection.
1. Brewer: *Up and Down in California*, p. 19.
2. Ibid., p. 213.

mapping, which required the analysis in depth of the various rock strata and their fossils. Though he could draw upon the Pacific Railroad Reports and the careful but limited charts of the Coast and Geodetic Survey, it soon became apparent that there existed no satisfactory base map on which he and his assistants could place their geological data. So, almost from the beginning, Whitney's parties engaged in topographic mapping along with their examination of the geological formations.

In many ways, topography became the most important concern of the California Geological Survey, and it was almost certainly one of its most significant achievements. The same could perhaps be said for the great national surveys which followed. First of all, to make it feasible to survey and map the rugged California terrain, improvement had to be made on the older techniques such as the chain and compass method used by the Land Office surveyors, and the base line and odometer-meander system used by the army engineers. Whitney had the answer. In his work on the Lake Superior copper fields he had experimented with the technique of using ordinary surveyor's "fixes" as a basis for the creation of a set of triangles that blanketed the region and measured its distances. Heights could be measured with barometers, and terrain sketched in and hachured on maps. It was a simple system, cheap, relatively accurate, and it made possible the surveying of the Sierras.

This system was not as original as Whitney and his topographer C. F. Hoffmann claimed, however. As early as 1850 Captain Howard Stansbury and Lieutenant John W. Gunnison had used a similar technique to map the Great Salt Lake and nearby Utah Lake.[3] On the Mexican Boundary Survey of 1850–57, Major Emory had brought mountain-peak triangulation to a high degree of refinement, even using night-time signal fires built atop the Southwestern peaks to guide his surveyors.[4] Actually Whitney's method was probably a refinement of the Coast Survey's triangulations as applied by the Army Topographical Engineers to the Lake Surveys. Whitney could have observed such triangulation techniques during his work on Lake Superior in the 1850's.[5] The Coast Surveyors doubtless gained their knowledge from French engineering techniques employed by Hassler and Bache.

3. See, for example, Howard Stansbury: "Report," pp. 151–217, 296–303.
4. William H. Emory: "Report."
5. For an example of the relationship of the Corps of Topographical Engineers to the Lake Surveys, see "Report of the Colonel of the Corps of Topographical Engineers," 31st Cong., 2nd sess., *Sen. Exec. Doc. 1* (1850–51).

C. F. Hoffmann's map of the region adjacent to San Francisco Bay. An example of the excellent topographical maps made for the California Geological Survey by a master of topography. *Courtesy Library of Congress*

Whatever its origin, Whitney's method made possible the later large-scale mapping of the West. It changed the Hayden Surveys and the Wheeler Surveys, and it was from the beginning employed by Clarence King and John Wesley Powell in their work. As such, it played an important part in the development of American science in the Far West.

4

As Whitney saw it, the scientific exploration of California should be divided into four great north-south reconnaissances. The first would encompass the Coast Range and its environs, incorporating the Coast and Geodetic Survey's maps of the harbors and inlets of the coast. The second would follow the western slope of the Sierras northward, concentrating on the mineral regions in that zone. The third followed the crest of the High Sierras; and the fourth, the big bonanza country of the eastern slopes of the mountains from Panamint in the south to Honey Lake in the north. If time and appropriations permitted, Whitney planned to carry the Survey eastward into Nevada, first to the Humboldt Range, then on to Austin and perhaps to Salt Lake in Utah.

During the winter of 1860–61 Whitney and his men tackled the easiest task first. They made Los Angeles their headquarters and explored outward in all directions, concentrating particularly on the country to the south, where they climbed their first mountain, the highest peak in the Santa Ana Range. Dragging their brass-encased barometers up its windswept slope, they began the scientific measurement of California. The view—150 miles in every direction—gave them an idea of the complicated terrain of desert and mountain and coastline that they would be required to map.[6]

Gradually, in the course of their work, Whitney's party took shape. Though they were not as tough or picturesque as the men of the California Boundary Survey, who were recruited from the slums of San Francisco and rode out into the Mojave Desert and Death Valley aboard a string of bellowing camels that same season, Whitney's New England academicians slowly but surely became Westerners.[7] They acquired flamboyant cowhide boots, rough flannel shirts, broad-brimmed hats, and on occasion they strapped on

6. Brewer: *Up and Down in California*, pp. 37–8. The first days of the California Survey are chronicled on pp. 11–41.
7. Ibid., p. 30.

guns. Brewer, in particular, learned the value of tough, durable trousers after several mountain excursions left his city pants an embarrassing heap of rags.[8]

They learned to sleep in the open, on an old oilcloth and a blanket; to cook out over an open fire, and eat almost anything. They also learned to pitch a Sibley tent and peg it with more guy ropes than the army manual specified. They acquired the skill to wash clothes in a muddy creek without falling in; to carry packs and delicate instruments up the steepest trails and the highest mountains in spite of weather conditions. They even learned to handle, and perhaps admire, the cantankerous California mule.

With Southern California mapped, and their team well formed, they headed up the coastline to Santa Barbara and beyond, mapping as they went. Near Santa Barbara, Brewer noted a great "asphaltum" deposit that spread out over the countryside and was used by the local people for making roofs on their adobe houses. It "will be the source of some considerable wealth," Brewer wrote, little realizing its implications for the future course of the California Survey.[9]

For most of the spring of 1861 they followed the Coast Road past Santa Inez, San Luis Obispo, and Carmel to Monterey. Then they surveyed the Salinas Valley, a hot dusty valley where scorching winds funneled down out of the mountains to the sea. Near San Jose they met a party of what must have been the very earliest California tourists heading for the nearby hot springs.[1] This was a most uncharacteristic experience for an explorer since two thirds of the party were ladies. Despite these distractions, they reached San Francisco, where headquarters was established in the old Montgomery Block Building, and from this point on, Brewer more and more assumed command of the field parties while Whitney commuted back and forth between the field encampments and the survey workrooms in San Francisco. Much of Whitney's time was of necessity spent in lecturing the state legislature on the value of his geological survey. And at the same time he also began conferring with state officials about the establishment of the new College of California to be dedicated to the useful sciences.[2]

8. Ibid., p. 37.
9 Ibid., p. 59.
1. Ibid., p. 98.
2. J. D. Whitney to W. D. Whitney, Placer County, April 29, 1861, Dardenelles Diggings; J. D. Whitney to W. D. Whitney, San Francisco, Feb. 12, 1862; J. D. Whitney to G. J. Brush, San Francisco, Feb. 20, 1860; J. D. Whitney to W. D. Whitney, San Francisco, Feb. 28, 1862; J. D. Whitney to G. J. Brush, San Francisco, June 11, 1862.

In July, Hoffmann officially joined the Survey and J. F. Cooper signed on as zoologist and collector. Most of the summer season was spent in examining the New Idria and New Almaden quicksilver mines and in exploring the approaches to San Francisco Bay.[3] Hoffmann set to work almost immediately on an official map of the Bay. In the fall, Brewer and his men explored the Monte Diablo Range, examining its Carboniferous formations as the key to Coast Range geology. Then, before winter, they visited northern California's Napa Valley and the Geyser region.[4]

In the early spring of 1862 disaster struck. Torrential, unremitting rains blanketed the state, causing immense damage. Sacramento looked like Venice, with the water nearly up to the second stories of the raw-pine buildings. Roads were impassable, mines unworkable, sluices swept away. Worst of all, for Whitney's Survey, the state treasury was emptied.[5] Though funds were appropriated, no money was forthcoming, and in the season of 1862 Whitney was forced to reduce operations drastically. Cooper was laid off. Ashburner resigned. Whitney and Brewer, however, still took to the field, financed by a loan from Whitney's father in Northampton.

In the summer of 1862 they explored the entire Monte Diablo Range south of San Francisco Bay, the Sacramento River country (in spite of the floods), and went as far north as Mount Shasta, where on September 12, 1862, after a difficult climb, they reached the fog-enshrouded summit. According to Brewer, it was "a mere pinnacle of lava shooting up into the air . . . and only reached with some daring."[6] Atop the mountain, they drooped with fatigue. Lips and fingernails turned blue from lack of oxygen. Several of the men fell sick. And due to the fog they gained only occasional glimpses of the landscape below. All in all, it was hardly the triumphant climb that romantics like John Muir or Frémont might have pictured. It was, rather, a difficult scientific achievement, and when

---

Also Brewster: *Josiah Dwight Whitney*, p. 241. See also voluminous correspondence between Whitney and Daniel Coit Gilman concerning the new College of California, Whitney Papers.

3. Brewer: *Up and Down in California*, pp. 135–66.

4. Ibid., pp. 191–237.

5. Ibid., pp. 241–53. See especially pp. 245–6 for a discussion of the state treasury. Also see J. D. Whitney to W. D. Whitney, San Francisco, March 10, 1862.

6. Brewer: *Up and Down in California*, pp. 255–323. See p. 315 for quote. Pages 315 ff chronicle the ascent of Mt. Shasta. Page 323 indicates something of the condition of the surveyors after the climb.

they finished they had measured the highest mountain then known in the United States.

The return march took them once again down the Sacramento and through the gold fields, where reckless miners and callous saloon keepers in time-honored fashion still shot, stabbed, and staggered one another regularly.[7] By December of 1862 Whitney and his men had made a great survey up and down the western half of the state, charting its mountain peaks, totaling its resources, and examining its mineral strikes. Brewer estimated that in 1862 alone he had traveled some 9,264 miles—2,067 miles of it on foot.[8] Moreover, along with Averill, Hoffmann, and the young paleontologist Gabb, he had survived the wreck of an excursion boat off Alcatraz Island and a major earthquake which had rocked the old Montgomery Block.[9]

5

The season of 1863, however, was even more important. Working now as an experienced team, Brewer and his men tackled the western slope of the Sierra from Tehachapi northward. Besides examining the chief mineral sites, they came into first contact with some of California's greatest natural wonders. They explored the Kern River and Walker's Pass, then the King's River with its towering canyons. Then they passed through the groves of Big Trees from Kaweah to Calaveras, measuring their height and marveling at their dimensions. According to Brewer, even the prostrate trees were impressive. One was hollow and so large that a man could ride some 80 feet along its central cavity. When they reached Yosemite, Brewer termed it "not only the greatest natural curiosity in this state, but one of the most remarkable in the world."[1]

The men of the California Survey were not the discoverers of Yosemite. In 1833 Joseph Reddeford Walker and his men had crossed over the Sierras along the Divide to the north of the valley, having learned of its existence from their Indian guides (see Chapter 5). Then in January of 1851 a party of ex-Texas Rangers, pressed into service as militia under the command of Major James D. Savage, a former mountain man, entered Yosemite proper in

7. Ibid., pp. 325–44. See especially pp. 330–1.
8. Ibid., p. 353.
9. Ibid., pp. 355–8.
1. Ibid., pp. 375–413. See especially pp. 399, 403.

pursuit of Chief Ten-ie-ya's band of Yosemite Indians who had been raiding white settlements. When from the plateau that forms Mount Beatitude they gained their first view of the valley and the stupendous cliffs of El Capitan, even the Texans were stunned. Dr. Lafayette Houghton Bunnell, chronicler of the Mariposa Battalion, remembered: "The grandeur of the scene was but softened by the haze that hung over the valley—light as gossamer—and by the clouds which partially dimmed the higher cliffs and mountains . . . as I looked, a peculiar exalted sensation seemed to fill my whole being, and I found my eyes in tears with emotion."[2] Presumably his ruder companions of the trail experienced similar emotions as they moved into the awesome Indian stronghold.

Though the men of Major Savage's Mariposa Battalion did not succeed in routing the Indians in the winter of 1851, they had in effect discovered and first explored what is now the national park. Moreover Dr. Bunnell, according to his own testimony, proposed that it should be named after their Indian adversaries—the "Yosemity"—a proposal that was adopted by a voice vote of the members of the battalion.[3] Subsequently, in 1852, Lieutenant Moore of the United States Army also led a military detachment into the valley and in the report of his campaign changed Bunnell's "Yosemity" to "Yosemite," a term acceptable to all.[4] Every year after 1852, except 1854, the Yosemite was visited by groups of explorers and curiosity-seekers. In 1855 J. M. Hutchings, the San Francisco journalist, climaxed these ventures by publishing an account of his trip to the natural wonderland, complete with an illustration of the towering Yosemite Falls.[5] For years afterward *Hutchings Illustrated California Magazine* devoted much of its space to publicizing the scenic marvels of Yosemite—a development that was paralleled by the sublime artistic representations of the region painted by Thomas Hill and Albert Bierstadt.

The new mountain men of the California Geological Survey, on the other hand, were not initially interested in the beauty of Yosemite. At first their attention was attracted by the scientific problem of the valley's geological formation. As such they searched out the marks of ancient glaciation and other evidences of the titanic

2. Lafayette Houghton Bunnell: *Discovery of the Yosemite and the Indian War of 1851 Which Led to that Event* (Los Angeles: G. W. Gerlicher; 1911), p. 63. See also pp. 78–9.
3. Ibid., p. 70.
4. Ibid., p. 71.
5. Ibid., p. 75.

earth-shaping processes that had created it. So enormous were these Merced River canyons that, trained geologist though he was, Whitney could never bring himself to accept the theory that they were created by glaciers and erosion alone. He believed that a series of catastrophes had taken place, and each time a great fault block had dropped out of the bottom of Yosemite, making the canyon floor sink lower and lower.[6]

Though Whitney was keenly interested in the geology of the Yosemite region, he too appreciated it as scenery. Indeed, in the California Surveys he regarded it as a public resource, something that must be preserved against private exploitation and opened up for the enjoyment of the people. Though no one can be certain of the exact genesis of the National Park idea, Whitney and the men of the California Survey were among the most influential of those who urged President Lincoln to grant the area to the state of California to be set aside for public enjoyment.[7] And when in 1864 Yosemite was so given to the state of California, Whitney, Brewer, and Hoffmann were prominent on the first board of trustees, of which Frederick Law Olmsted served as first chairman.[8] The preservation of regions of special beauty was a new concept of what constituted a natural resource, and in Whitney's published report of the California Survey in 1865 may perhaps be documented the first official use of these natural wonders in a direct appeal to tourists. In this sense, Whitney tied in the park idea with the practical search for new people and new capital that preoccupied California and other frontier societies of the day. This was the beginning of a regional pattern of thought that has persisted and grown to major proportions as a characteristic Western industry.

6

While in the Yosemite country, the California Survey party made its first contact with the High Sierras. Brewer and Hoffmann scaled Mount Dana and from its heights saw mountain peaks in every direction, most of which they named for the first time. Far in the distance to the east was Mono Lake, and Brewer and Hoffmann

6. Whitney: *Geology*, p. 421.
7. J. D. Whitney: *Yosemite Book* (New York: J. Bien; 1868), p. 10.
8. Ibid. See also *Report of the Commissioners to Manage Yosemite Valley . . . For the Years, 1866–67* (San Francisco: Towne and Bacon; 1867).

headed for it while Whitney went back to San Francisco for more funds to continue the field work.[9] By this time their labors had begun to reach the spectacular in achievement and excitement. From Mono Lake, which they mapped for the first time, the party headed north to the Washoe country on the eastern slopes of the Sierras and moved slightly beyond to Lake Tahoe and then back over the Sierra to the American River. In the first weeks of September, the party disbanded and Brewer took a river steamer out of Sacramento bound for San Francisco to secure more funds with which to continue his work. On that occasion he met Clarence King and James T. Gardner, fresh from Yale and looking for a California adventure.[1] They quickly agreed to join the Survey as volunteers, and when Brewer once again returned to the northern mines, King went with him. Together, on the twenty-sixth and again on the twenty-ninth of September 1863, they climbed the extinct cobalt cone of Lassen's Peak. Clearly visible through the cold frosty air on the twenty-ninth were the Coast Range, Mount St. Helena, St. John, the dim outline of Mount Diablo far away to the south of San Francisco Bay, and looming relatively nearby, the gray-blue mass of Mount Shasta.[2] On his first trip out with the California Survey, King had been treated to one of its greatest experiences.

From Lassen's Peak, Brewer and King moved westward, surveying all the counties of northern California as far as Crescent City on the shores of the Pacific. This task completed, they embarked on the steamer *Oregon* bound for San Francisco. By the end of November, they had reached headquarters and the conclusion of the season's labors. It was now winter and the time to prepare explications of the year's activities for the California legislature— a task no less formidable than the field surveys themselves.

7

Since, according to the California constitution, all offices created by the legislature automatically expired after four years, the winter legislative session of 1863–64 was an especially crucial one for Whitney. The entire future of the Survey, as well as his directorship, was at stake and he struggled mightily to maintain both. By

9. Brewer: *Up and Down in California*, pp. 408–12.
1. Ibid., pp. 415–52. See especially pp. 451–2 for Brewer's description of his meeting with King and Gardner.
2. Ibid., pp. 460–6.

1864, however, despite the heroic deeds of the explorer-scientists, enthusiasm for the Survey had lessened considerably. Whatever political patronage it afforded had already been dispensed and so it no longer attracted votes. Moreover, not many local California men had been chosen for work on the Survey in any case. The image of dominance by the Eastern colleges rankled many California citizens, and a number of men connected with the new California College in Oakland banded together in support of W. P. Blake, whom, though he was also a Yale man, they considered a local geologist and more deserving of the post of survey director.[3]

Still another group which opposed Whitney consisted of clergymen, some of whom had heard his strong defense of Darwinism and natural selection, delivered to the legislature the previous year. In their view, instead of revealing the mind of the Creator at work in the world, Whitney's surveyors were blaspheming His works and scrambling the order of creation by continually unearthing strange fossils.[4] As an additional argument against the Survey, they pointed out that the only publication produced by Whitney and his men was William Moore Gabb's *Paleontology*, an impractical and possibly blasphemous work.[5] Instead of turning his attention to matters of immediate economic concern to the state, ran the argument, Whitney had merely studied fossils. He had located no new mineral resources, and, what was worse, he had pronounced negatively on more than half the mineral strikes he and his men examined, thereby dashing hopes in many quarters. In so doing, it was thought, they had discouraged new capital from entering the state. Booming California, Whitney's detractors maintained, did not need a nay-sayer. It needed "positive thinking" to attract attention to state opportunities.[6] In Whitney's negative pronouncements and in his strong advocacy of conservation, there was more than a hint that he considered his role to be that of regulator as well as explorer. Strong regulation could hamper speculative opportunity for the expectant capitalist of the middle class. It was therefore intolerable to Californians, especially as administered by an outsider from the East.

In the face of mounting opposition, Whitney refused to compromise on his principles. He did not even bother to explain that

3. J. D. Whitney to Father, April 5, 1864, Whitney Papers.
4. Brewster: *Josiah Dwight Whitney*, pp. 299–300.
5. Ibid.
6. For an example of this type of criticism, see San Francisco *Daily Alta California*, March 6, 1864.

Gabb's work in paleontology, and his own work, had been directed toward pinpointing the exact strata in which the gold deposits occurred, thus facilitating their detection. Doubtless, there were few in his legislative audiences during the past years who even knew what he meant by "auriferous" deposits and strata, in any case. Yet the opposition to Whitney's Survey was not to be dismissed lightly. It was an important historical phenomenon in that it epitomized a Western structure of values that for the rest of the nineteenth century bred opposition to Western public works directed from the East. In less than twenty years, the Californians, who were themselves mostly immigrants, had developed a regional self-consciousness to the point where they were prepared actively to resist outside direction that did not seem to coincide with their immediate interests. Theirs might be considered a variety of Far Western anticolonialism that accepted the institutions of the East and the cultural benefits to be derived therefrom but which at the same time came more and more to insist that they work for the local rather than the national welfare. Weller's rebuke of the Topographical Engineers in 1856 and the reaction of the California legislature to Whitney in 1864 are clear indicators of this emerging attitude.

The result for Whitney and his men, therefore, was a partial but insignificant defeat. A new bill which sustained the Survey and Whitney was passed, but it markedly changed his duties. With his salary and appropriations cut in half, and the agricultural, botanical, and zoological work suppressed, Whitney was ordered to devote his time to "a thorough and scientific examination of the gold, silver, and copper producing districts of this State, and to make such scientific and practical experiments as will be of value in the discovery of mines and the working and reduction of ores."[7] He was thus to abandon scientific speculation and attend to the "practical" concerns of prospecting. Characteristically, Whitney did not waste time pondering the meaning of the new measure. As soon as funds were assured, he and his wife embarked on a steamer for New York. He wanted to see to the printing of his reports and to compare notes with his scientific colleagues in the East.

8

Despite the legislative reversals, the season of 1864 was perhaps the most spectacular for the Survey. Even before Whitney left for

7. Brewster: *Josiah Dwight Whitney*, p. 235.

the East, he had gotten the year's work underway. He sent King, Hoffmann, and Gabb on a scientific reconnaissance of the Yosemite. King returned with fossil specimens from the Mariposa region which provided the final and conclusive evidence for dating the gold-bearing slates in the Jurassic period and the auriferous gravels in the Pliocene—one of the most important discoveries made by the Survey.[8]

Also, before his departure for the East, Whitney took King with him on a survey of the Comstock Lode, and the country east of the Sierras. King's particular duties were to make barometer readings to determine the altitude of Lake Tahoe, and to run a survey as far east as the Humboldt Range in furtherance of Whitney's plans for extending his survey all across the Great Basin. While engaged in this independent assignment, King first got the idea for his own Fortieth Parallel Surveys, conducted later.[9] It is some indication of Whitney's incredible energy and dedication that he managed to see to all of these operations while at the same time doing constant battle with the legislature during the crucial spring period.

While Whitney was in the East, the Survey continued under Brewer's direction. With what was left of the annual appropriation, Brewer, King, Hoffmann, Gardner, and Richard Cotter carried out the first full-scale exploration of the High Sierras, in which, as a later writer remarked, they added an area to the map of California which was "as large as Massachusetts and as high as Switzerland."[1] Carrying their barometers and theodolites up the towering Sierras, they became latter-day mountain men of a wholly different sort, but nonetheless explorers and discoverers.

Brewer's party left J. Ross Browne's establishment near Oakland on May 25, 1864.[2] Their line of march took them south along the Bay to its head, then across Pacheco Pass and into the San Joaquin Valley. There for the next week they rode south across a parched and dreary wasteland blown by whirlwinds and dust devils and dotted with dead and dying cattle. At Visalia the soldiers eagerly volunteered as escorts to the expedition, to escape the awful valley heat. Once beyond Visalia, the scenery changed. The Big Trees

8. Whitney: *Geology*, pp. xiii–xiv.
9. Ibid., p. 224; King: *Mountaineering in the Sierra Nevada*, Thurman Wilkins, ed. (Philadelphia: J. B. Lippincott; 1963), p. 179; Thurman Wilkins: *Clarence King* (New York: The Macmillan Co.; 1958), pp. 61–2.
1. Brewster: *Josiah Dwight Whitney*, pp. 237–8.
2. Brewer: *Up and Down in California*, p. 505. The progress of the party is chronicled by Brewer on pp. 505–32.

became prominent, then the rushing mountain streams, then the high grassy meadows, and finally in the distance, the towering mountains.

From Thomas' Mill on the Kaweah the route was upward along the divide between that river and Boulder Creek. Upon ascending Mount Silliman, they could see, far ahead, their initial destination —a prominent peak, which was soon named Mount Brewer. From this point on, they struggled upward across rushing torrential streams and along huge moraines piled up by former glaciers along the mountain wall. By the first of July they were at the foot of Mount Brewer and ready for the ascent. Brewer and Hoffmann went up first—a long bitter climb which left them exhausted atop the mountain's summit at two o'clock in the afternoon. But the climb had been worth it, for from the top of Mount Brewer, over 14,500 feet high, they could see in all directions. Most important, they could see, five miles ahead and across an immense gorge to the east and south, a range studded with peaks higher even than Mount Brewer, upon which they stood at the cost of such great labor.[3]

When they returned to camp they were too weary to talk, but their very silence intrigued King, and Hoffmann's sketches of the distant peaks confirmed King's impressions gained in looking south from Mariposa the previous month. "I instantly recognized the peaks," he wrote, "whose great white pile had led me to believe them the highest points of California."[4]

The next day was July 4, 1864, and taking Richard Cotter with him, King decided to try for "the top of California."[5] Assisted by Brewer and Gardner, they first scaled the main ridge of Mount Brewer, where they were confronted by the great gorge and "the black granite walls, the thousand granite spires, the vast fields of snow and frozen lakes," and most of all, "the awful desolation."[6] The only way, as King saw it, across the gorge was a high narrow ridge that stood like a blade between the mountain ranges and divided the Kern and King's rivers. Across this ridge King and Cotter made their way. Sometimes they lowered themselves by ropes from ledge to ledge. At other times they cut steps on the ice, clawed niches out of the rock with their fingers, or made a quick glissade down a snow slide, tumbling over and over, packs and all. They spent a cold night camped out on a ledge of lumpy feldspathic

3. Ibid., pp. 524–5.
4. King: *Mountaineering in the Sierra Nevada*, p. 50.
5. Ibid.
6. Ibid., p. 51.

granite listening to rock slides rumbling ominously overhead. Then, the next morning at four, they began again climbing up a sheer wall, crevice by crevice, until at last they ascended a slender spire of ice and fell over onto the narrow crag near the summit. The rest of the climb was easy. They reached the crest at exactly twelve o'clock, King recorded. And though, as they could see from the summit, they had not yet reached "the top of California," for towering Mount Whitney lay still before them, they had come where no one else had ever come before them. In triumph King rang his hammer upon the topmost rock. "We grasped hands," he wrote, "and I reverently named the grand peak MOUNT TYNDALL."[7]

The descent and return from Mount Tyndall was more difficult still than the upward climb. Even allowing for King's embellishments in *Mountaineering in the Sierra Nevada*, it was one of the great mountain adventures.[8] When they arrived back at Brewer's camp five days later, King simply reported "twice on the way Cotter came within a hair's breadth of losing his life and once I almost gave myself up."[9] When informed of their feat, Whitney wrote: King "deserves a gold medal for his pluck."[1] Yet Whitney's failure to exploit such feats handicapped his survey before the legislature —a mistake that later government explorers and surveyors rarely made.

King's ascent of Mount Tyndall was not his only achievement during the expedition, however. While Brewer and Hoffmann and Gardner packed up and moved onto the South Fork of the King's River, King and Cotter made an unsuccessful attempt to scale Mount Whitney itself, which they recognized as the highest point of land in California. Before he could reach the summit, King was stopped by "a soaring wall, three or four hundred feet from the top." It was all he could do to hang out his barometer in the slashing wind and fight off the strange drowsiness that attacked him at that high altitude.[2]

While King and Cotter were making their assault on Mount Whitney, Brewer had led his men, including Hoffmann, who was now lame with painful rheumatism, through the gigantic gorge

7. Ibid., p. 75.
8. Ibid., pp. 76–93. Whitney: *Geology*, pp. 385 ff., contains a less dramatic version of King's feat.
9. Quoted in Whitney: *Geology*, p. 387. Also quoted in Wilkins: *Clarence King*, p. 70.
1. Quoted in Wilkins: *Clarence King*, p. 70.
2. Ibid., p. 73.

of the South Fork of King's River, up over what came to be called Kearsarge Pass and down past Inyo into Owen's Valley. From there their route was northward through Owen's Valley, their progress marked by ominous Indian signal fires.[3]

On the second of August they turned westward and recrossed the mountains at Mono Pass, from whence they descended with the greatest difficulty over the broken country along Mono Creek to the headwaters of the San Joaquin. By this time Hoffmann was in such pain and so helpless that he had to be tied to his horse. Whitney lost thirty pounds. Gardner too was exhausted. But at last they reached the rendezvous point at Galen Clark's ranch below the Yosemite. King had been waiting there for three weeks when they pulled in. "We were a hard-looking set," Brewer remembered, "ragged, clothes patched with old flour bags."[4] Thus concluded perhaps the most spectacular exploration ever made in the High Sierras. In the course of their adventures, the Brewer and King parties had managed not only to scale the heights. They had measured them, charted their position, sketched in the topography, and in so doing had changed the entire map of the West in a significant way. Scientists with an appreciation for the sublime as well as the exact in nature, they had been Ruskins on a grand scale, and most of their sentiments were crystallized in two great volumes —Whitney's *Geology*, which in spite of its sober scientific format still could not conceal their grand adventure, and King's classic *Mountaineering in the Sierra Nevada*, the prime Ruskinian document of the age. Like Irving's *Bonneville*, Frémont's *Narrative*, and Powell's *Colorado River*, King's *Mountaineering* had one of the great stories of Western exploration to tell, and it told it superbly well—so much so that it belongs with these other classics which helped forge an image of the West as an exotic place fit to match the imagination of a Moran or a Bierstadt.

9

In September of 1864 the governor of California signed a bill that officially accepted Yosemite for the state as a "public pleasure ground." By the time Brewer and his men reached San Francisco, then, a new task confronted them. An exact survey of Yosemite

3. Brewer: *Up and Down in California*, pp. 533–40.
4. Ibid., pp. 539–47. See especially pp. 546–7.

and its environs had to be made. So, with scarcely a week's rest, King and Gardner were ordered into the field to complete the work before the onset of winter.

King, Gardner, and Cotter set out on October 5th and when they reached Yosemite made their headquarters in two cabins near Black's Hotel.[5] Preliminary to beginning the exact survey of the valley, they scaled the heights—first the northern wall, then El Capitan, which looked 3,000 feet down onto the floor of the valley. King, with an eye to the total landscape, became interested in the larger problem of the origin of the whole Merced country rather than in the survey of the park boundary lines. As a result, Gardner did most of the topographical work and the mapping while King climbed the various domes and peaks and speculated about the actions of glaciers and the possibility of cataclysm in forming Yosemite's massive amphitheater.[6]

Before they finished the survey, winter set in with a tremendous snowstorm, and by the end of October it was all they could do to survive. Somehow, however, they ran the survey of the south boundary of the park, sketched in the valley floor (quite inaccurately, as it turned out), and made a final rendezvous at Galen Clark's ranch. So severe were their exertions that Cotter nearly perished and King had to carry him through the blizzard the final distance to the ranch.

While King was returning from the High Sierras, Brewer began sounding their depths. In November of 1864 he went to Virginia City, where for the first time he examined the mines in detail, noting that many of them had passed their peak of production. He descended some 500 feet into the Gould and Curry Mine in a small cage let down by a rope, and once underground, experienced a sensation that was exactly opposite from the heady freedom of the Sierras. "Here and there a candle sheds a feeble light," he wrote. "Long, dark galleries or 'drifts' run from the landing place, with narrow railroad tracks in them. . . ." He could hear the rumble of loaded ore carts, the clatter of picks and drills, and the ominous groan of a pump keeping back the water from the lower galleries.

Stage by stage they climbed back up the mine levels, sometimes wandering through the darkened galleries into the Savage Mine which adjoined the Gould and Curry deep underground. Once they

5. Wilkins: *Clarence King*, p. 78.
6. Ibid., pp. 78–80. Also see "Field Notes and Observations on the Yosemite Valley and Surrounding Country, Oct.–Nov. 1864," B-2, King Papers, Henry E. Huntington Library.

passed a little black hole that fell away some 115 feet. A miner's body had been recovered from it only a few days before. Everywhere water seeped in and only the timbers seemed to keep the whole earth from falling in upon them. It was a new kind of exploring experience for Brewer and he enjoyed it thoroughly.[7]

It was just as well that he visited Virginia City when he did, however, because it proved to be his last opportunity to do so. He received a professorship in the Sheffield Scientific School at Yale and his days as a Western explorer, though not ended, were to be ever afterward more restricted.[8] When he boarded the steamer on November 14, 1864, at San Francisco, it was his farewell to the California Surveys. With his last season a fitting climax to his great labors as a scientific explorer, Brewer went back East to another career at Yale. But he was not entirely finished with California or its problems.

10

While investigating the Comstock mines, Brewer met a New Havener who eventually became the nemesis of the California Survey. He was Professor Benjamin Silliman, Jr., a chemistry teacher at Yale, and the son of the founder of the Sheffield Scientific School. By 1864 Silliman had gained great fame both as a mining consultant and as the country's foremost expert on petroleum. Almost singlehanded, he had started silver rushes in Austin and Reese River, Nevada, but he was most famous as the man whose advice on the valuable illuminating properties of oil had prompted the New Haven Railroad conductor Daniel Drake to drill for oil at Titusville, Pennsylvania, in 1859, thereby starting a worldwide boom and a new industry. Suave, handsome, intelligent, Silliman belonged to what passed for New Haven aristocracy. He was a friend to the great on both sides of the Atlantic and he was a particular friend of men with money to invest. His entrepreneurial instincts brought him to the Comstock in 1864 on a rapid mineralogical survey of Nevada and California. Upon the completion of what proved to be a convivial reconnaissance, Silliman returned East and began to float a series of gigantic oil-prospecting companies based on the expectation of finding, as he put it, "fabulous

7. Brewer: *Up and Down in California*, pp. 551–9. See especially pp. 355–6.
8. Ibid., p. 548.

wealth in the best of oil."[9] According to Silliman, oil was so plentiful in California that it floated in the sea off Santa Barbara and rose to the surface inland at Ojai Ranch and numerous other places in great pools of "asphaltum" (see p. 341, Portfolio II). In Santa Barbara County, he wrote in one prospectus, "you have . . . a remarkable and almost unrivaled source of supply of mineral oil, favorably situated for cheap extraction and delivery on the seaboard."[1] To exploit these "deposits," many of which had been briefly worked and abandoned in Spanish days, Silliman was instrumental in floating at least three speculating companies, Pacific Coast Petroleum Company of New York (capital stock, $5,000,000), San Buenaventura Pacific Petroleum Company of New York, and the Philadelphia and California Petroleum Company.[2] Thus began what came to be known as the "Great California Oil Bubble."

Silliman's dramatic discovery of huge sources of untapped wealth in California was almost immediately a near-fatal blow to Whitney's survey. Why had not the state geologists in their excursions up and down the state found such resources?[3] Only the San Francisco *Bulletin* for February 10, 1865, and the *Mining Press* bothered to refute Silliman's claim (calling it a "swindle" and an "oily gammon").[4] And the bubble grew bigger as back East the Yale chemist made a specialty of giving deliberately restrained evening lectures on California oil to parties of credulous capitalists who sat captivated by the steady flickering light generated by a lampful of "pure" California oil.[5]

Whitney, caught off guard, sent William Ashburner, his chemist, into the oil region to investigate the claims, but so uncertain was he

9. *D.A.B.* For a detailed report on Silliman's promotional activities, see J. D. Whitney to W. D. Whitney, Boston, March 1, 1865; J. D. Whitney to W. D. Whitney, Boston, March 10, 1865; W. D. Whitney to J. D. Whitney, New Haven, March 24, 1865; March 28, 1865; April 9, 1865. Silliman's comment appears in Benjamin Silliman, Jr.: *Prospectus for the Pacific Coast Petroleum Co. of New York* (New York, 1865), Box 31, Brewer Papers, Yale Historical Manuscripts Collection.

1. Benjamin Silliman, Jr.: *Prospectus for the San Buenaventura Pacific Petroleum Co. of New York* (New York, 1865), p. 24, Brewer Papers, Yale Historical Manuscripts Collection.

2. *Document of Suit in Equity Against the Philadelphia and California Petroleum Company by R. L. Ashurst and E. Spencer Miller, Solicitors for the Complainants,* No. 53, January Term, 1867, Brewer Papers, Yale Historical Manuscripts Collection.

3. J. D. Whitney to W. D. Whitney, Boston, March 10, 1865; March 8, 1867.

4. J. D. Whitney to W. D. Whitney, Boston, March 10, 1865; March 20, 1865, Whitney Papers.

5. W. D. Whitney to J. D. Whitney, New Haven, March 24, 1865; March 28, 1865; April 9, 1865.

of the results that, as he later put it in a letter to his brother: "I concluded to turn my thoughts to Harvard."[6]

From New Haven, however, on March 21, 1865, Brewer dashed off a letter to the Springfield *Republican* exposing the oil scheme.[7] When Ashburner's analysis confirmed the earlier report of Humphrey Storer, the New Haven chemist to whom Whitney had sent his first oil samples in 1862—namely, that oil was not present in commercial quantities—both Whitney and Brewer stepped up the attack on Silliman.[8] In this they were aided by Whitney's brother, William, a professor of linguistics who was also on the Yale faculty. Together they gained wide access to newspapers and journals, including E. L. Godkin's *Nation*, the most respectable journal of its day.[9] Still the oil speculators held out, and Silliman's lawyers called on Bowles of the *Republican*, threatening suit.[1] Bowles replied by offering to send a representative into Connecticut to make the suit easier.[2]

In the summer of 1865, however, S. F. Peckham, a chemist, began an unspectacular but exhaustive eighteen months' survey of the "petroleum region," obtaining samples from the major sites at Cañada Lago, Pico Springs, and Simi (Ojai) Ranch, the latter being the major site of Silliman's venture. Peckham analyzed these samples carefully, comparing them with samples bearing Silliman's mark, and found that, strangely enough, Silliman's oil samples were different. They could not have come, as they were, from the California sites, where the oil was very crude, with a high specific gravity, and not well suited for either transportation by pipeline or illuminating purposes. As Peckham put it rather dryly: "These differences all point to the falsification of the oil examined by these gentlemen [i.e., Silliman and his partners] by admixture of light oil." He added that "the falsification consisted in the addition

6. J. D. Whitney to W. D. Whitney, San Francisco, March 8, 1867, Whitney Papers.
7. W. H. Brewer to Rossiter Raymond, undated, Box 31, Brewer Papers, Yale Historical Manuscripts Collection. This is a complete description, in two drafts, of the petroleum controversy, intended for publication in *The Nation*.
8. Ibid. Also W. H. Brewer, draft of a letter to the Springfield *Republican*, March 21, 1865. The letter appeared on March 24, 1865. See also J. D. Whitney to W. D. Whitney, Boston, March 1, 1865; March 10, 1865; March 20, 1865; April 2, 1865; March 8, 1867.
9. Ibid.
1. Samuel Bowles to W. D. Whitney, Springfield, Mass., Feb. 18, 1874, Whitney Papers.
2. Ibid. For further Bowles correspondence in the matter, see Bowles to W. D. Whitney, March 24, 1874, Springfield, Mass., Whitney Papers.

of an equal portion of refined Pennsylvania oil . . . to crude oil from the Cañada Lago Spring."[3]

Peckham's report, though scientifically persuasive, was not decisive. And it formed only a part of Whitney's campaign, which became highly personal. Eventually, alerted by the state geologist to the abysmal failure of Silliman's companies, investors became wary and uninterested. Lawsuits were instituted by disappointed stockholders and at least one suicide was laid at Silliman's door.[4] Suddenly the oil bubble collapsed, and the professor turned abruptly to mining ventures, where once again he found himself in jeopardy in the famous Emma Mine case.[5] In 1870 Silliman was dropped from the faculty of the Sheffield Scientific School and from the Yale College faculty because of his speculative activities.[6]

Whitney and Brewer had been vindicated. As state geologists and public servants, they had used their scientific knowledge to expose a possible swindle as large as the later, more celebrated Diamond Hoax. In so doing, they had assumed a quasi-regulative position, one in which they saw themselves as responsible overseers of investment in the mineral resources of the state. It was a daring extension of the explorer's role and one that was certain to clash with injured interests. Whitney, for one, did not shirk what he considered to be his duty, even though it was unpopular, and in 1874 he and his brother resigned from the National Academy of Sciences because it would not expel Silliman.[7]

Ironically, two years later the first successful commercial well

3. S. F. Peckham: "On the Supposed Falsification of Samples of California Petroleum," *American Journal of Science*, second series, Vol. 43 (1867), pp. 345–51.

4. *Document of Suit in Equity Against the Philadelphia and California Petroleum Company by R. L. Ashurst and E. Spencer Miller, Solicitors for the Complainants*, No. 53, January Term, 1867, Brewer Papers, Yale. See page 17a of this document: "Mr. William H. Storie committed suicide and his son attributed it to his severe disappointment and loss."

5. J. D. Whitney to W. D. Whitney, San Francisco, June 16, 1873. Also J. D. Whitney, San Francisco, Oct. 18, 1873, draft of a Proposal to the Council of the National Academy of Sciences, Whitney Papers.

6. See the *Yale University Catalogue for 1868–70*.

7. For correspondence concerning the impeachment of Silliman, see footnote 5 on this page. See also W. D. Whitney to J. D. Whitney, New Haven, Nov. 2, 1873; Silliman to National Academy, New Haven, Feb. 10, 1874; Julius Hilgard to W. D. Whitney, Washington, Feb. 19, 1874 (46 enclosures); W. D. Whitney to J. D. Whitney, New Haven, July 19, 1874; Joseph Henry to W. D. Whitney, Aug. 7, 1874; Julius Hilgard to W. D. Whitney, Washington, Dec. 2, 1874; Dec. 6, 1874; Dec. 19, 1874; J. D. Whitney to W. D. Whitney, Cambridge, Dec. 21, 1874; Dec. 28, 1874; Feb. 4, 1875. The last letter describes the circumstances of J. D. Whitney's resignation from the National Academy.

came through at Pico Springs and by a twist of technological fate Silliman, rather than Whitney, has seemed vindicated before the bar of history.[8] Yet—if the testimony of Brewer's son can be believed—long afterward, near the end of their lives, Brewer visited Silliman at his home at 34 Hillhouse Avenue and in a final reconciliation Silliman broke down and admitted that Brewer had indeed been right. Finishing the conversation with head bowed, Silliman confessed that at last "he knew much of the story of which he was previously in ignorance," and that "if everybody had been as honest and true a friend to me as . . . [Brewer had] been I would not today [have] been in this humiliating position."[9]

Somebody, perhaps some California oil speculator, had indeed switched samples on Yale's Professor Silliman.

11

Whitney returned to San Francisco in the autumn of 1865 and presented the first volume of his *Geology* to the legislature at the

8. Arthur B. Perkins: "Mining Camps of the Soledad," Pt. 3, *The Historical Society of Southern California Quarterly*, Vol. XL, No. 4 (Dec. 1958), p. 383.
9. Statement of Henry Brewer, Jan. 26, 1931, Box 31, Brewer Papers, Yale. This confirms Peckham's findings of 1867 (see footnote 3 on the preceding page).

Henry Brewer's account, based on his father's reminiscences, is, of course, not conclusive. It can, however, be checked against certain other references, such as the *Yale College Catalogues* for the period, S. F. Peckham's "Report" (my footnote 3, preceding page), and the versions presented by Josiah Dwight and William Dwight Whitney in the Whitney Papers at Yale. The Silliman Papers at Yale shed little light on the problem. John F. Fulton and Elizabeth Thompson, in *Benjamin Silliman* . . . (New York: Henry Schuman; 1947), pp. 240–1, present a completely erroneous account of the situation. They wrongly conclude that William Dwight Whitney and William H. Brewer invested in oil in California. Brewer's letter to the Springfield *Republican* of March 21, 1865, which touched off the controversy, makes his negative position clear, as do the extensive Whitney Papers. The Whitney Papers also refute the Fulton-Thompson claim that the dispute between Whitney and Silliman was really over whether the oil was in northern or in southern California. Whitney denied that there was commercial oil anywhere in California. And, finally, the Fulton-Thompson conclusion that "time has proved Silliman right, for California has been one of the most important oil-producing states in the nation and all of the production has come from the southern part of the state," overlooks the important historical fact that it took a new technology to locate the subsurface oil in southern California, and to make it really commercial. On the basis of genuine samples from Ojai Ranch, it was not, as of 1864–70, commercially useful, as the collapse of Silliman's oil ventures eloquently attested.

height of the petroleum controversy. Though it was an effective part of his campaign against Silliman and the speculators, however, neither it nor any of his other efforts stilled the mounting opposition to his scientific survey.

So tight were funds that when King and Gardner reported for work, having also returned from a sojourn in the East, they were assigned to General McDowell's military command in Arizona and ordered to make a survey across the Mojave Desert to the Colorado River and on to Prescott.[1] This was Indian country, and besides, the Apache, the Havasupai, the Hualpai, and most of the Colorado River tribes were on the warpath. I "only hope they will be prudent and not let the Apaches get their scalps,"[2] wrote Whitney.

They nearly did. On the twenty-fourth of January, King and Gardner had ridden far out ahead of their escort when suddenly they were surrounded by fifty menacing Indians. King attempted to distract them, and thus gain time, by showing them his equipment. But, while the leaders looked on impassively, the others began kindling a roasting fire, intending to dance "a veritable *can-can d'enfer*," as King once put it, around the explorers as they grilled them. King's delaying stratagem worked, however, as they had only stripped down to their leather breeches when the cavalry escort rode up and saved them.[3]

The Army was not always so dependable, however, and scarcely had they got to Camp Date Creek and set up their survey when the enlistments of the soldiers ran out and the whole work collapsed. King and Gardner returned to San Francisco without completing the assignment, but with a considerable knowledge of the desert country and the inhabitants of Arizona. They were then assigned to a summer survey of the Upper San Joaquin, the Merced, and Mount Ritter. While looking off across the great Nevada Basin from this vantage point, King finally made up his mind to strike out on his own.[4] When he returned to San Francisco he presented Whitney with his resignation and asked for Whitney's help in securing his own Interior Survey of Nevada and points East. Though he did not

1. Rositer W. Raymond: "Biographical Notice," *Clarence King Memoirs*, The Century Association (New York: G. P. Putnam's Sons; 1904), p. 330.
2. J. D. Whitney to W. D. Whitney, Dec. 24, 1865, Whitney Papers. Also quoted in Wilkins: *Clarence King*, p. 83.
3. Raymond: "Biographical Notice," pp. 330–2. King used the phrase "a veritable *can-can d'enfer*" to refer to the plight of a soldier who had perished in a similar situation, but it is applicable here.
4. Wilkins: *Clarence King*, pp. 91–2. Also see Gardner's version of their plans, in Raymond: "Biographical Notice," pp. 332–5; and King Papers, Folder A-3.

tell Whitney, he planned to parallel the new transcontinental railroad.[5] Whitney, however, refused his support, though he later gave
it, and King returned East with only an endorsement from the
military.[6] Colonel R. S. Williamson, the former Topographical
Engineer, had seen and liked his work.[7]

Gradually, however, the field work of the Whitney Survey declined. With Brewer at Yale and King and Gardner retired, Hoffmann partially disabled, and Rémond, his new topographer, dying
of consumption, Whitney was hard pressed to keep parties in the
field. Thanks to King's work at Yosemite, he was able to finish his
Guide Book to that region, but most of his time appears to have
been taken up with combating Silliman's oil claims, supervising
the drawing up of maps of San Francisco Bay and central California,
directing surveys of the mining regions of Plumas County, and examining the celebrated Calaveras Skull and the region in which it
was found. In the latter instance, Whitney fell victim to a famous
hoax, declaring the Calaveras Skull to be of ancient origin when in
actuality it had been planted deep in a mine by two men as a joke
on their employer.

In the summer of 1867, survey activity was stepped up. Hoffmann and an assistant mapped the Big Tree country and corrected
the errors in King's sketch of the Yosemite. They also made some of
the first photos of the High Sierras.[8] W. M. Gabb led a party out
across Nevada as far as the 116th degree of longitude, and he later
surveyed part of Death Valley.[9] D'Heureuse mapped Kern, Tulare,
and Inyo counties.[1] Wackenroder made still another survey of the
Central Sierras.[2] And Whitney himself spent the season touring
Oregon.[3] When he returned, he rode eastward into Nevada in an
attempt to join Gabb's party. Instead—as he wrote his brother—
just beyond Virginia City they "were gone through by the 'road

5. Ibid., p. 91.
6. Richard Bartlett: *Great Surveys of the American West* (Norman, Okla.:
Oklahoma University Press; 1962), p. 143 *n.* For Whitney's private feelings
about King's venture, see J. D. Whitney to W. D. Whitney, San Francisco,
April 29, 1867; May 9, 1867; June 8, 1867.
7. Wilkins: *Clarence King*, p. 92.
8. J. D. Whitney to W. D. Whitney, Sept. 17, 1867, Whitney Papers.
9. J. D. Whitney: *Letter of the State Geologist Relative to the Progress of the
State Geological Survey*, 8 vols. in one (San Francisco, 1862, 1863, 1866–67),
Report for 1866–67 (published 1867).
1. Ibid.
2. Ibid.
3. J. D. Whitney to W. D. Whitney, San Francisco, July 20, 1867, Whitney
Papers.

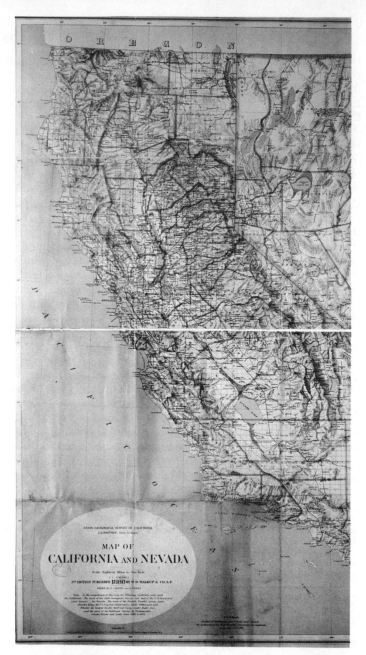

Map of California and Nevada, a later map drawn by cartographers
of the California Geological Survey. *Courtesy Library of Congress*

agents' . . . in the neatest and most scientific manner. . . ." He was left with only the survey instruments, and a serious shortage of funds.[4]

Despite the heightened activity of the summer season, the Survey was in a bad way. Sparked by the petroleum controversy and the disappointed oil promoters, the legislature of 1867–68 was distinctly hostile to Whitney. All of the factions of opposition came together. Consequently, though the legislature owed Whitney over $8,000, which he had paid out of his own pocket,[5] it adjourned that year without providing for the continuance of the Survey.[6] It was no longer possible for Whitney to defy the special interests of the state of California. And though he continued carrying on such survey work as publication of the *Yosemite Book* and the dispatch of an occasional cartographical field party, Whitney's State Geological Survey was to all intents and purposes dead as of 1868. Most scientists considered it a great loss, as did John Strong Newberry, who wired from Columbia College that he had heard the survey was dead and "I hope the despatch was a lie, both for your sake and the sake of science. . . ."[7]

Whitney continued to hope, however, and for six more years he

4. J. D. Whitney to W. D. Whitney, Sept. 17, 1867, Whitney Papers.
5. J. D. Whitney to Hon. A. L. Tubbs, Chairman, Finance Committee, Senate of California, San Francisco, Feb. 10, 1868.
6. J. D. Whitney to W. D. Whitney, San Francisco, March 29, 1868, Whitney Papers. Whitney's version of the defeat of his Survey is interesting: "The petroleum and other swindlers made a dead set on the survey and killed it, having malleable material to work with in the Democratic legislature. . . . We were especially unfortunate in having in the Senate a man, the fugleman of the Democracy, a veteran politician and a former United States Surveyor General, under whose administration the fraudulent surveys in the southern part of the state were made, and the character of which is being exposed as fast as our work covers the ground. Of course he fought against us with all his might."
   In a letter to W. D. Whitney from San Francisco, April 13, 1868, he added: "Petroleum is what killed us. By the word 'petroleum' understand the desire to sell worthless property for large sums and the impolicy of having anybody around to interfere with the little game. . . ."
   According to his biographer, Whitney attributed his defeat to "the general ignorance and indifference of the public concerning all scientific matters; the intrigues of various persons who foresaw advantage for themselves if the survey should be reorganized under another head; the hostility of a powerful group of speculators; and finally, rather perhaps an occasion than a cause, the personal enmity of Governor Booth." Brewster: *Josiah Dwight Whitney*, pp. 291 ff.
7. J. S. Newberry to J. D. Whitney, School of Mines, Columbia College, New York, April 6, 1868, Whitney Papers.

worked on, marshaling Eastern academic support and endorsements, but to little avail.[8] In the end, with a final appropriation of $48,000 for two years, he barely succeeded in gaining reimbursement for the funds that he had advanced the Survey.[9]

It is perhaps an easy matter to see the demise of the Whitney Survey as a simple example of the disinterested public servant pitted against "special interests." But the issue was more complex. Whitney and his fellow scientists represented an outside elite which had persuaded a small minority of "the better people" to embark on a bold and long-range scientific venture. The democracy, expecting a prospecting survey or at least an agency for promoting renewed California investment in the face of competition from other mineral regions, rejected it. They demanded "practical" things first, and while it is clear that the voters and the interests erred in failing to realize the relationship of paleontology to mining, it is not so clear that they were wrong in refusing to sponsor the publication of illustrated books on birds, or the surveys of Nevada desert and Oregon mountains.

Perhaps what they feared most was not the waste and apparent impracticality of Whitney's survey, however, but rather the new idea of conservation implicit in Whitney's every approach to his task. To the common man he appeared as a negative, a representative of some outside elite who had come to dampen enthusiasm, curtail the big bonanza, guard the public domain for the "better sort" and the "big interests" who knew better how to use it. He had come as a regulator to quash their hopes in the name of science. And if, as some writers maintain, the dream of the sturdy middle-class yeoman is pure myth,[1] Whitney in 1868 found that for him it contained a certain unyielding reality. He had been vanquished by a dream. And he had touched upon what was to be a central dilemma throughout the history of conservation. If efficiency and waste are the guiding lights, then how does one avoid an alliance between a knowledgeable elite and the highly organized upper class? In California, declining from its boom days in the 1860's, the problem became acute and it was settled for a time in favor of

8. For a statement of his plan of action, see J. D. Whitney to W. D. Whitney, Northampton, June 18, 1868, Whitney Papers. His activities for the period are described in his voluminous correspondence down to 1874, Whitney Papers.

9. J. D. Whitney to W. D. Whitney, San Francisco, March 9, 1872, Whitney Papers.

1. Smith: *Virgin Land, passim.*

the middle class. Whitney was never really aware of its complexity, though he and his survey became its victims.

For the Survey itself, there was much to be said. It marked a transition between the old general surveys and those which focused on specific problems like mountain-making and the age of gold-bearing strata. As such, it served as an almost unique training ground for civilian scientists in the West who were not under military supervision. Thus it formed a nucleus of civilian-oriented experts who staffed the later national surveys and ultimately helped upset army control of Western exploration. Often over-shadowed by the later, more famous national surveys, the California Survey was an institutional proving ground, a means of training able new scientists, a generator of new enthusiasms for a conservation approach to the West, and perhaps most of all a glorious adventure in a new dimension of exploration—the surmounting of the High Sierras and their incorporation into the horizon of human knowledge. But before the civilian scientific explorer, however heroic his feats, gained ascendency in the West, the military was once again to have its day in the sun.

CHAPTER XI

The Army Way

AFTER Appomattox, the United States Army once again faced West. Though greatly reduced in size as a result of the Army Act of 1866, the military was confronted in the postwar years by a series of Western problems that overshadowed anything it had faced before the war. A great rush of settlers had moved West, led by a horde of voracious prospectors who, in much greater numbers, duplicated the feats of the fur trappers of a bygone day in that they invaded every valley, gulch, and river bed in the mountain West in search of the big bonanza. Wherever they went, however unpromising and inaccessible the site, tent cities sprang up, and civilization came to the wilderness. With civilization came more population and an increasing demand for transportation, and by 1868 at least three railroad projects and several important wagon roads were underway, pushing out across the plains through the buffalo country and into the mountains. Inevitably they clashed with the Indian, brushing him aside, killing his buffalo, reducing his domain, threatening his very existence. As early as 1866, the great Indian wars had begun and the Army was faced with a new kind of conflict—a guerrilla war extending over vast distances and every conceivable kind of terrain. Moreover, the enemy was like nothing the civilized soldier had seen before—a mobile, resourceful fighter who knew the country and could live off the land no matter what the hardship. In addition, the Indian was not without allies. The Indian agents of the Interior Department who sold him guns and supplies had a certain cynical appreciation of him, and back in the East, groups of prewar Abolitionists turned from the South to the West with a newfound, vocal interest in the redman.

It was not only his resourceful enemies that complicated the soldier's task. Each false-front hamlet and tent metropolis demanded federal military aid, chiefly to subsidize its own somewhat premature economic enterprises. And when political representatives were unable to secure the desired military aid, the miners and settlers frequently created new rushes and even new Indian wars that forcibly commanded military attention. Just as the early fur trader had had the luxury of direct access to his government, so too did the sourdough and his frontier friends the itinerant lawyers and politicians. Caught between two fires, and with a force of only 45,000 men to guard the enormous Western frontier and garrison the conquered South, the Army's situation seemed precarious, if not almost hopeless. And yet, to the professional soldier, it also offered an opportunity. Threatened with displacement and alienation in the postwar rush to civilian industrial development, he could perhaps once again assume an important place in the social evolution of his time. The settlement of the West was a great and inevitable epic adventure. As part of it he could once again, as in the days before the war, become an important member of society. For some, with the bugle calls of Gettysburg and Cedar Creek and a hundred other battles still fresh in their ears, it offered a chance for glory. For others it was an opportunity for service.

2

Paradoxically, out on the pressurized postwar frontier, the first military necessity was accurate information. Despite the years of prewar experience in the West, and the monumental efforts of several generations of military and civilian explorers, there was still not enough useful and reliable geographical information about the country. As the settlers reached out into ever more remote regions, a demand arose for data concerning mountain passes, transportation routes, Indian strongholds, river courses, resources for farmer, miner, and railroader, and even such prosaic things as the degree of annual rainfall. New technology and new goals, not to mention new theaters of operations, demanded that fresh maps be drawn and new reports be submitted. Because of the Indian dangers and the lack of appropriate existing institutions with financial support, civilian agencies could not undertake the task. Thus the Army returned to conducting scientific explorations and surveys over the whole West, even to the extent of reviving in an informal manner the old Bureau of Explorations and Surveys under the Chief of Engineers.

This bureau was not the only, or even the major, means employed by the Army to gather information, however. The military employed at least three different institutional approaches to the problem. In the first instance, the Chief of Engineers assigned at least one of his exploration officers to each of the military departments in the West, where he served for all practical purposes as an intelligence officer, coordinating the field reports of various scouting parties onto a master map of his particular region, and often conducted field expeditions himself. Secondly, beginning in 1867, the Army employed Clarence King, formerly of the California Geological Survey, to conduct an extensive scientific reconnaissance of the 40th parallel from the California border to the Great Plains. His path was roughly one hundred miles wide, following the line of the transcontinental railroad, and was primarily oriented toward the location of resources which would sustain the railroad and its settlers. Third, in 1871, Lieutenant George Montague Wheeler, an ambitious officer of the Engineer Corps, commenced what came to be called the United States Geographical Surveys Beyond the 100th Meridian. Wheeler's Survey was an attempt to divide the West into ninety-four enormous geodetic quadrangles and within this framework to construct, in systematic fashion, a definitive map of the country. Each of these approaches, though necessarily involving a measure of duplication, was thought by the War Department to be important in its own right and the best service it could afford to the cause of Westward expansion. The fate of each of these operations constitutes in a very real sense the story of army exploration in the postwar West.

3

The most demanding of the explorers' functions fell on the engineer officers attached to the Western military departments. In the postwar West there were six major departments, each commanded by a major general. In 1866–67, for example, the following divisions existed: Dakota, commanded by General Alfred H. Terry; Missouri, under General W. S. Hancock; the Platte, under General Philip St. George Cooke; the Gulf, headed by General Philip Sheridan; California, under General Irwin McDowell; the Columbia, under General Frederick Steele; and the Arkansas, under General E. O. C. Ord. From time to time these departments were redrawn and their commanders changed, but the engineer officer's function remained the same. He had to serve at least two masters, the departmental commander, who might order him into the field at any time, and the Chief of Engineers, who demanded results in the form of maps, mineral surveys, and wagon-road estimates. In addition, his printed reports were closely scrutinized by a number of civilian critics including congressmen, territorial representatives, speculators, and members of the National Academy of Sciences. His position was indeed precarious and his role an exacting one, but by the same token the enormous range of his commitments made him an influential part of the Army's Western operations.

There is no systematic way to describe these far-ranging duties. For the most part they were somewhat loosely-coordinated on a national level, arising when the opportunity and/or the demand presented itself. Some of the earliest reconnaissances were conducted in the Department of the Pacific in an attempt to keep pace with prospectors branching out into the interior from California. In 1865 Colonel R. S. Williamson pioneered military roads from Susanville to Fort Bidwell in northern California and then on to Fort Klamath in Oregon. The following year he struck out into the Great Basin on a reconnaissance from Fort Churchill to Ruby Valley and Silver City, laying out a path for military detachments assigned to protect adventurous miners bent on exploiting the riches of eastern Nevada.[1] In 1866, too, as previously recounted, Clarence King and James Gardner accompanied a detachment of cavalry across the Mojave Desert to Fort Mojave on the Lower Colorado River. In the course of their march, they explored large portions of northwestern Arizona between Prescott and the Colorado River. Out of these ventures and Lieutenant Joseph C. Ives's 1857 expedition up the Colorado grew a marked concern for the exploration of that river.

The exploration of that unknown river and the location of north-south routes across the Great Basin became the two most important projects of the Department of the Pacific. By 1866 the Mormons had established an outpost at Callville on the north bank of the Colorado River just below the Grand Canyon, and from all directions prospectors were converging on that region. Arizona promoters, fresh from a minor mineral boom in that territory, had

1. Report of the Chief of Army Engineers, in "Annual Report of the Secretary of War," 40th Cong., 2nd sess., *H.R. Exec. Doc. 1* (1867), pp. 53–4.

initiated a new Colorado steamboat line that had pushed through Black Canyon, which Lieutenant Ives had assumed to be the head of navigation, and in 1866 Captain Rodgers on the *Esmeralda* reached Callville itself.[2] The Mormons, eager for explorers' aid in opening up the canyon region, advertised the Colorado River country above Callville as "better than the 100 miles just below," and Captain R. S. Mansfield, in his report to the Chief of Engineers, added soberly, ignoring the obvious, that there was "no reason to doubt" this information.[3]

Then, in the fall of 1867, a dramatic event occurred. One James White, a prospector, drifted into Callville aboard a crude log raft. He was dragged from the river, "a pitiable object, emaciated and haggard . . . his mental faculties, though still sound, liable to wander and verging on insanity."[4] When he could talk, he told his rescuers that he had drifted for fourteen days down the Colorado through canyons and whirlpools. He thus claimed to be the first man through the Grand Canyon. The military, as well as everybody else, were interested. Perhaps the best account of White's trip is contained in a letter he wrote to his brother some three weeks after his rescue:

Callville, September 26, 1867. Dear Brother it has been some time sence i have heard from you i got no ance from the last letter that i roat to you for i left soon after i rot i went prospected with Captin Baker and George Strole in San Won montin Wee found vry god prospeck but noth that wold pay then we store down the San Won river we travel down a bout 200 miles than we cross over on Calorrado and camp we lad over one day wee found out that he could not travel down the river and our horse was sore fite and we had may up our mines to turn back when wee was attacked by 15 or 20 utes indis they kill Baker and George Strole and myself took fore ropes off our hourse and a ax ten pounds of flour and our gunns wee had 15 miles to woak to Colorado we got to the river jest at night we bilt a raft that night wee got it bilt abot teen o clock tha night. wee saile all that night wee good sailing from three days and

2. Report of Chief of Army Engineers, in "Annual Report of the Secretary of War," 40th Cong., 3rd sess., *H.R. Exec. Doc. 1* (1868–69), p. 1188.
3. Ibid., p. 1189.
4. Statement of Dr. C. C. Parry, first published in the *Transactions of the Academy of Science of St. Louis*, Vol. II (1868), pp. 499–503, quoted in Dr. Harold A. Bulger: "First Man Through the Grand Canyon," *The Bulletin of the Missouri Historical Society*, Vol. XVII (July 1961), p. 324.

the fore George Strole was wash of from the raft and drown that left me aline i thought that it wold be my time next i then poul off my boos and pands i then tide a rope to my wase i wend over falls from 10 to 15 feet hie my raft would tip over three or fore times a day the third wee loss our flour and for seven days i had noth to eat to ralhide nife cober the 8–9 day i got some muskit beens the 13 days a party of indis frendey they wold not give me noth eat so i give my pistols for hine pards of a dog i ead one of for super and the other breakfast the 14 days i rive at Callville where I was tak carie of by James Ferry i was ten days with out pants or boos or hat I was soon burnt so i cold hadly walk the ingis tak 7 head horse from us jous i can rite you halfe i under went i see the hardest times that eny man ever did in the world but thank god that i got thrught safe I am well a gin and I hope the few lines will fine you all well I send my best respects to all.

Josh ance this when you git it P drech yor letter to Call ville Arizona.

Josh ass Tom to ancy that letter that i rote him several yeas a goe.

James White.[5]

Though White's story was believed by his contemporaries who had never seen the canyons of the Colorado nor tested its distances, a later generation of explorers and historians of the river has been almost unanimous in considering it a hoax. John Wesley Powell, who as the first official explorer of the Grand Canyon was hardly a disinterested observer, neglected to mention White at all in his report, though he had met and talked with him.[6] Frederick Dellenbaugh, participant and chronicler of the second Powell expedition, and historian of the river, called White's story "a splendid yarn" and White himself "a champion prevaricator," but Dellenbaugh appears to have based his comments on a later journalistic embellishment of White's rather simple narrative.[7] The most searching

5. Ibid., pp. 322–3.
6. William Culp Darrah: *Powell of the Colorado* (Princeton, N.J.: Princeton University Press; 1951), p. 109.
7. Frederick Dellenbaugh: *The Romance of the Colorado River* (New York: G. P. Putnam's Sons; 1906), p. 183. Dellenbaugh's account of White's voyage is on pp. 174–83, and it is clear that he based his analysis on Parry's report as touched up by William Bell in *New Tracks in North America*, second edition (New York: Scribner and Welford and Co.; 1871), rather than White's own story as reprinted in Bulger, "First Man," pp. 322–3, and in the present account.

analysis of White's story was conducted by another river explorer, Robert Brewster Stanton, who interviewed White in 1907 and in the course of the interview managed to reveal numerous instances of White's singular ignorance of the river.[8] No one had really improved on Stanton's analysis and his criticism of White based upon the prospector's numerous errors concerning the river itself and also upon the impossibility of his having made so long a voyage in the time alleged to have elapsed must thus stand as representative. Most damaging was the fact that it took the efficient John Wesley Powell over 42 days to cover approximately the same distance that White claimed to have progressed in 14. It is altogether possible, however, that White, delirious and starving, lost track of the time and indeed drifted in a comatose state for days through the canyons. Stanton concluded nevertheless that White had entered the Colorado south of the Grand Canyon and that his voyage had been a relatively short one of 60 miles downriver.[9]

A later generation of historians, notably R. E. Lingenfelter and Dr. Harold A. Bulger, have attempted to defend White.[1] Lingenfelter, like Stanton, suggests that White went south, not north, from the San Juan River, but that he entered the river near Navaho Creek above the Grand Canyon. Bulger, referring to a letter written by White when he was eighty, notes that White consistently maintained to the end of his life that he was north of the San Juan. Indeed, this appears to be the most consistent element in his story. Bulger, concentrating on the overland aspects of White's journey, carefully traces his route to White Creek Canyon on the Colorado north of the San Juan and south of Cataract Canyon. Then he accounts for the four days of placid sailing through comparatively quiet Glen Canyon, and numerous other discrepancies in White's story, in what is so far the most convincing case for the defense of the old prospector. Bulger did not manage to solve the time problem, nor did he adequately explain White's apparent ignorance of the lower river. Thus, like the equally intriguing mysteries of John Colter's exact route and James Ohio Pattie's trail to the Yellowstone, the precise achievement of James White must remain, at least for

8. Robert Brewster Stanton: *Colorado River Controversies,* James M. Chalfant, ed. (New York: Dodd, Mead and Co.; 1932), pp. 3–93. I have also examined Stanton's manuscript research notes and collected papers in the Historical Manuscripts Division of the New York Public Library. See also the Frederick Dellenbaugh Papers in the same repository.
9. Ibid.
1. See footnote 4, p. 394. Also see R. E. Lingenfelter: *First Through the Grand Canyon* (Los Angeles: G. Dawson; 1958).

the time being, a mystery. It seems clear, however, that he was not the d⌐liberate prevaricator that Dellenbaugh and others have labeled him, for, in contrast to Powell, he did very little to exploit his feat, beyond publishing his story in *Outing* magazine. He left that to creative writers like Dr. William Bell and the novelist John W. DeForest.[2]

Two tantalizing facts remain. White and his ill-fated companions were definitely known to have been in the San Juan region in the summer of 1867, and in September of that same year White was dragged from the Lower Colorado, the victim of what was obviously a harrowing experience. Clearly he had had more than a casual contact with the river and the unexplored canyons around it.

4

White's appearance at Callville, and the subsequent publication of Dr. C. C. Parry's interview with him in the *Transactions of the St. Louis Academy of Sciences,* made a marked impression on the army explorers.[3] Major Williamson enclosed Parry's account in his report to the Chief of Engineers and proposed two expeditions to probe the mysteries of the Colorado. The first was a cautious plan to ascend the river in stages, thereby avoiding any sudden confrontation with cataracts or whirlpools. This plan was later followed by Lieutenant George M. Wheeler. The second was a proposal to send a party from Virginia City via Paranagat to the Upper Colorado, where the explorers would then assemble a boat and float down the river, taking their chances with nature's hazards. Williamson himself volunteered to undertake this mission.[4] But by the end of 1868, when his report was submitted, it was too late. John Wesley Powell's Colorado venture was already underway. In his report for 1869 the Chief of Engineers declared: "The continuation of the exploration of this river above Callville, Utah, has been postponed in view of the enterprise now in progress under the direction of Professor Powell."[5]

2. Among the earliest accounts of White's trip was the one that appeared in William Bell: *New Tracks in North America.* In 1871 the Connecticut writer John W. DeForest utilized White's story as the basis for his lurid novel *Overland* (New York: Harper and Brothers; 1871).
3. Report of the Chief of Army Engineers, in "Annual Report of the Secretary of War," 40th Cong., 3rd sess., *H.R. Exec. Doc. 1,* Pt. II (1868), pp. 1190–4.
4. Ibid.
5. Report of the Chief of Army Engineers, in "Annual Report of the Secretary of War," 41st Cong., 2nd sess., *H.R. Exec. Doc. 1,* Pt. II (1869), p. 68.

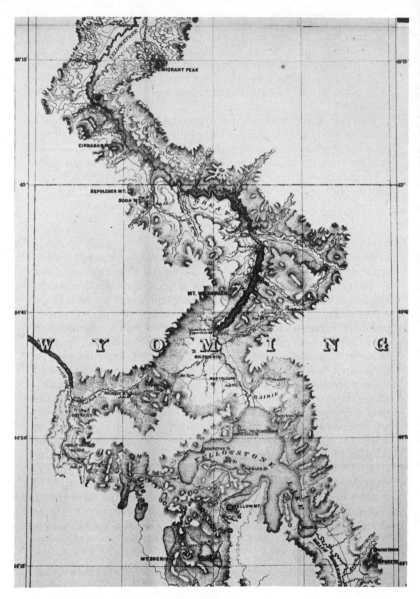

Map of the Yellowstone Park region drawn by Captains Barlow and Heap, 1871. *Courtesy University of Texas Library*

From the Lower Colorado the Department of the Pacific moved on to other enterprises. In 1869 Lieutenant George M. Wheeler led the first of his many expeditions into the West. Operating under direct orders from General E. O. C. Ord, Wheeler led an expedition southward from Camp Halleck, Nevada, on the Central Pacific Railroad line, along the eastern boundary of Nevada to the Mormon settlements near present-day Las Vegas in the southern part of the new state. Wheeler's mission was to search out a new military road over which troops could be moved from the Central Pacific to posts in Arizona and Nevada, where they could protect the mining camps from Indians and keep a watchful eye on the Mormons. His reconnaissance was a grueling one that lasted five months, or until the end of November 1869, but it was a noteworthy accomplishment. He had made the first north-south traverse of the Great Basin since the days of Peter Skene Ogden, and he had reached the Colorado River at Callville not long after Powell had completed his voyage at that point—thus making Wheeler one of the earliest of the latter-day explorers to enter the "Plateau Province." The young lieutenant derived further satisfaction from the fact that along the way, in eastern Nevada, he managed to name his first mountain after himself.[6]

5

Still another noteworthy project undertaken by the Department of the Pacific was the venture in 1869 by Captain Charles Raymond to far-off Alaska, America's newest territory. Not the earliest or the most significant of Alaskan explorations, Raymond's expedition is nevertheless indicative of the Army's pioneering role in opening up new territory and promoting new ventures in settlement. Raymond, born in Hartford, Connecticut, was one of a series of brilliant engineer officers developed as a result of the Civil War. He had attended Brooklyn Polytechnical Institute, then West Point, where in 1863, while still a cadet, he was commissioned an officer on the staff of General Darius N. Couch—himself a plant collector on the prewar frontier—and fought through the battle of Gettysburg. He then returned to West Point, where he was graduated at the head of his class in 1865. By 1867 he was a captain in the elite Corps

6. George M. Wheeler: *Preliminary Report Upon a Reconnaissance Through Southern and Southeastern Nevada, Made in 1869* (Washington, D.C.: U. S. Government Printing Office; 1875).

of Engineers. The Alaskan venture was his first major independent command.[7]

The expedition had been ordered in response to a particular demand. Far up on the Yukon River, which runs from east to west across central Alaska, the Hudson's Bay Company had established a fur-trading post on what was claimed to be American territory. Captain Raymond, as an expert in geodetics, was ordered north to determine the exact location of the post, and should it be on American soil, to take possession of it. He was to proceed from Fort Hamilton on the west coast of Alaska up the Yukon, and along the way make a general reconnaissance of the country, its resources, and the "number and disposition of the native tribes in its vicinity." He was also to determine the amount and nature of the British fur trade in the region, thus performing a duty similar to those performed by American explorers of an earlier day at Fort Astoria.

On April 6, 1869, accompanied by one assistant, John J. Major, he sailed from San Francisco aboard the brig *Commodore* bound for Sitka.[8] At Sitka he was joined by his escort, Private Michael Foley, 9th U. S. Infantry. By the first week in July they had reached Fort Hamilton on the Lower Yukon and the party had swelled to thirteen men. Appropriately, on July 4, 1869, they embarked in two whaleboats towed by a small river steamer which had been brought north aboard the *Commodore*. Twenty-seven days later, after a long trip up the twists and turns of the Yukon, they arrived at remote and slightly ramshackle Fort Yukon, which stood almost precisely on the Arctic Circle. Though they had not the luxury of a cabin accommodation, Raymond and his men had accompanied the first successful steamboat trip up the river.

They soon brought bad news for the British, as Raymond was able to determine, after elaborate astronomical observations, that Fort Yukon indeed stood upon American soil. He promptly took formal possession of the post and ordered the British traders out. They accepted like gentlemen, however, perhaps glad of the chance to leave their remote outpost, and whatever possibility had existed for America's first skirmish on the Arctic Circle disappeared in a burst of good fellowship. Raymond had done what he could for the American fur-trading interests. By September 27 he had come back down the picturesque river, past the Kaujuk Mountains, Horse

7. *D.A.B.*
8. Charles W. Raymond: "Report of a Reconnaissance of the Yukon River, July to September, 1869," 42nd Cong., 1st sess., *Sen. Ex. Doc. 12* (1870). Unless otherwise stated, my account is based on this source.

Island, and the Russian mission, and he embarked on that day for San Francisco.

Raymond's report was extremely competent, though it provided little in the way of original information. As he himself carefully pointed out, there had been at least seven expeditions into the region before his own, including one in 1863 by Ivan Lukeen, and another in 1866 by the scientists of the Western Union Telegraph Company, William Healey Dall and Frederick Wymper. The results of their labors had already been published in two books, Dall's *Alaska and Its Resources* and Wymper's *Travels in Alaska and on the Yukon.* Raymond's map, though more accurately determined than the others, was actually the fifth map of the region produced since 1842. More than anything else, Raymond's expedition represented the almost spontaneous, stimulus-response approach taken by the army departments and the Corps of Engineers to the need for information and aid to Western settlement. His expedition also keynoted the fact that though Alaska was a new, almost exotic possession, in the eyes of the military it was still part of the old frontier and would be treated in the same routine manner.

6

While the Department of the Pacific was turning its attention to remote Alaska, equally interesting developments were taking place in the Department of the Dakotas. These involved the official rediscovery of another exotic place—Yellowstone Park. Though numerous fur trappers, prospectors, and even missionaries since the days of John Colter had made their way into parts of Yellowstone, as late as 1866 it remained a mystery to scientific explorers—a mystery made all the more intriguing by the trappers' stories of fabulous geysers, smoking pools, multicolored lava pots, and burning rivers. In 1859–60 Captain William F. Raynolds, with Jim Bridger as his guide, had tried and failed to enter the park area by crossing the towering Absarokas, and he was forced to detour around it to winter quarters on the Oregon Trail. It thus remained a blank spot on the army maps.[9]

9. William F. Raynolds: "Report on the Exploration of the Yellowstone and the Country Drained by That River," 40th Cong., 2nd sess., *Sen. Ex. Doc.* 77 (1868). See also Raynolds's field notebooks for this expedition, and the reports of his subordinates, in Raynolds Papers, Yale Western Americana Collection.

By the mid-sixties this blank spot was becoming an increasing irritation. John Bozeman had opened his Powder River Trail to the Three Forks country, and swarms of miners invaded that region, where John Colter had run for his life scarcely fifty years before. At Alder Gulch they hit the bonanza and Virginia City sprang up, the fief of Henry Plummer, greatest of the Western desperados. It was typical Western El Dorado, which, despite or perhaps because of its unsavory reputation, daily attracted new swarms of prospectors. To the north in Montana, near strategic Bozeman Pass, the Army constructed Fort Ellis and stationed an infantry regiment to guard it and as many Montana inhabitants as possible. But to the south of Fort Ellis, and to the east of Virginia City, lay Yellowstone, another of those regions held in awe and respect by the Indian, which to the prospector offered an irresistible temptation. It was inevitable that sooner or later the Army must turn its attention to the exploration, and if necessary to the policing, of this territory.

As early as 1866, spurred on by rumors of Captain W. W. De Lacy's successful penetration of the region in 1863,[1] the citizens of Virginia City, Helena, and Bozeman began to think of a joint military-civilian expedition to the Upper Yellowstone, and by 1867 active efforts were being made to organize such a party. In 1867 and 1868 the effort failed, however, due to Indian outbreaks in the Gallatin Valley and the lack of troops necessary for the escort. Normally venturesome citizens, as one observer put it, suddenly found "pressing business engagements" which prevented their accompanying any expedition.[2] But in 1869, when the venture was revived, with its usual dismal result, three men—David E. Folsom, C. W. Cook, and a ranch hand named Peterson—decided to take the risk on their own. They provided themselves with horses, camping equipment, repeating rifles, Colt revolvers, and the inevitable and necessary pick, pan, and shovel. Setting out from Helena, they followed the Yellowstone River to its headwaters in Yellowstone

1. For an account of De Lacy's expedition, see Henry Gannett: "Geographical Fieldwork of the Yellowstone Park Division," in *Twelfth Annual Report of the United States Geological and Geographical Survey of the Territories*, 2 vols. (Washington, D.C.: U. S. Government Printing Office; 1883), Vol. I, pp. 464–5. Also see Walter W. De Lacy: "A Trip Up the South Snake River in 1863," Historical Society of Montana, *Contributions*, Vol. I (1876), pp. 113–43.

2. N. P. Langford: *The Discovery of Yellowstone Park* (privately printed, 1905), pp. ix–xx.

Lake and then crossed westward over the divide to the Madison River, which they followed up as far as present-day Excelsior Geyser. Then, by a route which is not precisely known today, they made their way out of the park area and returned to Helena. They had found no gold, but they had seen such marvels that they were reluctant to tell about them to an assembly of citizens unacquainted with their reputation for veracity.[3]

In 1870, however, Folsom prepared an account of his trip for the *Western Monthly Magazine* of Chicago, and though most of the copies of that journal were destroyed in a fire, their feat became common knowledge.[4] A larger follow-up expedition was planned for 1870, and N. P. Langford of Helena, soon to become the first director of Yellowstone National Park, went to St. Paul and approached General W. S. Hancock for a military escort. With popular enthusiasm at a high pitch, Hancock could hardly refuse, so once again the Army was committed to a Yellowstone venture.[5]

The civilian contingent of the second Yellowstone expedition consisted, in addition to Langford and General Henry D. Washburn, Surveyor General of Montana, of Cornelius Hedges, Samuel T. Hauser, Warren C. Gillette, Benjamin Stickney, Truman C. Everts, Walter Trumbull, Jacob Smith, Charles Reynolds, Elwyn Bean, and two Negro cooks.[6] When they arrived at Fort Ellis, they were with great reluctance provided with a meager escort of five men and one officer, the able Lieutenant Gustavus C. Doane. Lieutenant Doane's orders left most of his duties unspecified except those of escort and protection, though he was apparently selected for the expedition because of his knowledge of geology and geography.[7]

The combined party of nineteen men left Fort Ellis on August 22 and marched southeast toward the Yellowstone River. Their route required them to pass through hostile Indian country and they mounted guard duty every night. Numerous signs indicated that they were being carefully watched by Crow Indians, whose Absaroka domain they were entering, and by the time they reached the Yellowstone itself, signal fires appeared on neighboring mountain tops, marking their progress. On one occasion two strag-

3. Ibid., pp. x–xi.
4. Ibid., p. xi.
5. Ibid., p. xii.
6. Ibid. This volume contains Langford's diary of the Washburn-Doane expedition.
7. Gustavus C. Doane: "The Yellowstone Expedition of 1870," 41st Cong., 3rd sess., *Sen. Exec. Doc. 51* (1870–71).

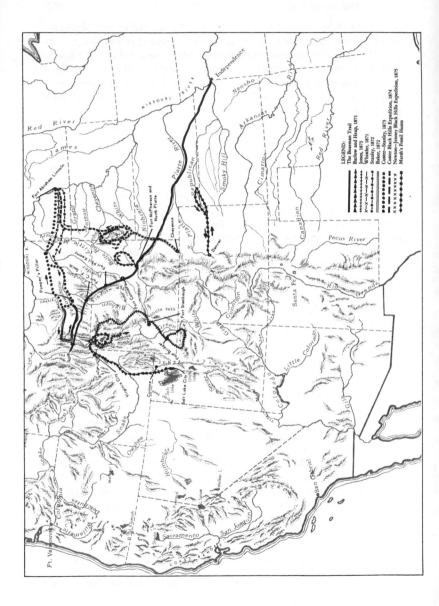

glers from the party sighted a band of more than one hundred warriors, just out of sight, following the main party. But the Crows had always been normally well-disposed toward the Americans, and by the last week in August the explorers reached the park area and Lake Yellowstone.

There a new reality confronted them. The stupendous canyons of the Yellowstone altered their imagination forever. And these were followed by the wild beauties of Yellowstone Lake and the towering mountains that overlooked it to the east—the mountains that had thwarted Captain Raynolds and Jim Bridger in 1860. Then came the thermal springs near West Thumb, the acres of dangerous lava encrustations that concealed the burning depths beneath, jets of steam, bubbling paint pots, and northwest, near the Firehole River, the giant geysers. Clearly the Indians were correct when they described this as a region left unfinished by the Creator. As others before them had observed, perhaps He left it so because it was the very entrance to the infernal regions. At least subconsciously, this must have seemed the case, for as the Washburn-Doane party rode through, giving names to landmarks never before christened, the name of Satan and the theme of hell predominated. One inspired exception, however, was the name they gave to one of the largest geysers—Old Faithful.

Besides the marvels, there was the wilderness, trackless uncharted miles of it in every direction, and its terrifying significance was made clear to them when one of the party, Truman C. Everts, became lost. After a week of searching the entire southern shore of Lake Yellowstone, the rest of the party reluctantly abandoned him to his fate and started for home, rations long since exhausted. Everts, as it turned out, gained more first-hand information about the wilderness than anyone else in the group, for he was lost some thirty-seven days, surviving on a few minnows, thistles, and bits of wild game. He was finally found by a rescue party far to the north, near Gallatin River.[8]

The most significant result of the expedition was the decision by all the explorers (save one) to abandon any thought of private and personal exploitation of the wonderland they had seen and, instead, at the suggestion of Cornelius Hedges, to work together in an effort to persuade the federal government to set aside the region as a national park.[9] Indeed, upon his return, Langford de-

8. Truman C. Everts: "Thirty-seven Days of Peril," *Scribner's Monthly*, Vol. III, No. 1 (Nov. 1871), pp. 1–17.
9. Langford: *Yellowstone*, pp. xix–xx.

voted his every effort to this end, lecturing widely in the East and publishing a number of colorful articles in national magazines. He soon became known as "National Park" Langford. After the publication of his report as a Senate Executive Document, Lieutenant Doane faded back into army obscurity, reappearing only temporarily as a messenger to the Barlow and Heap military expedition of 1871, and as part of the escort for Hayden's party of that same year.

It seems clear that Langford, Washburn, and the other Montana men realized not only the beauty of the Upper Yellowstone, but its real significance as an attraction to tourists which would lead to the eventual commercial development of the whole area. Jay Cooke's Northern Pacific Railroad was already pushing out across the Dakotas from Bismarck, and the Upper Yellowstone country offered one further attraction to settlers along the line of the proposed road. Langford himself even went so far as to lecture on the railroad's behalf at Cooke's Philadelphia home in the spring of 1871.[1] Further proposals for the scientific exploration of the Yellowstone were backed by Speaker of the House James G. Blaine, a noted friend of business.[2] In response to this demand, Congress authorized a large civilian expedition to be led by the famous geologist Ferdinand V. Hayden, who was currently the chief of the Interior Department's United States Geological Survey of the Territories. Hayden's expedition of 1871 was the most famous of all the explorations of the Upper Yellowstone and it undoubtedly contributed the most effective persuasion, in the form of William H. Jackson's photographs and Thomas Moran's gorgeous paintings, for the establishment of the national park in 1872. But Hayden's story is part of a larger episode in the history of Western exploration and will be considered more fully in a subsequent chapter.

7

While the Interior Department, a formidable and not altogether friendly rival of the Army, was preparing to explore the Yellowstone, General Sheridan was also ordering an expedition into the field, to maintain military predominance in exploration, if nothing else. On June 26, 1871, he ordered Captain J. W. Barlow, chief

1. William Turrentine Jackson: "Governmental Exploration of the Upper Yellowstone, 1871," *Pacific Historical Review*, Vol: XI (1942), pp. 188–9.
2. Ibid.

engineer of the Military Division of the Dakotas, "to proceed to the head-waters of the Yellowstone River." He was to head a small party of engineer-explorers who would take advantage of Hayden's large army escort, but who with a small personal escort of six men would operate independently and construct an accurate map of the region.[3]

Barlow's party consisted of Captain D. P. Heap of the Engineers; Mr. W. H. Wood, a topographer; and Mr. Thomas J. Hines, a photographer. They left by train from Chicago on July 2, 1871, and traveled to Ogden, Utah. After a short visit to Salt Lake City, they boarded a stagecoach which took them via Corinne, Utah, to Virginia City, and ultimately on a bouncing buckboard they reached Fort Ellis and joined Hayden's expedition at its staging area.

Delayed for one day after the departure of Hayden, Barlow took the field on July 16 at the head of a party of eleven men, including three civilian packers, two laborers, and a cook. Rendezvousing with Hayden's party at Boetler's Ranch just north of the present-day park region, Barlow abandoned his supply wagons and continued south along the valley of the Yellowstone in company with the larger party. (See map, p. 404.) Barlow's route was identical to that of the Washburn-Doane expedition, except that he turned west up Gardiner's River and discovered, as his first grand sight in the Yellowstone, Mammoth Hot Springs—already the solace of some semi-invalids who had come south to enjoy its waters. From Gardiner's River he moved southeast overland, and on July 24, from atop a ridge, he got his first view of the awesome canyon of the Yellowstone. They reached the river at a bridge built by C. J. Baronette, one of the rescuers of Everts the previous year. Then, turning south once again, they passed Tower Falls, Mount Washburn, which afforded them another magnificent view, the lower falls of the river, Mud Volcano, and eventually, on July 29, reached the shores of Yellowstone Lake.

After exploring parts of the lake, Barlow again parted company with Hayden's party and struck out westward for the East Fork of the Madison River and the geyser basins. Hayden, following a more direct route, broke a new trail to the basins. The first three days of August they spent at the Upper Geyser Basin and then on August 4 they moved on to Old Faithful and the Lower Geysers. Dazzled by the wonders he saw, even the sober military mind of Barlow could

3. J. W. Barlow: "Report of a Reconnaissance of the Basin of the Upper Yellowstone in 1871," 42nd Cong., 2nd sess., *Sen. Exec. Doc. 66* (1872).

only echo the purple phrases of Langford's earlier description. Much of his report was devoted to describing the "superbly beautiful" geyser basin, "with its thousand steam jets and graceful fountains scattered so lavishly along both sides of the river, and surrounded with high enclosing hills clothed with rich foliage." "No other locality," he concluded, "can be found which combines so many attractions. . . ."[4]

On August 7, Lieutenant Doane arrived from Fort Ellis with a small escort to replace Hayden's large company, and his expedition had to begin to turn toward home. Barlow's command headed for Lake Yellowstone and then, breaking entirely new ground, moved south to the Upper Snake River, discovering Heart Lake along the way. One of the most magnificent vistas of all was the view of the Grand Tetons to the south. Climbing mountains never before climbed, and penetrating the uncharted wilderness south of Lake Yellowstone and along the Upper Snake and the Yellowstone, Barlow spent the week of August 13–19 working his way eastward to the Absaroka rampart. In the course of his travels, he thoughtfully named mountains for all his superiors, Generals Sheridan, Hancock, and Humphreys.

By August 19 he had reached the southeast extension of Yellowstone Lake and was heading north for the lower falls of the river. Failing to cross the Yellowstone at Sulphur Mountain, Barlow took his party along the east bank of the river, once again into relatively new country, though once he crossed the Bannock Indian Trail leading to Clark's Fork of the Yellowstone he was in country traversed many years before by the indomitable John Colter, who was now forgotten by explorers. From Baronette's Bridge, the homeward trail was the same as the outward route and included a pause for a luxurious and colorful bath at the Mammoth Hot Springs. They reached Fort Ellis by the first of September.

Barlow's reconnaissance was by no means as spectacular as that conducted by Hayden. His modest report was published as a Senate Document and as such perhaps contributed to the establishment of the park. His great service, however, was in the direct line of the many contributions made by army engineers. With the help of Heap and Wood he constructed the first accurate map of the whole region. Sighting from mountain tops and taking innumerable astronomical observations, he corrected many of the errors in Hayden's more publicized maps. Moreover, he had explored

4. Ibid., p. 30.

country south of Yellowstone Lake which appeared on no other map. Such was the fate of the "army way," however, that all his elaborate notes, observations, meteorological data, and Hines's photographs arrived back in Chicago just in time for the great fire, and very little of it survived.[5]

8

With the creation of the Yellowstone National Park in 1872, much of the work of exploration reverted to civilian surveys, particularly those of F. V. Hayden. Little attention has been given to subsequent army efforts to continue exploration in the region. But there was at least one additional army venture of significance in that direction. In the summer of 1873 Captain W. A. Jones of the Corps of Engineers was ordered by his superior, General E. O. C. Ord, now commander of the Department of the Platte, to make a reconnaissance northward from Fort Bridger, Wyoming, to the Yellowstone region, in an effort to locate a military road that would proceed directly from the Union Pacific Line to the Park and the settlements north of it.[6] Already familiar with the opportunities afforded by such an assignment from his experience on the reconnaissance of the Uinta Mountains in 1871, Captain Jones assembled an elaborate party which included the geologist Theodore B. Comstock of Cleveland, Ohio; Dr. C. C. Parry as botanist; C. L. Heitzman, Assistant Surgeon, U. S. Army, as chemist; and Lieutenant S. E. Blunt, 13th Infantry, astronomer, and in addition four topographers, an astronomical assistant, a meteorological assistant, three general assistants, a chief packer, and two guides. There was also a large escort, a sizeable quartermaster and commissary staff —and later a tribe of unruly Shoshone Indian guides.

While preparing his force for the march north, Captain Jones sent his geologist Comstock and a small escort south from Fort Bridger to make a geological reconnaissance of the Uinta Mountains of Utah, which he had not been able to do in 1871. From the outset, then, Comstock was afforded a view of the geology from the

5. Ibid., p. 3. See also W. H. Jackson: *Time Exposure* (New York: G. P. Putnam's Sons; 1940), p. 203.
6. William A. Jones: *Report Upon the Reconnaissance of Northwestern Wyoming, Including Yellowstone National Park, Made in the Summer of 1873* (Washington, D.C.: U. S. Government Printing Office; 1875), p. 5. Unless otherwise stated, my account is based on this report.

Uintas northward to Montana, a strategic north-south section of the Rocky Mountain region. His report was thus destined to be an elaborate and important one.

On June 12, 1873, Jones led his cavalcade northward out of Fort Bridger and across the Black and Muddy Forks of Green River so long familiar to generations of mountain men (see map, p. 410). He crossed the Union Pacific Railroad line near Bryan and headed north across the red deserts of central Wyoming, aiming for the Wind River Mountains. On June 23 he had reached Fort Stambaugh at the southern extremity of that range. Along the way he passed the celebrated South Pass, coolly labeling it an "evident misnomer," since, as he observed, "the . . . road hardly crosses a hill of any magnitude."[7] From Fort Stambaugh his route took him east of the Wind River Mountains to the valley of the Popo Agie, now defiled by the picturesque settlement of Miner's Delight and the military post at Fort Brown.

On the thirteenth of July his entire cavalcade forded the Wind River, at a tortuous ford "lined with a motley crowd of soldiers, citizens, pack mules, and gaudily dressed Indians with their squaws, children, and numerous loose ponies."[8] From this point they crossed over the Owl Creek Mountains and entered the Big Horn Basin. When they reached the Stinkingwater River they turned west and followed John Colter's old Indian trail into the park. Like the others before him, Captain Jones was so overawed by the natural wonders of the park that he sent one of his assistants north to Fort Ellis for supplies so that he could extend his stay. After locating a trail down the Yellowstone Valley to Gardiner's River and Mammoth Hot Springs that completed for the time being his duties as a wagon road surveyor, Captain Jones turned south to Yellowstone Lake and the Geyser Basins to the West. In a reconnaissance not entirely devoid of humor, he followed a tourist trail into the Geyser Basins, but when he began the return to Yellowstone Lake, his Indian guides, being plains Indians after all, became lost and the command settled into some confusion. Eventually, however, they found their way to Yellowstone Lake, and on its south shore the entire command celebrated by staging a wild dance around two forlorn Sioux scalps given his Shoshone guides by a passing Crow warrior. Soldier and Indian alike vied in a contest of blood-curdling war whoops, to which the Captain apparently contributed his share. A

7. Ibid., p. 8.
8. Ibid., pp. 12–13.

few days later, however, the good relations between Indian and white deteriorated and the guides withdrew, leaving the soldiers stranded in the wilderness in the very shadow of General Sheridan's Peak.

Eventually most of the Indians returned to the fold after being plied with food and heightened respect. But the most important member, the only Indian who knew of a route out of the Yellowstone Basin to the south, continued to sulk. Desperate by now, Captain Jones, who appears to have mistrusted all redmen from the start, finally secured the recalcitrant Indian's aid by threatening to take him back to Fort Brown in irons. This simple stratagem had good effect, and thanks to the aid of that Indian, whose name was never mentioned in Captain Jones's report, they made the major discovery of the expedition—Togwotee Pass. This pass led south into Wind River Valley and afforded an excellent means of connecting the park with the Union Pacific Railroad. Succeeding, as he carefully pointed out, where the Astorian Wilson G. [sic] Hunt, Captain Bonneville, Captain Raynolds and Jim Bridger, and F. V. Hayden had all failed, Captain Jones had penetrated the great southern bastion of Yellowstone Park.

Published in 1875 as a government document, the report of the Jones expedition has been largely obscured by more elaborate civilian reports but, as it stood, it was impressive. Captain Jones's section of it consisted of some eighty pages on the itinerary of the party, the physical geography of the region, the new Yellowstone route to Montana, and a survey of mineralogy. In addition, Lieutenant Blunt published his astronomical calculations, Surgeon Heitzman reported on the chemistry of the mineral and thermal waters, Dr. Parry noted the discovery of ten new plant species, and J. D. Putnam described the insects collected. Most important, however, was Dr. Theodore Comstock's elaborate geological report and colored geological map, one of the first ever drawn of the Yellowstone-Uinta region. Far different from the geological reports of an earlier day, it was organized into topics of modern significance such as physical geology, stratigraphy, dynamical geology, chemical action, and a new subject recently made possible by Lord Kelvin's work, thermodynamics. Comstock also included a stratigraphic chart comparing the various observed strata and their fossils with those of "East North America," "West North America," and Europe. It was the first attempt at a comprehensive survey not only of the Yellowstone country, but of the Uinta Basin, only recently opened up by the paleontologists E. D. Cope and O. C. Marsh.[9] Little read in its own day, and ignored today, Comstock's report deserves more attention than it has received. It provided a cross section of the geological knowledge of the Western United States, circa 1873.

9

While army engineers were helping to reveal the wonders of Yellowstone Park, events of equal significance were taking place to the east, in the valley of the Lower Yellowstone. In 1869 the Philadelphia banker and financier of the Civil War, Jay Cooke, had agreed to back a Northern Pacific Railroad, and plans were immediately launched for a survey of the route between Bismarck and the Pacific Coast. As early as 1870 a civilian engineer, W. Milnor Roberts, surveyed a line from the Pacific Coast east to Bozeman, Montana, the strategic pass through which, it was agreed, the railroad must run.[1] He was unable, however, to continue his survey east of Bozeman because of the general hostility of the Sioux Indians in the valley of the Yellowstone. Military aid was needed.

The Department of the Dakotas responded to the call. In the later summer of 1871, Major J. N. C. Whistler escorted a civilian survey party east from Fort Rice near Bismarck, on the Missouri River, to the mouth of Glendive Creek in eastern Montana.[2] At the same time Captain Edward Ball, operating out of Fort Ellis, shepherded a detachment of surveyors down the Yellowstone some 140 miles. This party suffered great hardships in the early snowfall of that year and twenty-three soldiers returned to the fort in frostbitten condition.[3]

Signs of hostile Indians had been everywhere apparent, and to guard against the possibility of an uprising, the two survey parties of 1872 had large and elaborate escorts. Colonel D. S. Stanley led a party of 33 officers, 553 enlisted men, 13 Indians, and 5 scouts, plus two Gatling guns and a brass twelve-pound cannon out of Fort

9. Henry Fairfield Osborn: *Cope, Master Naturalist* (Princeton, N.J.: Princeton University Press; 1931), pp. 177–260; and Charles Schuchert and Clara Mae Le Vene: *Othniel C. Marsh, Pioneer in Paleontology* (New Haven, Conn.: Yale University Press; 1940), pp. 357–8, are the standard accounts of the work of these two great paleontologists in the Uinta Basin.
1. Mark Brown: *The Plainsmen of the Yellowstone* (New York: G. P. Putnam's Sons; 1961), p. 196.
2. Ibid.
3. Ibid.

Rice on July 26 on a direct line for the mouth of the Powder River, a shorter route than that taken by Major Whistler the previous year. Along the way he was continually menaced by hostile Indians of Chief Gall's band of Unkpapa Sioux. When they reached the mouth of the Powder, the Indians halted them and attempted an ambush under the guise of a parley. A short fight ensued and the Indians were driven off, but as the surveyors ran their line back downstream and down O'Fallon Creek, continual skirmishing occurred and three men were killed.[4]

To the west, on July 27, Major Baker, the commandant at Fort Ellis, led another strong party out along the Yellowstone in an effort to link up with Stanley's party. This group had reached a point just upstream from Pryor's Creek when the Indians surprised them in a night attack. Except for the vigilance of one of the prospectors accompanying the party, the Indians might well have massacred the whole command. About three in the morning of August 14, one Jack Gorman saw an Indian stealing up on the camp, and cocking his revolver, shot the marauder in the head. Instantly the camp awoke and the Indians began firing from all directions. Major Baker, thoroughly intoxicated from an all-night poker game, was unable to assume command, and his subordinate Captain Rawn formed up a skirmish line and drove the attackers off with significant losses. By seven o'clock the battle, which was at once dubbed "The Battle of Poker Flat" in Major Baker's honor, was over. Two men had been killed. In his report, Major Baker declared tersely:

> About 3 a.m. of the 14th the command was attacked by a band
> of Sioux and Cheyennes variously estimated at 400 to 1,000.
> The companies were promptly formed by their company com-
> manders and the Indians were easily repulsed.[5]

With that, the party moved downriver to the rough country near Pompey's Pillar, at which point "Colonel" Hayden, the civilian surveyor, rightly grew apprehensive over his protection and insisted that they conclude their work for the season. Accordingly, and with ostensible reluctance on the part of the military, they turned north to the Musselshell and followed that route back to Fort Ellis.[6] Turned back by the Indians on two fronts, the Army had failed in its mission to aid the railroad explorers and appeared, moreover, to have a genuine Indian war on its hands.

4. Ibid., pp. 202–3.
5. Ibid., pp. 201–2.
6. Ibid.

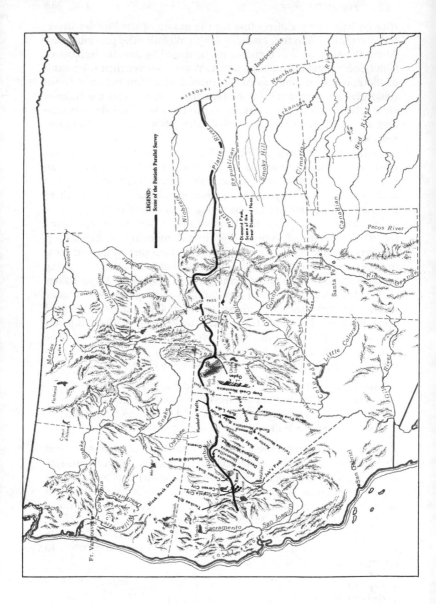

LEGEND:
——— Scene of the Fortieth Parallel Survey

10

In order to complete the railroad survey in the face of Indian hostility, it was obvious that a larger force would be needed. Accordingly, in the spring of 1873, the entire 7th Cavalry was moved to Fort Rice and detailed as part of Colonel Stanley's escorting force. Stanley's assignment, beyond conducting the railroad survey, was to make a reconnaissance, in force, of the Yellowstone country.[7] According to the newspaper correspondent attached to the party, Stanley was expected to (1) aid and escort the Northern Pacific Railroad Survey; (2) "subdue and intimidate" the Indians; (3) locate new military posts; and (4) make a scientific survey of the entire region.[8] Besides the 7th Cavalry, he had at his disposal four companies of the 17th Infantry, five companies of the 22nd Infantry, and a mixed battalion of the 8th and 9th Infantry. As an auxiliary, he was also given thirty Indian scouts, eight half-breeds, and "Lonesome Charlie" Reynolds, one of the most famous civilian scouts of the day. In all, Stanley's command numbered 1,900 men and 250 wagons. To help solve the supply problem, and also as part of the reconnaissance, Colonel "Sandy" Forsythe, the veteran of Beecher's Island, was to take a steamboat, the *Key West*, up the Yellowstone and establish a supply depot at the mouth of Powder River. He took along with him Luther S. "Yellowstone" Kelly, another famous civilian scout.[9]

The scientific party included J. A. Allen of the Cambridge (Massachusetts) Museum, who was in charge of zoology, botany, and paleontology; Dr. L. R. Nettre, geologist; W. R. Powell of Washington, D.C., photographer; Edward Konipucky of Cambridge, artist; and C. W. Bennet, taxidermist. There were also a number of adventurous British noblemen along for the sport, plus Custer's pack of excellent hunting greyhounds. On behalf of science, Sheridan's order particularly decreed that:

> All officers and persons on the expedition are charged with the duty of contributing as much as may be in their power to aid in the collection and preservation of . . . knowledge.[1]

7. New York *Daily Tribune*, Saturday, June 28, 1873, in *Custer's Yellowstone Expedition, 1873–74*, a collection of newspaper clippings in Yale Western Americana Collection. Also see D. S. Stanley: *Personal Memoirs* (Cambridge, Mass.: Harvard University Press; 1917), Appendix, pp. 238–71.
8. Ibid.
9. Brown: *Plainsmen*, p. 203.
1. New York *Daily Tribune*, Saturday, June 28, 1873.

General Terry, addressing the departing explorers, declared this to be "the most interesting of all the Indian campaigns,"[2] and one lieutenant wrote home to mother: "What with English lords, scientists, and outsiders of every military description, you would imagine it a big picnic. . . ."[3] The press, in the person of a special correspondent of the New York *Tribune,* was on hand to cover all aspects of the expedition.

The line of march took the cavalcade out along Major Whistler's route of 1871, where they crossed the Big Muddy on an ingenious pontoon bridge constructed of ninety-six whiskey kegs. (See map, p. 404.) Custer, ranging far out ahead with an elite detachment of the 7th Cavalry commanded by his brother Tom, reached the Yellowstone at the mouth of Glendive Creek on July 13 and the whole command went into bivouac. It was two weeks before the supplies were finally replenished and the troops ferried across the river, but at last, on July 27, the actual survey could start.

Custer, as usual, was in the van, relentlessly scouting ahead. Then, on August 4, six Sioux Indians suddenly appeared on the plain ahead, making rude demonstrations. Custer, with Moylan's squadron at hand, quickly gave chase, though he was ten miles ahead of the main command. The Indians retreated hastily, leading the troopers into an ambush near the mouth of Tongue River, close to present-day Miles City, Montana. Just in time, Custer sensed the ambush and dismounted his 80 men to receive a disciplined charge by a body of 250 mounted Indians. The correspondent from the *Tribune* declared of the Indian charge: "The 7th Cavalry could hardly have done it better. With painted faces, heads decorated with ribbons and fillets," he added, "they sallied out with loud-whoops."[4]

The fire from the dismounted troopers quickly shattered the Indian charge, and both sides settled down to a war of tactics. Led by Sitting Bull, the Indians deployed in a semicircle and kept a steady fire on the troopers. The battle lasted for nearly three hours, with few casualties on either side, but at the end of that time the soldiers had virtually run out of ammunition and the situation was becoming desperate. The Indians essayed a series of stratagems— first they tried to stampede the horses, but Custer himself foiled this attempt; then they set fire to the grass, but there was no wind

2. Brown: *Plainsmen,* p. 204.
3. Ibid.
4. New York *Daily Tribune,* article in *Custer's Yellowstone Expedition, 1873–74,* p. 20. My description of the battle of Tongue River is based on this account.

and the grass was green. Still, they advanced behind the smoke screen, drawing the last bit of cavalry fire.

With disaster looming greater at each rifle volley, Custer, through the haze and smoke, noticed far in the rear of the Indian lines some messengers riding from the direction of Stanley's command. Sensing that help was near and that this was the climactic moment of the battle, the boy colonel ordered his tired troopers to mount and charge. The Indians "turned like sheep and scattered in every direction," noted the *Tribune* writer, and the battle was won.[5] The only casualties were three stragglers from Colonel Stanley's main detachment, one of them the veterinarian, who had gone ahead to get his horse a drink of water.

Not content with his victory, Custer pursued the Indians for three days on a daring series of moonlight marches. On Sunday, the tenth of August, they reached the Yellowstone near the mouth of the Big Horn and found that the Indians had already crossed it. The weary men were granted a day's rest while Bloody Knife, the chief Indian scout, constructed bullboats to ferry the supplies across the river. At dawn on Monday morning, a few Indians appeared on the opposite bank. When the troopers rushed out to see them, a whole volley cut loose from five hundred yards away, across the river. The horses were ordered to the rear and one tardy trooper who affected nonchalance suddenly heard a loud sickening crash in the underbrush and found himself dragging a dead horse.[6]

The Indians, now massed strategically on the opposite bank to oppose the crossing, suddenly turned the battle into a sporting contest. One by one they leaped out to hurl insults, and the soldier sharpshooters did their best to pick them off. Private Tuttle, Custer's orderly and a renowned sharpshooter, "dropped" three Indians, but when he took aim on a fourth, he was "dropped" by a rifle bullet between the eyes. Downstream, the Indians crossed the river and attempted to outflank the soldiers. Two hundred dripping redskins hurled themselves on Lieutenant Braden's command of eighteen men. Braden himself fell, his leg shattered, but the veterans of the 7th held firm.

Once again, at the psychological moment, Custer turned to his favorite tactic. Let the *Tribune* correspondent tell it:

"Strike up Garry Owen," said he to the leader of the band. The familiar notes of the stirring Irish air acted like magic. If the

5. Ibid., p. 21.
6. Ibid., pp. 24–5.

commander had had a galvanic battery connecting with the
solar flexus [sic] of every man in the field, he could hardly have
electrified them more thoroughly. What matter if the cornet
played a faltering note and the alto horn was a little husky?
There was no mistaking its tune and meaning. "Forward!"
shouted the commanders, and away they went "pell-mell" . . .
like a whirlwind.[7]

The Indians ran for their lives, the shells from "Old Stanby" Stanley's artillery, which had just come on the field, exploding in their
midst. The battle was over in an instant. One last burst landed in
the midst of a huddle of squaws and old men who were watching the
sport. When the cloud of dust and debris cleared away, they were
all gone. The Battle of the Big Horn, as far as Custer was concerned,
had come to a satisfying conclusion.

The rest of the expedition was an anticlimax as the command
headed down the Yellowstone, except for one slight skirmish when
some Indians, not without a sense of grim humor, hid behind
Pompey's Pillar and let fly upon a company of bathing troopers.
After connecting with the last stake of Baker's survey on the Yellowstone, the command turned north to the Musselshell. Then it
divided, and Stanley returned to Glendive Creek via Porcupine
Creek while Custer rode overland. From that point they followed the
old trail to Fort Rice. It had been an interesting campaign, though
the effectiveness of the scientific explorers was severely limited by
the hostility of the Indians, who appeared neither "subdued" nor
"intimidated" by Stanley's command. Indeed, the savage strategists
appear to have learned far more about Custer's military habits than
he did about theirs—for in a similar decoy and ambush situation
a few years later on another Big Horn they proved far more skillful
than he.

As to the railroad, there was an interesting development. While
Baker, Stanley, and Custer were scouting the country and praising
its possibilities in their reports, a team of Austrian bankers was also
making a reconnaissance of the region. Upon their return, they
pronounced the Northern Pacific a "premature enterprise" and refused to subscribe to Cooke's bonds. Cooke in desperation threw
them on the open market for sale to widows and shopkeepers, using
the same technique with which he financed the Civil War. Unfortunately, however, it was 1873 and the general panic of that

7. Ibid., pp. 25–6. The quote appears on p. 26.

year caught up with him, causing the fall of the House of Cooke. To the dismay of the American widows and shopkeepers—not to mention the soldiers, like Custer, and the boosters, like Langford—the road did not get past Bismarck for some years.[8]

11

The collapse of the Northern Pacific Railroad did not daunt the military, however. By the summer of 1874 the officers of the Department of the Dakotas were occupied with a new problem in the southern part of their territory—the unexplored Black Hills country. Though the Black Hills were a familiar Western landmark since 1735, when the Vérendryes discovered them, they had not been successfully explored. In 1857 Lieutenant G. K. Warren of the Corps of Topographical Engineers had entered the region and had described Inyan Kara and other prominent features, but he was turned back by hostile Indians at Bear Butte.[9] By 1874 civilian miners had begun to approach and enter the Black Hills in search of precious metals—totally disregarding the fact that it was a favorite Indian sanctuary and hunting ground.

In the summer of 1874, in order to verify, or discount, the rumors of gold discoveries in the Indian sanctuary, the commanding general of the Dakotas ordered Colonel Custer to make one of his famous reconnaissances in force of the whole region. Custer's command included ten companies of the 7th Cavalry, two companies of Infantry, a battery of three Gatling guns and one Rodman gun, a detachment of Indian scouts and guides, and a military band—in all, over a thousand men. His train consisted of nearly a hundred wagons. In addition, he was assisted by a scientific staff consisting of Captain William Ludlow of the Engineers; W. H. Wood, topographer; Professor N. H. Winchell, the State Geologist of Minnesota; George Bird Grinnell of Yale, a paleontologist; and a photographer. Professor Winchell's task was the most demanding, for he was to report on the various auriferous strata and mother lodes observed.

With the usual ceremony, Custer's command left Fort Abraham Lincoln, near Bismarck, to the strains of "Garry Owen" on July 2,

8. Brown: *Plainsmen*, p. 120. Also see in *Custer's Yellowstone Expedition*, pp. 41–7, three articles: "The Northern Pacific Railroad," "The Suppressed Report of the Berlin and Vienna Experts," and "The Reply of the Company."
9. Warren: "Report." See my Chapter 9, p. 310.

1874.[1] On the advice of Lonesome Charlie Reynolds and the other veteran guides who accompanied the expedition, everyone was expecting an Indian attack before the march was over. Their general route was due west to the divide between the Missouri River drainage and that of the Little Missouri (see map, p. 404). In following this course, they struck the Heart River and then turned south, crossing the Cannonball and traversing the Bad Lands just east of the Little Missouri. On July 18, they crossed the Belle Fourche, or North Fork, of the Cheyenne on the edge of the Black Hills proper. They continued due south along the western margin of the Black Hills to the famous landmark of Inyan Kara, a high basalt dome that Lieutenant Warren had seen in September of 1857. From this point they followed Castle Valley southeast through great fields of lush grass and wildflowers. When they reached Harney Peak near the head of French Creek in the heart of the Black Hills, the main party went into encampment while Captain Ludlow led a rapid reconnaissance to the South Fork of the Cheyenne and back again. Custer and his men had now traversed the Black Hills from north to south and they paused to allow the miners and geologists time to prospect the promising ledges of French Creek.

On August 2, from his camp at Harney Peak Custer sent a dramatic overland dispatch to Fort Laramie reporting his progress and announcing "that gold has been found at several places, and it is the belief of those who are giving their attention to this subject that it will be found in paying quantities." He added: "Veins of what the geologists term gold-bearing quartz crop out on almost every hillside."[2]

When the colonel and his command turned north up the eastern edge of the Black Hills, they again paused at Bear Butte on Warren's trail of 1857 and Custer sent another dramatic dispatch, this time by Lonesome Charlie himself. He announced that "the mystery which has so long existed regarding the interior of the Black Hills has been dispelled." It was a lush region of wildflowers, good grass, water, timber, and most important: "On some of the water courses

1. Report of the Chief of Army Engineers, in "Annual Report of the Secretary of War," 43rd Cong., 2nd sess., *H.R. Exec. Doc. 1*, Pt. II (1874–75), Appendix KK: "Preliminary Report of Reconnaissance to the Black Hills, St. Paul, Minn., Sept. 7, 1874," p. 628. See also Jay Monaghan: *Custer* (Boston: Little Brown and Co.; 1959), pp. 353 ff. See also *Custer's Yellowstone Expedition*, pp. 54–9.
2. George A. Custer: "Order Book," MS., Yale Western Americana Collection. These are printed in 43rd Cong., 2nd sess., *Sen. Exec. Doc. 32* (1875), pp. 1–9.

almost every panful of earth produced gold in small, yet paying quantities."[3] The Black Hills were "ripe" for white civilization.

The return march to Fort Lincoln was uneventful and the entire command reached the fort on August 30, 1874. The reconnaissance had lasted exactly two months. And the real conflict arose when the party returned. Captain Ludlow, the chief engineer, by his failure to return an enthusiastic report, cast strong doubt on the gold discoveries;[4] and the geologist's report, though highly interesting in that it extended the Dakota Cretaceous much farther south than any geologist conceived it to be, failed completely to substantiate or even mention the discovery of gold in paying quantities.[5] In addition, Colonel William B. Hazen, the commandant at Fort Buford far to the north, used rainfall statistics collected from all the army posts in the region to call into question Custer's descriptions of the Dakotas as a lush country fit for agricultural settlement.[6]

The commanding general, Hancock, appears to have accepted Custer's telegraphed reports, but with some caution, as he submitted his formal report to the Secretary of War.[7] In addition, civilian scientists and would-be entrepreneurs were not entirely sure of gold in the Black Hills. They suspected Custer of attempting to revive the fortunes of the Northern Pacific Railroad and of loosely promoting settlement into the Dakota Indian lands. Meanwhile, the small prospectors headed in droves for the valley of French Creek, constructing a stockade in that area in the late fall of 1874. It was all the army could do to locate them and drive them out that winter and the following spring. Custer had almost singlehandedly begun a gold rush.

12

The Black Hills gold rush only compounded the government's difficulties with the Sioux Indians, however, since not only were

3. Ibid. See especially p. 8.
4. Report of the Chief of Army Engineers, in "Annual Report of the Secretary of War," 43rd Cong., 2nd sess., *H.R. Exec. Doc. 1*, Pt. II (1874–75), Appendix KK: "Preliminary Report of Reconnaissance to the Black Hills, St. Paul, Minn., Sept. 7, 1874," p. 630.
5. Ibid., pp. 631–2.
6. William Babcock Hazen: *Our Barren Lands: the Interior of the United States West of the One-Hundredth Meridian and East of the Sierra Nevadas* (Cincinnati, Ohio: R. Clarke and Co.; 1875). See especially pp. 11–28.
7. Report of the General of the Army, in "Annual Report of the Secretary of War," 43rd Cong., 2nd sess., *H.R. Exec. Doc. 1*, Pt. II (1874), pp. 24–5.

the Black Hills their favorite refuge, but they were also part of the official Sioux reservation. The problem of the Black Hills gold was thus turned over to the Indian Bureau, and certain members of Congress attempted to block the publication of anything that would advertise the region and its resources. The Secretary of the Interior, determined to get to the bottom of the gold rumors, ordered still another expedition into the Dakotas in the summer of 1875.[8] This one was to be a thoroughly scientific venture. At the suggestion of Professor John Strong Newberry of the Columbia School of Mines, and with the concurrence of Joseph Henry and the Smithsonian Institution, Walter P. Jenney was selected as geologist in charge of the expedition, and Henry Newton, Newberry's protégé, went as his assistant. Newton was an especially able man with some years of experience in the field of mineralogy. Others who accompanied the expedition were Newberry's son, C. G. Newberry, who gave out before the expedition reached the Black Hills and returned to Fort Laramie; Dr. V. T. McGillicuddy, topographer; Captain H. P. Tuttle of the Cambridge Observatory, astronomer; and a force of some eleven professional miners led by W. F. Patrick, E.M. Most of these miners later set up operations in the Black Hills and contributed to its colorful boom.

Because the Indians were expected to demonstrate against this newest invasion, the explorers were provided with an elaborate escort of some 400 soldiers and a train of 75 wagons—a cavalcade which almost matched in splendor that of Colonel Custer the previous year.

The whole party assembled at Cheyenne on April 25, 1875, and left shortly thereafter along the trail to the Spotted Tail and Red Cloud agencies, the easiest route to the Black Hills.[9] They entered the Black Hills from the south and during the four months and twenty days they were in the Indian sanctuary made a complete geological and mineralogical survey, working generally from south to north (see map, p. 404). It was a vast improvement on Winchell's survey of the previous year. On every hand, miners as well

8. See Walter P. Jenney: "The Mineral Wealth, Climate, Rainfall, and Natural Resources of the Black Hills of Dakota," 44 Cong., 1st sess., *Sen. Exec. Doc. 51* (1876).
9. Henry Newton and Walter P. Jenney: *Report on the Geology and Resources of the Black Hills of Dakota, with Atlas* (Washington, 1880), p. 19 and *passim*. This is the final report of the expedition, published by the United States Geographical and Geological Survey of the Rocky Mountain Region, under John Wesley Powell. It contains the most complete narrative of the Black Hills Survey. Hereafter referred to as Newton and Jenney: *Report*.

as geologists found evidences of gold and they fell to work with enthusiasm. Even the soldiers of the escort caught the spirit and neglected their duties to pan for gold. The chief result of the expedition appears to have been, not only the confirmation of gold deposits near French Creek, but the location of numerous other auriferous deposits in all parts of the Black Hills. Jenney, who seems to have devoted most of his time to the gold strikes, found at least six different geological sites for the precious metal (1) in veins of quartz traversing the Archean slates and schists; (2) in slates mineralized by water depositing silicon and iron pyrites (fool's gold); (3) in the conglomerates of the Potsdam Sandstone; (4) in trachytic porphyrites intruded at the time of the elevation of the hills; (5) in slates and schists of this later period; and (6) in the placer gravels resulting from the erosion of the previous formations in the Tertiary Period. He concluded:

> Compared with some of the world-renowned districts in California and Australia, the placers at present discovered are not remarkably rich, yet there are claims already opened and worked which are yielding a very good return for the labor employed. . . . [He added] There is gold enough to thoroughly settle and develop the country, and after the placers are exhausted, stock-raising will be the great business of the inhabitants who have a world of wealth in the splendid grazing of this region.[1]

He had thus confirmed Custer's report almost completely.

When the expedition returned to civilization, Jenney published his practical findings in a preliminary report that was distributed by the Interior Department in 1876. The other scientists, laboring more profoundly, produced a monumental report on the Black Hills which compared favorably with anything ever done by government explorers.[2] Newton unraveled the whole complicated geological history of the Black Hills in a very sophisticated study. He described the numerous sedimentary deposits, several periods of uplift and igneous intrusion, and he placed the present or last uplift of the Hills in the late Cretaceous or early Miocene period. Most interesting was his work in the river deposits, which outlined clearly the ideas of antecedent and consequent river erosion, a concept often attributed solely to Major John Wesley Powell. To cap his labors, Newton drew a spectacular topographical relief map which showed

1. Ibid., pp. 225, 300.
2. Ibid., *passim*.

the Black Hills to be an immense ring surrounding an uplifted plateau cut by numerous rivers and streams. It was one of the best pieces of topographical art ever done. (See p. 339 in Portfolio II.)

Other interesting contributions to the final geological report were a study of the paleontology by R. P. Whitfield, the botany by Asa Gray, the astronomy and barometric hypsometry by Captain Tuttle, and most important a treatise on microscopical petrography by John H. Caswell. Microscopical petrography, or the study of rock and mineral structures by means of microscopic slides, was a new technique devised in Europe and pioneered by Professor Ferdinand Zirkel of Leipzig, who had been brought by Clarence King to the United States and here did a volume in King's Fortieth Parallel series.[3] Caswell's study, published with the Jenney-Newton final report on the Black Hills, was thus the second such work to appear in America, and, but for an unfortunate circumstance, it might well have been the first.

After the preliminary publication of Jenney's report on the gold-bearing strata, certain forces in Congress again came to the fore and blocked the passage of the final report. Newton, distraught at the delay, hastened back to the Black Hills for more data, and there, on the fifth of August 1877, he died of typhoid fever.[4] When his work was finally published in 1880, it was prefaced by a tribute from his old mentor John Strong Newberry.

The importance of the Jenney study is suggested by the shift in emphasis between it and Custer's survey of the previous year. Whereas Custer's had been a military reconnaissance, the Jenney foray had been predominantly a civilian venture, sponsored by the Interior Department and staffed by experts from Eastern and national institutions. It keynoted the fact that by the mid-seventies, academic-oriented civilian scientists were definitely beginning to challenge the military for control of Western exploration. Indeed, the civilians had almost certainly begun to replace the soldiers.

3. See Ferdinand Zirkel: *Microscopical Petrography*, United States Geological Exploration of the Fortieth Parallel, Professional Papers of the Engineer Department, United States Army, No. 18, 7 vols. (Washington, 1870–1880), Vol. VI.
4. Newton and Jenney: *Report*, p. xi.

13

As if to heighten this contrast, there was still another series of military-supported, but civilian-controlled explorations that took place during this same period. These were the Yale College expeditions led by Professor Othniel Charles Marsh, the paleontologist.

Othniel C. Marsh was a product of the Yale Scientific School, where he studied under Benjamin Silliman and James Dwight Dana, the geologist to the Wilkes Antarctic Expedition.[5] After a year's supplementary study at Heidelberg and Berlin, he had returned to Yale as a professor of the new science of paleontology and director of a scientific museum which his uncle George Peabody was in the process of building for Yale. Almost immediately, Marsh entered the world of science from an established position, but his discovery of prehistoric fossil horses near Antelope Station, Nebraska, mentioned at the outset of this narrative, launched him on his special career as scientific paleontological prospector and explorer of the Old West.

After attending the Chicago meeting of the American Association for the Advancement of Science, in August of 1868, Marsh headed West. From the evidence he collected at his brief stop at a remote Nebraska stationhouse, and on subsequent Western expeditions made with military aid, Marsh was able to reconstruct the evolution of the horse all the way from three-toed Protohippus of the Pleistocene down to the modern, hooved variety. He thus demonstrated, among other things, that the horse had existed in North America long before the Spaniards arrived with their awesome beasts. But, most important, his reconstruction of the horse genealogy was the strongest argument yet produced to confirm the truth of Charles Darwin's theory of evolution. It supplanted Joseph Leidy's crude efforts of a decade earlier, and Darwin himself acknowledged it as the best support he had received since the publication of the *Origin of Species* in 1859.[6]

Eager to follow up his initial discoveries, Marsh planned another expedition into the West in 1869, but widespread Indian uprisings made it impractical. In 1870, however, with support from General

5. For biographical data on Marsh, see Schuchert and Le Vene: *Marsh*. See also O. C. Marsh: "Memoirs," MS., Yale Historical Manuscripts Collection. This last is a collection of five autobiographical chapters written by Marsh, and referred to by his official biographers as the "Howe Manuscript" since it was given to Yale by Mrs. Ernest Howe of Litchfield, Connecticut.
6. Ibid., p. 2.

Sherman, Marsh led an elaborate entourage of Yale graduate students on the first of a series of Western expeditions. Armed with pistols, fine rifles, hunting knives, and great quantities of camping paraphernalia, the Yale contingent left New Haven on the last day of June 1870. They proceeded out across Nebraska to Fort McPherson, near the railroad town of North Platte. There they picked up a military escort of veteran cavalrymen, two Pawnee Indian trackers, and the celebrated scouts Major North and Buffalo Bill.[7]

The route followed by the party of paleontologists and soldiers was due north across the Platte, over the blazing Sand Hills, where the temperature shot to 114 degrees, to the Loup Fork. Then they turned west along that river to its headwaters, at which point they again turned south and struck the North Platte River near the mouth of Bird Wood Creek. When their strange cavalcade of Indians, soldiers, and the by now shaggy paleontologists approached the town of North Platte, Nebraska, the entire population turned out, fearing Indians were swooping down in a raid.

Out on the Loup Fork, where the river had eroded away the strata, their scientific efforts had met with success. The soldiers stood guard while the Yale geologists, often on hands and knees, searched the stream beds for specimens of ancient fauna. Even the Indians joined in the fun of digging up the prehistoric beasts, and before they finished, the party had collected more primitive horses, miniature camels, and a mastodon.

Shortly after returning to Fort McPherson, Marsh and his men shifted their base of operations farther west, to Fort D. A. Russell in Wyoming. Here again they met with extraordinary success. In northern Colorado they located a Miocene formation which had never been seen before, south of the White River of South Dakota. It yielded great quantities of prehistoric turtles, rhinoceri, birds, rodents, and the curious remains of an oreodon, which C. W. Betts, the correspondent from *Harper's,* described as "a remarkable animal combining characteristics of the modern sheep, pig, and deer."[8] They also found a specimen of the gigantic horned Titanothere, whose jaw alone measured four feet in length.

The next phase of the expedition operated out of Fort Bridger, Wyoming, on the edge of the Uinta Mountains. Here Marsh helped

7. Ibid., pp. 101–3 ff. See also "Marsh Memoir," Marsh Papers, Yale Historical Manuscripts Collection.
8. C. W. Betts: "The Yale College Expedition of 1870," *Harper's New Monthly Magazine,* Vol. XLIII (June–Nov. 1871), p. 666. Pages 663–71 provide the best narrative of Marsh's expedition of that year.

to open up the Tertiary lake-bed formations that were to yield end-less specimens of dinosaurs and other ancient reptiles. He took his party across the Uinta Mountains at a pass 11,000 feet high, over a route recently opened by the army to supply the Uinta Indian Agency. In the course of their labors, he and his men narrowly escaped a shoot-out with the notorious Brown's Hole gang of desperadoes.[9]

After their arduous work in the Uintas, Marsh and his men turned to pleasure. They visited Salt Lake City, where the students admired Brigham Young's twenty-two daughters, and Marsh held earnest conversations with Young concerning the fossil horse. Marsh's discovery soon became celebrated throughout the desert Zion—not as a proof for Darwinian evolution, but as one more demonstration that the lost tribe of Mormon and Moroni had indeed existed in North America. It was clear to Brigham Young that Marsh had found the very ancient horses described in the Book of Mormon, which had previously been somewhat of an embarrassment to nineteenth-century Mormon Prophets.

After journeying to California, where they visited Yosemite, the Mariposa, and the geysers, Marsh and his students returned to the plains of Kansas and in bitter cold, mid-November weather they braved the hostile Cheyennes in one more search for fossils. It was a climax to the year's work. Escorted by cavalry, who protected them from Indian attack, they hunted buffalo with furious intensity and they held monumental prairie feasts punctuated by Yale College songs. They also found fossils. Among the most important of these were the mosasaurs, giant sea serpents thirty-five feet long, who lived in the warm seas of Kansas millions of years ago. Climaxing their endeavors, in the soft chalk along the river Marsh found a small hollow bone about six inches long, which was actually, as he later learned, the wing finger of a huge flying dragon, the reptile pterodactyl. The first such creature found in North America, it dwarfed anything found elsewhere in the world. It had a wing-spread of twenty feet, and yet weighed only about thirty pounds. It was an aeronautical and paleontological marvel.[1]

When Marsh and his students arrived back in New Haven in December, they came in triumph, bearing, not gold as was traditional in most prospecting expeditions of the day, but thirty-five boxes of fossil bones. This was the nucleus of exotic creatures

9. Ibid., p. 671.
1. "Marsh Memoir," Marsh Papers, Yale Historical Manuscripts Collection. Also see Schuchert and Le Vene: *Marsh*, pp. 119–20.

around which one of the world's great museums would be constructed. In contributing supplies and military escorts, the Army had helped to subsidize the climactic emergence of a new science in America.

Marsh continued to receive military cooperation and in the succeeding years, 1871, 1872, and 1873, he led his students and coworkers on a series of expeditions to all parts of the West, even journeying to Oregon, where he opened up the John Day River Basin, an immense fossil repository. Everywhere he went, too, Marsh established collectors, who continually shipped him trainloads of fossil specimens, until by the late seventies he became virtually the Andrew Carnegie of the paleontological world. His agents became notorious for their acquisitive instinct, and occasionally for their carelessness in recovering specimens. Marsh's own running feud with E. C. Cope, a Philadelphia paleontologist, was one of the celebrated scandals of the days of rampant robber-barons in science.[2]

Marsh was also a reformer, however, and on his last important Western expedition, in 1874, he met Chief Red Cloud at his Nebraska reservation. Learning that the Indian agent was cheating and profiteering from the redmen, Marsh went to Washington and initiated an investigation of the Indian Bureau which embarrassed the government and highlighted the Indians' plight. Primed with information obtained by army officers contemptuous of the Indian Bureau, Marsh succeeded finally in securing the resignation of Columbus Delano, the Secretary of the Interior.[3] In his own way,

2. See Osborne: *Cope;* and Schuchert and Le Vene: *Marsh, passim.* For Marsh's activities as a collector, see Schuchert and Le Vene: *Marsh,* pp. 169–225. They neglect to mention, however, that Marsh's field collectors, being unfamiliar with the scientific purposes of the fossils, often were extremely careless in removing the specimens from the rock matrices in which they were found. Cope's collectors were guilty of the same fault. See Michele La Clergue: "The Laramie Controversy in American Geology," unpublished paper presented to the Midwest Junto of the History of Science Society, April 2, 1965.

The climax of the Cope-Marsh feud came on Jan. 12, 1890, when the New York *Herald* published Cope's attack on Marsh, accusing him of plagiarizing from his assistants, and on Jan. 19, 1890, when it also printed Marsh's reply headed, "Marsh Hurls Azoic Facts At Cope." Perhaps Marsh's unkindest sally was the one in which he demonstrated that Cope had described the giant reptile *Elasmosaurus* "wrong end foremost." Cope apparently had mistaken the head for the tail and vice versa.

3. Schuchert and Le Vene: *Marsh,* pp. 139–68. Also see Marsh Papers, Yale Historical Manuscripts Collection, for letters from the military informing Marsh of the agency frauds. He was personally thanked by General George A.

the Yale paleontologist had helped the Army gain sweet revenge on its civilian tormentors, and he had helped Red Cloud, who became his fast friend, even to the extent of visiting Marsh's New Haven mansion. He had also become a famous figure in his own right, one whose importance in the world of civilian science would eventually have crucial, if ironic, significance for the fate of all army exploration in the West. The 1870's were, however, his great days as a field explorer. As the exotic shapes of prehistoric beasts began to be assembled for school children in Yale's Peabody Museum, it was clear that he had discovered a new Western horizon. He had in fact revealed and dramatized much of ancient America.

By the same token, the predominantly civilian character of Marsh's expeditions, and other simultaneous developments, made it clear that the days of the pure military reconnaissance were rapidly passing. By 1876 the Bureau of Explorations and Surveys, and the whole field intelligence division of the Army Engineers, was languishing for lack of funds. Congress had cut its appropriations and nothing that General Humphreys said in his plaintive annual reports had any effect. The emphasis had shifted to a more sophisticated approach to Western exploration. But though this phase of its activities had been curtailed, the Army played a great role for a time in developing the newer, more sophisticated academic approaches to scientific exploration in the West.

Custer in 1875. See Letters Received, 1875, Marsh Letterbooks, Peabody Museum, Yale University.

CHAPTER XII

The West of Clarence King

THE most noteworthy of Army-sponsored exploring achievements was Clarence King's Geological and Geographical Exploration of the Fortieth Parallel. A widely heralded venture of its day, King's survey, like that of Frémont in an earlier time, has rarely been viewed as a phase of military operations in the West. Henry Adams, for example, after terming the Congressional enabling act for the Survey, almost the "first modern act of legislation," took pains to emphasize that King had organized the Survey as "a civil—not military—measure."[1] However, King received his appointment as director of the Survey and the entire appropriations for the work, as a result of military rather than civilian backing.[2] Moreover he received his commission directly from Secretary of War Stanton and he regularly reported to and took orders from General Andrew Atkinson Humphreys, the Chief of Army Engineers.[3] To obscure this fact is to distort not only the nature of his survey, but the entire institutional relationship of government explorations in the post-Civil War West. In its sponsorship of the King Survey and its extreme hospitality to wide-ranging and even experimental scientific ventures, the Army proved actually to be on the side of progress rather than, as is commonly held, on the side of tradition and reaction. This perhaps explains the surprise and even indignation of the military when they were attacked by scientific men on these grounds in the late seventies.

1. Henry Adams: *The Education of Henry Adams*, Modern Library Edition (New York: Random House; 1931), p. 312.
2. See Chapter 10, p. 385. Also see Wilkins: *Clarence King*, pp. 94–5.
3. For evidence of King's working relationship with General Humphreys see "Letters Sent by Clarence King to General A. A. Humphreys, 1867–1879," Records of the United States Geological Exploration of the Fortieth Parallel, R.G. 57, National Archives.

But if the King Survey was military in origin and administration, it was, by the same token, decidedly different from
most army operations. King was allowed to write his own orders,
and to pick his own staff, all of whom were civilian scientists. His
parties included no officers of the Engineer Corps. The only direct
connection with the Army, once the Survey was in the field, was its
dependence upon military outposts and quartermaster depots for
supplies, the constant use of military escorts, whose value had
been demonstrated in the Arizona adventure of 1866, and King's
obligation to clear all of his activities with General Humphreys.
This freedom contributed in important ways, and not only to the efficiency and sophistication of his scientific work. It also resulted
in the gradual emergence of a spirit of independence among civilian explorer-scientists that eventually helped to overthrow army
rule in this field. Paradoxically, therefore, in attempting to range itself on the side of scientific progress and intellectual freedom, the
Army sowed the seeds of its own destruction as a factor in high-level
national science and exploration in the West.

The plan for a scientific survey of the Fortieth Parallel country took final shape in King's mind one brilliant autumn day in
1866 when he and James Gardner looked out from the sunny slopes
of Mount Conners across the Great Basin to the purple haze of
mountains beyond,[4] but he had been thinking about leading his
own grand survey of the Cordilleras and the Great Basin for some
time before that. While working on the Whitney surveys, as early
as 1864, he had whiled away his idle hours subconsciously designing emblems and badges for the various surveys which he planned
to lead. Once he even boldly printed in his notebook: "The U. S.
Interior Survey C. R. King, Supt."[5] Judging from Whitney's own
correspondence, he too believed King would eventually lead his
own survey of the arid basin regions southeast of the Sierras. What
surprised Whitney, and everyone else, was the magnitude and ingenuity of King's eventual plan.[6]

Anyone who knew Clarence King should not have been surprised, however. When Henry Adams, who always admired energy,
described him as an "Alcibiades or Alexander," the "best and brightest man of his generation," he was hardly exaggerating at all.[7]

4. Bartlett: *Great Surveys*, p. 141.
5. See, for example, "Field Notes and Observations on Yosemite, Oct.–Nov.
64," B-2, King Papers, Huntington Library, San Marino, California.
6. J. D. Whitney to W. D. Whitney, San Francisco, April 29, 1867, Whitney
Papers, Yale Historical Manuscripts Collection.
7. Adams: *Education*, pp. 311, 416.

Born in Newport, Rhode Island, in 1842, the son of a Canton trader who died shortly after his son's birth, Clarence King had always been an enthusiastic many-sided person.[8] Well reared, handsome, athletic, and yet of a speculative bent and immersed in the causes of the day, King gave the appearance, by the time he entered Yale in the fall of 1860, that he was destined for greatness. At Yale he found his opportunity. Scorning the traditional classical education offered by the college, he enrolled instead in the new Sheffield Scientific School and there allied himself with progress, success, and intellectual excitement.

The Sheffield Scientific School stood at the corner of Prospect and Grove streets, several blocks down College Street from the old Yale Fence, traditional heart of the campus. This was appropriate, because it occupied a rather anomalous place in the Yale education program. Since the college already had a scientific program staffed by many of its best professors, the Sheffield School served the function of a graduate school and a place for special advanced work with the great men of the day. There King worked with the chemist George Jarvis Brush, and with William H. Brewer. He also studied geology under James Dwight Dana, whose lectures, so full of fascinating stories about Dana's South Seas expedition with Wilkes, must have given King his first enthusiasm for the life of an explorer-scientist.[9] Among his classmates in scientific studies was Othniel C. Marsh soon to be his co-worker and benefactor. Brewer's letters from California, which Brush read him, inspired King to become a field geologist and go West.[1] Taking his boyhood friend and Yale classmate James Gardner with him, King set out across the country for California in 1862, and they had their historic meeting with Brewer on a Sacramento paddlewheeler in the fall of 1863.

The California Geological Surveys became King's graduate school and their formative relationship to his career is obvious. What is not so obvious, however, is the fact that as much as any-

8. The best biographical treatment of King is Wilkins: *Clarence King.* Also see *Clarence King Memoirs,* The Century Association (New York: G. P. Putnam's Sons; 1904), which contains important articles on King by a number of his closest friends. In addition, see Biographical Papers, A 1–6, King Papers, Huntington Library, and S. F. Emmons Papers, Boxes 30 and 31, Library of Congress.

9. See James Dwight Dana: "Lectures," MSS., Dana Papers, Beinecke Library, Yale University. See also Gardner's impression of Dana's lectures, quoted in Wilkins: *Clarence King,* p. 38.

1. Wilkins: *Clarence King,* p. 42.

thing else King's career was shaped and his opportunities created by his contact with the Yale scientists. European-trained and interested in the special problems of their new disciplines, the Yale scientists and their friends at Harvard and in Washington were men of power who came to play a vital role in the institutionalization of science in America. Able, sophisticated, full of energy and singleminded dedication, they virtually paralleled the captains of industry in their organizing abilities. King almost immediately became their favorite, and his outstanding success in California served to confirm their expectations. Thus, when he went to Washington in 1866, armed with Colonel R. S. Williamson's written support for his Fortieth Parallel Survey, he was also not without friends in the world of organized science. Agassiz of Harvard, Dana and Brewer of Yale, Baird of the Smithsonian Institution, and even Whitney of California stood ready to help him in some capacity. It was thus no real surprise when in the winter of 1867 he left Secretary of War Stanton's office, at the age of twenty-five, with an appointment in his pocket that was coveted, so Stanton said, by at least "four major-generals."[2]

When he chose his assistants for the Survey, King also chose men from the world of advanced science rather than the usual all-purpose naturalists of a bygone day. His first choice was of course James Gardner, who would serve as chief topographer. Thanks to his excellent training under Hoffmann on the Whitney Survey, Gardner had become one of the foremost field topographers in the country, and he refused the new chair of geodesy at Harvard's Lawrence Scientific School to join King. Excitable and somewhat egotistical, Gardner basked to a certain extent in the sunny light of King's personality. He did not like the Army with its red tape and its strong-minded officers, as he was to demonstrate later in his career. Moreover, he was a maverick with little sense of *esprit*, and as a leader he was far inferior to King and came near to wrecking the Survey during its first year in the field.[3] He was an able topographer, however, and a dedicated scientist.

For his geologists King chose two men with backgrounds almost identical if not superior to his own. They were the Boston-bred brothers James Duncan Hague and Arnold Hague. James D. Hague had attended the Lawrence Scientific School at Harvard, then the

2. *Clarence King Memoirs*, p. 385.
3. See, for example, William Whitman Bailey to Brother, Carson City, Feb. 19, 1868; Bailey to Lode, Carson City, March 1, 1868, Bailey Papers, Huntington Library.

University of Göttingen and the Royal School of Mines at Freiburg. King had known him since 1862, when they met at the Sheffield Scientific School. Arnold Hague had attended the Sheffield Scientific School, the universities of Göttingen and Heidelberg, and the Royal School of Mines. They were both good friends of King at the time of their selection as members of the party.[4]

In addition to these two geologists, King also selected a third, Samuel Franklin Emmons, who, after graduating from Harvard in 1861, had also found his way to the Royal School of Mines in Germany. There he had met and become fast friends with Arnold Hague, and Hague recommended him to King. Emmons, with his quiet competence and dedication, soon became one of King's life-long friends and one of the best of his field leaders.[5]

All of these men belonged to the newer generation of scientists. They were young men—J. D. Hague was thirty-one, Arnold Hague twenty-six, Emmons was also twenty-six, and King himself was only twenty-five. They came to their work with marks to make and unencumbered by the naturalist tradition of an earlier era.

As botanist on the Survey, King hired William Whitman Bailey, Jr., the son of the eminent professor of biology at West Point. The elder Bailey, long a close friend of John Torrey, was an expert in algae and microscopic biology and had been a pioneer in the technique of microscopy in the United States. He had had a long and close relationship with army explorations to the West and it was perhaps fitting that his son should accompany King's expedition as his introduction to a scientific career. After a year in the field, however, young Bailey's health gave way and he was replaced by Sereno Watson, another Yale man. Watson arrived in King's camp on the Truckee in the summer of 1867, a physical wreck. Very shy, tall and thin, with spectacles for his nearsighted eyes, Watson was past forty and a failure in the eyes of the world. He had journeyed to California with the idea of starting a new life as a scientific worker on the King Survey. He had come a good part of the way on foot, and when he arrived in the Survey camp, he looked it. King

4. The best short biographies of the brothers are in Bartlett: *Great Surveys*, pp. 147–8. See also *D.A.B.* In addition, see King to Humphreys, New Haven, April 6, 1867, Fortieth Parallel Survey Records, R.G. 57, National Archives. This letter also mentions Gardner's refusal of the chair of geodesy at Harvard's Lawrence Scientific School.

5. Bartlett: *Great Surveys*, p. 148. See also *D.A.B.*; and King to Humphreys, New Haven, May 8, 1867, Fortieth Parallel Survey Records, R.G. 57, National Archives.

hired him with no salary as a camp helper out of pity.[6] Before the
year was out, he had more than proven himself as a botanist, however, and his rival, the youthful Bailey, wrote home to his brother:
"My fellow botanist, Watson, is a most excellent worker, and makes
neat and admirable notes. He should have my place and I wish to
the Lord he had. I have felt discouraged ever since he came."[7]
Watson eventually did secure Bailey's place, and after the King Survey was over, he went on to become one of the outstanding botanists in the country and curator of the Gray Herbarium at Harvard.

To complete his team of outstanding assistants, King added
Robert Ridgway, a young amateur ornithologist from Mt. Carmel,
Illinois, who had become a protégé of Spencer Baird through correspondence;[8] Henry Custer, a Swiss and a veteran of the Army's
Northwest Boundary Survey under General John G. Parke; and
Timothy O'Sullivan, Matthew Brady's photographer with the Army
of the Potomac in the Civil War. O'Sullivan, of whom little is
known, was an outstanding photographer, and as a result of his
labors on the King Survey, and later on the Wheeler Survey, he
produced the first photographs of the Great Basin and the Grand
Canyon and Colorado Plateau country. Though the members of
the King Survey were often bored with his stories of the Civil War—
"one would think he had slept with Grant and Meade and was the
direct confidant of Stanton," wrote Bailey—still they remembered
him as "a good fellow."[9] He pulled his weight.

Besides these more famous men, there were others: F. A. Clark
and W. D. Wilson, topographers; and a number of teamsters and
camp men, and, once out in Nevada, Sergeant Edward Schwartz
and twenty men of the 8th Cavalry as escorts. All in all, it was an
able and professional group.

2

King's orders, which he wrote himself, suggest better than anything else the magnitude of the task he had undertaken and the
confident spirit with which he approached it. They were as follows:

6. Ibid., p. 150.
7. William Whitman Bailey to Lode, Big Bend of the Truckee, Nevada, Aug.
14, 1867, Bailey Papers.
8. Bartlett: *Great Surveys,* pp. 151–2.
9. William Whitman Bailey to Lode, Big Bend of the Truckee, Nevada, Aug.
14, 1867, Bailey Papers.

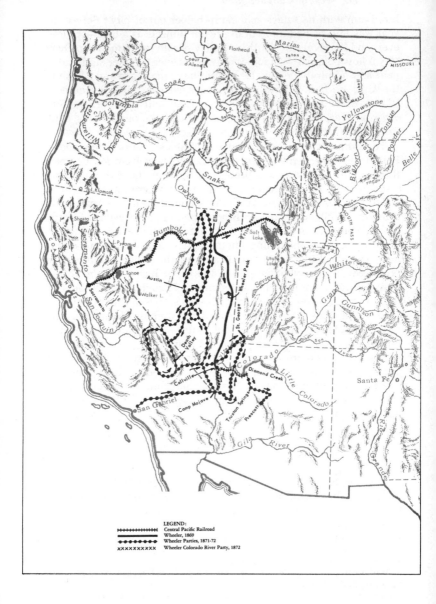

LEGEND:

+++++++++	Central Pacific Railroad
━━━━━━	Wheeler, 1869
●━●━●━●	Wheeler Parties, 1871-72
××××××××	Wheeler Colorado River Party, 1872

The object of the exploration is to examine and describe the
geological structure, geographical condition and natural resources of a belt of country extending from the 120th meridian
eastward to the 105th meridian, along the 40th parallel of
latitude with sufficient expansion north and south to include
the line of the "Central" and "Union Pacific" railroads and as
much more as may be consistent with accuracy and a proper
progress, which would be not less than five degrees of longitude yearly. The exploration will be commenced at the 120th
meridian where it will connect with the geological survey of
California, and should, if practicable, be completed in two
years. . . . It should examine all rock formations, mountain
ranges, detrital plains, coal deposits, soils, minerals, ores,
saline and alkaline deposits . . . collect . . . material for a topographical map of the regions traversed, . . . conduct . . . barometric and thermometric observations [and] make collections
in botany and zoology with a view to a memoir on these subjects, illustrating the occurrence and distribution of plants
and animals.[1]

He planned, in short, to make a sweeping but systematic reconnaissance across northern and central Nevada, Utah, Colorado, and
southern Wyoming from the Sierras of California to the front range
of the Rocky Mountains, encompassing the Great Basin and the
central Cordilleras. Only the Pacific Railroad Surveys and Henry
Engelmann's march westward with Captain James Simpson in
1857–59 had approached King's project in magnitude and scope.

He intended to survey the land forms of the region, map them
with a new degree of accuracy now made possible by methods developed on the California Survey, and he planned to examine
closely all the possibilities for economic development along the
line of the railroad, particularly those having to do with mining.
In addition, there was an added military increment not stated but
clearly in the minds of those who were concerned with subduing the
Indians and settling the West. General Sherman's overall military
policy for transforming the trans-Mississippi region depended
greatly upon pushing the railroad through the Indian country and
with it a wedge of settlers who would become self-sufficient and fan
out in ever increasing numbers, eventually overwhelming the red-

1. For evidence that King wrote his own orders, see Wilkins: *Clarence King,*
p. 96. For the orders, see Humphreys to King, March 21, 1867, Letters Received, Fortieth Parallel Survey Records, R.G. 57, National Archives.

men with civilization and sheer population.[2] King's survey contributed mightily to that long-range strategy. Even his scientific findings were directly relevant to military considerations.

3

After a farewell dinner at Yale College, the advance elements of King's staff sailed from New York on May 1, 1867, and King himself followed ten days later.[3] They crossed the Isthmus of Panama and coasted up the Pacific to San Francisco, where King and his group arrived on June 3. The advance corps had already moved on to Sacramento and there they were bivouacked in a field outside of town, practicing for the rugged months that lay ahead. Tents were pitched and saddles slung on racks outside the door. Then the men began the difficult work of breaking in the mules and then breaking the tenderfeet to the mules. "I take a little ride every day on mule back," wrote young Wiliam Bailey, "and am at present afflicted with a most grievous tail. What with my knife and six shooters, canteen, spurs, etc. I am quite a knight errant." Then he added slightly later, still in pain and less jaunty: "King says for my comfort there is no bum on earth but what will get hardened to it."[4]

On the third of July they started eastward on the difficult trek over the Sierras, eleven men on horseback, two freight wagons, an instrument cart, and a remuda of mules and spare mounts. They were bound for the Donner Pass. This was the route taken by the Central Pacific Railroad, and along the way straw-hatted coolie workers could be seen hewing a path for the road out of the solid rock of the Sierras.

The first base camp was established at Glendale near the site of modern Reno on the Truckee Meadows, thirty miles from sky-blue Pyramid Lake and an equal distance from the new town of Carson City. There King joined the party on the fifteenth of July and began to map his strategy for the assault on the alkali deserts and rugged mountains that stretched out endlessly before them. Though he had at first been reluctant to devote much of his energies to topog-

2. For General Sherman's policy, see Robert Athearn: *General William Tecumseh Sherman and the Settlement of the Far West* (Norman, Okla.: University of Oklahoma Press; 1956).

3. Wilkins: *Clarence King*, p. 98.

4. William Whitman Bailey to Lode, Camp 1, Sacramento, California, June 16, 1867; and Bailey to "Dear Bro," Camp 1, Sacramento, California, June 30, 1867, Bailey Papers, Huntington Library.

raphy, King soon saw that the first order of business was the construction of an accurate map upon which to register his geological and economic data. The Central Pacific Railroad's map drawn in 1864 was apparently unknown to him, or was considered inadequate, so he set his parties to work on a block of territory 150 miles in length and 100 miles wide between California's Sierras and the Shoshone Mountains to the east, an area of some 15,000 square miles.

King's method, as he himself admitted in the preface to the *Atlas* of the Survey, was that of a reconnaissance rather than a true geodetic survey. He worked on the base-line and triangulation method, using the sextant and the zenith telescope for astronomical checks on the work. This method, which depended largely on timing the period of immersion of the satellites of Jupiter and other similar astronomical phenomena, had been developed by the Corps of Topographical Engineers before the Civil War, particularly on the Mexican Boundary Survey. What made King's survey somewhat more effective, however, was the now perfected technique of using a lighter theodolite for observations from mountain peak to mountain peak as part of the triangulation process. This enabled his topographers to concentrate, as they did, upon the mountain ranges and cover relatively large areas of territory in a short time. It was also far more accurate than the old army method of gauging distance by means of an odometer pulled along the line of march on a one-wheeled vehicle. As a final check on the most difficult part of his topographic work, the longitude readings, King eventually was able to make use of the telegraph rather than the old-fashioned and delicate chronometers. This system, even today in Europe, is referred to as "the American system" of geodetic surveying.

On July 17 Sergeant Schwartz and the cavalry escort arrived—a tough lineup of troopers with knives stuck in their boots—and the actual surveying work could begin. After himself conducting a preliminary survey of Peavine Mountain, King dispatched a number of parties in different directions. Some studied the silver-bearing rocks of the Virginia Range. Emmons, Arnold Hague, and Henry Custer went west to the Hot Springs Range near Humboldt Sink. Gardner and Clark explored the Truckee Mountains, while King led the main party through the Canyons of the Truckee and down to its great bend, where, plagued by heat and mosquitoes, he established another camp. James Hague, Tim O'Sullivan, and Robert Ridgway were sent west to examine Pyramid Lake and while there they attempted to run the rapids of the Truckee for the first time in a small sailboat, only to meet disaster when the boat struck a rock. The only casualty, however, was O'Sullivan's pocketbook with 300 dollars in gold pieces in it, which was used to weight a line cast to the shore and fell into the turbulent Truckee. Pyramid Lake itself proved interesting but dangerous. The wildlife, especially the pelicans, were beautiful, but the rattlesnakes who dominated the island of the lake caused the explorers some consternation.[5]

Meanwhile, back on the Truckee, malaria began to strike down the members of the survey party. Bailey had been sick from the outset and he was glad when Watson showed up in camp to help him with his duties. King, too, was ill, and the rest of the party suffered intensely from the heat. Tempers grew short and at least one prostrate member of the party refused to ride in the wagon, declaring: "I'd go on foot sooner than accompanying the latter [Gardner] any day."[6] King decided to move out of the Truckee River country and the march grew more and more painful as malaria spread through the group. At Coffman Station they met a strange hermit who believed he was guarding Christ's mount of temptation, and he cheered them up by proclaiming "desolation thy name is Humboldt."[7] The heat became so intense that Emmons tried to squeeze into the shadow of a telegraph pole, while Bailey, with a naïveté perhaps induced by the sun, wrote his brother: "There are wells out here which are said to cause Gonnorhea," and apparently Professor Silliman later offered confirmation of the story.[8] Eventually they reached Parker's Station on the very edge of the Humboldt Sink, known to the local inhabitants as "the worst place between Missouri and Hell." By this time the explorers were in desperate straits, with most of the men down with malaria, and resolution fast failing. At the outset of his career, King was faced with disaster. There was nothing to do but move quickly, and he took his men into the mountains to the town of Oreana, hoping that the altitude would cure their ills. This did no good, however, and they

5. The best account of this phase of the Survey is John Sampson (T. O'Sullivan): "Photographs from the High Rockies," *Harper's New Monthly Magazine*, Vol. XXXIX, No. 232 (Sept. 1869), pp. 465–75. See also King to Humphreys, Camp 12, Truckee River, Nevada. Aug. 3, 1867, Fortieth Parallel Survey Records, R.G. 57, National Archives.

6. William Whitman Bailey to Lode, Big Bend of the Truckee, Nevada, Aug. 14, 1867, Bailey Papers.

7. William Whitman Bailey to Lode, Camp 18, West Humboldt Mountains, fifteen miles from Unionville, Sept. 6, 1867, Bailey Papers.

8. Ibid.

moved north to the little mining town of Unionville, another desolate place. There a hospital was set up in a building used as the
local jail, and the men convalesced while in the basement below
a murderer clanked in his chains.[9]

Faced with failure, King refused to give in, and almost immediately he took the remaining able-bodied men and marched south
to the Stillwater Ranges, just east of the Carson Sink. There, while
adjusting his theodolite atop Job's Peak, he was suddenly struck by
a bolt of lightning. "I was staggered and my brain and nerves [were]
severely shocked. The theodolite was thrown and badly injured,"
he reported to General Humphreys.[1] When Clark helped him to his
feet and back to camp, he discovered that his right arm and side
had turned brown. After a week he recovered enough to resume
work, and soon was enjoying the experience "immensely." During
this period he managed to complete the survey of the Silver Hill
and East Humboldt Range.[2]

Henry Custer, still suffering from "the mountain ail," had also
been in the saddle and at work. Although they did not reach their
objective, the Shoshone Range nearly halfway across Nevada, King
deemed that they had progressed for enough east and began to
work backward over the dreaded Humboldt and Carson Sink country. For the rest of the season they worked in a westward direction.
Emmons, now partially recovered, surveyed the Black Rock Desert
and mountain country in the northwest corner of Nevada. Custer
finished his work on the Humboldt River down as far as Oreana,
then collapsed again. Gardner returned to San Francisco to recu-
perate. O'Sullivan, Bailey, and Ridgway, the latter two still in bad
condition, marched from Unionville directly to rendezvous at Glendale. By mid-October, King and James D. Hague had completed
a survey of the mines in the Humboldt district, and then had
gone north to the Silver City, Idaho, silver fields on the edge of the
survey area.[3]

On November 26, the whole party reassembled at Glendale.
Gardner had returned to survey Winnemuca Lake, and the rest
of the men had recovered their health. They headed for winter

9. Bailey's letter to Lode (see footnote 7 on the preceding page) indicates the
degree of serious illness in the party.
1. King to Humphreys, Virginia, Nevada, Dec. 18, 1867, Fortieth Parallel
Survey Records, R.G. 57, National Archives. See also William Whitman Bailey
to Lode, Unionville, Nevada, Humboldt Mts., Sept. 29, 1867, Bailey Papers.
2. Ibid.
3. Ibid.

quarters, in comparatively good condition, most of the men going to cheaper lodgings in Carson City, while King, Gardner, and the geologists put up at Virginia City in the great silver-mining district.

From winter encampment at Virginia City, King reported the results of his year's work to General Humphreys. Though he estimated that at least twenty percent of his party's effectiveness had been wasted by the siege of malaria, still he had reason to be proud of his achievements. "We have covered a block of country extending from the one hundred and twentieth Meridian eastward to Long. 117° 30′ and reaching [from?] Lat. 39° 31′ to 41°." He added: "This is in every way the most difficult and dangerous country to campaign in I know of on the continent."[4]

In addition to the mapping and general geological reconnaissance, the explorers had collected some two thousand rock specimens, examined numerous mines, and established three hundred barometrical stations at which some two thousand observations were made. "Our economical results alone," King concluded, "I believe are worth to the Government all I have expended." They had, as King wrote, "turned a threatened failure into a very complete success."[5]

4

The winter of 1867–68 was an extremely severe one, with blinding rainstorms, floods, and heavy snowfalls, but King managed to turn the season to good account. During the day he and his geologists, Emmons and Hague, explored the Comstock, searching out the whole complex of tunnels and shafts that bored into the heart of Mt. Davidson. Tim O'Sullivan arrived from Carson City and took some magnesium-flare photos deep down in the stopes, the first such pictures ever taken underground in the United States. Working through all kinds of weather, they slowly gathered the geological and mechanical data that was to make their combined volume on the mining industry a classic. Down south in Carson City, the topographers worked over the huge maps drawn to a scale of two miles to the inch. And in the interim they all had their moments of relaxation in the boom-town atmosphere of Washoe. Bailey found

4. Ibid.
5. Ibid.

consolation in the young mistress of his boardinghouse and reported the dramatic shooting of the local sheriff,[6] while King in his
best Newport attire, including lemon-colored gloves, dazzled the
ladies of Virginia City.[7] They all felt a fresh enthusiasm for the
coming season's work. King's example created a new spirit. Once
again nothing was impossible.

5

The season of 1868 began on May 8 even before the snows had
cleared in the mountains. Two parties took the field. One under
Emmons and J. D. Hague journeyed first to Austin, Nevada, the
most recent of the great silver boom towns, and then eighty miles
southward to the Toiyabe Range and its mining outposts. Another
party, under Henry Custer and Sereno Watson, mapped the area
east of Unionville, and on June 22, two Humboldt River parties
worked eastward to the crest of the Shoshone Range. King remained
behind at Carson City to answer to a lawsuit over some hay his men
had "borrowed" from an irate Truckee farmer. In between legal
tangles, King managed to visit Pyramid Lake and finish up his
work on the Comstock. By a stroke of good fortune, he purchased
the underground notes for 1862, 1863, and 1864 from R. H.
Stretch, the former Mine Superintendent of the Comstock, and
these notes provided him with data on the rich upper portions of
the vein then caved in and inaccessible. With the notes, King concluded, "I can unhesitatingly say that we have the most thorough
account of any great silver mining district in the world."[8]

From the survey of the Comstock two important considerations
emerged. The geologists, all well trained in chemistry, noted that
over 40 million dollars' worth of ore had been wasted in the relatively short period of eight years, due to faulty smelting. James D.
Hague set to work on new formulas and processes that would
reduce this waste. King addressed himself to the question of ore
resources and concluded that, contrary to Whitney's pessimistic
report, signs indicated substantial further reserves at a greater

6. William Whitman Bailey to Brother, Carson City, Jan. 6, 1868; Feb. 19,
1868, Bailey Papers.
7. Wilkins: *Clarence King*, p. 113.
8. King to Humphreys, July 10, 1868, Camp near Austin, Fortieth Parallel
Survey Records, R.G. 57, National Archives.

depth.[9] This was confirmed by the great strike of 1874, the richest bonanza of all in the Comstock.

The field parties rendezvoused with King at Austin, and on July 3 he once again sent them out in four details. Gardner returned to the astronomical station at Job's Peak, and for most of the season he repaired the errors in his topographical work of the previous year. Hague and Clark moved east for forty miles north of the overland wagon road, as far as Ruby Valley. King and Custer paralleled them to the south. Emmons moved far ahead some two hundred miles to the ranges on the edge of the Salt Lake Desert.[1]

On August 10 they met at Fort Ruby near the Central Pacific line, and James D. Hague was sent to Colorado to make engineering studies of the mines in that region. In the month of July the whole middle section of topography had been worked up from the Shoshone Mountains eastward, and Emmons had covered the ranges on the edge of the Salt Lake Desert, including Don Don Pass, and then had worked backward to Fort Ruby. During this period one of the soldiers of the escort deserted and fled west. King, realizing what a blow to morale a successful desertion would be, gave chase for a hundred miles through northern Nevada. Finally, using a time-honored Western stratagem, he "headed him off at a pass" in the Havilah Mountains. Stealing up with drawn revolver, King surprised the deserter over a campfire. "I captured him in a hand to hand struggle in which I nearly lost my life," King reported, "and only saved myself by dodging his shot and cramming my pistol in his ear in the nick of time. I lodged him in Austin jail and the fact of his capture forever reduced the soldiers and the working men of the survey to obedience."[2]

Then the survey work went on. King explored the Ruby Range. Emmons worked up the country north of the Humboldt River, and Hague, moving on a belt to the south, covered all the country, as King put it, "lying in a triangle whose three points are Franklin Lake, Pilot Peak, and Humboldt Wells."[3] After a rendezvous at Humboldt Wells in eastern Nevada, they all turned their attention northward. Hague followed the railroad around the north end of

9. Ibid.
1. King to Humphreys, Aug. 13, 1868, Camp near Ruby, Nevada, Fortieth Parallel Survey Records, R.G. 57, National Archives.
2. "C.K.'s notes for biographical notice of him," Biographical Papers, A-3, King Papers, Huntington Library. Also quoted in Wilkins: Clarence King, pp. 118–19.
3. King to Humphreys, Newport, R.I., Nov. 14, 1868, Fortieth Parallel Survey Records, R.G. 57, National Archives.

the Salt Lake through a barren and waterless country. Emmons followed along just north of Hague, "thoroughly demolishing the so-called 'desert coal-field' which in reality," according to Emmons, "had no existence whatever."[4] King journeyed north to the awesome canyons of the Snake River, which he saw for the first time. He found it such an inspiring sight that he wrote an article on it for Bret Harte's *Overland Monthly*.[5] By October 14, all of the parties had finished their season's work and they converged on Salt Lake City. The property was stored and the horses left to the tender care of Porter Rockwell, the Mormon elder, better known as the notorious leader of the sinister Danite avengers. This was appropriate, for he was the kind of authentic Western character that King would have liked. On October 20 the explorers started East for a month's vacation.

King's second season had been an even bigger success than the first. Except for a short stretch south of the Great Salt Lake, he and his men had completed the topography and geology all across the Basin as far as the Salt Lake. It covered now a belt a hundred miles wide and over five hundred miles long. His collections ran to fifty large boxes, which were shipped to Washington and there dazzled Eastern scientists. Most important, however, were his studies of the silver mines and his first thoughts on the overall geological structure of the Great Basin region. The former was significant because it was the most complete study of its kind, particularly as it related to the Comstock sections. More than anything else, this impressed both scientists and business-minded Congressmen. King rightly recognized its importance and immediately put Emmons and J. D. Hague to work composing their volume, *The Mining Industry*, of which King's Comstock study formed one part. Doubtless remembering Whitney's mistake in publishing his "impractical" paleontology volume first, King saw to it that his series of publications got off on the proper useful level.

His other consideration was in the realm of theory, or historical geology. In crossing the Great Basin, he noted that it was not a single basin at all, but two basins, one just east of the Sierras in the Humboldt Sink region and one large area whose remnant was the Great Salt Lake. In between was a great upland plateau area some 6,000 feet high, studded with ancient mountains.[6] Topo-

4. Ibid.
5. "The Falls of the Shoshone," *Overland Monthly*, Vol. V (Oct. 1870), 379–85.
6. Wilkins: *Clarence King*, pp. 122–3.

graphically, this was not the new discovery King believed it to be, since Simpson and Engelmann had seen the basin in much these same terms on their prewar expedition. Their observations, however, were not to be published until 1875. What was new was King's recognition that both of these depressions had been ancient Pliocene lake beds later fed by the great mountain glaciers of the West at a time roughly contemporaneous with the coming of the polar ice cap to the East. Though he did not trace out the shoreline of the lakes with the exactness of Grove Karl Gilbert of the Wheeler Survey, King nevertheless succeeded in making a major contribution to the knowledge of Western geology. Gentleman that he was, however, King deferred to Gilbert, allowing him to publish his classic *Lake Bonneville* first, and thus Gilbert, whose work was more complete, received the honor of naming the ancient lake. and being acclaimed its "discoverer."[7] King gained some measure of satisfaction in that he "discovered" and named the other ancient lake, Lake Lahonton. In a typical stroke of the imagination, King followed Frémont's example on the Humboldt and named his lake after an explorer who never saw the Great Basin at all, but had at least imagined its waters.

It was well that King had produced these dramatic results. His appropriation was now exhausted and his two-year term was ended. He would have to wrestle Congress for survival. And Congress that year was feeling bearish on the subject of government surveys. With his usual skill, however, King went to Washington, set up headquarters, displayed his wares, and so thoroughly captured key Congressmen—including Ben Butler, who liked his survey because there were no West Pointers on it—that Congress passed a special appropriation for him attached to the Sundry Civil Bill.[8] Technically, he could, if he chose, move out from under the Army, but King remained loyal to the Engineers and went on with plans to work up his data under the usual military auspices.

6

Having received his appropriation, King returned to Salt Lake City, arriving on May 15, some days after his main party. As usual, he had several plans all operating at once. While he organized his

7. Ibid. See also Grove Karl Gilbert: *Lake Bonneville*, Monographs of the United States Geological Survey, Vol. I (Washington, 1890), p. 17.
8. *Clarence King Memoirs*, pp. 384–5.

parties for the field, replacing lost equipment and mapping his assault on the towering Wasatch Mountains, he also left James D. Hague back in Boston hard at work on his report on the mining industry, and Arnold Hague at Yale finishing up a chemical analysis of the ore-reduction process. Personally elated at the results achieved so far in this field, King wrote to General Humphreys:

> The chemical investigations have proved to be of greater value than we dared to hope: at first survey of results, it appears that we have discovered the great error of the silver process, and by a slight variation of the chemical conditions we have succeeded in raising the percentage of yield from 64 and 66 percent to 93 and 95 percent.[9]

He was cautious, however, and deferred public announcement of this breakthrough until he could test it in actual operation in a Nevada silver mill.

The task confronting the field parties for the summer of 1869 was that of carrying the Survey eastward through the Wasatch Mountains, and the tangled Uinta and Green River country beyond, to the Green River Divide, which King believed would mark the end of his labors. Accordingly, he moved his base camp to Parley's Park, twenty-five miles east of Salt Lake City, and sent three parties out on various missions. After finishing a study of the desert south of Salt Lake, Emmons proceeded via the Provo River eastward to the canyons of the Duchesne and then north to the Uintas, where he traced out the crest of that lofty range. King himself followed the railroad route through Echo Canyon and thence to the Bear River, and along it to its headwaters in the Uintas. Their most important work on this trip was the discovery of substantial coal formations in the Green River country east of the Wasatch Mountains. In his report King declared: "Our investigation of the complex question of the coal formation has been entirely settled, resulting in a full knowledge of the occurrence of the coal rocks and a most satisfactory estimate of the *unopened fields*." He also added that his geological samples and indeed his close examination of the Uintas provided "new data which will definitely complete the explanation of the great Cordillera mountain system."[1] He saw the Uintas as once towering mountains worn down to their present heights by

9. King to Humphreys, Salt Lake City, Utah, June 17, 1869, Fortieth Parallel Survey Records, R.G. 57, National Archives.
1. King to Humphreys, Aug. 26, 1869, Camp Parley's Park, Fortieth Parallel Survey Records, R.G. 57, National Archives.

the great glaciers whose meltwaters had flowed into the basin, forming Lake Bonneville. That summer, too, he devoted some time to examining the country to the north near Snake River in an effort to discover where the great Pliocene lake had emptied its waters into the sea. The outlet he located, however, was later proven, by G. K. Gilbert, to be incorrect.[2] These two kinds of observations by King, the one economic and the other in the realm of theory, illustrated quite clearly the dual emphasis of his work, and the one explains in a sense the acceptance of the other by Congressmen and the public at large.

While King and Emmons were threading the difficult country east of the Wasatch, another assistant, R. Davis, along with F. A. Clark, Sereno Watson, and Robert Ridgway, was engaged in a marine survey of the Great Salt Lake itself. The lake had risen nine feet since Stansbury's survey of 1850, and its entire outline had been changed. Some 600 square miles had been added to its area, thus necessitating a new mapping project. The task was made difficult by the sudden destruction of their party's boat when it struck a rock in the lake. Fortunately, however, they managed to cling to the capsized hull, their eyes stinging from the briny water, and they were ultimately rescued.[3]

By mid-August most of the new survey work for the year was completed. King returned to Salt Lake City, where he auctioned off his surplus equipment at a sale made picturesque by the presence of Brigham Young and a coterie of stern, hard-bargaining Mormon bishops. Emmons and Arnold Hague, who had rejoined the field party, returned back across the Basin, along the 40th parallel, to review the results. J. D. Hague restudied the Colorado gold fields, and Clark spent ten days examining the White Pine mining district in the middle of the Basin country. He was joined in that work by Hague.[4]

All of the parties met at Argenta, Nevada, at the end of September, thus officially closing the season. Ridgway headed back to Washington to work on his collections, and Watson, in company with Professor Daniel Cady Eaton, a Yale botanist who had been King's somewhat cantankerous guest for the summer, took the cars for

2. Wilkins: *Clarence King*, p. 126.
3. King to Humphreys, Salt Lake City, Utah, June 17, 1869; July 15, 1869, Fortieth Parallel Survey Records, R.G. 57, National Archives. Also see "Notes: Journey to Church, Gunnison and Frémont Islands, June 23, 1869," Scientific Papers, B-7, King Papers. Bartlett: *Great Surveys*, pp. 176–7.
4. Ibid.

New Haven. King and Hague headed for San Francisco, exhausted. The irrepressible King refreshed himself, however, by plunging into the artistic and literary life of San Francisco with his old friend Bret Harte of the *Overland Monthly*. Out in Utah, King had written of his "intense yearning" to complete his "analytical study of Nature and drink in the sympathetic side."[5] He had also demonstrated this facet of his personality by including the painter Gilbert Munger in his entourage of that year. As the explorers lounged about the meadows of Parley's Park, catching trout and observing the beauties of the mountain scenery, Munger transformed their scientific thoughts into huge, four-foot Ruskinian portraits of the grandeur and sublimity that surrounded them.[6] Out in San Francisco, King capped off all these sentiments with a literary breakfast at the Union Club in honor of his friend Bret Harte.[7] Then in late November he headed East and back to the world of science.

7

In the winter of 1869–70 it was clear that the mercurial King had grown tired of routine survey work, no matter what its momentary excitements. He now desired to settle back and work up his many findings into a grand synthesis that would make them more directly relevant to the science of the day. He also enjoyed the companionship of the great and near great in Washington, Boston, and New Haven, where he had finally established his headquarters. For the most part his work was done and he desired to reap its rewards.

With some dismay he received General Humphreys's orders to take to the field again. Nevertheless, he dutifully obeyed, sending his regrets to the Spencer Bairds that he could not summer with them in Woods Hole, and he then headed West once again, the victim of his own success.[8] Reluctant though he was to undertake new explorations, King soon conceived of a project that led to one of his greatest discoveries. He took the now completed railroad to

5. Wilkins: *Clarence King*, pp. 128–30. See also King to Humphreys, Camp near Argenta, Nevada, Oct., 1869, Fortieth Parallel Survey Records, R.G. 57, National Archives; and "Miscellaneous Notes, 1869," D-17, King Papers, Huntington Library.
6. Wilkins: *Clarence King*, p. 128.
7. Ibid., p. 130.
8. Ibid., pp. 133–4.

San Francisco, stopped off for another round of raconteuring with Bret Harte, and then headed north to Mt. Shasta, bent on a detailed study of mountain-making. Emmons, who went with him, was sent north to Mt. Rainier, while Arnold Hague went on to Mt. Hood. King's party headed up the Sacramento to the Shasta country, and on September 11 they climbed Mt. Shastina, a shoulder of the main peak, and looked down onto a field of ice. They had discovered the first active glacier in the United States. By taking a different approach to Shasta's solemn cone, King and his men had seen a sight no member of the California Geological Survey had ever seen, and it was a sight of crucial importance.[9] The discovery of the glacier added great support to King's reconstruction of Western geology, which depended to a large extent on the action of glaciers in the comparatively recent Tertiary times. It clearly gave him the upper hand in his scientific dispute with Whitney over the history of Yosemite. Emmons's and Hague's almost simultaneous discovery of glaciers farther north in Mts. Rainier and Hood also added weight to King's interpretation.

With the discovery of the glacier, King now reached a much wider audience upon his return to the East. There were the many people who disputed his claim, alleging that they, not he, had discovered glaciers many years before.[1]

Besides the glacier enthusiasts, there were those who urged King to popularize his exploits in a literary work. Foremost of these was James T. Fields of the *Atlantic Monthly*, who succeeded in persuading King to do a series of sketches for his magazine. Then King concluded an agreement with James R. Osgood for a popular book of fictionalized and semi-fictionalized stories about his experiences out West. Though he always affected surprise that his stories appeared one day in book form, King actually worked as hard at his literary tasks, and perhaps with greater enthusiasm, than he ever did at his scientific endeavors.[2] When *Mountaineering in the Sierra Nevada* finally appeared in February of 1872, it was the result of many hours of labor and long periods of self-doubt about his true merits as a man of letters. It was a great book and caught something no scientific report, however well written, could ever do. With his literary license, King not only presented the grandeur and the dangers of the High Sierras, but he also managed to re-

9. Ibid., p. 136. Also see King to Humphreys, Oct. 10, 1870, Fortieth Parallel Survey Records, R.G. 57, National Archives.
1. Ibid., p. 144.
2. Ibid., pp. 141–3.

capture the local color and exoticism of the disappearing frontier and its picturesque people. As well as anything in print could do it, King's stories of degraded redmen, California bandits, Nevada desperadoes, and the forlorn Newtys of Pike, brought the West and its people brilliantly to life. This was a side of his career that had not been revealed in the sober letters to General Humphreys, but as much as anything else he did, it represented King and his time.

8

Having risen to the heights in his discoveries of 1870, King desired to pursue his studies of mountain-making and vulcanism further in 1871. He even planned an expedition to Mt. St. Elias in Alaska, but he was sternly rebuked by General Humphreys, who ordered him back into the Rockies to finish his surveys as far as the Great Plains.[3] King did, however, manage to work in one trip to California, where, ironically enough, he made his erroneous ascent of Mt. Whitney, or rather Sheep Rock, which in a storm he mistook for that lofty peak.[4] Then he hurried back to Fort Bridger, Wyoming, arriving on June 27, in time to supervise the field-survey operations once again.

Perhaps the most difficult year of the survey was 1871. Forest fires, deserts, drought, and the rugged country between the Green River and the Front Range taxed all of the field parties under Emmons and Hague to the utmost. King himself was peripatetic. He saw to the surveys in June and early July. Then he rushed back to Washington to supervise the final work on the mining volume. By August he was in the mountains again, and in Estes Park, Colorado, he had his famous meeting with Henry Adams, the Harvard historian who would one day be the sole means of keeping his name alive.[5] Besides the meeting with Adams, King had one further adventure in 1871. In the autumn, as he was making his final survey of the Uintas, King sighted a large grizzly bear. He gave chase, and the bear led him for miles across sagebrush plains and sand dunes into a labyrinth of eroded gulleys. Suddenly the grizzly

3. King to Humphreys, New Haven, Conn., Jan. 23, 1871; Humphreys to King, March 28, 1871, Fortieth Parallel Survey Records, R.G. 57, National Archives.
4. Wilkins: *Clarence King*, p. 145.
5. King to Humphreys, Camp on Henry's Fork of Green River, Oct. 8, 1871, Fortieth Parallel Survey Records, R.G. 57, National Archives. Also see Adams: *Education*, pp. 310–13, for an account of the meeting.

452   EXPLORATION AND EMPIRE

disappeared. It was mid-morning before the hunters found him again, holed up in a cave. Daring what no mountain man would have even considered, King took his single-shot Ballard and crawled into the cave after the grizzly. All he could see were two glowing eyes in the dark, but he fired. Then abruptly he felt himself being dragged by the ankles face down on the cave floor and backward out of the opening. One of his hunters had, with some damage to King's features, rescued him. No irate bear emerged, and when they gingerly crawled back to see, they found him dead. King's bullet had entered his brain.[6]

9

After a brief respite in Hawaii with Arnold Hague during which he carefully examined the bubbling volcanic craters, even to the extent of descending into the cone of Mauna Loa, King returned to his duties with the Fortieth Parallel Survey.[7] The season of 1872 involved operations across the whole length of the parallel. King operated primarily out of California, in the vicinity of Mt. Humphreys, though he visited his field-survey parties in Nevada and Wyoming. Emmons, Wilson, and Hague set forth from Fort Fred Steele in Wyoming, and their task was to carry the topographical work ahead as fast as possible. All in all, it was a busy season that did not leave time for much else.[8]

In the spring and summer of 1872, however, a series of events were taking place that would come to a climax as the capstone of King's entire career. Early in 1872, two grizzled prospectors, Philip Arnold and John Slack, had appeared at a San Francisco bank and attempted to deposit a bagful of uncut diamonds. Having done so, they disappeared. But the diamonds came into instant prominence.[9]

6. *Clarence King Memoirs*, pp. 340–3; "Manuscripts and Correspondence by Contributors to Memoirs," A-3, King Papers, Huntington Library; Wilkins: *Clarence King*, p. 3.
7. Wilkins:*Clarence King*, pp. 155–7.
8. King to Humphreys, Fort Fred Steele, Wyoming, July 3, 1872, Fortieth Parallel Survey Records, R.G. 57, National Archives.
9. The most accurate account of the Diamond Hoax is in S. F. Emmons' Field Notebooks, "The Diamond Discovery of 1872," Acc. 1113, R.G. 57, National Archives. A typed copy of this is also in the Emmons Papers, Box 32, Library of Congress. King's account of the affair is in King to Humphreys, San Francisco, Nov. 27, 1872, Fortieth Parallel Survey Records, R.G. 57, National Archives. This version is less accurate than that of Emmons because it infers that King and Gardner *alone* had located the site of the diamond

They were shown to William Ralston, a director of the Bank of California, and then to a number of other capitalists in the city, who were all intrigued as to their origin. A search was instituted and Arnold and Slack were quickly located. When quizzed, they reported that they had found the diamonds at an undisclosed site. They consented to take a representative of the capitalists to the site, but insisted on blindfolding him first. After disembarking from the Union Pacific Railroad, they led General David Colton on a four-day trip through mountains and canyons to the site of their discovery, where he, too, found diamonds, and rubies, and a number of other precious stones.

Extremely cautious, the California businessmen then took Arnold and his diamonds to New York, where Charles Tiffany, upon examination, pronounced the gems "a rajah's ransom." They had, as one writer put it, discovered "the American Golconda"[1]—a vast field of gems virtually untouched by the hand of man, just waiting to be exploited by sound business enterprise. If they succeeded, Amsterdam itself might well move West. Immediately they formed a nationwide syndicate, the New York and San Francisco Mining and Commercial Company, which bought the rights to the diamond fields from Arnold and Slack for about $600,000, and they prepared to float a public stock issue of $12,000,000. To insure that every thing would be absolutely safe and sure, the syndicate hired the most cautious mining engineer in the West, Henry Janin, and he too examined and was dazzled by the diamond field, reporting in the public print that he had personally invested in it and that he considered "any investment at the rate of forty dollars per share or at the rate of four million dollars for the whole property, a safe and attractive one."

During this time, the syndicate had managed to keep the location of the diamond fields a strict secret, and as the news of the discovery leaked out, men with imaginations and the strong acquisitive instincts of the day went wild. Most people located Golconda in

---

fields. *The New York Times* for Nov. 27, Dec. 5, Dec. 6, Dec. 7, and Dec. 8, 1872, also carried reports on the hoax. The earliest full-length work on it is Asbury Harpending: *The Great Diamond Hoax and Other Stirring Incidents in the Life of Asbury Harpending,* James H. Wilkins, ed. (San Francisco: J. H. Berry Co.; 1915). This account is inaccurate. See also A. J. Liebling: "The American Golconda," *The New Yorker,* Vol. XVI (Nov. 16, 1940), pp. 40–8. The best modern accounts of the hoax are Bartlett: *Great Surveys,* pp. 187–205; and Wilkins: *Clarence King,* pp. 159–71. In general, I have followed Emmons, Bartlett, and Wilkins.

1. Liebling: "Golconda."

Arizona, others in Nevada, and almost every day prospectors wandered into Denver announcing they had found gems. Not since Coronado had followed Cibola halfway across North America had so many men so assiduously pursued windfall wealth. All along the transcontinental railroad, spies watched the trains for suspicious parties of prospectors. Even the telegraphers were not to be trusted.

King and the other members of the Fortieth Parallel Survey were of course fascinated by the rumors of the diamond discovery, particularly inasmuch as it very probably lay in the heart of country they had crossed many times. They were suspicious. Never in all the weary years of surveying and geologizing had they found gems or even a formation that looked as if it might contain such precious stones. When King visited Emmons and Wilson at camp near Fort Bridger in midsummer, they begged to be allowed to institute a search of their own for the stones, but King, with one eye on the War Department, put it off until the end of the season, when they had completed their routine work. Meanwhile he did some speculating on his own. The location of the diamond field could not be in Arizona, he knew, because the flooded condition of the Snake [Little Snake], Bear [Yampa], and Green rivers precluded any foray in that direction during the past summer. Piecing this fact together with Janin's description of the location of the field "upon a mesa near pine timber," King realized that "there was only one place in that country which answers to the description, and . . . that place lay within the limits of the Fortieth Parallel Survey."[2]

When King, Emmons, Gardner, and A. D. Wilson all met at the office in Montgomery Block on the eighteenth of October, they compared the results of their thinking and, King remembered: "Curiously enough Mr. Gardner and I had without formerly mentioning the subject reached an identical conclusion as to where the spot was."[3]

Actually, some ingenious detective work had been done by Emmons and Wilson, as well as Gardner and King. On the fifth of October, while on the westbound train just out of Battle Mountain, Nevada, Emmons and Gardner had noticed a party of Eastern surveyors who were joined at Alta Station in the Sierras by Henry Janin. They were obviously returning from the diamond fields, so Gardner and Emmons struck up a conversation and gleaned what

2. Wilkins: *Clarence King*, p. 162.
3. King to Humphreys, San Francisco, Nov. 27, 1872, Fortieth Parallel Survey Records, R.G. 57, National Archives.

bits of information they could. They didn't get much out of Janin and his friends, but they did learn that Janin's earlier trip to the diamond fields had taken only three weeks, not enough time to go to Arizona. A. D. Wilson, who had been in the Green River country that summer, reported that the party had disembarked from the train somewhere between Green River and Rawlins. Putting this together with the data about the flooded Green, Yampa, and Snake rivers, they narrowed the field of possibilities considerably. Emmons had further learned that Janin had camped at the foot of a pine-covered mountain which had snow on its slopes as late as June, and Gardner pried from his surveyor the observation that their camp had been on the northeast side of a mountain from which they could see no other high peaks either to the north or to the east. Emmons, Gardner, Wilson, and Hague, who joined the game, concluded that there was only one place the diamonds could be—a peak just north of Brown's Hole, some forty miles east of Green River, right in the country where Utah, Wyoming, and Colorado came together. King agreed completely, and they made plans for an immediate departure for the site.

Everything had to be kept secret, of course. King did not even inform General Humphreys. Instead, just before they boarded the train—in separate parties, with sieves and shovels—he sent a dispatch from Fort Bridger to the General, on October 28, telling him he was off on a reconnaissance of Brown's Hole.

They departed from Fort Bridger on a bitter-cold day. It was October 29. For the next few days they worked their way north through the most unpleasant, freezing weather imaginable. Emmons reported that the horses "became encased in balls of ice."[4] Four days out, they crossed the icy Green River and struck a deep gulley cutting into the side of the mountain they were aiming for. There, out of the biting wind, they made camp and the search began. A few hundred yards out of camp, they found a mark on a tree, then Henry Janin's official water claim, then more mining notices, and finally a small sandstone mesa stained with iron deposits. This must be the spot. Quickly they got down on hands and knees. They probed until dark, finding one diamond apiece on the first try. "That night," remembered Emmons, "we were full-believers in the verity of Janin's reports, and dreamed of untold wealth that might be gathered."[5]

4. Emmons: Field Notebooks. See footnote 9, p. 452.
5. Ibid.

The next day, ignoring the sweeping wind and the shriveling cold, they surveyed the entire area, picking up quantities of stones. They learned, however, that the diamonds did not occur anywhere else but in the mesa where they first found them. By the afternoon they began to get suspicious. King discovered that the gems were always found in a ratio of twelve rubies to one diamond. Then they noticed that most of the stones were in anthills and places where the earth had been ever so slightly disturbed. Their suspicions heightened when one man found a diamond delicately perched atop an anthill where, had it been there long, it would surely have been washed away. Later they found evidence that the stones had been pushed into the anthills with a stick, and some disturbed places even had human footprints around them, though this was not conclusive since Janin and others had worked the site. To be sure, on the third day they checked the stream beds and other places where diamonds must surely have settled, and they dug a deep pit far into the sandstone formation. All this yielded nothing. Golconda was a fraud.

Just as they concluded this, a stranger appeared. He was an unscrupulous New York City diamond dealer who had followed their labors for days through field glasses. When he learned that the diamonds were a hoax, he declared: "What a chance to sell short."[6] This reminded King of the grave responsibility they bore, and that night they made plans to slip out and beat the diamond dealer back to civilization. The next day King and Wilson left before dawn and rode all day, forty-five miles through the badlands, directly to Black Butte Station. They arrived just in time to catch the train for San Francisco.

In San Francisco, King first sought out his friend Janin and confronted him with the evidence. Then they went to the company directors, and King presented a letter with his findings. Ralston and Company stalled for time and begged King to keep quiet until they could sell out, but he refused. They did gain a few days, however, by persuading King to take Janin and the others to the diamond fields for a final check. When they returned, crowds had gathered outside the bank waiting for a dramatic announcement from Ralston. The San Francisco tycoons had been duped by Arnold and Slack and caught by King. There was nothing to do but reveal the whole story. Ralston and his partners published King's letter and the syndicate assumed full responsibility and repaid the stock-

6. Ibid.; Bartlett; *Great Surveys*, p. 199.

holders. There were many who still continued to believe, however, that the scheme had originated with the syndicate in the first place. Slack disappeared, and Arnold, back in Kentucky, bought a safe and coolly stored his loot. In 1879 he was shot in the back and the loot disappeared.

Meanwhile King was the hero of the hour. The San Francisco *Bulletin* called him "a cool headed man of scientific education who esteemed it a duty to investigate the matter in the only right way, and who proceeded about his task with a degree of spirit and strong common sense as striking as his success."[7] The Fortieth Parallel Survey as a scientific endeavor, according to the editor, had proven its practical value. Back East, Whitney, who was still fighting his own battle against the oil swindles, rejoiced at King's success. "Who's the King of Diamonds now?" he asked. "And isn't he trumps?"[8]

Unbelievably, however, General Humphreys was displeased. Upon receiving King's official report, he replied soberly: "As these Fields are situated within the limits of the Survey you have charge of, it was eminently proper that they should be included in your operations and an exhaustive examination of them be made." But, he added: "The manner of publicly announcing the results of the examination should I think have been different."[9] In short, King should have gone through channels. But perhaps General Humphreys's stiffness can be excused, for by 1873 the Army was beginning to feel the competition from rival civilian surveys under the Interior Department. In view of increased Congressional opposition, it had to be jealous of whatever laurels fortune cast its way.

10

During the winter of 1872–73 King rested from his labors of the previous season and enjoyed his heightened status in San Francisco society, where every notable from Ben Ali Haggin to George Hearst paid homage to him. Even more than this, he enjoyed the company of his literary friends, especially Horace F. Cutler, the "Batchelor of San Francisco," who shared his enthusiasm for Don Quixote, and for whom King wrote one of his most mem-

7. Quoted in Bartlett: *Great Surveys*, p. 203.
8. Wilkins: *Clarence King*, p. 171.
9. Humphreys to King, Jan. 10, 1873, Fortieth Parallel Survey Records, R.G. 57, National Archives.

orable stories, "The Helmet of Mambrino," a fictionalized account
of the search for the barber's basin worn by the valorous knight of
La Mancha.[1] In the summer of 1873, however, he went back to
work, combining private ventures in mine-consulting with a review
of the Fortieth Parallel geology. Part of the summer he spent in
the East, urging his men on in their various enterprises and touring the White Mountains with Emmons. In September, on the way
to Nevada, he met W. A. Goodyear and discovered his error in
climbing the wrong Mt. Whitney. He detoured south, and in one
easy afternoon's hike on September 18, he attained the long-elusive
summit of his favorite mountain, thus rectifying his last embarrassment as a Western explorer. On that trip, too, he crossed the Sierras
and prospected in California's Inyo and Owens Valley for the
Paleozoic fossils that would provide the last link in the chain of
evidence for his volume on the geology of the basin region. In this,
too, he was completely successful. All during the summer and fall
of 1873, however, he suffered recurring bouts of illness which made
his field work difficult. When he arrived in New York in November
of that year, he was happy to see that at last his labors in mountain
and desert were over.[2]

As a great and epic feat of exploration and adventure, the King
Survey surpassed everything else that had been done in the latter-
day West except perhaps Major Powell's dramatic descent of the
Grand Canyon. But the most important result of his adventures
was the monographs produced with incredible diligence and insight by King and the members of his staff. The keynote to his
scientific approach was contained in a letter to General Humphreys:
"The day has passed in geological science," he wrote, "when it is
either decent or tolerable to rush into print with undigested field
operations ignoring the methods and appliances in use among advanced investigators. It is my intention to give to this work a finish
which will place it on an equal footing with the best European publications, and those few which have redeemed the wavering reputation of our American investigators."[3] This he succeeded in doing.
His volumes on the Fortieth Parallel Survey, dealing with a massive

1. Wilkins: *Clarence King,* p. 174. "The Helmet of Mambrino" is included in
Clarence King Memoirs, pp. 5–115.
2. Wilkins: *Clarence King,* pp. 176–83. King to Humphreys, 47 Lafayette
Place, N.Y., Dec. 17, 1873, Fortieth Parallel Survey Records, R.G. 57, National Archives. In the latter, King discusses his Paleozoic and Azoic fossil
discoveries and also mentions his recurring illnesses.
3. King to Humphreys, Feb. 25, 1874, Fortieth Parallel Survey Records, R.G.
57, National Archives.

section of North American geology, were the first thoroughly professional studies of the Western environment, and they became a model for all others to follow.

For the completion of the volumes, he had the services of most of his original team. Gardner, however, having finished the huge Atlas of the Survey, resigned to join F. V. Hayden's Geological Survey of the Territories, and there he abruptly, and much to King's dismay, began a feud with his old employers, the Army.[4] Emmons journeyed to Europe to purchase microscopes with which to examine the rock samples, and he returned, at King's request, with Professor Ferdinand Zirkel of Leipzig, the foremost expert on the new science of microscopical petrography. Zirkel at once set to work examining the thousands of rock sections that the geologists had assembled. The result of his labors was Volume VI in King's series, *Microscopical Petrography*, which came out in 1876.[5] Imperfect though it was in certain instances, and paralleled to some extent by Caswell's work on the same subject, in the Black Hills Survey, whose publication was, however, held up by politics,[6] Zirkel's volume was nevertheless a pioneer work. Using new instruments which revealed a hitherto inaccessible microscopic world, Zirkel materially changed the direction of geologic studies in the United States.

Almost all the volumes produced by King and his men were impressive. Hague's and King's *Mining Industry* (1870)[7] had set the standard and appeared to quiet Congressional worries about practicality. Sereno Watson's *Botany* (1871)[8] almost immediately became a classic. It related the various forms of plant life to the immense variety of country Watson had traversed, and it included a substantial catalogue of plants worked up by such authorities as George Engelmann, Edward Tuckerman, and Daniel Cady Eaton. It was for years the only reference book on the flora of the Great Basin.

In 1877 Arnold Hague and S. F. Emmons produced their volume

4. See, for example, James T. Gardner to J. D. Whitney, May 7, 1874, Washington, Whitney Papers, Yale Historical Manuscripts Collection. Also see Wilkins: *Clarence King*, pp. 174–5
5. Ferdinand Zirkel: *Microscopical Petrography*, Professional Papers of the Engineer Department, U. S. Army, No. 18 (Washington, 1876).
6. See my Chapter 11, p. 424.
7. James D. Hague and Clarence King: *Mining Industry*, Professional Papers of the Engineer Department, U. S. Army, No. 18 (Washington, 1870).
8. Sereno Watson: *Botany*, Professional Papers of the Engineer Department. U. S. Army, No. 18 (Washington, 1871).

on the descriptive geology of the Fortieth Parallel.[9] In it they described in ordered fashion the main topographical features of the five major regions the Survey examined, which were the two basins and the plateau of Nevada and Utah, the country between the Wasatch and Green River, and the final section from Green River to the Front Range. It formed Volume II of the series.

The year 1878 saw the publication of Volume IV, which was actually three separate monographs.[1] There were two studies of paleontology. The first was written by the indefatigable Fielding Bradford Meek and dealt with invertebrate fossils from the Lower Silurian to the Tertiary. The second was a special study of the specimens from the Eureka and White Pine districts, by R. P. Whitfield and James Hall of Albany. Part III, written by Robert Ridgeway, was on ornithology, a study which delighted the naturalists of the day, particularly Ridgway's mentor, Spencer F. Baird. A final volume was completed in 1880. This was Professor Othniel C. Marsh's first full-length work, *Odontornithes: A Monograph on the Extinct Toothed Birds of North America.*[2] Marsh was a close friend of King's, and King had followed his pursuit of the ancient fauna of the West with great interest, dovetailing his own studies of the Bridger Basin, the Morrison Formation, and the John Day Basin with the findings of Marsh in these regions. During the course of administering the surveys, King had visited Marsh's collections at Yale many times. He was one of the first to view Marsh's fossil horse series. Though he frequently in jest warned Marsh that his extensive collections, coming to rest in New Haven, were threatening to tilt the continent, King had a great respect for the Yale paleontologist and counted it fortunate that he was able to include Marsh's volume in his series, with General Humphreys's permission.[3] Widely regarded as the "missing link" in Darwin's evolutionary series, Marsh's discovery of toothed birds in ancient America

9. Arnold Hague and Samuel Franklin Emmons: *Descriptive Geology*, Professional Papers of the Engineer Department, U. S. Army, No. 18 (Washington, 1877).

1. Fielding Bradford Meek: *Paleontology* (Part I); James Hall and R. P. Whitfield: *Paleontology* (Part II); Robert Ridgeway: *Ornithology* (Part III), Professional Papers of the Engineer Department, U. S. Army, No. 18 (Washington, 1878).

2. Othniel Charles Marsh: *Odontornithes: A Monograph on the Extinct Toothed Birds of North America*, Professional Papers of the Engineer Department, U. S. Army, No. 18 (Washington, 1880).

3. Wilkins: *Clarence King*, p. 207.

was a dramatic accomplishment that called forth great praise from European scientists. When Huxley came to America he went almost immediately to Yale to see Marsh's collections, and Darwin himself, besieged by critics, added his praise and thanks.[4]

Perhaps the two extremes of the survey results are represented by Gardner's *Atlas* and King's own volume, *Systematic Geology*.[5] The outstanding feature of the Atlas was the rapidity with which it was produced. Whereas engineer officers and even Whitney procrastinated for years over their maps, Gardner had his done almost as soon as the Survey was finished. The large octavo folio included one overall map of "The Cordilleras of the Western United States," a survey of the entire territory traversed, and ten smaller maps. The smaller maps, drawn originally to a scale of two miles to the inch and then photographically reduced to four miles to the inch, were arranged in two identical series. The first was a Topographical Series of the five sections represented in *Descriptive Geology*, namely the Rocky Mountains, the Green River Basin, the Utah Basin, the Nevada Plateau, and the Nevada Basin. The topographical maps concentrated chiefly on the mountains and the rivers, but the method of hachuring, a brush technique, though beautiful, was so vague as to somewhat obscure the sense of altitude and depth. The geological maps, covering the same regions, were better. A final inclusion was a series of general geological cross-sections of the kind that were traditional in geological reports. A handsome production, Gardner's *Atlas* appears nevertheless not to have been the outstanding contribution to geography it might have been, perhaps due to his haste in compiling it.[6]

11

The capstone of the entire series was King's *Systematic Geology*.[7] Disdaining a mere report of his findings in the field, King attempted to be truly scientific, and out of his many samples and field observations to compose a history of Cordillera geology that would reveal

4. Ibid., p. 208.
5. Clarence King: *Systematic Geology,* Professional Papers of the Engineer Department, U. S. Army, No. 18 (Washington, 1878).
6. See Introduction to *Atlas*, Professional Papers of the Engineer Department, U. S. Army, No. 18 (1878).
7. See footnote 5 on this page. Unless otherwise stated, my description is based on this work.

the laws and principles of geologic science. It was a vast improvement on Whitney's comparable study.

He began chronologically with the earliest period, the Archean or Pre-Cambrian Period, in which a whole continent now hidden but similar in topographical features with that of the present day rose up, its dominant features lofty mountains rising to Himalayan heights of 30,000 feet, with solid escarpments rising as much as 10,000 feet. And in between were profound valleys rapidly being filled by a process of erosion on a massive scale. Then the Pre-Cambrian continent sank. In the East it was a gradual process, but in the West the drop was sudden. There followed a long period of Paleozoic immersion in which a great sea washed over most of Western America and the lofty Wasatch became a mere atoll barely showing above the billowing salt sea. During this period, King reasoned, great climatic changes and periods of emergence and subsidence must have occurred, for there were six different layers of sedimentary deposition, including the Wasatch Limestone, the Weber Quartzite, and the Upper Coal Measures of the swampy Carboniferous. Some of these layers, deposited over a long period of time, were as much as 12,000 feet thick, and between the 105th and the 112th meridian they thickened from 1,000 to 32,000 feet. At the close of the Paleozoic, the West sank again, breaking off at the Wasatch Fault, and the sea deepened, while to the east a mediterranean ocean appeared on the site of the Great Plains. As this shallow sea washed westward, gradually rising and subsiding, it formed the Rocky Mountain Red Beds of the Triassic, and then the Jurassic, in whose Morrison and Cañon City formations of central Wyoming Marsh had found gigantic dinosaurs. Then came the Cretaceous. A warm shallow sea advanced and retreated at least four times, leaving behind fossil mollusks and cephalopods. It was the last great ocean to cover the Rocky Mountains. Beyond the Wasatch, however, the Paleozoic seas remained undisturbed throughout the Mesozoic Era.

Then suddenly at the end of the Cretaceous, the last period of the Mesozoic Era, the Great Plains abruptly domed and the mountains arose, "causing the sea to retire altogether from the interior of America, absolutely obliterating the mediterranean ocean which had divided the eastern and western land masses . . . since the close of the carboniferous."[8] Later, as G. K. Warren had pointed out, the whole region tilted some 7,000 feet, draining off all water into the

8. Ibid., p. 356.

Gulf of Mexico, and, King dramatically observed, "not a species remained."[9]

The next great period was the Cenozoic Period, in which during the Eocene huge fresh-water lakes appeared in the heart of the Rocky Mountains along the Green River Basin. They extended through parts of New Mexico and Colorado as far south as Arizona. In the subsequent Miocene Period the lakes multiplied and spread, introducing entirely new forms of fresh-water life. And just at the close of the Miocene two new basins began to appear along the Wasatch and Sierra fault lines. This was a period of what King called "orographical displacement."[1] Mountains rose. The "crust yawned and enormous volumes of lava rolled out, overwhelming neighboring lands."[2] Especially along the fault lines east and west, the Miocene and Pliocene periods saw tremendous explosions and fracture and fire. They were, King concluded, "immense exhibitions of telluric energy."[3]

This was followed by the glaciers, not the tremendous grinding Greenland Cap to the east, but rather a series of local glaciers that scooped out the V-shaped valleys of the Uintas and the Sierras. In between, there were raging torrents of meltwater that poured down through the mountain valleys carrying boulders as big as houses that swept everything before them. And then another glacial period followed. In all, King concluded, there were "two periods of precipitation with a drier interval."[4] The two lakes, Lake Bonneville and Lake Lahonton, originally formed in the Pliocene period, sank deeper into the floor of the Great Basin at this time. Then during the period of dryness they all but disappeared—only to be filled by the furious cascades of the second period of glacial disintegration. During this time the Western mountain topography took its present form, and since the last glacial era, the region appeared to be in the midst of another long dry period. It was this condition which caused King and his colleagues, not to mention the generations of previous Argonauts who inched across the vast dreary wastes, so much difficulty and travail. With the publication of King's *Systematic Geology*, the Great Basin in all its complex history had at last been dis-

9. See King's restatement of this point in Clarence King: "Catastrophism and the Evolution of Environment," A Commencement Address to the Sheffield Scientific School, June 26, 1877 (n.p.). Copy in Yale University Library. p. 19. This address is a first, and shorter, version of *Systematic Geology*.
1. King: *Systematic Geology*, pp. 435–6.
2. See footnote 9 on this page.
3. Ibid.
4. King: *Systematic Geology*, pp. 478, 487.

covered and incorporated into the sophisticated world of science. It was a story only a trifle less dramatic than Genesis.

In the midst of composing his great synthesis of Western geology, King had an opportunity to draw even more profound conclusions from his work, which placed it in the mainstream of scientific speculation. He was asked to deliver the commencement address to the class of 1877 of the Sheffield Scientific School. King used this occasion to launch a sweeping attack on the whole school of Uniformitarian geologists and biologists who, since Darwin, had come to dominate American and European science. The address, entitled "Catastrophism and the Evolution of Environment,"[5] sprang directly from his observations of the countless instances of catastrophe in the geologic history of the West, and he used his dramatic American evidence to confront the followers of Lyell, and indeed all the British Uniformitarians and their disciples, whom he termed "an army of scientific fashion-followers."[6] With an eloquence that echoed the futile rhetoric of his friend Louis Agassiz, King unfolded his Western story to an audience which included not only the students of Sheff, but O. C. Marsh, his friend, and one of the great Darwinians of his time.

The disagreement between Uniformitarians, who were "imprisoned" in the present, and Catastrophists, who reached all the way back to the sudden primordial terrors of primitive man, was simply a debate over the rate of change in the environment, King argued. Given this basic difference, the Uniformitarians, seduced by biology and mesmerized by the iron logic of Malthus, had failed completely to note the geologic record. Looking only at fossil links, they had not noted the "mechanical rupture, displacement, engulfment, crumbling and crushing of the rocky surface of the globe."[7] The result was that they had projected the gradual change observable in the present into the geological past, ignoring great changes in the rate of energy and accelerations which must have been felt by every living and perishing species in the ancient past. Carrying the argument directly to Marsh, King told his audience: *"Between each two successive forms of the horse there was a catastrophe* which seriously altered the climate and configuration of the whole region in which these animals lived."[8] He added that "Huxley and Marsh assert that the bones *prove descent.* My own work proves that each

5. See footnote 9 on the preceding page.
6. Clarence King: "Catastrophism and the Evolution of Environment," p. 10.
7. Ibid., p. 26.
8. Ibid., pp. 36–7.

new modification succeeded a catastrophe."[9] The only species that survived, in King's view, were those which were extremely "plastic"[1] and could change with the sudden catastrophes that destroyed their more rigid brethren. He concluded with a resounding statement that echoed Agassiz at his best: "A mere Malthusian struggle was not the author and finisher of Evolution. . . . He who brought to bear that mysterious energy we call life upon primeval matter, bestowed at the same time a power of development by change, arranging that the interaction of energy and matter which make up the environment should, from time to time, burst in upon the current of life and sweep it onward and upward to ever higher and better manifestations. Moments of great catastrophe, thus translated into the language of life, become moments of creation, when out of plastic organisms something new and nobler is called into being."[2]

King's brave sally was for the most part greeted by his scientific friends with embarrassment, though Henry Adams came to base much of his philosophy of history upon it.[3] King had dramatically demonstrated in the long view the relatively sudden local changes in the environment, using as examples his Western discoveries, and to this extent evolutionists might be forced to make minor concessions. But his terminology caught him on the horns of the same cruel dilemma that had vanquished Agassiz a decade before. Did he mean by "plastic" those species which most readily adapted to the environment? If so, he had offered no real challenge to Darwin's theory. If not, he was forced into a kind of teleological Lamarckianism in which the Creator caused certain species—the giraffe perhaps, or the cephalopod, or even Henry Adams's favorite, the Eocene lemur—to change characteristics overnight in order to stay alive through the basaltic floods or the long glacial winters. It appeared that in the heightened emotion of a June afternoon's commencement, King, a humanist at heart, had overreached himself. Fortunately Marsh and his Darwinian peers recognized the brilliant achievements of his work on the Fortieth Parallel Survey, and the Yale address passed by, a minor friendly skirmish in the war between science and theology. Instead of condemning him, by 1879 they all combined to propel him to the pinnacle of success, the first directorship of the United States Geological Survey.

9. Ibid., p. 37.
1. Ibid., p. 34.
2. Ibid., p. 37.
3. Henry Adams: *Education*, pp. 224–36, 312–13, 399–402.

The significance of King as a Western explorer is not difficult to estimate. Working within the traditional army framework, he had brought discovery to a new height. By carefully surveying the whole vast basin and range country, he had not only located new resources and suggested ways of adjusting to a non-agricultural frontier. He had also made Western exploration a newer, more exciting, more exact science. Abandoning the purely descriptive, which he loved, he devised laws and rules of environmental development. He outlined scientific sequences of cause and effect. And he utilized all the latest scientific theories and techniques, such as Richthofen's mathematical law of eruptive sequences and Zirkel's microscopical petrography. Moreover, he assembled a nucleus of brilliant professionals who were interested in the specific problems of Western geology, from volcanoes to glaciers, men who could and would continue on in their own right. Thus, his glamorous example, and his very demonstration of the whole horizon of possibilities and opportunities for highly trained academicians in the West, contributed as much, if not more, than anything else to the rapid displacement of the soldier-engineer as the key figure in Western exploration. Above all, he had incorporated the West into the realm of academic science.

CHAPTER XIII

The Last Stand of the Army Explorer

THE third phase of post-Civil War army exploration in the West was Lieutenant George Montague Wheeler's Geographical Surveys of the Territories of the United States West of the 100th Meridian. Comparatively little-known and largely uncelebrated, Wheeler's surveys represented an attempt by the Army to instill a professional spirit in its Western exploring activities to the point where it could regain scientific prestige in its own right, and with it control over all geographical activity in the Far West.

Wheeler, who graduated sixth in the class of 1866 at West Point, was a soldier born a generation too late.[1] Ideally, he belonged with the old prewar Corps of Topographical Engineers, but he came into the world in Hopkinton, Massachusetts, in 1842, the very year of John C. Frémont's first dramatic trip to the Rocky Mountains, and he began his work as an explorer just as John Wesley Powell was completing his voyage through the last completely unopened region of the West. By the time Wheeler was graduated from West Point, where he had spent the war as a cadet, the Army was in eclipse, and he was a newly minted second lieutenant at a time when experienced officers were the most abundant commodity on the national labor market. Thus, as a soldier he was one among many, and as an explorer he was simply too late. Perhaps it was only his West Point record and his fortunate marriage to the daughter of Francis Preston Blair, Jr., that saved him from a career of monotonous garrison duty and made him, in spite of all odds, an explorer after all.

As a second lieutenant, he was soon assigned to General E. O. C. Ord's command in California, where, working under the influential

1. *D.A.B.* Also see obituary in *The Army and Navy Journal*, May 6, 1905, which was taken from *The New York Times* of May 5, 1905.

Colonel R. S. Williamson, who had put Clarence King on the path to fame, he learned the exacting trade of military topographer. By 1869, as was previously related,[2] he had gained promotion to first lieutenant and led his first independent expedition—an old-style reconnaissance south from Fort Halleck on the Central Pacific line through eastern and southern Nevada. His diligence in the 1869 expedition, which lasted for five grueling months, and covered 82,000 square miles, plus his great ambition, which prompted him to project even grander reconnaissances than any of his fellow officers, placed him almost immediately in the forefront of new army explorers in the West. His work in 1869 was in the forbidding southwestern desert regions of Nevada and Utah, south of the Fortieth Parallel Surveys, where Josiah Dwight Whitney had expected Clarence King to concentrate his operations after his 1866 venture into that region. The area, though penetrated many times by previous explorers, had never been, as Wheeler put it, "instrumentally explored." In 1867–68 Williamson and others had been interested in the Colorado River, particularly after James White's appearance, but upon receiving orders from higher up, they had reluctantly abandoned the area to Powell's civilian operation.[3]

But even given the success of Powell's civilian voyage, Wheeler, as a military explorer, was responding to another and different set of needs peculiar to the Southwest. Not only was he interested in an area largely bypassed by most surveys of his day, and avoided by experienced officers as the Botany Bay of military banishment, but he was also, as an explorer and topographer, in a position to provide something vitally needed by Lieutenant Colonel George M. Crook's command, accurate geographical maps of the rugged Apache and Paiute country. From a military standpoint, a large-scale mapping venture in the Far Southwest was of the greatest necessity. Wheeler, eager and anxious to create a career for himself in the grand tradition of prewar explorers, was willing to provide for this necessity, whatever the monotony, risk of exposure to desert elements, and danger from the Indians.

Several other elements contributed to Wheeler's spectacular rise. Though King's survey was clearly under military jurisdiction, it consisted almost entirely of civilian academicians and as such offered little in the way of career opportunities to peacetime sol-

2. See Chapter 11, p. 394.
3. See Chapter 11, p. 397.

diers. Moreover, the sudden emergence of the Powell and Hayden surveys under the auspices of the rival Interior Department presented a serious threat to military leadership. This rankled the officers of the regular army like General Humphreys, and he used every power at his command to promote Wheeler's proposals. Second, Wheeler was able to capitalize, paradoxically enough, on the backing of the scientists, who supported King on a *quid pro quo* basis, as his correspondence with King's patron, Professor O. C. Marsh of Yale, clearly indicates.[4] Thus, though he lost all priority in the "Plateau Province" to Powell, by 1871 Wheeler, scarcely thirty years of age, emerged as leader of his own elaborate survey. This survey, thanks to his efforts in the next two years, gradually took form and became the important "United States Geographical Surveys West of the 100th Meridian." By dint of two years of hard work in the field, Wheeler became head of an entire bureau of exploration in his own right. And with him he carried the Army's hopes for survival in competition with the able captains of civilian science.

2

What contributed most to Wheeler's sudden success as a Western explorer was his spectacular exploration of 1871. Under orders from General Humphreys, he was sent to explore and map "those portions of the United States territory lying south of the Central Pacific Railroad, embracing parts of Eastern Nevada and Arizona."[5]

"The main object of this exploration," General Humphreys explained patiently, "will be to obtain topographical knowledge of the country traversed by your parties, and to prepare accurate maps of that section. . . . It is at the same time intended that you ascertain as far as practicable everything relating to the physical features of the country, the numbers, habits, and disposition of the Indians who may live in this section, the selection of such sites as may be of use for future military operations or occupation, and

4. G. M. Wheeler to O. C. Marsh, Washington, D.C., March 4, 1871, Marsh Letterbooks, Peabody Museum, Yale University. For Humphreys's pride in army achievements, see A. A. Humphreys to James A. Garfield, Washington, D.C., Feb. 5, 1873, Humphreys Papers, Pennsylvania State Historical Society.
5. Capt. George M. Wheeler: *Preliminary Report Concerning Explorations and Surveys Principally in Nevada and Arizona* (Washington, 1872), pp. 11–12.

the facilities offered for making rail or common roads, to meet the wants of those who at some future period may occupy or traverse this part of our territory."[6] In his spare time he was to survey the mineral resources of the country, the geological formations, the vegetation, its suitability for agriculture, the weather, and establish a number of astronomically observed points of latitude and longitude. The detail included in General Humphreys's orders indicated clearly that he had high hopes for the results of Wheeler's expedition.

To accomplish his many objectives, Wheeler assembled an excellent force. He recruited Lieutenant D. A. Lyle of the Second United States Artillery from as far away as Alaska, and after a frustrating tangle with his regional commander, Lieutenant D. W. Lockwood of the Engineers reported for duty in August. Wheeler also secured the services of Acting Assistant Surgeon Walter J. Hoffman, due to the good offices of Spencer F. Baird at the Smithsonian. Timothy O'Sullivan, of the King Surveys, served as photographer. In addition, Wheeler took along Grove Karl Gilbert, one of the greatest of all American geologists, and his friend Archibald Marvine from the University of Pennsylvania. The expedition of 1871 was Gilbert's first extensive experience in the West, and from his observations of the barren lake-bed landscapes of the Great Basin, he conceived his idea of the configuration of ancient Lake Bonneville.[7] Finally, in addition to topographical assistants, packers, and men of the cavalry escort, Wheeler introduced a new figure—a type that was to play an increasingly important role in the publicity-conscious efforts of the new explorers. He was a reporter, Frederick W. Loring of Boston, Massachusetts. Noting the singular success of Powell, Hayden, and King in the field of public relations, Wheeler hoped that O'Sullivan's photographs and Loring's articles would dramatize his work in the Southwest.

The various parties assembled on May 3 at Halleck Station on the Central Pacific Railroad, thirty men in all. After an initial move west to Carlin, Nevada, Wheeler divided his forces up into various survey parties who zigzagged southward, east, and west across Nevada, visiting mining districts at Battle Mountain, Bull Run,

6. Ibid.
7. G. K. Gilbert: "Report on the Geology of Portions of Nevada, Utah, California, and Arizona, Examined in the Years 1871 and 1872," *Report Upon the Geographical and Geological Explorations and Surveys West of the One Hundredth Meridian* (Washington, D.C.: U. S. Government Printing Office; 1875), Vol. III, Pt. I, p. 19.

Eureka, Belmont, Pioche, and the Paranagat Valley.[8] Frederick W. Loring enlivened the march with his satirical observations of Cowitch, the Shoshone chief who wanted "muck-a-muck" for his braves, and knew "a heap." He also told stories about Brigham Young, who wore a pair of light-gray trousers "stained in one or two places," and "a heavy cloak, which partially hid his obesity," and of the old California scout who was proud of the fact that a friend of his, aged forty, had just married a girl of eight.

"Well," said the old scout in one of Loring's articles, "we develop early here in California. There air seven or eight children married in Owen's Valley; and one gal of twelve has been divorced from her first husband, and married her second." (Spit) "We develop in California—we do."[9]

Neither Loring's jaunty manner nor the scientists' preoccupation with their many duties could relieve the difficult conditions under which they all labored, however. Miles of arid waste and volcanic rubble passed underfoot. The heat rose to 118 degrees. And in July the worst was to come. The various field parties converged on Death Valley from Camp Independence, Owens Valley, and from the Armagosa River. On the twenty-fourth and twenty-fifth of July, Lieutenant Lyle's party lowered themselves down rocky Break Neck Canyon in the Panamint Range and set out across the upper end of Death Valley from Last Chance Spring to Gold Mountain. Their guide, a prospector named Charles Hahn, deserted them on the first day and was never seen again, though a body believed to be his was later found. Following Lieutenant Lyle, Wheeler, with the main body, also lost his guide [Wm. Egan], but on August 23 Wheeler too managed to make his way across the valley to Furnace Creek in the Funeral Mountains.[1]

Lyle and Wheeler were not the first men to enter and explore Death Valley. A band of California-bound gold seekers had wandered into its gloomy wastes in December of 1849. Lost and in danger of starvation, they had split up into a number of bands, each desperately seeking a route across the Panamint Range on the far side of the valley. Three men perished, as one by one each of the parties, Jayhawkers, Mississippians, Georgians, Bennetts, and

8. Wheeler: *Preliminary Report, passim.* My account is based on this source, unless otherwise stated.
9. See Frederick W. Loring: "A Council of War," p. 183; "A Glimpse of Mormonism," p. 215; "Into the Valley of Death," p. 574, *Appelton's Journal of Science, Literature and Art,* Vol. VI (Aug. 12 and Nov. 18, 1871).
1. See "Report of Lt. D. A. Lyle, Second United States Artillery," in Wheeler: *Preliminary Report,* Appendix B, pp. 80–3. See also pp. 16–17.

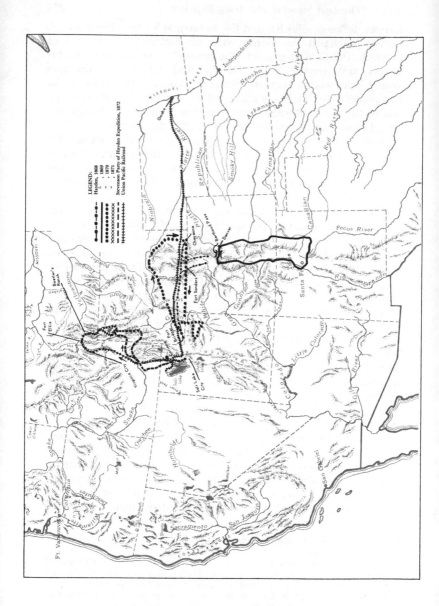

Briers, made their way in different directions up out of the desert. When the last party, the Briers, crossed over the divide of the Panamint Range, they had looked back over the scene of their prolonged hardships and in a burst of true inspiration called out "Goodbye Death Valley," thus affixing its name forever.[2]

Later other men had entered the valley, lured by a piece of solid silver alleged to have been discovered there by one of the original Argonauts and used for a gunsight. Dr. E. Darwin French, one of the silver seekers in search of the lost "Gunsight Mine," explored the valley in 1850 and again in 1860. He was perhaps the first man to use its picturesque name in print.[3] And in 1861 Dr. J. R. N. Owen led a team of the California Border Survey across its dazzling alkali flats. The Owen expedition was distinguished chiefly by the presence of three camels, Maya, Touli, and Catchouk, who stood the trip in splendid fashion.[4]

But though the valley had been traversed before, the Wheeler expedition found it nonetheless difficult. The thermometer reached 120 degrees, and even Loring's jauntiness was gone as he nearly succumbed to sunstroke. Wheeler devoted only a paragraph to his experience in Death Valley, but it was revealing.

> The route lay for more than 39 miles in light, white, drifting sand, which was traversed between 5 am and 6 pm., the center of the desert being reached about meridian. The stifling heat, great radiation, and constant glare from the sand were almost overpowering, and two of the command succumbed near nightfall, rendering it necessary to pack one man on the back of a mule to the first divide on the route, where a grass sward was reached at the end of the long sandy stretch, while the second, an old and tried mountaineer, became unconscious for more than an hour in nearly the same locality.[5]

It was in the best tradition of army exploration, and in retrospect Wheeler must have enjoyed it. The California newspapers, how-

2. Carl I. Wheat: "Trailing the Forty-Niners Through Death Valley," *Sierra Club Bulletin*, Vol. XXIV, No. 3 (June 1939). Also see William Lewis Manly: *Death Valley in '49* (San Jose, Calif.: Pacific Tree and Vine Co.; 1894).

3. Wheat: "Pioneer Visitors to Death Valley After the Forty-Niners," California Historical *Quarterly*, Vol. XVIII, No. 3 (Sept. 1939), pp. 195–214.

4. See Arthur Woodward: *Camels and Surveyors in Death Valley*, Publication No. 7, Death Valley '49ers, Inc. (Palm Desert, Calif.: Desert Printers, Inc.; 1961).

5. George M. Wheeler: *Report Upon United States Geographical Surveys West of the One Hundredth Meridian* (Washington, D.C.: U.S. Government Printing Office; 1889), Vol. I, p. 45. Hereafter cited as Wheeler: *Final Report*.

ever, found Wheeler and his party something less than heroic. They accused the lieutenant of abandoning the two guides in the desert to die, or perhaps murdering them. He was also reported to have hung up a local Indian boy by his thumbs from a wagon tongue, and on another occasion he was accused of having staked out four more redmen in the desert until they sold him their mules at a fair price. Wheeler was no lover of the Indians. He referred to them as "barbarians," and "savage assassins," and he deplored the peace policy so often urged by the Interior Department. Yet it is difficult to believe the newspaper picture of him, particularly since Egan, the guide reported murdered, apparently later reappeared in the mining district of St. George in southern Utah, a deserter and nothing more. Still, as Clarence King's near disaster of 1866 demonstrated, they were in dangerous country and, out of fear, may perhaps have resorted to stern measures.[6]

Having sounded the depths of Death Valley, Wheeler turned to his next objective, the exploration of the Colorado River upstream from Camp Mojave. Since Powell had already coursed down the river, with its roaring rapids, in 1869, and in 1871 was just completing a second, more scientific survey of the river, Wheeler's plan seems at first somewhat quixotic—especially as he intended to go *upstream*, fighting the terrible rapids all the way. He had his reasons, however. From the time of James White's emergence from the river at Callville in 1868, and even before that, as early as the Ives expedition of 1857, the Army had been concerned with three basic aspects of the river country: the possibility of extending the head of navigation far up into the canyon country as a means of supplying troops in that forbidding region; the location of transportation routes and wagon roads into the same area that would facilitate communication between the Central Pacific Railroad and the Far Southwest; and finally the assessment of the possibilities of the river for irrigation and reclamation purposes. A rapid cruise down the river could accomplish none of these objectives—so Wheeler adopted the army way, and went upstream.

His expedition was an elaborate one. Lieutenants Lockwood and Lyle made for St. George, Utah, and established two supply bases on the north side of the river, one at Pah-Koon Springs, and the other at Grand Wash. Along the way they explored parts of the Virgin River and the whole area around present-day Hurricane Mesa and Zion National Park. Then Lieutenant Lockwood crossed

6. Bartlett: *Great Surveys*, pp. 343–4.

over the river and established another supply base between Truxton Springs, Arizona, and Diamond Creek, the objective of Wheeler's river party. The geologist Gilbert accompanied this party for a time and thus was afforded an opportunity to examine the plateau country and the great volcanic cone of the San Francisco Mountains to the south. It was Gilbert who first applied the name "Colorado Plateau" to all the north rim country.

Wheeler journeyed due east from Death Valley to Camp Mojave near the present-day Needles, California. There he secured three riverboats and a barge, and assembled a party consisting of Gilbert, Dr. W. J. Hoffman, Tim O'Sullivan, E. M. Richardson, Frank Hecox, F. W. Loring, six boatmen, one sergeant and five privates from Company C, 12th Infantry, and the Mojave chief "Captain" Asquit and thirteen of his braves.

They set out from the landing at Camp Mojave on September 16, 1871, with O'Sullivan on one of the boats, appropriately named "The Picture," already at work with his wet-plate apparatus photographing their departure.[7] Slowly they made their way upriver, through Painted Canyon, around the Big Bend, and into Black Canyon (see map, p. 436). Dazzled by its vertical walls and romantic vistas, Wheeler nevertheless soberly concluded that "although [it was] interesting in the extreme," it did not "equal in grandeur what was expected of it from the description given in Ives' Report."[8] No canyon scenery, however, could have matched Egloffstein's Dorésque visions which illustrated Ives's Report.

On September 25, they passed the deserted site of Callville, then Las Vegas Wash, making camp at the foot of Boulder Canyon. By this time they had begun the heavy labor of towing the boats against the strong current. Above the Virgin River they entered Paiute country, and the Mojaves began to grow apprehensive, since this was the stronghold of their traditional enemies. Wheeler, however, succeeded in securing a truce between the tribes, and the expedition struggled on, past Grand Wash and up to the Grand Canyon proper.

At the Ute Crossing, just below Grand Canyon, they paused for a day to regroup for the final dash to Diamond Creek. Then, taking fifteen days' rations, they continued up the river, with Gilbert scouting ahead, to gain time to make his sketches of the great geological sections made visible by the action of the river. Soon they

7. Wheeler: *Final Report*, pp. 156–70. Unless otherwise stated, my account is based on this source. For the name of the boat "Picture," see p. 158.
8. Ibid., p. 159.

began to hit the rapids, which were, in Wheeler's restrained language, "more formidable than any yet seen."[9] On October 21 they passed a rock which marked the supposed upriver progress of the Mormon scout O. D. Gass and four men in 1864. At Vernal Falls two boats capsized and the party broke up into sections, each making dreary wet camps along the riverbank. Two men were injured, and the difficulties mounted. Wheeler wrote: "I have several times during the day despaired of reaching Diamond Creek in time to join the relief party there, as each rapid in turn seems to be more powerful than the last. . . ."[1]

At Disaster Rapids another boat capsized and was wrecked spilling its contents, including Wheeler's valuable notes, into the muddy Colorado. It took three precious days to work the boats around this point, and Wheeler's notes and collections were never recovered. By October 15, having lost some of their provisions in the marine disaster, Wheeler and his men were on emergency rations. There was no game to replenish their supply, and the river was proving more formidable than ever. Wheeler wrote hopefully on October 17: "Speculations are rife to-day as to the prospect of either want and starvation and inability to get out of the cañon, and yet I believe there will be some loophole in event of the utmost emergency."[2] Even the Indians became discouraged at being sealed in by the towering canyon walls with little or no food, leaking boats, and only the surging river ahead of them. Desperate by now, Wheeler dispatched Hecox and Roberts overland for the relief party, while Gilbert calmly observed the planet Venus.

The next day, in a last effort, led by Wheeler and Gilbert personally, they reached the mouth of Diamond Creek at last. There a fishing pole and line indicated that the rescue party was indeed alerted and ready with the much-needed supplies. On the twentieth of October the rendezvous was made and they were saved. Wheeler had at least duplicated Ives's feat of 1857 and he had done it the hard way, by water. Wheeler and his scientific party left the river at Diamond Creek and headed overland to Truxton Springs. The rest of the men and Indians were left behind, to cruise back downstream at their leisure, or perish, and they fade from history at this point.

What Wheeler had accomplished by his river trip is difficult to say. Long before he reached Diamond Creek, he had passed the

9. Ibid., p. 163.
1. Ibid., p. 164.
2. Ibid., p. 167.

head of navigation, and his men were far too busy staying alive on the turbulent waters to locate wagon trails. Even the imperturbable Gilbert had his difficulties in making geological and astronomical observations along the way. O'Sullivan's pictures and the crude map which Wheeler produced are perhaps the main additions to knowledge, and spectacular as they were, they hardly seemed worth the effort of the river hardships.

One further note of disaster punctuated the expedition. Three members of the party, Frederick Loring, William Salmon, and P. W. Harnel, started for California via the overland stage and on Sunday, November 5, they were attacked by a band of Apache Indians near Wickenburg, Arizona, and all but two occupants of the stagecoach were killed. Loring's career as a publicist for the Wheeler expedition was thus abruptly terminated and Wheeler was left with the melancholy duty of communicating the sad news to Loring's father in far-off Boston.[3] As late as 1889, when he finally published his report on the expedition, Wheeler was outraged at Loring's death. It was, he concluded, "one of the evidences of the mistaken zeal, of the then peace-at-any-cost policy, that was for so long a time applied to the settlement of the Indian problem. Unfortunately, the bones of murdered citizens cannot rise to cry out and attest the atrocious murders. . . ." He noted, however, with grim satisfaction, that the "redskin assassins" had ultimately been found and punished by General Crook.[4]

3

In his report for 1871, Wheeler recognized that "the day of the path-finder has sensibly ended," and he proposed a broad plan for the "complete reconstruction of the engineer map of the Western Territories," which ultimately led to the complete change in his surveys by 1873.[5] Yet in 1872 his field operations were still largely of the pathfinding or reconnaissance variety, rather than the accurate surveys of broad regions he was proposing. And though he recognized the value of base-line and trigonometrical surveys, and actually established six astronomical stations that year, his chief concern seems to have been to meet his competition by reexploring the Colorado Plateau and Grand Canyon region. The most interest-

3. Ibid., p. 35; Bartlett: *Great Surveys*, p. 348.
4. Ibid.
5. Wheeler: *Preliminary Report*, pp. 60–1.

ing results of this work were the photographs of William Bell and the drawings of John E. Weyss, the former Mexican boundary topographer and Civil War mapmaker who accompanied the field parties. Weyss's views of the Grand Canyon country, such as his famous portrayal of "The Crossing of the Fathers," though hardly in a class with W. H. Holmes's remarkably accurate studies of the same mesa and canyon country, nevertheless were impressive renderings of that remote locality visited by Escalante nearly one hundred years before.

In his prospectus for 1873, Wheeler again declared that "the time has come to change the system of examination, from that idea of exploration which seems to attach itself to a linear search for great and special wonders, to a thorough survey that shall build up from time to time, and fortify our knowledge of the structural relation of the whole."[6] By this he meant that the day of the great individual explorers in the manner of Frémont (or Powell) was over.

As early as the summer season of 1873, he had two distinct parties in the field beginning work on a systematic trigonometrical and astronomical basis. One party, which he led, operated out of Southern California, while the other party, commanded by Lieutenant W. L. Marshall, began its work from Denver, Colorado, having as its duty the survey by triangulation of Colorado south of the Union Pacific line and west of the front range.[7] But that summer in Colorado, near the headwaters of the Arkansas, Lieutenant Marshall ran into parties of the Hayden Survey. Before long, four out of five of Hayden's geological field parties were operating in the Twin Lakes region.[8] Thus the absurd spectacle presented itself of two surveying parties, their instruments placed on the same remote mountain peaks, surveying the same wilderness territory. Congress, however, saw no humor in the situation at all.

4

In 1874 the Townsend Committee on Public Lands of the House of Representatives met to consider the problem of duplication in

6. Wheeler to Humphreys, Washington, D.C., Feb. 3, 1873, in Wheeler: *Notes Relating to Surveys in the Western Territories of the United States* (n.d., n.p.), Yale Collection of Western Americana, p. 7.
7. Statement of Lt. W. L. Marshall, March 1, 1874, in 43rd Cong., 1st sess., *H. R. Report* 612 (1874), pp. 71–2. Hereafter cited as *Townsend Report*.
8. Ibid.

Western surveys, which by this time had become acute. The investigation was instigated by the War Department in an effort to assert its authority over all the surveys, and thereby check the advances made by the Interior Department, but the political pressure was by no means one-sided. According to Wheeler's geologist H. C. Yarrow, Hayden declared in 1873: "You can tell Wheeler that if he stirs a finger or attempts to interfere with me or my survey in any way I will utterly crush him—as I have enough congressional influence to do so and will bring it to bear."[9] Hayden did indeed have enormous influence in Congress. His letter files reveal that for several years he had been supplying members of Congress with that explorer's equivalent of the railroad pass—free sets of lavishly illustrated books, geologists' reports of value to would-be prospectors, and sets of sun pictures and stereopticon slides of the marvels of the West enough to delight anyone's favorite nephew.[1] Indeed, throughout the seventies the various surveys vied with one another in these lavish photographic productions for propaganda purposes.[2] Then, too, he could bring to bear against the Army an impressive backing by the various scientific and academic pressure groups, all of which had something to gain if purely civilian enterprise prevailed.

To this end, Hayden and Gardner, who had joined his survey, by 1874 began to assail the major scientific centers in the country with promotional material. In May of 1874 Hayden wrote to Josiah Dwight Whitney on behalf of his cause: "The friends of Civilian Science must now come to the rescue. This cause appeals to every scientific school in the land. Ask all your friends to write to such members of Congress as they know protesting. . . ." He added: "It is a fight for dear life with the odds against us but Congress is evidently in our favor, and there the work must be done."[3] By May 13 Gardner was applying even more direct pressure. "It is a great crisis for the science of the country," he wrote with almost evangelical zeal. "There must now be decided whether civilians who have de-

9. Ibid., p. 63. Dr. F. Kampf also supported this testimony.
1. For many examples of this practice, see Letters Received File, United States Geographical and Geological Survey of the Territories (Hayden Survey), Interior Department Records, R.G. 57, National Archives.
2. Wallace Stegner: *Beyond the Hundredth Meridian* (Boston: Houghton Mifflin Co.; 1954), pp. 174–91. Wheeler also produced three collections of photographs, which he distributed to interested parties. See Wheeler Papers, Yale Western Americana Collection.
3. F. V. Hayden to J. D. Whitney, Washington, D.C., May 3, 1874, Whitney Papers, Yale Historical Manuscripts Collection.

voted years to science are to direct the scientific work of the country. Can you not write an article on the general principles involved and get *The Nation* to print it? I hope Yale and Harvard will speak up nobly in this crisis. It is no time for trimming and we shall remember the friends that stand by in this awful struggle. The weak-backed men will be marked by the stand they take."[4] Then, in another hurried letter, that same day he added: "It is a great issue for science and you have given us much help in this time when we are strained to the utmost. Hayden ordered 600 of the large sized photographs to be sent to you as soon as they can be printed."[5] Whitney, who regarded Hayden as "an enthusiastic man, ignorant of course," and did not trust him personally, nevertheless fell into line.[6]

In the 1874 hearings the Army was immediately put on the defensive. It was clear to most observers that Wheeler had been deliberately surveying areas already covered by previous parties in an obvious attempt at empire building. Moreover, Wheeler's haughty refusal to testify on matters of War Department policy did nothing to aid his cause, and his intemperate exchange with Hayden caused them both to be censured for bad manners in the committee report.[7] Most of the civilian scientists—some of whom had quarreled with Wheeler while serving under him—now stood together against the military. The issues of the power struggle were clearly focused for them, and they felt that the Western surveys could better be staffed by their protégés than by men from West Point who kept the civilian scientists subordinate to their authority.[8]

Powell, deliberately picking the worst example of Wheeler's work, declared flatly that his maps were inaccurate and useless for geological purposes.[9] Hayden asserted that "there is not a single square mile of the Rocky Mountain region sufficiently accurate and in detail on the engineer maps that we could use for geological purposes."[1] And Gardner alleged that Wheeler had "marched around and looked into but did not enter . . . great regions as large

4. James T. Gardner to J. D. Whitney, Washington, D.C., May 13, 1874, Whitney Papers, Yale Historical Manuscripts Collection.
5. James T. Gardner to J. D. Whitney, Washington, D.C., May 13, 1874, Whitney Papers, Yale Historical Manuscripts Collection.
6. J. D. Whitney to W. D. Whitney, Cambridge, May 13, 1874, Whitney Papers, Yale Historical Manuscripts Collection.
7. *Townsend Report,* p. ⁻⁸
8. Ibid., pp. 73–7.
9. Ibid., p. 51.
1. Ibid., p. 39.

as Connecticut and Rhode Island together," so that perforce "a large amount of the topography" had to be "left to the imagination of the draughtsmen."[2]

Based on half-truths and differences of opinion, these were nevertheless stunning blows to Wheeler's survey, the more so because they were backed up by numerous academic letters of protest. The most prominent of these was from Yale College, signed by President Noah Porter, O. C. Marsh, and all the scientists except James Dwight Dana, who was under some obligation to Wheeler since he had received permission to incorporate Wheeler's (and Gilbert's) researches into his new textbook of geology.[3]

In 1874, however, Wheeler mustered enough strength to survive, undoubtedly because he enjoyed the support of President Grant.[4] And, in fact, all the surveys were left in the field stronger than ever. The Yale letter was quietly replaced by another which denied opposition to Wheeler,[5] and the Townsend Committee concluded that, though the Hayden and Powell surveys were more accurate, "there is an abundance of work for the best talents of both the War and Interior Departments in the scientific questions of the Western Territories for many years to come." Characteristically for its time, it felt that there was a public value in encouraging unrestrained competition between the various branches of government service.[6] Looking back on the Congressional struggle of 1874, Wheeler must have felt some disappointment at his failure to assume control of all Western exploration, but it must also have been with relief and no little gratitude that he named the highest mountain peak that year for James G. Blaine.[7] Survival, next to complete success, was most important.

2. Ibid., p. 59.

3. Ibid., pp. 73–7. For the Wheeler-Dana relationship, see Wheeler to Gen. A. A. Humphreys, Washington, D.C., Nov. 11, 1873, Wheeler Papers, Yale Western Americana Collection. Wheeler granted Dana permission to publish his material in preliminary reports in journals and "for insertoin [sic] in a new edition of his work on Geology."

4. See "Message of the President," May 2, 1874, 43rd Cong., 1st sess., *H.R. Exec. Doc. 240* (1874).

5. See Exhibit No. 11, "Disclaimer of Faculty of Yale College Concerning Geographical and Geological Surveys West of the Mississippi," June 9, 1874, 43rd Cong., 2nd sess., *H.R. Report 149* (1874).

6. *Townsend Report*, pp. 16–18.

7. Wheeler to Hon. James G. Blaine, Washington, D.C., Feb. 8, 1875, Wheeler Survey Records, R.G. 77, National Archives.

5

In response to the charges brought out in the hearings, Wheeler paid more attention to the latest scientific techniques in his surveys. He set up three separate astronomical observatories, including one housed in a specially constructed brick building in Ogden, Utah. He abandoned the meander system, based on measurement by odometers, in favor of base-line and trigonometric triangulation entirely, and he began experimenting with contour maps instead of representing topography in vague, hachured sketches. He further addressed himself to problems of agricultural settlement in the arid lands, branching out into irrigation surveys and attempts at land classification and the redirection of settlement patterns, clearly anticipating by several years John Wesley Powell's celebrated and influential *Report on the Lands of the Arid Region,* published in 1878. In concerning himself with these matters Wheeler was no pioneer, however, since as far back as Kearny's Mexican War reconnaissance of 1846, Lieutenant William Hemsley Emory had looked at the dry Southwest and called for new settlement patterns based on the realities of topography and watercourses rather than on the 160-acre grid pattern of the public-land surveys.[8]

6

Each year, from 1874 on, the Wheeler Surveys became more extensive and his atlas of maps increased. In 1874 itself, there were two field divisions operating in California and Colorado.[9] But under each of these divisions there were two and five field parties, respectively, including one that provided the paleontologist E. D. Cope with the opportunity to make his greatest discovery, the Eocene beds of northern New Mexico, with their distinctive remains of early mammals.[1] Along with Dr. Oscar Loew, he also discovered and explored some of the half-hidden citadels of the vanished Indian cultures along the San Juan River.[2]

8. See my Chapter 7, pp. 256–7.
9. Wheeler: *Annual Report,* 1875.
1. E. D. Cope to Father, Sept. 14, 1875, Cope Papers, American Museum of Natural History, New York. Cope's field diaries for the period are also in this collection. The letter of Sept. 14, 1874, is also quoted in Osborne: *Cope,* pp. 200–1.
2. Wheeler: *Annual Report,* 1875, pp. 166–78.

In 1875 seven parties were in the field, including a special expedition operating out of Santa Barbara which uncovered a new archaeological horizon and forwarded rich collections to the Smithsonian Institution.[3] That same year Lieutenant Hoffman Birnie led another expedition into Death Valley, exploring it from north to south as well as from east to west, thereby completing the accurate mapping of that remote region.[4] In 1876 Wheeler's work became more "practical," as one of the six field parties concentrated on a detailed study and map of the Comstock Lode, though King's survey had already produced its classic work on the subject, and Dan De Quille's *Big Bonanza*, surely a more famous work, came out that same year (1876). Another of the parties "explored" and remapped Lake Tahoe and Carson City, suggesting that they were beginning to run out of wildernesses to conquer.[5]

In 1877 and 1878, in an operation perhaps grown too elaborate for its own good, Wheeler sent nine parties into the field in three divisions: Colorado, California, and Utah. His surveyors triangulated from five separate base lines, checking their results against those obtained at astronomical observatories in Ogden, Utah; Fort Bliss, Texas; and the Dalles in Oregon. Survey parties covered the entire eastern slope of the California Sierras and moved north into Oregon, while other groups surveyed parts of Idaho, Wyoming, Colorado, Nebraska, Montana, and New Mexico.[6] So eager was Wheeler to complete the mapping of the West that he proposed to General Humphreys that he be allowed to keep his parties in the field the year round. In the winter season the men could be shifted south to the Mexican border country and thus lose no time.[7]

By 1878, however, his men no longer precisely shared his enthusiasm. Their waning excitement was evident in the decline in quality of their reports. Lieutenant Symons, exploring in northern California, began one section of his report with the memorable travelogue phrase: "Bidding adieu to Rabbit Creek and its myriads of little scampering inhabitants. . . ."[8] A journalist accompanying one of the Colorado divisions described how they all kept busy study-

3. Wheeler: *Annual Report*, 1876, pp. 312–28. Also see Wheeler: *Final Report*, Vol. VII, pp. 1–292.
4. Ibid., p. 132.
5. Wheeler: *Annual Report*, 1877.
6. Wheeler: *Annual Report*, 1878, 1879.
7. Wheeler: *Annual Report*, 1878, pp. 101–2.
8. Wheeler: *Annual Report*, 1879, p. 215.

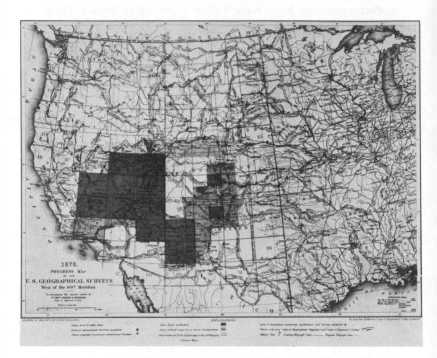

The progress of the Wheeler Surveys to 1876. This map indicates Wheeler's division of the West into ninety-four quadrants similar to those later employed by the United States Geological Survey. *Courtesy National Archives*

ing "a sprightly humming bird [which] stole among the flowers and robbed them of their honey with his dainty bill."[9]

Thus, in the spring of 1878, the House Committee on Appropriations, noting that all the Western surveys were growing at a rate somewhat greater than Parkinson's Law, refused to vote funds for their continuation until an investigation was made of the possibilities for their consolidation and condensation.[1] This was really a vote of no confidence in Wheeler's work, and it marked the beginning of the end of large-scale army exploration in the West.

Nevertheless, as commander of the Surveys West of the 100th Meridian, Wheeler could look back with some pride at his achievements in promoting the study and settlement of the West. At a total cost, by his own estimate, of some $496,895.51, he had surveyed over a third of the country west of the 100th meridian. He had been one of the first (though admittedly in no case *the* first) scientific explorers of Nevada, Arizona, and the Plateau Province of southern Utah, and western Colorado. His astronomical work, which involved literally thousands of observations, even Powell admitted deserved to be "ranked with the best that has ever been done." By his own count, Wheeler had supervised some twenty-five publications, including his extensive annual reports and seven large volumes of final reports on geography, astronomy, geology, paleontology, zoology, botany, archaeology, and history. By the time he finished, he had produced some seventy-one maps, including a geological as well as a topographical atlas, seven economic or land-use maps, and special maps of the Comstock and the Grand Canyon.[2] To be sure, many, though not all, of these maps were on too large a scale to be useful for recording geological formations. But Wheeler's survey, as the title implied, was a geographical rather than a geological survey, and the geologists were, more often than not, auxiliaries to the main parties of topographers, which perhaps

9. William Henry Rideing: "The Wheeler Expedition in Southern Colorado," *Harper's New Monthly Magazine*, Vol. LII (May 1876), p. 800. Rideing, an English journalist, later published a book about his experiences with the Wheeler Survey in the West. See Rideing: *A-saddle in the Wild West* (London: J. C. Nimmo and Bain; 1879).

1. Wilkins: *Clarence King*, p. 233. Between 1867 and 1878 Congress appropriated the following amounts to the four surveys: Hayden, $690,000; Wheeler, $550,000; King, $387,000; and Powell, $259,000. See William Culp Darrah: *Powell of the Colorado* (Princeton, N.J.: Princeton University Press; 1951), p. 243.

2. Wheeler to Humphreys, April 28, 1878, Wheeler Survey Records, R.G. 77, National Archives. Powell's admission of the excellence of Wheeler's astronomical work appears in *Townsend Report*, p. 51.

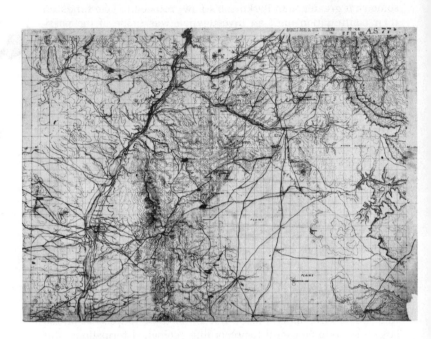

One of Wheeler's topographical maps, with contour lines. This refutes the charges made by Powell and Hayden that Wheeler did not make maps with contour lines. *Courtesy National Archives*

explains their frequent dissatisfaction with his surveys. For military operations and for a general basis of information leading to settlement, Wheeler's geographical approach and his topographical maps were more than adequate. In addition to this, his artists and photographers made some of the best of all the pictures of the Old West; and the Smithsonian Institution profited richly by the 43,759 specimens of natural history received from his collection parties.[3]

Individually the geological work of Gilbert, the paleontological discoveries of Cope, and the archaeological publications of Cope and Loew were of first-rate importance; and the geological work of J. J. Stevenson, the zoology of Coués, and the Santa Barbara ethnology of Yarrow were by no means unimportant. In a modest way, Wheeler himself had been a pioneer, though not an innovator in advocating land-classification and planned settlement in the West. Along with Whitney in California, he was the first man to point up the public implications of Western resources. Like the California geologist, he regarded the vast mineral deposits, the timber stands, and the rivers as too valuable to be left completely in private hands without some federal supervision. They belonged ultimately to the people and it was the government's job, in his view, to control them.[4] In this sense he went far beyond his contemporaries in Western exploration, and had his surveys not died in 1879, a new Western policy might well have arisen from his work.

Nevertheless, as of 1879, Wheeler's survey, scientifically speaking, was out of date. Though he tried to modify the old army way and incorporate the lessons and techniques learned on the King, Hayden, Whitney, and Powell surveys, his work was essentially only another great reconnaissance reminiscent of pre-Civil War days. As such, it was clearly overshadowed by the more skillful, practical and theoretical work of better-educated scientists from other surveys who had moved past geography and were interested in the particular and profound problems of an age of increasing specialization. Wheeler's work, in the last analysis, was too broad and superficial. In a tactical sense, it represents a false tunnel, one

3. Wheeler to Humphreys, April 28, 1878, Wheeler Survey Records, R.G. 77, National Archives.
4. Wheeler: *Annual Report,* 1876, pp. 75–7; *Final Report,* pp. 173, 179–81, 194, 223–7. See also Wheeler to Dr. J. O. Rothrock, March 22, 1880, Wheeler Survey Records, R.G. 77, National Archives. Note that Wheeler's earliest comments on irrigation, and the idea that water rights should go with the land, precede those of Powell. With regard to mining, see Wheeler to A. A. Humphreys, Jan. 23, 1872, Wheeler Papers, Yale Western Americana Collection.

of the abandoned mine shafts of learning—a clear case, for the most part, of the discontinuous and the non-cumulative aspects of science.

Despite the fact that the Army continued to send out the usual Western scouting parties (many of which produced important local results), all official large-scale army exploration in the West, except for Alaska, where the military played a prominent role, ended in 1879 with the consolidation of the Western surveys under Clarence King as director of the United States Geological Surveys. By 1878 President Grant was gone, and the military lost whatever preponderance it had in Washington. No Western party, or so-called "land ring," wished to defend the army surveys, though the Western politicos likewise disapproved of the centralized and federalized Geological Survey.[5] Times had changed, and Wheeler and his surveys and the Army suffered a signal defeat at the hands of Powell, King, and the special committee of the National Academy of Sciences picked to recommend a consolidation policy to Congress. That committee produced a report that condemned the Wheeler Surveys and called for centralized civilian control of the Far West, its exploration, and indirectly its exploitation and settlement.[6] In accordance with American tradition, the military gave way before the civil, and the scientific patronage of the Western surveys—though ultimately not of the Public Land Office Surveys—was placed firmly in the hands of the Academy. Perhaps, as far as the Army was concerned, this was all for the best. The "starving time," when the West was sparsely settled and the danger from Indians still necessitated the clanking cavalry escort, was over. As some of the other explorers' accounts were already suggesting, and perhaps as a result of their influence, the day of the spa and the tourist was about to begin.

5. Darrah: *Powell of the Colorado*, p. 248. See also the speeches by Western congressmen: Martin Maginnis (Montana), Thomas M. Patterson (Colorado), D. C. Haskell (Kansas), and John D. C. Atkins (Tennessee), Feb. 18, 1879, *Cong. Record*, 45th Cong., 3rd sess., Vol. VIII, Pt. 2, pp. 1202–11.
6. "Report of the Committee of the National Academy of Science, Nov. 6, 1878," 45th Cong., 3rd sess., *Sen. Misc. Doc. 9* (1878–79). The members of the committee were: O. C. Marsh, James D. Dana, William B. Rogers, J. S. Newberry, W. P. Trowbridge, Simon Newcomb, Alexander Agassiz. See also J. W. Powell to O. C. Marsh, Sept. 24, 1878, Marsh Letterbooks, Peabody Museum, Yale University, which reveals Powell's attempt to influence Marsh's committee; and J. W. Powell to Secretary of the Interior Carl Schurz, pp. 971–75, Letters Sent, Jan. 2–Dec. 31, 1878, Rocky Mountain Survey, Interior Department Records, R.G. 57, National Archives, in which Powell actually edits Marsh's report.

CHAPTER XIV

F. V. Hayden
Gilded Age Explorer

DURING the last days of army exploration in the Far West, the military explorer, as has been apparent, came to be faced with severe competition from other branches of the federal government. The surveyors of the Public Land Office had crossed the Mississippi and with chain and compass were gradually inching westward, applying their gigantic grid pattern in regular fashion upon the flat contours of the Great Plains. One weakness, however, of the Public Land Survey, and there were many, was its very mechanical and abstract quality. All lands—hills, river bottoms, deserts, badlands—everything in its path was to be laid out in base lines and staked off in unrealistic grid patterns. This was its primary function, and it left little room for speculation as to proper use of the land. Moreover, its progress was such that it actually pushed the frontier before it as adventurous prospectors, cattlemen, and squatters moved on ahead to choice lands where they could have preemption rights when the public surveyors finally did arrive. What was needed was a team of explorers who could range out ahead of the land survey and the pioneers, and quickly open up the new country, locate its resources, classify its lands for proper settlement, and thus point the way for rational and efficient use of the country.

In 1869 such a team was formed. It was called the United States Geological Survey of the Territories, and it became an agency of the Interior Department. As such, it competed directly with the army surveys, forming the means whereby the soldier-explorer was gradually replaced and the civilian scientist assumed full control of Western exploration. The story of the Interior Department Surveys, which constitutes the bulk of the next two chapters, has many similarities to the story of the military surveys, but the civilian operation went far beyond the military one. Conceived and executed as direct aids to the settlement and conquest of the wilderness, as were the military surveys, the Interior Department Surveys had, in addition, a profound effect upon institutions back home. The discoveries made in the great Western laboratory, the rivalries generated, the unusual and startling confrontations with undreamed-of reality all wrought great changes in the national approach to the West, and in the end effected on the highest level the complete institutionalization of natural science in its approach to Western America. This was a decisive chapter in the history of science as well as a crucial episode in the conquest of the frontier.

2

One of the two men who brought the Interior Department Surveys into national prominence was a curious self-made man of science named Ferdinand Vandiveer Hayden. Born in Westfield, Massachusetts, in 1829, he was sent by his widowed mother, like some child out of a Victorian novel, to live with an uncle on a farm near Rochester, New York.[1] While growing up on the farm, Hayden apparently dreamed of greater things, for when he reached the age of sixteen he refused his uncle's offer of adoption and set off on his own to become "a professional man." He taught school for two years, then realizing the deficiencies of his education, he made his way to Oberlin, Ohio, and there, penniless but eager for knowledge, he persuaded the president of Oberlin College, the Reverend Charles Grandison Finney, to allow him to work his way through to a degree. Finney, the greatest revival preacher of his day, was a leader in the abolitionist movement, and his convert Theodore Dwight Weld had led a revolt against the Lane Theological Seminary of Cincinnati in 1833 which eventually resulted in the transfer of the entire body of student abolitionists to Oberlin. By 1847, when Hayden arrived, Oberlin was the leading center of this activity. Hayden, however, seemed some-

1. John Wesley Powell: "Ferdinand Vandiveer Hayden," *Ninth Annual Report of the United States Geological Survey to the Secretary of the Interior 1887–88* (Washington, D.C.: U.S. Government Printing Office; 1889), pp. 31–8. See also Charles A. White: "Memoir of Ferdinand Vandeveer Hayden, 1829–1887," National Academy of Sciences *Biographical Memoirs* (Washington, D.C.: National Academy of Sciences; 1893), Vol. III, pp. 395–413. Unless otherwise stated, biographical details on Hayden are based upon the above.

what oblivious to the idealistic movements surrounding him and instead appears to have pursued his regular studies with a single-mindedness that led his teachers and classmates to view him as an "enigma." He was "the boy of the class," no espouser of social causes, "an enthusiastic dreamer, who would never conquer in practical life." The class historian wrote of him some twenty years after graduation that, despite his remarkable persistency and hard study, no one prophesied success for him.[2]

But Hayden had other interests. While at Oberlin he studied most closely with the young geologist John Strong Newberry, and Newberry urged him to continue his studies with his own mentor, James Hall of Albany. Thus, already imbued with the desire to become a geologist-naturalist, Hayden enrolled in the Albany Medical College and in 1853 was granted an M.D. Much of his time, however, was spent with Hall, who was then at work on his monumental *Palaeontology of New-York*, the model for all subsequent state surveys. Hayden soon became Hall's protégé and even lived in Hall's house. Upon his graduation in 1853, Hall sent him on his first geological expedition.

In 1849 Dr. John Evans had explored the Dakota Badlands and had written a report on their rich fossil deposits which was published by David Dale Owen in 1852. It then attracted Hall's attention.[3] Involved in the Pacific Railroad Surveys of 1853, and fancying himself the geologist of the nation, Hall decided to dispatch Hayden to Dakota to make fossil collections. In the spring of that year Hayden, accompanied by the paleontologist Fielding Bradford Meek, ascended the Missouri River on a steamboat to Fort Pierre and then made an overland trip to the Badlands. From the outset Hayden ran into difficulties. The Culbertson-Evans Northern Pacific Railroad Survey expedition attempted to keep him from leaving St. Louis, on the grounds that he was poaching on their discovery. Then they attempted to break up his expedition by hiring Meek. In a heated exchange, which was finally resolved by the forthright honesty and patience of Meek and the good offices of George Engelmann and Louis Agassiz, who happened to be in St. Louis at the time, Hayden was thoroughly chastened, but allowed to conduct his expedition.[4]

2. Powell: *Ninth Annual Report*, p. 32.
3. Merrill: *Geology*, pp. 501–4.
4. Major portions of the correspondence concerning this affair are in Merrill: *Geology*, pp. 699–707. See also F. B. Meek to James Hall, St. Louis, May 19, 1853, Box 5, James Hall Papers, New York State Museum, Albany, N.Y. In

When Hayden returned to Albany, he broke with Hall and began his own independent career.[5] In 1854, sponsored by the Chouteau family and various learned societies, he returned to the Dakotas and spent the next two years exploring alone through the Indian country from Fort Pierre in South Dakota to Fort Benton in Montana, and down the Yellowstone to the Big Horn. During this time he covered most of the important sites between the Missouri and the Yellowstone, and his collections relating to the Cretaceous strata began a new chapter in the history of Western geology. His work in the Near Northwest was the beginning of the concentration on particular rather than general problems by Western geologists. (See Chapter 8.)

Collaborating closely with Meek, who told him where to look and what to look for,[6] Hayden had spectacular success, and the team of Hayden and Meek achieved sudden prominence—so much prominence, in fact, that Meek, too, moved out of Dr. Hall's house and went to work for the Missouri State Survey. Later Meek went to Washington, where in 1859 he set up bachelor quarters in a house of low repute with John Strong Newberry.[7]

By 1856 Hayden's reputation had grown to the extent that Lieutenant G. K. Warren eagerly solicited him as geologist to his Dakota expedition of that year. He also accompanied Warren on his abortive Black Hills expedition of 1857.[8] Hayden's discoveries and Meek's evaluations took on greater importance as their knowledge accumulated with repeated expeditions. Modeling their work after that of James Hall, they assembled a stratigraphic column ranging from the lowest level of Azoic or Granite Rocks through the Potsdam Sandstone, which they were the first to discover in Western America, to the latest or Quaternary Age. This established the first such standard stratigraphic model for the West. Newberry himself, in his exploration of the Grand Canyon, related his find-

---

addition, see F. B. Meek: "Field Notebook, 1853," and Vol. III, Fielding B. Meek Papers, Smithsonian Institution.

5. White: "Memoir of Ferdinand Vandeveer Hayden"; Merrill: *Geology,* p. 502.

6. For example, see Meek to Hayden, Albany, May 4, 1854, Hayden Survey Letters Received, R.G. 57, National Archives.

7. John Strong Newberry to Hayden, Washington, D.C., Jan. 12, 1860, Hayden Survey, L.R., R.G. 57, National Archives. For evidence of Meek's troubles with Hall, see Meek to Hayden, Albany, May 4, 1854; Columbia, Missouri, Aug. 13, 1854; May 8, 1858, Hayden Survey, L.R., R.G. 57, National Archives.

8. See G. K. Warren: *Preliminary Report;* and Merrill: *Geology,* p. 711.

ings to it, as did Henry Engelmann in his transcontinental march with Captain Simpson in 1857–59. In addition to creating the earliest fundamental order in Western geology, Hayden, always with Meek's guidance, produced a geological map of the Yellowstone–Upper Missouri country that was far superior to any of its predecessors.[9]

Then, narrowing their sights somewhat, Hayden and Meek made two further discoveries of prime importance. They located five separate layers of Cretaceous horizon which became the standard for all future geologists.[1] They followed Hall's example and cut loose from European terminology and analogies, naming the Cretaceous sections after the localities where they were discovered: "Fort Pierre Group," "Fort Benton Group," etc. In this way they began a sequential chain that was not related to global or cosmic geology but was a simple picture of American reality as they saw it. It thus constituted a great scientific step forward. All of this required the utmost precision in the study of the characteristic invertebrate fossils of the Cretaceous Period, and the major share of the credit clearly belongs to Meek, for this was preeminently his field. His letters indicate that he provided most of the guidance for Hayden, but they also indicate quite clearly that he could not have functioned without him, for he deeply respected Hayden.[2] Thus, the criticism leveled at Hayden by Powell on this count in 1878 would appear to be uninformed, if not viciously unfair.

So adept did Hayden and Meek become in their study of fossil stratigraphy that by 1857, in the Dakotas, they had also discovered the existence of numerous fresh-water lakes and estuaries of the Eocene Period, thus antedating by a decade King's later discoveries of the same horizon in the Rocky Mountains.[3] In 1858, on a joint trip to Kansas, they also helped to clarify the discovery of the great beds of the Kansas Permian later made famous by Professor Hawn.[4]

9. For the stratigraphic column and the geological map, see Warren: *Preliminary Report*, p. 63, and *passim*.
1. Ibid.
2. See the nearly 300 letters in the Hayden-Meek correspondence, Meek Letterbooks, Meek Papers, Smithsonian Institution, for an idea of the close working relationship that existed between these two men.
3. Warren: *Preliminary Report*, p. 65; Merrill: *Geology*, p. 508; Powell: *Ninth Annual Report*, p. 37.
4. F. B. Meek: Field Notebook, Nos. 5 and 6 (1858, 1859), Fielding B. Meek Papers, Smithsonian Institution.

In addition to their work with invertebrate fossils, Hayden and Meek, and Hayden in particular, collected numerous specimens of vertebrates which they shipped back to Dr. Joseph Leidy at the University of Pennsylvania. As the Dakota specimens poured in, Leidy was kept busy producing descriptive papers for the Philadelphia Academy of Natural Sciences. Before he was finished, he and his co-workers had firmly established the science of vertebrate paleontology in America. His greatest work bore the romantic title "The Ancient Fauna of Nebraska," but included the Dakota specimens. In it he revealed the existence of great varieties of ancient life—camels, elephants, rhinoceri—all species thought to have been confined to the "older" parts of the world.[5]

Leidy's greatest discovery was the early horse. Long before Professor Marsh put together his sequence, Leidy had already established the existence of the horse in North America, tracing its fossil ancestors back into the Miocene and Pliocene.[6] His study was almost contemporaneous with the appearance of Darwin's great work and did not receive the acclaim due it because, unlike Marsh's work, the Darwinian controversy had not yet arisen to draw attention to it. A primitive step in the direction of Darwinian synthesis, Leidy's work, like that of Meek and of Hayden, was actually the first attempt at an American series of causally related developments in this field and furthered the scientific revolution wrought by the Dakota expeditions. By 1860, when Hayden completed his last prewar expedition to the Yellowstone and Wind River Mountains with Captain Raynolds, the science of geology in Western America had broken loose from classical European models and was now firmly established in local induction. It had become a true science.

One of the important factors in this scientific breakthrough may well have been the education of Hayden, Meek, and Leidy. Unlike Agassiz, Whitney, King, Marsh and the later professionals, they had not received extensive scientific training in Europe. Instead, Hayden and Meek worked with Hall and absorbed the local lessons of the New York State Survey. Leidy was an M.D. and a teacher

5. Joseph Leidy: "The Ancient Fauna of Nebraska," *Smithsonian Contributions to Knowledge*, Vol. VI, Art. 7 (Washington, D.C.: Smithsonian Institution; 1853).
6. See Joseph Leidy: "On the Fossil Horse of America," *Proceedings of the Academy of Natural Sciences of Philadelphia*, Vol. III (1857), pp. 262–6. Also see Henry Fairfield Osborne: "Biographical Memoir of Joseph Leidy," National Academy of Sciences *Biographical Memoirs*, Vol. VII (1913), pp. 339–96. See especially pp. 344, 356–68.

in Philadelphia, and though he had numerous European contacts, he stayed close to the local scene and the evidence presented by his gigantic specimens. Whitney's comment on Hayden's lack of education, related earlier, was therefore misleading. His local background in naturalism had, it was true, certain shortcomings that became apparent in his later work, but it had advantages that far outweighed the disadvantages. He was by no means "ignorant and uneducated." He merely represented a different scientific circle with a different background.

3

With the outbreak of the Civil War, Hayden turned to his medical practice and in 1862 was appointed an acting assistant Surgeon of Volunteers, in which capacity he served throughout the war.[7] By 1866 he had resigned his commission, accepted a professorship in absentia at the University of Pennsylvania, and returned to the Badlands of the Dakotas for more fossils.[8] All through the long hot summer of that year he labored with a team of volunteer diggers to unearth prehistoric turtles and other fantastic specimens. Unlike the military explorers, he had nothing to fear from the Indians. They held him in awe, calling him "the man that picks up stones running."[9]

By the end of 1866, however, except for his appointment at the University of Pennsylvania, Hayden was unemployed. It was obvious that he could not continue his free-lance expeditions indefinitely. He needed some visible means of support. And in 1867 Spencer Fullerton Baird of the Smithsonian Institution came to his rescue. He informed Hayden that the new state of Nebraska had a certain sum of federal money left over from its territorial days which had been granted to the state by Congress for a geological survey to be conducted under the auspices of the General Land Office.[1] This was a break from precedent and it offered Hayden the chance to lead his own survey. Quickly he marshaled support from Generals Warren and Humphreys, the already powerful O. C. Marsh, and from the Smithsonian Institution. Perhaps his most effective backing came from General "Black Jack" Logan, the po-

7. Powell: *Ninth Annual Report,* p. 35.
8. Ibid.
9. Bartlett: *Great Surveys,* p. 4.
1. Ibid., p. 10.

litical boss of Illinois, who, representing Chicago interests, had an obvious concern with developing the resources of the hinterland soon to be tapped by railroads operating out of that city.[2]

Hayden's first survey, which he made with the help of James Stevenson, his longtime comrade, F. B. Meek, and Dr. C. A. White, the state geologist, bore many of the characteristics of his later work.[3] It was a county-by-county examination of the resources of Nebraska, supplemented by a broad range of technical geological observations. His interests ranged from the location of coal and limestone deposits to observations on the cultivation of farms and fruit trees. Almost anything that constituted an economic resource he highlighted in glowing terms calculated to please the local inhabitants. Even the barren stretches of western Nebraska he predicted would have "a fine stock-growing" future. From the outset, too, he stressed a favorite theory borrowed from British and French scientists such as Sir John F. W. Herschel and M. Boussingault, that with cultivation and the planting of trees on the plains would come increased rainfall.[4] This observation, actually a European idea, and its more detailed promulgation by Professor Cyrus Thomas in his reports for subsequent years, became known as the "rain-follows-the-plow" theory, and caused Hayden no little scientific embarrassment in later years, though it mightily pleased Nebraska boosters.[5]

Hayden's first report, a pamphlet of some fifty-nine pages, was so well received that the copies were all distributed and it had to be reprinted in 1873.[6] In 1868 he received a further appropriation of $5,000, this time attached to the Sundry Civil Bill, and he extended his surveys out beyond Nebraska to the Rocky Mountain region. This was his chance, as he later put it, to examine "those sections which appeared at the time to be the chief objective points

2. See "General Letters Received," 1867–69, Hayden Survey Records, R.G. 57, National Archives. Also see Powell: *Ninth Annual Report*, pp. 42–3.
3. See F. V. Hayden: "First Annual Report of the United States Geological Survey of the Territories Embracing Nebraska" (1867) in *First, Second, and Third Annual Reports of the United States Geological Survey of the Territories* . . . (Washington, D.C.: U.S. Government Printing Office; 1873), pp. 5–64.
4. Ibid., p. 15.
5. See Henry Nash Smith: "Rain Follows the Plow: The Notion of Increased Rainfall for the Great Plains," *Huntington Library Quarterly*, Vol. X (Feb. 1947), pp. 169–94.
6. See footnote 3 on this page. Hayden: "Prefacatory Note," *First, Second, and Third Annual Reports*.

of emigration and improvement."[7] In general he followed the line of the Union Pacific Railroad, beginning at Cheyenne and working west toward Fort Bridger, but along the way he made digressions. In August, accompanied by Louis Agassiz and James Hall, he followed up the Little Laramie across the Wyoming–Colorado border to the Snowy Mountains, noting the existence of the now familiar Cretaceous beds even in the mountains. Along the way, the party paused to examine the gold diggings in the Medicine Bow Mountains, and to remark upon the great future of lumbering in the mountain region.[8]

On a second side trip, this a hunting expedition with Francis Preston Blair, Jr., he left Fort Sanders and journeyed south via the Big Laramie to North Park, Colorado, where he observed "myriads of antelopes quietly feeding in this great pasture-ground like flocks of sheep." Then in September he continued westward from Fort Sanders to the end of the line, or Separation Point, near Fort Bridger, thus concluding his year's labor.[9] He had seen a great deal of country that was new to him and he had made significant collections on which he planned to base a new geological map of the West. He had also pointed out the attractions of Wyoming and Colorado.

4

Once again the government was pleased, and in 1869 Hayden received a doubled appropriation of $10,000 to continue his work. This time, too, he was removed from the jurisdiction of the General Land Office and required instead to report directly to the Secretary of the Interior.[1] His survey became officially known as the United States Geological Survey of the Territories. His plans for 1869 were much more extensive than ever before. Assembling a party which included James Stevenson; the artist Henry W. Elliott; Reverend Cyrus Thomas, entomologist; Persifor Frazer, Jr., mining engineer; E. C. Carrington, zoologist; and B. H. Cheever, along with three teamsters, a cook, and a laborer, he set out to explore all along the

7. Hayden to Columbus Delano, Washington, D.C., April 25, 1874, Letters Sent, Hayden Survey Records, R.G. 57, National Archives.
8. For an account of the 1868 expeditions, see Hayden: *First, Second, and Third Annual Reports*, pp. 67–102.
9. Ibid., pp. 86–102. The quote appears on p. 87.
1. Bartlett: *Great Surveys*, p. 16. See also *U.S. Statutes at Large*, Vol. XV, p. 306.

mountain wall from Denver over Raton Pass and into Santa Fe.[2] Then his itinerary included a return via Taos, the San Luis Valley, and the famous South Park (see map, p. 472). As usual, his objectives were mixed, but practical considerations predominated. He highlighted such things as the evidences of the fresh-water lake beds of the Tertiary, and he made huge collections of fossils, including that most famous of Western specimens Inoceramus, but he also noted the location of coal beds and iron ore that promised to make Colorado the Pittsburgh of the West. The Reverend Thomas developed his "rain-follows-the-plow" thesis at greater length, giving careful consideration to possible land classification and irrigation, and Persifor Frazer wrote a special detailed report on the mines and minerals of Colorado.[3]

The report of 1869 was so well received that the 8,000 copies printed were all distributed in three weeks. In fact, Hayden was left without a personal copy. Thus the pattern for his future successes was set. Using the reconnaissance technique and depending upon army posts for supplies, he could cover an immense amount of territory each year, combining his geological pleasures with the serious pursuit of practical prospecting in the public interest. So wide was his range that nothing escaped his attention. If the country was too mountainous for settlement, he stressed its scenic beauty and picturesqueness, and Elliott made drawings to document his observations. In remote corners, mineral springs would attract tourists, and game would attract hunters and sportsmen. All the while, such basic things as timber stands, farm and pasture lands, precious mineral veins, rivers, coal and lignite beds, and iron deposits occupied his full attention. Geology was important insofar as it contributed to these objectives and as it served a basic educational function, for Hayden was a product of his age. No radical or reformer, or even a giant intellect, not one of the professional elite, but a self-made man, he was par excellence the businessman's geologist.

5

By 1870 his appropriation had grown to $25,000, and in a behind-the-scenes political struggle he had managed to defeat Gen-

2. Hayden: *First, Second, and Third Annual Reports*, pp. 103–251. For the organization of the survey, see p. 105.
3. Ibid., pp. 236–8, 229–51, 201–28.

eral Land Office Commissioner Joseph B. Wilson, preventing him
from launching a rival survey,[4] though he was not able to impede
the meteoric rise of John Wesley Powell.

Hayden's expedition of 1870 was the largest to date. It included
twenty men, four heavy wagons, and two army ambulances. In
addition to his usual assistants, Hayden also took along Sanford
Robinson Gifford, a noted Hudson River landscape painter, and
William Henry Jackson, the greatest of all Western photographers.[5]

Jackson had been born in Keeseville, New York, in 1843 and very
early had displayed great artistic talent.[6] By the time he was in his
teens, he was working as a touch-up man and background illustrator for photographers in upstate New York and nearby Vermont.
Little by little he mastered the art of photography. His early self-
portraits, depicting among other things his extreme youth, are
testimonials to the rapidity with which he learned his trade. After
serving as a combat artist during the Civil War, he returned home,
but a quarrel with his fiancée caused him to change his life. In
1866 he headed West, first as a bullwhacker to Salt Lake City, then
on with a wagon train to California. He returned eastward to Julesburg, Colorado, in 1867 with a herd of wild horses.

The following year, in partnership with his brother, he bought
a photography studio in Omaha, Nebraska, where, though two
photographers before him had sold out in disgust, he soon had a
thriving business. Many of the earliest street scenes and interiors
of Omaha, now displayed in that city's Joslyn Art Museum, were
the work of Jackson. In his spare time he went with the local missionaries to Indian villages and acquired the patience and techniques required for photographing the redmen.

In 1869 he initiated two momentous enterprises. First he married
Mollie Greer, and then, after a six-day honeymoon on a slow-mov-
ing Missouri River steamer, he left his bride and set out along the
Union Pacific Railroad to photograph it for the first time. These
early photographs along the railroad line, often taken from a haz-

4. For evidence of this struggle with Wilson, see Spencer F. Baird to Hayden,
Oct. 29, 1870, and Nov. 10, 1870, Letters Received, Hayden Survey, R.G. 57,
National Archives.
5. F. V. Hayden: *Preliminary Report of the United States Geological Survey
of Wyoming* (Washington, D.C.: U.S. Government Printing Office; 1871),
pp. 3–8. Hereafter cited as *Fourth Annual Report*.
6. Biographical details for William H. Jackson taken from William H. Jackson: *Time Exposure* (New York: G. P. Putnam's Sons; 1940). Also see Le
Roy R. and Ann W. Hafen: *The Diaries of William Henry Jackson, Frontier
Photographer* (Glendale, Calif.: The Arthur H. Clark Co.; 1959), pp. 11–20.

ardous perch on the cow-catcher of engine #143, gained him fame overnight. Somewhere along the line in Wyoming he met Hayden, who was impressed enough by his work to make a special trip to Omaha to secure his services for the 1870 expedition.[7]

In appointing Jackson to his survey, Hayden was not just attempting to use the dramatic new medium to publicize his work, though throughout the years of his surveys he came to employ Jackson's photos more and more as propaganda, presenting them as gifts to compliant congressmen. In the main, Hayden was interested in using whatever artistic means he could to convey the complex reality of the West. Elliott's drawings had been excellent, but nothing could match the new measure of accuracy afforded by the camera. It could be argued that Jackson's ability to capture the many scenes of sublime beauty in the West on his photographic plates and stereopticon slides did more than anything else to publicize the "tourist's West." It also had the effect more than once of causing Hayden to focus upon isolated and beautiful natural phenomena in his expeditions rather than upon more scientifically valuable objectives. But in the long run Jackson's photos entailed far more advantages than disadvantages. His views of exposed rock strata aided the geologist, and his photography of barren, jagged landscapes gave planners a new and more realistic view of the problems confronting the Western settler. And, finally, his portraits of the surviving Indians were among the few means available for conveying a picture of the aborigines as they really were. In short, Jackson, like the avant-garde writers, the scientists, and even the local colorists of his time, was helping to usher in a new era of realism that would in part replace and at the same time, as far as subject matter was concerned, parallel the romanticism of an earlier day.

Hayden's party assembled at Camp Carlin, near Fort D. A. Russell, in early August of 1870.[8] They followed the line of the Union Pacific Railroad, keeping first to the north via Red Buttes, Sweetwater River, and South Pass to Fort Bridger (see map, p. 472). Then they turned south and explored Henry's Fork, parts of the Green River, the Uinta Mountains, Brown's Hole, Bridger's Pass, the Medicine Bows, and then headed on to Cheyenne. They were hardly traversing new country, for Hayden and his men had seen

7. Jackson: *Time Exposure*, pp. 186–7.
8. Hayden: *Fourth Annual Report*. Unless otherwise stated, the following account is based on this source.

most of it before, and Clarence King's parties were engaged in exploring the same region. Still, this journey provided excellent opportunities for making useful geological and economical observations, and it gave Jackson a marvelous chance to photograph new country. In the course of his hurried reconnaissance, Hayden was, as usual, extremely perceptive. He pointed out the Tertiary lake beds of the Rocky Mountains almost at the same time that King did, and in the Medicine Bows he noted evidence of the existence in centuries long past of great glacial action and then the furious melting which caused erosion on a scale that could not be duplicated by present forces. But whereas such evidence led King to a catastrophist position, Hayden took time into consideration and remained a more scientifically correct uniformitarian.

The report of the season's activities [*The Fourth Annual Report*] ran to some 501 pages of text, nearly ten times the size of Hayden's previous reports, and it was a proper reflection of his achievements. Adopting a diary or itinerary style for his work, Hayden sacrificed organization for speed in placing his miscellaneous observations before the public.[9] Unlike King, who preferred to digest his findings in his carefully considered *Systematic Geology*, Hayden believed in getting as much scientific data before the world as quickly as possible. Without Meek's theoretical structure, which had reinforced his earlier work, Hayden's later reports declined in quality, though they invariably contained so much fascinating material that they are of interest to geologists even to the present day. As Hayden saw it, revealing the wonders and resources of the West to the widest possible audience, scientific and non-scientific, of his day had become his life's work. "Never has my faith in the grand future that awaits the entire West been so strong as it is at the present time," he wrote in the preface to his report for 1870, "and," he continued, "it is my earnest desire to devote the remainder of the working days of my life to the development of its scientific and material interests, until I shall see every Territory, which is now organized, a State in the Union."[1]

To this end, he worked with businessmen—whom he went out of his way to praise and thank—politicians, soldiers, scientists, school children, emigrants, and anybody else who had any connection with Western development, and thus his reports had to be

9. Ibid., *passim.*
1. Ibid., p. 7.

written honestly, but favorably whenever possible, and in layman's language.[2] It is not surprising that they did not please reformers like Powell, and the highly trained professionals of the National Academy. Still, if the report of 1870 is any measure, they had their value.

His book stands as a prime example of a miscellaneous and positive approach to the West. It included two sections on the general geology of the region traversed by the Survey, a long report by Cyrus Thomas on the agricultural possibilities of each region, including reflections on the cattle industry and the land-grant system, a list of new species of orthoptera, a paleontological report by Meek, a study of the "Tertiary Coals of the West" by James T. Hodge, John Strong Newberry's first important work on the ancient lakes of Western America, a paper by Leidy on vertebrate fossils, one by Leo Lesquereux on fossil plants, and another by E. D. Cope on the fossil reptiles and fishes from Kansas to Wyoming. The work concluded with R. S. Elliott's "Report on the Industrial Resources of Western Kansas and Eastern Colorado," and six catalogues of specimens collected by the party. It was obvious that not all of these papers were the work of Hayden and his surveyors. Some, such as Lesquereaux's, were written by Eastern specialists and included by Hayden in the manner of the old Topographical Engineers and their reports. He had thus padded his volume with materials of uneven quality, so that it really formed a kind of annual scientific journal. The main advantage of this was that he was able to secure the services, prestige, and loyalties of many otherwise unavailable scientific giants of his day. His lack of discrimination and his pretention in these reports, however, made him extremely vulnerable to critics. But in 1870 there were few if any critics on Hayden's horizon, and his survey, increasing in size, importance, and popularity, was heading for its greatest days.

6

Perhaps the most famous expedition of Hayden's career was generated by an event that took place somewhat to the north of the scene of his previous season's exploration. In the summer of 1870 the Washburn-Doane expedition had begun the rediscovery of the Yellowstone wonderland as described in a previous chapter.[3] Its

2. Ibid., pp. 7–8.
3. See Chapter 11, pp. 403–6.

adventures and striking discoveries, not to mention the harrowing experience of Truman C. Everts, who was separated from Washburn's party for over a month, were relayed to the public in every conceivable manner. Articles appeared in the newspapers. *Scribner's* published an account of the trip. Langford lectured in the East and buttonholed Congressmen. And Lieutenant Gustavus Doane published an admirable brief report in the government document series which was short enough to be read by all, and vivid enough to call attention to the long-concealed beauties of the Yellowstone. All of this had immediate appeal to Hayden, who planned to carry his surveys north into the, to him, familiar Upper Missouri country anyway. So, with the help of James G. Blaine and his own large following in Congress, Hayden secured an appropriation of $40,000 to finance an official exploration of the Yellowstone.[4]

James Stevenson hurried out to Ogden to begin organizing the expedition as quickly as possible. Hayden, Jackson, Elliott, and the others followed, making a rendezvous in early June.[5] Along the way Hayden acquired several new men, among them A. C. Peale, a mineralogist, and Antoine Schoenborn, a topographer and an old friend from the prewar days of the Raynolds expedition. Schoenborn, who unfortunately committed suicide in Omaha on the return trip, was the first professional topographer employed by Hayden since the outset of his survey. One further addition to his party, and an extremely valuable one, was the great landscape painter Thomas Moran. A vastly underestimated painter, Moran was a colorist and a romantic whose gigantic canvases, along with those of Albert Bierstadt, did much to create the legendary West of vivid contrasts and enormous expanses that became so appealing to the succeeding generation of nature lovers and tourists who came in the wake of the public surveys. Moran always believed he was painting the truth in nature, but his primary achievement went beyond simple depiction and deserves greater attention today. He painted, quite literally, the sublime psychological reality of the West, in which if a mountain was larger than life, a cloud formation somewhat overdramatic, and the rainbows seemed artificial, still it all added up to a portrayal of the impact of the magnificent scenery on those who were viewing it for the first time. Like the paintings of Bierstadt and Church, Moran's canvases called up in the viewer inner

4. William Turrentine Jackson: "Government Exploration of the Upper Yellowstone, 1871," *Pacific Historical Review*, Vol. XI (June 1942), pp. 187–200. Also see Bartlett: *Great Surveys*, p. 40.

5. Bartlett: *Great Surveys*, pp. 40–1; Hayden: *Fifth Annual Report*, p. 3.

feelings of the sublimity of nature and the inconsequence of man. These were true emotions, recognized even by the roughest of Western veterans, who, critical of sham and unreality in portraits of the West, were among his greatest admirers.

Hayden's expedition, composed of seven wagons and thirty-four men, departed from the Mormon city on June 11, 1871.[6] They were headed for Fort Ellis, far north in Montana territory, above the park area. Their route took them over the Snake River scablands, along trails blazed by mountain men and Hudson's Bay brigades so many years before. Then they headed for Virginia City in Alder Gulch, virtually a ghost town, now picked over by forlorn Chinese coolies. From there the way lay through the rocky, timbered region that had once been the domain of the warlike Blackfeet. At last, in the first week of July, they reached Fort Ellis. There they found the Barlow-Heap military expedition (see Chapter 11) preparing for its own reconnaissance of the Upper Yellowstone. They decided to join forces whenever possible, but on July 15, one day before Barlow and Heap were ready, Hayden and his men left Fort Ellis with their wagon train and headed for Boetler's Ranch in the valley of the Yellowstone, three days' journey away.

At Boetler's Ranch they again rendezvoused and discarded the cumbersome wagons, somewhat to the disadvantage of Jackson, who had to pack all his photographic equipment on muleback. On July 20 the joint expedition departed from the ranch and started up the Yellowstone River. The first night out, two mountain hunters regaled the explorers gathered around the campfire with tales of the "old days" in Yellowstone, which included all the unbelievable accounts of its marvels that Hayden had heard from Jim Bridger years before. The next day's march took them past the first of these sites, the iron-red Cinnabar Mountain, then the Devil's Slide, a great hill intersected by two perfect walls of lava. By the end of the third day they reached the dazzling multicolored pools of Mammoth Hot Springs, where their hopes of being its discoverers were somewhat dashed by the presence of some anonymous invalids who were calmly taking the mineral baths. So impressive was the site, however, that Moran produced one of his greatest paintings from sketches made on the spot. In addition Jackson's dramatic view of

6. The organizational details and narrative of Hayden's Yellowstone expedition are in Hayden: *Fifth Annual Report.* See also Hayden to Columbus Delano, Ogden, Utah, June 8, 1871; Bottler's Ranch, Emigrant Gulch, Yellowstone River, July 18, 1871; Yellowstone Lake, W.T., Aug. 8, 1871; Ft. Hall, Idaho Territory, Sept. 20, 1871; Bottler's Ranch, Emigrant Gulch, Yellowstone R., Aug. 28, 1871, Letters Sent, Hayden Survey, R.G. 57, National Archives.

the frail but dashing Moran peering into the deep cerulean blue of a steaming pool is one of the best photographs he ever made.

Along the way, Hayden filled his notebook with geological observations, as he made the first such professional examination of the complex formations of the park. Very quickly it became apparent, if the Devil's Slide and the Mammoth Springs hadn't already indicated so, that the Yellowstone country was perhaps the best place in the world to study incipient volcanic activity and igneous intrusion. Vast floods of basalt were interspersed with layers of Cretaceous strata, and they were often folded into the anticlinal wrinkles that signal the mountain-making process. Metamorphic rocks abounded as in no other place in the West, and great canyons cut by the rivers revealed entire ages and geologic horizons. The Yellowstone was indeed a perfect laboratory for the geologist. Unfortunately Hayden could pause only briefly at each of the exposures, and his was perforce only a superficial surface reconnaissance of an enormously complicated region, but one that raised numerous questions for future geologists.

Returning to the Yellowstone from Gardiner's River, they passed Tower Creek, a region of "wonderful ravines and canyons," and began the ascent of Mt. Washburn. From atop Mt. Washburn, Hayden got a different view, that of the topographer. "We caught the first glimpse of the great basin of the Yellowstone, with the lake," he wrote, "which reminded one much, from its bays, indentations, and surrounding mountains, of Great Salt Lake. To the south are the Tetons, rising above all the rest, the monarchs of all they survey, with their summits covered with perpetual snow."[7] Within his 360 degree view, too, were the Madison Mountains, the Gallatins, Emigrant Peak, and, far off, the distant ridges of the Big Horns.

From Mt. Washburn the party made its way down into the Yellowstone Basin, which, as Hayden saw it, had been in Pliocene times "one vast crater," the scene of "as great volcanic activity as that of any portion of the globe."[8] Out of the thousands of vents and fissures the fluid interior of the earth had once poured in a long catastrophic night of volcanic violence and horror.

The falls of the Yellowstone were something else again. From out of a green meadow the falls dropped abruptly in two great cascades, the mass "detached into the most beautiful snow-white, beadlike drops" which struck the basin below and ricocheted some two hundred feet. The whole presented, in Hayden's inadequate prose,

7. Hayden: *Fifth Annual Report*, p. 80.
8. Ibid., p. 81.

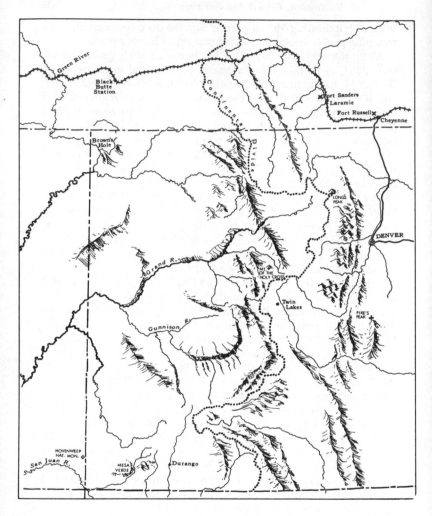

The scene of Hayden's Colorado Surveys

"the appearance of a mass of snow-white foam." For Jackson this was the pictorial climax of the entire expedition. Elliott and Moran sketched for hours, while he and a local photographer, J. Cressman of Bozeman, took pictures from every angle, Cressman using Jackson's camera after his own toppled from a windblown precipice into the roaring cataract below.

From the falls the party pushed on past the sulphur springs to Yellowstone Lake and made camp on its shores. A collapsible boat was assembled, and its two makeshift masts and ragged canvas sail were somehow picturesque on the long-undisturbed waters of the mountain lake. The boat was christened the *Anna* after the daughter of Massachusetts Senator H. L. Dawes, one of the backers of Hayden's expedition. Besides using it to map the irregular shores of the lake, Jackson also sailed aboard the fragile craft with his precious camera equipment and made photographs from otherwise impossible angles. Only one thing disturbed the explorers' idyll—the beautiful trout of Lake Yellowstone were filled with worms and thus were inedible. It was somehow appropriate that this flawed region should also contain unnatural creatures.

Traveling around the lake proved exceedingly difficult. Autumnal fires swept the dense forests. Tangled undergrowth blocked the explorers' path and caught the wheels of the awkward odometer. The mules had to be driven head down through the brush, scraping their loads against trees and bushes. But by establishing a series of base camps at West Thumb and other places, they managed to reconnoiter the western side of the lake and map its shores, though somewhat inadequately.

On July 31, Hayden, Schoenborn, Elliott, and Peale struck out to the northwest, bound for the Firehole Geyser Basin. They traveled some thirty-one miles through a rough country of rocks and fallen timbers before they reached a stream, which turned out to be the Madison. There they discovered what is now known as the Upper Geyser Basin. Following the east fork of the Madison, they eventually reached the Firehole River and the Lower Geyser Basin, where the bubbling and steaming of the hundreds of vents in the morning air called to Hayden's mind Langford's earlier image of a factory village.

Along the way they passed every geyser formation the imagination could conceive of. Some were flat, deep pools falling in greens and blues down to the center of the earth. Others were vulgar grunting and sucking mud caldrons—traps for unwary animals down through the ages. Great red, yellow, and green pools flowed in sheets across the rocky landscape and then tumbled with hisses of steam into the swift-flowing Firehole River. Fountains abounded, and domes, minarets, and half-ruined sculptures of purest white silica stood out against the pines. It was a kaleidoscope, wrote Hayden. "The decorations on the sides of the basin are lighted up with a wild, weird beauty, which wafts one at once into the land of enchantment; all the brilliant feats of fairies and genii in the Arabian Nights' Entertainments are forgotten in the actual presence of such marvelous beauty. . . ."[9] And over such terrestrial marvels as the Punch Bowl, the Dental Cup, and the Bath Tub towered the giant water spouts—Grand Geyser, the Giant and Giantess, and of course, Old Faithful. What a misfortune that Jackson and Moran were not along on that first visit to capture that dazzling sight!

The rest of the trip was anticlimactic. From the Geyser Basin they moved eastward to Hot Springs Camp on Lake Yellowstone, where they were joined by Lieutenant Doane, who brought orders recalling their military escort to Fort Ellis. The major part of the expedition was thus concluded. Elliott and Carrington surveyed the rest of the lake from the *Anna*. Stevenson went back to Boetler's Ranch for more supplies. And Hayden led the remainder of the party around the southern and eastern shore of the lake, where the views from the mountainsides helped fill in the rest of the topographic picture. Eventually they followed Pelican Creek to the East Fork of the Yellowstone and then crossed over the river at Baronet's Bridge, finally making their way back to Boetler's Ranch. According to Hayden, they had been just thirty-eight days in the wonderland, though Jackson later claimed it was "exactly 40."[1]

The results of Hayden's expedition of 1871 were mixed. On the practical level, Hayden joined forces with the Northern Pacific interests and Langford's Montana group and at their suggestion lobbied vigorously and with success for the establishment of the Yellowstone region as a national park.[2] He personally approached his many friends in Congress and contributed an article to *Scribner's*.[3] He also distributed Jackson's photographs and stereopticon slides to virtually everyone within reach of the mails. The result was that on March 1, 1872, by order of Congress and President Grant, the

9. Ibid., p. 121.
1. Ibid., *passim*. See also Jackson: *Time Exposure*, p. 202; Bartlett: *Great Surveys*, p. 56.
2. Bartlett: *Great Surveys*, p. 58. William Turrentine Jackson: "The Creation of Yellowstone National Park," *MVHR*, Vol. XXIX (June 1942), pp. 187–206.
3. F. V. Hayden: "The Wonders of the West. II. More About the Yellowstone," *Scribner's Monthly*, Vol. III, No. 4 (February 1872), pp. 388–96.

Yellowstone became a national park, modeled directly after California's state-governed Yosemite. Though Hayden ever afterwards claimed almost exclusive credit for the park idea, the men of the 1870 Washburn-Doane expedition, and officials of the Northern Pacific, were its real originators. Clearly, though, the passage of the park bill owed as much to Hayden's influence and efforts as it did to any other single cause. And the publicity attending the park bill at the time called attention to Hayden's survey, making it the best known of the postwar surveys, and the richest.

In other areas, too, Hayden and his assistants made notable contributions. Sketchy and disorganized though his own work was, Hayden was the first geologist to study the problems of the park region, and if he did not solve them, he at least raised most of the important questions that would occupy geologists for years to come. The rest of his report was a compendium of sub-reports and miscellaneous papers more or less relating to the Survey. Professor Cyrus Thomas wrote seventy-five pages on the "Agricultural Resources of the Territories," emphasizing the surprising amount of available fertile land, and for the first time calling for some plan to conserve timber resources from exploitation.[4] He also anticipated John Wesley Powell's later report on the "Arid Lands of the West" by advocating a planned system of irrigation in the dry regions. "We . . . know," he wrote, "from the history of those counties where irrigation is extensively practiced that it is absolutely necessary that the State shall take more or less control of this matter, upon which its prosperity, and, in fact, perpetuity rests."[5] Beyond this, he called for a system in which the "General Government" would grant to the states and territories in regions west of the 100th meridian every alternate section of public land, to be used for the construction of canals and irrigation ditches. "And the law making such grant should expressly reserve water priviledges to those who may settle upon and occupy the remaining sections."[6] Thus, by 1871, most of the important concepts of land classification, conservation of public resources, both aesthetic and economic, and state control of irrigation and water rights were clearly formulated and commonly upheld by scientific men who explored the West, whether military or civilian.

In the field of purer science, paleontology was best represented with extensive papers by Leidy, Meek, Cope, and Lesquereux. The

4. Hayden: *Fifth Annual Report*, pp. 205–69. See especially pp. 218–25.
5. Ibid., p. 226.
6. Ibid.

latter, continually breaking new ground with his studies of fossil plants, provided perhaps the widest-ranging and most exciting speculations. In his summary he concluded, among other things, that "some types of the North American Tertiary and Cretaceous flora appear already in the same formations of Greenland, Spitzbergen and Iceland; the derivation of these types is therefore apparently from the arctic regions . . . the relation of the Tertiary flora of Greenland and Spitzbergen with ours indicates, at the Tertiary and Cretaceous epochs, land connection of the northern islands with our continent."[7] He failed, however, to speculate about the relationship of northern ice floes and glaciers to the distribution of plants in those ancient geologic times.

Cope devoted one of his papers to the exotic fauna of ancient Kansas. Speaking of the continental sea, he wrote: "Far out on its expanse might have been seen in those ancient days a huge, snake-like form which rose above the surface and stood erect, with tapering throat and arrow-shaped head; or swayed about, describing a circle of twenty-feet radius above the water. Then it would dive into the depths and naught would be visible but the foam caused by the disappearing mass of life. Should several have appeared together, we can easily imagine tall twining forms rising to the height of the masts of a fishing fleet, or like snakes twisting and knotting themselves together. . . . This is . . . Elasmosaurus platyurus Cope, a carnivarous sea-reptile."[8] And then there was the flying saurian, Ornithochirus harpyia Cope—Marsh's Pterodactyl (Cope claimed discovery and refused to use Marsh's name). "These strange creatures flapped their leathery wings over the waves," so Cope imagined, and often plunged into the sea to seize an unsuspecting fish. "Or," Cope wrote, "soaring at a safe distance [they] viewed the sports and combats of the more powerful saurians of the sea. At nightfall we may imagine them trooping to the shore, and suspending themselves to the cliffs by the claw-bearing fingers of their wing-limbs."[9]

Thus dramatically the ancient world came to life under the artistic imagination of the scientists in a way that paralleled or even surpassed the gorgeous canvases of a Moran or the dazzling plates of Jackson. These efforts at creativity had less immediate impact than did those of the artists and photographers, however. They only became apparent as the great museums of America

7. Ibid., p. 317.
8. Ibid., p. 320.
9. Ibid., p. 323.

began to grow and the enthusiasm of science filtered down to a popular audience and became a part of education.

On all levels, then, Hayden's survey, even when it acted as a clearing house for casual papers by friends from the East, served the cause of civilization. His greatest asset, his imagination was also his greatest weakness, however. Everything was appealing. Everything had possibilities and must be included, the shoddy and the brilliant alike. Hayden was the type of person who never threw anything away. Like the age he lived in, he was eclectic, and his researches and reports amount to a veritable explosion. Figuratively speaking, they rival the riotous contours of the then fashionable "Queen Anne" house. In all of this only a faint order was discernible. Significantly, though he had promised the Secretary of the Interior a "fine set of maps," his surveys to date lacked a competent topographical and systematic base. It is to Hayden's credit that he recognized this and in his plans for the following year he added four topographers. He intended to return to Yellowstone to finish the work he had begun.

7

The expedition of 1872 included some sixty-one men divided into two parties. One was led by Hayden and took the usual route through Fort Ellis and Boetler's Ranch back into Yellowstone.[1] The other, captained by James Stevenson, headed for Fort Hall in Idaho, then moved on to Henry's Fork of the Snake and Pierre's Hole.[2] There it paused to explore the old haunts of the mountain men, and a party led by Stevenson and Langford attempted the ascent of the Grand Teton (see map, p. 472). But though Stevenson reported a successful ascent to the summit to Secretary of the Interior Delano, and Langford publicly proclaimed it, even to the point of giving out a (totally false) description of the summit, other members of the party and the local inhabitants were skeptical. The William O. Owen party who climbed the mountain in 1898 refuted their claim entirely, and in 1926 the legislature of Wyoming, on

1. Hayden: *Sixth Annual Report*, p. 1. See also Hayden to Columbus Delano, Bottler's Ranch, July 23, 1872, Letters Sent, Hayden Survey, R.G. 57, National Archives.
2. Hayden: *Sixth Annual Report*, p. 2. See also James Stevenson to Columbus Delano, Ft. Hall, Idaho, Oct. 16, 1872, Letters Sent, Hayden Survey, R.G. 57, National Archives.

the advice of competent authorities, awarded the honor of "first climb" to Owen rather than Stevenson.[3]

From the Tetons, Stevenson's party moved north to a rendezvous with Hayden's party at the Firehole Geyser Basin. They did not cross over the mountains into Jackson's Hole, but instead, on the advice of their guide Beaver Dick Leigh, they moved north out of Pierre's Hole and crossed via "Tyghee" (Togwotee) Pass directly over to the Firehole. Within a few days, both parties were reunited. When the expedition ultimately broke up, Hayden headed back the conventional way, while Stevenson led his men south through Jackson's Hole to the headwaters of the Snake, and along its course to Fort Hall. In Jackson's Hole they found and named all of the beautiful lakes—most of them after "Beaver Dick" and his family. It was a refreshing departure from the almost automatic system of congressional-patron nomenclature.

Several aspects of Hayden's 1872 expedition are important. For one thing, it was greatly increased in size, with new men such as the botanist John Merle Coulter and C. Hart Merriam, an ornithologist. The four topographers—Gustavus Bechler, Henry Gannett, Frank Bradley, and W. H. Holmes—were men of ability. Competent, though somewhat inexperienced, they had their futures before them. Gannett, who later became the chief topographer for the United States Geological Survey, had been trained by Hoffmann, of the Whitney Surveys, who was teaching at the Lawrence Scientific School at Harvard. Gannett was one of that group of Hoffmann's protégés which included King and Gardner, who came to have such an important role in systematically mapping the West.

William H. Holmes was perhaps the greatest artist-topographer and man of many talents that the West ever produced. Born in 1846, Holmes lived for ninety-three years, a central figure in the development of so many scientific surveys, bureaus, and art galleries that his career is a palimpsest of the cultural and institutional

3. Bartlett: *Great Surveys*, pp. 67–8. See also James Stevenson to Columbus Delano, Ft. Hall, Idaho, Oct. 16, 1872, Letters Sent, Hayden Survey, R.G. 57, National Archives. N. P. Langford: "The Ascent of Mount Hayden: A New Chapter in Western Discovery," *Scribner's Monthly*, Vol. VI, No. 2 (June 1873), pp. 129–37; Frank H. Bradley: "Explorations of 1872: United States Geological Survey of the Territories, under Dr. F. V. Hayden, Snake River Division," *American Journal of Science and Arts*, third series, Vol. VI, No. 33 (Sept. 1873), p. 198 *n*. Bradley's account of the Teton expedition is in Hayden, *Sixth Annual Report*, pp. 208–31. See especially the map showing the supposed line of ascent, p. 221, and the description of the summit, p. 222. Also see Nolie Mumey: *The Teton Mountains: Their History and Tradition* (Denver, Colo.: The Artcraft Press; 1947), pp. 371–81.

history of late-nineteenth-century America.[4] His greatest talent was drawing, and it was as an artist that he first attracted enough attention to secure a post on the Hayden survey. His artistic technique was like no other's. He could sketch panoramas of twisted mountain ranges, sloping monoclines, escarpments, plateaus, canyons, fault blocks, and grassy meadows that accurately depicted hundreds of miles of terrain. They were better than maps, and better than photographs because he could get details of stratigraphy that light and shadow obscured from the camera. The hundreds of panoramas and sketches that he did for the Hayden Survey, and his later illustrations for Dutton's *Tertiary History of the Grand Canyon District,* are masterpieces of realism and draftsmanship as well as feats of imaginative observation.

In Hayden's survey, Holmes also developed into a first-class geologist and anthropologist, and in later years he headed the Bureau of Ethnology and directed the Smithsonian Institution's researches in anthropology. But he never lost his love for art. His topographical sketches reappear as illustrations for his book on the Armour Expedition to Yucatan in 1895, and the fabulous cities of Palenque, Uxmal, and Chichen Itza are portrayed in imaginative panoramas that have never been surpassed.[5] At the close of his career, he became director of the National Collection of Fine Arts, and today he is an almost forgotten figure, obscured by an affluence which he helped to create and the rushing tides of modern art which, though he would not have appreciated the comparison, his own work so clearly foreshadowed.

Notwithstanding the competent crew, the results of Hayden's topographic mission of 1872 were undistinguished. He clearly lacked the ability to organize his men for a basic purpose of this kind, and the topographers functioned as illustrators more than as draftsmen that year, through no fault of their own.

4. John R. Swanton: "William Henry Holmes," National Academy of Sciences *Biographical Memoirs,* Vol. XVII (Washington, D.C.: National Academy of Sciences; 1937), pp. 223–37. Also see William Henry Holmes: "Biography [sic] of William H. Holmes," *Random Records of a Life in Art and Science,* Vol. I. The Random Records are composed of some sixteen volumes of letters, memoirs, newspaper clippings, articles, descriptive anecdotes, and photographs assembled by Holmes in preparation for his autobiography. They are now in the library of the Smithsonian Institution. I have commenced work on a biography of this important artist, scientist, and federal administrator.

5. See W. H. Holmes: *Archeological Studies Among the Ancient Cities of Mexico. Pt. I. Monuments of Yucatan* (Chicago: Field Columbian Museum; 1895).

Another unpleasant aspect of Hayden's later efforts was his tendency to include the sons of Congressmen and Senators in his parties. Though Powell, and Hayden's other detractors, generally overestimated this practice, the roster of 1872 indicates that two relatives of "Black Jack" Logan went along, including his son, who served as Hayden's general assistant.[6] Representative Kellogg also sent his son and had plans of accompanying the Survey himself.[7] Some of these well-placed persons were guests, or "pilgrims," as the regular personnel called them. Others were hard-working regulars, as William Logan's accounts of his tedious dealings with the drunken Major Baker at Fort Ellis attest.[8] It is difficult, then, to assess the effect of Hayden's practice. His motives, however, seem clear.

On the scientific side, discoveries continued to mount. Cope worked the Bridger Basin and the Bitter Creek region that year and made valuable finds, including the giant rhinoceros-like Eobasileus, which Cope called "the most extraordinary fossil mammal found in North America." In all, Cope's work of the summer of 1872 yielded some fifty new species of fossil quadrupeds, birds, crocodiles, lizards, snakes, turtles, and fishes, as the Eocene horizon of the Rocky Mountains came to life at the touch of his paleontologist's hammer. Then, at the height of his work he fell grievously ill of mountain fever and spent the winter in a desperate battle for his life.[9]

Joseph Leidy, too, was in the mountains, and so was Meek, and

6. Hayden: *Sixth Annual Report*, p. 5.
7. Rep. L. M. Kellogg to Hayden, House of Representatives, April 27, 1872, L.R., Hayden Survey, R.G. 57, National Archives.
8. William A. Logan to Hayden, Bozeman, Montana Territory, July 1, 1872, L.R., Hayden Survey, R.G. 57, National Archives.
9. E. D. Cope to Hayden, Green River City, Aug. 27, 1872; Green River, July 31, 1872; Ft. Bridger, Wyo., Oct. 9, 1872; Annie Cope to Hayden, Ft. Bridger, Wyo., Sept. 22, 1872, Sept. 26, 1872, Letters Received, Hayden Survey, R.G. 57, National Archives. See also E. D. Cope: "Field Notebook, 1872"; and Cope to Brig. Gen. E. O. C. Ord, Ft. Bridger, Wyo., June 22, 1872; to Father, Camp on Cottonwood Creek, July 17, 1872; to Brother, Camp near Church Buttes, Wyo., July 28, 1872; to Father, Camp on Green River at Mouth of Fontenelle Creek, Sept. 8, 1872; to Sister, Ham's Fork, Sept. 15, 1872; to Father, Ft. Bridger, Oct. 12, 1872; to Brother, Ft. Bridger, Oct. 19, 1872, in E. D. Cope Papers, American Museum of Natural History, New York City. Parts of all these letters are quoted in Osborne: *Cope*, pp. 183–94. See especially p. 193 for Cope's first sketch of Eobasileus, the "Dawn Emperor" of Wyoming. See also Cope's report in Hayden: *Sixth Annual Report*, pp. 545–649.

all their findings appeared as contributions to Hayden's survey.[1] Lesquereux, in his own quiet manner, began one of the major controversies of the day with his exhaustive treatise on the Laramie lignite beds of the West. He concluded that they were of Tertiary age, rather than Cretaceous as most of the other paleontologists held.[2] In spite of their opposition, Lesquereux held his ground. The flora, he asserted, were characteristic of the Tertiary, a later period than the Cretaceous. This controversy lasted for years, until a new scientific generalization had been established, namely that the flora of an age persist longer than the fauna. In the case of the lignite beds, Cretaceous flora had persisted all through the lower Tertiary, while due to some unknown cause the fauna died out and were replaced.[3] The implications of this seemingly esoteric quarrel were vast. For one thing, nobody could be quite certain why the flora persisted and the fauna died out, since climatic conditions must have changed very little. In addition, if the flora persisted through several geologic eras while the fauna were confined to relatively short periods, it appeared that the fauna offered greater opportunities for precision in stratigraphical dating than did the flora. These were among the many questions of scientific import raised by Hayden's survey and its publications.

8

An important turning point in the history of the Hayden Surveys was reached in 1873. Shifting his attention from the spectacular but overworked Yellowstone region, Hayden proposed to revert to more practical activities and focus on the promising territory of Colorado, which lay directly in the path of settlement and which in the 1870's was in the midst of a mining boom. In a letter to his superior, Secretary of the Interior Columbus Delano, Hayden stated his reasons for this change.

1. Joseph Leidy to Hayden, Ft. Bridger, Wyo., July 24, 1872; F. B. Meek to Hayden, Salt Lake City, Aug. 16, 1872, L.R., Hayden Survey, R.G. 57, National Archives. Leidy's "Remains of Primitive Art in the Bridger Basin of Southern Wyoming," appears in pp. 651–54 of Hayden: *Sixth Annual Report.* For Meek's work, see pp. 429–520 of Hayden: *Sixth Annual Report.*
2. Leo Lesquereux: "Contributions to the Fossil Flora of the Western Territories, Part II, The Tertiary Flora," *Report of the United States Geological Survey of the Territories,* Vol. VII (Washington, D.C.: U. S. Government Printing Office; 1878), pp. 21–31. See especially pp. 30–1.
3. Ibid.

For the last two years the survey has operated about the sources of the Missouri and Yellowstone Rivers; but the expenses of transportation, subsistence, and labor are so great that it seems desirable to delay the further prosecution of the work in the Northwest until railroad communication shall be established. The Indians, also, are in a state of hostility over the greater portion of the country which remains to be explored. It seems desirable, therefore, to transfer the field of labor, for the coming season, to the eastern portion of the Rocky Mountain range, in Colorado and New Mexico.

And he added:

There is probably no portion of our continent, at the present time, which promises to yield more useful results, both of a practical and scientific character. This region seems to be unoccupied at this time, as far as I am aware, by any other survey under the Government, and the prospect of its rapid development within the next five years, by some of the most important railroads in the West, renders it very desirable that its resources be made known to the world at as early a date as possible.[4]

Thus, once again, Hayden had hewed close to the practical, business-oriented line, and based his project on the imminent approach of railroads to Colorado. In this case his work clearly served a useful purpose and he was awarded, not the $100,000 appropriation he asked for, but the substantial sum of $75,000, enough to put a large staff in the field.[5]

Actually, though his printed letter did not state it as such, Hayden proposed to carry his surveys southward from the southern boundary of King's Fortieth Parallel Surveys to the southern boundary of the United States, between longitude 104°, or the Front Range, and the line of the western boundary of Colorado.[6] In some instances he would, of necessity, overlap King's survey and at times duplicate the work of Powell. And, though he stated to the contrary, he must have known his work would conflict to a large extent with

4. Hayden to Columbus Delano, Washington, D.C., Jan. 27, 1873, L.S., Hayden Survey, R.G. 57, National Archives. Also reproduced in altered form in Hayden: *Seventh Annual Report*, p. 1.
5. Ibid.
6. See Hayden to Columbus Delano, Washington, D.C., Jan. 27, 1873, L.S., Hayden Survey, R.G. 57, National Archives.

the operations of the Wheeler Survey in the Southwest. At any rate, his final project was narrowed down to a survey of Colorado, perhaps the best service that he could have performed.

In large measure the new focus of the Hayden Survey was due to James Gardner, who joined his staff in 1873. The Survey of Colorado was modeled after the King and Whitney surveys, in which the aimless rambling of the geologist had been systematized by basing the geological work upon a previously worked-out topographical survey. In 1872 Hayden had been unable to coordinate his topographers' activities, but when Gardner took over, assisted by A. D. Wilson, also of King's survey, his expeditions assumed some plan and system, hence were of greater value. It may also have been at Gardner's instigation that Hayden initially proposed to move toward the Southwest, where the army topographers were working. Be that as it may, Hayden's survey from 1873 until the end of 1875, when Gardner completed his work, was a far different operation than it had previously been.

The Survey party assembled in Denver in the spring of 1873, set up a base camp outside of town, and began its labors in almost military fashion. Six separate parties, or divisions, were organized. The first, headed by Gardner, was the chief triangulation party, which had the job of ranging out ahead and making the primary triangles, or demarcations, of the regions to be explored and surveyed by the other parties. For this reason, Gardner's group took the field first, tracing out a six-mile base line, just outside Denver, on which all of the other primary triangles would rest. Then he moved off into the mountains to the west.[7]

The other divisions included three field survey parties to carry out the detailed work in the areas assigned for the year: Middle Park, South Park, and the San Luis District. Each division included a topographer, a geologist who worked closely with him, several naturalists and assistants, and two laborers and a cook. The first year, the three divisions were headed, respectively, by Archibald Marvine, who had come from Wheeler's survey, by Henry Gannett, and by A. D. Wilson.[8]

Besides these, there were two other parties, a photographic party under Jackson which roamed over the whole territory, making photos of whatever seemed interesting, and a quartermaster corps

7. Hayden to Columbus Delano, Colorado, July 1, 1873, L.S., Hayden Survey, R.G. 57, National Archives. Also see Hayden: *Seventh Annual Report*, pp. 1–8.
8. Ibid.

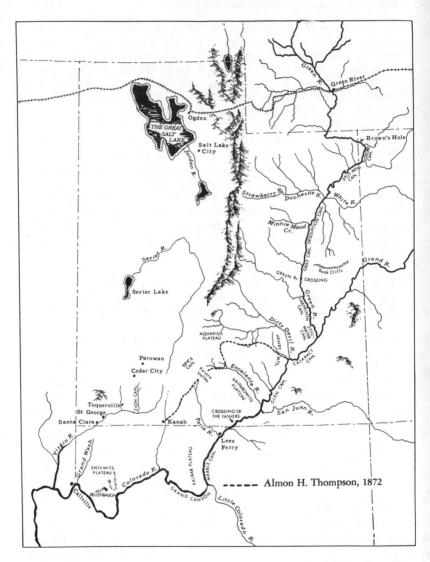

The Colorado River and the Plateau Province of John Wesley Powell

under the direction of James Stevenson which saw to the supplying of all the field divisions.[9] Hayden acted as supervisor and impresario for the entire organization. In this capacity he devoted the major portion of his time to administrative work, but he also managed to get out into the field and visit the more complex geological regions, which demanded his personal attention.

This was the overall pattern of operations, and each year Hayden's parties, sometimes increased to seven or eight divisions, took the field and labored with great enthusiasm from June to October.[1] Building on Gardner's topography and on the work of Gannett, Wilson, Bechler, and Holmes, the geologists sketched in the rock formations, located valuable mineral deposits, and examined all the mining operations from Cherry Creek in northern Colorado to the far-off San Juan strike in the southern part of the state. Occasionally they ran into trouble, as in 1873, when they confronted Wheeler's parties in the Twin Lakes region and precipitated the Congressional crisis of 1874.[2] At other times nature provided her own difficulties. Forest fires, sweeping through miles of timber, threatened them and made mountain-peak observations all but impossible. Lack of water in the dry country of the Far Southwest nearly destroyed at least one division. Others became lost in the intricate canyons of the San Juan and La Plata country. Snow and cold impeded progress, and once a Congressman's son came down with mountain fever and almost died.[3] On another occasion, near Godwin Creek in central Colorado, on a peak nearly 14,000 feet high, Wilson's party was caught in an electrical field and nearly perished. The tripod began to "click like a telegraph machine," pencils in their hands chattered, and their hair emitted a sound "like frying bacon." The triangulation work, Franklin Rhoda later reported, was "getting exciting. . . . When we raised our hats our hair stood on end, the sharp points of the hundreds of stones about us each emitted a continuous sound, while the instrument outrang everything else." Soon the "terrible humming" increased and lightning began to crash all around them. Just in time they finished their

9. Ibid.
1. See Hayden: *Seventh, Eighth, Ninth Annual Reports.*
2. See Chapter 13, p. 478. Also see William H. Holmes to Hayden, Pueblo, Colo., June 13, 1875, L.R., Hayden Survey, R.G. 57, National Archives, which indicates that the rival field parties were on good terms by the summer of 1875.
3. Hayden to Columbus Delano, Elk Mountains, Colo., Sept. 6, 1874, and Twin Lakes, Colo., Sept. 19, 1874, L.S., Hayden Survey, R.G. 57, National Archives.

work. Wilson, braving a severe shock, seized the surveying instrument, and Rhoda the sizzling brass barometer, and together they slid down the mountain to safety just as a tremendous lightning bolt struck the bald summit where they had been.[4]

Then there were the Indians. Most of Colorado was peaceful, but in 1873, when because of a mining boom the Utes were dispossessed of the lands along the San Juan, they became surly and dangerous. They refused to pose for Jackson's pictures, fearing further bad luck, and in the summer of 1875 they tried to prevent Holmes from taking his survey into their territory. They suspected him of being the government surveyor come to demark the boundaries of their reduced domain.[5] Chief Ouray, however, remained nominally friendly and finally aided the Survey by furnishing guides and some protection through his territory.[6] But he had no control over all the Utes, and many who regarded him as a figurehead began harassing the Hayden parties. In 1875, along the Dolores River in the Sierra la Sal country of southwestern Colorado, the combined parties of Gardner and Gannett were attacked by a band of Indians and besieged on a wide sagebrush plain near the base of the Colorado Plateau. With the Indians growing stronger every hour, they were in desperate straits. The only way out was a scramble up the steep escarpment to the plateau, and at dawn Gardner mounted his men and made a dash for safety. The Indians followed, firing their rifles in an attempt to trap them against the cliff. At last a deer trail was located, and one by one the scientists struggled to comparative safety, leaving behind four dead mules and most of their instruments, and other valuable equipment.[7]

At approximately the same time, two other parties were threatened, one back on the Dolores. And several weeks later, near Mesa Verde, William H. Jackson had to run for his life before a band of howling savages. No one heard from him for weeks, and the entire Survey had given him up for lost when he finally reappeared in good condition.[8]

4. Hayden: *Eighth Annual Report,* pp. 456–8.
5. William H. Holmes to Hayden, Camp on the La Plata, June 29, 1875, L.R., Hayden Survey, R.G. 57, National Archives. Hayden: *Ninth Annual Report,* pp. 237–8.
6. Hayden to Zachariah Chandler, Secretary of the Interior, Cheyenne, Wyo. T., Oct. 2, 1876, L.S., Hayden Survey, R.G. 57, National Archives.
7. Bartlett: *Great Surveys,* pp. 95–6. Gardner's account of the Indian skirmish appears in *The Rocky Mountain News,* Sept. 5, 1875. See also Holmes: *Random Records,* Vol. II.
8. Ibid., p. 97; Jackson: *Time Exposure,* pp. 240–1.

Since Hayden had made a point of scorning Indian dangers and decrying the necessity for military escorts for surveys in the West, these episodes had serious implications for him. Coming just after the 1874 dispute with the Army, they cast a shadow on his statements about the lack of danger from Indians. Indeed, they appeared to strengthen the Army's hand in its contest with the Interior Department. Hayden was understandably distressed when Gardner almost immediately related his adventures to *The Rocky Mountain News* of Denver, which brought them out in sensational installments in early September 1875.[9]

Henry Gannett, too, felt that Gardner had "made himself and all of us ridiculous enough." In a letter to Hayden, on October 15, 1875, from the comparative safety of Bath, Maine, he waxed somewhat bitter over the Interior Department's attempt to cover up the whole incident. "As I understand it," he wrote, "the Department is trying hard to persuade themselves that those Indians simply played a game of bluff on us; that they, while they wanted our property, wouldn't have harmed a hair on our heads on any account. This is all very reasonable and agrees perfectly with the facts, doesn't it?"[1] Gardner, whether from anger at being reprimanded for his articles, or from fear of the Indians, quit the Survey at the end of 1875 and went on to safer work as the chief topographer for the new survey of the State of New York.[2] Fortunately for the Hayden Survey, by 1876 the Indians were all under control, and the work progressed to its conclusion.

9

Besides its pragmatic achievements, and its various difficulties, Hayden's Colorado Survey had another side to it. As in Yellowstone, Hayden was concerned to reveal the wonders of the West to the outside world, and this he did with spectacular success. From the beginning, Jackson's photos and stereo slides were distributed all over the country. After 1872, Holmes's panoramas also became famous. And in 1870, thanks to a newer and cheaper process of photo reproduction, Hayden brought out one of his most famous volumes, *Sun Pictures of Rocky Mountain Scenery*, profusely illus-

9. See footnote 7 on the preceding page.
1. Henry Gannett to Hayden, Oct. 15, 1875, Bath, Maine, L.R., Hayden Survey, R.G. 57, National Archives.
2. Bartlett: *Great Surveys*, p. 103.

trated with Jackson's photographs.[3] H. R. Townsend of the House Committee on Appropriations, in the critical year of 1874, received a sun picture of the Mount of the Holy Cross; and just a bit earlier, in January, President Grant was presented with a copy of Hayden's *Sun Pictures*. . . .[4] Well aware of the value of these strategic gifts, Hayden had a larger purpose in mind. He loved the West and its fantastic beauty, and being a self-made man, he regarded it as mandatory to share these marvels with the people. It was part of the democratic process of education. It was also progress through new technology, and, of course, it invited the people to come West.

In a sense, the capstone of Hayden's career came in 1873 and 1874, respectively, when he or members of his party revealed for the first time to a wide audience the twin wonders of Colorado's Mount of the Holy Cross and the mysterious, ancient cliff dwellings of the vanished peoples of Mesa Verde. The "discovery" of the Mount of the Holy Cross took place in July of 1873, when Hayden, Gannett, Jackson, and others of his survey, along with William Dwight Whitney, the Yale philologist and brother of Josiah Dwight Whitney of California, went north from Twin Lakes, across the Tennessee Pass and Eagle River, and after two days of rugged climbing saw the great snowy cross radiating in the Colorado sun. Jackson was the first to see it as he struggled with his heavy camera equipment across the shoulder of Notch Mountain. "I emerged above the timberline, and the clouds," he remembered years later, "and suddenly, as I clambered over a vast mass of jagged rocks, I discovered the great shining cross there before me, tilted against the mountainside."[5]

As all the parties assembled for a view of the awe-inspiring spectacle, a rainbow suddenly appeared, in one of those sublime moments so sacred to the nineteenth-century romantic imagination. Holmes recaptured the experience in a sketch—mountains, cross,

3. See F. V. Hayden: *Sun Pictures of Rocky Mountain Scenery* (New York: Julius Bien; 1870).
4. W. Townsend to Hayden, House of Representatives, Jan. 12, 1874; Orville E. Babcock to Hayden, Executive Mansion, Jan. 22, 1873, L.R., Hayden Survey, R.G. 57, National Archives.
5. Jackson: *Time Exposure*, p. 217. Also see Holmes: *Random Records*, Vol. II, p. 54; Clarence S. Jackson and Lawrence W. Marshall: *Quest of the Snowy Cross* (Denver, Colo.: University of Denver Press; 1952); and W. D. Whitney letters in *The Rocky Mountain News*, Aug. 31, 1873. Also see Hafen and Hafen: *The Diaries of William Henry Jackson*, pp. 249–51, in which Jackson does not mention sighting the Holy Cross. Instead he records: "Clouds hung about all the summits and we could not see the top of the Holy Cross at all" (pp. 250–1)

rainbow, and all—and later, inspired by Jackson's subsequent photograph, Moran came West to paint the cross, in one of his greatest canvases. Trivial though it seems as a discovery per se, the Mount of the Holy Cross had meaning for all the many thousands who saw its various representations. To the religious mind of the day it was worth as much as all the moving sermons delivered by Henry Ward Beecher. Nature itself had spoken and, curiously enough, to Hayden, who was himself a notorious unbeliever.

The other great "discovery" of the Hayden Survey had a more durable significance. In September of 1874 William H. Jackson and his photographic party headed south from Denver into the San Juan country, intending to photograph the peculiar land configurations and the silver-mining districts of that region. They made their way via Cochetopa Pass into the valley of the Upper Del Norte and then pushed on to the wide-open mining towns of Silverton and Durango along the Animas in what had been known since 1860 as Baker's Park. At this point they intended to turn west to the La Plata mining region, but they met Captain John Moss, who changed their plans. Moss, an itinerant miner and an old California hand, was the "boss" of the La Plata district, and he persuaded Jackson and his men to take the route via the Mancos River, where they would see the Indian ruins and cliff dwellings long rumored to exist in the hidden canyons of the Mesa Verde. If indeed they did exist, they would make remarkable subjects for the camera, so Jackson employed Captain Moss to lead them to the ruins.

At first they found little that was impressive—a few moldering adobe ruins partially covered by mounds of soil, and broken potsherds, black on white, none of which was larger than a half dollar. Then they found a fresh Indian trail and followed it down the Mancos canyon. Soon they came upon the stone ruins of a city, then more evidence of primitive inhabitants, walls, crevice-like niches with dressed stones in front of them, and pieces of pottery. On the ninth of October they made camp in a clump of cedar trees just below one of the highest walls of the canyon. Jackson noted in his diary: "Had found nothing that really came up to my idea of the grand or picturesque for photos and began to feel a little doubtful and discouraged."[6] They made supper, and afterward, sitting around the fire, they began to josh one of the younger members of the party about the steep climb up the cliff that faced him the next day if he wanted to photograph any houses. Jackson remembered:

6. Hafen and Hafen: *The Diaries of William Henry Jackson,* pp. 261–334. The quote appears on p. 309.

He asked us to point out the spot [for the climb]. The Captain pointed at random. "Gee," says he, "I see it." I beheld upon my close observation there was something that appeared very like a house, the doors and windows could be seen. We all started at once to investigate. The side of the cañon was formed of successive tables, or benches of sandstone rising perpendicularly one above the other to a total height of about 800 feet. One house was upon the last one and below it the precipice was fully 100 feet above the narrow bench at its foot. Half way up, the others, with the exception of Mr. Ingersol and myself, were satisfied and did not care to go any farther as they were afraid of darkness overtaking them before they could get back. We determined to see all there was to be seen that night so as to know how to approach it on the morrow. Found a tree and a series of crevices by which, with a little trouble, we reached the plateau upon which the houses stood. Then, perched away in a crevice like a swallow's or a bat's nest, [there] it was, a marvel and a puzzle. Its total height was about 12 or 14 feet, divided into two stories, and each floor into two rooms. . . . The material was a sandstone, the same as the rocks among which it nestled. It had been truly dressed, and upon the outward wing, covered with a plaster or kind of stucco. Inside, the walls had been plastered and colored red.[7]

This was Jackson's first view of the spectacular cliff dwellings of the Mesa Verde, an inspiring moment in the history of exploration. The next day they managed to haul the camera equipment up the cliff to a point where it was possible to photograph the ruin. The result was one of Jackson's best pictures. Then they pushed on down the valley, sighting ruins at every hand. In addition to the high cliff houses, there were town sites all along the Mancos, and here and there, circular stone towers that must have served as lookouts. More than once Jackson and his men risked their lives crawling out along twenty-inch ledges hundreds of feet high to investigate some ancient family's precarious perch, or crossing the treacherous Mancos to examine a ruin still standing out on the

7. Ibid. See also William H. Jackson: "First Official Visit to the Cliff Dwellings," *Colorado Magazine of History*, Vol. I, No. 4 (May 1924), pp. 151–9. W. H. Jackson: "Ancient Ruins in Southwestern Colorado," in Hayden: *Eighth Annual Report*, pp. 369–81. Ernest Ingersoll, a journalist who accompanied the party, also contributed an account to the New York *Tribune* for Nov. 3, 1874.

plain.[8] They never paused, however, to investigate any of the numerous side canyons that branched off from the Mancos, and thereby missed the opportunity of discovering the great cliff palaces of Mesa Verde. It was not until 1888, when a cowboy named Bob Wetherill and his partner Charles Mason rode down into a canyon chasing some lost stock, that the mighty Cliff Palace ruin, the famous landmark of Mesa Verde, was discovered.[9] Jackson and his party marched down the Mancos, cut across to the McElmo, then Aztec Spring and the Hovenweep (missing the ruins there), and made a complete circuit of the Mesa Verde. He then retraced his previous route back to the Del Norte and went on to Denver.

The following year, 1875, and again in 1876, both Jackson and William H. Holmes returned to Mesa Verde and made extensive surveys of the Mancos Valley. Holmes's report for those two years is a careful, yet dramatic, presentation of the cliff ruins and the semicircular walled towns that stud the Mancos Valley.[1]

He also included reproductions of ancient Indian drawings of men and horses and strange creatures long vanished from the arid Southwest. One picture shows what had obviously been a hunt, with weird distorted representations of men and animals. Another depicts a stately procession of beasts, some of which clearly resemble deer, elephants, gigantic birds, and crocodiles. (See p. 352 in Portfolio II.) So interested in archaeology did Hayden become as a result of these marvelous discoveries that in 1876 and 1877 he sent Holmes and Jackson on a survey of all the Southwestern ruins from the San Juan to Canyon de Chelly, the Chaco Canyon, and the Pueblo Pintado, to the existing Moqui Villages near the Colorado River. Their reports, including diagrams, sketches, illustrations of pottery, and precise descriptions, constituted a landmark in the history of Southwestern archaeology and started Holmes on virtually a new career.[2] True, they had discovered nothing that Captain Moss and the local miners, or Captain John N. Macomb on his trip down the San Juan in 1859, or for that matter the Mormon scouts of 1854, had not seen before. But Holmes and Jackson made a detailed survey, with photographs and drawings which dramatized

8. Ibid. See especially Hayden: *Eighth Annual Report,* pp. 375–6.
9. See *Mesa Verde National Park . . . Colorado* (Denver, Colo., 1940), p. 8. This is the official park guidebook put out by the Department of the Interior.
1. See Hayden: *Tenth Annual Report,* pp. 381–450. This includes the reports of both Holmes and Jackson for 1875, 1876, and 1877.
2. Ibid.

the cliff dwellings and made them known to the outside world. For the Philadelphia Centennial of 1876, Jackson made models of the major ruins he had seen, and these were featured as part of the Interior Department's exhibition.[3] These models were later distributed to leading institutions of learning throughout the country, where they served an educational purpose. Besides the geysers and multicolored pools of the Yellowstone, and the awe-inspiring Mount of the Holy Cross, Hayden and his men had revealed an entire lost civilization that for centuries had lain buried in the heart of the Rocky Mountains.

10

By 1877, however, Hayden's vast operation was running into difficulties. Powell, who regarded ethnology and the study of Indians as his own province, wrote to Carl Schurz, the new Secretary of the Interior, proposing that Hayden and his men leave their work in this field while he in turn would give up geology.[4] In a letter of August 2, 1877, Schurz forwarded his proposal to Hayden with the comment: "This proposition appears to me frank and fair and you are therefore directed to make your choice accordingly. . . ."[5] With some regrets, Hayden chose geology, and in the seasons of 1877 and 1878 turned his attentions once again northward to Idaho, Wyoming, and the Yellowstone.[6] His final report was a two-volume, exhaustive treatise on the Yellowstone that attempted to encompass a systematic geological survey of the region which he had failed to achieve in 1871 and 1872.[7] But the days of the spectacular discovery were over, and so too were the great days of the Hayden Survey. In 1878 began the institutional battle that resulted in the unification of the Western surveys under the single United States Geological Survey, after which Hayden became a mere employee of the Geological Survey, his autonomy and authority gone. He continued to work in the West as a government geologist, however,

3. Bartlett: *Great Surveys*, p. 117. See also Holmes: *Random Records*, Vols. II and IV, which contains illustrations of the models prepared for the Philadelphia Centennial.
4. Schurz to Hayden, Dept. of the Interior, Washington, D.C., Aug. 2, 1877, L.R., Hayden Survey, R.G. 77, National Archives.
5. Ibid.
6. Hayden to Schurz, Washington, D.C., Sept. 28, 1877, and Nov. 15, 1877, L.S., Hayden Survey, R.G. 77, National Archives.
7. Hayden: *Twelfth Annual Report*, 2 vols. (1878).

until 1883, when he retired because of ill health, and he eventually died in Philadelphia of locomotor ataxia in 1886.

11

Evaluating Hayden and his surveys is a difficult task. Unquestionably, in his own disorganized way Hayden was one of the country's most brilliant and imaginative geologists. In his prewar work he had helped to bring about a revolution in Western geology, though much of his success was due to Meek and Leidy. In almost every postwar field report, he contributed new insights and vast quantities of information, and gave focus to new geological problems not conceived of by other geologists. That he rarely paused to develop any of his ideas is one of the tragedies of his hasty drive for success and national prominence.

The Survey of Colorado, systematized by Gardner, was an outstanding success, and an important contribution to the development of that state. It represented what had always been Hayden's prime objective—the bringing of science to the practical aid of Western settlement. In an age when pragmatism was just beginning to be formalized into a philosophy, Hayden epitomized its methods in his approach to his scientific work in the West. To locate coal deposits, mineral veins, mines, timber stands, agricultural resources, grazing lands, water, irrigation sites, and tourist spas was, to him, the duty of the territorial geologist. And, being no reformer, he worked with businessmen and politicians in indiscriminate fashion, always willing to help whoever was interested. His popularity was inevitable, and to his way of thinking, it was honestly earned.

Not the least measure of his labors was the vast archive of publications he assembled. His survey alone produced four different sets of works. Each year for eleven years he issued substantial annual reports running to hundreds of pages. Then, at Cope's urging,[8] he began issuing in 1873, on short notice, a series of bulletins that enabled the scientists connected with his survey to get instant credit for their discoveries. The Hayden bulletin, often criticized by other scientists, was actually a new scientific journal that made it possible for his men to break the monopoly on scientific publication

8. Cope to Hayden, Nov. 28, 1873, L.R., Hayden Survey, R.G. 57, National Archives. See also L. F. Schmeckebier: "Catalogue and Index of the Publications of the Hayden, King, Powell, and Wheeler Surveys," *Bulletin No.* 222, U.S. Geological Survey (1904).

held by *The American Journal of Science* and its backers in Eastern academic circles. Careless as it often was, the Hayden bulletin served a useful purpose, and the proof that it was needed lies in the vast quantity of material submitted to it.[9] In addition, along with his annual reports and bulletins, Hayden began to publish "final reports, or monographs"—great definitive tomes by Cope, Lesquereaux, Meek, and others, which were major contributions to their respective sciences, and rivaled the best publications of the other surveys.[1]

In mapping, Hayden scored fewer successes. *The Atlas of Colorado,* drawn by Gardner and illustrated with Holmes's marvelous panoramas, was as good as the Atlas of the King Survey and far better than those produced by Powell and Wheeler.[2] Jackson's photographs, and the landscape work of Holmes, need no further word. They helped to create a new world for millions of Americans. Finally, not the least of Hayden's achievements stemmed from his love for the scenic beauty he observed on every hand out West. This fostered his ability to dramatize the Rocky Mountain West, and his own work in it, to the point where all America recognized it, not as a dreadful place to get across, but as a wonderland of nature to be lived in and enjoyed.

Educated himself under the apprentice system, and having absorbed his greatest lessons from the example provided by James Hall's New York State Survey, Hayden in his own survey provided a matchless training ground for the promising young men who would be the scientific leaders of the country for the next generation. By the same token, the Hayden Survey also educated the public to appreciate and enjoy the romantic labors of the working scientist. With each new dramatic discovery, his men assumed larger stature in the public eye at a time when science and efficiency,

9. Schmeckebier: "Catalogue," pp. 21–30. These included papers by Holmes, Jackson, Cope, Lesquereux, A. S. Packard, Elliott Coués, H. C. Yarrow, C. A. White, David Star Jordan, Samuel H. Scudder, Asa Gray, Joseph Hooker, and A. R. Grote, among others.

1. Ibid., pp. 20–1. E. D. Cope's *The Vertebrata of the Tertiary Formations of the West* (1883) ran to some 1,009 pages and became known in the scientific world as "Cope's Bible." This book, along with the volumes on fossil flora by Lesquereux and one volume on invertebrate fossils by F. B. Meek, were the most impressive of the "Final Reports."

2. F. V. Hayden [and Gardner and Holmes]: *Geological and Geographical Atlas of Colorado and Portions of Adjacent Territory* (New York and Washington: Julius Bien; 1877). A second edition was printed in 1881. Hayden also produced a number of separate map sheets that were often more useful than his Atlas. See Schmeckebier: "Catalogue," pp. 35–7.

under the impetus of Darwinism, were moving rapidly to the fore. Every schoolchild saw his sun pictures and stereopticon slides, learned something of natural history from his popular writings, and visited museums created by the labors of his men.

Hayden was thus a towering but typical figure of his time. Careless, wasteful of his talent, undisciplined, eclectic, indiscriminating, one part sham and much of a showman, he was nonetheless a serious, able, and dedicated man who gave his life to his work. If in the eyes of others he pursued the cult of success too assiduously, it must at least be said that he worked very hard in the pursuit, and deserved more than most whatever acclaim he attained. Possibly because he was so much in the public eye, he received disproportionate criticism during his career, but as this history of Western exploration has shown, he was not alone in his drive for the top. Almost all his rivals equaled him in ambition, though only one overshadowed him in success. He was a one-armed man with the same self-made background and with the same zest for outdoor adventure and the pursuit of knowledge in the service of the country—John Wesley Powell, conqueror of the Colorado.

CHAPTER XV

John Wesley Powell
The Explorer as Reformer

MONUMENTAL though the achievements of the other explorers of the day might have been, the greatest explorer-hero since the days of Frémont was one-armed Major John Wesley Powell. A casually educated, self-made scientist with a driving ambition, Powell was perhaps the outstanding representative of a breed of political men who came to the fore in the late nineteenth century. Displaying no less talent for organization and concentration, no less political acumen or knowledge of the levers of power than their notorious counterparts, the better-known captains of industry, Powell and those like him labored primarily in the cause of reform. They were intellectuals, which made their work harder, and scientists, which made their concepts often difficult to understand. Their weapon was knowledge gained by hard experience as field explorers. And if their manner often seemed overconfident, at times overbearing, as they unrolled their maps before Congressional committees, published their massive, erudite tomes proudly in obscure series, or jabbed at their adversaries with sobering facts, they nevertheless had the good of the country and its people on their minds. Theirs was a serious mission in the American tradition, and it is perhaps one of the more notable failures of our popular historians that the details of their activities have been obscured by the adventures of the robber barons and the politicos.

As scientists and public men, Powell and his circle sought to put the explorer's experience to practical use in promoting the fair, efficient, and socially useful development of the West. And for every disappointment or failure, they left behind a record of large vision, new ideas, and concepts that would one day change the face of the land. Long before Theodore Roosevelt and the Progressives ushered in an era of conservation and reform, these government men had already laid down the guidelines along which such reform could be accomplished. They had erected the structure of bureaus and commissions and trained the staffs of experts whereby the major reform ideas as they related to the West could get into the mainstream of American thought. Significantly, too, theirs was not a clear-cut or unambiguous achievement. It was carried out with plain scientific labor, but it was also built on bitterness, intrigue, jealousy, class conflict, professional and political struggle, and economic infighting. Curiously, those few historians who have concerned themselves with the career of Major Powell and his associates have tended to minimize these aspects of their lives, with the result that Powell and his men seem almost simple figures grappling heroically, if futilely, with the vast forces of nineteenth-century political and economic darkness that surrounded them.[1] Perhaps this accounts for their relative obscurity.

2

Powell's background and education bore many similarities to Hayden's, but diverged in several significant ways. Born in Mount Morris, New York, on March 24, 1834, he spent much of his early life on a series of back-country farms.[2] His father, a strict Methodist preacher, regularly rode the circuit, in addition to tending the farm and trying his hand in a modest way in the business of tailoring. In 1841 the family moved to Jackson, Ohio, at the height of the abolitionist controversy. As a preacher and staunch abolitionist, Joseph Powell was not precisely welcome, and John Wesley in his

1. The best biographies of Powell are Darrah: *Powell of the Colorado;* and Wallace Stegner: *Beyond the Hundredth Meridian* (Boston: Houghton Mifflin Co.; 1954). Accounts of his life by contemporaries are G. K. Gilbert, ed.: *John Wesley Powell: A Memorial to an American Explorer and Scholar* (Chicago: Open Court Publishing Co.; 1903); and W. M. Davis: "John Wesley Powell, 1834–1902," National Academy of Science *Biographical Memoirs,* Vol. VIII (Washington, D.C.: National Academy of Sciences; 1915), pp. 11–86. See also Elmo Scott Watson, ed.: *The Professor Goes West* (Bloomington, Ill.: Illinois Wesleyan University Press; 1954); Leonard Wibberly: *Wes Powell: Conqueror of the Grand Canyon* (New York: Farrar, Straus and Cudahy; 1958); Thomas Manning: "A History of the United States Geological Survey," unpublished manuscript in Dr. Manning's possession; and Richard A. Bartlett: *Great Surveys.*
2. Biographical data on Powell are based on the sources given in the preceding footnote, unless otherwise stated.

school days gained his first experience in the difficult ways of the reformer. He fought regularly at school and at such a disadvantage that he was finally withdrawn and sent to the small tutoring establishment of a neighbor, George Crookham. Crookham, a Calvinist like John Wesley's father, was regarded as something of an eccentric, for he preferred not to work, and instead built a two-room log-cabin school and laboratory where he indulged himself in his twin hobbies of natural history and pedagogy. Though Powell was the only minor in Crookham's small class, he appears to have engaged most of the master's attention. In addition to wide, almost random reading in the classic treatises of the day, Powell studied nature at first hand on field trips with Crookham. On other occasions they constructed crude chemical apparatus and repeated the experiments that others learned about only in books. Thus very early Powell learned about facts and induction. He also gained a postgraduate lesson on the lot of the intellectual when one day Crookham rushed up to the house with the sad news that local bullies had burned his school and with it all his books, apparatus, and specimens. Class was dismissed, and the Powells eventually moved on in 1846 to a farm in Walworth County, Illinois, where John Wesley grew into manhood.

His first job was as a teacher in a country school in Jefferson County in southern Wisconsin at a salary of $14 a month. From Jefferson County he went on to teach in Clinton, Decatur, and Hennepin, Illinois, and in between he enrolled for brief stretches of instruction at Illinois Institute (Wheaton College), Illinois College at Jacksonville, and Oberlin (Hayden's alma mater). He began to make natural-history excursions, once trekking across Michigan to collect specimens and to visit his mother's long-lost brother. Between 1852 and 1861 he also made long trips down the Ohio, the Illinois, the Des Moines, and the Mississippi all the way from St. Paul to New Orleans. This was valuable experience for his later career, and so great was his local reputation as an explorer and collector (he had six thousand plants in his personal herbarium) that he was elected secretary of the Illinois Natural History Society. By 1860 he was lecturing on the lyceum circuit in Tennessee, Kentucky, and Mississippi, and he became principal of public schools in Hennepin, Illinois.

While he was thus engaged, the first opportunity came to put his reformer's principles into action. Because he believed that slavery could only be abolished by war, he answered Lincoln's first call for volunteers, signing on as a private in the 20th Illinois Volunteer

Infantry. He took his duties as a soldier as seriously as he did everything else, and rose rapidly to sergeant, then to lieutenant. On a short leave in Chicago, he was outfitted with a new uniform and purchased Mahan's book on military engineering and Vauban's treatise on fortifications. With the help of these he was able to supervise the construction of fortifications at Cape Girardeau, Missouri.

Eventually he was transferred out of his Illinois regiment at the request of its commander and placed on special duty as an engineer. It was then that he met General Grant and became his friend. On a special furlough granted him by the general, he journeyed to Detroit to marry his cousin Emma Dean (the daughter of his mother's long-lost brother). When he returned, it was as commander of his own battery of the 2nd Illinois Artillery. A perfectionist and a disciplinarian, Powell had his battery ready when he was ordered into the bloody battle of Shiloh, and his battery made a stand in the crucial center of the line in a peach orchard called the "Hornet's Nest." There it helped hold the Confederates at bay long enough for Grant to re-form his army. But Powell himself was wounded by a half-spent Minié ball and sent to the rear on General Lew Wallace's own horse. Behind the lines, with his wife standing by, Powell's right arm was amputated.

Despite this crippling injury, Powell continued on in active duty, his wife, by means of a special pass from General Grant, accompanying him wherever he went. He rose to the rank of major and brevet lieutenant colonel, taking a prominent part in the siege of Vicksburg (where he took time off to look for fossil shells in the trenches), the Nashville campaigns, under Thomas, and the march on Atlanta with Sherman. At Vicksburg he served under General "Black Jack" Logan of Illinois, with whom he would have many dealings in later life. As a commander of artillery in Sherman's Atlanta Campaign, he had the misfortune to see his brother Walter captured by the Confederates. Walter was sent to a Southern prisoner-of-war camp and in an attempted escape became completely deranged. He was eventually exchanged and mustered out but never fully recovered his health. By the time Powell ended his military service, he had seen much of the country and made contact with many of America's future leaders, and he had experienced personal pain and anguish and given his all for the cause he believed in. Most important for his later career, he learned the difficult ways of massive bureaucracy.

3

When he arrived back home in Wheaton, Illinois, Powell determined to continue his twin careers of science and education. He
declined to run for minor political office, and instead accepted a
post as professor of natural history at Illinois Wesleyan College.
His teaching load was substantial, including instruction in botany,
zoology, comparative anatomy, practical entomology, natural philosophy, the logic of natural science, and geology.[3] In covering this
incredible range of material, Powell utilized Crookham's method
and wherever possible took his students into the field or laboratory
for practical experience. Though it has been claimed that Powell
was an innovator in this teaching technique,[4] it is clear from the
long line of naturalists and geologists trained in state and national
surveys and in the laboratories of Europe, whose activities have
previously been described, that he was only practicing the standard
techniques of the better teachers of his day. At the frontier college
of Illinois Wesleyan, this was no mean accomplishment.

Powell, however, was not satisfied with his modest though demanding post. He was interested in going West to explore the
Rockies. With this ultimate objective in mind, he shifted to Illinois
Normal University, and persuaded the officials of that institution,
Illinois Wesleyan, and the State Natural History Society to back his
proposals for a state natural-history museum in Bloomington. With
this support he journeyed to Springfield and secured an appropriation of $1,500 from the state legislature, establishing the museum.
Naturally he was appointed the first curator, and, in the bargain,
he was authorized to use $500 of the appropriation to finance a
collecting trip to the Rocky Mountains.[5]

This was not enough backing, however, and Powell eventually
secured further support from the Illinois Industrial University, the
Chicago Academy of Sciences, the Union Pacific Railroad, the
Chicago, Alton and St. Louis, the Pittsburgh, Fort Wayne and Chicago, and the Chicago and Rock Island railroads. Then he went
to Washington and obtained General Grant's support, which enabled him to draw rations on a cost basis from various army posts

3. Darrah: *Powell of the Colorado*, pp. 74–6.
4. Ibid., pp. 76–7.
5. Ibid., pp. 77–81.

in the West and to secure a military escort out of Fort Laramie. Joseph Henry, at the Smithsonian Institution, provided him with instruments and advice. The remainder of the expenses Powell made up out of his own pocket.[6] Thus, his first scientific venture might be classified as a "mixed enterprise." Funds and support came from a variety of sources, including state and federal institutions, private business, and Powell himself. It was not, however, an official government expedition.

The personnel of his party consisted of college students, amateur naturalists, teachers, and relatives, including his indefatigable wife Emma. The most important member of this group, next to Powell, was his brother-in-law Almon H. Thompson, a teacher in Bloomington. This was Thompson's first venture into the West, but under Powell's supervision he eventually became an able explorer and mapmaker and the chief topographer of the Powell Surveys.

The expedition assembled at Council Bluffs and on June 1, 1867, Powell and his party took their departure, heading westward across the plains.[7] On General Sherman's advice they steered clear of the Dakota Badlands, where Indians were on the prowl, and headed for Denver, joining up with a wagon train at Fort McPherson. On July 1, Powell rode on ahead into Denver and made the fortunate acquaintance of William N. Byers of *The Rocky Mountain News*. Byers introduced him to Oramel G. Howland, his printer, who was something of an amateur explorer himself, and also recommended that he contact his (Byers') brother-in-law Jack Sumner, who had a cabin in Colorado's Middle Park, the objective of Powell's excursion. Thanks to Powell's advance planning, his expedition was already well known by the time it reached Denver, as Byers gave it full publicity in his newspaper.

Out of Denver, Powell's party took a little-used and difficult trail over the Rampart Range and into Bergen's Park. At this site they remained for nearly a month, making collections and examining the surrounding countryside. On July 27 they began the ascent of Pike's Peak, reaching the top about 3 p.m. that same day. Later it was claimed that the intrepid Mrs. Powell had been the first woman to ascend the peak, but historical research has revealed that Julia Holmes, a "bloomer girl" from Kansas, out on a lark one day in

6. Ibid., pp. 81–2. Also see Watson: *The Professor Goes West*, pp. 1–2.
7. Ibid., pp. 82–90. Watson: *The Professor Goes West*, pp. 2–11, reprints first-hand reports of the expedition by J. C. Hartzell, which appeared in the Bloomington, Illinois, *Pantagraph*.

1858, had preceded her, and somewhat later two other women described as "denizens of Golden" also climbed the peak.[8]

From Pike's Peak the naturalists moved leisurely into South Park and over snowy Berthoud Pass. Then they returned to South Park for three weeks before heading back to Denver by way of Central City, whose mineral strikes the Major wished to study. While the main contingent disbanded in Denver, Powell and his wife remained behind for two months to explore the Grand River as it ran through Colorado. Already the Major was making plans to descend the Grand the following summer as far as its junction with the Colorado. This idea was apparently suggested to him in conversations with Jack Sumner, whom he had met in Middle Park as arranged and who assisted his party in their travels. It was the beginning of Powell's greatest work as an explorer.

4

Upon his return to Bloomington, Powell demonstrated the particular enthusiasm and ability which carried him on to success as an organizer and administrator. He deposited his collections at the museum, lectured widely and dramatically to public and student audiences, and without telling anyone in Bloomington, he accepted a tentative appointment as professor at Illinois Institute.[9] Then he went to Washington, where again with Grant's help, and that of Senator Trumbull of Illinois and Representatives Cullom and Garfield, he secured government supplies for a party of twenty-five men.[1] By this time, too, he had the wholehearted backing of Joseph Henry of the Smithsonian Institution, who was intrigued by Powell's plan to explore the little-known Colorado River country, as well as by his plan to scale Long's Peak to the top for the first time.

With the backing of Illinois state institutions, including this time the State Board of Education, Powell assembled a party of twenty-one at Denver, including W. N. Byers of *The Rocky Mountain News*. They trekked over Berthoud Pass to Hot Sulphur Springs on Grand River in North Park. There Powell established his headquarters and was joined by Jack Sumner, Gus Lanken, Oramel Howland, and

8. See Watson: *The Professor Goes West*, p. 8 n. Also see Agnes Wright Spring, ed.: *A Bloomer Girl on Pike's Peak* (Limited Edition, published by the Western History Dept., Denver Public Library, Denver, Colorado, 1949).
9. Darrah: *Powell of the Colorado*, p. 92.
1. Ibid., pp. 92–3.

Billy Rhodes Hawkins, the latter a fugitive from justice back in Missouri.[2]

They remained in Middle Park for three months, collecting specimens of the flora and fauna and whatever fossil remains they could find. Powell also examined the nearby mountains, particularly the Colorado Range and the Gore Range, whose highest peak was Mt. Lincoln, some 14,300 feet in altitude.

In August they were visited by a party of summer tourists which included the Speaker of the House of Representatives, Schuyler M. Colfax, soon to be Grant's vice-president. Also with the Colfax party were Samuel Bowles, editor of the Springfield, Massachusetts, *Republican*, one of the most influential newspapers in the country, and Colfax's political manager. Bowles, who was also a friend of Josiah Dwight Whitney, was keenly interested in the future of the West, as his two books, *Across the Continent* . . . and *The Switzerland of America* . . . , clearly indicated. He was much impressed with Powell, too, and took pains to describe the expedition and its objectives in dispatches to his newspaper. The Major's ultimate intention, he observed, was "to explore the Upper Colorado River and solve the mysteries of its three hundred mile canyon." He found this prospect exciting: "Here are seen the central forces that formed the continent; here more striking studies in physical geography, geology, and natural history, than are proffered anywhere else." Powell he described as "well-educated, and enthusiastic, resolute, a gallant leader."[3] With Byers and two correspondents to Chicago newspapers as members of his expedition, and with the additional help of Bowles, Powell and his men were assured of maximum publicity—a distinct aid to their cause in future years.

On the twentieth of August, Powell, his brother Walter, L. W. Klepinger, Samuel Gorman, Ned Farrell, Jack Sumner, and William Byers set out to ascend Long's Peak for the first time. It took two days of difficult travel to approach the peak so that they were in a position to make the climb. Even at that, on the afternoon of the twenty-second they were camped above the timberline in virtual despair of ever reaching the top when Klepinger made a daring reconnaissance alone and located a feasible route. He had thought to make the first ascent unaided, thereby gaining a "scoop," as he put it, over the rest of the party, and had climbed up past the

2. Darrah: *Powell of the Colorado*, pp. 95–9.
3. The meeting with Colfax and the opinions of Bowles are chronicled in Wallace Stegner: *Beyond the Hundredth Meridian*, pp. 30–4. See especially p. 32 for the Bowles quotation.

famous notch, but the footing became precarious and darkness was fast approaching. Reluctantly he began the descent and reached camp after nightfall, following Jack Sumner's signal fires.[4]

On August 23, the whole party made the ascent to the summit, and stood on the bald mountain top of Colorado, from which they could see the parks spread out in all directions before them, and beyond that, the mountains of the Continental Divide. Someone produced a bottle of wine, which was drained by all but Gorman and Klepinger, and the latter sought to preserve the memory of the occasion by enshrining one of the Major's indifferent camp biscuits in a baking-powder can atop the summit. Powell, conscious of his own dignity and the solemnity of the occasion, removed the biscuit and made a speech instead.[5] He had not quite reached the romantic and symbolic grandeur of Frémont on the Wind River Divide in 1842, but it is obvious that he was conscious of the role.

From Middle Park Powell's party made their way with great difficulty along the Berthoud–Bridger Trail across the Divide to the West and then moved downstream to the lower stretches of the White River 150 miles above its junction with the Green. The trek was an adventurous one. F. M. Bishop, sent back for supplies, became lost along the Yampa River and struggled into camp ragged and worn out some five weeks later. Gus Lanken, one of the mountaineers, deserted, taking with him a mule and supplies. He made for a cabin which he had nearby and upon reaching it stood off pursuing members of Powell's party with his rifle. The explorers decided to abandon the mule, though Klepinger took revenge by carving in a tree: "Gus Lanken is a mule thief. Klepinger says so, this 14th day of September 1868."[6]

On the White River bottoms, 150 miles from its junction with the Green, Powell and his party constructed three log cabins which the Major proposed to use as his headquarters for a winter reconnaissance of the Colorado. By now he was seriously preparing to make the descent of the unexplored river by boat, and he needed as much information about its canyons as he could gather. He had previously studied all available accounts of the river, such as Lieutenant Ives's detailed narrative of his expedition upriver to Black Canyon and his descent into the Grand Canyon near Diamond

4. See W. N. Byers's account of the ascent in *The Rocky Mountain News*, Sept. 1, 1868. More accurate is L. W. Klepinger's account in "First Ascent of Long's Peak," *The Trail*, Vol. VII, No. 8 (Jan. 1915), pp. 13–15.
5. Klepinger: "First Ascent," p. 15.
6. Darrah: *Powell of the Colorado*, p. 103.

Creek, and also Newberry's careful geological notes. He also consulted Gunnison's volume of the Pacific Railroad Survey *Reports* and Warren's map of 1857, on which the Colorado was a great unknown. The results of Macomb's expedition to the Green and Grand were not available to him, since the report was not published until 1875. The only information on that region was the word of an enterprising Western editor who told him he had once laid out a city on the fertile bottoms along the junction of the Green and Grand but was run off by Indians—a story that Powell would have good reason to doubt less than a year later.[7] Gorlinski's Land Office Map of 1868 was his most reliable source of information but, like the army maps, it too left the Colorado region largely blank.

Then there was James White, whose story in the interview with Dr. C. C. Parry had been made public. Before he left on his canyon voyage, Powell sought White out and heard his story first hand, but considered his account too vague to be of much help. A final source was the Indians. During the months they were encamped along White River, Powell studied the local Utes closely, learned much of the lore of their tribe, and listened to their opinion of the river. They even had a legend about the disappearance of an Indian family and its canoe in the turbulent waters below White River. Curiously, Powell knew very little of the mountain men and their adventures along the river. He had heard of Ashley, for example, but he knew almost nothing of his 1825 voyage down the Green.[8]

After camp was established, the Major left Mrs. Powell, Walter, and several of the other hardier members of the party behind, and trekked out around the Uintas with the rest of the group, who were bound for home and civilization. Later, with Sumner, Howland, and others, he returned after exploring the Uinta Mountains and Brown's Hole. Much of the winter he spent studying the White River Utes and planning his forthcoming canyon voyage.

When spring came, floods inundated their cabins, forcing the whole party to higher ground. Dissension broke out and it was evident that the time to return home was fast approaching. In March, though it was still cold and the snow was deep in the mountains, they began to pack out for civilization. Their course took them via the Yampa, Brown's Hole, and Fort Bridger to Granger Station on the Union Pacific line. From there they returned to Chicago, and

7. Ibid., p. 109. See Darrah, ed.: "J. C. Sumner's Journal," *Utah Historical Quarterly*, Vol. XV (1947), p. 115.
8. See Powell: *Exploration of the Colorado River of the West and Its Tributaries* (Washington, D.C.: U. S. Government Printing Office; 1875), pp. 26–7.

Gorlinski's Land Office map of 1867. This was the map Powell used to prepare for his canyon voyage of 1869. It indicates what was known about the
canyon country before his trip. *Courtesy Library of Congress*

Emma Powell went on to visit relatives in Detroit. The Major headed for Washington to prepare for his harrowing descent of 1,500 miles of unexplored Colorado River. It was to be the climactic event of late-nineteenth-century exploration, and would mark the opening up of the last completely unknown territory in the continental United States.

5

In Washington, Powell again secured authorization to draw government rations, but little else besides the best wishes of the Smithsonian Institution. Before going East, he had commissioned a Chicago boatbuilder named Bagley to construct four special craft for his proposed voyage. Three of them were to be twenty-one feet long and built of oak, with watertight compartments at either end to assure buoyancy even in the roughest of water. The fourth was made of light pine and was only sixteen feet long. It was to serve as a pilot boat for the others and was designed to float in otherwise inaccessible places. In designing these boats, Powell drew not only on his personal knowledge of the Colorado and its specific problems, but also on his years of river experience. They were good craft, and before he loaded them on a flatcar for Green River Station on May 4, 1869, the Major had personally tested them in a cruise on Lake Michigan.

The chief source of financial support for the Colorado River voyage was again Powell himself. Other contributors were Illinois Normal, Illinois Industrial University, and the Chicago Academy of Sciences, and also the Union Pacific and Burlington railroads. For his team of nine explorers Powell chose a curious collection of men. Walter Powell, enormously strong and completely loyal, went along of course. Jack Sumner, Oramel Howland, his brother Seneca, Bill Dunn, a mountain hunter, and Billy Rhodes Hawkins—all men from the previous year's campaign—also signed on. Then there was Andrew Hall, a young plainsman and Indian fighter with a lively sense of humor, and George Bradley, a soldier whom the Major had met at Fort Bridger in 1868, who said he "would explore the river Styx" if it would get him out of the Army. This the Major easily accomplished with the aid of his friend General Grant. To round out the original ten, there was Frank Goodman, one of that ubiquitous breed of nineteenth-century English sportsmen who seemed almost as numerous in the mountain West as the Indians.[9] All these men agreed to work for little or no pay, and the Major, of course, put money into the venture, so that it was an amateur undertaking in the best sense of the word. It has been observed that on this crucial voyage Powell failed to take any scientific men along, though many were available, especially through his contacts at the Smithsonian. This seems a serious omission, especially as his surviving correspondence gives no indication that he even tried to secure the services of anyone trained in natural history, except perhaps Dr. Vasey of Bloomington, who accompanied him on his first trip West.

Most of the men were already assembled at Green River City when the Major arrived on May 11. While they were waiting for Powell, they were accosted one day by a curious character named Captain Samuel Adams who claimed he had congressional authorization to take charge of the river trip. He borrowed money from members of the party, who remained skeptical of his story and waited in nearby Bryan for the arrival of Powell. When he told his story to the Major and produced his worthless credentials, he was sent packing. Adams later turned up, however, in Middle Park, Colorado, where his fallacious stories of having already navigated the Colorado River gained him the backing for a disastrous competing voyage down the Grand River. While Powell and his men were somewhere below the junction of the Green and the Grand, Captain Adams smashed his last vessel—a homemade raft—on the rocks of Cedar Canyon, and the walk back to civilization concluded his exploring activities.[1]

The next few weeks at Green River were weeks of training and preparation for Powell and his men. They learned to handle the boats, and Powell devised a system of flag signals to be sent back by the lead boat to warn of impending difficulties. Some of the men also learned to handle such instruments as the sextant and the barometer. Oramel Howland acquired the techniques of charting the river's course by the meander system and he was assigned this task on the trip. Supplies were assembled, tools stowed away, and on May 24, 1869, with jaunty cries of departure, they pushed away from the bank about noon and began their dangerous voyage. They

9. For biographical data on the members of the first Powell Colorado River expedition, see Darrah: "Biographical Sketches and Original Documents of the First Powell Expedition of 1869," *Utah Historical Quarterly*, Vol. XV (1947), pp. 29–30, 89, 93–4, 106–8, 109–12.
1. Stegner: *Beyond the Hundredth Meridian*, pp. 50–3, 77–84.

had only a rough idea of what lay before them down the unknown river and its canyons, and many fantastic tales of gloom and disaster to reflect upon as they rowed away.

They made a picturesque fleet as they drifted along.[2] Powell, with Jack Sumner and Bill Dunn, led in the light boat, christened the *Emma Dean,* and then came Walter Powell and George Bradley in the *Kitty Clyde's Sister,* Andrew Hall and William Rhodes Hawkins in the *Maid of the Canyon,* and the Howland brothers and Frank Goodman in the *No Name.* The first day they made eight miles before stopping to make camp. But the second day three of the boats ran aground on a sandbar and the difficulties of the voyage had properly begun. No one was to hear from them again for thirty-seven days, or until they reached the Ute Indian Agency below the Uinta Mountains, which lay directly across their path. In the meantime interest in their expedition had been heightened all over the country by reports in the newspapers of Omaha, Springfield, and Chicago of their demise in the crushing rapids of the Upper Green River. A confidence man named John A. Risdon made a brief career out of posing as the only survivor of the wreck, until he was exposed by Emma Powell, who never doubted for her husband's safety despite the dire reports.[3]

Meanwhile, the Major and his men traversed the fairly easy stretches of the Upper Green, where, though the river wound through cliffs 1,200 feet high, it was, according to George Bradley, "deep and calm as a lake."[4] When they reached the Flaming Gorge just below Henry's Fork, however, the rapids began and stayed with them all through the Uintas. They passed Flaming Gorge, Horseshoe Canyon, Kingfisher Canyon, Red Canyon, and came into the

2. Unless otherwise stated, this account is based on Powell: *Exploration*; and Darrah: "Biographical Sketches and Original Documents of the First Powell Expedition of 1869," pp. 9–148. This last includes the edited texts of the George Y. Bradley Journal, the letters of Major Powell to the Chicago *Tribune,* the letters of W. H. Powell to the Chicago *Evening Journal,* the letters of O. G. Howland to *The Rocky Mountain News,* J. C. Sumner's Journal, Major Powell's Journal, and geological notes by Major Powell. The original manuscript of the George Y. Bradley Journal is in the Library of Congress, and I have studied it. A copy of J. C. Sumner's Journal is in the Robert Brewster Stanton Collection of the New York Public Library, and I have also consulted it. Another manuscript copy of the Sumner Journal and several loose sheets from what are apparently Sumner's original notes can be found in the Smithsonian Institution.

3. Darrah: *Powell of the Colorado,* p. 129.

4. Darrah, ed.: "Bradley Journal," *Utah Historical Quarterly,* Vol. XV (1947), p. 32.

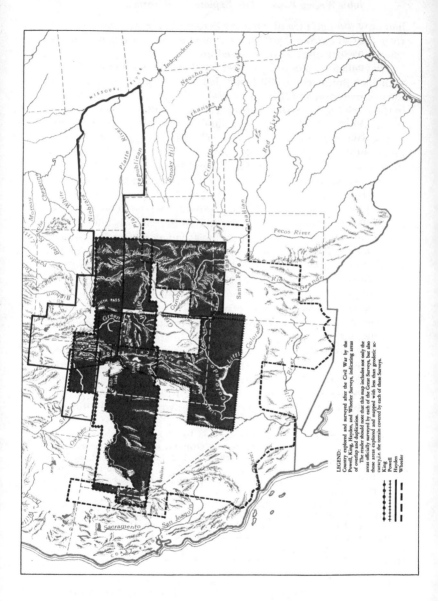

LEGEND:
Country explored and surveyed after the Civil War by the Powell, King, Hayden, and Wheeler Surveys, indicating areas of overlap and duplication.

The reader should note that this map includes not only the areas officially surveyed by each of the Great Surveys, but also those areas explored and mapped with less than geodetic accuracy, i.e. the terrain covered by each of these Surveys.

King
Powell
Hayden
Wheeler

valley of Brown's Hole. Whole days were spent in shooting the rapids. At times they had to let the boats down the roaring currents by means of ropes. At other times they laboriously unloaded the heavy boats and portaged them around rough spots. On June 1 they reached a particularly difficult obstruction—a series of falls in Red Canyon—and found painted on a prominent rock in midstream: "Ashley 1825." Powell, who misread the date as 1855, believed Ashley to be a prospector who came to grief at this point on the river, after which he trekked out to Salt Lake City and assisted in the building of the Mormon Temple to earn money for his passage home.[5] Like the exploits of the old Spaniards, the achievements of the fur-trade explorers less than fifty years before were already fading from memory.

They named the falls Ashley Falls, appropriately enough, and spent most of the day lining around them. Whenever he could, Powell left the boat camp and climbed out of the canyons for a look at the plateau country. At this point his side trips and the delays to take measurements did not irritate his men, but later, as the food supply ran low, they became a source of discontent. Near the foot of Brown's Hole, Powell climbed out on the plateau overlooking the entrance to forbidding Lodore Canyon. Its height above the river was over 2,000 feet, and he wrote, in a letter to the Chicago *Tribune* that was later incorporated into his final report on the canyon voyage, that he and some of his men had walked to the edge of the canyon and looked down 2,000 feet below. "I can do this now," he wrote, "but it has taken several years of mountain climbing to cool my nerves, so that I can sit with my feet over the edge, and calmly look down a precipice 2000 feet. And yet I cannot look on and see another do the same. I must either bid him come away, or turn my head."[6]

Always aware of the sublime beauty of the scenery as well as the mysteries that lay ahead, Powell reported, in the characteristic romantic fashion of his day, his impressions on facing the Canyon of Lodore:

> This evening as I write, the sun is going down, and the shadows are settling in the cañon. The vermillion gleams and roseate hues, blending with the green and gray tints, are slowly changing to somber brown above, and black shadows are

5. See footnote 8, p. 539. Also see Darrah, ed.: "Major Powell's Letters to the Chicago *Tribune*," *Utah Historical Quarterly*, Vol. XV (1947), p. 78.
6. Ibid., p. 80.

creeping over them below; and now it is a dark portal to a region of gloom—the gateway through which we are to enter on our voyage of exploration tomorrow. What shall we find?[7]

On June 7, in Lodore Canyon, the first major accident occurred. Riding ahead in the *Emma Dean,* Powell saw a particularly difficult fall. He signaled the boats behind, but Oramel Howland failed to see his frantic gestures in time. He was just a few seconds too late in pulling in for shore, and as a result, the boat and its three men shot over the falls and into the boulder-torn rapids. Rearing and pitching, sometimes lost in the foam, the boat glanced off one rock, jammed briefly, then slipped off and headed two hundred yards downstream to a second rapid, where it crashed broadside into a boulder and broke in half. The men were thrown like dolls into the river. Powell and the others ran along the bank, powerless to help. Fortunately, no one perished. O. G. Howland swam to an island in the middle of the river, as did his brother Seneca. Frank Goodman clung desperately to a slippery rock downstream, the water washing over him. They were finally rescued, but the boat was completely wrecked, with Powell's precious barometers in it.[8] Gloom settled over the camp that night and Powell debated with himself whether to cross overland to Salt Lake City for more barometers or go on without them. They named the rapids "Disaster Falls."

The next day, however, they found part of the boat still intact, and Sumner rescued the barometers and with them a keg of whiskey which Howland had smuggled aboard.[9] After that, Disaster Falls had more pleasant connotations. Lodore Canyon, nevertheless, proved continuously difficult. There were rapids throughout, and no relief in sight for days. On one occasion they nearly lost another boat, the *Maid of the Canyon,* as it slipped from their grasp and went down the rapids alone, and miraculously was unharmed. There were few comfortable campsites and Bradley commenced to grumble in his secret diary.[1] When they did find a campsite, a brush fire roaring down to the water's edge caused the loss of valuable equipment and nearly trapped them. But finally, on June 18, they broke free of Lodore and sailed out into the comparative tranquillity of Echo Park, near the junction of the Yampa. Eight days later they were in Uinta Valley near Berthoud's crossing and the

7. Ibid. Also see Powell: *Exploration,* p. 21.
8. Darrah: "Major Powell's Letters," pp. 80–1; Powell: *Exploration,* pp. 24–5. See also Darrah: "Bradley Journal," p. 36.
9. Darrah: "Major Powell's Letters," pp. 80–1.
1. Darrah: "Bradley Journal," p. 37.

site of Escalante's crossing nearly a hundred years before. There they paused for several days to trek out to Pardyn Dodd's Ute Agency up the Uinta for supplies and to send their first letters home. It was only then that the people back home knew for sure that Risdon's announcement of their death had, in Mark Twain's terms, been "a little premature."

Frank Goodman left the party at the Ute Agency, having seen enough of the river. And the men grew impatient to continue the voyage. Supplies, because of the overturning of the boats, the fire, etc., had grown dangerously low and the Ute Agency had very little to spare. But Powell took his time, deliberately making observations and overhauling the gear. He was a careful man, and he was on a scientific mission. By July 6 he was ready, and they finally sailed off down the river.

Danger in every form accompanied them. On July 8, Powell climbed a steep cliff along the river and was trapped on a ledge, unable to go backward or forward, with only the rocks and the river below. He held on to the cliff with the frantically clutching fingers of his one arm, but these began to cramp and lose their grip. Above him Bradley coolly considered a means of rescue and hit upon the expedient of lowering his long underwear down to the Major. In one desperate gamble Powell let go of the rocks and as he started to teeter backward grasped hold of the dangling longjohns. Bradley pulled him up to safety.[2]

For the next week they swept on down the river through Desolation Canyon, then Cool or Gray Canyon, which cuts across the Tavaputs Plateau. Suddenly they were out of the canyons and drifting past Gunnison's Crossing. But this was only a brief respite. Past the San Rafael Valley, they turned into Labyrinth Canyon and then its successor Stillwater Canyon. On the seventeenth of July they reached the junction of the Grand River, a point surrounded by towering walls, broken spires, and eroded canyons, clearly not a site where anybody had ever laid out a city. They had come 538 miles.

The next few days were spent in exploring this strategic junction. Powell climbed the heights, from which he could trace the winding courses of the Green and the Grand. "Away to the west," he wrote, "are lines of cliffs and ledges of rock—not such ledges as you may have seen where the quarryman splits his blocks, but ledges from which the gods might quarry mountains . . . and . . . cliffs where

2. Ibid., p. 46; Powell, in *Exploration*, pp. 33–4, describes this incident as having taken place on June 18.

the soaring eagle is lost to view ere he reaches the summit."[3] To the east he could see the Sierra La Sal, the site of Captain Moss's silver rush. "Wherever we look there is but a wilderness of rocks; deep gorges, where the rivers are lost below cliffs and towers and pinnacles; and ten thousand strangely carved forms in every direction; and beyond them the mountains blending with the clouds."[4] Out of all this scenic grandeur Powell was also fashioning a scientific view of the river and canyon country. No other locality in the world presented such an opportunity for the study of geologic processes, and even in the rush of his adventure Powell did not neglect the opportunity.

Below, the men caulked the boats, made new oars, and grew impatient at the delay. Food was running low and time was precious. On July 21, they started again. Almost immediately they hit rough water as they shot through Cataract Canyon. By July 28 they were past its termination, marked by Mille Bend Crag. Then another canyon, deep and narrow, appeared, then the Dirty Devil River, so named by Bill Dunn because of its sulphurous odor. Below the Dirty Devil they struck massive Glen Canyon, the Henry Mountains not quite visible to the west. On the twenty-ninth of July they had sighted up along the red canyon walls just above Glen Canyon a ruined cliff dwelling some two hundred feet above the river.[5] Parts of the walls of what had been a three-story dwelling still stood, lost in the depths of the canyon and undisturbed for centuries. On the wall below were hieroglyphic inscriptions scratched on the rock, and above, on the rim of the canyon, stood a ruined watchtower, its rickety ladder still more or less intact. Powell had discovered the Far Western limits of the Cliff Dwellers' culture that Macomb had observed along the San Juan in 1859 and that was to prove so startling and romantic to Jackson and Holmes at Mesa Verde a few years later.

At the end of July they reached the San Juan, and a day later the Paria where it flows into the Colorado at Lee's Ferry. Along the way they passed the site of Escalante's crossing on his return from Utah in 1776. Ahead of them, bounded by the Vermilion and Echo cliffs, was beautiful Marble Canyon, perhaps the most dangerous run of all. In Marble Canyon the river narrowed and the walls

3. Powell: *Exploration*, p. 58.
4. Ibid.
5. Ibid., p. 68. See also Darrah: "Bradley Journal," p. 56; and "J. C. Sumner's Journal," pp. 116–17.

seemed to grow higher. There were few good camping places, and even the gorgeous scenery grew monotonous. On August 10 they reached the Little Colorado, which marks the entrance to the Grand Canyon itself. Their last big trial was ahead of them. In his entry for August 13 Powell grasped the drama of the occasion:

> We are now ready to start on our way down the Great Unknown. Our boats, tied to a common stake, are chafing each other, as they are tossed by the fretful river. They ride high and buoyant, for their loads are lighter than we could desire. We have but a month's rations remaining. . . . We are three quarters of a mile in the depths of the earth, and the great river shrinks into insignificance as it dashes its angry waves against the walls and cliffs that rise to the world above. . . .
>
> We have an unknown distance yet to run; an unknown river yet to explore. What falls there are, we know not; what rocks beset the channel, we know not; what walls rise over the river, we know not. Ah well! we may conjecture many things. The men talk as cheerfully as ever; jests are bandied about freely this morning; but to me the cheer is somber and the jests are ghastly.[6]

Down they plunged into the Grand Canyon for days, through stupendous cataracts that swamped their boats, past unyielding granite boulders with the walls rising higher and higher until they towered over a mile above the river. There was little time now for side trips or scientific observations. One bone-jarring crash followed another and entire days were spent lining past impossible points, or gambling with the current when there was no foothold along the sheer indifferent walls. Rain and floods and rushing freshets complicated their work. On August 16 they pulled in at Bright Angel Creek and there found mealing stones and more Indian ruins, proof that someone sometime had survived in that fearsome gorge. By August 21 the dreaded granite was past them except for occasional patches, but the river was still swift and the marble walls sheer. Lava intrusions began to appear and volcanic cores were

6. Powell: *Exploration*, p. 80. Bradley wrote in his journal for August 13: "We camp tonight at the head of the worst rapid we have found today and the longest we have seen on the Colorado." Referring to James White's claim, he added: "I am convinced that no man has ever run such rapids on a raft, though it is possible he might pass along the shore and build another raft below and so work his way out but I pay little heed to the whole story." Darrah: "Bradley Journal," p. 63.

visible on the south shore. On the twenty-fifth they made thirty-
five miles, and Powell recorded the simple word "Hurrah!"[7] The
next day: "A few days like this and we are out of prison."[8] But the
last stretch proved to be the worst. On August 27 they were stopped
by a series of rapids that began with a fall of eighteen to twenty
feet. To continue seemed impossible, but as they went into camp,
the Major determined to try it in the morning.

That night after supper Oramel Howland announced his intention to leave the river and walk out over the Shivwits Plateau to
the Mormon settlements. Bill Dunn stuck with him, as did his
brother Seneca, with some reluctance. The others, canvassed by
Powell, agreed to try the river with the Major. By his calculations,
their destination, the Virgin River settlement of Callville, was less
than ninety miles ahead. Nothing could dissuade the Howlands and
Dunn, however, and the next morning they took their departure
in a sad, friendly farewell while the Major and his men faced the
river in the two remaining boats.[9]

7. Powell: *Exploration*, p. 95.
8. Ibid., p. 96.
9. Ibid., pp. 98–9. Stanton and Chalfant, in *Colorado River Controversies*,
seriously question the veracity of Powell's report of the expedition, in particular of his implication that Dunn and the Howland brothers deserted the
river party at Separation Rapids. They assert that Powell ordered or forced
Dunn, whom he disliked, to leave the party and that the Howlands went
with him. The chief evidence for this thesis consists of two accounts, one
by the embittered Jack Sumner in 1907, and another by Billy Rhodes Hawkins
in the same year. Hawkins also produced the life preserver that Powell
allegedly wore on his canyon trip. See Stanton and Chalfant: *Colorado
River Controversies*, pp. 135–232. A picture of the life preserver appears
opposite page 224. Credence is lent to Stanton's account by the excellent
work that he did in demonstrating (see pp. 97–137) that Powell had used
materials from his 1871–72 expedition in his report of the 1869 voyage in
such a way as to make it seem that they were part of the first trip. Stanton
also pointed out that Powell suppressed all mention of the second river
expedition in his famous report of 1875.
However, Stanton appears to have been piqued because Powell either
ignored or spoke disparagingly of his Colorado River expedition of 1889–90,
and hence cannot be considered entirely impartial. Moreover, in his journal
entry for Aug. 28, 1869, Bradley mentions no mutiny or bitterness, but simply
states: "Three men refused to go farther (two Howlands and Wm. Dunn)
and we had to let them take to the mountains. They left us with good feelings
though we deeply regret their loss for they are as fine fellows as I ever had
the good fortune to meet." (Darrah: "Bradley's Journal," p. 70.) Jack
Sumner is less helpful. His journal for Aug. 28 states: "O. G. Howland and
W. H. Dunn decided to abandon the outfit and try to reach settlements on the
head of the Virgin River." (Darrah: "J. C. Sumner's Journal," p. 122.) Both
of these are at variance with Stanton's account and tend to support Powell,

The plan was to line the boats down as far as possible in two stages, then to trust to the current for the rest. Bradley's boat went first and the line was slowly paid out to its limit, but the foaming, rushing river pulled him ahead and the boat swung like a battered pendulum at the end of the line. With all hope lost, Bradley reached for his knife to cut the line, but suddenly the stern post tore loose from the boat and it shot down the cataract. Calmly taking the stern oar, Bradley gave one, two, three strokes, turning the boat with the current, which shot him past the rocks and into the waves and foam. "Bradley is gone so it seems," wrote Powell, remembering his thought on the occasion,[1] but then out of the waves the craft emerged, and there stood Bradley on his half-submerged boat, waving his hat in triumph. Sumner and Powell ran along the cliff, while Walter Powell, Hawkins, and Hall tumbled into the remaining boat and in helter-skelter fashion, broadside and tumbling, they too ran the last great rapid of the Colorado.

Three days later they rounded a bend in the river and came upon some Mormons fishing. It was a father, his two grown sons, and an Indian boy, and they had been alerted by Mormon authorities to watch for debris and other telltale signs of Powell's expedition, which it was feared had perished somewhere on the river above. But Powell and his loyal men had survived and reached their destination at Callville. They had done what no other men had ever done before. They had dared the river and they had won, and in so doing they dispelled the last great mystery of the American West. But not without cost. As they sat on the shore of the Colorado at the little Mormon camp, restoring their worn-out bodies with delicious melons brought down by the people of St. Thomas, their companions of the river, Oramel Howland, his brother Seneca, and Bill Dunn, lay dead somewhere out on the Shivwits Plateau, felled from behind by Indian arrows.

6

Powell returned to civilization a hero. Newspapers all over the country carried accounts of his stirring voyage, and the death of

though the circumstances under which the entries were written are unknown. Because the journals were written at the time of the events and before any post-expedition recriminations arose, I have accepted the Bradley-Sumner journal versions and hence Powell's own version of the affair at Separation Rapids.

1. Powell: *Exploration*, p. 102.

the three unfortunate mountaineers served to heighten the story. In the fall and winter of 1869 the Major lectured all over the Midwest from Detroit, where he was reunited with his wife, to the Illinois towns where he had worked as a teacher. As he repeated his experiences before lyceum audiences, Powell gradually refined his ideas about the canyon country and improved his oratorical style until he became a polished performer. As his biographer, William Culp Darrah, has pointed out, Powell had a good deal more to say in the way of scientific generalizations about his voyage than most historians have been willing to admit.[2] However, compared to the later clarifications and precise definitions of his official report of 1875, his early impressions of the Plateau geology seem slight, though they contain some of the seeds of his later work. In Detroit he lectured on the concept of erosion, comparing the Colorado to the Mississippi and estimating that it had taken 60,000,000 years to make the present canyon passage. Then, as a reporter for the Detroit *Post* observed, "He dwelt at some length on the formation of lakes and streams at altitudes above the timberline and the clouds; also their influence on the surface as their streams washed down century after century. . . ."[3]

Almost immediately after returning, he was persuaded by Dr. William A. Bell to submit an account of his voyage to the Royal Geographical Society.[4] This became Powell's first written report, but it was not published by the Royal Society. It appeared as an appendix to Dr. Bell's popular book, *New Tracks in North America,* which also carried the story of James White's canyon trip.[5] In this account, too, Powell briefly alluded to the various processes of erosion, though he dwelt primarily on his adventurous experiences and descriptions of the scenery.[6] Likewise, his geological field notes which have survived appear to be more descriptive than conceptual, so that one must conclude that the precise ideas that Powell later advanced about the canyon country were perhaps present after his first voyage, but only dimly and imperfectly formed.[7] Moreover, he had little to bring back, and most of the astronomical data concerning the upper river had been lost in the massacre of Oramel

2. Darrah: "Geological Notes by Major Powell," *Utah Historical Quarterly;* Vol. XV (1947), pp. 132–3.
3. Quoted in Darrah: *Powell of the Colorado,* p. 147.
4. Dr. William A. Bell to Powell, London, Nov. 18, 1869, L.R., Powell Survey, R.G. 57, National Archives.
5. See Bell: *New Tracks,* p. 560.
6. Ibid.
7. Darrah: "Geological Notes," pp. 134–9.

Howland, for Powell had inadvertently given him both sets of notes on the first phase of the trip through July 2. Thus, it was already clear to the Major that another, more thorough study of the river and its canyons and plateaus would be necessary.

This time, however, when he went to Washington he was much better received, and Congress appropriated $10,000 for a "Geographical and Topographical Survey of the Colorado River of the West."[8] Out of this appropriation Powell received no salary, and he continued to hold his professorship at Illinois Normal, but at last he had formed a survey that was "official" and in some way comparable to the other great national surveys of the day. Taking his cue from King, whose operation he considered the best of its kind, Powell very early decided that his next explorations should not be just another river-plateau reconnaissance, but should be firmly based on an accurate topographical survey of the whole region. There was no other way to acquire a sense of geological order from the mass of fantastic shapes and complicated forms that had confronted him in the Plateau Province. The study of the techniques of topographical mapping involved long and difficult work for Powell and his men, but from the first the value of these efforts was never doubted, and topography even more than geology became basic to Powell's approach to the West for the rest of his long career.

7

In the late summer of 1870 Powell went West to begin preparations for a second expedition down the river. He arrived in Salt Lake City on August 20 with F. M. Bishop and Walter Graves, who were to act as topographers in the exploration of the plateaus north of the Grand Canyon. Powell had two chief objectives: to find a way to bring supplies down to the river so that he and his men would not have to face starvation as before; and to learn more precisely the fate of his lost men. Aided by Hamblin, he gained the confidence of the Shivwits and learned that they had killed his men by mistake, after confusing them with a party of prospectors who had killed one of their women.[9] In talking with the Shivwits, the Major be-

8. Darrah: *Powell of the Colorado*, pp. 152–3.
9. Paul Hyde Bailey: *Jacob Hamblin*, pp. 289–306; Powell: *Exploration*, pp. 106–32; Powell: "An Overland Trip to the Grand Canyon," *Scribner's Monthly*, Vol. X (Oct. 1875), pp. 659–78; Charles Kelly, ed.: "Capt. F. M. Bishop's Journal," *Utah Historical Quarterly*, Vol. XV (1947), pp. 159–62.

came fascinated with their culture and their legends. This represented a further heightening of that interest in ethnology that became Powell's prime interest in later life. He also developed, along with a sensitivity for their culture, a compassion for their wretched situation that deeply stirred him.

With Hamblin as his guide, Powell crossed the Shivwits Plateau, climbed Mt. Trumbull, from which he overlooked the whole canyon country, and then made a difficult descent due south via the Pa-ru-nu-weap and Mu-koon-tu-weap canyons of Zion to the banks of the Colorado in lower Grand Canyon. (See map, p. 518.) Then he returned to Kanab and began preparations for another expedition.[1] Again with Hamblin as leader, he headed due east to the Paria, where he located a good supply base for the coming year at what soon became Lee's Ferry. Then, crossing the Colorado in an improvised boat, Powell, Hamblin and their party moved on to what Powell called "the Ancient Province of Tusayan," or the Hopi Villages in northwestern Arizona.[2] Oriabi and its six sister villages had been familiar territory to Hamblin since he visited them twenty-two years before,[3] but to Powell they were endlessly fascinating. The scene of a disastrous Spanish defeat which the Indians still remembered in inscriptions, and visited by Lieutenant Ives in 1858,[4] they meant even more than that to Powell. They were the living successors to the mysterious structures which he had encountered in the canyon voyage and along the Vermilion Cliffs bordering the Paria and Kaibab plateaus.

Slowly an ethnological picture began to grow in his mind as he linked them with the Utes and Paiutes to the north and the ruins encountered by explorers to the east. On the basis of the Hopis' own legends, and their present-day conflicts with the Navaho and Apache, he reasoned that a great civilization had once existed in the valleys of the Colorado and its tributaries, but slowly, under the pressure of warlike northern invaders (the Athabascan Apache, for example), the town dwellers had retreated into mountain fortresses, where they struggled with the hostile environment for survival and gradually died out, or moved southward.[5] It was the beginning of Powell's matchless comprehension of Indian ethnol-

1. Bailey: *Jacob Hamblin*, pp. 289–306.
2. Ibid., pp. 317–18. Also see John Wesley Powell: "The Ancient Province of Tusayan," *Scribner's Monthly*, Vol. XI (1876), pp. 193–213.
3. Ibid., pp. 195–206.
4. See Chapter 9, p. 308.
5. Darrah: *Powell of the Colorado*, p. 158.

ogy, a subject which appealed to him far more than did geology. Almost immediately he became aware of its practical utility, for in early November he went with Hamblin to Fort Defiance, New Mexico, and helped conclude the first treaty between the nomadic Navahos and the Pueblo towns.[6] By the time he returned to Salt Lake City, Powell was quite ready, from all points of view, to launch his second river expedition and his comprehensive survey of the Plateau Region.

8

Realizing that the scientific results of his first river voyage were inadequate, Powell projected his second expedition on a much broader scale. He delegated problems of supply to Jacob Hamblin and the Mormon scouts, and much of the topographic work of the river survey to A. H. Thompson and F. M. Bishop, and he himself made only part of the river trip of 1871–72.[7] At intervals he crossed

6. *Ibid.*, pp. 158–9.

7. The most complete published narrative of Powell's second Colorado River expedition is Frederick Dellenbaugh: *A Canyon Voyage*, published by G. P. Putnam in 1908 and reprinted by the Yale University Press in 1926 and 1962. This was for a long time the only published account of the expedition, since Powell chose to ignore it in his official report of 1875. In 1939, however, J. Cecil Alter and Herbert E. Gregory edited the "Diary of Almon Harris Thompson" for the *Utah Historical Quarterly*, Vol. VII (1939), pp. 3–140. In 1947, William Culp Darrah and others began publishing the remaining primary materials relating to the second river trip of 1871–72. This series of publications has become the most important source of information concerning the trip. See Darrah: "Major Powell Prepares for a Second Expedition"; Ralph V. Chamberlin: "Francis Marion Bishop (1843–1933)"; Charles Kelly, ed.: "Capt. Francis Marion Bishop's Journal," and "Letters of Capt. F. M. Bishop to the Bloomington *Pantagraph*," in *Utah Historical Quarterly*, Vol. XV (1947), pp. 149–255. Also see "The Exploration of the Colorado River and the High Plateaus of Utah in 1871–72," *Utah Historical Quarterly*, Vols. XVI–XVII (1948–49), pp. 1–540, which contains biographical sketches of the members of the expedition and reprints the journals of Stephen Vandiver Jones, John F. Steward, W. C. Powell, W. C. Powell's description of the Hopi Towns, and three letters by Andrew Hall. E. O. Beaman's journal was published as "The Cañon of the Colorado, and the Moqui Pueblos" in seven installments, running from April 18, 1874, to May 30, 1874, in *Appleton's Journal*, Vol. XI (1874), pp. 481–4, 513–16, 545–8, 590–3, 623–6, 641–4, 686–9.

In addition, see the Frederick Dellenbaugh Papers, New York Public Library, for Dellenbaugh's manuscript Diary, and those of Almon Harris Thompson, Mrs. Almon Harris Thompson, and Stephen V. Jones, and a copy of the John F. Steward Diary originally presented to the Chicago Historical Society. The Walter C. Powell Diary is to be found in the museum at

and recrossed the Plateau Province between the Colorado and Salt Lake City, carefully studying the terrain, much of which was not visible from the depths of the river canyons. He also went to Washington to secure further aid for the Survey, and to purchase a house—symbol of his determination to hold and maintain what, after his resignation from Illinois Normal in early 1872, was to become a permanent government position.

Significantly, Powell's operations from 1871 to 1874 involved a much more informal relationship with the government than any of the other surveys. Through a clerical error, but perhaps too as a result of Powell's deliberate strategy, his survey was not at first under the control of the Interior Department. He was required to report only to the Smithsonian Institution.[8] In addition to saving him the tedious labor of clearing everything through essentially nonscientific channels, this also made him a special protégé of the professional and academic scientists, who, congregating around the Smithsonian, were fast coming to dominate official scientific activity in the West. These were important advantages for Powell, and he made good use of them for the next three years.

In many ways the expedition of 1871 was anticlimactic. Its itinerary was too complicated to make it dramatic, and as Wallace Stegner has astutely observed, its special glories really belong to the Major's second-in-command, A. H. Thompson.[9] As in the first expedition, Powell largely ignored the world of professional scientists in choosing his crew, and of the first group only Jack Sumner was asked to accompany the 1871 party.[1] Sumner was unable to do so, however, and so the personnel of the 1871 expedition was made up of relatively inexperienced nonprofessional friends and relatives.

Grand Canyon National Park. Another relevant source of information is the Robert Brewster Stanton Collection, also in the New York Public Library. This collection contains not only material from Stanton's Colorado River expedition of 1889–90, which is beyond the scope of the present book, but also the extensive material collected by Stanton as background for his book *Colorado River Controversies,* much of which bears directly on the Powell expedition, as discussed above, in footnote 9, pp. 550–1. The Still Pictures Section of the National Archives contains an extensive collection of the photographs taken on the expedition by Beaman and Hillers. Unless otherwise stated, my account is based on the above sources, and the excellent secondary works of Stegner, Darrah, and Bartlett already cited.

8. Darrah: *Powell of the Colorado,* p. 205.
9. Stegner: *Beyond the Hundredth Meridian,* pp. 136–45.
1. Darrah: *Powell of the Colorado,* p. 163.

It was in keeping with the practices of the day, when nepotism reached even into the office of the President, but it was hardly ideal for scientific purposes.

The most important member was Almon H. Thompson, who as the Major's brother-in-law had accompanied his first expedition in 1867. Thompson, a teacher of mathematics, was at the time superintendent of schools in Bloomington, Illinois. And though he was to become an expert topographer through hard experience in the field, at the outset he had no qualifications whatsoever, either as a draftsman or as a riverboat man. Assisting Thompson were Stephen Vandiver Jones, principal of the Washburn, Illinois, schools, and John F. Steward, a war veteran, inventor, and amateur student of geology whom the Major had met in the trenches at Vicksburg, where both had been searching for fossil-shell specimens. Still another academician was F. M. Bishop, once a Powell student and more recently a teacher at Illinois Normal. Bishop had accompanied Powell on the Plateau expeditions of 1870 and could thus be considered more experienced than most.[2]

Then, in imitation of Hayden and Wheeler, Powell included a photographer, E. O. Beaman, who had been recommended by the New York photographic supply firm of E. and H. T. Anthony Company.[3] Beaman was not the Major's first choice for the job, but at least he was a professional and had some experience in the field in the Middle West, so he was signed on. The artist of the expedition was Frederick Dellenbaugh, seventeen years old, and an able, enthusiastic youth who besides his brief art training in Paris had also his family relationship to A. H. Thompson to recommend him. Dellenbaugh, in the course of the 1871 expedition, painted the first pictures of the Grand Canyon and he likewise proved to be the most accomplished of Thompson's assistant topographers. For the rest of his life Dellenbaugh, who became a professional explorer and globetrotter, counted the 1871 canyon voyage as his most memorable experience, and his exciting book, *A Canyon Voyage*, was for a long time the only published account of the expedition.[4]

The other members of the party were Andrew Hattan, the cook; John K. Hillers, a teamster who eventually became the expedition's photographer; Frank Richardson, who deserted soon after the

2. Biographical data derived from *Utah Historical Quarterly*, Vols. XVI–XVII, cited in footnote 7, pp. 555–6.
3. Ibid.
4. Ibid.

group got underway; and Walter Clement Powell, the Major's first cousin.[5]

Later, out in Utah, two more men joined the party, James Fennemore, a photographer from Savage's Photography Studio in Salt Lake City, who replaced Beaman for a short time, and William Derby Johnson, a graduate of the University of Deseret, who along with Dellenbaugh came to serve as one of Thompson's topographic assistants.[6]

This then was the colorful party which assembled at Green River City in the spring of 1871 and climbed aboard the three new boats that the Major had had once again especially constructed. These boats, named the *Emma Dean*, the *Nellie Powell*, and the *Cañonita*, were decided improvements over the first vessels. They had the added advantage of a watertight compartment amidships, which increased dry-storage space, added buoyancy, and contributed to the broadside strength of the craft. At the last minute, the Major decided to lash a chair to the middle deck of his boat, the *Emma Dean*, and for most of the voyage there he sat, alternately staring intently down the river and reading aloud to his men from volumes of poetry which he carried along to relieve the monotony of the voyage.

On the twenty-second of May 1871, under a "brilliant sun" and a "sky of sapphire," as Dellenbaugh described it, the travelers packed the last of their gear into especially designed waterproof bags, waved goodbye to the little knot of well-wishers, and pushed out into the Green.[7] It was as if Lindbergh had taken off a second time alone in *The Spirit of St. Louis* for Paris—a daring second contest with fate, and as such it did not seem any the less dangerous to the men because it had been done before. "Read Jack Sumner's Journal . . ." wrote Walter Powell. "Tis enough to make one's hair stand on end."[8]

The itinerary of the trip is very difficult to follow (see map, p. 518). From May 22 to July 7, 1871, they coursed down the upper stretches of the Green from Flaming Canyon to the foot of Lodore. At this point Powell left the river party and headed overland, intending to meet them at the mouth of the Uinta, a rendezvous which he was unable to keep. After waiting at the Uinta [Duchesne]

5. Ibid.
6. Ibid.
7. Dellenbaugh: *A Canyon Voyage*, p. 9.
8. *Utah Historical Quarterly*, Vols. XVI–XVII (1948–49), pp. 259–60.

for twenty-two days, from July 14 to August 5, the river party, with Thompson in command, pushed off downstream and reached Gunnison's Crossing on August 29, at which time they were reunited with Powell.[9] The Major accompanied the river survey as far as the Crossing of the Fathers, which they reached on October 10, and then he again departed on a survey of the surrounding Plateau country, which took him as far as Kanab. There he established a base camp for the winter phase of the operation. The river men ran Glen Canyon and reached Lee's Ferry at the mouth of the Paria on October 23. No great disaster had occurred, but they had all had their fill of river travel. For several weeks the prospect of starvation had faced them, until Pardyn Dodds of the Ute Agency showed up at the Crossing of the Fathers with supplies, and even then they were reduced to wearing rags and battered shoes which afforded no protection from either sun or rocks. Jones had suffered a badly wrenched leg. Hillers was bitten by a scorpion; Bishop and Steward began to feel their old war wounds; and the *Cañonita* had been abandoned up north at the desolate mouth of the Dirty Devil. All told, it had not been an easy trip, and they were glad to leave the river at this point.

By December they had all settled into camp near Kanab and begun the serious work of topography.[1] The first task was laying out the nine-mile base line along the earth's surface from which the primary triangulation could be conducted. Then the surveyors split up into teams which ranged over the Kaibab Plateau and extended as far west as Hurricane Mesa. At this time Powell conducted his exploration of present-day Zion National Park, which he described in his official report as having taken place not in 1872, but as part of his trek of 1870.[2] It seems clear that he predated this exploration to heighten the romanticism of the *Scribner's* magazine articles on which the report was based. It is also quite possible that he wished to appear to have anticipated Wheeler's parties which had entered the region in 1871 while conducting their abortive ascent of the Colorado River.[3]

In February, Powell left for Washington after securing Thompson's agreement that he would work through to spring with or

9. Alter and Gregory: "Diary of Almon Harris Thompson," pp. 25, 27–31, 41–2.
1. Dellenbaugh: *A Canyon Voyage*, p. 165.
2. Stegner: *Beyond the Hundredth Meridian*, pp. 148–9.
3. See Chapter 13, pp. 475–6. Also Stegner: *Beyond the Hundredth Meridian*, p. 149.

without pay.[4] With the Major gone, the men worked on as usual, except that Steward was forced to retire due to pain from his war wounds, and E. O. Beaman resigned to conduct his own independent expedition south across the Colorado to Oriabi.[5] No one knew quite what the Major's plans were, and Thompson's correspondence with his chief indicates that he, too, was not a full party to Powell's considerations.[6] Much of Thompson's time seems to have been taken up with the training of a new photographer. Fennemore proved to be an indifferent hand. Walter Powell had failed miserably as Beaman's assistant and then had grown extremely jealous when Jack Hillers emerged as an outstanding practitioner of the wet-plate trade.[7]

By the end of May 1872 Thompson and his men had completed a preliminary map of the Grand Canyon region, and the Professor, as he was called, set off on an overland march of his own (see map, p. 518). Taking Dellenbaugh and several other men, he made a reconnaissance north from Kanab past the White Cliffs and Kaiparowits Peak into Potato Valley, in search of the Dirty Devil River. At this point they discovered a new river, the Escalante, the last unknown river in the United States. Then they moved on, north and east across the Aquarius Plateau and around the Henry Mountains, which they also discovered, to Crescent Wash near the mouth of the Dirty Devil. There they reclaimed the *Cañonita,* and Dellenbaugh, Hillers, Johnson, and Fennemore rode the boat downstream to Lee's Ferry while Thompson retraced his steps back across the mountains and plateaus to Kanab.[8]

Although Thompson's exploration received little publicity in Powell's report, it was one of the most important conducted in the course of Powell's survey. Besides ranging over much unknown country, and underscoring its agricultural possibilities, Thompson

4. Stegner: *Beyond the Hundredth Meridian,* p. 139. See also J. Cecil Alter and Herbert E. Gregory: "The Diary of Almon Harris Thompson," p. 63. Powell made the agreement with Thompson regarding pay on Tuesday, Dec. 12, 1871.

5. Stegner: *Beyond the Hundredth Meridian,* p. 140; Alter and Gregory: "The Diary of Almon Harris Thompson," p. 67. See also E. O. Beaman: "The Cañon of the Colorado, and the Moquis Pueblos," *Appleton's Journal,* Vol. XI (May 2, 1874), p. 548.

6. See A. H. Thompson to Powell, Kanab, Feb. 7, 1872; Feb. 8, 1872; Winsor, A.T., March 11, 1872, L.R., Powell Survey, R.G. 57, National Archives. Also see Darrah: *Powell of the Colorado,* p. 180.

7. See letters cited in the preceding footnote. Also see Darrah: *Powell of the Colorado,* p. 173.

8. Dellenbaugh: *A Canyon Voyage,* pp. 195–214.

had laid the groundwork of data for the later geological studies of Clarence Dutton on the High Plateaus of Utah, and Grove Karl Gilbert's monumental *Geology of the Henry Mountains*.

Dellenbaugh and the others waited at Lee's Ferry for several weeks, observing the fanatical leader and his family hard at work in Lonely Dell. They did what they could to help him and wondered secretly if it were possible that this mild-mannered old man had engineered the notorious Mountain Meadows massacre of westbound Missouri emigrants.[9] By August 17 the whole party, with the exception of Bishop and Beaman, was assembled at Lee's Ferry. Powell, Dellenbaugh, Walter Clement Powell, Jones, Hutton, Hillers, and Thompson then started down the river through dreaded Marble Canyon. The water was much higher in the summer of 1872 and the traveling was exceedingly difficult. The boats moved so fast that it sometimes became impossible to control them. At least once the Major was heard to utter: "By God, boys, we're gone," as the boats plunged down the foaming cataracts.[1] On another occasion Hillers almost drowned in a raging whirlpool, and but for his life preserver Powell would have perished in the same treacherous vortex. When on September 7 they reached Kanab Canyon, where Jacob Hamblin was waiting for them, Powell decided that they had explored the river far enough, and the second canyon voyage was officially ended. Though the data on the lower stretches of the Grand Canyon was extremely meager, due to his harrowing experiences in this region in 1869, Powell decided to rely on Ives's map as far as Diamond Creek, and on his own notes and whatever could be gained from a land survey.[2] It was the only time in his life that Powell backed off from a challenge, but in this instance it probably saved the lives of all of his men and with them the future of the Powell Survey. From the advantage of hindsight, it was a wise decision.

From September to December of 1872 Powell and his men reexplored the Shivwits Plateau, mapping the lower canyons by land, and then at the end of the year they returned to Kanab to finish Thompson's map. On February 16, 1873, Dellenbaugh, after a difficult trek through the wintry snows of central Utah, arrived in Salt Lake City with the completed map encased in a homemade tin tube.[3] It was forwarded on to Washington, where Powell was al-

9. Ibid., pp. 210–14.
1. Ibid., pp. 215–41. The quote appears on page 221.
2. Ibid., pp. 242–3.
3. Ibid., pp. 250–9, 262–7.

ready hard at work promoting further appropriations for his now famous survey.

9

The significance of Powell's exploration of the Colorado and the plateaus and mountains of Utah went far beyond mere adventure into the unknown. Not only had he and his men conquered the long mysterious river and discovered the last unknown river (the Escalante) and mountain range (the Henry) in the continental United States;[4] they had also made their work meaningful in every conceivable way by focusing upon particular problems of social and scientific significance. As Powell himself remarked in 1874: "Exploring expeditions are no longer needed for general purposes."[5] In contrast to his rivals in the West, he confined his activities to those subjects that interested him. Taking his cue from Clarence King, Powell quickly grasped the fact that no survey of the country was really valuable unless it was based on accurate topography, and Thompson's maps became the keystone of his enterprise. Thus, in contrast to Hayden, who realized the importance of topography much later, Powell saw the complex canyon and plateau country in an orderly fashion. Facts were clearly related, the land and its features laid out in a rational manner before him, and one generalization led in a logical sequence to another.

Unlike the other survey operations, Powell did not attempt to cover all fields of knowledge. He all but ignored botany and zoology except as they related to his main interests in geology and ethnology. He made no attempt, moreover, to survey mining regions, to experiment in metallurgy or chemistry, or to contribute practical data to eager businessmen. Powell remained a scientist with a remarkably clear view of the single, central problem that lay behind all his study of the West, namely the problem presented by the environment to people who wished to settle in the West and make use of it. Adaptation, a good Darwinian word, was the key to most of his thought, and unlike many of his contemporaries, he learned from the people who had already experienced the problems of the West, particularly the Mormons and the Indians. A central theme

4. This has been pointed out by Wallace Stegner, editor of *The Exploration of the Colorado River* (Chicago, Ill.: University of Chicago Press; 1957), p. xiii.
5. Powell to Secretary of the Interior, April 24, 1874, in George M. Wheeler: *Notes Relating to Surveys in the Western Territories of the United States* (n.p., n.d.), Yale Western Americana Collection.

runs through all of his thought: institutions and techniques devised in what he called the humid Eastern sections of the United States could not be successfully transplanted to the new and challenging Western environment. His mission, as he saw it, was to describe accurately the new environment and point up its lessons for the onrushing tide of civilization. It was a pedagogical mission, appropriately enough, and as civilization and its spokesmen gradually invested the West, it ultimately became a reforming mission.

Building on Thompson's maps and his own extensive explorations in the field as the Powell Survey continued from 1871 to 1879, the Major produced two important works of geology: the second half of his *Exploration of the Colorado River of the West* (1875), and the *Report on the Geology of the Eastern Portion of the Uinta Mountains* (1876). Despite dry-sounding, academic titles, these are two of the most exciting Western books ever written and formed the basis for the development of an altogether new approach to geology. Here paleontology, which had preoccupied most of the other scientific explorers in the West, was passed over in favor of structural geology and, most important of all, an examination on a grand scale of the vast earth-shaping processes that produced the canyon and plateau country. A confirmed uniformitarian, Powell was less interested in the geological past as reconstructed and "philosophical" history than he was in what could be learned for the present and the future from a study of the processes of change that had shaped the past. It was a subtle but important distinction that permeated every page of his geological writing.

Both of his geological books are in the realm of descriptive geology, but out of the multitude of his scientific experiences of the Western landforms, he devised a series of basic definitions that have stood the test of time. The most important of these are the concepts of base level of erosion, which is the lowest point of erosion in the region and the level toward which the streams and rivers are trending; antecedent valleys, or valleys carved in periods prior to the present erosion system; and consequent valleys, or those carved in more recent times after a period of uplifting and folding. Like the good teacher that he was, Powell whenever he could devised precise terms that defined and clarified the phenomena he was describing. Transverse valleys, longitudinal valleys, and their variations such as diaclinal, cataclinal and monoclinal valleys, are some of the precise terms applied by the Major to landforms that had appeared merely picturesque to other scientific explorers.[6]

6. See Powell: *Exploration*, p. 160.

And, with his definitions and diagrams in mind, he was able to reconstruct the process that created the Plateau Province in spectacular fashion. Most famous was his description of the relationship of the Colorado River to the Uinta Mountains.

> Again, the question returns to us, why did not the stream turn round this great obstruction, rather than pass through it? The answer is that the river had the right of way; in other words it was running ere the mountains were formed; not before the rocks of which the mountains are composed, were deposited, but before the formations were folded, so as to make a mountain range.
>
> The contracting or shriveling of the earth causes the rocks near the surface to wrinkle, or fold, and such a fold was started athwart the course of the river. Had it been suddenly formed, it would have been an obstruction sufficient to turn the water in a new course to the east, beyond the extension of the wrinkle; but emergence of the fold above the general surface of the country was little or no faster than the progress of the corrasion of the channel. We may say, then, that the river did not cut its way *down* through the mountains, from a height of many thousand feet above its present site, but, having an elevation differing but little, perhaps, from what it now has, as the fold was lifted, it cleared away the obstruction by cutting a cañon, and the walls were thus elevated on either side. The river preserved its level, but mountains were lifted up; as the saw revolves on a fixed pivot, while the log through which it cuts is moved along. The river was the saw which cut the mountains in two.[7]

7. Ibid., pp. 152–3. For a modern interpretation of the geologic history of the Colorado Plateau country, see Charles B. Hunt: *Cenozoic Geology of the Colorado Plateau,* Geological Survey Professional Paper 279 (Washington, D.C.: U. S. Government Printing Office; 1956). Hunt is in general agreement with the Powell thesis that the Colorado River was antecedent to the main uplifting of the plateau, though he sees the situation as being more complex. He substitutes the concept "anteposition," which "refers to the arching of a canyon so that a stream becomes ponded and deposits sediment upstream from the arch. When downcutting is resumed, a new superposed course is developed in the stretch represented by the reservoir. But the low point on the rim of the reservoir is the raised portion of the old valley; this becomes the new spillway and downstream from this point the new valley has the aspects of antecedence" (p. 1). See also pp. 73–87, in which Hunt develops this thesis more extensively and presents a diagrammatic history of the Colorado Plateau. By demonstrating that the various canyons of the Colorado are of different ages, Hunt appears to have modified Powell's "log and saw"

It is instructive to compare this clearly reasoned uniformitarian description with Clarence King's poetic and spectacular generalizations about nature's grand catastrophes in the Rocky Mountains, or Josiah Dwight Whitney's persistent refusal to admit that the Yosemite was not formed one day, eons of years ago, when the valley floor suddenly collapsed and fell several thousand feet. King and Whitney, however, ran counter to most geologic thinking of the day, which in 1870 was predominantly uniformitarian, and it is misleading to magnify Powell's work, as some writers have done, by using this contrast to make his theories seem more revolutionary than they really were.[8] Powell's great strength was the masterful clarity and precision of his descriptions of earth processes which had been taken for granted for some time by less perceptive geologists. Patiently and simply he explained uplift, synclinal and anticlinal folding, faults, lateral displacement, and cliff erosion until they almost seemed to be his own concepts, though all these phenomena had been observed and described by others. Uniformitarianism itself seemed almost his own invention. Hear him now instructing his public:

> Thus it is that the study of the structural characteristics of the valleys and cañons teaches us, in no obscure way, the relation between the progress of upheaval and that of erosion and corrasion, showing that these latter were *pari passu* with the former, and that the agencies of nature produce great results—results no less than the carving of a mountain range out of a much larger block lifted from beneath the sea; not by an extravagant and violent use of power, but by the slow agencies which may be observed generally throughout the world, still acting in the same slow, patient manner.[9]

Or climb with him to the cliff at the end of Labyrinth Canyon "and look over the plain below, and you see vast numbers of buttes scattered about over scores of miles, and every butte so regular and beautiful that you can hardly cast aside the belief that they are works of Titanic art. . . . But no human hand has placed a

---

concept in the direction of Newberry's earlier view that the river was ponded and spilled over obstacles in its path, creating the canyons. See Chapter 9, p. 319, of the present work.

8. See, for example, Darrah: *Powell of the Colorado*, p. 217; Stegner: *Beyond the Hundredth Meridian*, p. 118.

9. Powell: *Exploration*, p. 162.

block in all those wonderful structures. The rain drops of un-
reckoned ages have cut them all from solid rock."[1]

It was no wonder that, with his maps and colorful diagrams, or
even with a blackboard and a piece of chalk, the Major made an
irresistible teacher, one who could sway lyceum audiences and
congressional committees alike. He was a scientist of brilliant lucidity with the imagination of a conjurer. When his first major
report was published in 1875, it sold out immediately.

10

As the Powell Survey continued through the seventies, other
able geologists joined his staff. In 1873 the Major succeeded in
winning Grove Karl Gilbert away from Wheeler's survey—an act
for which Wheeler harbored bitter resentment, though he continually proclaimed that his venture was not a geological one.[2] Gilbert, like Powell and Hayden, was a product of local scientific
training and apprenticeship.[3] He graduated from the University
of Rochester, worked for a time in Ward's Natural History Establishment, which furnished specimens for school laboratories, and
then joined the State Geological Survey of Ohio, under John Strong
Newberry. Due to the influence of Archibald Marvine, he secured a
place with Wheeler's survey in 1871 and accompanied the army
explorer across the West from Death Valley to the canyons of the
Colorado. Gilbert's great work on ancient Lake Bonneville, as previously mentioned, began as a monograph publication of Wheeler's
survey. But by 1873 Gilbert had felt the restriction of army discipline and army command and, perhaps chafing a bit under the
leadership of young Wheeler, resigned to join Powell.

As chief geologic assistant to Powell, he published his classic
book *The Geology of the Henry Mountains* in 1877. The Henry
Mountains project had originally grown out of Thompson's discovery in 1872, but Gilbert soon made it his own. In the Henrys
assisted by William H. Holmes, he formulated the laccolith or dome
principle, which proposes that the mountains were created by a

1. Ibid., p. 174.
2. Wheeler to G. K. Gilbert, Washington, D.C., June 7, 1874, L.S., Wheeler
Survey, R.G. 77, National Archives.
3. See Stegner: *Beyond the Hundredth Meridian*, pp. 155–8; and William
M. Davis: "Biographical Memoir of Grove Karl Gilbert, 1843–1918," National
Academy of Science *Biographical Memoirs*, Vol. XXI (1927)

huge bubble of lava that did not come to the surface but instead bowed up the layers of rock above it into a gigantic dome or laccolith. This was an entirely new theory of mountain-making.

In 1880 came Gilbert's final treatise on Lake Bonneville, published by the United States Geological Survey under Powell's direction. But before that he made important contributions to the study of erosion, rainfall, and the measurement of the lake beds in Utah.[4] These were practical contributions that called for great ingenuity in devising schemes to measure river flow and lake-bed expansion and in the construction of workable rain gauges. More than anyone else, Gilbert followed in the direct line of Powell's environmentalism.

Another of Powell's important assistants who kept the Survey work going while the Major was in Washington was, paradoxically, an army man, Captain Clarence Dutton. Dutton was a Yale graduate and of the same school and type as Clarence King, who graduated two years later.[5] He was in the same class as the powerful O. C. Marsh—a factor which aided Powell in the struggle over the consolidation of the geologic surveys in 1879. Dutton, an obscure and forgotten figure on the Yale campus today, was one of the school's many prominent nineteenth-century scientists. He stayed in the Army after the Civil War and found himself stationed at the Watervliet Arsenal in West Troy, New York, with a great deal of time on his hands, whereupon he began studying the new Bessemer steel process. Occasionally he published a paper on the subject, and conversed with James Hall of Albany, who had already promoted so many scientific careers. By 1871 Dutton had been transferred to Washington and in the meetings of the local philosophical society met most of the prominent Washington scientists of the day. In 1874 Powell offered him a place on his survey, and with Joseph Henry's help a special act of Congress was passed assigning Dutton to the Survey staff on detached duty. He remained with the Major for fifteen years.

Dutton was a scientist, but like King, he had a bent for artistic expression that made his reports read like poetic travelogues. He was an artist with words whose sensitivity for nature rivaled that

4. Ibid. See also the chapters by Gilbert in Powell: *Report on the Lands of the Arid Region of the United States*: Chapters IV, "Water Supply," and VII, "Irrigable Lands of the Salt Lake Drainage System."
5. See biographical sketch in Stegner: *Beyond the Hundredth Meridian*, pp. 158–74. Also see George F. Becker: "Obituary of Major C. E. Dutton," *American Journal of Science*, fourth series, Vol. XXXIII. No. 196 (April 1912), pp. 387–8.

of the best painters of the day, and his work could be compared, as Wallace Stegner has compared it, only with the spectacular landscape diagrams of William H. Holmes.[6] The two men, who later worked together on Dutton's major work, *The Tertiary History of the Grand Canyon District*, developed superb accuracy in noting the features of the land. In Dutton's case this took the form of romantic word pictures, and in Holmes's it resulted in panoramas of canyon and mesa (see pp. 336–9 in Portfolio II).

Dutton's chief books were the *Tertiary History of the Grand Canyon District* (1882) and *The High Plateaus of Utah* (1880). The 1880 work was a detailed study that filled in the earlier observations of Powell and extended them into the beautiful park-like region that rises above the canyon country as a capstone to the Plateau Province. Dutton was also interested in technical problems. He wrestled for a time with the theory of isostasy, the idea that as the ocean floors sank under a load of sediment the land masses gradually rose and bent or cracked, causing displacement of the kind observed in the Plateau Province. He also studied vulcanism, traveling over much of the world observing lavas and comparative volcanic action, and in passing he made a study of the Charleston earthquake of 1884.[7] No one since Richthofen, with his ideas of the sequence of lava flows, had contributed so much to the study of vulcanism as Dutton. Moreover, by the end of Dutton's career, he had even improved on the great Richthofen, whom King and Whitney had so admired.

Gilbert and Dutton, like Thompson, were only two of the many scientists Powell helped to train in the course of his surveys. They were, however, characteristic of the many leaders of science who derived from their relationship with Powell a greater enthusiasm for science and an enhanced understanding of its meaning for man.

11

In keeping with his fundamental utilitarian and environmental approach to the West, Powell also extended his studies to the science of man. Inspired by the ancient ruins along the Colorado

6. Ibid.
7. Ibid. The Western photographer Jack Hillers accompanied Dutton to Charleston in 1884 and made some of his most spectacular photographs of the earthquake and its aftermath. See Hillers: Photograph Collection, Still Pictures Section, National Archives.

which he had observed on his canyon voyages, and by the pathetic and yet exotic tribes he had encountered in the Plateau Province—Paiutes, Shivwits, Unikarits, Utes, and Mokis—Powell very early began serious researches into Indian ethnology. From the beginning he had a way with Indians, a tolerance for their way of life and a respect for their customs. He disdained the use of military escorts as he traveled through the Indian country, and on numerous occasions blamed much of the difficulty with the redmen on the threatening presence of military garrisons in their territory.[8] Rather than mistrusting the Indians, he learned all he could about them, as on his 1870 excursion among the hostile Shivwits who had murdered the Howlands and Bill Dunn. On that occasion he succeeded in persuading the Shivwits to trust him, so much so that they explained their mythology and their carefully guarded tribal lore to him.

Vocabularies were the Major's constant interest, and under his direction over 200 such word lists were compiled. Powell himself became fluent in most of the primitive plateau languages. One of his most significant works was the *Introduction to the Study of Indian Languages*, which he published in 1877 after consultation with Professor William Dwight Whitney of Yale, the foremost scientific philologist of his time.[9] It was a manual, for the use of field ethnologists, which standardized the procedure for collecting tribal vocabularies.

So familiar with the problems of the plateau Indian was Powell that in 1873, along with G. W. Ingalls, he was appointed a special commissioner to investigate the conditions of these tribes and to make recommendations concerning their fate. In the summer of that year, the Major journeyed to Utah in company with the painter Thomas Moran, and for several months crossed and recrossed the plateaus and mountains, studying the tribes and investigating white claims of Indian depredations. In August, a huge council was held in Salt Lake City in which most of the depressed tribes agreed to move to reservations if they could be secured from the government.[1]

8. See J. W. Powell's testimony before the Townsend Committee on May 18, 1874, in Wheeler: *Notes Relating to Surveys in the Western Territory of the United States*, p. 52. This document is actually 43rd Cong., 1st sess., *H.R. Doc. 612* (1874), p. 52.

9. John Wesley Powell: *Introduction to the Study of Indian Languages* (Washington, D.C.: U. S. Government Printing Office; 1877).

1. See J. W. Powell and G. W. Ingalls: *Report on the Conditions of the Ute Indians of Utah; the Pai-Utes of Utah, Northern Arizona, Southern Nevada, and Southeastern California; the Go-Si-Utes of Utah and Nevada; the North-*

Powell went to Washington, his reformer's spirit thoroughly aroused, to report in person the scandalous and fraudulent treatment the Indians had received at the hands of the various Rocky Mountain agents. This was the beginning of a continuous series of investigations which eventually culminated in the Marsh exposé of 1875 and the resignation of Secretary of Interior Columbus Delano.

The report on the tribes which Powell and Ingalls issued in 1874 was one of the most constructive studies ever made on the Indian problem. Firmly convinced that a policy of military policing was wrong, Powell advocated moving the tribes to selected reservation sites which, as he said, should not be "looked upon in the light of a pen where a horde of savages are to be fed with flour and beef, to be supplied with blankets from the Government bounty, and to be furnished with paint and gew-gaws by the greed of the traders, but that a reservation should be a school of industry and a home for these unfortunate people."[2]

Within this simple statement, Powell incorporated a key concept which it is now apparent that imperial powers of the nineteenth century largely overlooked, and that was the idea that the country owed more to its primitive subjects than simple subsistence. It owed them the means of education whereby they might, if they chose, better their lot, and bring themselves into closer parity with the rest of the country. Along these lines, Powell advocated an eight-point program for the reservation:

1. All bounties should be used to induce work.
2. The Indian should not be supplied with ready-made clothing, but the materials to make their own garments.
3. They should not be furnished with tents as it encouraged their nomadic way of life.
4. Each family should be supplied with a cow, on the theory that property ownership, however limited, breeds respect for the property of others.
5. The reservation farms should be irrigated, and expert farmers sent to teach the Indian husbandman.
6. Each reservation should have a blacksmith, carpenter, and saddle- and harness-maker, and each should employ several Indian

western Shoshones of Idaho and Utah; and the Western Shoshones of Nevada (Washington, D.C.: U. S. Government Printing Office; 1874). See also Darrah: Powell of the Colorado, pp. 194–204.
2. Powell and Ingalls: Report on Conditions of the Ute Indians of Utah. . . . , p. 23.

apprentices and should consider it an important duty to instruct
them.

7. Each reservation should have an efficient medical department.
8. Schools should be established and the English language taught
to all pupils as a means of breaking the tribal culture and conveying some understanding of the white man's ways.[3]

The Major's approach to the Indian problem is a recognizable
version of the nineteenth-century position that the primitive cultures should somehow be civilized, or "Americanized," and as part
of this process they should become self-reliant. Powell's plan was a
sophisticated and responsible version of the Protestant work ethic
and as such fitted the Indian cultures into a traditional framework.
In later years Powell became friendly with the ethnologist Lewis
Henry Morgan and almost totally absorbed his thesis, expressed
in the classic *Ancient Society* (1877), that all peoples evolved
through successive stages of savagery, barbarism, and civilization.
Powell incorporated this Darwinian point of view into the methods
and approaches used by the Bureau of Ethnology, which he established in 1879. He even appropriated Morgan's very terms, using
them in his public lectures on Indians, but he added a final stage
which he called "enlightenment," or the rationally governed scientific society.[4] At this point he was not far in advance of a contemporary European theorist who also used Morgan's ideas to formulate
a concept of inevitable evolution to the perfect society of scientific
socialism, Friedrich Engels.[5]

3. Ibid., pp. 24–5.
4. See, for example, Powell: "From Savagery to Barbarism," *Transactions
of the Anthropological Society of Washington*, Vol. III (1895), pp. 173–96;
and "From Barbarism to Civilization," *American Anthropologist*, Vol. I
(1888), pp. 97–123; Powell: "Mythologic Philosophy," *Popular Science
Monthly*, Vol. XV (1879), pp. 795–808, and Vol. XVI (1880), pp. 56–66.
For his appreciation of Lewis Henry Morgan, see Powell: "Sketch of Lewis
H. Morgan, President of the American Association for the Advancement of
Science," *Popular Science Monthly*, Vol. XVIII (1881), pp. 114–21. On May
25, 1877, Powell wrote to Morgan: "After reading your book, I believe you
have discovered the true system of social and governmental organization
among the Indians." Quoted in Bernhard J. Stern: *Lewis Henry Morgan:
Social Evolutionist* (Chicago: University of Chicago Press; 1931), p. 194.
5. Carl Resek: *Lewis Henry Morgan: American Scholar* (Chicago: University
of Chicago Press; 1960), pp. 160–2. In 1884 Friedrich Engels published *The
Origin of the Family, Private Property and the State*, with the subtitle "In
the Light of the Researches of Lewis Henry Morgan." In it he declared that
"Morgan in his own way had discovered afresh in America the materialistic
conception of history discovered by Marx forty years ago, and in his comparison of barbarism and civilization it had led him, in the main points, to

12

Powell was also concerned for the future of white settlement in the lands of the arid West. As early as 1873, in his annual report on the Surveys of the Plateau Province, Powell stressed the extreme aridity of the region and the necessity for some sort of rational land-classification system.[6] Then in 1878, as part of his campaign for the consolidation of the various government surveys and land-office projects under one responsible civilian authority, Powell published his most famous work, the *Report on the Lands of the Arid Regions of the United States.*[7] It was the first modern treatise on political reform as it related to the Far West. In it he pointed up a reality that was fast being obscured by the boomers and boosters of the West, namely that much of the West was unsuitable for settlement and farming along the patterns devised in the comparatively humid East. Two fifths of the United States was, in fact, arid. What was needed was a scientific and environmental approach to the West and its resources. First the country must be mapped, and the lands classified as mineral lands, coal lands, pasturage lands, timber lands, and irrigable lands. Then Powell proposed two new land laws which would organize irrigation districts and pasturage districts. As stated, the bills involved a sweeping change of the existing land laws. No longer would the traditional Land Office grid pattern with its 160-acre farms be mechanically laid down across the West. Instead settlement would be in irrigation districts similar to the Mormon colonies Powell had observed in Utah. The unit of each irrigated farm would be, not 160 acres, but 80, and all water rights would inhere in the land. Groups of farmers would be encouraged to come together to form irrigation cooperatives, thereby sharing the enormous expense of the required dams, flumes, and ditches. They would be governed democratically and, if possible, locally, in the public interest.

Grazing, he further proposed, should be organized in units of 2,500 acres, 20 acres of which might be irrigated farmland to be

---

the same conclusions as Marx." (Quoted in Resek: *Lewis Henry Morgan*, p. 161.)

6. Powell: *Report of Explorations in 1873 of the Colorado River of the West and Its Tributaries, Under the Direction of the Smithsonian Institution* (Washington, D.C.: U. S. Government Printing Office; 1874), p. 14.

7. Powell: *Report on the Lands of the Arid Regions of the United States,* second edition (Washington, D.C.: U. S. Government Printing Office; 1879). The material that follows represents an analysis of this document.

used for growing winter hay and various necessities. Again all water rights would inhere in the land, and the cattlemen were encouraged to cooperate in forming grazing districts of adjoining and unfenced land.

These proposals, the capstone of Powell's years of work as a Western explorer, were designed to prevent a number of evils which he had observed in the West. Principal among these was the monopoly of water rights, which according to traditional settlement patterns and Anglo-Saxon law was perfectly possible under present conditions in the West. At first, individuals settled on the streams and water holes and dammed up the flow for their own use. Then, because of the expense involved, water companies were formed, and using loopholes in the Timber Culture Act of 1873 and the Desert Land Act of 1877, they were able to get monopolies on much of the available water in the West. They could waste it, use it for hydraulic mining, sell it to the highest bidder, or use it to force the settlers out of a given region. With irrigation districts, and water rights inhering in the land, in Powell's view, this was not likely to happen.

In addition he attacked the Public Land Office Surveys for employing the contract system of surveying, in which an individual was employed as a surveyor and paid according to the amount of territory surveyed. This led, he asserted, to inefficiency and, even worse, to further corruption and dishonesty.[8] Surveyors could survey people off their lands, redistrict territory in such a way as to cut off water, and alter claims to favor the highest bidder. The corrupt surveyor in the employ of a land ring was a prominent figure in the West. And, though Powell barely alluded to it, surveyorships, with their rich rewards, were among the most prominent forms of political patronage in the West. If an honest and responsible federal authority could be established to carry on this work, it followed that important reforms would be effected.

Powell's arid-lands report was one of the most important books ever to come out of the West. It focused on basic regional problems and, what was more unusual, provided creative answers. Although it was commonly held to be original in pointing up the problems of the arid region, however, it was hardly so, nor was it the all-encompassing bible that many made it out to be. As this study has indicated, as far back as Lieutenant Emory's march to the Pacific with Kearny in 1846, men had speculated on the new settlement

8. Ibid. See especially Chapter II.

patterns needed for the West. Lieutenant Wheeler had pointed up the problem of irrigation and water control, as had General William B. Hazen in his pamphlet debate with Custer in 1873. Even Cyrus Thomas, often blamed for the "rain-follows-the-plow" theory, devoted many pages of his reports for the Hayden Survey to a consideration of land classification, irrigation, and water-rights control. He even carried the question into an area Powell largely ignored, timber conservation.[9] The Major himself observed that mining camps, with their rudely established common law and common water rights, provided a model of what he had in mind.[1] And, as one writer has recently pointed out, the Texas Republic from the beginning based its laws on the Spanish colonial approach to the arid lands, and provided for homestead units of 4,470 acres. In 1880 the remaining public domain was divided into agriculture, grazing, and forest lands.[2] It is thus not so much because of the originality of the ideas that the arid-lands report is important, but rather because of its broad comprehension of the problems involved, the precision and clarity with which they were outlined and defined, and the fundamental sense of organization and rationality which Powell brought to the problems and to their possible solutions. As stated in Powell's report with brilliant lucidity, the program of irrigation districts, grazing districts, dams, reservoirs, and mountain catch basins, provided a clear blueprint for the next hundred years, and one whose details, even with the vast programs of the Reclamation Service, and the New Deal, have not yet been fully realized.

Despite its importance, and its fundamental rationality, however, Powell's report was not well received by Westerners. It was at the time, and has been since, a program which appealed primarily to Easterners, though there were many exceptions in that day and later. Essentially, it ran counter to what Professor Henry Nash Smith has outlined as the myth of the yeoman farmer.[3] To many small Western farmers it seemed to close much of the public domain to opportunity, particularly if one had to wait for government land classification before taking possession of one's fee-simple prop-

9. See Chapter 14, p. 509.
1. Powell: *Report on the Lands of the Arid Regions of the United States,* Chapter II.
2. Wallace Stegner, ed.: *Powell Report on the Lands of the Arid Regions of the United States* (Cambridge, Mass.: Harvard University Press; 1962), p. 33 n. See also Walter P. Webb: *The Great Plains,* pp. 426–7.
3. Smith: *Virgin Land, passim.*

erties. To others it seemed to favor the large cattlemen, giving them more land, water titles, and allowing them to coalesce in powerful grazing groups that kept settlers out of their particular valley.[4] Then, too, some asked to what extent reorganization would be involved? Would someone in Washington decide to move them off their land, like destitute Indian tribes, because the area was not "irrigable" and "suitable only for grazing"?[5] And how was a man to start as a small rancher and work up to 2,500 acres if he didn't begin with a few cows and a farm?

There were some, seduced by the temporary wet cycles of the seventies, and others who were successful dry farmers, who disputed the Major's data and asserted that experience was more important than Washington science.[6] Many of the middle class felt, and with a measure of truth, that Powell had overemphasized the agricultural aspects of Western life, and that in so doing he had discouraged all settlement. It must be admitted that Powell, with his farm background, had largely overlooked the mining and mercantile and timber frontiers, and had stressed the theory of division of labor in one context but ignored it in another. He had not seen the possibility that the West could trade its minerals for foods raised in other sections. In a measure, this was due to his implicit assumption of environmental determinism and his failure to grasp the implications of the technological revolution of his day. Still, what he had to say regarding fundamental agricultural problems was largely valid, the more so when applied to the Great Plains and the Dust Bowl west of the 100th meridian. His feel for the land, and people like himself who had worked the land, was matchless and noble in spirit.

And his prescience and virtue were made to seem more so in his own day because of the attacks directed against him by spokesmen of land rings, water monopolists, cattle combines, speculators, railroad promoters, mining tycoons, phony irrigation societies, frightened local politicians, and the fatuous forerunners of the chamber of commerce booster. Eventually his program went down in defeat, but only to reemerge in what Powell would surely have thought of as a more enlightened era, though one not completely divested

4. See the speeches by Congressmen Martin Maginnis (Montana), Thomas M. Patterson (Colorado), D. C. Haskell (Kansas), of Feb. 18, 1879, in *Cong. Record,* 45th Cong., 3rd sess. (1879), Vol. VIII, Pt. 2, pp. 1202–11.
5. Ibid.
6. Darrah: *Powell of the Colorado,* pp. 310–14.

of darkness.[7] He would not have been satisfied even with this, however, for Powell implicitly envisioned the perfect society, scientifically and rationally organized, with man working in harmony with his environment. He was no limited reformer, nor even a pragmatist, for he had long-range goals toward which his passion for order propelled him. In a cynical age he stood out in the great American tradition. Like the Puritans who came to the New World to organize their model society, the City on the Hill, Powell went into the dreaded canyons of the Colorado and among the spires and dry landscapes of the Plateau Province and emerged with his own vision of the perfect society. The age was different but the aim and the impulse were the same.

But his adventures, achievements, and lofty ideals as of 1878 are only part of the story. In the 1870's and 1880's Powell played a role in government that was no less revolutionary or controversial. No account of his career, or for that matter of the total impact of exploration on American life in the nineteenth century, is complete without some attention to the bloody battlegrounds of institutional Washington where Powell became a leader with far mcre responsibilities than ever faced him at Vicksburg or Shiloh or Atlanta.

7. Powell's ideas reemerged, for example, in the Newlands Reclamation Act of 1902, the Taylor Grazing Act of 1934, and the Tennessee Valley Authority of 1933.

CHAPTER XVI

Epilogue

Beyond the Explorer's Frontier

BY the end of the 1870's exploration in the West had moved past
its age of discovery. Powell's two canyon voyages and Thompson's
plateau reconnaissances had revealed the last unknown regions
in the United States, and during the course of Powell's survey they
had been mapped and described so completely as to become part
of the familiar geography of the Western region. Institutional individualism, however, had replaced the solitary explorer, and in a
duplication of the entrepreneurship of the world around them, the
leaders of the four great postwar surveys built their exploring teams
into elaborate organizations. Engaged in serious public service
which produced important contributions to science as well as to
Western settlement, the survey leaders, Powell, King, Hayden, and
Wheeler, by their very earnestness and dedication were plunged
into a long and bitter rivalry which, as the acrimonious debates
unfolded, somewhat obscured their achievements. It was comparatively easy in the heat of debate to overlook, for example, Hayden's
brilliant insights into paleontology, easy to discount Wheeler's extensive mapping operations as "superficial and military-oriented," a
simple matter to dismiss King's great monographs as slight work
done by an "overrated" catastrophist, and it was even disconcert-
ingly easy to see Powell, not as the great geologist that he was,
but as a mere organizer—a bureaucrat bent on becoming a "captain"
of science and government. Nevertheless, the rise of institutional
rivalries, the Congressional clashes, the bitter letters and behind-
the-scenes maneuvering that accompanied the rise of the explorers'

empires is likewise an important part of their story, and a vital chapter in the history of science in America that must be considered by all students of the relation of organized knowledge to culture.

2

The conflict among the great surveys had its official beginnings in the summer of 1873 'when the parties of Wheeler and Hayden met in the Twin Lakes region of southern Colorado and commenced in all belligerence to map each other's territory.[1] Actually, however, tremors of friction could be detected as far back as 1869 when Powell's amateur voyage down the Colorado disrupted army plans to accomplish the same feat.[2] And Powell later claimed that, when Wheeler's men entered southern Utah in 1871, they were duplicating his own labors.[3] Likewise, continuous bad relations existed between the army explorers in Montana and the Dakotas and the men of the Hayden Survey, stemming primarily from the basic conflict between the War Department and the Interior Department over general Indian policy. As early as 1871 Captains Barlow and Heap saw to it that the army interests in Yellowstone Park were represented, though they were outwardly cooperative with Hayden, and in 1872 the men of the Hayden Survey found it difficult to get proper supplies from the commandant at Fort Ellis.[4]

In 1874, however, the Congressional debate over the Twin Lakes dispute brought all the rivalries and animosities into public focus.[5] Often mistakenly attributed to the machinations of Powell, the 1874 controversy was primarily a clash between the Army and the Interior Department, initiated by the military in an effort to maintain its preeminence in the field of Western exploration before it was too late.[6] Hayden was, somewhat dubiously, cast as the repre-

1. See Chapter 13, p. 478.
2. See Chapter 11, p. 397.
3. Powell to the Secretary of the Interior, April 24, 1874, in Wheeler: *Notes Relating to Surveys in the Western Territory of the United States*, Yale Collection of Western Americana. Also 43rd Cong., 1st sess., *House Report 612* (1874), p. 47.
4. William A. Logan to Hayden, Bozeman, Montana Territory, July 1, 1872, Letters Received, Hayden Survey, R.G. 57, National Archives.
5. This was reflected in the Townsend Committee of the House of Representatives investigation of the public lands in May of 1874. See 43rd Cong., 1st sess., *House Report 612* (1874), hereafter cited as *Townsend Report.*
6. See William Dwight Whitney to Josiah Dwight Whitney, Northampton,

sentative of civilian science. Through his wide correspondence, and with the energetic assistance of James Terry Gardner, he managed to secure the support of the major scientific institutions of the country.[7] In creating a scientific Armageddon in 1874, Gardner and Hayden thus managed to crystallize for the first time a self-awareness among the nation's professional scientists of their status and power in official Washington. The National Academy of Sciences and the Washington Philosophical Society, along with the major universities, such as Yale, Harvard, and Columbia, became linked in a self-conscious alliance which, joined with the Smithsonian Institution, made them an important factor on the national political scene.

Powell managed to use the 1874 episode as a platform for his ideas, which because they were so creative, and in such contrast to the absurd bickerings of Wheeler and Hayden, made him seem in retrospect quite the most important of the combatants. Like King, however, he maintained a certain aloofness from the basic struggle. A representative of the Smithsonian Institution rather than the War or Interior Departments, he was not forced to bear the standard of any political branch of the government. Instead, he appeared as an outside observer—a solid friend of professional science who criticized the shoddy in both camps, and interjected whatever positive and constructive suggestions that were made. His comments were consistently unfair to the military in the matter of mapping, in that he insisted that Wheeler's maps were done by meander methods and were superficial, when in fact Wheeler was actually far ahead of Powell in mapping techniques and employed better and more experienced topographical assistants.[8] Nevertheless, as a result of his comments both rival surveys improved their work after 1874.[9] Likewise, in bringing the matter of land classification before

Mass., May 12, 1874, and James T. Gardner to Josiah Dwight Whitney, Washington, March 5, 1874, May 13, 1874, Whitney Papers, Yale Historical Manuscripts Collection.

7. Ibid. See also F. V. Hayden to Josiah Dwight Whitney. Washington, May 3, 1874; Gardner to Josiah Dwight Whitney, Washington, May 7, 1874; Hayden to Josiah Dwight Whitney, Washington, May 8, 1874; Hayden to Josiah Dwight Whitney, Washington, May 12, 1874; May 13, 1874; Gardner to Josiah Dwight Whitney, Washington, May 13, 1874; May 14, 1874; May 23, 1874; June 5, 1874, Whitney Papers, Yale Historical Manuscripts Collection.

8. *Townsend Report*, pp. 47–54.

9. In 1874 Hayden had already begun his survey of Colorado with Gardner as his topographer. Thereafter his improved maps began to appear. For the

the public, Powell appeared as the innovator, when both Wheeler and Hayden had all along asserted the value and necessity for such work. Yet it was Powell who brought their ideas and his to public focus, thereby changing the orientation of survey work.

After the resolution of the 1874 dispute, which left all the surveys in the field, including Powell's, stronger than ever, the conflict continued to smolder. Marsh's exposure of the Red Cloud Indian frauds had involved military cooperation, and he was personally thanked by General Custer, never the favorite of the civilian agents.[1] The departure of Secretary of Interior Columbus Delano was a temporary victory for the military, and the alliance between the War Department and professional science seemed established, especially after Marsh agreed to add his monograph on Odontornithes to the publications of the King Survey. Meanwhile, wasteful duplication and overlap in the surveys continued. Publications and sun pictures came off the Government Printing Office presses in ever-increasing volume, and Powell opened up a number of new areas of scientific interest.

With the accession to office of President Rutherford B. Hayes, however, the climate changed. Reform and retrenchment again preoccupied Washington officials. Carl Schurz became Secretary of the Interior, and appropriations grew more difficult to manage through a reluctant Congress. The Grant era and all it stood for was at last ended.

In January of 1877, Powell was fighting for the life of his survey. On January 25 of that year he thanked John Strong Newberry of Columbia University for writing to Congressmen Abraham Hewitt and James Garfield on his behalf.

> I fear that it will be a tight squeeze for us this year but hope
> to get through all right. While I know the Appropriation Com-

improvement in Wheeler's work, see Wheeler: *Annual Report*, 1875, 1876, 1877, 1878. In 1875 he established an elaborate astronomical station at Ogden, Utah, and three other, less elaborate stations at Las Vegas and Cimarron, New Mexico; Sidney Barracks and North Platte, Nebraska; and Julesburg, Colorado. The results of field operations were related to base lines at these main stations by means of triangulation, and then longitude positions were checked by the newest, or Western Union Telegraph, method. The use of the telegraph by Wheeler as early as 1874 put him clearly in advance of Powell with regard to geodetic accuracy. See Wheeler: *Annual Report 1875*, pp. 7–14.

1. Custer to Marsh, N.Y., Oct. 4, 1871, Marsh Letterbooks, Peabody Museum, Yale University. Also see the many letters Marsh received from merchants and soldiers during the Red Cloud fight, in Marsh Papers, Yale Historical Manuscripts Collection.

mittee and especially the Chairman will attempt to cut off Western work, I think that the greater body of Congressmen are in favor of my work. Especially is this true with a few of the most influential men, such as Mr. Seelye, Mr. Garfield, Mr. Randall, and Mr. Hewitt.[2]

And, indeed, Newberry had gone far not only to promote Powell's cause, but to destroy his rival, Hayden. In duplicate letters to Garfield and Abraham Hewitt, he praised Powell and his assistants as "men of first rate ability . . . inspired by true scientific enthusiasm." Hayden, he declared, "has come to be so much of a fraud that he has lost the sympathy and respect of the scientific men of the country." And he added: "It may well be questioned whether he and his enterprises should be generously assisted as they have been." Among the charges leveled at Hayden by Newberry, his one-time friend and protégé, were that he had become "simply the political manager of his expeditions"; he "had in some way accumulated a handsome property" in Washington; he distributed photographs and reports with an eye to political effect; he hired relatives of Congressmen for similar political effect; his survey had deteriorated because his best men had either died or deserted him; and his publications were irrelevant ones "prepared by experts from materials obtained through his collectors." The latter of course referred to the work of E. D. Cope, always a black sheep in the family of official science.[3]

Newberry's letter, which purported to represent disinterested scientific opinion, was clearly devastating, and it had to be, because Powell and like-minded scientists feared that Congress was about to authorize a consolidation of the Western surveys under Hayden. Such a consolidation did not occur, but in the summer of 1877 Schurz ordered a clear division of labor between his two Interior Department surveys. At Powell's suggestion, possibly a desperate remedy to stave off disaster, Hayden was given the choice of working either in geology or in ethnology, two fields where he had scored signal success.[4] Hayden took geology, testily replying: "I would therefore respectfully suggest that Major Powell be desired to de-

2. Powell to John Strong Newberry, Jan. 25, 1877, L.S., Powell Survey, R.G. 57, National Archives.

3. Newberry to James Garfield, Jan. 20, 1877; Newberry to Abraham Hewitt, Jan. 20, 1877, copies in L.S., Powell Survey, R.G. 57, National Archives.

4. Carl Schurz to Hayden, Washington, D.C., Aug. 2, 1877, L.R., Hayden Survey, R.G. 77, National Archives.

vote himself exclusively to Ethnographic work and its cognate branches after the present year. . . ."[5]

In accordance with the agreement, Powell began taking his best men, including Dutton and Gilbert, off geological work in 1877, though he insisted on their right to bring their present labors to completion and publication under his aegis. But instead of turning to ethnology, Powell turned his attention to irrigation and the problems of settlement in the arid lands. It was at this time that he and Gilbert began work on the *Report on the Lands of the Arid Regions*. Land reform and settlement had long been his basic interest anyway, and a widely distributed public report—a dramatic program or plan of action—would serve as a means of circumventing his inferior institutional position at the same time that it would bring an important question to national attention.

The climax to this behind-the-scenes struggle came in the spring of 1878. At the behest of the House Appropriations Committee, Powell, Hayden, and Wheeler submitted reports on all their surveying activity in the West to date. Of these, Powell's was clearly the most able. He reported in detail on the work of his survey, and then with the precision that always characterized his work he carefully defined the areas of duplication and overlap that existed between his rival surveys. Then, turning to a comparison of their respective maps, Powell, with scrupulous fairness, defined the achievements of each survey, even emphasizing the fact that both Wheeler and Hayden were now producing contour maps, albeit on a different scale from his own.[6]

By contrast, Hayden's report was an argumentative and intemperate plea for the status quo, and coming in the wake of Newberry's letter to Congressman Hewitt, who was a member of the Committee, served to demonstrate Powell's privately stated opinion of him.[7]

Out of this Appropriations Committee came the key proposal. Congressman Hewitt, perhaps on his own, but probably with some prompting by King, suggested that the National Academy of Sci-

5. Hayden to Schurz, Washington, D.C., Nov. 15, 1877, L.S., Hayden Survey, R.G. 77, National Archives.
6. For the Powell and Hayden Reports, see 45th Cong., 2nd sess., *H.R. Exec. Docs*. 80 and 81 (1878). Darrah, in *Powell of the Colorado*, pp. 242–3, declares that Powell appeared in person before the House Committee and delivered a strong condemnation of his rivals' work. I could find no evidence of this.
7. Ibid., especially *Doc. 81*.

ences be authorized to review the whole subject of the unification of the surveys and submit a report incorporating its specific recommendations to Congress.[8] This was an important proposal because when accepted by Congress it virtually meant the doom of both the Wheeler and the Hayden surveys. In May of 1878 Joseph Henry, the president of the National Academy, had died, and O. C. Marsh, the vice president, had hurried home from Europe to take over. Since 1874, when Hayden had tried virtually to blackmail him into endorsing his stand against Wheeler, Marsh had disliked him.[9] Moreover, E. D. Cope, Hayden's paleontologist, was Marsh's hated rival. Both Hayden and Cope, though members of the Academy, stood outside the select circle of acceptable American scientific leadership, and they knew it. By the same token, since 1874 official science had frowned on red-tape army leadership, and though it lent its support to King's army survey, it did so because he was not under the direct jurisdiction of field engineers.

The makeup of the Academy's committee was revealing.[1] Marsh presided. Then there were James Dwight Dana of Yale, William B. Rogers, John Strong Newberry, W. P. Trowbridge, Simon Newcomb of the Naval Observatory, and Alexander Agassiz of Harvard. Only Trowbridge had attended West Point. The rest were all opposed to army surveys and strongly in favor of civilian-dominated science. Moreover, Marsh, Newberry, Newcomb, Dana, and Agassiz were personal friends of Clarence King, who by this time was allied with Powell. Agassiz, in fact, was a silent business partner with King in

8. See Henry Nash Smith: "Clarence King, John Wesley Powell, and the Establishment of the United States Geological Survey," *MVHR*, Vol. XXXIV, No. 1 (1947), p. 43. See also Stegner: *Beyond the Hundredth Meridian,* p. 233. Stegner points out that Hewitt took credit for suggesting that the Academy's help be sought in the consolidation question, whereas S. F. Emmons credited King with the idea. It seems most likely to me that the idea originated with King, who was on very good terms with the members of the Academy, particularly Marsh. King, in turn, must certainly have made his proposal to his friend and business partner Hewitt, who based his claim for credit on his role in Congress. There is no evidence to suggest that Powell originated the proposal. For the King-Hewitt business relationship, see footnote 4, p. 584. Emmons, who was also a business partner, was in the best possible position to know of King's relationship with Hewitt.

9. See F. V. Hayden to O. C. Marsh, Washington, D.C., April 20, 1874, and O. C. Marsh to Hayden, draft in reply, no date, Marsh Letterbooks, Peabody Museum, Yale University.

1. See O. C. Marsh: "Letter from the Acting President of the National Academy of Sciences Transmitting a Report on the Surveys of the Territories," 45th Cong., 3rd sess., *H.R. Misc. Doc.* 5 (1878), p. 5.

the ND Ranch, a vast spread near Cheyenne, Wyoming, entered under the name of N. R. Davis, King's former field assistant.[2] Another ranching partner of King's was none other than Abraham Hewitt, who had officially proposed the committee in the first place.[3] In 1879, during the consolidation fight, together with Gardner and Edward Cooper, the mayor of New York City, King and Hewitt formed the Lakota Company Ltd., capitalized at $100,000. In all, Hewitt was associated with King in three large ranching ventures during this period.[4]

A confusing but tangible alliance began to emerge. On one level was official science led by Marsh, Dana, Whitney, Agassiz, and other friends of Clarence King and John Wesley Powell. All were unalterably opposed to army-dominated science and "upstart" science of the kind represented by Hayden and Cope. On another level were the business friends of Clarence King, who, after they read Powell's *Report on the Lands of the Arid Regions*, which he delivered to them as soon as it was printed, must have been delighted at his proposals for 2,600-acre grazing-lands classification. With his system, the one-horse outfits and the sodbusters would be classified right off the range, along with the troublesome local Land Office rings. Sensible and sound Eastern big business of the kind Hewitt represented would be encouraged.

Finally, too, there were the scientists, officials, and Congressmen who, at intimate parties at Henry Adams's house on H Street, or in meetings of the Philosophical Club, or at other Washington receptions, came to know and admire both King and Powell.[5] There is only indirect evidence that King and Powell met before 1878, or that they were seen much together.[6] However, Marsh at Yale, and Hewitt and Garfield in Washington, provided a clear link in the alliance. Army officials, always sensitive to Washington currents, grasped the situation immediately and virtually retired from the

2. Wilkins: *Clarence King*, pp. 217–20, 223.
3. Ibid., p. 223.
4. Ibid. King actually had interests in four ranching ventures: the ND Ranch in partnership with Davis, Emmons, Gardner (and after 1878, Alexander Agassiz); the Dead Man Ranch, a large spread in western Nebraska entered under the name of E. B. Bronson, King's secretary; the Lakota Co. Ltd.; and the Rocky Mountain Cattle Company, formed in 1880 in partnership with Hewitt and Henry Cabot Lodge. See Wilkins: *Clarence King*, pp. 217–29.
5. Wilkins: *Clarence King*, p. 238.
6. David H. Dickason: "Henry Adams and Clarence King," *New England Quarterly*, Vol. XVII (March–Dec. 1944), p. 239.

field. General Humphreys, in what Newcomb referred to as "hari-kari," resigned from the National Academy, though his resignation was not accepted.[7] As the survey fight developed, he swung in behind Marsh, King, and Powell.

The eventual outcome of the Academy's deliberations should not have been surprising to anyone, though Hayden, Cope, and most of the Western politicians continued to fight. In November of 1878 Powell forwarded a formal report to the National Academy of Sciences which attacked the Public Land Office and by implication the Hayden and Wheeler surveys. The main burden of his report, however, called for a bold new reorganizing of the Western public-lands policy as well as a consolidation of the various Western surveys under one civilian authority.[8] The Academy incorporated Powell's program virtually intact in its report to the Secretary of the Interior in November 1878, and later, after the fight was won, rewarded King with the directorship of the newly formed United States Geological Survey—a post which, contrary to most historical opinion, and King's own public statements, he eagerly sought.[9]

But though the forces were marshaled, the struggle over Powell's program was not as easily won as logic suggested it should have been. Powell's program (and the Academy's) was controversial. It divided the Western surveys into two categories: (1) "Surveys of mensuration," and (2) "Surveys of geology and economic resources of the soil." Then it made four major recommendations: (1) All land-mensuration systems should be combined under one federal agency, the United States Coast and Interior Survey. (2) The present Western surveys should be combined under a single United States Geological Survey. (3) Both the Coast and Interior Survey and the Geological Survey should be placed under the authority of the Interior Department. (4) A commission of agents should be established, "who shall take into consideration the codification of the present laws relating to the survey of the public domain, and who shall report to Congress within one year a standard of classi-

7. Simon Newcomb: *Reminiscences of an Astronomer* (Boston: Houghton Mifflin Co.; 1903), pp. 256–7; A. Hunter Dupree: *Science in the Federal Government*, p. 208; Schuchert and Le Vene: *Othniel C. Marsh*, p. 254.
8. Powell: *Report to the Secretary of the Interior On the Methods of Surveying the Public Domain, at the Request of the National Academy of Sciences* (Washington, D.C.: U. S. Government Printing Office; 1878).
9. See footnote 1, p. 583. See also Clarence King to O. C. Marsh, Jan. 2, 1878, Jan. 15, 1878, Marsh Letterbooks, Peabody Museum, Yale University; Darrah: *Powell of the Colorado*, p. 251.

fication and valuation of the public land, together with a system of land-parceling survey."[1]

The first provision removed all authority from the Public Lands Office and placed the local surveys in federal hands, while the fourth provision made certain that the demise of the Land Office would be complete. This raised a much greater opposition than the proposals relating to the geological surveys, because it struck at the heart of local control of affairs, whether honest or corrupt. Rallying to the side of Hayden, who had always been a booster of local territorial progress, every Western Congressman and Senator, with the exception of two, opposed the Academy's recommendation and its proposal as set forth in the form of a bill written by Powell himself.

Hewitt, realizing that the bill was doomed to failure in the Public Lands Committee dominated by Western men, saw to it that the measure was reported into the House by the friendly Appropriations Committee of which he was a member and Atkins of Missouri the chairman.[2] By the time it reached the floor for debate on February 10, 1879, Powell's bill, thanks to the work of Marsh, had the unqualified endorsement of such public figures as President Hayes, Secretary of Interior Schurz, General William T. Sherman, and Superintendent Patterson of the Coast Survey.[3] It was ably defended on a bipartisan basis by Peter Wigginton of California, James A. Garfield of Ohio, and in a particularly eloquent speech of February 11, 1879, by Hewitt himself.[4]

Still, despite this powerful backing, the bill ran into determined opposition from the Western bloc in Congress. Much of their opposition stemmed from the "myth of the yeoman farmer," or a belief that Powell's program was designed to exclude settlers from the West. Other Western politicians probably, though not certainly, had nefarious interests such as land rings and water companies to protect. But basically their arguments took two forms. They saw the potential land-reform program as described in Powell's *Arid Lands Report* as one which favored the big cattlemen, who could afford to utilize 2,600 acres, over the small cattleman who was just getting started. No one quarreled with Powell's

1. See footnote 1, p. 583.
2. Smith: "Clarence King, John Wesley Powell, and the Establishment of the United States Geological Survey," p. 47; Stegner: *Beyond the Hundredth Meridian*, p. 237.
3. Ibid.
4. Ibid. Hewitt's speech can be found in *Congressional Record*, 45th Cong., 3rd sess., Feb. 11, 1879, pp. 1203–7. Garfield's remarks are on pp. 1209–10.

contention that water rights should inhere in the land. They concentrated rather on the problem of size. "It is claimed," declared Representative Martin Maginnis of Montana, "that we must divide up this land into larger parcels in order that stockmen and graziers may occupy it. I think that is one great cause for this agitation. I think the great stockmen of Colorado and California would like to have the pre-emption and homestead system broken up, which limits farms to one hundred and sixty acres each so that they may obtain vast tracts of three, four, and five thousand acres and cover our territories with small editions of the Spanish land grants of California. . . ."[5]

Other Western men were opposed to federal interference in local affairs—at least on this occasion. Patterson of Colorado addressed himself to Hewitt: "If it is necessary to codify all the laws of the land system and suggest new methods, why is there any greater necessity for calling in a crowd of strangers to do this work than for seeking the aid of outsiders upon a thousand and one other matters of legislation that constantly arise here?"[6] Haskell of Kansas went even further. Probably inspired by Hayden and Cope, he spoke of the "scientific lobbyists" in Washington, comparing them to the big city machines of his day. "It is very natural," he declared, "that any particular class of men who have been educated to scientific pursuits and have been engaged on governmental work until they have become gray-headed should be very anxious to perpetuate their reign. And that is where the scheme originated."[7]

Generally dismissed by historians as ignorant, venal men who were tools of unnamed but certainly questionable interests, these Western spokesmen nevertheless expressed a point of view which represented a distinct if not profound dislocation in American society. They spoke for the frontier and its climate of expectant capitalism—a Jacksonian phase through which the Eastern half of the country had already passed decades before. And they demanded the freedom of economic opportunity which older sections had enjoyed previously, without fully realizing that increased capacities for industrial and capital organization, of the kind that Hewitt with his New York financial connections and his huge Wyoming ranches knew so well, had already made this difficult, if not impossible. In addition, and with some justification, they

5. *Congressional Record*, 45th Cong., 3rd sess., Vol. VIII, pt. 2, p. 1202.
6. Ibid., p. 1203.
7. Ibid., p. 1211.

placed no confidence in elite reformers of the kind represented by Marsh, Powell, and Hewitt. To place their trust in an outside scientific elite appeared to remove whatever local control the Western men had over their own destinies, leaving no assurance that the rapacious and power-grasping groups that were so much feared would not themselves come to dominate official Washington. It was a dialogue as old as democracy and as fundamental as the frontier.

Armed with these arguments, the Westerners, mostly Republicans, resisted Powell's measure, until Page of California broke the deadlock by proposing a compromise that retained the United States Geological Survey but left the land system as it was.[8] The compromise measure passed by a close vote in the House—98 to 79—but in the Senate, where the West was stronger, the whole bill failed.[9] Hewitt, however, managed to secure its transfer to a conference or joint committee of the House and Senate of which he was a member. Then, in the closing days of the session, he saw to it that, in modified form, which included only the provisions for consolidation of the geological surveys and a commission to study the public lands, the bill was reported out of committee and attached to the Sundry Civil Expense Bill, where it passed by 148 to 107 in the House and 35 to 24 in the Senate.[1] It was thus only a partial victory for the forces of reform.

Historical opinion has differed as to who was primarily responsible for even this partial victory in achieving the final consolidation of the Western surveys.[2] It seems clear, however, that,

8. Smith: "Clarence King, John Wesley Powell and the Establishment of the United States Geological Survey," p. 51.
9. Ibid.
1. Ibid., p. 52.
2. Smith, in "Clarence King, John Wesley Powell and the Establishment of the United States Geological Survey," credits Powell with being the prime mover in the consolidation struggle (see p. 57). Wallace Stegner, in *Beyond the Hundredth Meridian*, follows the Smith account very closely and stresses Powell's role, to the exclusion of Hewitt and King. Darrah, in *Powell of the Colorado*, provides very little information on the consolidation but is in general a supporter of Powell in this matter. A. Hunter Dupree, in *Science in the Federal Government*, concurs, and generally follows Smith. Thurman Wilkins, in *Clarence King*, places King in the key role, as does David Dickason, in "Henry Adams and Clarence King, the Record of a Friendship," and Henry Adams in *The Education of Henry Adams*. Samuel F. Emmons, in "Clarence King Geologist," *Clarence King Memoirs*, who was closer to the event than anyone else, asserts that King was primarily responsible for the consolidation, especially in the crucial recommendation for referral to the National Academy

whatever the reason, King and Powell were both prime movers in the consolidation struggle. The plan was Powell's, and he took the lead in advancing the cause in the press, in writing letters to influential Congressmen or causing such letters to be written by his scientific colleagues, and in providing a consistent flow of facts and sober reflections that gave direction to the much-needed reform. He was most effective in public appearances, particularly before congressional committees. There he was at his best, calmly explaining the most difficult questions, and dramatizing with his maps and blackboard diagrams what might otherwise have been the dull subject of Western public-lands policy.

King's role must not be discounted, however. By virtue of the fact that he was the friend of Marsh and most of the other important powers in the scientific establishment, King was most important in winning their allegiance to Powell's plan. Likewise, his connections in official Washington, and among the business-oriented Congressmen of the day, were much more extensive than Powell's. He was thus able to use political, social, and financial ties in a way that would have been impossible for Powell. As Yale man, adventurer and clubman, littérateur, scientist, and exposer of the Diamond Hoax, he stood as the symbol of that peculiar alliance between very big business, the socially acceptable intellectuals, and the advocates of limited reform who came to support Powell's plan. As such, he was a logical choice for director of the United States Geological Survey.

---

of Sciences. Abraham Hewitt, in his speech of Feb. 11, 1879, claimed credit for his own part in the plan; Simon Newcomb, in *Reminiscences of an Astronomer*, places King in the forefront. Richard Bartlett, in *Great Surveys of the American West*, feels that Hayden has been treated unfairly by all authorities on the consolidation struggle, particularly by Smith.

I am persuaded by the Emmons account, the letters of Clarence King and Major Powell to O. C. Marsh in the Marsh Papers, and the material in Wilkins's *Clarence King* concerning King's role as partner in the cattle business with Hewitt and Emmons, largely derived from the King Papers. These make clear that King had a role in the consolidation struggle fully as important as that of Powell, as I have indicated here. To conclude this, however, is not in any way to denigrate Powell's leading role in the reform movement. It is rather to attempt to present a balanced picture of an event which has been somewhat distorted by the exigencies of a biographical approach to history. See footnote 8, p. 583.

3

The battle thus shifted to a struggle over the appointment of a director for the Geological Survey. Hayden, with widespread Western political connections and massive popular support, seemed certain to gain the appointment, particularly since mail from his partisans flooded President Hayes's office in the White House. But again the scientific alliance swung into play. As early as January 2, 1879, before the bill had finally passed, Clarence King wrote his friend Professor Marsh, asking for help in gaining the nomination.

> I have received a round about and private notice that it is time to put in my credentials. Harvard is going to write a sort of general letter which various professors will sign. Now I am going to get you to confer with President Porter and Brush and get up a letter for me at the earliest possible moment which being a Yale letter will be my chief credential.
>
> It should, beside any generalities which might read well in my obituary notice, harp somewhat on my fifteen years continuous geological service, twelve being in charge of the 40th Parallel Survey. In geology the main point to be insisted on is that I have a practical and intimate knowledge of economic geology. Also that I have enough executive faculty to manage the business. Lastly that my relations to the scientific men of the land are such that I can gain the cooperation of good men. Privately I can tell you and my Yale friends that I shall have Pumpelly, the two Hagues, Emmons, Powell, and Siebert. . . .
>
> Besides that, I want a letter of general recommendation for the place of Director . . . to be signed by the members of the Committee of the National Academy who made the report.[3]

Powell contributed mightily to King's cause by writing a long and detailed letter to Garfield reducing all of Hayden's accomplishments to ashes.[4] Then he wrote to Atkins, calling upon him

3. See footnote 9, p. 585.
4. Powell to Garfield, draft n.d. [1878], Powell Survey, Letters Sent, R.G. 57, National Archives. See also Powell to Garfield, March 7, 1879, Office of Secretary of the Interior, Letters Received, Concerning the Geological Survey, R.G. 57, National Archives.

to support King directly by approaching Schurz and Hayes, which he did, and Schurz swung in behind King.[5]

Virtually the entire scientific community came to King's aid. Recommendations poured in from Yale, Columbia, Johns Hopkins, New York University, the American Museum of Natural History, and the State Museum at Albany, and from every member of the Academy Committee except Dana.[6] On the local scene, Simon Newcomb remembered, "the movers in the matter divided up the work, did what they could in the daytime, and met at night at Wormley's Hotel to compare notes, ascertain the effect of every shot, and decide where the next one should be fired."[7] They also met at Major Powell's newly founded Cosmos Club, a scientific social organization which the Major had founded in 1878 to replace the old Philosophical Club. The ultimate stroke that secured King's appointment, however, was a personal visit from Marsh, Brewer, and Newberry to President Hayes in which Brewer carefully explained King's work in California and along the Fortieth Parallel, and Newberry gave his strongest support. As geologist of the State Survey of Ohio, Newberry carried great weight with the Ohio President.[8] After a final consultation with Schurz, Hayes made his decision. King received the appointment, and at last the battle was almost over.

"Now that the battle is won," Marsh wrote to Powell jubilantly, "we can go back to pure science again."[9]

For Powell, however, the survey struggle was the beginning rather than the end of a career. In the same session that passed the Survey Bill, another measure was passed establishing a National Bureau of Ethnology. It was the first such governmental institution established for the scientific study of man, and Powell throughout the remainder of his career served as its chief. He also served on the Irrigation Commission of 1879, as provided in Hewitt's bill, but with less success. After a hard year in the field making irrigation surveys, etc., the Commission was totally ignored by Congress when it presented its recommendations. The great battle had indeed resulted in only a partial victory.

5. Darrah: *Powell of the Colorado*, p. 351; Smith: "Clarence King and John Wesley Powell in the Establishment of the United States Geological Survey," pp. 52–3.
6. Wilkins: *Clarence King*, p. 241.
7. Newcomb: *Reminiscences of an Astronomer*, p. 259.
8. Ibid.; Wilkins: *Clarence King*, p. 242.
9. Darrah: *Powell of the Colorado*, p. 252.

4

Though the United States Geological Survey continued to send expeditions into the West, they no longer had as their objective to discover the unknown, but rather concentrated on an assessment of the nation's resources. The formation of the Survey in 1879, therefore, marks the end of an era of American Western exploration—an era that began with Lewis and Clark's epic march to the Pacific at the opening of the nineteenth century and concluded with Powell and King's institutional victory over the forces of frontier individualism. Nevertheless, though a detailed examination of the history of the Geological Survey is beyond the scope of this book, a brief study of its activities down to the resignation of Major Powell as director in 1894 is necessary to indicate something of the impact and influence of the ideas of this last great generation of Western explorers.

When Clarence King took office as first director of the Geological Survey in March of 1880, he did so with some misgivings. There were two fundamental legal ambiguities in the definition of his duties as director, and one personal ambiguity not often noted even by his closest friends. The legal ambiguities, as he pointed out in his first annual report, involved the scope of the Survey. Was he responsible for surveying and classifying the agricultural lands of the West and certifying them for settlement in advance of the Land Office Survey? And did his duties and those of his staff extend to the entire national domain, or just the Western territories?[1] In approaching these questions, King chose to remain conservative. He ignored any land-classification function and he left the national-domain question in abeyance, though he did organize under Raphael Pumpelly an informal bureau with headquarters in Newport, Rhode Island, whose duty it was to look into the mining industry of the Eastern United States.[2] He also organized several regional survey districts in the Eastern part of the country that could be activated if Congress chose to inter-

1. King: *First Annual Report of the United States Geological Survey* (Washington, D.C.: U. S. Government Printing Office; 1880), p. 6. For an astute comparison of the policies of King and Powell with respect to the Geological Survey, see Thomas G. Manning: "The Influence of Clarence King and John Wesley Powell on the Early History of the United States Geological Survey," *Interim Proceedings of the Geological Society of America*, Report of April 1947, pt. 2.
2. Ibid., pp. 47–8, 57–60.

pret the national-domain clause freely.[3] In addition, he observed that the interstate-commerce clause and the taxing powers, granted the national government under the Constitution, provided all the legal authority needed for an expansion of the Survey into the older states.[4]

Fundamentally, however, King's concept of the Geological Survey was limited. With a modest budget of $100,000, he had to confine his activities to the West, and within that sphere to specific projects. Unlike Powell, he believed that mining and technology, rather than agriculture, were the keys to Western development. Always abreast of the latest European innovations, King was never an environmentalist, but rather an advocate of the Industrial Revolution and big business. Accordingly, he divided his Western work into four districts and within each authorized a detailed study of mines and mining industries as the major task of the division chief. Emmons was placed in charge of the Rocky Mountain District and there began his classic study of Leadville, Colorado. Dutton continued to work in the Plateau Province, with W. H. Holmes as his assistant. G. K. Gilbert had the Great Basin as his province and continued his work on ancient Lake Bonneville. His work represented the closest anyone came to an irrigation survey under King's leadership. And even then in that district Arnold Hague conducted a special intensive survey of the Eureka Mining District. The Far Western, or Coastal, District was placed under G. F. Becker, who devoted his major efforts to an examination of the Comstock Lode. And his assistant, a survey clerk named Elliot Lord, began writing his famous history of that region.[5]

In addition, King also employed his official staff of thirty-eight men, and a host of local temporary assistants, in compiling a census or inventory of the mineral resources of the United States. The statistical publications that resulted were of major importance to the eventual development of the mineral industries of the country.[6] If he had achieved nothing else, King had at least brought a semblance of overall order to what had been a haphazard, individually organized enterprise. Moreover, the monographs that came out of these first years, including Dutton's *Tertiary History of the Grand Canyon District*, Emmons's *Lead-*

3. Ibid., pp. 6, 8.
4. Ibid., p. 78.
5. Ibid., pp. 6–8.
6. Ibid., pp. 52–6.

594 EXPLORATION AND EMPIRE

ville, Colorado, Lord's *Comstock Mining and Miners,* Becker's *Comstock Lode,* Hague's *Geology of Eureka Mining District,* Gilbert's *Lake Bonneville,* and Marsh's *Dinocerata,* all attest to the excellence of King's leadership and the quality of his men.

Nevertheless, King has suffered somewhat in comparison with Powell because he was a creature of his time, not a reformer. He considered himself as an auxiliary to the development of major private wealth-producing industries in the United States. Fundamentally he was a Whig who conceived of the government as a means of helping business, which, since it produced wealth and exploited technology and innovation, helped the country. Given the circles King traveled in, this was an inevitable point of view, but in many ways it led nowhere and lacked the challenge of Powell's reforming mission.

Having set up the Survey to his satisfaction, King grew bored with routine. At heart he, too, wished to be a captain of industry, and so, during the crucial months in 1880 when he should have been in Washington fighting for increased appropriations for his survey, King was in Arizona and Mexico looking after his private mining interests. His Wyoming cattle empire, too, demanded attention at this time, forcing King to resolve the personal conflict that plagued him as director.[7] Under the terms of his appointment he could have no pecuniary interest in the lands or minerals that came under his jurisdiction, and he could accept no fees for outside mining consultation.[8] The latter he relinquished with some reluctance, as it was a major source of income. The former he had not fully decided on by 1880. Finally, however, in that year he determined to resign the Directorship of the Survey. Shortly afterward, he sold out the cattle business to Hewitt, just in time to avoid the winter disasters of 1882; and he decided to set off in search of a fortune as a mining entrepreneur.[9] In short, he succumbed to the major tides of the nineteenth century. The rest of his story is pure tragedy: repeated mining failures, mental and physical illness, a clandestine marriage, and at last, undeserved obscurity and a pathetic death of tuberculosis in Arizona in 1901. His own university refused, despite efforts by Henry Adams and S. F. Emmons, to accede to his last pitiful request and grant him an honorary degree at its bicentennial celebration in

7. Wilkins: *Clarence King,* pp. 260–2.
8. Kin͠g: *First Annual Report of the United States Geological Survey,* p. 3.
9. Wilkins: *Clarence King,* pp. 228, 260, 267–82.

1901.[1] It missed an excellent chance, for as Adams once said, King was "the best and brightest man of his generation."[2] And from a man who was so much a part of his generation, what more could have been expected than that he be "the best and brightest" —one of the nineteenth century's grandest but most tragic figures?

5

Powell, on the other hand, took office as Director of the Survey with a vigor and enthusiasm that challenged his time. His main focus was, as usual, rooted in the land as an environment for living. Mining and technology interested him far less than agriculture and irrigation.[3] He was likewise not concerned by legal ambiguities or supposed limitations on his survey. Almost immediately he combined the Bureau of Ethnology with the Geological Survey, expanded the staff dramatically by adding part-time auxiliary workers, more than doubled the budget, and set out to construct a topographical map of the entire United States. He also set up a chemistry lab in Washington, and by special arrangement, with the help of his good friend Professor Marsh at Yale, who was appointed to his staff, he added the study of paleontology to the Survey duties.[4]

One objective, however, remained always before him, and that was reform of the land system. The topographical map series in quadrant sections, perhaps his most useful innovation, was one step toward this objective. When his survey came under fire by the Allison Commission appointed to look into expanding federal agencies in 1884, Powell refused to retreat, and instead took the offensive. Day after day, in testimony before the Commission, he unrolled his maps, brought out startling statistics about aridity and settlement, and challenged the Land Office Survey at every point. He concluded by calling for a National Department of Science governed by the Regents of the Smithsonian Institution, a

1. King to S. F. Emmons, Pasadena, Calif., Aug. 29, 1901, Box 30, Emmons Papers, Library of Congress.
2. Adams: *Education of Henry Adams*, p. 416.
3. Darrah: *Powell of the Colorado*, pp. 273–86. See Manning: "The Influence of Clarence King. . . ."
4. Ibid.

proposal the Commission also backed, in modified form, without success.[5]

In 1888 his big chance came. The blizzards of 1886–87 had virtually destroyed the cattle industry and the droughts of the following summer had forced farmers into considering irrigation. Irrigation congresses sprang up all over the United States, and the government was called upon to do something. Western legislators, led by William Stewart of Nevada, in temporary alliance with Powell, pushed through as part of the Sundry Civil Bill authorization for an Irrigation Commission designed to locate water resources and classify irrigable basins. Powell as director of the Geological Survey was to be in charge of the Irrigation Survey, and much was expected of him.[6] As desperate Westerners saw it, he would rush teams of men into the field, and, as it were, scientifically prospect for water sites, which the local communities would then develop. In anticipation of his success, a water-company boom ensued, and thirty-three companies were chartered in New Mexico alone.[7]

The Stewart forces, and those associated with them, including an irrigation group headed by Francis M. Newlands, were not entirely looking for the public plunder that many have subsequently supposed, however.[8] Mixed in with private ambitions were schemes to turn over water companies to public communities or states, along the lines that Powell advocated all along, though in most cases the communities were too impoverished to float large irrigation schemes and capitalistic enterprise was the only possible way. Curiously, water companies and cattlemen's associations in which large numbers of stockholders were represented, though they were private capital ventures, were actually organized and

5. Powell: On the Organization of Scientific Work of the General Government (Washington, D.C.: U. S. Government Printing Office; 1885). This volume is largely made up of Powell's extended testimony before the Allison Commission in the winter of 1884–85. See p. 27 for Powell's plan for a National Department of Science.
6. Darrah: Powell of the Colorado, pp. 299–314. Also see E. W. Sterling: "The Powell Irrigation Survey, 1888–1893," MVHR, Vol. XXVII (1940), pp. 421–34. Sterling pointed out that "Stewart's constituents were at the time seeking to guard against the encroachments of large California cattle interests, particularly the Lux and Miller outfits, who were grabbing all the water holes." (See p. 421.)
7. Sterling: "The Powell Irrigation Survey, 1888–1893," p. 427.
8. See William Lilley: "The Early Career of Francis Newlands," unpublished doctoral dissertation, Yale University.

carried out many of Powell's plans. The Major, however, never recognized them as doing so.

From the beginning, the Irrigation Survey got off to a bad start. Powell chose not to proceed in haste to survey the most obvious sites, but instead began a general topographical survey of the whole region and its interrelated watersheds.[9] It was the work of a decade at least, and duplicated much of what King had done years before, especially in the Great Basin. To Western communities impatient for relief, and on the verge of disaster, his pace seemed agonizingly slow and his project too large. His depreciation of artesian-well schemes, and his forthright declaration to irrigation congresses that most of the land was too arid to be settled in any case, seemed to be an attempt to classify settlers out of farming entirely—which in retrospect might have been a good idea.

What made the situation most acute, however, was that the Authorization Act for the Irrigation Survey included a clause that suspended all settlement in the West pending proper classification by Powell.[1] The Major himself did not realize the extent of his powers until, in 1889, the Land Office began questioning it, and upon a ruling by President Harrison was forced to invalidate all claims after 1888.[2] By accident Powell had gained complete control over settlement in the West.

But with this immense power, the Major suddenly became a target for all the combined Western interests, led by Stewart of Nevada, who felt he had been duped by the Washington bureaucrats. Strengthened by the addition of twelve new Western Senators from six newly admitted states, Stewart and his constituents were able to stop Powell cold in 1890 by reducing the Irrigation Survey budget to $165,000, which made it impossible to continue the work.[3] After 1890 they continued to hammer away at Powell and the Geological Survey. Using Marsh's paleontological works as the butt of their attacks, the Western bloc in congress cut $90,000

9. Darrah: *Powell of the Colorado*, pp. 306–7.
1. Ibid., pp. 305–6.
2. Stegner: *Beyond the Hundredth Meridian*, p. 320.
3. Ibid., pp. 328–45. Also see Darrah: *Powell of the Colorado*, pp. 336–49. Another contributory factor in the demise of the Irrigation Survey was E. D. Cope's attack on O. C. Marsh in the New York *Herald* on Jan. 12, 1890. This highlighted the role of paleontology in the Survey and made it an easy target for "practical-minded" Congressmen and Senators. See Stegner: *Beyond the Hundredth Meridian*, pp. 324–8; Darrah: *Powell of the Colorado*, pp. 336–45.

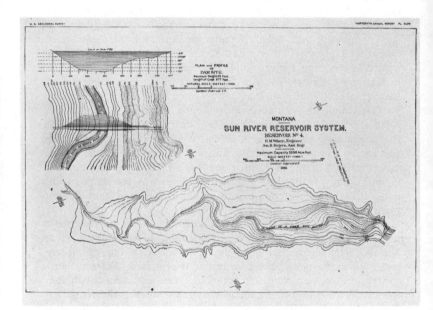

One of Powell's Irrigation Survey maps, 1889. *Courtesy Library of Congress*

off the budget in 1891, and in 1892 slashed it so drastically that many of Powell's employees had to work on for nothing, or "con amore" as he called it.[4] Thus by 1893 Powell, who had risen to the heights of power and ambition, found himself suddenly laid low. He could no longer serve the cause of reform. On May 4, 1894, he dictated his formal letter of resignation as Director of the Geological Survey, though he continued to supervise the Bureau of Ethnology until his death in 1902.[5] It was truly the end of an era, the end of the last generation of great explorers, men who had gazed upon the unknown in the West and then, as they had for decades, put their impressions and their knowledge to work for the country. Somehow it was appropriate that Powell, the last of these great Western men, should retire in 1894, because a new age had come into being, symbolized by the Columbian Exhibition in Chicago in 1893. Though Powell's ideas had portent for the future, he was nevertheless a figure of the romantic past.

Even as Powell was pondering his resignation, a young historian from Wisconsin arose at the meeting of the American Historical Association in Chicago in 1893, and calling attention to the fact that the Census Bureau Report of 1890 had declared the continuous frontier to be officially ended, brilliantly and poetically ushered the frontier era, of which Powell had been so much a part, into the realm of history. "Stand at the South Pass of the Rocky Mountains," Frederick Jackson Turner bade his audience, "and watch the procession of civilization pass by."[6] And if anyone had looked closely, he would have seen each successive wave of civilization led by the explorers—Lewis and Clark, Zebulon Pike, John Colter, Peter Skene Ogden, William Ashley, Jedediah Smith, Benjamin Bonneville, Frémont, the scouts and wagon masters, the Topographical Engineers, the railroad surveyors, state geologists, cavalry officers, obscure prospectors, missionaries, surveyors, and geologists from Ferdinand V. Hayden to Powell himself.

In 1800 the United States was an underdeveloped land with a wilderness spread out before it, its destiny as part of the Union still uncertain. It was the explorers, as much as anyone, who

---

4. Darrah: *Powell of the Colorado*, pp. 347–8. See also United States Geological Survey: *15th Annual Report*, p. 7.
5. Darrah: *Powell of the Colorado*, pp. 347–8.
6. Frederick Jackson Turner: "The Significance of the Frontier in American History," *The Frontier in American History* (New York: Henry Holt and Co.; 1920).

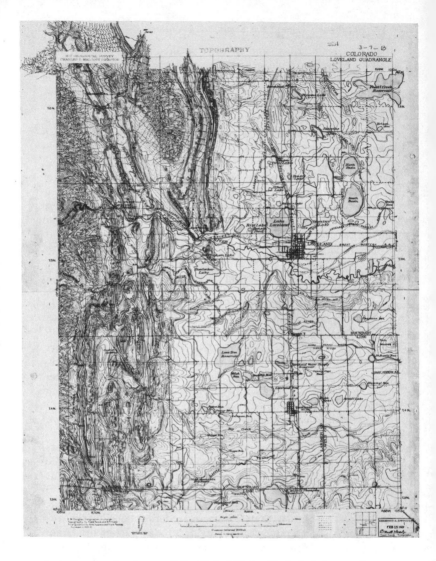

A modern quadrant map of the United States Geological Survey. *Courtesy National Archives*

helped first to secure it from international rivals, then to open it up for settlement, to lay out the lines of primary migration, locate its abundant resources, and then inquire into and point up the complex problems involved in the administration of one of the largest inland empires in history. And at the same time that the explorers assisted in the transformation of an underdeveloped wilderness into a rich and powerful country, they increased the stature of civilization itself. Out of the wilderness experience, out of the great natural frontier laboratory, came one of the finest chapters in the history of science, and with it the growth of modern institutions dedicated to the endless conquest of knowledge. From the Dakota Badlands, the arid escarpments of the Great Basin, the gorgeous depths of the mad Colorado, and the silver mountains of California and Nevada came entirely new branches of science, whole new agencies of government and political techniques, even bureaus for the study of man himself· and his ultimate environment. Commission government, land reform, conservation, resource management, scientific mineralogy, expertise and expert men to direct an ever growing, complex society were brought into being. In 1893 their day seemed over, but within a few short years their impact on the twentieth century would make itself felt. Their explorations, and the knowledge derived from them, would help to produce an empire—a democratic empire larger than anyone could ever have imagined.

Images of Progress

The Camera Becomes Part
of Western Exploration

THE development of portable wet-plate camera equipment and the means of reproducing photographs for mass publication and distribution signaled a new era in the art of Western exploration. Not only was greater accuracy in reporting and a more candid portraiture possible, but in some cases the camera could go places and see things that the painter or artist could not. Moreover, the apparent realism of camera studies made it a dramatic and convincing new means for bringing the wonders of the West and the work of the explorer to the attention of the public and the public's representatives in Congress. Every major explorer in the post-Civil War West, therefore, made certain to include a photographer in his entourage. Competition between the Great Surveys made the inclusion of this novel means of advertising a virtual necessity which was not overlooked.

Even before the Civil War, there had been attempts to employ cameras on exploring expeditions. The painter John Mix Stanley, who accompanied the Isaac I. Stevens Northern Pacific Railroad Survey, made some successful pictures, which are now apparently lost. Albert Bierstadt, accompanying the Frederick West Lander expedition in the same period, also attempted photography. Frémont took S. N. Carvalho into the southern Rockies with him in 1853, and Carvalho, standing waist deep in snowdrifts, also shot scenes which are now lost. Lt. Joseph Christmas Ives, on his Colorado River expedition of 1857, made one signal attempt to photograph the Lower Colorado, but a gust of wind blew over his canvas tent, camera, and apparatus, and he gave up in disgust. If he had persevered, the Grand Canyon would have been first photographed at the same time that it was first represented by an artist. It was not, however, until the perfection of field photography in the Civil War that any great strides were made in the use of the camera as an adjunct to exploring operations.

In the 1860's, the great photographers of the American West began to put their skills to use on a broad scale. Timothy O'Sullivan, who had worked with Matthew Brady, came West to join Clarence King's Fortieth Parallel Survey, and later the Wheeler army surveys. John Wesley Powell employed a number of photographers: E. O. Beaman, Walter C. Powell, James Fennemore of Savage's Studio in Salt Lake City, and eventually the self-taught Jack Hillers. F. V. Hayden was fortunate in securing the services of the greatest of all Western photographers, William Henry Jackson. And even Custer was not without photographic assistance, as W. H. Illingworth of St. Paul accompanied his expedition to the Black Hills. Several military expeditions, notably Ludlow's, Ruffner's, and Barlow's, also included a photographer. On several occasions he was the unlucky W. T. Hines, whose work seemed destined always to be destroyed in one way or another. Once he lost his camera as it toppled into a gorge. Later a set of his photographic plates burned up in the great Chicago fire. Still he persevered, and perhaps some day remnants of his work will come to light.

Photography in the mountains and deserts of the Far West was not easy. In the first place, "portable" was a relative term. It usually took at least two men to carry all the equipment, and more assistance than that to hoist it up to the rugged mountain peaks which afforded the best vantage points for spectacular shots. Note the material taken by Jackson on his first trip out with the Hayden surveys in 1870, as recorded by Robert Taft in *Photography and the American Scene*.

> "*Stereoscopic camera with one or more pairs of lenses*
> *5 x 8 Camera box plus lens*
> *11 x 14 Camera box plus lenses*
> *Dark tent*
> *2 Tripods*
> *10 lbs. Collodion*
> *36 oz. Silver nitrate*
> *2 qts. Alcohol*
> *10 lbs. Iron sulfate [developer]*
> *Package of filters*
> *1 ½ lbs. Potassium cyanide [fixer]*
> *3 yrds. Canton flannel*
> *1 Box Rottenstone [cleaner for glass plates]*
> *3 Negative boxes*
> *6 oz. nitric acid*
> *1 qt. Varnish*
> *Developing and fixing trays*
> *1½ doz. bottles of various sizes*
> *Scales and weights*
> *Glass for negatives, 400 pieces*"

Much of this was fragile or perishable equipment that required special packing and handling. Often the greatest hazard to successful photography was the very human, if perverse, desire of the mule packers to jettison the heavy equipment in some convenient gulch. The mules, too, frequently refused to cooperate and in various ways placed the equipment in jeopardy.

Once the cameras were set up, the photographer had to contend with mountain haze, the blazing desert sun, uncertain and tricky light, and the demands of time and schedule. According to Jackson, it took about thirty minutes to take a picture, working fast—and most of that time was spent unpacking the gear and setting it up. Once exposed, the glass negative had to be washed over gently with various chemicals in a delicate operation which made patience perhaps the most necessary quality for good photography. However, the great photographers persisted and the result is a magnificent record of late-nineteenth-century Western exploration and development, some examples of which make up this portfolio.

The first section of pictures presented here is a sampling of the varieties of Western scenic experience captured by the photographers. Every kind of Western landscape is represented: mountains, deserts, canyons, mighty rivers and waterfalls, and the fantastic geysers of Yellowstone. It is a kaleidoscope of experience in nature similar to that which dazzled parlour viewers of Victorian America. At first, the photographers chose scenes that might have been selected by earlier landscape painters (as many of them indeed were) and composed their pictures like paintings on canvas. At this, Jackson proved to be a master. He could place his camera so that it would sweep over the landscape like the brushes of Bierstadt or Moran, and he produced an old artistic image in a new medium. While artists like Moran were influenced by the photograph, by the same token the photographers, in the choice of subjects and composition, were influenced in turn by the landscape artists. The first photographs in this series are examples of this.

In addition, though the photographers only gradually became aware of it, the camera provided a medium for social realism. Unwittingly, O'Sullivan's spectacular pictures, taken hundreds of feet underground in the Gould and Curry Mine, dramatized the fearful plight of the mine worker. And Hillers' photos of Indians, though at first romantic, gradually took on the quality of the Stieglitz pictures of emigrants. They were used by the reformer John Wesley Powell to show the miserable condition of the redmen, who, after the camera revealed them in their natural state, could by no stretch of the imagination be considered "noble savages." Powell used the camera to take up where Catlin had left off decades before, but this was a far more effective means of documentation.

Finally, with the camera's facility for portraiture, the explorer emerged from pictorial obscurity for better or for worse. He became a part of the Western scene in visual terms, and an authentic hero to generations of schoolchildren brought up on the widely distributed photographs, sun pictures, and stereopticon slides of the various expeditions. As for the explorer himself, the graphic revolution had begun and the opportunities for self-advertisement were irresistible—for which the cultural historian can only be thankful. Seldom if ever has an era of high adventure been so vividly and artistically documented.

I

The Camera and the Painter's Eye

Mount of the Holy Cross in Western Colorado. W. H. Jackson, 1873. *Courtesy National Archives*

Yellowstone forest ranger Harry Yount and the view north from Berthoud Pass. W. H. Jackson, 1874. *Courtesy National Archives*

Cottonwood Canyon, Wasatch Mountains. Timothy O'Sullivan, circa 1869. *Courtesy National Archives*

Hayden's Cathedral, Uinta Mountains. W. H. Jackson, 1870. *Courtesy National Archives*

The Falls of Yosemite. C. E. Watkins, 1860's. *Courtesy Yale Western Americana Collection*

Grand Canyon of the Yellowstone from East Bank. W. H. Jackson, 1874.
Courtesy National Archives

Gardner's River Hot Springs (Mammoth Hot Springs). W. H. Jackson, 1872. W. H. Holmes adds that the figure is Thomas Moran. *Courtesy Smithsonian Institution, National Collection of Fine Arts*

Beehive group of geysers from opposite side of Firehole River. Jack Hillers, circa 1880. *Courtesy National Archives*

Mud geyser in action. W. H. Jackson, 1871. Jackson has caught the geyser in mid-eruption, creating an effect similar to a painting by Turner or Whistler. *Courtesy National Archives*

On the edge of a glacier. Timothy O'Sullivan, 1868–69. *Courtesy National Archives*

Camp at the falls of the Snake River. Timothy O'Sullivan, 1868–69. *Courtesy National Archives*

Wagon of the King Survey on sand dunes of the Carson Desert in the Great Basin. Timothy O'Sullivan, 1867. *Courtesy National Archives*

Cliff ruins, Mancos Canyon, Colorado. W. H. Jackson, 1875. *Courtesy National Archives*

Distant view of ancient ruins in Cañon de Chelly, N.M. Timothy O'Sullivan, 1871–72. *Courtesy National Archives*

Near the foot of Toroweap, Grand Canyon. W. H. Jackson, 1875. *Courtesy National Archives*

Devil's Anvil, Shivwits Crossing, Grand Canyon. William Bell, date uncertain. This is a photographic counterpart to the drawings of Gustave Doré. *Courtesy Library of Congress*

The Grand Canyon of the Colorado from below. William Bell. *Courtesy National Archives*

Quarrying granite for the Mormon Temple. W. H. Jackson, 1872. *Courtesy National Archives*

Virginia City, Nevada, at the height of the silver boom. Timothy O'Sullivan, 1867. *Courtesy National Archives*

The Gould and Curry Mine. Timothy O'Sullivan, 1867. This was one of the largest and most famous mines of its day. Note the extremely neat operation. *Courtesy National Archives*

II

An Underground Landscape

The following five pictures were taken deep down, hundreds of feet below the earth, in the Gould and Curry Mine. The first pictures ever taken underground in the confining stopes of a mine, they represent an innovation in photography. In 1866, according to Robert Taft, Charles Waldack of Cincinnati had photographed the vast interior of Mammoth Cave, Kentucky. Possibly influenced by this experiment, Timothy O'Sullivan took his camera 300 feet deep into the Gould and Curry Mine, and using magnesium flares, caught the frightening everyday life of a Western silver miner. His astonishing pictures are published here for the first time.

Loading ore cart at the foot of the elevator shaft. Timothy O'Sullivan, 1867.
Courtesy National Archives

623

Mining the lode. Timothy O'Sullivan, 1867. Note the timbering. *Courtesy National Archives*

Rough times in rough places: miner at at work at the end of a shaft. Timothy O'Sullivan, 1867. The tiny candle provides the only light for the miner on his twelve-hour day underground. *Courtesy National Archives*

Stalactites in the stopes. Timothy O'Sullivan. This is the way a shaft looked as the miner moved down it on his way to work. *Courtesy National Archives*

Cave-in. Timothy O'Sullivan, 1867. The booted leg at the right undoubtedly belongs to the guide, not to a victim of the cave-in. *Courtesy National Archives*

III

From Romanticism to Realism in Indian Portraiture

The next four pictures were made by Jack Hillers of the Powell Plateau Survey in the 1870's. They document Powell's interest in Indian life and indicate the miserable conditions he found among the tribes of the Colorado Plateau country. In creating the Bureau of Ethnology in 1879, Powell attempted to fashion an agency to help the Indian, and he used these pictures to make his point. The first photo is a deliberately romantic odalisque. The other three provide a sorry contrast to it.

627

Indian odalisque. Jack Hillers. *Courtesy Yale Western Americana Collection*

Paiute men gambling. Jack Hillers. *Courtesy Yale Western Americana Collection*

Paiutes at home. Jack Hillers. Compare this with Alfred Jacob Miller's pastoral scene on p. 209 in Portfolio I. *Courtesy Yale Western Americana Collection*

More Paiutes at home. Jack Hillers. The wickiup was their year-round home. Note the woman grinding corn. *Courtesy Yale Western Americana Collection*

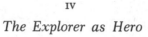

IV

The Explorer as Hero

Custer expedition assembling for the march to the Black Hills. W. H. Illing-worth, 1874. *Courtesy National Archives*

Indian's eye view of Custer Expedition entering the Black Hills. W. H. Illingworth, 1874. *Courtesy National Archives*

"Our First Grizzly," killed by General Custer and Colonel Ludlow. W. H. Illingworth, 1874. Custer is in a characteristically heroic pose, and with him is Ludlow. On the left is Bloody Knife, the scout who died with Custer at the Little Big Horn. *Courtesy National Archives*

The Yale man as explorer: Clarence King in camp at Salt Lake City. Timothy O'Sullivan, 1868–69. *Courtesy National Archives*

Clarence King, mountaineering. Timothy O'Sullivan, 1867. *Courtesy Bancroft Library, University of California*

Wheeler Grand Canyon Expedition starting from Camp Mojave on the Colorado River. Timothy O'Sullivan, 1871. *Courtesy National Archives*

Wheeler Expedition camp in Painted Canyon, Colorado River. Timothy O'Sullivan, 1871. Wheeler is in foreground. *Courtesy National Archives*

On the floor of the Grand Canyon. Timothy O'Sullivan, 1871. Grove Karl Gilbert is pondering a geological problem. The Mojave guides nap during the noon rest, giving the photographer a chance to sidestep their superstitious fear of photography. *Courtesy National Archives*

Wheeler and his men at Diamond Creek on the floor of the Grand Canyon. Timothy O'Sullivan, 1871. This is as far as Wheeler and his men made it up the river, but they had the satisfaction of reaching the point where Lt. Ives had descended to the floor of the canyon in 1857. They got there the hard way, by lining upstream against the current. *Courtesy Library of Congress*

Hayden Expedition entering Yellowstone. W. H. Jackson, 1871. *Courtesy National Archives*

Hayden's hunters in the Yellowstone: José, and Joe Clark. W. H. Jackson, 1872. *Courtesy National Archives*

The Cook

peale   gannett   Hayden
amelung   Cooper   Holmes

Hayden party in Yellowstone Park, 1872

Hayden's party encamped in the Yellowstone. W. H. Jackson, 1872. Note
the geyser basin in the background. Gannett and Hayden are in the center
rear. Holmes is on the extreme right. *Courtesy Smithsonian Institution, National Collection of Fine Arts*

Triangulation operations at the summit of Silverton Mountain, San Juan, Colorado. W. H. Jackson, 1874. The artist, probably W. H. Holmes, is seated. *Courtesy National Archives*

W. H. Jackson starting out with his man Dixon. Self-portrait by W. H. Jackson, 1875. *Courtesy Smithsonian Institution, National Collection of Fine Arts*

W. H. Jackson's photographic party, San Juan country, 1875. Self-portrait by W. H. Jackson, 1875. This party had a narrow escape from warlike Ute Indians. *Courtesy Smithsonian Institution, National Collection of Fine Arts*

First pictures of cliff ruins at Mancos Valley, 1874. W. H. Jackson, 1874. Seated is the journalist Ernest Ingersoll. Standing is the guide and discoverer of Mesa Verde, John Moss. *Courtesy Smithsonian Institution, National Collection of Fine Arts*

Powell's second Colorado River expedition starting out. E. O. Beaman, 1871.
Courtesy National Archives

Professor Almon Harris Thompson on the trail. Jack Hillers, 1873. *Courtesy National Archives*

Jack Hillers at work on the Aquarius Plateau. Self-portrait by Jack Hillers, 1873. *Courtesy National Archives*

Professor Almon Harris Thompson and family at a Colorado pueblo. W. H. Jackson, 1875. This is a crossing of explorers' trails: Hayden's crew, under Jackson, encounters Thompson's survey on the Colorado Plateau. *Courtesy Smithsonian Institution, National Collection of Fine Arts*

John Wesley Powell. Jack Hillers, 1873. *Courtesy Yale Western Americana Collection*

A Note on the Sources

The materials on which this book is based include virtually every printed work relating to American exploration in the nineteenth century, numerous general and specialized works in the history of science and on various phases of Western and United States history, comparative studies of exploration conducted by other countries in other parts of the globe, and extensive manuscript and archival collections. It is, therefore, not possible to present here a complete bibliography of the materials consulted, particularly the secondary materials or authorities, since this would entail a separate bibliographical volume of interest primarily to specialists in the field of exploration and Western history. Instead, I have attempted to list most of the immediately relevant works in my footnotes, which appear at appropriate points in the book. The function of the essay that follows is to present as complete a guide as possible to the manuscript and archival collections used, since these are the most difficult for researchers to locate, and in addition to make a series of general comments on the various kinds of printed sources available to scholars and interested readers who wish to proceed beyond the beginning that I have made.

I. Manuscript and Archival Sources

The manuscript and archival sources available for a study of American exploration in the nineteenth century are surprisingly abundant. Much of the exploration was official exploration, or was institutionally oriented, so that the letters and journals and field notebooks of the explorers were very often preserved either in governmental institutions or in the seats of higher learning. To a surprising degree also, however, the letters and journals of unofficial explorers such as the mountain men were also preserved. Very possibly this came about because the unofficial explorers, as well as the official explorers, were conscious of their role in history, particularly their part in the epic movement represented by the settlement of the American West. The list of relevant manuscript sources that follows is as complete as memory permits.

1. The National Archives

A. Record Group 77, Office of the Chief of Engineers. This also includes the records of the Chief of Topographical Engineers, and part of the records of the Bureau of Explorations and Surveys. It is the most extensive collection of materials available for the study of nineteenth-century military exploration in the West. Of special interest are the recently acquired records of the United States Geographical Surveys West of the 100th Meridian. At the time I examined them, shortly after their arrival from Stanford University, they consisted of four packing cases of materials, including field notebooks, meteorological records, personnel records, seven volumes of letters-received registers with index, seven volumes of letters sent with index, seven volumes of letterpress books, and many other miscellaneous documents. This collection constitutes approximately one half of the Wheeler Survey papers known to be in existence. The other comparable collection is in the Western Americana Collection of Yale University. For more detailed information on this Record Group, see Goetzmann: *Army Exploration in the American West*, pp. 461–2. The researcher should be informed that much of the material listed in De Grange's Index to this Record Group is no longer in existence. This has caused some confusion among students of Western exploration.

B. Record Group 94, Adjutant General's Office. See especially the Bonneville File, and materials on W. A. Jones, G. A. Custer, and William Ludlow.

C. Record Group 46, Records of the Senate. See especially the Bonneville File.

D. Record Group 59, State Department Records. Chiefly important for materials on the Mexican and Northwest Boundaries, and for correspondence concerning Oregon, Texas, and the Mexican War.

E. Record Group 48, Interior Department Records. See the letterbooks concerning the Pacific Railroad Surveys, letters received by the Bureau of Explorations and Surveys, Mexican Boundary Survey correspondence, the records of the Wagon Roads Office, and the letterbooks of the Secretary of the Interior.

F. Record Group 49, General Land Office Records.

G. Record Group 57, Geological Survey Records. A most important collection, this contains the major records of the Hayden Survey, Clarence King's correspondence with General A. A. Humphreys, and the official records of the Powell Survey in fourteen volumes of letters, also a small collection of George M. Wheeler papers.

H. The Still Pictures Section. This is a massive archive of the photographic work of Jackson, Hillers, O'Sullivan, Beaman, Fennemore, Illing, and other lesser-known picture-makers of the Old West.

I. The Cartographic Records Section. This is of vital importance to any study of Western exploration, since the originals of many of the government and territorial maps are preserved in this collection. Also included are some of the original drawings made by the explorers.

2. The Library of Congress

Nicholas P. Trist Papers, William B. Franklin Papers, James Buchanan Papers, John N. Macomb Papers, Dr. William Lee Papers, the Journals of Titian Peale, the Diaries of Charles Preuss, Carl Schurz Papers, Simon Newcomb Papers, Cooper-Hewitt Papers, S. F. Emmons Papers, George F. Becker Papers, George P. Merrill Collection, George Y. Bradley Diary. Also see the Prints and Photographs Collection for materials on the Western Surveys.

3. The Smithsonian Institution

Fielding B. Meek Papers, also William Henry Holmes: "Random Records of a Lifetime in Science and Art," sixteen volumes of assorted diaries, letters, pictures, and reminiscences collected by Holmes in preparation for his autobiography, Smithsonian Institution Correspondence Files. Other materials, chiefly Powell's field notes, are in the Bureau of American Ethnology.

4. Yale Western Americana Collection

William Hemsley Emory Papers, William F. Raynolds Papers, Elwood Evans Papers, Fort Sutter Papers, I. I. Stevens Papers, George Suckley Papers, George Gibbs Papers, Clinton Gardner Papers, George F. Emmons Papers, Henry Eld Journal, Paul Max Engle Papers, R. H. Kern Letter, Thomas Hempstead Letterbook, Alexander Ross MS. of "Fur Hunters of the Far West," Robert Stuart Journal and Travelling Memoranda, George M. Wheeler Papers, Frederick Dellenbaugh Papers, De Zahara Collection, John Jacob Astor Letters, Henry Atkinson Journal, Escalante Journal, Bent Papers, Lewis and Clark Papers, George M. Colvocoresses Diary, James G. Cooper Letter, Francis Vinton Greene Papers, Samuel T. Hauser Diary, Joseph Heger Drawings, Alfred Jacob Miller Paintings, Osborne Russell MS. of "Journal of a Trapper," Samuel Seymour's watercolors of the Long Expedition, James S. R. Wilson Journal of a Trip to Yellowstone Park, Henry Atkinson Journal, James Wilkinson Letter, Jean Luis Berlandier Papers, and George A. Custer, Black Hills Expedition, Order and Dispatch Book.

5. Yale Historical Manuscripts Collection

Benjamin Silliman Papers, Journal of Anthony Glass, John Maley Journal (both in Silliman Papers, along with related correspondence), Benjamin Silliman Jr. Papers, George Jarvis Brush Papers, William Henry Brewer Papers, Whitney Family Papers, O. C. Marsh Papers, James Dwight Dana Papers, Daniel Cady Eaton Papers, Correspondence File American Journal of Science, Barna Upton Papers.

6. Yale Peabody Museum

O. C. Marsh Letterbooks.

7. New York Public Library

Washington Irving Papers, Frederick Dellenbaugh Collection (the latter includes the Journals of Almon H. Thompson, Mrs. A. H. Thompson, and Stephen V. Jones, plus a photostatic copy of the John F. Steward Diary), George Gibbs Papers, Robert Brewster Stanton Collection (also includes a copy of J. C. Sumner's Journal), Henry D. Mansfield Letters.

8. American Museum of Natural History

Edward Drinker Cope Papers.

9. Butler Library, Columbia University

Edwin James Journals and Notebooks, 1820–27.

10. New York Botanical Gardens

John Torrey Papers.

11. New York State Museum
   James Hall Papers.

12. New York State Library
   Gouverneur Kemble Warren Papers.

13. The American Philosophical Society
   Thomas Nuttall Diary (photostat), Zebulon Pike Papers, George Hunter Papers (including Louisiana Journals), William Dunbar Journals, Edwin James Letters, Andrew A. Humphreys Letters, Alexander von Humboldt letter to Frémont (Oct. 7, 1850), F. V. Hayden Letters, James D. Hague Letters, Wallace Stegner Collection of John Wesley Powell Materials, William H. Emory Letters, J. J. Abert Letters, Ferdinand Hassler Papers, Edwin James Letters.

14. Pennsylvania State Historical Society
   Andrew Atkinson Humphreys Papers, Isaac Roberdeau Papers, George Gordon Meade Papers, James Buchanan Papers, Daniel Parker Papers.

15. Philadelphia Academy of Natural Sciences
   S. W. Woodhouse Journals, R. H. and E. M. Kern Drawings and Sketches, Miscellaneous Correspondence of the Society.

16. John Carter Brown Library
   John Russell Bartlett Papers.

17. Gilcrease Institute
   Jean Luis Berlandier Papers, Ranald Slidell McKenzie Letterbooks, R. H. Kern letter to George R. Gliddon (Nov. 1, 1851), Corporal Thoma Sketchbook, Josiah Gregg Journals and Letters.

18. Oklahoma State Historical Society
   Amiel Weeks Whipple Papers, Heinrich B. Möllhausen Drawings, D. S. Stanley Diary, T. B. Wheelock Letters and Journal.

19. Kansas State Historical Society
   Jedediah Smith Papers, including photostat from Floyd Risvold Collection.

20. Missouri Historical Society
   Charles Geyer Papers, J. N. Nicollet Papers, William Clark Papers, Manuel Lisa Papers, James Kennerly Papers, William H. Ashley Papers (including Journals of Harrison G. Rogers on Jedediah Smith Southwest Expeditions, 1826, May–July 1828), Andrew Drips Papers, Robert Campbell Papers, David Adams Papers, Vasquez Family Papers, George and John C. Sibley Papers, Santa Fe Papers, Stephen W. Kearny Journals, William L. Sublette Papers (including Ashley Diary), Indian File, A. W. Doniphan Papers, Chouteau Family Papers (a very extensive and excellent collection), John Jacob Astor Papers, Kenneth McKenzie Papers, Bent, St. Vrain and Co. Folder, John Dougherty Papers, John O'Fallon Collection, Theodore and Wilson Price Hunt Papers, Mexican War File, Western Travel File, Dobyns Family Papers, Astorians Folder.

21. Texas State Historical Society
Thomas Rusk Papers.

22. Bancroft Library
Thomas Salathiel Martin "Narrative," George Horatio Derby Papers, William Fayel "Narrative of Col. Robert Campbell's Experiences in the Rocky Mountain Fur Trade from 1825–1835" (copy loaned to author by Dale L. Morgan).

23. Huntington Library
Clarence King Papers (this is the most important collection of King Papers), William Whitman Bailey Papers, John W. Gunnison Papers.

24. Newberry Library
F. W. von Egloffstein Drawings.

25. St. Louis Botanical Gardens
George Engelmann Papers.

26. Jocelyn Art Museum
Prince Maximilian of Wied-Neuwied Collection.

27. Ministerio de Relaciones Exteriores de Mexico
General García Condé Papers and Records of the Mexican Boundary Survey.

28. William Robertson Coe Library, University of Wyoming
James Bridger Map, Richard "Beaver Dick" Leigh Journal.

The following libraries and museums contain scattered items of some relevance to this book: New Mexico Historical Society Museum, Rosenberg Library, Houston Public Library, Panhandle Plains Historical Museum, Grand Canyon Museum, Yellowstone Park Library and Museum, West Point Museum, Jackson Hole Museum (privately owned, in the town of Jackson Hole), Yale Geological Library, New-York Historical Society, Arizona Pioneers Historical Society, Washington State Historical Society, Denver Public Library, Manuscript Division, University of Oklahoma Library, the United States Geological Survey, Washington and Denver Branches. Some of the family papers of James W. Abert are in the possession of his granddaughter, the Marquesa de Zahara, who generously loaned them to me, along with the Diaries of Captain Albert Barnitz, which she has since presented to the Yale Western Americana Collection.

II. Printed Sources

The printed sources for the history of nineteenth-century Western exploration are very extensive. They fall into three general groups, which are considered separately below: United States Government publications; books and articles published in the nineteenth century; source materials edited and published at a later date.

A. United States Government Publications

The United States Government Publications can be broken down into several categories: the House and Senate Document Series, published continually from the birth of the republic, but for the first fourteen Congresses published retrospectively and called *The American State Papers;* publications by the various government bureaus, departments, and agencies such as the United States Geological Survey and the Office of the Chief of Engineers; and the *Congressional Globe* and *Congressional Record.*

There are a number of guides and indexes to these publications, all of varying quality. See A. M. Boyd, ed.: *United States Government Publications: Sources of Information for Librarians;* H. S. Hirshberg and C. H. Melinant: *Subject Guide to United States Government Publications;* A. W. Greeley, ed.: *Public Documents of the First Fourteen Congresses 1789–1817,* published as *Sen. Doc. 428,* 56th Cong. 1st sess. Also see American Historical Association *Report for 1903;* B. P. Poore, ed.: *Descriptive Catalogue of the Government Publications of the United States* (index defective); J. G. Ames, ed.: *Comprehensive Index to the Publications of the United States Government, 1881–1893* (listing of documents incomplete); M. A. Hartwell, ed.: *Checklist of United States Public Documents, 1789–1890, Congressional: to the Close of the Sixtieth Congress; Departmental: to the End of Calendar Year 1909,* third edition (Washington, 1911), one of the most useful guides. Adelaide Hasse: *Reports of Explorations Printed in the Documents of the United States Government* (1899), is most useful. L. F. Schmeckebier: "Catalogue and Index of the Publications of the Hayden, King, Powell, and Wheeler Surveys," *Bulletin* 222 of the United States Geological Survey (Washington, 1904), is indispensable.

The House and Senate Documents Series contains abundant material on both the official and the unofficial exploration. In the former category, of particular relevance are the annual reports of the Secretary of War, which include the sub-reports of the Chief of Topographical Engineers, the Chief of Engineers, and the reports from the generals commanding the various Western Military Districts. Especially lengthy or important reports of exploring expeditions, such as those by Frémont, Stansbury, Ives, Emory, Simpson, Sitgreaves, Abert, Doane, Barlow, Powell, and Raynolds, were published as separate documents, as were the important reports of the Mexican Boundary Survey and the Pacific Railroad Surveys of 1853. The annual reports of the Wheeler Surveys and the King Surveys were also published in the Document Series as parts of the Report of the Secretary of War. And the reports of the Hayden Survey were published as parts of the Annual Report of the Secretary of the Interior, another series of important documents.

Separate sets of official reports, monographs, and maps were also published by the Office of the Chief of Engineers, the Smithsonian Institution, Wheeler's United States Geographical Surveys West of the 100th Meridian, Hayden's United States Geological and Geographical Survey of the Territories, Powell's United States Geographical and Geological Survey of the Rocky Mountain Region, King's United States Geological Exploration of the Fortieth Parallel, and after 1879 the United States Geological Survey. See Schmeckebier for a complete list of their very extensive publications. The annual reports of Whitney's California Geological Survey were published by the state of California.

The *Congressional Globe* and *Congressional Record,* poorly indexed, can be found in virtually any library. They are important chiefly in tracing debates over the purposes, nature, and impact of exploration. For example, the important points of view concerning the formation of the United States Geological Survey, and Powell's conduct of that agency, can be found in these volumes. Not to be neglected are the individually published reports of the National Academy of Science, the reports of the Townsend Committee of 1874, the Atkinson Committee of 1878, the Allison Commission of 1884–86, and the various committee hearings on Powell's irrigation survey in 1890.

B. Books and Articles Published in the Nineteenth Century

Here the literature is vast. It includes travel books, explorers' accounts, journals of trappers, scientists, emigrants, reporters, soldiers, and soldiers of fortune, and the various kinds of promotional literature, company reports, exposé pamphlets, political memoirs, campaign biographies, emigrant guidebooks, semi-fictionalized adventure stories, fact-based fiction such as Stewart's *Altowan* and Ruxton's *Fur Hunters of the Far West*, scientific articles and important reviews of all of the above materials. Unfortunately, there is no sure guide through all this material, and perhaps there never can be, since the relevance of much of these works depends largely on the project at hand. However, two bibliographies constitute an indispensable beginning for the student of Western exploration: Henry Raup Wagner and Charles Camp: *The Plains and the Rockies* (here a new edition is needed); and Max Meisel: *A Bibliography of American Natural History*, 2 vols. (Brooklyn, New York: The Premier Publishing Co.: 1924). Meisel's is a monumental work that lists not only the major scientific reports stemming from various Western expeditions, but also the papers published by the various learned societies. Both books are vital for any researcher in the field of Western exploration.

An important component of the nineteenth-century literature of exploration is the popular periodicals. Some of the most significant accounts of expeditions were published in *Scribner's Monthly*, *Appleton's Monthly*, *Harper's Monthly Magazine*, *Overland Monthly*, *Popular Science Monthly*, and the *Century Magazine*. Likewise, the reports to scientific journals such as *The American Journal of Science*, the *Transactions of the Philadelphia Academy of Natural Sciences*, and the *Transactions of the St. Louis Academy of Science*, represent a body of significant information that should not be overlooked. Newspapers, such as *Niles' National Register*, the New York *Herald*, *The Rocky Mountain News*, and all the various early Missouri newspapers, are of prime importance. The Yale Western Americana Collection contains a masterful selection of the most important items, culled from early frontier newspapers by Dale L. Morgan, which has been particularly useful to me.

C. Source Materials Edited and Published at a Later Date

This is the pride of Western historiography. The work of generations of patient, scholarly editors has made my present study possible. Concerned with preserving the record of the Westward movement have been local and national historians, antiquarians, and editors, some individually, some with federal, state, or private help. They have collected and preserved enough authentic raw materials to make it feasible at this point in the evolution of Western historiography to begin to attempt new interpretations and new syntheses similar to those launched by American colonial historians some years ago which have caused a renaissance in that field at the present time.

Though it would be impossible to name all the people and institutions who have pioneered in this editing work, some individuals and institutions merit special attention. For example, Reuben Gold Thwaites, whose *Early Western Travels Series, Jesuit Relations,* and *Lewis and Clark,* are of prime importance; Elliott Coués, editor of Pike's Journals, Alexander Henry's Journals, and numerous other volumes; Ralph P. Bieber and A. B. Bender, editors of *The Southwestern Trails Series;* Le Roy and Anne Hafen, editors of *The Far West and Rockies Series;* Milo Milton Quaife, editor of Polk's Diary and a long series of Lakeside Classics of the early West; Archer B. Hulbert, for his *Overland to the Pacific Series;* Carl I. Wheat, whose *Mapping the Transmississippi West* is a major work in the field of Western Americana, in an area where it was badly needed; The Hudson's Bay Record Society, The Champlain Society, Clarence Carter's *Territorial Papers of the United States,* the Exploration and Travel Series of the Oklahoma University Press, Maurice S. Sullivan and H. C. Dale on Jedediah Smith, Charles Camp on James Clyman, Herbert Bolton on the Spanish Southwest material, Abraham Nasatir, whose *Before Lewis and Clark* is a classic, the Quivira Society, William Culp Darrah and Herbert Gregory on Powell, Paul C. Phillips on Warren Ferris, Phillip A. Rollins on Robert Stuart, the pioneer collections of the Missouri Historical Society, and the many works of Dale L. Morgan, who is an institution unto himself.

The following Western journals and historical quarterlies, in addition to the particular items cited above, contain the bulk of the source materials on the Old West: *Mississippi Valley Historical Review, Arizona and the West, Southwestern Historical Quarterly, Montana, the Magazine of Western History, Pacific Historical Review, Pacific Northwest Quarterly, The American West, The Beaver (Hudson's Bay Company), Frontier Times, Agricultural History, Amerindian, Sierra Club Bulletin, New York Posse Westerners' Brand Book, Seattle Posse Westerners' Brand Book, Chicago Posse Westerners' Brand Book, Denver Posse Westerners' Brand Book, Arkansas Historical Quarterly, Annals of Iowa, Iowa Journal of History and Politics, Palimpsest, Chronicles of Oklahoma, Colorado Magazine of History, Colorado Quarterly, Illinois State Historical Society Journal, Historical Society of Southern California Quarterly, Kansas Historical Quarterly, Louisiana Historical Quarterly, Missouri Historical Society Bulletin, Missouri Historical Review, Minnesota History, Nebraska History Magazine, New Mexico Historical Review, North Dakota Quarterly, Oregon Historical Quarterly, Utah Historical Quarterly, Wisconsin Magazine of History, Idaho Yesterdays, Los Angeles County Museum Bulletin, Nebraska State Historical Newsletter, North Dakota History, South Dakota Historical Society Collections, South Dakota University Museum News, Gilcrease News, El Paso Historical Society Password, California Historical Society Quarterly, The Canadian Historical Review, The Trail.*

Much of this book is quarried out of the files of these Western publications. Regrettably, there is no feasible way to comment in detail on the source material contained in these journals, or on the vast numbers of authoritative articles in them, or for that matter on the secondary literature of books and pamphlets concerning the Old West and its explorers. To comment on this literature in detail would be to comment on the literature of nineteenth-century America itself, for as this narrative has suggested, the regional and the national culture cannot be separated. The West has so often mirrored the East in all its complexity that the regional historian must to some extent take cognizance of the literature, values, and institutions of both.

Index

A NOTE ABOUT THE AUTHOR

WILLIAM H. GOETZMANN was born in 1930 in Washington, D.C., and attended Yale University, where he received his B.A. in 1952 and his Ph.D. in 1957. He taught history and American studies at Yale from 1955 to 1964, and in September 1964 he became Director of the American Studies Program at the University of Texas. Mr. Goetzmann was awarded the John Addison Porter Prize of Yale University for his doctoral dissertation, which was later published by Yale University Press as *Army Exploration in the American West*.

NINETEENTH AND TWENTIETH CENTURY
AMERICAN HISTORY IN NORTON PAPERBACK

Francis Jennings *The Invasion of America: Indians, Colonialism and the Cant of Conquest* N830

Gabriel Kolko *Railroads and Regulation, 1877–1916* N531

Stanley I. Kutler *Privilege and Creative Destruction: The Charles River Bridge Case* N885

Howard Roberts Lamar *The Far Southwest, 1846–1912: A Territorial History* N522

Peggy Lamson *The Glorious Failure: Black Congressman Robert Brown Elliott and the Reconstruction in South Carolina* N733

Richard P. McCormick *The Second American Party System: Party Formation in the Jacksonian Era* N680

William S. McFeely *Grant: A Biography* 30046

William S. McFeely *Yankee Stepfather: General O. O. Howard and the Freedmen* 00537

Robert C. McMath, Jr. *Populist Vanguard: A History of the Southern Farmers' Alliance* N869

Herbert S. Mitgang *The Man Who Rode the Tiger: The Life and Times of Judge Samuel Seabury* N922

Burl Noggle *Teapot Dome* N297

Douglass C. North *The Economic Growth of the United States, 1790–1860* N346

Nell Irvin Painter *Exodusters: Black Migration to Kansas After Reconstruction* N951

Robert E. Quirk *An Affair of Honor: Woodrow Wilson and the Occupation of Veracruz* N390

James L. Roark *Masters Without Slaves: Southern Planters in the Civil War and Reconstruction* N901

Richard H. Sewell *Ballots for Freedom: Antislavery Politics in the U.S.* N966

Bernard W. Sheehan *Seeds of Extinction: Jeffersonian Philanthropy and the American Indian* N715

Kathryn Kish Sklar *Catharine Beecher: A Study in American Domesticity* N812

John W. Spanier *The Truman-MacArthur Controversy and the Korean War* N279

Sarah Stage *Female Complaints: Lydia Pinkham and the Business of Women's Medicine* N038

Ida M. Tarbell *History of the Standard Oil Company* (David Chalmers, Ed.) N496

Tom E. Terrill and Jerrold Hirsch, Eds. *Such As Us: Southern Voices of the Thirties* N927